THE ROUGH GUIDE TO

Istanbul

This third edition updated by

Terry Richardson and Rhiannon Davies

ROUGH GUIDES

roughguides.com

Contents

OPPOSITE BLUE MOSQUE PREVIOUS PAGE HAGHIA SOPHIA

Introduction to
Istanbul

Istanbul is unique. The only city in the world to straddle two continents and to have played capital to consecutive Christian and Islamic empires, its location at the crossroads of Europe and Asia has helped it shape the region's history for over 2500 years. Built on seven hills, the city (in its former guise of Constantinople) was the centre of the Byzantine Christian world from the fourth to the fifteenth centuries AD – the formidable six-kilometre-long land walls, the imposing bulk of the church of Haghia Sophia, and the delicate frescoes in the Kariye Museum are just some of the wonderful remnants of this period. The Ottomans, who famously conquered the city in 1453, have left an even more impressive legacy, and it is the domes and minarets of their many mosques that dominate the skyline of the old city, endowing it with the "oriental" exoticism that so enthrals Western visitors.

With a **population** estimated at seventeen million and rising, Istanbul is a metropolis going on megalopolis, a teeming, vibrant urban centre that can make other European cities seem dull in comparison. A city this size may seem an anomaly in a country where half the populace still work the fields in remote villages, but in many ways booming Istanbul is Turkey. Although stripped of its capital status in 1923, Istanbul exerts a powerful, almost mystical hold on the psyche of the nation and remains its cultural, economic and intellectual heart.

No one could deny that Istanbul has its concerns. A city whose population has increased at least twelvefold since the establishment of the Turkish Republic in 1923 is bound to have suffered. Traffic congestion, pollution, rising crime rates and water shortages are just some of the problems successive Istanbul mayors have had to deal with. Not to mention the Gezi Park protests in the heart of Istanbul in spring 2013 that brutally exposed the schisms in a society undergoing rapid change, shaking the image of both city and country worldwide.

ABOVE AN İZNİK TILE; DAILY PRAYERS IN EYÜP; APPLE TEA IN HAYDARPAŞA

BLACK SEA

KİLYOS

RUMELİ FENERİ

ROAD UNDER CONSTRUCTION

GARİPÇE

ANADOLU
FENERİ

3rd Bosphorus Bridge
(under construction)

POYRAZKÖY

BELGRADE
FOREST

BAHÇEKÖY

Üzün
Kemer

Büyük
Bend

KEMER BURGAZ

Rumeli Kavağı

SARIYER

Anadolu Kavağı

Bosphorus

ANADOLU KAVAĞI

Anadolu Kavağı

Sadberk Hanım
Museum

Sarıyer

BÜYÜKDERE

ÇAYIRBAŞI

ORTA ÇEŞME

BEYKOZ

Tarabya

TARABYA

TARABYA YENİKÖY CAD

YENİKÖY

Sait Halım Paşa Yalı

Yeniköy

PAŞABAHÇE

EMİRGAN

Sakıp Sabancı Museum

Emirgan

KANLICA CAD

Hıdıv Kısrı

Kanlıca

FATİH SULTAN MEHMET ACCESS ROAD

0-2

KAĞITHANE

LEVENT

Borusan Contemporary Gallery
Rumeli Hisarı

Bosphorus

ANADOLU HİSARI

ETİLER

Bebek

Küçüksu Kısrı

Anadolu Hisarı

BEBEK

Hıdıv
Sarayı

Kandilli

MECİDİYEKÖY

Arnavutköy

KANDİLLİ

FATİH SULTAN MEHMET ACCESS ROAD

YILDIZ

0-1

CUMHURİYET CAD

ARNAVUTKÖY

Vaniköy

Küleli Naval College

Çengelköy

ORTAKÖY

Teşvikiye

ÇIRAĞAN

Ortaköy

ÇENGELKÖY HAVUZBAŞI

EYÜP

HASKÖY

BEŞİKTAŞ

Naval Museum

Beşiktaş

Beylerbeyi

BEYLERBEYİ

ÇAMLICA

TAKSİM

BEYOĞLU

Kabataş

Kuzguncuk

Büyük
Çamlıca Hill
(262m)

Television
Tower

Golden Horn

KARAKÖY

Tophane

Üsküdar

KUZGUNCUK

UMRANİYE

FATİH

Karaköy

Eminönü

ÜSKÜDAR

SALACAK

BAĞLARBAŞI

ALTUNİZADE

0-2

Land
Walls

EMİNÖNÜ

Harem

Florence Nightingale Museum

SULTANAHMET

Ahırkapı
Lighthouse

HAREM

SELİMİYE

BOSPHORUS BRIDGE ACCESS ROAD

KUMKAPI

HAYDARPAŞA

ACIBADEM

Haydarpaşa

KADIKÖY

KOZYATAĞI

Kadıköy

KIZILTOPRAK

ERENKÖY

SEA OF MARMARA

FENERBAHÇE

CADDEBOSTAN

Caddebostan

SUADİYE

BOSTANCI

Suadiye

0   5
kilometres

N

THE BOSPHORUS

Geographically, historically and strategically, **the Bosphorus** – the thirty-kilometre strait dividing Europe from Asia – is one of the world's crucial waterways. With a medley of tankers, ferries and fishing boats weaving their way up, down or across its glittering blue waters, it is also one of its most visually stunning.

The river derives its name ("Ford of the Cow") from one version of a **Greek myth** in which Zeus seduces the beautiful Io. Zeus's jealous wife, Hera, suspects the lovers, so Zeus turns the unfortunate Io into a cow to disguise her. Pursued by an angry horsefly, Io swims the straits to flee her tormentor. Were Io to attempt her escape today, she'd most likely be mown down by one of the eighty thousand or so ships that pass through each year. In ancient times, ships laden with Scythian grain from the Black Sea hinterland sailed through en route to the bread-hungry citizens of Pericles's Athens. Today, Russian tankers filled with oil and liquefied gas ply the same route into the Mediterranean and fuel-starved Europe, helping make the Bosphorus the second busiest waterway in the world – so busy there are plans to build a mega-canal, a second Bosphorus, to alleviate the problem (see p.153).

Despite the problems, there's a buzz and confidence to Istanbul. **Foreign investment** has poured in over the last decade, particularly from the Gulf States, tourism is booming and the city is home to the Istanbul Biennial, an established arts festival of worldwide importance. It's little wonder that support for EU accession is dropping; Istanbulites know that their vital metropolis can, if necessary, stand alone and take full advantage of its unique position between Europe and the Middle East.

What to see

For most visitors, Istanbul is a city of two halves: the **old city**, sited on a triangular peninsula pointing across the Bosphorus towards Asia, and the lively districts of Beyoğlu and Galata, north of the Golden Horn. Most of the major sights are in the former, within a remarkably compact area that's easily explored on foot. At its heart is **Sultanahmet**, an historic area of twisting, cobbled lanes, overhung by quaint old wooden houses, and studded with landmark buildings from the powerful Byzantine and Ottoman empires: the **Haghia Sophia**, **Hippodrome**, **Topkapı Palace** and **Blue Mosque**.

West of Sultanahmet, the university district of **Beyazıt** is dominated by the **Grand Bazaar**, an exotic "shopping centre" that has been doing business for over five hundred years; while to the north, nudging up to the waters of the Golden Horn, lie bustling **Sirkeci** and **Eminönü**, the former famous for its grandiloquent station, the latter for the olfactory delights of the Ottoman-era **Spice Bazaar**.

The atmospheric **northwest quarter** boasts the wonderful Byzantine church of St Saviour in the Chora, now the **Kariye Museum**, and, a little beyond it, the mighty **land walls** of Theodosius. It's in the backstreets here, particularly around the ultra-orthodox **Fatih** district, where visitors will find the "traditional" Istanbul of young women garbed in headscarves and skull-capped men sipping sweet black tea while waiting for the next call to prayer. Across the Golden Horn lies the old "European" quarter of **Beyoğlu**, an

THE ORIENT EXPRESS

Immortalized in Graham Greene's *Stamboul Train* and Agatha Christie's *Murder on the Orient Express*, the train that linked Paris and Vienna with Istanbul became a metaphor for style, opulence and, of course, intrigue. The eastern terminus for the Orient Express was **Sirkeci Station**, opened with great fanfare in 1888. Designed by Prussian architect August Jachmund, it was an oriental fantasy, with a Parisian-style dome, minaret-like turrets and Moghul-influenced windows.

The *Orient Express* connected Europe with the capital of the Ottoman Empire, but across the Bosphorus in Asia another temple to travel arose: **Haydarpaşa**. Completed in 1908, this German-built station, a monumental, mock-castle structure with stunning views back across the water to the domes and minarets of the old city, is even more splendid than Sirkeci.

area of graceful nineteenth-century apartment blocks that has become the nerve centre of a booming arts, cultural and nightlife scene, focused on Istanbul's major shopping street, **İstiklal Caddesi**.

Recent improvements in the city's transport mean it's relatively easy to get from one sightseeing area to another. The far-flung sites in **Asian Istanbul** are now linked to the old city by the Bosphorus metro tunnel, opened in 2013, and by ferry. Beyoğlu and Galata are also well connected to Asian Istanbul by ferry. The boat trip alone makes a cruise across worthwhile, with the nightlife of **Kadıköy** and the Ottoman architecture of **Üsküdar** the major attractions.

North of the city centre, the Bosphorus is lined on either side with swish villages-cum-suburbs; these are best seen from the decks of the **Bosphorus Cruise**, which zigzags between Europe and Asia as it heads up the strait towards the Black Sea. Under an hour's boat ride south of Istanbul, out in the Sea of Marmara, the charming **Princes' Islands**, with their horse-drawn carriages, *fin-de-siècle* wooden villas, pine forests and beaches, have long provided a summer retreat from the bustle of the city – and are cheap and quick to reach by ferry. There's plenty to see **the city**, too: **Edirne**, a former Ottoman capital; legendary **Troy**; the World War I battlefields of **Gallipoli**; "Green" **Bursa**, draped across the slopes of towering Uludağ; and the laidback, rural retreat that is lakeside **İznik**.

When to go

Istanbul has a relatively damp **climate**, with hot, humid summers and cool, rainy winters with occasional snowfalls. The city is at its best in May and June, then again in September and October, months that offer the perfect combination of dry, warm weather and long daylight hours. July and August can be sweltering in the daytime, though by way of compensation the night-time dining and drinking at the city's numerous pavement and rooftop bars and restaurants is a delight. In January, February and even into March, it can be very chilly, with winds whipping down the Bosphorus from the Black Sea and fog rolling in from both the strait and the Sea of Marmara, though periods of bright, sunny weather punctuate the grey, and the city takes on an ethereal beauty in the snow.

Author Picks

Terry has a passion for uncovering this unique city's lesser-known historical treasures on foot; Rhiannon makes a point of seeking out the latest buzzing nightlife haunts and galleries. Both share a love of Istanbul's great cuisine. Here are a few of their personal highlights.

On your bike The busy streets of the metropolis are a challenge for cyclists, so head out to one of the traffic-free Princes' Islands in the Sea of Marmara, the nearest one only a half-hour sea-bus ride away. Rent a bike and shake off the city grime among pine-scented hills and wave-lapped shores. p.158.

Least-known Byzantine mosaics Virtually every visitor admires the Haghia Sophia's glittering mosaics and the stunning collection in the Kariye Museum. Just as impressive are those in the side-chapel of the former Church of Theotokos Pammakaristos, attached to the Fethiye Camii in the seldom-visited district of Fatih. p.94.

Best walk A stroll alongside the mighty land walls of Theodosius is one of the most satisfying outings in the city. Churches, mosques, traditional houses – even the remnants of a palace – dot the line of the fortifications that stretch over six kilometres between the Sea of Marmara and the Golden Horn. p.101.

Eat, drink and be merry *Meyhane*s are an Istanbul institution best enjoyed on a Friday or Saturday night, when crowds of locals while away the evening over an endless stream of *meze* (starters), appetizers and grilled fish, accompanied by copious amounts of wine, beer or *rakı* (aniseed spirit). Try *Ali Haydar* in Samatya (p.188), *Refik* in Beyoğlu (p.190) or *Safa* in Yedikule (p.188).

Gallery Hopping Buzzing Beyoğlu is home to loads of cool, free art galleries, all within easy walking distance of each other. Try SALT Beyoğlu (p.124 & p.208) for exhibitions with challenging social and political themes, Arter (p.123 & p.207) for well-known, often controversial domestic and international artists, and Mısır Apartmanı (p.124 & p.208), a fine Art Nouveau apartment block honeycombed with small galleries.

> Our author recommendations don't end here. We've flagged up our favourite places – a perfectly sited hotel, an atmospheric café, a special restaurant – throughout the Guide, highlighted with the ★ symbol.

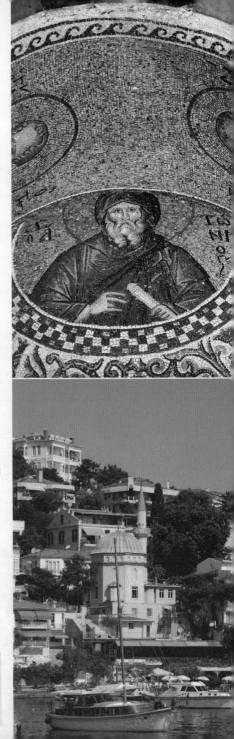

21
things not to miss

It's not possible to see everything Istanbul has to offer in one trip – and we don't suggest you try. What follows is a selection of the city's highlights, including spectacular architecture, outstanding museums and culinary treats. All entries have a page reference to take you straight into the Guide, where you can find out more. Coloured numbers refer to chapters in the Guide section.

1 **HAGHIA SOPHIA**
Page 45

The most important Byzantine building in the world – as the Hagia Sophia or "Church of the Divine Wisdom", it was the heart of eastern Christendom for close on a millennium.

2 **BASILICA CISTERN**
Page 61

It's hard to believe that something so prosaic as an underground cistern could be so fascinating, but combine Roman engineering and craftsmanship with contemporary lighting and you get one of the city's most impressive remains.

3 **DESSERT TIME**
Page 180

Join the sweet-toothed Turks and tuck into some *baklava*, preferably accompanied by real Turkish Maraş ice cream, in the famous *Karaköy Güllüoğlu* (see p.182).

9 MEYHANE CULTURE
Page 177

No visit to Istanbul is complete without a no-holds-barred night out at a lively *meyhane* (tavern).

10 SELİMİYE CAMİİ, EDİRNE
Page 270

The dome of this sixteenth-century mosque appears to float effortlessly above the faithful praying below.

11 HIPPODROME
Page 63

The arena of the Roman, then the Byzantine city, the Hippodrome is now an open park area still boasting the Egyptian Obelisk.

12 DOLMABAHÇE PALACE
Page 131

The late-Ottoman Dolmabahçe Palace in Beşiktaş dominates the Bosphorus waterfront.

13 THE ARCHEOLOGY MUSEUM
Page 58

Discover Istanbul's fascinating history in this superb museum.

14 TOPKAPI PALACE
Page 50

The symbolic and political centre of an empire that stretched from the Balkans to Arabia and the Russian steppes to North Africa.

ISTANBUL MODERN
Page 115
Istanbul's answer to London's Tate Modern.

 TROY
Page 259
A giant wooden horse guards the entrance to the ancient remains at Troy.

 FOOTBALL
Page 225
Football in Turkey is dominated by Istanbul's "Big Three": Beşiktaş, Fenerbahçe and Galatasaray.

 KARIYE MUSEUM
Page 94
This fine museum contains some of the best Byzantine mosaics and frescoes in existence.

 SÜLEYMANİYE MOSQUE COMPLEX
Page 82
This mosque complex combines sanctity and architectural merit in equal measure.

 VISITING A HAMAM
Page 227
Istanbul's historic *hamams* provide a relaxing way to round off a day's sightseeing.

NIGHTLIFE
Page 197
The Beyoğlu area of the city is justly famed for its bars and clubs.

18

19

20

21

Itineraries

There's so much to see and do in Istanbul that it is difficult to know where to start. That's why we have come up with these four itineraries. The first and third may be done on foot, the second requires the judicious use of one of the city's vintage trams.

DAY 1

The heart of the old city, Sultanahmet, is the obvious place to begin your exploration of Istanbul.

❶ **Basilica Cistern** An eerily beautiful subterranean reminder of the city's fascinating Byzantine past. **See p.61**

❷ **Haghia Sophia** The vast interior of the domed Church of the Holy Wisdom is as breathtaking today as it was in its sixth-century heyday. **See p.44**

❸ **Lunch** Grilled-meatball specialist *Tarihi Sultanahmet Köftecisi* is so good it draws droves of locals. **See p.178**

❹ **Blue Mosque** This colossal testament to Sultan Ahmet I is a cascade of domes and semi-domes; inside it has over 5000 beautiful blue İznik tiles. **See p.64**

❺ **Hippodrome** This former chariot-racing and circus arena is today a pleasant open space dominated by a hieroglyph-covered Egyptian obelisk. **See p.63**

❻ **Church of St Sergius and Bacchus** A mosque since the Ottoman conquest of 1453, this domed gem was an important church in the Byzantine period. **See p.66**

❼ **Sokullu Mehmet Paşa Camii** Older and more intimate than the Blue Mosque, this elegant place of worship is the work of master architect Sinan. **See p.66**

DAY 2

On this day of marked contrasts, we visit what was once the home of Ottoman sultans, then cross the Golden Horn to hip Galata.

❶ **Topkapı Palace** Set in a series of walled gardens, these splendid pavilions, once the nerve centre of the Ottoman Empire, can easily take up the entire morning. **See p.50**

❷ **Spice Bazaar** Down on the waterfront, the five-hundred-year-old Spice Bazaar and bustling streets around it are the place to find all manner of comestible delights. **See p.72**

❸ **Lunch** Stroll across the 1.5km Galata Bridge to Karaköy Fish Market, where a few cheap-eat joints dish up delicious fresh fish sandwiches and platters at bargain prices. **See p.71**

❹ **Ottoman Bank Museum/SALT** A towering, Neoclassical building on Bankalar Caddesi is home to this fascinating museum and cutting-edge exhibition space. **See p.112**

❺ **Galata Tower** Head up the Art Nouveau-style Kamondo Steps to this fourteenth-century tower and ascend it for superb panoramic views. **See p.112**

❻ **İstiklal Caddesi** Grab a well-earned coffee or beer in one of the many cafés and bars in and around the city's premier shopping street, or ride the nostalgic tram up to Taksim Square. **See p.119**

ABOVE TOPKAPI PALACE AND THE BOSPHORUS RIVER

HILLTOP ISTANBUL

In its former incarnation as Constantinople, this city was proud to have been built, like Rome, on seven hills. This fascinating stroll through the backstreets will take you up three of them.

❶ Süleymaniye Complex Dominating the city's third hill, this beautiful complex, complete with mosque, baths, religious schools, hospital, library and shops, is named after the Ottoman Empire's greatest ruler, Süleyman. **See p.82**

❷ Vefa Bozacısı This Istanbul institution has been serving up the delicious fermented-millet drink *boza* at this building since 1896. Its health-giving properties will help you on your way. **See p.179**

❸ Aqueduct of Valens This great example of late-Roman engineering reaches a height of 18m, where it crosses busy Atatürk Bulvarı. **See p.84**

❹ Lunch Ringing the lively Women's Bazaar are a number of Kurdish restaurants – try *Siirt Şeref Büryan* for lamb cooked in a clay *tandır* oven. **See p.188**

❺ Fatih Camii The fourth hill is crowned by the "Mosque of the Conqueror", built in 1463 on the site of an important Byzantine church; it's at the heart of what is, today, the city's most conservative district. **See p.92**

❻ Yavuz Selim Camii The austerely beautiful prayer hall of this early sixteenth-century mosque is topped by an elegant shallow dome; the views over the Golden Horn are equally beautiful. **See p.92**

❼ Fener Greek Patriarchate The interior of the Patriarchate's Church of St George features glittering gilt iconostases and frescoes. **See p.99**

❽ Golden Horn Stroll along the shores of the Golden Horn, past the cast-iron Church of St Stephen of the Bulgars, to quaint Ayvansaray pier and catch a ferry back to the Galata Bridge. **See p.100**

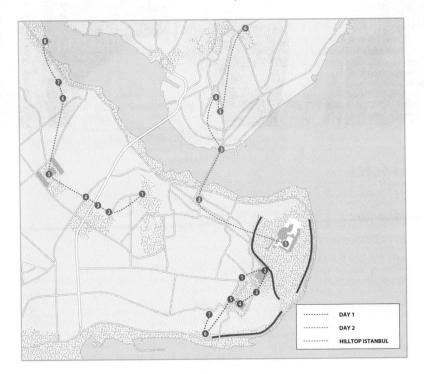

Basics

Getting there

Flights to Istanbul from the UK and Ireland take between three and a little over four hours depending on your starting point. Only two carriers fly direct from the US and Canada, so most North Americans reach Istanbul via a European gateway airport. Many travellers from Australia and New Zealand use a Round-the-World (RTW) ticket that includes the city, but there are direct flights from South Africa. Note that there are two international airports in Istanbul (see pp.23–24), with a third scheduled for completion in 2018.

Making an early booking, being flexible and (especially if flying from the US) avoiding weekend flights are the keys to getting the best deal regardless of season. There's not necessarily a big difference in price between summer and winter, though as most people tend to visit Istanbul in the warmer months (April–Oct), seat demand is consequently higher and prices tend to jump alarmingly unless you book very early. Christmas and New Year, Easter and other school holidays, not to mention Turkish national and religious holidays, also see hikes in seat prices.

Travelling overland by train, bus or car from Britain or elsewhere in Europe is just about feasible, but takes far longer than flying and will most likely cost more.

Flights from the UK and Ireland

Three **budget airlines** fly to Istanbul. Return flights from Stansted with Pegasus (Ⓦflypgs.com) to Sabiha Gökçen start as low as £95 in winter (Nov–March), rising to over £300 for late, summer-season bookings. easyJet (Ⓦeasyjet.com) fly from Luton year-round to Sabiha Gökçen starting at £30, and rising to £250 for late, summer-period bookings; from April to November they also fly from Gatwick for similar prices. Atlas Jet (Ⓦatlasjet.com) flies daily from Luton to Atatürk Airport for around £250 return in summer, £130 in winter.

Book early and scheduled flights can be very good value and often leave at more sociable hours. However, cheaper fares often have strict restrictions on date changes or refunds.

The widest choice of scheduled flights from the UK is with the Turkish national carrier, Turkish Airlines (THY; Ⓦturkishairlines.com). THY links London Heathrow with Istanbul five times daily with fares from £155 low season, and upwards of £300 in high. There are two flights daily from Manchester (£218 low season) and one daily from Edinburgh (around £210 low season) and Birmingham (£180 low season). British Airways (Ⓦbritishairways.com) has three daily services from London Heathrow to Istanbul from £175 low season.

From Belfast, there are year-round daily scheduled services with British Airways, involving a stop in London or Manchester, prices start from £270 low season. From Dublin, direct daily flight are operated by Turkish Airlines, starting at €200 in low season.

Flights from North America

The cheapest way to reach Istanbul from North America is to pick up a bargain transatlantic fare to Europe, then arrange the final Istanbul-bound leg of the journey yourself (for onward flights from the UK, see p.21).

Turkish Airlines (THY; Ⓦturkishairlines.com) is the only carrier flying direct year-round **from the US**, operating three daily flights (twice daily in winter) from New York (JFK), several weekly from Los Angeles and Washington DC and daily out of Chicago. Delta Airlines (Ⓦdelta.com) fly out of JFK daily in the summer, several weekly in the winter, using various European hubs. United Airlines (Ⓦunited.com) generally has the cheapest stopping fares, via Frankfurt. European carriers, such as British Airways (Ⓦbritishairways.com), Air France (Ⓦairfrance.com), KLM (Ⓦklm.com), Alitalia (Ⓦalitalia.com) and Swiss (Ⓦswiss.com), route through **European hubs** such as London, Paris, Frankfurt, Milan and Zürich, with the best choice probably being Lufthansa (Ⓦlufthansa.com) via Frankfurt.

A BETTER KIND OF TRAVEL

At Rough Guides we are passionately committed to travel. We believe it helps us understand the world we live in and the people we share it with – and of course tourism is vital to many developing economies. But the scale of modern tourism has also damaged some places irreparably, and climate change is accelerated by most forms of transport, especially flying. All Rough Guides' flights are carbon-offset, and every year we donate money to a variety of environmental charities.

Fares for direct flights (valid for a month) out of New York with THY start from US$860 in the winter low season and up to US$2000 in the summer peak season (return). Indirect flights start from around US$730.

There is only one direct flight **from Canada** to Turkey, with THY flying daily between Toronto and Istanbul; low-season fares start from Can$1090. Otherwise, several airlines fly from Canada to Istanbul via major European hubs, with winter prices from Can$690.

Flights from Australia, New Zealand and South Africa

There are no direct flights from **Australia or New Zealand** to Turkey. However, several weekly scheduled flights will get you there after either a plane change or short layover in the airline's hub city – typically Bahrain, Bangkok, Singapore or Milan – before the final leg of the journey. A marginally less expensive, but far more time-consuming strategy would involve taking a flight to London and then proceeding from there with, say, easyJet (w easyjet.com).

Two-stop itineraries from Sydney range from around Aus$2180 in low season to Aus$2800 in high season with Turkish Airlines via Seoul. From **Auckland**, Lufthansa (w lufthansa.com), Singapore Airlines (w singaporeair.com) and Emirates (w emirates.com) fly to Istanbul from NZ$2300 year-round.

Round-the-World (RTW) tickets including Turkey use a combination of airlines, and could be worth considering for a long trip taking in many destinations; generally, some free stopovers are allowed, with low-season fares starting at Aus$2850, NZ$2400.

From **South Africa**, Turkish Airlines (w turkishair lines.com) run direct flights five times a week from **Johannesburg** to Istanbul with low-season prices starting around ZAR10,900. There are also flights from **Cape Town** with several airlines. South Africa Airways (w flysaa.com) flies daily via Frankfurt or Munich, but these are longer and more expensive, with winter prices starting from ZAR6350.

By train

As travelling to Istanbul **by train** is both slow and expensive it will largely appeal to rail buffs or those wishing to stop off en route. Given ongoing transport infrastructure works in and around Istanbul (see p.27), the best route **from the UK** is: London–Paris–Munich–Bucharest–Turkish border–Istanbul, with overnight trains between Paris and Munich, and Munich and Bucharest, and the stretch from the border to the city done by bus. Unfortunately, trains from Europe no longer run directly to Istanbul's historic Sirkeci station, which has been demoted to a stop on the new Marmaray metro line (see p.27). On completion of this metro line (date uncertain), trains from Europe should start running to Halkalı (16km west of the city centre), from where it will be a short metro ride to the city centre.

Each leg for the train journey from the UK needs to be booked separately, so you can stop off in any of the cities where you change trains, but the cost, a minimum of £265 one way, makes the purchase of an InterRail pass advisable.

InterRail passes

The best train deal is provided by an **InterRail pass** (w interrail.eu), which offers unlimited travel (except for express train supplements and reservation fees) on a zonal basis within thirty European rail networks. These passes are only available to European residents, and you must provide proof of residency to purchase one. To reach Turkey via the route described above, you need a Global Pass. For under-26s, you're looking at €442 (£369) for a pass valid for one month's second-class travel covering thirty countries, including Turkey; this costs €668 (£558) if you're over 26. A cheaper alternative is their five-days-travel-within-ten-days option – €184 (£153) for under-26s, or €281 (£234) for over-26s. It's possible to travel first class on an over-26s' pass at a considerably higher cost.

InterRail passes do not allow free travel between Britain and the Continent, although InterRail pass holders are eligible for discounts on rail travel in Britain and Northern Ireland, the cross-Channel ferries, and the London-to-Paris Eurostar service.

Packages and special-interest holidays

Although it's easy enough to sort out your own flight to, and accommodation in, Istanbul, many people still prefer to book a package, partly to avoid the hassle but also because they can actually work out cheaper than a DIY visit. A three-night city break to Istanbul starts at around £230 for three-star B&B accommodation, including flights. A stay of the same duration in one of the city's classic luxury hotels will cost upwards of £1100. The determining price for city breaks is the departure airport – the cheapest options from the UK take advantage of easyJet's Luton– or Gatwick–Istanbul runs. **Specialist holidays** focusing on Byzantine art, Ottoman architecture and the like, which rely on the services of a guest lecturer, are much more expensive, costing upwards of £1900 for a week.

AGENTS AND OPERATORS

Adventure World Australia ☎ 02 8913 0755 or ☎ 08 9226 4524, Ⓦ adventureworld.com.au; New Zealand ☎ 09 524 5118, Ⓦ adventureworld.co.nz. Tours of western and central Turkey, which include Istanbul and also the Gallipoli landing sites.

Anatolian Sky UK ☎ 0121 325 5500, Ⓦ anatolian-sky.co.uk. Turkey specialist offering city breaks in classic hotels in Istanbul.

Andante Travels UK ☎ 01722 715 800, Ⓦ andantetravels.co.uk. Relaxed one-week guided tours of Istanbul's Byzantine and Ottoman heritage, with a specialist guide-lecturer, plus fascinating week-long off-the-beaten-track explorations of lesser-known sites by foot and using public transport.

Cachet Travel UK ☎ 020 8847 3846, Ⓦ cachet-travel.co.uk. Three-day breaks in a couple of decent hotels in Sultanahmet, with additional nights' option.

Cultural Folk Tours US ☎ 1 800 935 TURK or ☎ 858 566 5951, Ⓦ boraozkok.com. Up to nine annual departures by this 1978-established San Diego-based company, led (and musically accompanied) by Bora Özkök. Offers several bus tours that get off the beaten track, but will arrange private tours in Istanbul and environs for interested parties.

Martin Randall UK ☎ 020 8742 3355, Ⓦ martinrandall.com. Offers an interesting week-long art history-orientated itinerary in Istanbul, visiting all the major sites.

North South Travel UK ☎ 01245 608291, Ⓦ northsouthtravel .co.uk. Flight agency offering discounted fares – profits are used to support projects in the developing world, especially the promotion of sustainable tourism.

Rosetta Travel Northern Ireland ☎ 028 9064 4996, Ⓦ rosettatravel.com. Reliable flight and holiday agent, offering low flight prices out of Belfast (and Dublin), with city breaks in Istanbul.

STA Travel Canada ☎ 1 888 427 5639; Australia ☎ 134 782; New Zealand ☎ 0800 474 400; South Africa ☎ 086 178 1781; UK ☎ 0800 819 9339; US ☎ 1 800 781 4040; Ⓦ statravel.com. Worldwide specialists in low-cost flights and tours for students and under-26s. Also student IDs, travel insurance, car rental, rail passes and more.

Sun Island Tours Australia ☎ 02 9283 3840, Ⓦ sunislandtours .com.au. Specialize in eastern Mediterranean destinations, with several options in Turkey, the most pertinent of which combines Istanbul with ANZAC (Gallipoli).

Trailfinders Australia ☎ 1300 780 212; Republic of Ireland ☎ 01 677 7888; UK ☎ 020 7628 7628; Ⓦ trailfinders.com. One of the best-informed and most efficient agents for independent travellers.

Travel Cuts Canada ☎ 1 800 667 2887; US ☎ 1 800 592 2887; Ⓦ travelcuts.com. Canadian student-travel organization.

Tulip Holidays UK ☎ 020 8211 0001, Ⓦ tulipholidays.com. Turkey and North Cyprus specialists, offering city breaks in a range of hotels in both Sultanahmet and Taksim. A good bet for combining the metropolis with a beach holiday on the Med or Aegean.

Wilderness Travel US ☎ 1 800 368 2794 or ☎ 510 558 2488, Ⓦ wildernesstravel.com. Offers two eleven-day trips, each including two days in Istanbul: one encompasses Istanbul, Cappadocia and the Aegean, the other follows a similar geography but the Aegean section is by yacht. Both allow three-day add-ons in Istanbul.

RAIL CONTACTS

Euro Railways Ⓦ eurorailways.com. Really good all-in-one outlet for all sorts of passes and tickets, though you have to book tickets either stage by stage or buy a travel pass.

The Man in Seat 61 Ⓦ seat61.com. This essential, non-commercial site is full of practical advice and planning on any train journey from the UK to just about anywhere in Eurasia (including Turkey). You can't buy tickets here, but all the necessary contacts are provided.

Arrival

Istanbul's main points of arrival are Atatürk International airport on the European side of the city (used by the majority of scheduled airlines), and Sabiha Gökçen, across the Bosphorus in Asia (used mainly by budget European carriers). Once the Marmaray metro line is completed (see p.27) trains from Europe should arrive at Halkalı, 16km from the city centre, from where the metro will take passengers to Sirkeci station in Eminönü, a short hop from lively Beyoğlu and Taksim, and the heart of the old city, Sultanahmet.

By plane

Istanbul's **Atatürk International airport** (Atatürk Hava Limanı; ☎ 0212 465 3000, Ⓦ ataturkairport .com) is 24km west of the centre at Yeşilköy, near the Sea of Marmara. It has two connected terminals, a ten-minute (covered) walk apart: international (*dişhatları*) and domestic (*içhatları*). The Havataş **bus service** (Ⓦ havatas.com) runs from both terminals to the Turkish Airlines (THY) office on the north side of Taksim Square (every 30min; 4am–1am; ₺10); journey time into Istanbul is thirty minutes to an hour, depending on traffic. For Sultanahmet and the old city, get off at the earlier Aksaray stop, from where it's a five-minute walk north and uphill to the T1 tramline (see pp.26–27), which runs east to Sultanahmet, **Eminönü** and across the Golden Horn to Galata. Alternatively, a **taxi** from the airport should cost around ₺40 to Sultanahmet and ₺50 to Taksim; make sure the driver uses the meter. Note that many old city hotels provide free shuttle-bus collections for guests staying more than three nights.

The M1 **Metro** (see p.27) runs from Atatürk International airport to the city centre (6am–midnight; every 6min). To reach it, follow signs for "Metro/Rapid Transit" and go down the escalators; you'll need to buy two *jetons* (small plastic tokens; ₺4 each) from a vending machine. Alternatively it's possible to buy the Istanbulkart (see p.25), for ₺10, also from a vending machine near the barriers, and top it up with travel credit at another machine. The M1 metro connects with the T1 tramway at Zeytinburnu; alight here and walk the short distance to the Zeytinburnu tram stop (this is where the second jeton is required). The tram runs to Sultanahmet: the entire journey from the airport is 30–45min. Alternatively take the M1 Metro to its terminus in Yenikapı, change to the Marmaray line and go one stop to Sirkeci, in the heart of the old city. For Galata and Beyoğlu change from the M1 to the M2 metro at Yenikapı and take the train across the Golden Horn to Şişhane or Taksim.

The city's second airport, **Sabiha Gökçen** (☎0216 585 5000, ⍟sgairport.com), used by easyJet and other low-cost European airlines, is out beyond the suburb of Pendik, in Asia. Shuttle buses run to Taksim Square (4am–1am every half-hour; ₺13), taking at least an hour. Taxis to Taksim cost around ₺75. The cheapest option is to take city bus #E/3 to Levent Metro, then the M2 Metro to Taksim – electronic tickets are available from a kiosk behind the Havataş bus stand. An alternative if you arrive in daylight hours and are travelling light is to take either the frequent #E/10 or #E/11 bus to Kadıköy (tickets sold at the kiosk behind the Havataş bus stand) on the Asian shore. Buses drop you right by the Turyol private ferry boat pier, from where ferries run approximately every twenty minutes to both Eminönü (old city) and Karaköy (Galata and Beyoğlu). Tickets are ₺4, the journey takes around fifteen minutes and the ferries run 6.45am–9.30pm daily. Reaching the European side of the city by sea is a perfect intro-duction to Istanbul.

By train

Owing to engineering works between Istanbul and the Turkish–Bulgarian frontier, and ongoing transport infrastructure work within the metrop-olis, at the time of writing all trains from Europe were terminating at the border, with onward bus travel to Istanbul provided (see p.22). The former terminus of the famed Orient Express, Sirkeci station, is now solely a stop on the Marmaray metro line. The city's other great old station, **Haydarpaşa**, on the Asian side of the Bosphorus, has been similarly sidelined by the Marmaray project (see p.27) and trains for Anatolian Turkey are likely to leave from suburban Pendik on its completion. Completion dates are being constantly revised and set back – see ⍟seat61 .com for updates.

By bus

There are two major **otogars** (bus stations) in Istanbul: Esenler (also known as Büyük Otogar) is 10km northwest of the centre on the E800 (Istanbul–Edirne toll road); Harem is on the Asian side between Üsküdar and Kadıköy. All national bus services stop at both, regardless of destination, and both are open 24 hours.

Esenler bus station (☎0212 658 0505, ⍟esenler iotogari.com) is well organized, and some 150 companies have numbered ticket stands here. Most companies run free buses to and from Taksim, or can arrange for you to travel on one run by another company. To get to Sultanahmet from Esenler, take the M1 Metro (6am–midnight; every 6min) from the metro stop in the centre of the *otogar* to Aksaray and switch to the T1 tram to Sultanahmet. Taxis into town cost around ₺25. Travelling from the city centre to Esenler by metro, remember to get off at *otogar*, not Esenler station. There's a (free) shuttle service from Taksim or Sultanahmet to Esenler (usually 1hr before departure) for tickets booked through a travel agent or bus company's city offices.

Arriving in Istanbul by bus from Asia, it's worth disembarking at **Harem bus station** (☎0216 333 3763), saving a tedious journey to Esenler through terrible traffic snarl-ups. From Harem, regular ferries cross the Bosphorus to Sirkeci (daily 7am–10.30pm; half-hourly), while private operators run boats to Beşiktaş and Kabataş. Dolmuşes depart every few minutes for Kadıköy and Üsküdar, leaving from the south side of the complex, beyond the ticket offices. From either of these suburbs, ferries cross to Eminönü, and from Üsküdar to Beşiktaş as well (for Taksim), as do buses (try the #110) and dolmuşes. Taxis are available everywhere, but you must pay the bridge toll (₺4.25) on top of the fare.

By ferry

Car ferries, operated by IDO (Istanbul Deniz Otobüsleri; enquiries on ☎0212 444 4436,

@ido.com.tr), cross the Bosphorus from Harem to Sirkeci (daily 7.00am–10.30pm; half-hourly). **Sea bus**, car and passenger services from Yalova, Bandırma (on the İzmir–Istanbul route) and Güzelyalı (Bursa) arrive at the **Yenikapı ferry terminal**, off Kennedy Caddesi just south of Aksaray. From here, catch the Marmaray metro one stop east to Sirkeci (for Sultanahmet and the old city) or the M2 metro north to Şişhane (for Galata and Beyoğlu or Taksim).

Cruise-ship arrivals will go through customs and immigration procedures at **Karaköy International Maritime Passenger Terminal**, across the Galata Bridge from Eminönü. From here (Karaköy-Galata) take the tram to Sultanahmet, the Tünel up to Beyoğlu, or the tram to Kabataş then the modern funicular to Taksim; alternatively, take a taxi (around ₺9 to Taksim, ₺8 to Sultanahmet).

City transport

Istanbul has a wide choice of transport, from a modern metro and tram network through ferries and catamarans to a period underground funicular. With over eleven million commuters a day, all public transport tends to be overcrowded, and pickpocketing is a concern, so use your common sense when travelling.

The tramway links most parts of the city that you're likely to want to visit, and is by far the easiest way to negotiate certain sections of the city. The metro system had been much improved by the opening of the tunnel under the Bosphorus and bridge across the Golden Horn; the bus system is daunting; while taxis and dolmuşes (shared taxis) are very reasonably priced, with knowledgeable – if not necessarily good – drivers. Ferries across the Bosphorus and up the Golden Horn are also a great way of getting around – the year-round Bosphorus Cruise (see p.147) is a favoured way of seeing the sights.

Traffic jams are unavoidable in Istanbul, though the historic Sultanahmet district is relatively traffic-free and easily explored on foot, as is most of Beyoğlu. Otherwise, expect to spend some time in tailbacks as you travel to and from other areas of interest – it can take an hour by road from Sultanahmet to Ortaköy, for example. Where possible, travel by tram, metro or ferry, though these can all be jam-packed at peak times. Kids under 6 travel free on city transport. A useful public transport journey planning website is @buradanoraya.com.

Buses

Istanbul's **buses** (otobüs in Turkish) come in a range of colours; the red-and-cream, green, and green/blue municipality buses all have "IETT" written on them. There are also a substantial number of privately run buses, mainly light blue. The main bus stops boast large route maps and lists of services. Most buses run daily from 6.30am to 11.30pm, though last buses depart from the outlying suburbs

ISTANBULKART – THE SMART-CARD WAY TO TRAVEL

An **Istanbulkart** (a credit-card-sized smart card) is a must if you're staying for a few days and want to travel around the city using public transport. The card costs a refundable ₺6 from kiosks in busy hubs such as Eminönü, Sultanahmet, Sirkeci, Beyazıt/Grand Bazaar and Aksaray, though some vendors may charge a small mark-up. Alternatively you can buy it for ₺10 from machines with touch-screen instructions located close to major transport stops, which includes ₺4 credit. You "charge" the card with travel credit at either the kiosks or at a machine labelled "Elektronik bilet ve dolum cihazı" (electronic ticket top-up machine); there are on-screen instructions in English and German as well as Turkish. Machines accept ₺10, ₺20, ₺50 and ₺100 notes, but badly creased ones are often rejected. The passes are accepted on all municipal and some private buses, sea buses, ferries, the metro and the tram.

At the entrance to tram, metro, train and ferry transport stops there are turnstiles; hold the Istanbulkart against the receptor and the journey cost (₺2.15) is deducted. For journeys taken with 90min of the last the fare is only ₺1.45. As the alternative ticket option, a jeton, costs ₺4 per journey, it's easy to see how much you can save by using this travel card. Note that the Istanbulkart can be used by several people – there's no need to buy one card per person if you're travelling around as a couple or group, though you will have to swipe it for each person travelling.

The Istanbulkart is an updated version of the akbil system (which worked in the same way but used a metal disc held in a plastic key) and you'll see many locals using the old devices. It's important to know this as many places selling and charging the Istanbulkart advertise themselves only with a sign reading "Akbil dolum merkezi" or "Akbil dolum bayii".

much earlier. Either use an Istanbulkart (see p.25) or buy an electronic ticket in advance from one of the white kiosks next to the main bus, tram or metro stops (↜4), which you swipe across the screen next to the driver on boarding.

On the European side, the **main bus terminals** are at Eminönü, Vezneciler (Beyazıt), Taksim Square, Beşiktaş and ˙Aksaray; and on the Asian side, at Üsküdar and Kadıköy. No buses pass through Sultanahmet, so walk, or catch the tram three stops, down the hill to the bus station at Eminönü (in front of the ferry terminal). From **Eminönü**, there are buses to Taksim, west-bound services to Aksaray and Topkapı, and services to the Bosphorus shore, through Beşiktaş, Ortaköy and Arnavutköy to Bebek, where you'll have to change to continue on through the suburbs as far as the village of Rumeli Kavağı. Buses from **Taksim Square** head through Mecidiyeköy to the northern suburbs, down along the Bosphorus through Beşiktaş, Ortaköy and Aranvutköy, and across the Horn to Topkapı and Aksaray. The

Metrobus system, where buses use dedicated lanes, have speeded things up for commuters but the routes are of little interest to visitors.

Trams

The **main tram** service, or T1 *tramvay* (see box, p.29 for the **antique tram**) runs from Zeytinburnu via Topkapı to Aksaray (where it connects with the M1 Metro (or *hafif* metro), Laleli/Üniversite, Beyazıt, Cemberlitaş, Sultanahmet, downhill to Eminönü, and across the Galata Bridge to Karaköy (Galata), Tophane, Fındıklı and Kabataş. It is the most useful mode of transport in the city for the majority of visitors, linking the old city (Sultanahmet and the Grand Bazaar) with the cultural and nightlife hub of Beyoğlu across the Golden Horn. Trams are frequent and operate from 6am to midnight. Approaching trams signal their arrival with a bell, and passengers must wait on the concrete platforms, placed at regular intervals along the tracks. Note that the tram stops are marked, confusingly, by the same "M"

USEFUL BUS ROUTES

If you can get the hang of it, buses are an OK way to travel around the city, and for some locations are the only feasible option, short of an expensive taxi ride. For information in English on all routes, check Ⓦ iett.gov.tr/en.

ASIAN SIDE
#12 and **#14** Kadıköy to Üsküdar.
#15 Üsküdar up the Bosphorus to Beylerbeyi and Kanlıca.
#15/A Beykoz to Anadolu Kavağı.

EUROPEAN SIDE
#22 Kabataş up the Bosphorus including Beşiktaş, Ortaköy, Kuruçeşme, Arnavutköy, Bebek, Emirgan and İstinye.
#25/A Haciosman Metro to Maslak, Tarabya, Sariyer and Rumeli Kavağı.
#25/E Kabataş to Sariyer via Beşiktaş, Ortaköy, Arnavütköy, Bebek and Emirgan.
#28 Edirnekapı to Beşiktaş via Fatih, Eminönü, Karaköy, Tophane and Kabataş.
#28/T Topkapı to Beşiktaş via Fatih, Eminönü, Karaköy, Tophane and Kabataş.
#30/D Yenikapı to Ortaköy via Unkapanı/Atatürk Bridge, Karaköy and Beşiktaş.
#36/V and **#37Y** Vezneciler (Beyazıt) to Edirnekapı via Fatih/Yavuz Selim Camii (city land walls and Kariye Museum).
#38/E Eminönü to Edirnekapı (city land walls) via Unkapanı/Atatürk Bridge and Fatih.
#40 Taksim up the Bosphorus including Beşiktaş, Kuruçeşme, Arnavutköy, Bebek, Emirgan, İstinye, Tarabya and Sariyer.
#43 Taksim to Beşiktaş via Nişantaşı and Maçka.
#54/HT Taksim to upper Golden Horn (for Miniatürk, Rami Koç Museum and Santralıstanbul).
#54/EB Beyazıt to Eyüp via Aksaray, Fatih and Edirnekapı (for Northwest Quarter and land walls).
#55T Taksim to Balat and Eyüp.
#80T Taksim to Yedikule (city land walls).
#87 Taksim to Edirnekapı (city land walls and Kariye Museum).
#96T Taksim to Atatürk airport.
#151 Sariyer to Kilyos (Black Sea) via Rumeli Fener.
#830 *Otogar* to Taksim via Fatih, Unkapanı and Tepebaşı.

THE MARMARAY PROJECT

In the winter of 2013, the sections of tubing forming the Bosphorus **tunnel** were finally opened to the public and an underwater link between European and Asian Istanbul, an idea that first hit the drawing board back in the Ottoman period, had finally become a reality. The tunnel forms part of a rail line that will eventually stretch some 76km, from Halkalı on the European side to Gebze in Asia, and will link the city's two international airports, Atatürk and Sabiha Gökçen. The section running through the old city, from Sirkeci west to Yenikapı and onto Kazlıçeşme, is underground. From Sirkeci the line goes east under the Bosphorus; the first stop on the Asian side is Üsküdar. The public opening was originally scheduled for 2011, but work was delayed by the unearthing of many important archeological finds during construction, notably a massive Byzantine harbour, complete with more than thirty ships, at Yenikapı. A purpose-built museum was being constructed at Yenikapı at the time of writing to exhibit ships and other artefacts. The new rail link integrates with the rest of the city's transport system, and on completion it should be the linchpin between the European and Asian rail networks.

sign as the Metro. *Jetons* (₺4) can be bought at *Jetonmatik* machines located near most tram stops and are deposited in turnstiles on entry. Better, use an Istanbulkart (see box, p.25).

The Metro

There are now several Metro lines in the city, though only the M1, M2 and Marmaray lines (see transport map) will be of interest to the vast majority of visitors. The M1 Metro, or *hafif* metro, runs west from Yenikapı via the inter-city *otogar* near Esenler, to Atatürk International airport. Only small sections of this line run underground. The M2 Metro runs from Yenikapı on the shores of the Sea of Marmara north under the historic peninsula on which the old city stands before crossing the Golden Horn by a controversial bridge. It then goes back underground, with the first stop at Şişhane, at the Tünel end of İstiklal Caddesi, before continuing north to Taksim Square, Omsmanbey, Şişli, Gayrettepe Levent, and right out to Haciosmanbey.

The Marmaray metro line will eventually run from Halkalı, 16km west of the centre, to Gebze, 68km southeast of the centre in Asia. At the time of writing, the line runs from Kazlıçeşme near the land walls of Theodosius, via Yenikapı to Sırkeci, then under the Bosphorus to Üsküdar.

Metro trains run approximately every six minutes between 6am and midnight; *jetons* (₺4) are inserted in turnstiles on entry, or use the Istanbulkart.

Funiculars and the cable car

The **antique funicular** between Karaköy and İstiklal Caddesi in Beyoğlu is known as the **Tünel**, and connects with the antique tram (see p.29) on İstiklal Caddesi. A **modern funicular** (F1 on the Public Transport map) links Kabataş, at the northern end of the tram line, with Taksim Square (and the M2 Metro). The **cable car** linking the southern shore of the Golden Horn in Eyüp with the *Pierre Loti* café and Eyüp cemetery does not link with the rail or tram systems, but does save your legs. Use your Istanbulkart (see p.25) or buy a *jeton* for all of these.

Dolmuşes

Dolmuşes are shared taxis (usually in the form of a minibus) running on fixed routes, departing only when full ("dolmuş" means "full"). Services on longer routes tend to run along main arteries and depart according to a schedule known only to their drivers. Dolmuşes display their destination in the window. A flat **fare** (fixed by the municipality) is levied: watch what Turkish passengers are paying – usually a little more than a municipality bus – shout your destination to the driver and pay accordingly, passing the money via other passengers. Dolmuş stands at points of origin are denoted with a signposted "D". Services can be hailed at any point along the route; they're most frequent during rush hour and operate later than the regular buses, sometimes until 2am. To get off, call: "*müsait bir yerde*" or "*inecek* (pronounced "inejek") *var*".

The only dolmuş routes of interest to most visitors are the yellow minibuses departing from the northern end of Tarlabaşı Bulvarı, just below Taksim Square, which run across into the old town and along the Sea of Marmara to the city land walls near Yedikule, or those running up the Asian side of the Bosphorus between Kadıköy and Üsküdar and beyond.

PUBLIC TRANSPORT WHO'S WHO

Metro and tram services are operated by Istanbul Ulaşım (**w** Istanbul-ulasim.com .tr), as are the Piyerloti cable car and F1 funicular. Istanbul Elektrik Tramway ve Tünel (IETT; **w** iett.gov.tr) operate most city buses, historic trams and the nineteenth-century Tünel funicular. Fast ferries and sea buses (catamarans) are run by Istanbul Deniz Otobüsleri (IDO; **w** ido.com.tr), slower public ferries by Şehir Hatları (**w** sehirhatlari.com.tr).

Taxis

Taxis are ubiquitous, with over nineteen thousand legal *taksici* (taxi drivers) in the city. They are invariably painted yellow. **Fares** are reasonable, with rates around ₺2.7 per km, with an extra toll of ₺4.25 when crossing either of the Bosphorus bridges. All taxis are equipped with **meters**, but check that the driver switches it on to avoid arguments later. If there's any trouble, start discussing the *polis*, especially at any suggestion of a flat fare or if you think the driver has taken the longest possible route (both distinct possibilities), and if necessary note the registration number and call the Tourist Police (see p.35). To get an idea of fares before making a journey check **w** taksiyle.com, a site with a useful fare calculator and city map, or check (or book) through your hotel. Unregistered cabs are a major headache, with some ten thousand working the streets.

Ferries, sea buses and water taxis

The main **ferry** company is the efficient Sehir Hatları (City Lines; ☎ 444 1851, **w** sehirhatlari.com .tr). A timetable, available from the ferry terminals and from tourist offices and their website, is essential so that you can be sure when the last ferry back departs, as timings do change. On the busiest routes – such as Karaköy to Haydarpaşa and Kadıköy, there are generally three to five ferries an hour between 6am and midnight; all have a flat fare of ₺4 each way. For both ferries and the faster sea buses (see pp.28–29), buy a *jeton* and deposit it at the turnstile on entry, or use your Istanbulkart. The busiest routes are also served by several other small, privately run ferries, many under the umbrella of

the cooperative **Turyol**. Most Turyol boats leave from a terminal just west of the Galata Bridge in Eminönü, or over the water in Karaköy, again just west of the Galata Bridge, the destinations being Haydarpaşa and Kadıköy, respectively; tickets are sold at kiosks on the quayside, and from machines.

At the main **City Ferry Terminal** at Eminönü – between Sirkeci station and the Galata Bridge – there's a line of ferry quays or terminals (*iskelesi* in Turkish). On the west side of the Galata Bridge is Yemiş İskelesi, for Haliç ferries up the Golden Horn to Eyüp via Kasımpaşa and Ayvansaray (roughly hourly 7am–8pm). The ferry actually originates across the Bosphorus in Üsküdar so on the return journey make sure you get off at Eminönü. The terminal nearest to (the east side of) the Galata Bridge is Boğaz İskelesi, from where Sehir Hatları ferries run up the Bosphorus to Rumeli Kavağı (see box, p.147). Ferries from the terminal just east of this, the Hezarfen Ahmet Çelebi, cross to Üsküdar (daily 6.35am–11.30pm), while east of this the Evliya Çelebi terminal has boats crossing to Kadıköy (daily 7.30am–9pm). The Katıb Çelebi terminal is a book store and information point; east of it is the IDO car ferry terminal for Harem (daily 8am–9.30pm).

Regular Sehir Hatları ferries link Karaköy (on the other, north side of the Galata Bridge) to Kadıköy (daily 6.30am–midnight), some ferries also stop at Haydarpaşa. From Kabataş, ferries cross the Bosphorus to Kadıköy (Mon–Fri 7.20am–7.30pm), with a daily service (7am–9pm) from Beşiktaş to Üsküdar and to Kadıköy (8.15am–9.45pm). There are also regular ferries to the Princes' Islands from Kabataş (daily 6.50am–midnight, less frequent in winter; see p.159).

From Boğaz İskelesi, Sehir Hatları operates the popular daily **Bosphorus Cruise** (Boğaz Hatti; see box, p.147), a boat trip to Rumeli Kavağı and Anadolu Kavağı, the most distant villages up the Bosphorus on the European and Asian sides respectively (June–Oct daily 10.35am and 1.35pm).

Fast **sea buses** (*deniz otobüsleri*) run by İDO (Istanbul Deniz Otobüsleri; ☎ 0212 444 4436, **w** ido .com.tr) run from Kabataş, at the eastern end of the tramway, across the Bosphorus and into the Sea of Marmara, though these run less frequently except at peak commuter times. Sea-bus fares are a flat ₺10 for the Princes' Islands (6–12 daily), those to Yalova and other places on the south shore of the Sea of Marmara, which vary according to demand and how far you book in advance start from ₺9. There are numerous other sea-bus routes, including Bakırköy to Bostancı via Kadıköy and Yenikapı (hourly 7.30am–10pm). **Timetables** are available from all sea-bus terminals and online. If you're heading for İznik via Yalova or Bursa, sea buses and the slightly quicker *hızlı feribot* (fast ferries) depart frequently from the terminal in Yenikapı, a stop on both the M2 and Marmaray metro lines.

Water taxis (*deniz taksi*) are massively oversubscribed so, unless the fleet is considerably increased, don't bank on whizzing up and down the Bosphorus in one. Theoretically, you call ☎444 4498, give your name and your pick-up, drop-off points and a water taxi will collect you from one of the 27 designated docks, which include the Princes' Islands as well as numerous stops on both sides of the Bosphorus as far up as Rumeli Kavağı. Unless you are a Turkish speaker, the Ⓦ deniztaksi.com website is of little use, so use your hotel to book one. There's a ₺40 standing charge per journey, ₺25 per sea mile after that.

Driving

Driving in Istanbul is extremely hazardous – after South Korea, Turkey has the second highest fatality rate in the world (with 77 deaths per 100,000 vehicles on the road; by comparison, the UK has 13 deaths for the same number of vehicles) – and should be avoided unless you're a very experienced driver, and have the wherewithal to negotiate a strange, traffic-choked metropolis with poor signposting and few parking spaces. The only time it would make any sense is if you're circling the Sea of Marmara to take in Edirne, Gallipoli, Troy, Bursa and İznik. If you're still determined to drive in the city, you need to be at least 21 years old (27 for Groups E and above) to rent a car, with a **driving licence** held for at least one year. An **International Driving Permit**, from the RAC or AA in Britain/Australasia or the AAA/CAA in North America, is not essential – your own home licence will do at a pinch – but is very helpful, especially at traffic-control points (show the police your IDP, not your main home licence, in case they decide to keep it for any reason). **Rental rates** are quite high due to expensive vehicle prices in Turkey, and the high accident rate. The agencies below have pick-up points at Atatürk International airport and (bar Europcar) Sabiha Gökçen, and offices elsewhere in Istanbul – check their websites for working hours. Expect to pay around ₺120 a day for a week's rental (ten percent more for daily rental), depending on the car.

When checking a car out, agency staff should make a thorough diagrammatic notation of any **blemishes** on the vehicle – it's in your interest to make sure they do this, otherwise you might be blamed for something you didn't do. If you have an accident serious enough to immobilize you and/or cause major damage to other people's property, the traffic police will appear and administer alcohol tests to all drivers, results of which must also be submitted along with an official **accident report** (*kaza raporu*) in order to claim insurance cover. It's an offence to move a vehicle involved in a crash involving more than a minor bump before the police give the all-clear – leave it where it is, even if you're blocking traffic, otherwise all drivers involved risk an on-the-spot fine.

Fuel costs are very high because of government taxes; diesel (*mazot* or *dizel*) is ₺4.5 per litre, lead-free (*kurşunsuz*) around ₺5.15 per litre. Many of

---

TRAVEL NOSTALGIA: THE TÜNEL AND THE ANTIQUE TRAM

The easy way to make the long haul up the hill from the Golden Horn onto İstiklal Caddesi, Istanbul's premier shopping street, is via the **Tünel** (every 15min; Mon–Sat 7am–10.45pm, Sun 7.30am–10.45pm; ₺4 or ₺2.15 with the Istanbulkart). This one-stop funicular railway opened in 1875 and is the world's third-oldest passenger underground. The lower Tünel station is in Karaköy, just across the Galata Bridge, from where it takes a matter of minutes to whisk you to the upper station, at the bottom (southern) end of İstiklal Caddesi; use the Istanbulkart (see p.25) or purchase an electronic ticket from the machine just inside the Tünel building before boarding – discounted multi-use passes are available. The Rahmi M Koç Industrial Museum in Hasköy (see pp.116–117) has a restored nineteenth-century Tünel car on display, worth seeking out if you're a period-transport or nostalgia buff.

The **antique tram** rattles its way along the 1.5-kilometre length of İstiklal Caddesi from the upper Tünel station to Taksim Square (every 15min; daily 9am–9pm; ₺4), with three stops en route. Electronic tickets can be purchased in the Tünel building; the Istanbulkart is also accepted. With its turn-of-the-century look (drivers are adorned in vintage costumes) and smart red-and-cream livery, it lends pedestrianized İstiklal Caddesi a certain period charm – as well as saving your legs.

the major arteries around Istanbul are toll-only and vehicles rented from agencies at the airports are fitted with an electronic strip which is automatically read at the toll booths. On returning the vehicle the rental agency will deduct the amount of toll you have used from your credit card. There are plenty of filling stations on all major – and many minor – highways and at numerous points across Istanbul. **Credit and debit cards** (Visa Electron, Visa, Master-Card, American Express) are widely honoured for fuel purchases. As with most card transactions in Turkey, chip-and-PIN protocol is the norm. Car **repair workshops** and spare-part dealers are located in industrial zones called *sanayis* on the city's – and other town – outskirts.

CAR RENTAL AGENCIES

Avis ⓦ avis.com.
Budget ⓦ drivebudget.com.
Europcar ⓦ europcar.com.
Hertz ⓦ hertz.com.

Tours

It's worth considering a **city tour** if you're pushed for time or just don't want to plan an itinerary yourself. The more specialist options offered by Fest (see p.30) take you to some little-known sites that you may struggle to find yourself, and provide an expert guide to interpret them for you.

TOUR AGENCIES

Backpackers Travel Yeni Akbıyık Cad 22, Sultanahmet ☎ 0212 638 6343, ⓦ backpackerstravel.net. Conveniently located agency offering half- and one-day tours of the city.
Big Bus City Istanbul Aya Sofya Karşısı 1, Sultanahmet ☎ 0212 283 1396, ⓦ bigbustours.com. Big Bus offers two hop-on, hop-off open-top bus itineraries departing opposite the Haghia Sophia, one concentrating on the old city and Golden Horn, the other crossing both the Golden Horn and the Bosphorus bridge to Asia.
Fest Travel Barbaros Bul 74, Balmucu ☎ 0212 216 1036, ⓦ festtravel.com.tr. Fest has been running a variety of cultural tours around the city for 22 years, and is the official operator for the Istanbul Foundation for Culture and Arts (IKSV). Their regular programme includes a half-day on the Bosphorus, an Islamic cultural tour, a Jewish heritage day and a hop-on, hop-off bus tour of the main sites. More interesting are the walking tours where the guides, usually specialist lecturers in their field, take you to out-of-the-way, little-known sites in various quarters of the city.
Istanbul Tour Studio Halaskargazi Cad 6, Şişli ☎ 0533 355 3049, ⓦ Istanbultourstudio.com. Innovative agency offering all the standard tours plus more unusual options like cycling on the Asian shore, rowing on the Golden Horn, a street art tour and sailing trips to the Princes' Islands.

Istanbul Walks Şifahamamı Sok, Sultanahmet ☎ 0212 516 6300, ⓦ Istanbulwalks.net. A varied programme of walks running most days of the year, with licensed guides. Separate walks include the classic sites on both sides of the Golden Horn.
Kirkit Voyage Amiral Tafdil Sok 12, Sultanahmet ☎ 0212 518 2282, ⓦ kirkit.com. Very reliable company offering a variety of walking tours of the city – one concentrates on Byzantine Istanbul, another the palaces of the Bosphorus – using knowledgeable, professional guides. Also does tailor-made tours. The office is handily located if you're staying in Sultanahmet.
Turista Divan Yolu Cad 16, Sultanahmet ☎ 0212 518 6570, ⓦ turistatravel.com. Very reliable, bustling general travel agency in the heart of the old city, for everything from daily Istanbul tours to plane and train tickets and car rental.

The media

Newspapers and magazines weren't even allowed in the country until the middle of the nineteenth century; since then, however, lost time has been made up for with a vengeance.

Nearly forty mastheads, representing the full gamut of public tastes from elevated to gutter, compete for readers' attention. The airwaves were controlled exclusively by the government until the late 1980s, but with satellite dishes and overseas transmitters widely available, a vast quantity of private, cable and digital stations now flourishes across Turkey.

Turkish-language publications

Around seventy percent of the **newspapers** sold nationally are produced by two giant media conglomerates, the Doğan and Sabah groups. Three titles – *Sabah*, *Hürriyet* and *Milliyet* – dominate the middle market; slightly to the left of these stands *Radikal*, the best paper to pick up in Istanbul for listings of cinema, exhibitions and concerts. *Taraf* is more radical than *Radikal* and incurs establishment ire on virtually a daily basis. The only high-end newspaper, *Cumhuriyet*, founded as the mouthpiece of the Turkish Republic in 1924, mixes conservative nationalism with old-style socialism. Turkey's Islamist papers generally give intelligent and thoughtful coverage – of the biggest sellers, *Yeni Şafak* and *Zaman*, the former is a strong supporter of the Justice and Development (AK) Party elected to power in 2002, 2007 and 2011, while the latter takes a more independent line. The principal weekly **magazines** are the picture-driven *Tempo* and *Aktüel*, which serve up a diet of showbiz gossip, news and features.

English-language publications

The longest-running English-language **newspaper**, widely available across central Istanbul, is the *Hürriyet Daily News* (⊚ hurriyetdailynews.com). The weekend edition, covering both Saturday and Sunday, has more features and less up-to-date news than the daily. Every edition has a listings page devoted, in the main, to Istanbul. *Today's Zaman* (⊚ todayszaman .com), the English-language offshoot of *Zaman*, is backed by the controversial figure of Fetullah Gülen, an Islamic scholar/businessman currently in exile in the US and whose "Service" movement members were being purged from the judiciary, police and other Turkish institutions by the government at the time of writing. It's glossier than the *HDN* and has more features written by expats than its rival. Broadly speaking, the *HDN* follows the secular/nationalist line and *Today's Zaman* is liberal/Islamic. Both have online versions, as does new boy on the block, the dull, blatantly pro-AKP government *Daily Sabah* (⊚ daily sabah.com).

Glossy **magazines** include the bimonthly *Istanbul: The Guide*, sold at newsstands (₺10) or available free in many of the city's larger hotels. It's fine for listings of shops, restaurants, cafés and the like and has some good features; check its online version at ⊚ theguideistanbul.com for what's on listings. *TimeOut Istanbul* (⊚ timeoutIstanbul.com) the local imprint of the London listings magazine, has an eighty-page English edition (₺6) of what's-on listings and useful coverage of new bars, clubs and restaurants. The bimonthly *Cornucopia*, an expensive (£10), glossy upmarket magazine, sometimes has interesting features on Istanbul, as well as general pieces on everything from carpets to property renovation. Its website (⊚ cornucopia .net) has an online "what's on" Istanbul arts diary.

Easiest to find of the **international papers** are *The Guardian* (European edition), the *International Herald Tribune* and *USA Today*, though many other titles can be found in Sultanahmet and in Taksim/Beyoğlu.

Television

In the early 1980s Turkey had just one, closely controlled, state-run **television channel**. There are now a plethora of national channels and many more regional ones.

Turkish channels include several state-owned TRT (Turkish Radio and Television) channels where programming veers between foreign historical drama and American films (both dubbed into Turkish) and talking-heads panel discussions,

MEDIA MANIPULATION

In the wake of accusations of government bribery and corruption, in late 2013 **Twitter** was banned in Turkey for "spreading false information". **YouTube**, not for the first time, was also banned for a short period around the same time when a video posted on it showed top officials apparently discussing an undercover attack on neighbouring Syria. Both bans were lifted by the courts in 2014, though media-savvy locals had already found many ways to circumvent the restrictions.

punctuated by classical Turkish music interludes. Glossy Turkish soaps and serials are immensely popular not only in Turkey, but also in the Balkans and Middle East, with tourists from the latter especially flocking to Istanbul to see the locations where they were shot.

TRT Müzik features traditional Turkish music, while TRT-6 made history in 2009, becoming the first state-run TV channel broadcasting in the Kurdish language, a tongue banned for political reasons until the 1990s. Commercial channels offering light entertainment, film reruns and current affairs, Show, Star, ATV and Kanal D are the most popular. Music-orientated channels devoting their time mainly to Turkish pop videos and short youth-related features include Kral and Power Turk.

There are several **English-language channels** shown on the nation's digital provider, Digiturk, which most mid-range-and-above Istanbul hotels offer. CNBC-e, a joint venture with America's NBC, devotes evenings and weekends to a mix of films and US TV comedy and drama shows. Its rival, E2, has a similar mix, and both are in English with Turkish subtitles. BBC Entertainment is anything but, with a tedious mix of home makeover, cooking programmes and mainstream comedies, though the post-10pm schedule is much better. Also available are CNN, BBC World, Euronews and Al-Jazeera, as well as Eurosport, National Geographic and the History Channel.

For football, Digiturk is the main provider and live Turkish Premier League football is exclusive to its Lig TV channel (look for the banners advertising it outside bars and cafés). English Premier League matches are screened on Lig TV2, available wherever Lig TV is showing; other matches, including the English Championship, are on a separate provider, D-Smart. If you really want to watch any major (and many minor) televised sporting event from around the world, the *Port Shield* sports bar in Sultanahmet (see p.196) is conveniently located.

Radio

Frequency-crowding means even popular channels are almost impossible to pick up without interference. Of the four **public radio stations**, Radyo Üç (The Third Programme or TRT-3), most commonly found at 88.2, 94 and 99MHz, broadcasts the highest proportion of Western music.

For Western music, Açık Radyo (FM 94.9) provides a mixed diet of rock, jazz and soul, while Radyo Blue (94.5FM) specializes in dance, electronica and blues. Other big names offering Western music and production values include Capital FM (99.5), Kiss FM (90.3) and Metro FM (97.2). For Turkish music, the best stations are Kral (92.0) and, naturally enough, Best FM (98.4).

Festivals and cultural events

Despite the secular nature of the Turkish Republic, the nation's three major festivals are Muslim: Ramazan (Arabic Ramadan), Şeker Bayramı (Eid ul-fıtr in Arabic) and Kurban Bayramı (Eid al-Adha), the latter two of which are major holidays as well. Otherwise, there's just a handful of festivals in and around Istanbul, notably the gypsy festival in Thrace and the oil-wrestling festival outside Edirne, though the city has an impressive cultural-events calendar.

Religious festivals

The religious festivals observed all over the Islamic world on dates determined by the Muslim Hijra calendar are celebrated in Istanbul, and two of the most important, the Şeker and Kurban bayrams, are public holidays. As the Islamic calendar is lunar, the dates of the four important religious festivals drift backwards eleven days each year (twelve in a leap year), relative to the Gregorian calendar. However, future dates of festivals as given on Islamic websites are provisional, owing to factors such as when the moon is sighted and the international dateline, so expect variance of a day or so in the ranges in the lists below.

Ramazan, although it is not a public holiday, is arguably the most important Muslim festival, if you can call a month of daylight abstention from food, water, tobacco and sex a festival. It is not a public holiday, and working life carries on as normal despite the fact that much of the population, even in Istanbul, is fasting from sunrise to sunset. Try to avoid the roads during the hour leading up to the breaking of the fast (known as *iftar*), as tired, hungry and thirsty drivers rush home for much-needed refreshment. Few restaurants in Istanbul close for Ramazan but, particularly if you are in more conservative areas of the city such as Fatih, be discreet about eating, drinking and smoking in public during fasting hours. On the positive side, every night of Ramazan has become like a mini-holiday for many Istanbulites, with free meals doled out to the less well off from soup kitchens across the city, and a (very restrained) carnival-like atmosphere in places like the Hippodrome in Sultanahmet, where hundreds of stalls are set up for the entire month, selling everything from candy-floss and *gözleme* to Turkish coffee and *köfte*. It's very much a family occasion, and a great place to visit to see how the more conservative Istanbulites enjoy themselves – and to try some good-value, Turkish speciality foods. Also note that trying to find a seat in a restaurant at *iftar* can be tricky.

Kadir Gecesi (The Eve of Power) takes place between the 27th and 28th days of the month of Ramazan, the time when Mohammed is supposed to have received the Koran from Allah. The mosques – even more brilliantly illuminated than usual for the whole month – are full all night, as it's believed that prayers at this time have special efficacy; those who can't make it out tend to stay home reading the Koran and praying. On **Arife**, the last day of Ramazan, it is customary to visit the cemeteries and pay respects to departed ancestors; many rural restaurants are shut that evening.

The three-day **Şeker Bayramı (Sugar Holiday)** is held at the end of Ramazan, though it often stretches into a week-long break if the three crucial days fall in the middle of the working week. It is celebrated by family get-togethers and the giving of presents and sweets to children, and restrained general partying in the streets and restaurants; on the first night after Arife, you will have to book well in advance for tables at better restaurants.

The four-day **Kurban Bayramı (Festival of the Sacrifice)**, in which the sacrificial offering of a sheep represents Abraham's son Ishmael (a Koranic version of the Old Testament story), is marked by the slaughter of over 2.5 million sheep. It is even more important than Şeker Bayramı, with the head of the household beholden to sacrifice a sheep or goat on the main day of the festival.

During both Şeker and Kurban bayrams, which are also public holidays (see p.39), travel becomes almost impossible: from the afternoon leading up to the first evening of the holiday (a Muslim festival is reckoned from sunset) – and on the first and last days themselves – public transport is often completely booked up. If you're planning to head out of Istanbul, you'll struggle to get a seat on any long-distance coach, train, plane or ferry unless you book well in advance. Some shops and all banks, museums and government offices close during the holiday periods (although corner grocery stores stay open). The demographic balance of the city shifts, too, with millions departing the metropolis to visit relatives elsewhere in the country and visitors from all over Turkey and the Middle East heading into Istanbul.

PROVISIONAL ŞEKER AND KURBAN BAYRAMS DATES

2015 Şeker July 17–19; **Kurban** Sept 24–27
2016 Şeker July 4–7; **Kurban** Oct 12–15
2017 Şeker June 25–27; **Kurban** Sept 1–4
2018 Şeker June 15–17; **Kurban** Aug 21–24

Cultural festivals

The annual festival calendar is pretty full – at least between April and October, when most of the best events take place. The highlights are detailed below; for more information, consult the city tourist offices or the Istanbul Foundation for Culture and Arts (Ⓦiksv.org). Tickets for most events can be bought online from Ⓦbiletix.com.

February

!f Istanbul International Independent Film Festival
Ⓦifİstanbul.com. This annual two-week event brings together film buffs from around the world with a programme of screenings, concerts, talks and other parallel events around the city.

April

Istanbul Film Festival Ⓦfilm.iksv.org. Turkish, European and Hollywood movies premiere at Istanbul's cinemas, mainly in Beyoğlu, plus the best of the non-English-speaking world's releases from the previous year and new prints of classic films. Gala performances attended by directors and actors sell out well in advance.

Tulip Festival Two-week-long festival honouring the national flower, including concerts, arts events and competitions at different locations around the city. Over fifteen million bulbs flower across the city, planted by the municipality, best seen in parks such as Emirgan and Gülhane early in the month.

May

Babylon Soundgarden Ⓦbabylon.com.tr. One-day festival organized by the city's best club, *Babylon*; in 2014 it took place for the second time at open-air venue Parkorman, headlined by the Pet Shop Boys.

Chill-Out Ⓦchilloutfest.com. One-day dance, pop and electronica festival that saw sets in 2014 by Goldfrapp, Brandt Brauer Frick and twenty other artists, held in the green and pleasant surroundings of the fifteen-thousand capacity Life Park in Belgrade Forest.

Conquest Celebrations Ⓦibb.gov.tr. Week-long celebration of the Ottoman conquest of old Constantinople (May 29, 1453) – concerts by the Ottoman Mehter military band, fancy-dress processions and fireworks.

International Theatre Festival Ⓦtiyatro.iksv.org. Biennial event (next up in 2016), showcasing the best Turkish plays (by both local avant-garde and established theatre groups), and performances by leading foreign companies, which in the past have included the Royal Shakespeare Company. Some plays enacted at open-air venues such as the Rumeli Hisan, others in the Kenter Theatre.

June/July

Istanbul Music Festival Ⓦiksv.org. Concerts, recitals, dance and opera – this hugely successful festival was launched in 1973 to celebrate fifty years of independence and brings top-notch orchestras and soloists from all over the world to perform in such atmospheric venues as the church of Haghia Eirene. Organized by the Istanbul Foundation for Culture and Arts (IKSV), it lasts most of the month.

Kırkpınar Oil Wrestling Festival The premier festival for this still-popular traditional sport (see p.271), attracting big crowds to the fascinating border town of Edirne.

One Love Ⓦonelove.com. Moderately alternative weekend-long festival held at Parkorman in Belgrade Forest, with plenty of DJ-led dance sets and performances from international bands such as Basement Jaxx and Mogwai as well as local acts.

July/August

Istanbul Jazz Festival Ⓦcaz.iksv.org. Two weeks of gigs and jamming sessions from world-class performers, who in 2014 ranged from Chick Corea and Katie Melua to Angelique Kidjo and Jon Batiste. Outdoor venues include the Cemil Topuzlu Açık Have Tiyatrosu.

Rock N' Coke Ⓦrockncoke.com. A weekend of Western and Turkish rock held alternate years (the Arctic Monkeys headlined in 2013), usually held on an airfield 50km to the west of the city; buses run from Taksim.

September

ArtInternational ⓌIstanbulartinternational.com. Demonstrating the rise of Istanbul on the international contemporary art scene, this annual large-scale art fair was established in 2013 and held in the Haliç Congress Centre. Aiming to act as a bridge between the East and West it attracts some big players from around the globe.

Istanbul Biennial Ⓦbienal.iksv.org. Multimedia contemporary arts festival that usually runs mid-Sept to the first week in Nov (see box, p.209), held on odd-numbered years.

October

Akbank International Jazz Festival ⓦ akbanksanat.com.
Two-week festival concentrating on traditional jazz. Events include film screenings, informal jamming sessions and drum workshops. Varied venues include the Byzantine church of Haghia Eirene and the Babylon Performance Centre in Beyoğlu.

International Puppet Festival ☎ 0212 232 0224,
ⓦ kuklalstanbul.org. A celebration of Turkish Shadow Theatre, or *karağöz* – silent puppets tell their tale behind a two-dimensional screen. One venue is the Kenter Theatre (see p.206).

November

Contemporary Istanbul ⓦ contemporaryistanbul.com.
Week-long exhibition in the Lütfi Kırdar Congress and Exhibition Centre, showcasing Turkish and international artists. Art Istanbul runs parallel to it with events around the city (ⓦ artIstanbul.org).

Istanbul Marathon ⓦ Istanbulmarathon. Runners from around the world compete in this trans-continental marathon (see p.227).

Travel essentials

Climate

Istanbul has a relatively damp **climate**, with hot, humid summers and cool, rainy winters. July and August are usually sweltering, while May, June, September and October offer the perfect combination of dry, warm weather and long daylight hours. Winter – during January and February – can be very chilly in the city.

Costs

The Turkish **lira** is relatively stable, with inflation in 2014 a little under ten percent. At the time of going to press there were ₺2.9 to the euro, ₺3.64 to the pound and the dollar was ₺2.14. Costs are reasonable by most European standards, though certain items are as expensive, if not more so, than elsewhere, notably alcoholic beverages and fuel.

Stay in a hostel dormitory, eat in local workers' cafés or restaurants, avoid alcohol and the most expensive sites such as the Topkapı Palace and Haghia Sophia and you could get by on ₺75 a day.

MUSEUM PASSES

It's possible to make a saving on museum entry fees by purchasing a three- or five-day **Istanbul Museum pass** issued by the Ministry of Culture and Tourism. The three-day pass costs ₺85 and gives entry to Haghia Sophia, Topkapı Palace and Harem, Archeology Museum, Mosaic Museum, Museum of Turkish and Islamic Art and History of Science and Technology in Islam Museum. If you visited all of them you'd save over ₺40. The ₺115 five-day version adds five more museums, including the Kariye Museum. A major advantage of a pass is **fast-track entry** to sites – a worthy consideration given the sometimes massive queues at Haghia Sophia and Topkapı in particular. The passes are available from the first four museums listed above, and the Kariye Museum, as well as online from ⓦ muze .gov.tr. You can also buy single-entry tickets from the website in order to avoid queues.

Double that and you could stay in a modest hotel, see the sights and have a beer or two with your evening meal. Equally, a night out on the town in the entertainment hub of Beyoğlu could easily set you back well over ₺120, more if you head up to the chic rooftop bars or venture down to the swanky places on the Bosphorus.

Crime and personal safety

Istanbul is undoubtedly far safer than most large European or North American cities, and cases of mugging and assault against tourists are rare. Having said this, the crime rate is rising, due in part to the increasing disparity between rich and poor. Take the same precautions you would in any European city and you should be OK. Bear in mind that all police are armed and, despite recent improvements in training and transparency, are generally feared by the locals.

AVERAGE MONTHLY TEMPERATURES AND RAINY DAYS

	Jan	Feb	Mar	Apr	May	Jun	Jul	Aug	Sep	Oct	Nov	Dec
Max/min (°C)	8/3	8/3	11/4	15/7	21/12	25/17	28/21	82/21	23/16	19/13	14/8	9/5
Max/min (°F)	46/37	46/37	52/39	59/45	70/54	77/63	82/70	28/70	73/61	66/55	57/46	48/41
Rainy days	18	15	14	11	9	6	6	5.5	7	11	14	17

Trouble

For the average visitor, **pickpocketing** is the main cause for concern: be particularly careful around Sirkeci station, the Eminönü waterfront, the Grand Bazaar, Aksaray, Taksim (especially at night) and the city land walls around dusk. You should also be careful on public transport, particularly when it is crowded. Single women should take care in Taksim and Beyoğlu at night, and both sexes should be aware of the bad reputation of Tarlabaşı (which parallels İstiklal Caddesi in Beyoğlu), where poverty and crime go hand in hand and sexual harassment (to women from men; to men from some transvestites and transsexuals) is a problem.

Lone males heading out for the night should be wary of **confidence tricksters**. The usual scenario is to be approached by a friendly Turkish male, who'll suggest a good club or bar to go to. In the bar, there are (surprise, surprise) some attractive females, who your "friend" suggests buying drinks for. When the bill comes (to you), it can run into hundreds of euros. Even if you don't have enough cash on you, you'll be forced to pay with your credit card. In cases like this, it is very difficult to prove criminal intent – use your common sense and avoid the situation arising. The **spiking of drinks** is also a possible risk: make sure you buy your own drinks if you have any doubts at all about the person you're with.

To avoid the wrath of the local populace (and possibly the police as well) **never insult Atatürk or Turkey**, and don't deface, degrade, or tear up currency or the flag. Public drunkenness in general is frowned upon and will be considered an aggravating, not a mitigating, factor should you run into trouble. Try not to be drawn into **serious disputes**, since while things rarely turn violent in Turkey, when they do they can turn *very* violent.

Political demonstrations quite often get out of hand, as the Gezi Park protests (see box, p.127 and p.299) of 2013 starkly showed. The sight of riot police with helmets, batons and guns, as well as water cannon, are a common sight on Istanbul's protest heartland, which also happens to be the city's main shopping street, the upper section of İstiklal Caddesi, between Galatasaray Meydanı and Taksim Square. Most demonstrations pass off peaceably, but take care if there is one in progress.

Police

The police you're most likely to have any dealing with are the blue-uniformed **Polis**, the main force both in Istanbul and in towns and cities across the country. There's a tourist police centre at Yerebatan Cad 6 (☎0212 527 4503) in Sultanahmet with some English-speaking officers. The **Trafik Polis**, recognized by their white caps and two-toned vehicles, are a branch of this service and their main responsibility seems to be controlling intersections and doing spot-checks on vehicles at approaches to towns. Istanbul has a rapid-response squad of red-and-black-uniformed motorbike police known as the **Yunus Polis**; they are generally courteous and helpful to tourists and may speak some English. In the towns, you're also likely to see the **Belediye Zabıtası**, the navy-clad market police, who patrol the markets and bazaars to ensure that tradesmen aren't ripping off customers – approach them directly if you have reason for complaint.

In general, Turkish police have had a bad reputation, but things are beginning to change. Once low-paid and ill-trained, their pay has risen substantially (reducing corruption) in recent years, and graduate-intake programmes have raised the overall level of education of the police force. The "glass-walls" policy (designed to make the police more accountable for their actions) was introduced, at least partially, to satisfy the Europeans as Turkey strives for full EU membership, and as a result, attitudes towards suspects have improved considerably. Old habits die hard, however, as police over-reaction to the Gezi Park demonstrations of 2013 showed all too vividly (see box, p.127) with images of police firing tear gas canisters at peaceful protestors at point-blank range, and kicking demonstrators knocked to the ground by water cannon broadcast worldwide. **If you are arrested** for any reason, stay polite and be patient – getting irate tends to be counterproductive. You have **the right to make a phone call** to a friend, hotelier or consul.

Note that it is obligatory to **carry ID** at all times – for locals and foreigners alike – so if you are concerned about having your passport stolen (or losing it) while out and about, at least carry a photocopy of the pages with your details and Turkish entry stamp on your person.

Electricity

Turkey operates on 220 volts, 50 Hertz so most European appliances will work here. Plugs are European-style two-pin, so UK visitors should bring an adaptor. American appliances will need both an adaptor and a transformer.

Entry requirements

To enter Turkey, you'll need a full passport with at least six months' validity, and many countries require tourist visas. These must now be bought in advance of arrival in Turkey – e-visas are available online from ⓦevisa.gov.tr. It's a simple process to fill in the online form; payment is by Mastercard or Visa debit/credit card. The visa will be emailed to you; print it out and take it with you to the point of entry. **Visas** are multiple entry and, for most visitors, including citizens of the UK, Ireland, the US, Canada and Australia, are valid for 90 days in 180 days from the date requested on your e-visa application. Visas for citizens of the UK, US and Ireland cost $20, Australia and Canada $60. New Zealanders are not required to have a visa; South African visas are valid 30 days in 180 and are free. Note that entry requirements can and do change; check what's required well before your intended departure date with the Turkish Ministry of Foreign Affairs at ⓦmfa.gov.tr. To stay longer than three months you will need to apply for a residence permit (see p.43).

TURKISH EMBASSIES AND CONSULATES ABROAD

Australia 60 Mugga Way, Red Hill, Canberra ACT 2603 ☎ 02 6234 0000.
Canada 197 Wurtemburg St, Ottawa, ON K1N 8L9 ☎ 613 244 2470.
Ireland 11 Clyde Rd, Ballsbridge, Dublin 4 ☎ 01 668 5240.
New Zealand 15–17 Murphy St, Level 8, Wellington ☎ 04 472 1290 92.
South Africa 1067 Church St, Hatfield 0181, Pretoria ☎ 012 342 5063.
UK 43 Belgrave Square, London SW1X 8PA ☎ 020 7393 0202.
US 2525 Massachusetts Ave NW, Washington, DC 20008 ☎ 202 612 6700.

CONSULATES IN ISTANBUL

Australia Asker Ocağı Cad 15, Elmadağ, Şişli ☎ 0212 243 1333.
Canada 16th Floor, Tekfen Tower, Büyükdere Cad 209, Levent 4 ☎ 0212 385 9700.
New Zealand İnönü Cad 48/3, Taksim ☎ 0212 244 0272.
South Africa (Honorary Consul) Alarko Centre, Musallim Nacı Cad 113–115, Ortaköy ☎ 0212 260 378.
UK Meşrutiyet Cad 34, Tepebaşı, Beyoğlu ☎ 0212 334 6400.
US İstinye Mahallesi, Kaplıcalar Mevkii No.2, İstinye ☎ 0212 335 9000.

Customs and border inspections

You are permitted to bring one litre of spirits or two of wine, and six hundred cigarettes into Turkey duty free; there are no limits on the amount of foreign currency you can bring in. If you haven't exploited your allowance at your departure airport, you can usually buy duty-free goods at your Turkish port of arrival.

Few people get stopped departing Turkey, but the guards may be on the lookout for **antiquities** and **fossils**. Penalties for trying to smuggle these out include long jail sentences, plus a large fine. What actually constitutes an antiquity is rather vague (see p.214), but it's best not to take any chances.

Health

Turkey does not have reciprocal health arrangements with other countries, making health insurance mandatory. There are no vaccination requirements as such, though you should consult your doctor before travelling.

It's quite possible you'll suffer a mild bout of diarrhoea in Istanbul, particularly (though not only) if you eat from street stalls. **Tap water** is heavily chlorinated but best avoided – stick to bottled water. Lomotil or Imodium, trade names for the antiparastaltic diphenoxylate, are easily available in Turkey, though they block you up rather than kill the bug that ails you. Flagyll, on sale locally, is good if you go down with a more virulent stomach bug, but avoid drinking alcohol when taking it. In restaurants, avoid dishes that look as if they have been standing around and make sure meat and fish are well grilled. Avoid stuffed mussels in summer as they go off very quickly. If you're struck down, the best thing is to let the bug run its course and drink lots of fluids, including re-hydrating salts (Geo-Oral is a locally available brand). Eating plain white rice and yoghurt also helps. Stubborn cases will need a course of antibiotics – pharmacists are trained to recognize symptoms and you don't need a prescription for antibiotics. In theory, a state clinic (Develet Polykliniği) will treat foreigners for a very small fee.

Rabies is prevalent in Turkey, and Istanbul has its share of street dogs and cats. Be wary of any animal that bites, scratches or licks you, particularly if it's behaving erratically. First aid involves flushing a wound with soap and water after encouraging limited bleeding. Then go straight to a state clinic (within 72hr), where you should be given an injection (free of charge), the first of six, most of which you will probably need to have back in your home country.

Medical treatment

There are thousands of **pharmacies** (eczane) across Istanbul. Staff may know some English or German and are trained to diagnose simple complaints, take blood pressure, and the like. They also dispense medicines that normally require a prescription, such as antibiotics. Medication prices are low, but bring your prescription to find the (probably locally produced) drug that best matches your needs. Pharmacies also sell **birth-control pills** (doğum *kontrol hapı*), **condoms** (*preservatif*; the slang term is *kılıf*) and **tampons** (Orkid is the best domestic brand). **Night-duty pharmacies**, often found near main hospitals, are known as *nöbetçi*; a list of the current rota is posted in Turkish in every chemist's front window, as "Nöbetçi Eczaneleri". For more serious ailments, you'll find well-trained **doctors** in Istanbul and the larger towns and cities. As the state sector hospitals are overcrowded and under-funded, it's preferable to go to an *Özel Hastane* or private hospital, where consultations start around ₺200.

HOSPITALS

Alman Hastanesi (German Hospital) Sıraselviler Cad 119, Taksim ☎ 0212 293 2150, ⊚ almanhastanesi.com.tr. Reliable and well-run hospital, which also has a dental and eye clinic. Staff are proficient in English.
Amerikan Hastanesi (American Hospital) Güzelbahçe Sok 20, Nişantaşı ☎ 0212 444 3777, ⊚ amerikanhastanesi.org. Very good reputation, long established and with good equipment and well-trained staff, it also has a dental clinic.
Cerrahpaşa Hastanesi Koca Mustafapaşa Caddesi, Cerrahpaşa ☎ 0212 414 3000, ⊚ ctf.edu.tr. A well-regarded teaching hospital in the old city.
Sen Jorj Avustrya Hastanesi (St George's Austrian Hospital) Bereketzade Medresesi Sok 7, Galata ☎ 0212 292 6222, ⊚ sjh.com.tr. Decent hospital, handily located right in the heart of Galata.

DENTISTS

Alternatives to the practices in the German and American hospitals (see p.37 or see above), both with English-speaking staff, are:
Prodent-Can Ergene Valikonağı Cad 109/5, Nişantaşı ☎ 0212 230 4635.
Reha Sezgin Halaskargazi Cad 48/9, Harbiye ☎ 0212 240 3322.

Insurance

There are not yet any reciprocal health-care privileges between Turkey and the EU, so it's essential to take out an insurance policy before travelling, to cover against theft, loss, illness or injury. Before paying for a new policy, however, check whether you are already covered: some all-risks homeowners' or renters' insurance policies may cover your possessions when overseas, and many private medical schemes (such as BUPA and WPA) offer coverage extensions for abroad.

A specialist travel insurance company can sell you a suitable policy, or consider the travel insurance deal we offer (see box below). A typical travel insurance policy usually provides cover for the loss of baggage, tickets and – up to a certain limit – cash, cards or travellers' cheques, as well as cancellation or curtailment of your journey.

Many policies can be chopped and changed to eliminate coverage you don't need – for example, sickness and accident benefits can often be excluded or included at will. If you do take **medical coverage**, ascertain whether benefits will be paid as treatment proceeds or only after your return home, and whether there is a 24-hour medical emergency number. When securing baggage cover, make sure that the per-article limit – typically under £500/€750 – will cover your most valuable possession.

If you need to make a medical **claim**, you should keep receipts for medicines and treatment, and in the event you have anything **stolen or lost**, you must obtain an official statement from the police (or the airline that lost your bags). In the wake of growing numbers of fraudulent claims, most insurers won't even entertain a claim unless you have a police report.

Internet

The number of internet cafés in the city has declined massively as ever more Istanbulites have computers at home, laptops or broadband mobile-phone access. Fortunately, virtually all hotels and hostels in the city have internet access – often both terminals and wireless, and wi-fi is invariably free apart from at the top-end business hotels, where a steep charge is sometimes levied. Many cafés also have wi-fi. Rates in internet cafés, most of which have ADSL connec-

ROUGH GUIDES TRAVEL INSURANCE

Rough Guides has teamed up with WorldNomads.com to offer great travel insurance deals. Policies are available to residents of over 150 countries, with cover for a wide range of adventure sports, 24hr emergency assistance, high levels of medical and evacuation cover and a stream of travel safety information. Roughguides.com users can take advantage of their policies online 24/7, from anywhere in the world – even if you're already travelling. And since plans often change when you're on the road, you can extend your policy and even claim online. Roughguides.com users who buy travel insurance with WorldNomads.com can also leave a positive footprint and donate to a community development project. For more information, go to ⊚ roughguides.com/travel-insurance.

tions, tend to be ₺2 per hour. The Turkish-character keyboard you'll probably be faced with may cause some frustration. Beware in particular of the dotless "ı" (confusingly enough found right where you'll be expecting the conventional "i") which, if entered by mistake, will make an email address invalid – the Western "i" is located second key from the right, middle row. The @ sign is usually on the "Q" key; press the "Alt Gr" key then "Q" to type.

Laundry

Most hotels have a laundry service, and some of the major hotels offer services to non-guests, at a price – the one at the *Ceylan Intercontinental* in Taksim (☎0212 368 4444) is 24-hour. There are no coin-operated laundries in the city, but there are plenty of dry cleaners, some of which will do your laundry.

Left luggage and lost property

There are left-luggage (*emanet*) facilities at Atatürk and Sabiha Gökçen international airports (₺18 for 24 hours for a normal-sized bag).

If you lose, or have something stolen, report it to the tourism police at Yerebatan Cad 6 (☎0212 527 4503) in Sultanahmet.

Mail

Mail is handled by the state-run PTT (Post Telegraf Telefon; ☮ptt.gov.tr). Istanbul's central post office is on Büyük Postane Caddesi (☎0212 5261200; daily: post 8.30am–7pm; bank 8.30am–4.30pm; phone calls and stamps 24hr) in Eminönü, an imposing early twentieth-century building not far from Sirkeci station, is the most use to visitors staying in the old city. There's also a major post office at Yeniçarşı Caddesi, off İstiklal Caddesi and opposite Galatasaray Lycée (Mon–Fri & Sun 8.30am–5.30pm; ☎0212 251 5150). If you're staying in Taksim, the post office on Cumhüriyet Cad 2 (Mon–Sat 8.30am–5.30pm; ☎0212 243 0284) is the most convenient. Stamps are only available from the PTT.

Airmail (*uçakla*) rates to Europe are ₺2.50 for postcards and letters up to 20g. Delivery to Europe or North America can take seven to ten days. A pricier express (APG or *acele*) service is also available, which cuts delivery times for the EU to about three days. When sending items through the post, it's best to leave the envelope or package unsealed as post office staff may ask to see what's being sent.

Posting slots are clearly labelled – *yurtdışı* for overseas, *yurtiçi* for within Turkey, *şehiriçi* for local.

Alternatively, for letters and parcels, private Turkish courier companies include Aras (☎444 2552, ☮araskargo.com.tr) and Yurtiçi (☎444 9999, ☮yurticikargo.com), both of which are very efficient, comparable in price to the PTT and have offices all around the city.

Maps

The maps included in this guide should be enough for most purposes, but there are a number of other decent maps available if you're looking for something to complement these. The cheapest option is the free city map dished out by the tourist offices in Istanbul; other maps can be bought from kiosks around the touristy parts of the city, including the clear and accurate (though it only covers a small part of the Asian side of the city) Keskin Colour's *Istanbul Street Plan 1*. A little dearer and better is Net Maps' *Istanbul* which shows more of the Asian side and has detailed maps of the Princes' Islands.

Money

Turkey's currency is the Turkish Lira (Türk Lirası) or ₺ for short. It is divided into smaller units, kuruş, which come in coin denominations of 1, 5, 10, 25 and 50 and ₺1. Notes are in denominations of 5, 10, 20, 50, 100 and 200. The ₺ symbol was introduced in 2012 to reflect the growing stature of the currency. Many establishments, however, continue to price their goods and services according to the

---

KDV: TURKISH VAT

The Turkish variety of VAT (*Katma Değer Vergisi* or **KDV**), ranging from 8 to 23 percent depending on the commodity, is included in the price of virtually all goods and services (except car rental, where the fifteen percent figure is usually quoted separately). Look for the notice *Fiyatlarımız KDV Dahildir* ("VAT included in our prices") if you think someone's trying to do you for it twice. There's a VAT refund scheme for large souvenir purchases made by those living outside Turkey, but it's such a rigmarole to get that it's probably not worth pursuing; if you insist, ask the shop to provide a *KDV İade Özel Fatura* (Special VAT Refund Invoice), assuming that it participates – very few do, and they tend to be the most expensive shops.

TIPPING

A service charge of ten to fifteen percent is levied at the fancier restaurants, but as this goes directly to the management, the waiters and busboys should be left five percent again if they deserve it. In some places, a mandatory tip (*garsoniye*) accompanies the service charge. Round odd taxi fares upwards (you may not have a choice, as the driver may genuinely not have small change); hotel porters should be tipped appropriately.

old system, with the price suffixed by the letters TL, as in 10TL.

Rates for foreign currency are always better inside Turkey, so try not to buy much lira at home. It's wise to bring a fair wad of **hard currency** with you (euros are best, though dollars and sterling are often accepted), as you can often use it to pay directly for souvenirs or accommodation (prices for both are frequently quoted in euros), though make sure you know the current exchange rate. **Travellers' cheques** are, frankly, not worth the bother as exchange offices (see p.29) and some banks refuse them, while those that do accept them charge a hefty commission on transactions.

Exchange services

Unless things change dramatically, the lira's new-found stability means that you can change large amounts of cash in one go without worrying that inflation will erode its value. You should, though, try to keep all foreign-exchange slips with you until departure, if only to prove the value of purchases made in case of queries by customs.

The state-owned Ziraat Bankası, open Monday to Friday, 8.30am to noon and 1.30 to 5pm, gives a good rate of exchange, does not charge commission and usually has a dedicated currency exchange (*döviz*) counter. Queues, however, can be long. Take a ticket from the machine and wait for your number to appear on the digital display. It's also possible to change money at PTT (Post Offices), again commission-free. *Döviz*, or exchange houses, are common in the city, with several on Divan Yolu (old city) adjacent to the tram stop and İstiklal Caddesi (Beyoğlu). They buy and sell foreign currency of most sorts instantly, and have the convenience of long opening hours (usually Mon–Sat 9/10am–8/10pm, but some open daily) and short or non existent queues. Few now charge commission but the rate is less than banks or the PTT.

Credit/debit cards and ATMs

Credit cards are widely used in hotels, shops, restaurants and entertainment venues and with no commission (though many hotels offer discounts for cash payments). Don't expect, however, to use your card in basic eating-places or small corner shops. Swipe readers plus **chip-and-PIN** protocol are now the norm in most of Turkey.

The simplest way to get hold of money in Istanbul and its environs is to use the widespread **ATM** network. Most bank ATMs will accept any debit cards that are part of the Cirrus, Maestro or Plus systems; you can also use Visa and Master-Card, but American Express holders are currently restricted to Akbank ATMs. Screen prompts are given in English on request. The daily ATM withdrawal limit for most cards is about £250/€375 equivalent (or £80–200/€120–300 per transaction), depending on the bank or even individual ATM.

Opening hours and public holidays

Shops are usually open daily from 9am to 6pm, though many open on a Sunday as well. **Grocers** open daily from 8am to 8pm (sometimes earlier to later) and supermarkets often stay open until 10pm. **Banks** and **government offices** open Monday to Friday 8.30am to noon and 1.30pm to 5pm. **Museum, site and gallery** opening hours also vary quite markedly. Most open from 8.30 or 9am until 5 or 6pm, though some close earlier and the biggest sights stay open until 7pm in summer. All sites and museums are closed on the mornings of public holidays, while Istanbul's palaces are generally closed on Mondays and Thursdays. **Mosques** are theoretically open from dawn (first call to prayer) until nightfall (last call to prayer). However, some of the mosques most visited by tourists, such as the Blue Mosque, do not welcome non-Muslim visitors during prayer times. Unfortunately, mosques in less touristy areas present a different problem in that they are often locked between prayer times for security reasons, so this is the only time you're likely to be able to visit; be discreet when doing so. For more specific opening hours, refer to the relevant Guide chapters.

Public holidays

Banks, schools and government offices all close on five of the holidays listed below: New Year's Day, Independence/Children's Day, Youth and Sports Day, Victory Day and Republic Day.

January 1 Yılbaşı New Year's Day.

April 23 Ulusal Egemenlik ve Çocuk Bayramı Independence Day, celebrating the first meeting of the new Republican parliament in Ankara, and Children's Day.

May 19 Gençlik ve Spor Günü Youth and Sports Day, also Atatürk's birthday.

July 1 Denizcilik Günü Navy Day.

August 26 Silahlı Kuvvetler Günü Armed Forces Day.

August 30 Zafer Bayramı Celebration of the Turkish victory over the Greek forces at Dumlupınar in 1922.

October 29 Cumhuriyet Bayramı Republic Day commemorates the proclamation of the Republic by Atatürk in 1923. Parades through the streets, mainly by school kids banging drums and blowing trumpets.

November 10 The anniversary of Atatürk's death in 1938. Observed at 9.05am (the time of his death), when the whole country stops whatever it's doing and maintains a respectful silence for a minute. It's worth being on a Bosphorus ferry on this morning, when all the engines are turned off, and the boats drift and blow their foghorns mournfully.

Phones

Turkey uses a system of eleven-digit **phone numbers** nationwide, consisting of four-digit area or mobile-provider codes (all starting with "0") plus a seven-digit subscriber number. Numbers on the European side of Istanbul all begin with ☎0212, on the Asian side with ☎0216.

Given the Turkish penchant for chatting, **mobile phones** ("cep telefonu" or "pocket phones") are essential accessories in Istanbul (and beyond). Assuming that you have a roaming facility, your home mobile will connect with one of the local network providers. Charges, though, are high (up to £1.30/min to the UK), and you pay for incoming calls as well.

Mobile phones are expensive in Turkey, due to government taxes. To stop floods of cheap second-hand phones coming in from abroad a Turkish **SIM card** will only work in a non-registered phone for around ten days before the phone is blocked for use in Turkey. The three mobile phone companies are Turkcell (☎turkcell.com.tr), Vodafone (☎vodafone .com.tr) and Avea (☎avea.com.tr). All have outlets at both Atatürk and Sabiha Gökçen airport arrival areas as well as at many mobile phone outlets around the city. Vodafone offers SIM packages for ₺120, which includes ₺70 credit and 2GB of internet use. To register your phone you must visit a tax office to pay the ₺150 tax. Take your tax-paid receipt and passport to an outlet of the company you purchased your SIM package from and register your phone – it should take 24 hours to activate. The alternative is to buy a cheap handset, available at the airport or from shops around Sirkeci station in

---

EMERGENCY NUMBERS

Ambulance ☎112
Fire ☎110
Police ☎155
Tourist Police ☎0212 527 4503

---

the old city, and insert a Turkish SIM, with no tax or registration problems.

Calling home from Turkey

To call home from Turkey, dial ☎00 followed by the relevant international dialling code (see below), then the area code (without the initial zero if there is one), then the number.

Australia ☎61
Ireland ☎353
New Zealand ☎64
South Africa ☎27
UK ☎44
US & Canada ☎1

Smoking

The old saying "smokes like a Turk" is backed up by figures to prove it is a fairly accurate assessment, with over forty percent of the adult population (around 25 million) indulging the nicotine habit. Yet things are changing. Smoking was banned on public transport and in airports, bus terminals and train stations back in 1997, and, much to everyone's surprise, the law is, more or less, adhered to. From July 2009, it was prohibited in all public buildings, and all enclosed public spaces including bars, cafés, restaurants, clubs and the like. This latter ban is widely flouted in many bars and clubs, especially in and around the nightlife quarter of Beyoğlu, as well as in working men's tea shops and the like. *Nargile* (hookah) cafés get around the ban with semi-open verandas and roof terraces.

Time

Turkey is two hours ahead of GMT, seven ahead of EST and ten ahead of PST. It is in the same time zone as South Africa, and seven hours behind Perth, nine behind Sydney and eleven behind Wellington. Daylight saving runs from the last Sunday in March to the last Sunday in October.

Toilets

In the majority of Istanbul homes, **Western-style toilets** are the norm – this is also true of those in most cafés, restaurants, bars, clubs, cinemas, tourist sites and so on. The only difference between them and the ones you're used to at home is the small pipe fitted at the rear rim of the basin – which serves the same purpose as a bidet. The tap to turn it on is usually awkwardly located, at low level, on the wall behind the loo. The waste bins provided are for "used" toilet paper – blockages are not uncommon.

In poorer, less-visited neighbourhoods, however, **squat toilets** are still the norm. This is particularly true of those attached to mosques – in out-of-the-way parts of the city, the only "public" toilet you'll be able to find. There's always a tap and plastic jug right next to the toilet for washing the unmentionables but be warned that few provide paper, so carry some around with you. An attendant at the entrance will divest you of a lira (occasionally a little less) on your way out and, in return, give you a tissue and splash of cologne on your hands.

Note that cheaper bars and clubs around Beyoğlu sometimes have only one, unisex toilet.

Tourist information

Istanbul has six **tourist offices**. Most convenient for the majority of visitors is the one in Sultanahmet, near the Hippodrome at Divan Yolu 3 (daily 9am–5pm; ☎0212 518 8754), which has English-speaking staff and is moderately helpful. Other possibly useful offices are located in the *Hilton* on Cumhüriyet Caddesi near Taksim (daily 9am–5pm; ☎0212 233 0592) and on Beyazit Meydanı, just west of the Grand

Bazaar (daily 9am–6pm; ☎0212 522 4902). If you can resist the temptation to get into the city centre as soon as possible, there's another in the arrivals terminal at Atatürk International airport (24hr; ☎0212 465 3151). The tourist office in Karaköy Kemankeş Caddesi (daily 9am–5pm; ☎0212 249 5776) is really aimed at cruise-ship passengers disgorging from the nearby dock; the one in the entrance of Sirkeci station in Eminönü (daily 9am–5pm; ☎0212 511 5888) offers little except a few brochures.

TOURIST INFORMATION OFFICES ABROAD

ⓦ tourismturkey.org.
Australia Room 17, Level 3, 428 George St, Sydney, NSW 2000 ☎02 9223 3055, ⓔ turkish@ozemail.co.au.
Canada Constitution Square, 360 Albert St, Suite 801, Ottawa, ON K1R 7X7 ☎613 230 8654.
Ireland Refer to the embassy at 11 Clyde Rd, Ballsbridge, Dublin 4 ☎01 668 5240.
New Zealand Refer to the embassy at 15–17 Murphy St, Level 8, Wellington ☎04 472 1290.
UK First Floor, 170–173 Piccadilly, London W1V 9DD ☎020 7766 9300.
US 821 United Nations Plaza, New York, NY 10017 ☎212/687 2194; 2525 Massachusetts Ave NW, Washington, DC 20008 ☎202 612 6800.

Travellers with disabilities

Both Atatürk International and Sabiha Gökçen airports have wheelchairs and wheelchair-accessible

---

MOSQUE MANNERS

Strolling around the tourist-thronged sites of Sultanahmet, or striding down the premier entertainment and shopping street of İstiklal Caddesi, it's sometimes hard to remember that you are in a Muslim city. Istanbul may be Turkey's most cosmopolitan, forward-looking urban centre, but a fair proportion of its inhabitants are both conservative and devout. Bear this in mind particularly when visiting a mosque. All those likely to be of interest to a foreign visitor (and many more besides) display some kind of "conduct" notice at the door outlining the **entry rules** – which are simple:

· Cover your head (women) and shoulders/upper arms (both sexes)
· No shorts or miniskirts
· Take off your shoes before entering, and make sure you don't tread on the ground outside in your bare or stockinged feet before stepping over the threshold. Many mosques provide a plastic bag to carry your shoes around in. Alternatively, place your footwear on the shelves provided inside the mosque.

Especially if you are in a very devout area such as Fatih, try to avoid your visit coinciding with **noon prayers** – particularly those on a Friday – the most important prayer session of the week. Once inside the mosque, you're free to wander around, take photographs and admire the interior – but keep your voice down (there are often people praying or reciting the Koran outside of the five daily prayer times) and don't take pictures of worshippers unless they give their permission. Although the *imam* is a state-paid official, upkeep of the building is down to charity, so you may want to put a **donation** in the collection box.

ISTANBUL ON THE NET

There are many Istanbul-related sites on the internet. A good general introduction to the country and Istanbul can be gained from the official **Ministry of Culture and Tourism** site (Ⓦgoturkey.com).

GENERAL

Ⓦ**turkeytravelplanner.com** Very informative site, regularly updated, dealing with travel in Istanbul and all over the country.
Ⓦ**turkishculture.org** Not terribly innovative – but it does give a useful rundown on everything from architecture to ceramics, literature to music and lifestyles to cuisine – with plenty of photographs and illustrations.
Ⓦ**wittIstanbul.com** Useful website connected to the hotel of the same name, containing lots of information for first-time visitors.

ANTIQUITIES AND ARCHITECTURE

Ⓦ**exploreturkey.com** Excellent background on the country's historical monuments, written by an archeologist, with much information on Istanbul, and some on İznik, Bursa, Troy and Edirne to boot, though last updated in 2004.
Ⓦ**muze.gov.tr** Government website with information on the country's state-run museums, including the latest opening hours and admission fees.
Ⓦ**patriarchate.org** Literate coverage of Istanbul's numerous Byzantine monuments.

LISTINGS

Ⓦ**biletix.com** This online booking agency is the major outlet for virtually all concerts, sporting events and shows.
Ⓦ**iksv.org** Website for the Istanbul Foundation for Culture and Arts, with information on the city's major music, arts and theatre events– an excellent site for arts lovers.
Ⓦ**Istanbuleats.com** Fascinating blog-cum-guide to the city's food scene – especially off-the-beaten-track, salt-of-the-earth places.
Ⓦ**pozitiflive.com** Listings site for contemporary music and arts events.
Ⓦ**theguideIstanbul.com** Regularly updated, sassy guide to Istanbul life, including restaurant and exhibition reviews and events listings.
Ⓦ**timeoutIstanbul.com** Well-known listings site for finding out what's going on in the city.
Ⓦ**yabangee.com** The site of choice for young, literate expats, with listings, features and blogs.

---

toilets. **Getting around** Istanbul by the Metro and tram is possible, as they are, at least theoretically, wheelchair friendly, although at peak times the carriages are terribly crowded and getting access to some of the stations can be tricky. Some of the more modern buses have a ramp and low door but again can be very overcrowded and the drivers less than patient. The Metro running from Taksim Square north is the most wheelchair accessible, but of little interest to most visitors to the city. Public transport is theoretically free for disabled travellers but in practice, given the language barriers, may be difficult to obtain. Many of the city's pavements are broken and uneven, or cobbled, making things awkward – not to mention the number of steep hills.

The most **accessible sites** for the physically impaired are the Rahmi Koç Industrial Museum (see pp.116–117), Istanbul Modern (see p.115) and the Pera Museum (see p.123). The Topkapı Palace (see pp.50–57) and Haghia Sophia (see pp.45–49) are partially accessible, the Blue Mosque (see pp.64–65) and Basilica Cistern (see pp.61–62) impossible.

Women and sexual harassment

Turkish women occupy all positions in society, from headscarved housewives and devout Muslims robed head to toe in the all-enveloping *çaşaf* to secularized and "liberated" doctors living a single and independent life and high-school girls in short skirts and Converse baseball boots. Taking away the extremes, however, this is a socially conservative society and its women reflect this. Few go out to bars or clubs on their own, and though they may wear tight jeans and singlets, miniskirts and the like are still relatively rare. Wear jeans, trousers or sensible skirts, avoid eye contact with men, and try and look as confident and purposeful as possible. In conservative areas and when entering mosques or churches, make sure you're appropriately covered (see box, p.41).

If you do get harassed, don't suffer it alone – make a public scene to elicit the support of bystanders. Using Turkish to get your message across, such as "Ayıp!" ("Shame!") or "Beni rahatsız ediyorsun" ("You're disturbing me"), or the stronger "Defol!" ("Piss off!") or "Bırak beni" ("Leave me alone") may help in theory, but only if you don't mangle the pronunciation. "İmdat!" ("Help!") is more straightforward and should enlist you some aid.

Working in Istanbul

Most of the foreigners working in Istanbul are **teaching English** as a foreign language in a private school or college. There's a big demand for teachers in these schools, partly because of the high status accorded to learning English, and also because working conditions are not great and foreign-staff turnover tends to be high. Teaching posts for the bigger outfits are advertised in *The Guardian*'s educational section and the *Times Educational Supplement* in the UK, in the *International Herald Tribune* and the *Hürriyet Daily News* in Turkey, or check the expat website ⓦmymerhaba.com. The pay is adequate (usually around ₺2500/month) but free accommodation is the norm, as is health care. The school or language school should also get, and pay for, your residence and work permits. In all but the top schools, students tend to be rather spoilt and lacking in motivation and the management dictatorial and far more concerned with keeping parents, rather than their staff, happy. In language schools it all depends on the motivation of your students.

There are jobs other than teaching, but only where the employer can prove that the prospective foreign employee will be doing a job a native cannot do. Again wages are generally low.

The days of being able to leave the country every three months and come straight back in again for another three months have disappeared since the introduction of visas valid for 90 days in 180 (see pp.35–36). For stays of longer than three months you have to apply for a residence permit. The system has been reformed several times in recent years and remains in a state of flux. Basically you need to prove that you have savings in a Turkish bank equivalent to $6000 per annum, or an income of $500 coming in per month, a valid house rental agreement and proof you are paying into a health scheme – the state option is around ₺200 per month. You'll also need plenty of patience when visiting the Security Police (Emniyet Müdürlüğü) on Vatan Caddesi, A Blok, in Fatih, who issue the permit. For the latest Information see ⓦe-randevu .iem.gov.tr/yabancilar or ⓦyabangee.com/2014/06 /how-to-get-a-turkish-resident-permit.

BENEATH THE DOME OF HAGHIA SOPHIA

Sultanahmet

The heart of old, imperial Istanbul, compact Sultanahmet is home to the city's best-known attractions. Here, commanding a magnificent position overlooking the Bosphorus and Sea of Marmara stands the Topkapı Palace complex, once the heart of the powerful Ottoman Empire. Nearby is another fabulous Ottoman relic, the monumental Blue Mosque, whose name derives from the thousands of beautiful tiles adorning its airy interior. This working mosque, with its six slender minarets, mighty dome and cascade of semi-domes, proudly faces another monument, the former church of Haghia Sophia. This, the greatest legacy of the Byzantine Empire, is now the Haghia Sophia Museum, home to a wonderful series of glittering figurative mosaics.

Further legacies of the Byzantine era lie just north of the Blue Mosque. The **Hippodrome**, where chariots raced and mobs rioted, is one of the oldest monuments in the city, while the **Basilica Cistern** and **Cistern of 1001 Columns** were part of a superb water-supply system that ran right across the city. There are some excellent museums here, too, notably the **Archeology Museum**, featuring a superb array of finds from both Anatolia and former Ottoman domains, and the **Museum of Turkish and Islamic Art**, housed in the former palace of İbrahim Paşa.

South of the major sightseeing area, the steep, narrow streets running down from Cankurtaran to the Sea of Marmara are noteworthy for their surviving Ottoman houses, while a little to the southwest are a couple of minor architectural masterpieces: the **Church of St Sergius and Bacchus** and a fine mosque, **Sokollu Mehmet Paşa Camii**.

Sultanahmet attracts millions of visitors annually and tourism is now its raison d'être. Parting visitors from their hard-earned cash has become something of an art form here – be prepared to fend off the subtle but persistent **hustlers** who gather around the Hippodrome and Divan Yolu, whose main aim is to draw you into one of the many carpet shops. Few locals still reside in Sultanahmet and virtually every business here caters to the tourist trade, so a meal or drink out here inevitably means sharing it with hordes of fellow visitors. For a more Turkish night out, head across the Galata Bridge to Galata and Beyoğlu (see pp.109–129).

Haghia Sophia

Aya Sofya • Sultanahmet Meydanı 1 • Tues–Sun: April to Oct 9am–7pm; Oct to April 9am–5pm; last entry one hour before closing • ₺30 • W ayasofyamuzesi.gov.tr

For almost a thousand years, **Haghia Sophia** (Aya Sofya) was the largest enclosed space in the world, designed to impress the strength and wealth of the Byzantine emperors upon their own subjects and visiting foreign dignitaries alike. Built on the ancient acropolis, the first of Constantinople's seven hills, the church dominated the city skyline for a millennium. Following the Ottoman Turkish conquest of 1453, the domes and minarets of the city's mosques began to challenge its eminence.

Brief history

Haghia Sophia, the "Church of the Divine Wisdom", is the third church of this name to stand on the site. The first, a wooden basilica built in 360 AD, was totally destroyed during a riot. The second, a grandiose marble structure of which fragments remain, was erected under Theodosius II in 415. Like its predecessor, this too was razed to the ground. The current church was commissioned in the sixth century by Emperor Justinian, who was determined his creation would exceed the Temple of Solomon in Jerusalem in size and splendour.

Prior to the pioneering work of the architects Justinian appointed to realize his dream, **Anthemius of Tralles** and **Isidore of Miletus**, most churches followed the pattern of the rectangular, pitch-roofed Roman basilica or meeting hall. Anthemius and Isidore were to create a building of a type and scale hitherto unknown in the Byzantine world, and no imitation was attempted until the sixteenth century. The vast thirty-one-metre-diameter dome, which seems to hover over a seemingly empty space rather than being supported by solid walls, was unprecedented. The work was completed in 537 and Haghia Sophia was dedicated by Justinian on December 26th of that year.

In 558, part of the great dome collapsed in an earthquake. During reconstruction the height of the external buttresses and the dome was increased, and some of the windows blocked, resulting in an interior much gloomier than originally intended. The dome collapsed again in 989 and was rebuilt by an Armenian architect, Tridat. The worst desecration, however, was in 1204, when it was ransacked by Catholic soldiers during the **Fourth Crusade**. Mules were brought in to help carry off silver and gilt carvings and a prostitute was seated on the throne of the patriarch. In 1452, far too late to save it, the Byzantine Church reluctantly accepted union with the Catholics in the hope that Western

SULTANAHMET

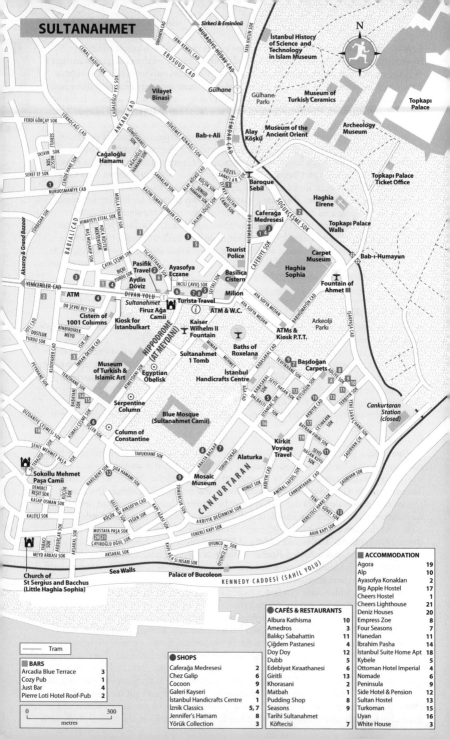

N

Sirkeci & Eminönü

İstanbul History of Science and Technology in Islam Museum

Topkapı Palace

Gülhane

Vilayet Binası

Gülhane Parkı

Museum of Turkish Ceramics

Bab-ı-Ali

Alay Köşkü

Museum of the Ancient Orient

Archeology Museum

Cağaloğlu Hamamı

Baroque Sebil

Haghia Eirene

Topkapı Palace Ticket Office

Caferağa Medresesi

Topkapı Palace Walls

Bab-ı-Humayun

Tourist Police

Carpet Museum

Pasifik Travel

Ayasofya Eczane

Basilica Cistern

Haghia Sophia

Fountain of Ahmet III

Aydın Döviz

Milion

ATM

Sultanahmet Firuz Ağa Camii

Turista Travel

ATM & W.C.

Arkeoloji Parkı

Cistern of 1001 Columns

Kiosk for İstanbulkart

Kaiser Wilhelm II Fountain

Baths of Roxelana

ATMs & Kiosk P.T.T.

HIPPODROME (AT MEYDANI)

Sultanahmet 1 Tomb

Başdoğan Carpets

Museum of Turkish & Islamic Art

Egyptian Obelisk

İstanbul Handicrafts Centre

Serpentine Column

Blue Mosque (Sultanahmet Camii)

Column of Constantine

Cankurtaran Station (closed)

Kirkit Voyage Travel

Sokollu Mehmet Paşa Camii

Arasta Bazaar

Alaturka

Mosaic Museum

CANKURTARAN

Church of St Sergius and Bacchus (Little Haghia Sophia)

Sea Walls

Palace of Bucoleon

KENNEDY CADDESİ (SAHİL YOLU)

Tram

BARS

Arcadia Blue Terrace	3
Cozy Pub	1
Just Bar	4
Pierre Loti Hotel Roof-Pub	2

0 _____ 300
metres

SHOPS

Caferağa Medresesi	2
Chez Galip	6
Cocoon	4
Galeri Kayseri	4
İstanbul Handicrafts Centre	1
İznik Classics	5, 7
Jennifer's Hamam	8
Yörük Collection	3

CAFÉS & RESTAURANTS

Albura Kathisma	10
Amedros	3
Balıkçı Sabahattin	11
Çiğdem Pastanesi	4
Doy Doy	12
Dubb	5
Edebiyat Kıraathanesi	6
Giritli	13
Khorasani	2
Matbah	1
Pudding Shop	8
Seasons	9
Tarihi Sultanahmet Köftecisi	7

ACCOMMODATION

Agora	19
Alp	10
Ayasofya Konakları	2
Big Apple Hostel	17
Cheers Hostel	1
Cheers Lighthouse	21
Deniz Houses	20
Empress Zoe	8
Four Seasons	7
Hanedan	11
İbrahim Pasha	14
İstanbul Suite Home Apt	18
Kybele	5
Nomade	9
Ottoman Hotel Imperial	4
Peninsula	9
Side Hotel & Pension	12
Sultan Hostel	13
Turkoman	15
Uyan	16
White House	3

powers would come to the aid of Constantinople against the Turks. On May 29, 1453, those who said that they would rather see the turban of the Turk than the hat of a cardinal in the streets of Constantinople got their way when the city was captured. **Mehmet the Conqueror** rode to the church of Haghia Sophia and stopped his troops looting the holy building. He then had it cleared of relics and said his first prayer there on the following Friday; this former bastion of the Byzantine Christian Empire was now a mosque.

Extensive restorations were carried out on the mosaics in the mid-nineteenth century by the Swiss **Fossati brothers**, but due to Muslim sensitivities the mosaics were later covered over again. The building continued to function as a **mosque** until 1932, when further renovations were carried out, and in 1934 Haghia Sophia opened as a **museum**.

INFORMATION
HAGHIA SOPHIA

The courtyard

Before entering the building from the west, which has always been the main entrance to the church, it's worth remembering that where you are standing was once a great, enclosed forecourt to the church. Scattered around here are some interesting archeological fragments, including a carved-marble **ambo** (Byzantine pulpit) and many beautifully carved capitals. Beyond the café is a collection of fallen masonry, with marble blocks elaborately carved in the late Roman style, once part of the classical temple-like facade of the second incarnation of Haghia Sophia. In the sunken pit to the left of the doorways is the stepped base of this second church, along with a series of blocks with relief-carved sheep symbolizing the Twelve Apostles. The depth of the pit also gives a clear indication of how far the ground level has risen over the centuries.

The narthexes

Five large portals pierce the western wall of the building. The central one, known as the **Orea Porta** or "Beautiful Gate", was reserved for the imperial entourage. Beyond it is the **outer narthex** or vestibule, a long cross-vaulted corridor which today contains a series of display boards, running from left to right along the length of the narthex, outlining the history of the site from the early Byzantine period through to the Ottoman period and beyond. It's well worth looking at this display for the cross sections, ground plans and reconstructions, which show how the building developed over the centuries. Also of interest here is a porphyry font to the left of the main portal and, to the right of it, the large marble sarcophagus of Empress Irene.

Five further doors lead through into the **inner narthex**, with a vaulted ceiling covered in gold mosaic and walls embellished with beautiful marble panels. The central portal to the nave is the **Imperial Gate**, again reserved for the emperor and his entourage only. The Byzantines believed it was made with wood from Noah's Ark, but of more interest is the superb mosaic set in the half-moon-shaped recess (lunette) above the door. It depicts a seated **Christ Pantocrator** (the All Powerful) holding an open book showing a Greek inscription that reads "Peace be upon you, I am the light of the world ". Grovelling to Christ's right is Emperor Leo IV, begging forgiveness for having married more times than was permitted under Church law.

The nave

Entering the nave through the Imperial Gate, it is hard, even for the least spiritual of visitors, not to be awed by the sheer sense of space created by the heavenly dome, some 32m in diameter and 55m above floor level. Pierced by forty windows, its scale is cleverly

1

exaggerated by the addition of half-domes to the west and east. The tympanum walls to the south and north of the central dome also emphasize the height of the building, especially as they are studded with rows of large, arched windows. At each corner of the nave are semicircular niches (*exedrae*). The galleries, which follow the line of these *exedrae* around the building, are supported by rows of columns and by four massive piers, which are the main support of the dome. The columns supporting the galleries are green antique marble, while those in the upper gallery are of Thessalian marble.

Worth noting in the northwest corner of the aisle is the **weeping column**. A legend dating from at least 1200 tells how St Gregory the Miracle-worker appeared here – the moisture subsequently seeping from the column has been believed to cure a wide range of conditions. Diagonally opposite, to the right of the apse, the circular marble-inlay panel in the floor is the **omphalos**, marking the spot where Byzantine emperors were crowned. The huge semi-dome of the apse itself contains a ninth-century **mosaic of the Virgin Mary**, Christ seated on her lap.

Byzantine **mosaics** were designed to be seen by lamp- or candlelight, which shows off the workmanship to its best advantage: flickering light reflected in pieces of glass or gold, which had been carefully embedded at minutely disparate angles, gives an appearance of movement and life to the mosaics. What remains of the **abstract mosaics**, and of the large areas of plain gold that covered the underside of the dome and other large expanses of wall and ceiling, dates from the sixth century.

Following the building's conversion to a mosque, several new features were added to suit its new purpose. Still visible today are the *mihrab*, slightly offset in the apse, a *mimber*, a sultan's loge, and the enormous wooden plaques that bear sacred Islamic names of God,

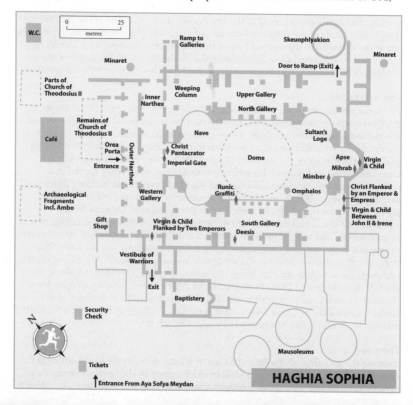

the Prophet Mohammed, the first four caliphs and the prophet's grandchildren Hassan and Hussein. These and the inscription on the dome by the calligrapher Azzet Efendi all date from the time of the restoration by the Fossati brothers.

The upper galleries
To reach the galleries, head for the northern end of the inner narthex, from where a sloping ramp leads up to the upper gallery. The logical way to proceed is across the western gallery, stopping to note the circle of green Thessalian marble that marked the **throne of the empress**, before turning left and passing through the gap in a carved marble screen into the south gallery. All the **figurative mosaics** in Haghia Sophia date from after the Iconoclastic era (726–843). One of the best is a **Deisis** scene to the right of the marble screen, depicting Christ, the Virgin and St John the Baptist. Although this mosaic is partly damaged, the three faces are all well preserved: that of John the Baptist is especially expressive, betraying great pain and suffering, while the Virgin has downcast eyes and an expression of modesty and humility. Opposite this, scratched into the balustrade running around the inside of the gallery, is some Viking **runic graffiti**. It was probably left by one of the members of the Varangian Guard, a unit recruited from Scandinavia which acted as personal bodyguards for later Byzantine emperors.

On the east wall of the south gallery, contiguous with the apse, is a **mosaic of Christ flanked by an emperor and empress**. The inscriptions over their heads read "Zoë, the most pious Augusta" and "Constantine in Christ, the Lord Autocrat, faithful Emperor of the Romans, Monomachus". It is believed that the two figures are Constantine IX Monomachus and Empress Zoë, who ruled Byzantium in her own right with her sister Theodora before she married Constantine, her third husband.

The other mosaic in the south gallery, dating from 1118, depicts the **Virgin and Child between Emperor John II Comnenus and Empress Irene**, and their son Prince Alexius, added later. This is a livelier, less conventional work than that of Zoë and Constantine, with faces full of expression: Prince Alexius, who died soon after this portrait was executed, is depicted as a wan and sickly youth, his lined face presaging his premature death.

To exit the galleries, you must head to the northeast corner of the north gallery, from where a ramp leads back down into the nave.

The Vestibule of Warriors
Today's exit from the building is from the southern end of the inner narthex, through a door leading into the **Vestibule of Warriors**. In the Byzantine period, this provided an alternative imperial entrance to the church and was where the emperor left his sword and crown. As you pass from the inner narthex into the Vestibule of Warriors, a large mirror reminds you to turn around and look upwards to see the most impressive mosaic of all, a **Virgin and Child flanked by two emperors**. Dated to the last quarter of the tenth century, it shows Emperor Justinian, to the right of the Virgin, offering a model of Haghia Sophia, while Emperor Constantine offers a model of the city of Constantinople.

Carpet Museum
Halı Müzesi • Bab-ı Hümayün Caddesi • Mon–Fri 9am–noon; 1–5pm • ₺10 • ⓦ halimuzesi.com
Some three hundred years after the conversion of the Haghia Sophia into a mosque, an *imaret* or soup kitchen was built at the northeast corner of the complex, reached through an elaborate Baroque gateway. In 2013 these splendid domed structures became home to a well-organized **Carpet Museum** displaying collection of carpets and kilims woven as long ago as the fourteenth century, and as recently as the twentieth. The collection is well labelled and explanatory boards give information on the symbolism of the various geometric motifs woven into the rugs.

1

Fountain of Ahmet III

Ahmet III Çeşmesi • Bab-ı Hümayün Caddesi

The Rococo-style **Fountain of Ahmet III** stands opposite the equally ornate gateway to the Carpet Museum. Dating to the eighteenth century, this square structure is surmounted by exaggeratedly overhanging eaves above which sprout five small domes. At each corner are fancy marble grilles from which water and, on special occasions, **şerbert** drinks were handed to passers-by. There were also four taps, one on each side, from which locals could draw water. Above the taps, in stylized, gilded Arabic, are verses from the famous poet, Seyit Vehbi Efendi.

Soğukçeşme Sokağı

Sandwiched between the bulk of Haghia Sophia to the west and the perimeter wall of the Topkapı Palace to the east, the narrow pedestrianized **Soğukçeşme Sokağı** or "street of the cold fountains" contains virtually all that's left of the area's once abundant wooden houses. Most of them, attractively painted in pastel colours, date to the late nineteenth or early twentieth centuries, but are identical in style to their predecessors, destroyed in one of the waves of fires that engulfed the city in Ottoman times. They were heavily restored (cynics may argue completely rebuilt) in the 1980s, and most have the overhanging upper floors (*cumba* in Turkish) which were so typical of Ottoman-era houses. Take the first left just past the Haghia Sophia onto Cafériye Sokağı and on the right is an exquisite domed building with a courtyard, the **Caférağa Medresesi**. Built by Ottoman master-architect Sinan, this former religious school is now home to traditional craft workshops and a pleasant café (see p.220).

Topkapı Palace

Topkapı Sarayı Müzesi • **Palace** Mon & Wed–Sun: April–Oct 9am–7pm; Nov–March 9am–5pm; last entry one hour before closing • ₺30; free to enter the first court • **Haghia Eirene** Mon & Wed–Sun 9am–4pm • ₺20 • **Harem** Mon & Wed–Sun 10am–4pm • ₺15 • Ⓦ topkapisarayi.gov.tr

Topkapı Palace (Topkapı Sarayı) was both the symbolic and political centre of the Ottoman Empire for nearly four centuries, until the removal of the imperial retinue to Dolmabahçe, by Sultan Abdülmecit I in 1853. It's a beautiful setting in which to wander and contemplate the majesty of the Ottoman sultanate, as well as the cruelty exemplified by institutions such as the Harem and "the Cage".

Originally known as *Sarayı Cedid*, or New Palace, Topkapı was built between 1459 and 1465 as the seat of government of the newly installed Ottoman regime. It was not at first a residence: Mehmet the Conqueror had already built what would become known as the Old Palace on the present site of Istanbul University (see p.86) and even after he himself moved, his *harem* stayed on at the old site.

In accordance with Islamic tradition, the palace consists of a collection of buildings arranged around a series of courtyards, similar to the Alhambra in Granada or a Moghul palace in India. Although this creates an initial impression of disorder, in fact the arrangement is meticulously logical. The **first court** was the service area of the palace and open to all, while most of the second court and its attendant buildings were devoted to the Divan, or Council of State, and to those who had business with it. The pavilions of judges were located at the **Ortakapı** (the entrance to the palace proper, between the first and second courts), in accordance with the tradition that justice should be dispensed at the gate of the palace.

The **third court** was mainly given over to the palace school, an important imperial institution devoted to the training of civil servants, and it is only in the **fourth court** that the serious business of state gave way to the more pleasurable aspects of life. Around the attractive **gardens** here are a number of pavilions erected by successive emperors in celebration of their victories. Here, the glorious views and sunsets could be enjoyed in privileged retreat from their four-thousand-member retinue.

The various adjustments made to the structure and function of the buildings were indicative of the power shifts in the Ottoman Empire over the centuries. During the "Rule of the Harem" in the sixteenth century, for example, a passageway was opened between the Harem and the Divan. In the eighteenth century, when the power of the sultan had declined, the offices of state were transferred away from the "Eye of the Sultan" (the window in the Divan through which a sultan could monitor proceedings) to the gateway that led to the palaces of the grand vizier, known as the Sublime Port.

INFORMATION   TOPKAPI PALACE

Tickets The ticket office for the Topkapı complex is situated to the right of the path as it approaches the second gate; that to the Harem, which charges a further admission, is in the second courtyard, meaning you can't visit the Harem without paying for entry to the palace.

Visiting tips Much of your time exploring (and you will need at least half a day) will be spent outside, either in the court gardens or walking between separate buildings, so try

to pick a dry day. Should your visit coincide with large parties of cruise-ship passengers, or mostly charming but always noisy groups of Turkish school children, the queues to some rooms, especially the Imperial Treasury and Room of the Relics of the Prophet in the third court, can be interminable.

Eating Apart from a small café in the second court, there's only the expensive *Konyalı Café* for food, so it's best to eat before entering.

First court

Most visitors approach the palace by entering the first court through the great defensive imperial gate of Mehmet the Conqueror, the **Bab-ı Hümayün**. Once through the gateway you are in the first courtyard. In the Ottoman period this was the palace's service area and open, as it is today, to the general public every day except Tuesday. The long-defunct **palace bakeries** are behind a wall to the right of the courtyard and the buildings of the **imperial mint and outer treasury** (all currently closed) are behind the wall north of the church of **Haghia Eirene**. In front of Haghia Eirene were located the quarters of the straw-weavers and carriers of silver pitchers, around a central courtyard in which the palace firewood was stored.

Haghia Eirene

Haghia Eirene (Aya İrini), "the Church of the Divine Peace", was originally constructed in the reign of Constantine (reigned 306–337), making it one of the city's oldest churches. It was rebuilt along with Haghia Sophia after being burnt down in the Nika riots of 532. The entry fee is steep considering visitors are confined to the narthex of the church, but as it's one of the most important Byzantine churches in the city viewing is essential for anyone with more than a passing interest in the period. Around the semicircular apse is the only **synthronon** (seating space for clergy in the apse of a church) in Istanbul to have survived the Byzantine era. It has six tiers of seats with an ambulatory running behind the fourth tier. The majority of the interior is now plain, exposed brickwork; most interesting is the simple mosaic in the apse, a plain black cross outlined against a gold background. This mosaic, completed when the church was repaired following an earthquake in 740, is typical of the Iconoclastic period (see box, p.282) when figurative images were prohibited. Interestingly, the church was never converted to a mosque, though it served as an arsenal for much of the Ottoman period, and in the nineteenth century as a depot for archeological treasures. Entry to the church may be restricted when it is being used for occasional music performances, particularly during the International Istanbul Music Festival (see p.33).

Ortakapı, the second court and the Divan

To reach the second court you pass through the Bab-üs Selam, "the Gate of Salutations", otherwise known as the **Ortakapı**, or middle gate. In the Ottoman period, only the sultan was allowed to ride through here, everyone else had to

1

TOPKAPI PALACE

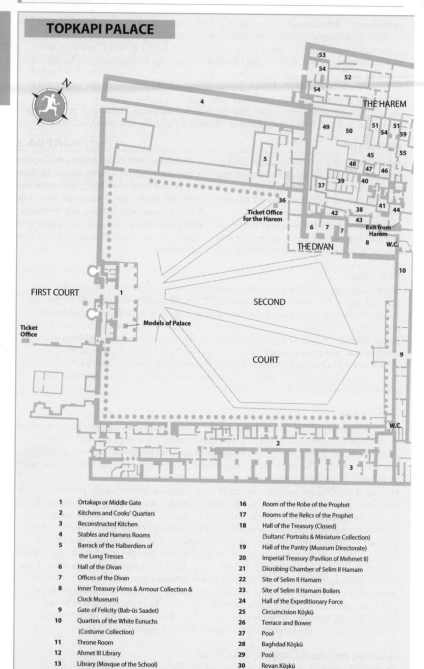

THE HAREM

53
54
52
54

49   50   51   51
         54   59

48   47   45   55
   46

37   39   40

Ticket Office
for the Harem   36

42   38   41   44
6   7   7   43
THE DIVAN   Exit from
                                    Harem
                              8   W.C.

FIRST COURT   10

Ticket
Office   1

      Models of Palace   SECOND

                              COURT   9

                                           W.C.

            2

            3

1	Ortakapı or Middle Gate	**16**	Room of the Robe of the Prophet
2	Kitchens and Cooks' Quarters	**17**	Rooms of the Relics of the Prophet
3	Reconstructed Kitchen	**18**	Hall of the Treasury (Closed)
4	Stables and Harness Rooms		(Sultans' Portraits & Miniature Collection)
5	Barrack of the Halberdiers of	**19**	Hall of the Pantry (Museum Directorate)
	the Long Tresses	**20**	Imperial Treasury (Pavilion of Mehmet II)
6	Hall of the Divan	**21**	Disrobing Chamber of Selim II Hamam
7	Offices of the Divan	**22**	Site of Selim II Hamam
8	Inner Treasury (Arms & Armour Collection &	**23**	Site of Selim II Hamam Boilers
	Clock Museum)	**24**	Hall of the Expeditionary Force
9	Gate of Felicity (Bab-üs Saadet)	**25**	Circumcision Köşkü
10	Quarters of the White Eunuchs	**26**	Terrace and Bower
	(Costume Collection)	**27**	Pool
11	Throne Room	**28**	Baghdad Köşkü
12	Ahmet III Library	**29**	Pool
13	Library (Mosque of the School)	**30**	Revan Köşkü
14	Harem Mosque	**31**	Tulip Gardens of Ahmet III
15	Court of the Room of the Robe	**32**	Mustafa Paşa Köşkü

0		20
	metres	

33	Physician's Tower	**51**	Apartments of Senior Women
34	Mecidiye Köşkü	**52**	Court of Women's hospital
35	Third Gate	**53**	Hospital Hamam
36	Entry to the Harem (Carriage Gate)	**54**	Hospital Kitchen Quarters
37	Mosque of the Black Eunuchs	**55**	Sultan Ahmet Kiosk
38	Court of the Black Eunuchs	**56**	Harem Garden
39	Barrack of the Black Eunuchs	**57**	Valide Sultan's Court
40	Princes' School	**58**	Valide Sultan's Dining Room
41	Quarters of the Chief Black Eunuchs	**59**	Valide Sultan's Bedroom
42	Quarters of the Treasurer	**60**	Valide Sultan's Hamam
43	Quarters of the Chamberlain	**61**	Kadin's Quarters
44	Aviary Gate (Kuşhane Kapısı)	**62**	Golden Road
45	Courtyard of the Women of the Harem	**63**	Ahmet III Dining Room
46	Kitchen of the Women	**64**	Throne Room Within
47	Hamam of the Women	**65**	The Sultan's Hamam
48	Stairs to Bedrooms	**66**	Osman III Terrace
49	Laundry	**67**	Terrace of Selâmlik Garden
50	Women's Dormitory	**68**	Apartment of the Selamlik (Sultan's Rooms)

1

dismount. Surmounted by attractive octagonal towers, it marks an imposing entrance to the main part of the complex. Today, the ticket turnstiles and security checks are located in this gateway.

Immediately to the right after passing through the security check are a couple of glass cases containing scale-models of the palace complex, useful for orientation. To the left and hidden from view down a hill are the **Privy Stables of Mehmet II**, which are used for temporary exhibitions. Diagonally left are the buildings of the Divan and the Inner Treasury and the entrance to the Harem. Opposite the Divan, on the right side of the courtyard, is the kitchen area, while straight ahead is the gateway to the third court.

The gardens between the paths radiating from the Ortakapı are planted with ancient cypresses and plane trees, rose bushes and lawns. Originally, they would also have been resplendent with peacocks, gazelles and, most importantly, fountains. This **second court** was the scene of pageantry during state ceremonies, when the sultan occupied his throne beneath the Bab-üs Saadet. At all times, even on one of the three days of the week when the courtyard was filled with petitioners to the Divan, silence reigned here, as people obeyed the rules of conduct imposed in the presence – actual or potential – of the sultan.

As you enter the buildings of the **Divan** you'll see the metal grille in the Council Chamber (the first room on the left), called "the Eye of the Sultan". Through this he could observe the proceedings of the Divan, where the eminent imperial councillors sat in session, and which took its name from the couch running around the three walls of the room. The building dates essentially from the reign of Mehmet the Conqueror, and the Council Chamber was restored to its sixteenth-century appearance in 1945, with some of the original İznik tiles and arabesque painting. The other two rooms of the Divan have retained the Rococo decorations of Ahmet III. The **Divan tower**, rebuilt in incongruous Neoclassical style in 1825, rises above the council chamber, but is not currently open to visitors.

THE CAGE

The Cage was adopted by Ahmet I as an alternative to fratricide, which had become institutionalized in the Ottoman Empire since the days of Beyazıt II. To avoid wars of succession, Beyazıt ruled that a sultan should execute his brothers upon his accession to the throne. The Cage was introduced as a way around this practice, but in the event proved a less than satisfactory solution. After the death of their father, the younger princes would be incarcerated along with deaf mutes and a *harem* of concubines, while their eldest brother acceded to the throne. They remained in the suite of rooms of the Harem known in Turkish as **Kafes** (the Cage) until such time as they were called upon to take power themselves. The concubines never left the Cage unless they became pregnant, and great care was taken to prevent this, either by the removal of their ovaries or by the use of pessaries, since if it did occur they were immediately drowned.

The decline of the Ottoman Empire has in part been attributed to the institution of the Cage. The sultans who spent any length of time there emerged crazed, avaricious and debauched. Osman II, for example, enjoyed archery, but only when using live targets, including prisoners of war and his own pages. He was assassinated by the janissaries, to be replaced by Mustafa I, who had all but died of starvation in the Cage and was even madder than his predecessor. He, too, was assassinated. The worst affected of all, however, was İbrahim, better known as **Deli İbrahim** (İbrahim the Mad). He spent 22 years in the Cage, and when they came to take him out he was so sure he was about to be assassinated that he had to be removed forcibly. His reign was characterized by sexual excess and political misrule (his mother, Köşem, once complained that there was not enough wood for the Harem fires and he responded by having his grand vizier executed). Eventually, in response to a rumour of *harem* intrigue, İbrahim had all bar two of his 280 concubines bound in sacks and thrown into the Bosphorus. According to one version of events, only one survived; wriggling free of her bonds, she was rescued by a passing French ship and taken to Paris.

Next to the Divan is another building from Mehmet the Conqueror's original palace, the **Inner Treasury**, a six-domed hall preceded by a double-domed vestibule and supported internally by three piers. The former treasury is now the Armoury Museum and houses an impressive collection of (mainly) Ottoman arms and armour. Look out for the curved sword of Mehmet the Conqueror inscribed with the words "may the necks of the enemies of Sheriat become the scabbards of this sword", and all the usual paraphernalia of late medieval warfare, from maces and axes to bows and shields. Kids may be intrigued by the hologram room, with flickering 3D representations of Ottoman janissaries and cavalry. Next to it is the Clock Museum, which contains some 380 clocks assembled by the Ottoman imperial family over a period of 400 years.

Across the courtyard from the Divan are the **palace kitchens and cooks' quarters**. Much of this complex was destroyed by fire in 1574, though the chimneys were stylishly reconstructed by Mimar Sinan, as were eight of the ten domes behind them (the two southernmost domes date back to the reign of Mehmet the Conqueror). The ten kitchens, which had a staff of 1500, all served different purposes; they are closed to visitors.

Third court

As you pass through the **Bab-üs Saadet**, "the Gate of Felicity", the **Throne Room** is immediately in front of you. This building, mainly dating from the reign of Selim I, was where the sultan awaited the outcome of sessions of the Divan in order to give his assent or otherwise to their proposals. This courtyard was also home to the Enderun or Palace School, making it arguably the most important courtyard in the palace, as it was here that the administrators, soldiers, artisans and artists who formed the backbone of the whole imperial Ottoman edifice were trained.

The grey marble building at the centre of the third courtyard, the **Ahmet III Library** is restrained and sombre compared to his highly decorative fountain outside the gates of the palace. To the right of the gate, behind the colonnade running around the southern edge of the courtyard, is the **Hall of the Expeditionary Force**, sometimes referred to as the Hall of the Campaign Pages (*Seferli Koğuşu*), which houses a collection of embroidery and a very small selection from the imperial costume collection. The latter includes a charming little outfit of Selim I's – red with yellow circles – prompting the question of where he could have acquired his epithet "the Grim".

Imperial Treasury

The **Imperial Treasury** is housed in the rooms that once functioned as the Pavilion of Mehmet II, which takes up most of the southeast side of the third courtyard, to the right of the entrance. The first two rooms – the right-hand one of which was used as the *camekan* or disrobing chamber of the *hamam* of Selim II – are beautifully proportioned and domed.

The first room contains a number of highly wrought and extremely beautiful objects, including a delicate silver model of a palace complete with tiny birds in the trees, a present to Abdülhamit II from Japan. The big crowd-puller in room two is the **Topkapı Dagger**, which starred alongside Peter Ustinov in the Sunday-matinee classic *Topkapi*. A present from Mahmut I to Nadir Shah that was waylaid and brought back when news of the shah's death reached Topkapı, the dagger is decorated with three enormous emeralds, one of which conceals a watch. In the third room, the **Spoonmaker's Diamond**, the fifth-largest diamond in the world, is invariably surrounded by a gawping crowd, which perhaps gives some impression of the effect it must have had during its first public appearance, adorning Mehmet IV's turban at his coronation in 1648.

The fourth room boasts a bejewelled throne and the hand and occipital bone of John the Baptist, but otherwise it's a relative haven of restraint, with ivory and sandalwood objects predominating.

1

Across the courtyard from the Imperial Treasury, the Pavilion of the Holy Mantle houses the **Rooms of the Relics of the Prophet**, holy relics brought home by Selim the Grim after his conquest of Egypt in 1517. The relics were originally viewed only by the sultan, his family and his immediate entourage on days of special religious significance, but were opened to the public in 1962. They include a footprint, hair and a tooth of the Prophet Mohammed, as well as his mantle and standard, swords of the first four caliphs and a letter from the Prophet to the leader of the Coptic tribe. The most precious of the relics are kept behind glass, attractively arranged and lit.

Fourth court

The **fourth court** consists of several gardens, each graced with pavilions. The **Baghdad Köşkü**, in the northeast corner of the tulip gardens laid out under Sultan Ahmet III, was built by Murat IV to celebrate the conquest of Baghdad in 1638. The exterior and cool, dark interior are tiled in blue, turquoise and white, and the shutters and cupboard doors are inlaid with tortoiseshell and mother-of-pearl. The **Circumcision Köşkü**, in the Portico of Columns, a short way west of the Baghdad Köşkü, also dates from the reign of İbrahim the Mad. Outside, it's covered in İznik tiles of the sixteenth and early seventeenth centuries. Any number of different patterns are represented in the eclectic design, but they include some of the most beautiful panels from the very best İznik period. Between these two beautiful *köşk*s is a terrace graced by a small gilt canopy, the İftariye, built by İbrahim the Mad in 1640 to celebrate the breaking of the fast during Ramadan. From here, the views up the Golden Horn, across to Galata and towards the Bosphorus, are superb. At the other end of the Portico of Columns is the **Revan Köşkü**, built to commemorate the capture of Erivan in the Caucasus by Mehmet IV.

The **Mecidiye Köşkü** – the last building to be erected at Topkapı – commands the best view of any of the Topkapı pavilions. It now houses the *Konyalı Café*. On a clear day from its garden terrace you can identify most of the buildings on the Asian shore of the Bosphorus.

Harem

The entrance to the **Harem** is in the second court. The word "harem" means "forbidden" in Arabic; in Turkish, it refers to a suite of apartments in a palace or private residence where the head of the household lived with his wives, odalisques (female slaves) and children. The Harem in Topkapı lies between the sultan's private apartments and the quarters of the Chief Black Eunuch. It consisted of over four hundred rooms, centred on the suites of the sultan and his mother, the valide sultan. Around these, in descending order of rank, were the apartments of the wives, favourites, sultan's daughters, princes, housekeepers, maids and odalisques.

Carriage Gate

The Harem was connected to the outside world by means of the **Carriage Gate**, so called because the odalisques would have entered their carriages here when they went on outings. To the left of the Carriage Gate as you enter the Harem is the **Barracks of the Halberdiers of the Long Tresses**. Blinkered to ensure the privacy of the women, they carried logs and other loads into the Harem, as well as serving as imperial guardsmen. The Carriage Gate and the Aviary Gate were both guarded by black eunuchs, who were responsible for running the *harem*, but only allowed to enter in daylight hours. At night, the female housekeepers took charge and reported any unusual occurrences to the Chief Black Eunuch.

The rooms of the Harem

The *Altın Yol*, or **Golden Road**, ran the entire length of the Harem, from the quarters of the Black Eunuchs to the fourth courtyard. Strategically located at the beginning of this passageway were the **apartments of the valide sultan**, also rebuilt after 1665.

THE WOMEN OF THE HAREM

The concept of the *harem* has long held a grip on the Western imagination. The most famous product of the Topkapı *Harem* was Haseki Hürrem, or Roxelana, wife of Süleyman the Magnificent. Prior to their marriage, it was unusual for a sultan to marry at all, let alone to choose a wife from among his concubines. The marriage, and the subsequent installation of the *harem* women in the palace, established the women of the *harem*, and especially the **valide sultan** (the mother of the reigning sultan), in a position of unprecedented power and enabled women to take more control over affairs of state.

Roxelana began this new order in characteristic vein: she persuaded Süleyman to murder both his Grand Vizier, İbrahim Paşa, and his son, the heir apparent, Mustafa – the latter in order to make way for her own son, Selim the Sot. The favourite of Selim the Sot, **Nur Banu**, made a significant change to the layout of the Harem when she became valide sultan in her turn. She moved her suite of apartments from one end of the Golden Road to the other, so that it was located next to that of her son, Murat III. This also meant she was lodged near to the entrance of the Divan and could easily listen in on affairs of state. Nur Banu encouraged her son in debauchery (he fathered a total of 103 children, 54 of whom survived him) and persuaded him to murder his most able minister, the Grand Vizier Sokollu Mehmet Paşa.

The number of **odalisques** (female slaves) employed in the *harem* increased steadily with the decline of the Ottoman Empire, and by the reign of Abdülaziz (1861–76) there were 809 in Topkapı. Many were imported from Georgia and Caucasia for their looks, or were prisoners of war, captured in Hungary, Poland or Venice. Upon entering the *harem*, they would become the charges of the *haznedar usta*, who would teach them how to behave towards the sultan and the other palace inhabitants. The conditions in which the majority of these women lived were dangerously unhygienic and many of them died from vermin-carried and waterborne diseases, or from the cold of an Istanbul winter. The women who were chosen to enter the bedchamber of the sultan, however, were promoted to the rank of imperial odalisque, given slaves to serve them, and pleasant accommodation. If they bore him a child, they would be promoted to the rank of favourite or wife, with their own apartments. If the sultan subsequently lost affection for one of these women, he could give her in marriage to one of his courtiers.

They include a particularly lovely domed dining room. A passageway leads from her apartments to those of the women she controlled, the senior women of the court. These compact areas had an upper gallery, in which bedding was stored, windows and a hearth.

Beyond the valide sultan's apartments, to the north, are some of the most attractive rooms of the palace. These were the apartments and reception rooms of the *selamlık*, the sultan's own rooms. The largest and grandest of them is the **Hünkar Sofrası**, the Imperial Hall, where the sultan entertained visitors. Another important room in this section is a masterwork of the architect Sinan: the **bedchamber of Murat III**, covered in sixteenth-century İznik tiles and kitted out with a marble fountain and, opposite, a bronze fireplace surrounded by a panel of tiling representing plum blossom.

The northernmost rooms of the Harem are supported by immense piers and vaults, providing capacious basements that were used as dormitories and storerooms. Below the bedchamber is a large indoor **swimming pool**, with taps for hot and cold water, where Murat is supposed to have thrown gold to women who pleased him. Next to the bedchamber is the light and airy **library of Ahmet I**, with windows overlooking both the Bosphorus and the Golden Horn; beyond this is the **dining room of Ahmet III**, whose walls are covered in wood panelling painted with bowls of fruit and flowers, typical of the extravagant tulip-loving sultan. To the southwest of the bedchamber are two rooms originally thought to be the notorious **Cage** (see box, p.54), though this is no longer believed to be the case – the Cage was actually situated in various rooms on the floor above. The exit from the Harem is the **Aviary Gate**, or Kudhane Kapısı, which brings visitors into the third court.

1

Gülhane Parkı and around

Gülhane Parkı surrounds Topkapı Palace on all sides. Once the extended gardens of the sultans, it is now a public park with mature trees, home to nesting herons in spring. It's a good place for kids to run off steam, though there's little play equipment. For tea and sustenance, the *Set Üstü Çay Bahçesi* (see p.179) in the northeast corner of the park is excellent; from here you can admire the **Goth's Column**, erected in the third or fourth century to commemorate a victory over the Goths, and views over the Bosphorus. The park stays open until well after dusk during the summer months, though the security guards are vague about exact closing times. The entrance to the History of Science and Technology in Islam is inside the park, and one approach to the wonderful Archeology Museum complex is also through the park.

Bab-ı-Ali

Heading downhill along the line of the tram from Sultanahmet, past the entrance to Gülhane Parkı, you'll see on the left an ornamental gateway, the **Bab-ı-Ali** or Sublime Porte. It marked the entrance to the administrative centre of the Ottoman Empire where, from the mid-seventeenth century onwards, the vizier presided over the day-to-day running of the empire. The Baroque-style gate, only erected in 1843, seems rather grandiose for its present-day purpose, marking the back entrance to the **Vilayet Binası**, the local government headquarters for the province of Istanbul.

Alay Köşkü

Opposite the Bab-ı-Ali, built into the high stone walls of Gülhane Parkı, part of the outer defences of the Topkapı Palace built by Fatih Mehmet II around 1465, is the **Alay Köşkü**. From this raised gazebo, sultans could watch official parades pass by, or, as was the wont of the more suspicious rulers, keep an eye on who was passing in and out of the Bab-ı-Ali across the road. One, Murat IV, kept his subjects on their toes by firing crossbow bolts at them from up here. The sloping ramp allowing sultans to reach the lookout on horseback is reached from inside Gülhane Parkı, a short way back up the hill.

Istanbul History of Science and Technology in Islam Museum

Istanbul İslam Bilim ve Teknoliji Tarihi Müzesi • Gülhane Parkı • Daily except Tues 9am–5pm • ₺10 • W ibttm.org

In the old imperial stables in Gülhane Parkı, built against the northwestern walls of the park, is the **History of Science and Technology in Islam Museum**. It houses a series of replicas of inventions by Islamic scientists between the eighth and sixteenth centuries. Purists may decry the absence of genuine artefacts but the models, produced at the Johann Wolfgang Goethe University in Frankfurt, are extremely well crafted and were based on genuine source material. They are beautifully displayed and certainly belie the West's often patronizing attitude towards science and technology in the Muslim world. Exhibits include a model of a planetarium based on the tenth-century works of the Islamic astronomer as-Siğzi, and a model based on a twelfth-century water-powered clock, shaped like an elephant.

Archeology Museum complex

Arkeoloji Müzesi • Osman Hamdi Bey Yokuşu, Gülhane • Enter either through Gülhane Parkı or from the first courtyard of the Topkapı Palace • Tues–Sun: April to Oct 9am–7pm; Nov to March 9am–5pm; last entry 30min before closing • ₺15 • W Istanbularkeoloji.gov.tr

The **Archeology Museum** complex, comprised of three separate buildings, contains a stunning array of finds from Anatolia, the Middle East and Istanbul itself. One of the city's most underrated sights, it attracts none of the crowds of the Topkapı Palace or the Haghia Sophia. The museum was established in 1875 in the **Çinili Köşk** (Tiled Pavilion), which still forms part of the museum complex. In 1891 a purpose-built Neoclassical pile, designed by the French architect Alexander Vallaury (also responsible for the *Pera Palace* hotel, see p.123), was completed opposite the Çinili Köşk to house the

CLOCKWISE FROM TOP BLUE MOSQUE (P.64); BASILICA CISTERN (P.61); ENTRANCE TO SOKOLLU MEHMET PAŞA CAMİİ (P.66)>

1

rapidly expanding collection. Today this is home to the majority of objects on display here, along with a smaller building, the **Museum of the Ancient Orient**, which houses the oldest finds. The museum was established as a direct response to the Western powers removing shiploads of antiquities from the Ottoman Empire to stock museums in London, Paris, Berlin and elsewhere. Given that the former Ottoman domains included lands home to some of the world's most exciting ancient civilizations, from the Assyrians to the Hittites, Egyptians to the Greeks and Romans to the Byzantines, it's hardly surprising that this museum complex contains so many world-class exhibits. Note that work to earthquake-proof the main building was ongoing at the time of writing and may result in the temporary closure of some sections.

The Museum of the Ancient Orient

The entrance to the **Museum of the Ancient Orient** (Eski Şark Eserleri Müzesi) is just to the left as you pass through the complex's ticket barrier. Housed in a fine Neoclassical building built in 1883, which was formerly a fine arts school, it contains a small but dazzling collection of Anatolian, Egyptian and Mesopotamian artefacts. The superbly preserved, late Hittite basalt lions flanking the entrance date from the ninth century BC, and give a taste of the incredible state of preservation of some of the exhibits inside.

One of the most interesting exhibits is the oldest peace treaty known to mankind, the **Treaty of Kadesh** in Room 7, found at the Hittite capital Hattusa. Written in cuneiform script, it was signed in 1274 when a battle fought on the River Orontes (today's Ası Nehri in Anatolia), between Pharaoh Ramses II and the Hittite king Muvatellish, ended in stalemate. The treaty includes a ceasefire agreement and pledges of a mutual exchange of political refugees, and was originally engraved onto silver tablets. It is the world's first known peace treaty, and a copy has pride of place in the United Nations' headquarters in New York.

The blue-and-yellow **animal relief** in the corridor beyond Room 1 dates from the reign of Nebuchadnezzar (604–562 BC), the last hero-king of Babylonia, when it would have lined the processional way in Babylon. Other exhibits were taken from Nebuchadnezzar's palace-museum, located at the Ishtar Gate. Another massive relief, in Room 8, depicts a three-times-life-sized **Hittite king Urpalla** presenting gifts of grapes and grain to a vegetation god. This is a plaster copy of a relief found at İvriz Kaya near Konya, dating from the eighth century BC.

Other exhibits include a **Sumerian** love poem and a tablet of Sumerian proverbs dating from the eighteenth century BC. In Room 7, the figure of a Babylonian duck was actually a **standard weight** belonging to a priest called Musallim Marduk: it weighs about 30kg and dates from around 2000 BC, making it the oldest known standard measure.

The Archeology Museum

One of the catalysts for the construction of the main building of the complex was to provide a home for the stunning sarcophagi uncovered by Osman Hamdi Bey, the Director of Ancient Antiquities, during excavations at Sidon in 1887. There is much else to see, however, in this wonderful museum, making it a must for anyone interested in the history of this city and the lands over which it once ruled.

The **Sidon Sarcophagi**, can be found in Rooms 9, 8 and 7 (to reach them turn left at the main entrance). Chief among them is the **Lycian Sarcophagus**, depicting centaurs, sphinxes and griffons, as well as scenes from Greek mythology. It is in the Lycian style, but the carvings show a Peloponnesian influence in the stocky bodies and broad faces of the human figures. In the same room are the anthropoid sarcophagi from Sidon, which illustrate the fifth-century BC fashion for Egyptian models in Greek sculpture. The **Tabnit Sarcophagus**, the oldest Sidon discovery, is in fact Egyptian in origin. A hieroglyphic inscription on the chest of this alabaster mummy-case states that it belonged to an Egyptian commander named Penephtah.

Dating from the end of the fourth century BC, the fabulous **Alexander Sarcophagus** is so called because it is covered with scenes of Alexander the Great hunting and in battle. It is ascribed variously by different sources to a ruler of the Seleucid dynasty or to the Phoenician Prince Abdolonyme. The metal weapons originally held by warriors and huntsmen on the sarcophagi were stolen prior to the excavations of Hamdi Bey, presumably when the burial chambers were looted.

The Ionic architecture of another of the Sidon sarcophagi, the **Sarcophagus of the Mourning Women**, shows eighteen members of the *harem* of King Straton (who died in 360 BC) in various poses of distress and mourning. From Room 7 you can continue round into the northeast wing of the museum, where there are several rooms containing more funerary relics. Right of the entrance, Rooms 13–20 contain a comprehensive collection of statuary dating from the Archaic through to the Roman period, much of it of superb quality. Room 16 exhibits a vivid statue of a young Alexander the Great, carved in the stylized manner popular at Pergamon, on Turkey's Aegean coast, in the second century BC.

The new wing, to the rear of the main body of the museum, contains exhibits from the **Thracian and Bithynian civilizations**, but of most interest is the **Byzantine collection**. A small but beautifully lit collection of artefacts that highlights the successful transition between Classical Roman and Christian Byzantine art, it includes a relief-carved plinth decorated with Nike, the winged goddess of victory, once topped by Constantinople's greatest charioteer, Porphyrius, which used to stand in the Hippodrome (see p.63).

On the first floor, the **Istanbul through the Ages** exhibition is rather dated but gives a superb overview of the city's complex history. The actual exhibits are small scale but carefully chosen – don't miss the case containing the bronze serpent's head, knocked off the fifth-century BC Serpentine column (see p.63) in the Hippodrome, or the section of the chain used to block access to the Golden Horn to enemy ships during the Byzantine period.

The next level up is devoted to the **Anatolia and Troy through the Ages** collections, well worth seeing, especially if you have either been to or are planning to visit the legendary city of Troy (see pp.259–261). The exhibits include a range of artefacts unearthed by Heinrich Schliemann and his successor, Dorpfield, at Troy, including much gold jewellery. On the third floor, **Neighbouring Cultures of Anatolia** concentrates on the ancient civilizations of Syria, Cyprus and Palestine and includes the famous Siloam inscription, a votive tablet dating back to the eighth century BC written in Paleo-Hebraic.

The Museum of Turkish Ceramics

The graceful **Çinili Köşk** or Tiled Pavilion – a few metres north of the Museum of the Ancient Orient – was built in 1472 as a grandstand, from which the sultan could watch sporting activities such as wrestling or polo. It now houses the **Museum of Turkish Ceramics**, displaying tiles of equal quality to those in Topkapı Palace and Istanbul's older mosques, along with well-written explanations of the different periods in the history of Turkish ceramics. Look particularly for polychrome tiles of the mid-sixteenth to mid-seventeenth centuries, dating from the longest and most successful period of tile production. Interesting exhibits include a mosque lamp from the Sokollu Mehmet Paşa Camii (see p.66), a ceramic coffee-cooler in which beans were placed after roasting and before grinding, and Murat III's attractive little fountain in the wall of the last room of all, after the İznik collection.

Basilica Cistern

Yerebatan Sarnıcı • Entrance on Caferiye Sokak • Daily 9am–7pm • ₺20 • ⓦ yerebatan.com

The **Basilica Cistern** (Yerebatan Sarnıcı) is one of many underground cisterns scattered throughout the city. This one, buried under the very core of Sultanahmet, is the first to have been extensively excavated. Although generally crowded, it is surprisingly spectacular and well worth seeing.

1

Probably built by the Emperor Constantine in the fourth century, and enlarged by Justinian in the sixth, the cistern was supplied by aqueducts with water from the Belgrade Forest. In turn, it supplied the Great Palace and later Topkapı Palace. The cistern fell into disuse after the Ottoman conquest and its existence was only brought to public attention in 1545 by the Frenchman **Petrus Gyllius**. He had been led to it by local residents, whose houses were built over the cistern and who had sunk wells into it. They even kept boats on the water from which they could fish its depths – Gyllius' interest was first aroused when he found fresh fish being sold in the streets nearby.

In 1987, fifty thousand tonnes of mud and water were removed, the walls were covered to make them impermeable, and eight of the columns were sheathed in concrete to fortify the structure. The construction of raised pathways to replace the rowboats used by early tourists may seem a desecration, but they do facilitate a leisurely examination of interesting bits of masonry, as does the careful spotlighting. Despite the piped muzak, the cistern is deeply atmospheric, with carp swimming lazily through the floodlit waters and water dripping steadily from the vaults above.

The largest covered cistern in the city, Yerebatan held eighty thousand cubic metres of water. The small brick **domes** are supported by 336 columns, arranged in 12 rows of 28, many of which have Corinthian capitals. The columns' varied styles probably indicate that they were made from the recycled remnants of earlier structures. One, decorated with a tear-drop relief-carved pattern, looks like it came from the triumphal Arch of Theodosius in Beyazıt (see p.85). The two **Medusa-head capitals** supporting a couple of columns in the southwest corner are also clearly relics from an older building. Part of the 1963 James Bond classic *From Russia with Love* was filmed here.

Divan Yolu

The main approach from Sultanahmet to Beyazıt (see p.85) is **Divan Yolu**, a major thoroughfare that gained its name because it was the principal approach to the Divan from the Topkapı Gate. Hordes of people would pour along it three times a week to make their petitions to the court. In Roman and Byzantine times, this street was the Mese or "Middleway" and ran from a triumphal arch known as the **Milion**, a marked fragment of which remains at the eastern end of Divan Yolu, westwards through the city – eventually linking in with the great Roman road system to reach as far as the Adriatic. Today it remains a crucial part of the city's transport network.

THE "WORLD FAMOUS" PUDDING SHOP

Back in the heady days of the 1960s, when Flower Power ruled and kaftans, Afghan coats and Jesus sandals were seen as serious fashion statements, every right-thinking young person wanted to head east to India. That meant an arduous overland trip from Europe – via Istanbul. In folk memory at least, the so-called **Hippy Trail** was one long procession of VW campervans daubed with peace logos and spaced-out hitchhikers wondering whether they were in Brussels or Belgrade. **The Pudding Shop** (or, to give it its proper name, the *Lale* (*Tulip*) *Restaurant*; see p.178) became the gathering point for those travellers setting out on the most difficult leg of the trail – across Anatolian Turkey and into Iran, Afghanistan and Pakistan and on to the fabled land of India.

The **Çolpan brothers**, İdris and Namik, having established their restaurant on Sultanahmet's busy Divan Yolu in 1957, were surprised to find it becoming *the* place where hippies met to swap stories and arrange onward transport. With typical Istanbulite business savvy, they put up a bulletin board where travellers could post a note offering a ride to Kathmandu or a message for a long-awaited travelling companion. Business boomed and the sales of rice pudding (one of the desserts on offer that gave the *Lale* its "unofficial" moniker) soared.

The Hippy Trail may have gone the same way as the Afghan coat, but the *Pudding Shop* continues to thrive. It is still run by the Çolpan brothers and, many redecorations later, the hippies' bulletin board – the original travellers "blog" – is preserved as a reminder of a bygone era.

Cistern of a Thousand and One Columns

Binbirdirek Sarnıcı • İmran Ökten Sokak • Daily 9am–8pm • ₺10

Off a narrow street running south from Divan Yolu Caddesi is the **Cistern of a Thousand and One Columns**. At 64m by 56m, this is the second largest cistern in the city and is accessible via an entrance in its impressively thick retaining wall on İmran Ökten Sokak. The structure is now bone dry and half its former height due to a false floor; originally, the hall was over 12m high, as can be seen from the small area of four columns excavated to the original floor. The cistern is thought to have been built under the palace of Philoxenus, one of the Roman senators who accompanied Emperor Constantine to the city. It dried up completely around the fifteenth century and was later used as a spinning mill until the early twentieth century.

Hippodrome

The arena of the **Hippodrome**, formerly the cultural focus of the Byzantine Empire, is today the **At Meydanı** ("Square of Horses"). Completely repaved in 2011, it is flanked to the northwest by the Museum of Turkish and Islamic Art, and to the southeast by the Blue Mosque.

A stadium was first constructed here by the Roman Emperor Septimius Severus in 203 AD and later enlarged by Constantine the Great for the performance of court ceremonies and games. Estimated to have held up to 100,000 people, the original orientation and dimensions of the 480-metre-long arena have been more or less preserved by the present-day square. Even after the fall of Constantinople in 1453, the Hippodrome continued to be a focus of state ceremony for the Ottoman sultans.

Assuming entry from the northeast end of the square, where it opens out onto Divan Yolu/the tram line, the first point of interest is a pretty domed structure, the **Fountain of Kaiser Wilhelm II**, a gift to Sultan Abdülhamit II from the German emperor, in town in 1898 to drum up support for his grandiose Berlin–Baghdad railway scheme. The fountain is built on the line of the original gateway to the arena for chariots and spectators. Continuing southwest down the square, you'll reach the **Egyptian Obelisk**. Originally 60m tall, only the upper third survived shipment from Egypt in the fourth century. The obelisk was commissioned to commemorate the campaigns of Thutmose III in Egypt during the sixteenth century BC, but the scenes on its base commemorate its erection in Constantinople under the direction of Theodosius I. The northeast side depicts the emperor watching from the imperial box as the obelisk is erected, on the northwest he watches vanquished foes parade past, on the southwest he is enjoying a chariot race, while on the southeast Theodosius wreathes the victors.

Continue down to the **Serpentine Column**, which comes from the Temple of Apollo at Delphi, where it was dedicated to the god by the 31 Greek cities that defeated the Persians at Plataea in 479 BC. The column was brought to Constantinople by Constantine the Great; the three intertwining bronze serpents originally had heads, which splayed out in three directions from the column itself. The jaw of one of the serpents was lopped off by Mehmet the Conqueror on his arrival in Constantinople as an act of defiance against such symbols of idolatry and the remaining heads were probably removed in an act of vandalism at the beginning of the eighteenth century – one of them is on display in the Archeology Museum (see pp.58–61).

The third ancient monument on the *spina* is the so-called **Column of Constantine**, a 32-metre-high column. In the tenth century the Emperor Constantine Porphyrogenitus restored the pillar and sheathed it in gold-plated bronze – an ornamentation that was taken and melted down by the Crusaders during the sacking of Constantinople in 1204. These three monuments are the sole survivors of the array of obelisks, columns and statues that originally adorned the *spina*, the raised central axis of the arena, around which chariots raced.

1

CROWD TROUBLE IN CONSTANTINOPLE

The crowds who attended the chariot races and other events held at the Hippodrome were split into two factions, the **Blues** and the **Greens**. The former were generally upper class, politically conservative and orthodox regarding religion; while the latter were from the lower classes and more radical in their political and religious views. Rivalry between them was every bit as rabid as that between present-day UK football-team supporters, often bubbling over into hooliganism and riots.

In 532, the rivalry was forgotten when members of the Blue faction combined forces with the Greens against Emperor Justinian in protest at heavy taxation, and in the resulting **riots** – which derived their name from the battle cry Nika (Victory) – much of the city, including the church of Haghia Sophia, was destroyed. It was the former courtesan, Empress Theodora, who eventually shamed Justinian into action and, as a result, thirty thousand Greens and a few hundred Blues were trapped and massacred by the forces of General Belisarius in the Hippodrome. Chariot racing was banned for some time after this, and it was a number of years before the Greens recovered to the extent that they could compete in either the sporting or the political arena.

The great curved end of the chariot racing track, the **sphendrome**, has been subsumed by a neo-Ottoman building, but its massive retaining wall can be seen by exiting the southeast corner of the square and following Naklibent Sokak around to the right.

Blue Mosque

Sultanahmet Camii • Sultanahmet Meydanı • Mon–Thurs, Sat & Sun closed to non-Muslims at prayer times, Fri 9am–noon

On the southeastern side of the Hippodrome is the **Blue Mosque** (Sultanahmet Camii). Its instantly recognizable six minarets, imposing bulk and prominent position on the Istanbul skyline combine to make it one of the most famous and visited monuments in the city. Despite this, many architectural historians compare it unfavourably to the earlier works of the master architect, Mimar Sinan (see box, p.82). From the outside, the building is undeniably impressive, particularly on the all-important approach from the Topkapı Palace along Bab-ı Hümayün and Kabasakal *caddesi*s. Above the level of the courtyard, the mosque is a mass of shallow domes and domed turrets, hardly broken by a single straight line.

Before construction began, in 1609, objections were raised to the plan of a six-minareted mosque. It was said to be unholy to rival the six minarets of the mosque at Mecca, and perhaps more pertinently it would be a great drain on state revenues. The true cause of the objections, however, probably had more to do with the need to destroy several palaces belonging to imperial ministers to make way for construction.

Inside the mosque, four **"elephant foot" pillars** (so called because of their size) of 5m in diameter impose their disproportionate dimensions on the interior, appearing squashed against the outer walls and obscuring parts of the building from every angle. But it's the predominantly blue colour of the internal decoration that is the biggest draw, from which the name "Blue Mosque" is derived. The **tiles** – over twenty thousand of them – constituted such a tall order that the İznik kilns were practically exhausted. Still in evidence are the clear bright colours of the best period of İznik ware, including flower and tree panels as well as more abstract designs.

Outside, at the northeast corner of the complex, is the **royal pavilion**, approached by a ramp and giving access to the sultan's loge inside the mosque – the ramp meant that the sultan could ride his horse right up to the door of his chambers. Below the mosque to the southeast is the **Arasta Bazaar**. Built at the same time as the mosque itself, rents from this charming double row of little shops were put towards the maintenance of the Blue Mosque. After decades of neglect the shops were refurbished in the 1980s and today are a major attraction for souvenir hunters (see p.214).

INFORMATION   **BLUE MOSQUE**

Entrance The mosque is best approached from the attractive northwest, Hippodrome-facing side, from where a graceful portal leads into the beautiful courtyard. This is surrounded by a portico of thirty small domes and has the same dimensions as the mosque itself. It's also possible to enter the courtyard from the Haghia Sophia side of the

mosque, through the northeast portal. Unless you are a practising Muslim, you are forbidden from entering the mosque itself via the main northwest facing door but must head around to the southwest entrance where there are often long queues. Here you must remove your shoes and put them in a plastic bag (provided).

Baths of Roxelana
Ayasofya Hürrem Sultan Hamamı • Kabasakal Caddesi

The attractive double-domed building flanking the south side of the square between the Haghia Sophia and Blue Mosque is the **Baths of Roxelana** or Ayasofya Hürrem Sultan Hamamı. Named after the favourite wife of Sultan Süleyman the Magnificent it was built in 1556 by Sinan (see box, p.82) to serve as the baths for the Haghia Sophia mosque complex. After many years of renovation it is again open as a working *hamam* (see p.227).

Museum of Turkish and Islamic Art
Türk ve Islam Eserleri Müzesi • Meydanı Sok 46 • Tues–Sun: April to Oct 9am–7pm; Nov to March 9am–5pm; last entry 30min before closing • ₺20

The **Museum of Turkish and Islamic Art** is an attractive, well-planned museum, containing one of the best-exhibited collections of Islamic artefacts in the world. The sixteenth-century setting of cool, darkened rooms around a central garden courtyard obviates the need for expensive technology to keep the sun off the remarkable exhibits, which highlight the wealth and complexity of Islamic art and culture.

The palace partially survived the periodic fires that swept through the city and – in 1843 – it was rebuilt in stone to the original plan. Originally completed in 1524 as a wedding present for İbrahim Paşa, Süleyman the Magnificent's newly appointed grand vizier, the palace (known as the İbrahim Paşa Sarayı in Turkish) is a fitting memorial to one of the most able statesmen of his time, whose abilities were matched only by his accumulation of wealth and power. His status can be judged from the proportions of the palace's rooms and by its prominent position next to the Hippodrome: later sultans were to use its balconies to watch the festivities below. İbrahim controlled the affairs of war and state of the Ottoman Empire for thirteen years and fell from grace partly as a result of the schemings of Süleyman's wife, Roxelana. Even so, it doesn't seem unreasonable that Süleyman should distrust a servant who could say to a foreign ambassador: "If I command that something should be done, and he [the sultan] has commanded to the contrary, my wishes and not his are obeyed." In 1536 the strangled body of İbrahim Paşa was found in a room of the Topkapı Palace; almost certainly executed on Süleyman's orders. İbrahim Paşa was buried in an unmarked grave and his possessions, not least the palace, reverted to the Crown.

The museum exhibits
The main concentration of permanent exhibits deals with Selçuk, Mamluk and Ottoman Turkish art, though there are also several important Timurid and Persian works on display.

The **Selçuk Empire**, centred in Konya, preceded that of the Ottomans in Anatolia, and it is interesting to trace influences from one to the other. Ceramic techniques, for example, were obviously well developed by the Selçuks, judging from the wall tiles on display in the museum, and the woodcarvings from Konya also suggest a high level of craftsmanship and artistry, which may have influenced later Ottoman work.

Other impressive exhibits include sixteenth-century Persian miniatures, which like many Ottoman works defy the Islamic stricture against depicting human or animal forms. Pictures in lacquer and leather-bound Persian manuscripts feature a tiger

1

ripping into an antelope and another of a dancing girl dated 1570. The tiny Sancak Korans were meant for hanging on the standard of the Ottoman imperial army in a jihad (holy war), so that the word of God would precede the troops into battle.

The **Great Hall** of the palace is occasionally devoted to special exhibitions about aspects of Islamic art, but more usually it houses a collection of **Turkish carpets** that is among the finest in the world. These range from tattered remains dating from the thirteenth century to carpets that once adorned Istanbul's palaces, some weighing thousands of kilograms. On the basement floor, there's an exhibition of the **folk art** of the *Yörük* tribes of Anatolia, which includes examples of a *kara çadır* (literally "black tent", a domicile woven from goat hair that can still be seen in central and eastern Anatolia) and a *topakev* (a tent constructed around a folding frame, used by nomads in Anatolia and Mongolia for over a thousand years).

Sokollu Mehmet Paşa Camii

Mehmet Paşa Yokuşu, Kadirga • Theoretically open at prayer times only, but the caretaker is usually around to unlock it during the day

A pleasant couple of minutes' walk from the southwest corner of the Hippodrome leads down the steep Mehmet Paşa Yokuşu to **Sokollu Mehmet Paşa Camii**. This, one of Mimar Sinan's (see box, p.82) later buildings (1571), is a seldom-visited gem. Sokollu Mehmet Paşa, who commissioned the mosque, was the last grand vizier of Süleyman the Magnificent and it was his military expertise that later saved the Ottoman Empire from the worst effects of the dissolute rule of Selim the Sot. He was eventually assassinated as a result of the intrigues of Nur Banu, the mother of Murat III, who was jealous of his power.

The large mosque **courtyard** is surrounded on three sides by the rooms of the *medrese*, now occupied by a boys' Koran school. The **interior** of the mosque is distinguished by the height of its dome and the impressive display of İznik tiles on its east wall. These are from the best period of Turkish ceramics: the white is pure, the green vivid and the red intense. Calligraphic inscriptions are set against a jungle of enormous carnations and tulips, and the designs and colours are echoed all around the mosque and in the conical cap of the *mimber*, the tiling of which is unique in Istanbul. While the stained-glass windows are copies, some of the original, extremely delicate **paintwork** can be seen in the northwest corner below the gallery and over the entrance. Embedded in the wall over the entrance and above the *mihrab* are pieces of the Kaaba, the cuboid building at the heart of the Islam's most sacred mosque in Mecca.

Church of Sts Sergius and Bacchus

Küçük Ayasofya Camii • Küçük Ayasofya Caddesi, Sultanahmet • Daily 7am–dusk • Donation

Located some 500m below the Blue Mosque is the often-overlooked but well-restored **Church of Sts Sergius and Bacchus**. It was built between 527 and 536 to service the palace of Hormisdas, and was originally named after two Roman soldiers, **Sergius** and **Bacchus**, who were martyred for their faith and later became the patron saints of Christians in the Roman army. The church was converted into the **Küçük Ayasofya Camii**, the "small mosque of Aya Sofya", early in the sixteenth century.

Like most Byzantine churches of this era, its **exterior** is unprepossessing brick, and only inside can the satisfying proportions be properly appreciated. It is basically an octagon with semicircular niches at its diagonals, inscribed in a rectangle. As the first domed church, just preceding Haghia Sophia, it is of great significance in the development of Byzantine architecture.

The original marble facing and gold leaf have vanished, but a frieze honouring Justinian, Theodora and St Sergius runs around the architrave under the gallery. Opposite the mosque entrance is a former religious school, the courtyard of which now serves as a shady tea garden.

Sea walls

At the Church of St Sergius and Bacchus, you're almost down at the Sea of Marmara and close to the best-preserved section of the **sea walls**, built in 439 by Cyrus, prefect of the East. They are a surviving part of the walls which ran right around the historic peninsula, a distance of around 15 kilometres, joining up to the land walls of Theodosius at both their northern and southern termini, ringing Constantinople with a virtually impregnable barrier. The best-preserved remains are the stretch of a couple of kilometres between Ahır Kapı and Kumkapı, with a walkway along Kennedy Caddesi.

Palace of Bucoleon and the Great Palace

About halfway between Küçük Ayasofya Camii and the southern end of the walls of the Topkapı Palace, the facade of the **Palace of Bucoleon**, a seaside annexe to the **Great Palace of the Byzantine emperors**, is one of the most melancholy and moving survivors of Constantinople. The Great Palace was an immense complex of buildings, and included the Palace of Bucoleon and the Magnaura Palace, rather than a single structure, covering around five square kilometres from Sultanahmet to the sea walls.

Set back from the road, all that's left of the **Palace of Bucoleon** is a section of wall pierced by three enormous marble-framed windows. Below the windows, marble corbels give evidence of a balcony that would have projected over a marble quay (the waters of the Marmara once reached almost as far as the palace walls). For the rest of the Great Palace, you'll need a lively imagination, though an impressive complex of vaulted basements can be reached via the **Başdoğan carpet centre** on Kutluğun Sokak, or the *Albura Kathisma* restaurant (see p.186) on Akbıyık Caddesi. Further sections of the palace exist under land belonging to the *Four Seasons Hotel* (see p.169). At the time of writing this large area of land was undergoing excavation/renovation and will open as an "archeological park" when the work is complete – there is a display board about the park opposite the south corner of Haghia Sophia.

Mosaic Museum

Büyüksaray Mozaik Müzesi • Torun Sok 113 • Tues–Sun: April to Oct 9am–7pm, Nov to March 9am–4pm; last entry 30min before closing • ₺8

The other substantial reminders of the Great Palace (see above) are the mosaics displayed in the **Mosaic Museum**, 500m inland from the Palace of Bucoleon. To reach it requires running the gauntlet of salespeople in the **Arasta Bazaar** – a renovated street-bazaar selling tourist gifts, whose seventeenth-century shops were originally built to pay for the upkeep of the nearby Blue Mosque.

Many of the mosaics in the museum are presented *in situ*, so that some idea of their original scale and purpose can be imagined. The building has been constructed so that some of the mosaics are viewed from a catwalk above, but can also be examined more closely by descending to their level. Smaller surviving sections of mosaic, each square metre of which contain some forty thousand tesserae, have been wall-mounted. All these remains were once part of a large mosaic decorating the palace's peristyle (an open courtyard surrounded by a portico). The scenes depicted by the mosaic artists, probably dating from Justinian's rebuilding programme of the sixth century, are extraordinarily vivid and give a valuable insight into everyday Byzantine life. On one, a man with a staff leads a camel surmounted by two riders; on another, a herdsman pulls an unwilling goat. In another fine scene, four boys drive hoops along with sticks – two of them have their tunics edged in blue, the other two in green, touching proof that rivalry between "the Greens" and "the Blues" in the Hippodrome did not preclude friendship (see p.64). Despite the Christian nature of the Byzantine world, scenes from classical mythology also abound – check out the hero Bellerophon battling the fire-breathing monster known as the Chimera.

Sirkeci, Eminönü and Tahtakale

Heading north, down from the tourist fleshpots of Sultanahmet towards the Golden Horn, there's a gradual change from tourism to commerce. Offices still fill the upper storeys of the fine buildings lining the bustling streets of lower Sirkeci and Eminönü, while shopkeepers selling everything from trainers to electrical appliances vie for business at street level. Istanbulites outnumber visitors and many of them depend on each other, not tourism, for their livelihoods, particularly in the bazaar quarter of Tahtakale. There are plenty of worthwhile attractions; Sirkeci station, once the eastern terminus of the Orient Express; the charming Ottoman-era Spice Bazaar; the Yeni Camii, a mosque as popular with hawkers and pigeons as it is with worshippers; and the Rüstem Paşa Camii, a mosque famed for its glorious İznik tiles.

By tram and train The T1 tram from Sultanahmet stops in both Sirkeci and Eminönü before snaking its way across the Galata Bridge to Beyoğlu. Sirkeci station is a stop on the Marmaray metro line linking it westwards to Yenikapı and Kazlıçeşme (for the land walls of Theodosius) and east via a tunnel under the Bosphorus to Üsküdar in Asia.

Sirkeci

Once workman-like **Sirkeci** is gradually giving way to the demands of tourism; its northern fringes, abutting Sultanahmet, have been the first to succumb, with the streets either side of the tram line full of hotels, restaurants and cafés. Closer to the waterfront, however, approaching the once opulent Sirkeci station, it remains largely a transport and commercial area. The area has, unsurprisingly, a largely transient population – its estimated permanent population of thirty thousand swells to some two million souls thronging the daytime streets and/or working in the multitude of local businesses. The city's seemingly unstoppable tourism boom is rapidly accelerating the gentrification of the area.

Sirkeci station
Ankara Caddesi

World-famous **Sirkeci station** (see box, p.8), a stone's throw from the waters of the Golden Horn, is best reached on foot by following the tram line downhill from Sultanahmet. Opened with great fanfare in 1888, right in the heart of imperial Istanbul, this grandiose temple to steam was once the eastern terminus for the famed Orient Express, the train that linked Paris and Vienna with Istanbul – and became a metaphor for style, opulence and, of course, intrigue. Designed by Prussian architect August Jachmund, the station was an Oriental fantasy, with a Parisian-style dome, minaret-like turrets and Moghul-influenced windows. The station retains a faded grandeur despite the passage of time – make sure you wander around to the building's north facade, facing the Golden Horn, as this was the original entrance – but the glamour days are long gone. In 2013 it stopped serving overground trains and became instead a stop on the Marmaray metro (see p.27) and today serves grumpy Istanbulites commuting between Europe and Asia via the Bosphorus tunnel rather than the socialites and spies of its heyday. For a glimpse of its past, however, visit the small railway museum inside the station, the **Sirkeci Garı Demiryolları Müzesi** (Tues–Sat 9am–5pm; free). On display is everything from silver cutlery from the Orient Express to vintage typewriters. Adjacent is the atmospheric *Orient Express* restaurant (see p.187).

Eminönü

Eminönü fronts the ferry-choked waters of the Golden Horn, the curving inlet that cleaves the European shore. The historic Mısır Çarşısı or **Spice Bazaar** is the district's major draw, though the **Yeni Camii** or "New Mosque" runs it a close second.

Given its role as one of the city's major transport hubs, it's no surprise that the area bustles with activity from dawn until the late evening. One almost obligatory rite here is to partake of a fish sandwich for around ₺5. They are best bought from the *Tarihi Eminönü Balık Ekmek*, just to the left of the Galata Bridge, where all day long and on into the evening chefs in gilt-brocade faux-Ottoman waistcoats grill the fish in front of your eyes. To the north, small boats moored to the dockside bob up and down in the swell, hawkers whizz remote-controlled cars through the legs of potential punters, and *simit* (a sesame-coated bread ring) sellers are kept busy by those who don't fancy fish or the other Eminönü delicacy, a carton of pickled vegetables. If you can find a peaceful spot among the mayhem, the views north across the Golden Horn and the **Galata Bridge** to Galata, and west to the equally busy waters of the Bosphorus, are fabulous. Underground, the **subways** are home to hordes of shops selling fake designer clothing, cheap trainers, battery-operated dancing giraffes, and a lot more. Despite the hassle,

2

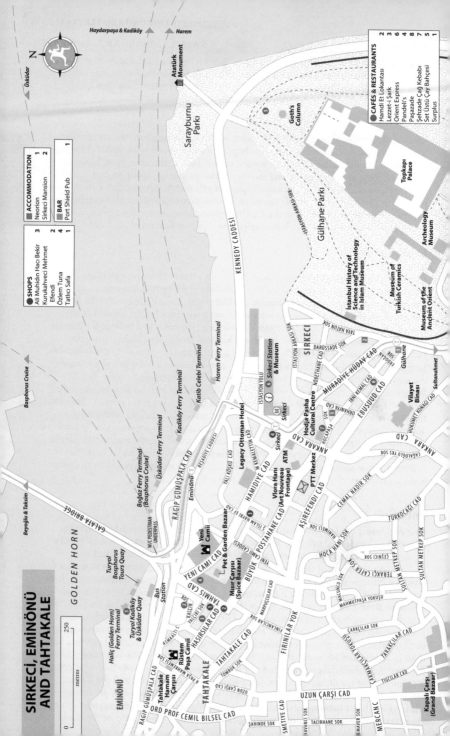

SIRKECİ, EMİNÖNÜ AND TAHTAKALE

0 ————— 250
metres

Haydarpaşa & Kadıköy   **Harem**

Üsküdar

N

Atatürk
Monument

GOLDEN HORN

Sarayburnu
Parkı

Bosphorus Cruise

Beyoğlu & Taksim

GALATA BRIDGE

Turyol
Bosphorus
Tours Quay

Halic (Golden Horn)
Ferry Terminal

Turyol Kadıköy
& Üsküdar Quay

Bus
Station

EMİNÖNÜ

Tahtakale
Hamam
Çarşısı

Goth's
Column

Gülhane Parkı

Topkapı
Palace

Archeology
Museum

İstanbul History of
Science and Technology
in Islam Museum

Museum of
Turkish Ceramics

Museum of the
Ancient Orient

KENNEDY CADDESİ

Boğaz Ferry Terminal
(Bosphorus Cruise)

Üsküdar Ferry Terminal

Kadıköy Ferry Terminal

Katib Çelebi Terminal

Harem Ferry Terminal

İSTASYON YOLU

Sirkeci Station
& Museum

SİRKECİ

İSTASYON ARKASI SOK

TAYA HATUN SOK

DARÜSSADE SOK

NÖBETHANE CAD

MURADİYE-HÜDAV CAD

Gülhane

Sultanahmet

Vilayet
Binası

HUKUMET KONAĞI CAD

ANKARA CAD

CAĞALOĞLU YKS SOK

EBUSUUD CAD

İBNİ KEMAL CAD

ORHANİYE CAD

ANKARA CAD

HOCA

Hodja Pasha
Cultural Centre

Sirkeci

Legacy Ottoman Hotel

HAMİDİYE CAD

HALİL RÜŞDÜ CAD

BEŞADİYE CADDESİ

RAGİP GÜMÜŞPALA CAD

Eminönü

W/C PEDESTRIAN
UNDERPASS

Vlora Hani
(Art Nouveau
Frontage)

PTT Merkez

ASİREEFENDİ CAD

POSTAHANE CAD

ATM

Yeni
Camii

Pet & Garden Bazaar

Mısır Çarşısı
(Spice Bazaar)

YENİ CAMİ CAD

YENİ CAMİ CADDESİ

MARPUÇCULAR CAD

TAHMİS CAD

HASIRCILAR CAD

Rüstem
Paşa Camii

TAHTAKALE

TAHTAKALE CAD

ASMAALTI C

TELLAL SOK

TACIRLAR SOK

P. PAŞA MAHKEMESİ SOK

RAGİP GÜMÜŞPALA CAD

ORD PROF CEMİL BİLSEL CAD

UZUN ÇARŞI CAD

ŞAHİNDE SOK

TACIRHANE SOK

HAVANCI SOK

SMETİYE SOK

MERCANC

MAHYER SOK

TIGCILAR CAD

ÇANKAKÇILAR YOKUŞU

TARAKÇILAR CAD

ÇARKÇILAR SOK

Kapalı Çarşı
(Grand Bazaar)

FINCANCILAR SOK

MAHMUTPAŞA YOKUŞU

MAKUROĞLU SOK

HOCA HANİ SOK

BÜYÜK

İSLAM HAYRİ ET CAD

FIRINLILAR YOK

TERAKÇİ CAFER SOK

SULTAN METKEP SOK

ÇEŞNİCİ SOK

HANIMELİ SOK

CEMAL NADİR SOK

TURKOCAĞI CAD

SULTAN METKEP SOK

TABLE LEGEND:

● SHOPS
Ali Muhidin Hacı Bekir	3
Kurukahveci Mehmet Efendi	2
Özlem Tuna	4
Tatlıcı Safa	1

■ ACCOMMODATION
Neorion	1
Sirkeci Mansion	2

■ BAR
Port Shield Pub	1

● CAFÉS & RESTAURANTS
Hamdi Et Lokantası	2
Lezzet-i Şark	3
Orient Express	6
Pandeli's	4
Paşazade	8
Şehzade Çağ Kebabı	7
Set Üstü Çay Bahçesi	5
Surplus	1

however, they're a far better choice than trying to negotiate the road and tram track separating the quayside from the rest of the area.

PTT Merkez
Büyük Postahane Caddesi

The **PTT Merkez** (Central Post Office) was designed by Vedat Tak and has been used as a post office since 1909. Tak, the first Turkish architect to study abroad, was a pioneer of the First National Architectural Movement which, following the formation of the Turkish Republic in 1923, aimed to blend contemporary European architecture with traditional Turkish styles and create something fitting for the new, progressive country. The structure is certainly monumental, with a sweeping facade split by two towers that were originally planned to hold clocks – one Ottoman in style, the other European. The interior is cavernous, its rather gloomy atmosphere enlivened by neo-Ottoman floral murals, aged and nicotine-stained wooden counters and original 1920s light fittings.

Vlora Han
Cnr Muhzirbadı Sokak and Büyük Postahane Caddesi

The wonderfully ornate Art Nouveau apartment building situated just across from PTT Merkez (see above) was formerly the **Vlora Han**. Stylized rosebud-relief plasterwork and whiplash wrought-iron work make this one of the most obvious Art Nouveau buildings in the city – if not the most artistic (that accolade goes to the Botter House in Beyoğlu; see p.122). Unfortunately, it's looking rather neglected and the lower storeys are marred by billboards.

Legacy Ottoman Hotel (Vakıf Han)
Hamidiye Caddesi

Even more monumental than the PTT Merkez (see above), the **Legacy Ottoman Hotel** (originally the Vakıf Han) was built in 1912, a colossal office block that paid testament to the wealth of the area and its commercial importance in the early twentieth century. Another example of the First National Architectural Movement, its reinforced-steel frame and cut-stone facade show a European influence, the tiled panels and domes that of an Ottoman past.

The Galata Bridge

The vast majority of visitors to Istanbul cross the **Galata Bridge** at least once during their stay. It won't win any architectural prizes, but the link between the two sides of European Istanbul, separated by the waters of the Golden Horn, is undeniably a city landmark and has been immortalized in Geert Mak's wonderful book *The Bridge* (see p.311). The noise from the trams, cars, trucks and buses crossing over the bridge, the ferries docking beside and passing under it, and the gabble of the tidal wave of milling pedestrians is deafening. The views from here, however, down the Golden Horn and into the Bosphorus itself, are superb, particularly at sunset. The upper deck is always lined with anglers, their numbers swelling to ludicrous proportions on a Sunday, and you have to pick your way carefully through bait buckets and strands of tangled line, sinkers and hooks.

The current bridge, built in 1994, is its fifth incarnation – the first was constructed in 1845 during the reign of Sultan Abdülmecit. The bridge has always had a symbolic significance, linking as it did the old, imperial and Islamic part of the city with the largely Christian, "Europeanized" area of Beyoğlu – home to foreign traders, diplomats and the like. To some extent, this gulf persists, with the old city's (the area on the historic peninsula, contained by the city land walls) curious mix of foreign visitors and conservative Muslim inhabitants contrasting with the vibrant nightlife and upwardly mobile, progressive residents of Beyoğlu.

2

Yeni Cami
Yeni Camii Caddesi

The **Yeni Cami**, or "New Mosque", is a familiar city landmark, sited across the busy road from Eminönü's ferry terminal. An imposing building, most visitors admire it only from the outside, though the interior is open to all. The last of Istanbul's imperial mosques to be built it was, like all such mosques, part of a complex that included a hospital, *hamam*, fountains and a market.

The only imperial mosque to be built during the reign of Mehmet III, the site chosen by Safiye, the Queen Mother, was regarded as wholly inappropriate. It occupied a slum neighbourhood inhabited by a sect of Jews called the Karaites, who were relocated across the Horn to Hasköy; a synagogue and church had to be demolished to make room for it. The site was also dangerously close to the water's edge, and the building programme was constantly plagued by seepage from the Horn.

Although work began in 1597, its construction was continually plagued by court politics. The original architect was executed for heresy and the work was interrupted again by the death of Mehmet III and the banishment of his mother to the Old Palace. Construction had reached as far as the lower casements when it was halted, and the Karaites returned to camp out in the rubble. The building wasn't completed until 1663, under the auspices of Valide Sultan Turhan Hatice, mother of Sultan Mehmet IV.

The mosque was designed by a pupil of Sinan (see box, p.82) and is generally considered to lack the grace of the great master's works. It is, nonetheless, an attractive mosque, built on a cruciform plan, with a large central dome surmounting four semi-domes. Entry is from a fine courtyard surrounded by porticoes, with an attractive octagonal *şadırvan* in the centre. As in most Ottoman mosques, the portico, running at right angles across the entry wall, has a raised platform used as an overspill prayer area when the mosque is full, or by late arrivals. Two attractive *mihrab*s puncture the wall either side of the main portal, embellished, like the doorway itself, with a finely carved stalactite design. The wooden doors are inlaid with mother-of-pearl, and the main *mihrab*, again with a stalactite design, is heavily gilded.

Spice Bazaar
Mısır Çarşısı • Daily 9am–7pm

The most atmospheric part of the Yeni Cami complex is the **Mısır Çarşısı**, the "Egyptian Bazaar", which is better known as the **Spice Bazaar**. The origins of the name are uncertain. In the Byzantine era, the site of the bazaar was the corn-trading centre, and "Mısır" means both "corn" and "Egypt" in Turkish. On the other hand, the name may derive from the fact that many of the Ottoman Empire's spices were imported from Egypt and were flogged in the "new" spice bazaar, or from the fact that it was endowed with customs duties from Cairo. Completed a few years before the Yeni Camii, this L-shaped bazaar has 88 vaulted rooms and chambers above the entryways at the ends of the halls. One of these, over the main entrance opposite the ferry ports, now houses the Greek restaurant, *Pandeli's* (see p.187).

THE GOLDEN HORN'S PLACE IN HISTORY

The history of the Golden Horn is inextricably linked with the fate of the city. In 1203–04, Crusaders took the Horn and proceeded to besiege Constantinople for ten months, until they breached the sea walls separating the inlet from the city. In 1453 Mehmet the Conqueror, prevented from entering the Horn by a chain (links of which can be seen in the Archeology, Military and Naval museums), built a pontoon bridge across the inlet and used it to ferry troops and supplies to his army camped in front of the land walls.

2

ROUND THE HORN – BY FERRY

Eminönü fronts the Golden Horn, known in Turkish as *Haliç* ("estuary"), one of the finest **natural harbours** in the world. It was terribly polluted until the noughties but recent years have seen huge improvements, much to the delight of fishermen and cormorants, both of whom prey on the fish that have returned to its relatively clean waters. Major plans announced in 2013 will see part of the inlet become a plush yacht marina by 2017.

The best way to experience the Golden Horn is to take the **Şehirhatları Haliç ferry** (see Ⓦ sehirhatlari.com.tr for timetables and prices) from either Eminönü or Karaköy to the last stop of Eyüp, near the head of the inlet – a forty-minute trip costs just ₺4, less with the Istanbulkart. Look out to the south and the whole skyline of the old city unfurls, dominated by the domes and minarets of major mosques. To the north, the trendy area around the Galata Tower gives way to a grittier area of docks and low-rent housing. The ferry is often packed with headscarved women making the pilgrimage to Eyüp (see pp.107–108), one of the holiest shrines in the Islamic world. Check the ferry timetable (approximately hourly between 8am and 8.30pm) carefully before departure and you can use it to stop off at various points en route. Disembark at Hasköy pier on the north side of the inlet to visit the excellent Rahmi M Koç Industrial Museum (see pp.116–117), Ayvansaray on the south shore to explore the terminus of the land walls of Theodosius (see pp.101–107) and the Kariye Museum (see pp.94–98) or Sütlüce for the scale-model theme park Miniatürk (see p.117).

Look out for the stubs of the early twentieth-century, cast-iron Galata pontoon bridge near Hasköy, its central sections occasionally towed into position so the bridge can be used when one of the other bridges across the inlet is closed for repairs. It was towed upstream from its original position in Eminönü in the mid-1990 when the new bridge was built. Just south of it is the Seabird (Ⓦ flyseabird.com) sea plane terminal – watching the planes take off and land is an exciting spectacle. Planes head out to Bursa (see pp.240–253) and other destinations south of the city, but they also offer an aerial tour of Istanbul.

Despite its name, the range and quality of spices in the bazaar is not what it was and prices aren't cheap – the shops in the surrounding maze of alleys are usually much better value than what's on offer inside. Of more interest in the bazaar itself are the varieties of *lokum* (Turkish delight) and the many bizarre concoctions being passed off as aphrodisiacs.

Around the Spice Bazaar

Running alongside the western wall of the Spice Bazaar is **Tahmis Caddesi**, lined by hole-in-the-wall shops stocking a wonderful array of cheese, olives, dried fruit, spices, dried meats and all manner of delectable foodstuffs at bargain prices. Running west at right angles from this strip of shops is **Hasırcılar Caddesi** (Street of the Strawmakers) where there are yet more speciality shops, including, on the corner, *Kurukahveci Mehemet Efendi* (see p.217), a coffee emporium in a fine Art Deco building, with perpetual queues outside.

Another interesting place to explore is the **garden/pet bazaar** on the east side of the Spice Bazaar. It's not a place for the sentimental: chicks and ducklings cluck frantically in open-topped cardboard boxes, while goldfinches flit from side to side of their tiny bamboo cages. There's even a leech doctor, the tools of his trade wriggling uninvitingly in an enormous glass jar. More prosaic, though, are the bags of seeds and decorative bamboo plants on sale here.

Tahtakale

Tahtakale ("Wooden Castle"), the incredibly busy traditional bazaar quarter west of Sirkeci and northwest of Eminönü, is lifted from mundanity by the presence of one of the city's best small mosques, the **Rüstem Paşa Camii**. Mosque aside, there's little to do except wander the cobbled streets, watching the few surviving *hamals* (stevedores;

hamal is derived from the Arabic for camel) bent double under their loads, or wonder at just who is going to buy the mountains of brushes, pans, coat hangers and other cheap plastic household paraphernalia on sale here. There are a few locally made items, such as hand-carved wooden spoons, on display, but the majority of stuff is imported from the Far East. One building of note is the **Tahtakale Hamam Çarşısı** dating back to the early years of the Ottoman conquest of the city in the fifteenth century. Built as a *hamam*, it continues to serve the local community – but as yet another shopping centre rather than a bath-house.

2

Rüstem Paşa Camii
Hasırcılar Çarşısı

Rüstem Paşa Camii is one of the most attractive of Istanbul's smaller mosques and very welcoming to visitors. Built for Süleyman the Magnificent's grand vizier, Rüstem Paşa (who was responsible, along with Roxelana, for the murder of the heir apparent Mustafa), the mosque dates from the year he died, 1561, and was probably built in his memory by his widow Mihrimah, Roxelana's daughter.

Designed by Sinan (see box, p.82) on an awkward site, the mosque is easy to miss as you wander the streets below. At ground level on the Golden Horn side, an arcade of shops occupies the vaults. Pass east through a small courtyard below the level of the mosque and turn left to reach the steps leading up to the mosque's terrace. The mosque is fronted by a double porch; the eaves of the outer one are lined with eight tile roundels on which are written the names, in Arabic, of Allah, Mohammed, the first four caliphs and the Prophet's two grandsons. The main entrance is on this facade; the one for visitors is on the left as you look at the mosque, just beyond a small stall selling guidebooks, İznik-tile fridge magnets and the like.

The **tiles**, inside and out, are among the best in any mosque in Turkey. They date from the finest period of İznik tile production, when techniques for producing tomato-red – slightly raised above the other colours – had been perfected. Designs covering the walls, piers and pillars, and decorating the *mihrab* and *mimber*, include famous panels of tulips and carnations and geometric patterns. Inside are galleries supported by pillars and marble columns and about as many windows as the structure of the mosque will allow.

The Grand Bazaar and around

The city's Kapalı Çarşı, known to most foreigners as the Grand Bazaar, was the prototype of today's shopping malls, and is the best-known and largest historic covered bazaar in the world. Understandably, most visitors to Istanbul opt to spend some time wandering its myriad alleyways and soaking up the atmosphere. The other major attraction in this sprawling district is Istanbul's finest mosque complex, the Süleymaniye, majestically situated atop the old city's third hill. Viewed from afar, it is one of the most distinctive silhouettes on the city's skyline; up close, it still exudes an air of sanctity and learning. The areas around the Grand Bazaar and the Süleymaniye are well worth exploring, although few visitors venture beyond the key sights.

East of the bazaar, on either side of Divan Yolu, historically the main artery through the Byzantine and then Ottoman city, are the famed **Column of Constantine**, and the **Çemberlitaş Hamamı**, one of the city's most popular and atmospheric Turkish baths. To the northwest, below the Süleymaniye, is a wonderfully well-preserved stretch of the fourth-century **Aqueduct of Valens**, spanning one of the old city's busiest thoroughfares, Atatürk Bulvarı.

Just west of the bazaar, the **Beyazıt Meydanı**, a busy square dominated by the Beyazıt Camii, one of the city's earliest imperial mosques, attracts itinerant vendors and students streaming in and out of the main gates of Istanbul University. Further west are **Laleli** and **Aksaray**, adjacent districts that have acquired a certain notoriety in recent years but have an atmosphere all of their own and contain some worthwhile Byzantine and Ottoman monuments – as well as some interesting places to eat. Running steeply down to the Sea of Marmara south of the bazaar, the narrow streets of **Gedikpaşa** and **Kumkapı** are scattered with churches of various denominations and a notable Ottoman *hamam*.

ARRIVAL

THE GRAND BAZAAR AND AROUND

By tram Take the T1 tram from Sultanahmet and get off at either Çemberlitaş or Beyazıt (for the Grand Bazaar or Süleymaniye complex), or Laleli (for the Şehzade and Laleli mosques, or an alternative route to the Süleymaniye complex).

By metro From Galata, Beyoğlu or Taksim take the M2 metro to Vezneciler, from where it's a few minutes' walk southeast to Beyazıt Square.

Grand Bazaar

Kapalı Çarşı • Mon–Sat 9am–7pm

With 66 streets and alleys, over four thousand shops, numerous storehouses, moneychangers and banks, a mosque, post office, police station, private security guards and its own health centre, Istanbul's **Grand Bazaar** is said to be the largest enclosed bazaar in the world. Complementing the retail outlets, humming workshops around the bazaar produce some of the goods sold there.

The bazaar, known in Turkish as the Kapalı Çarşı ("Covered Bazaar"), was built on the site of an earlier Byzantine trading area soon after the Ottoman conquest of the city in 1453. Originally, a particular type of shop was found in a certain area, with street names reflecting the nature of the businesses. Many of these distinctions are now blurred as the trade in certain goods has moved on, while that of others has expanded to meet new demands. In Ottoman times, bazaars throughout the empire consisted of both a covered and an open area centred on a *bedesten*, a domed building where foreign trade took place and valuable goods were stored. In Istanbul, the commercial centre was based around two *bedestens*, both inside the covered bazaar: the **İç Bedesten** (Old Bazaar; also known as the Cevahir Bedesten or "Jewellery Bazaar") probably dates from the time of the Conquest, while the **Sandal Bedesteni** was added in the sixteenth century to cope with the quantity of trade in fine fabrics that the capital attracted. The bazaar actually extends well beyond the limits of the covered bazaar and the whole area was once controlled by strict laws laid down by the trade guilds. These rules reduced unhealthy competition between traders and similar unwritten laws control market forces among traders in the Grand Bazaar even today.

Whether you actually enjoy wandering around here is very much a matter of temperament and mood; you'll either find the hassle from traders intolerable – though the many **cafés** in the bazaar (see pp.179–180) do offer a welcome respite – or you'll be flattered to be paid more attention in one afternoon than you've received in your entire life. Receiving the sales patter from a persuasive trader or three is part of the Grand Bazaar experience but remember one golden rule – once you have agreed a price for an item you are morally obliged to purchase it. The Society of Kapalı Çarşı Traders polices the area, issuing warnings to those deemed too intimidating, so if you find yourself uncomfortably targeted look around for one of the maroon-uniformed security guards.

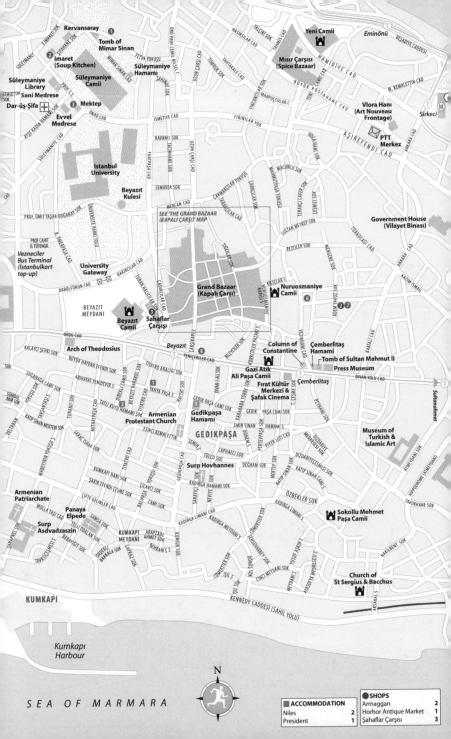

Kervansaray
Tomb of
Mimar Sinan ①
İMARET SOK
İMARET SOK
İMARET SOK
İMARET SOK
SÜLEYMANİY
②
Imaret
(Soup Kitchen)
Süleymaniye
Hamamı
MİMAR SİNAN SOK
ORD. PROF. CEMİL BİLSEL C.
FETVA YOKUŞU
UZUN ÇARŞI CAD
TAHTAKALE CAD
TOMRUK SOK
HASIRCILAR CAD
YALÇIN SOK
TAHMİS SOK
Yeni Camii
Eminönü
REŞADİYE CADDESİ
Misir Çarşısı
(Spice Bazaar)
BÜYÜK POSTAHANE CAD
HAMİDİYE CAD
M. KEMALETTİN CAD
Süleymaniye
Library
Süleymaniye
Camii
Süleymaniye
Sani Medrese
ŞEMSETTİN
SOK
Dar-üş-Şifa ✚
Evvel
Medrese
Mektep ③
SÜLEYMANİYE CAD
PROF. SS.
AYŞE KADIN HAMAMI SOK
ONAD CAD
İSMETİYE CAD
ŞAHİNCİ SOK
HAVANCI SOK
TAKRİHANE SOK
FUATPAŞA CAD
UZUN ÇARŞI CAD
FİRİNLAR YOK
HOCA HANI SOK
FİNCANCILAR YOKUŞU
MARPUÇULAR C
YENİ CAMİ MEYDANI
Vlora Hanı
(Art Nouveau
Frontage)
Sirkeci
M
PTT
Merkez
AŞİREFENDİ CAD
ANKARA CAD
MİMAR KEMALETTİN CAD
Istanbul
University
Beyazıt
Kulesi
SEMAVER SOK
MERCAN CAD
TACCILAR SOK
SEE 'THE GRAND BAZAAR
(KAPALI ÇARŞI)' MAP
ÇAKMAKÇILAR YOKUŞU
ÇARIKÇILAR SOK
MAHMUTPAŞA YOKUŞU
MACUNCU SOK
SULTAN METKEP SOK
MENGENE SOK
TERMAÇ CAFER SOK
YOS DİNEŞ
Government House
(Vilayet Binası)
TÜRKOCAĞI CAD
ANKARA CAD
KAZIM İSMAİL
PROF. ÜMİT YAŞAR DOĞANAY SOK
PROF. CAHİT
O. TÜTENGİL
İ. ÖMERPAŞA SOK
ÜNİVERSİTE PARKI YOLU
BAKIRCILAR CAD
TURAN HALICILAR CAD
ÇADIRCILAR CAD
BEZCİLER SOK
KILIÇCILAR S
VEZİRHANI CAD
Nuruosmaniye
Camii ⑥
② ⑦
ADLİYE SOK
Vezneciler Bus Terminal
(İstanbulkart
top-up)
University
Gateway
DARÜLFÜNUN CAD
BEYAZIT
MEYDANI
Beyazıt
Camii
Grand Bazaar
(Kapalı Çarşı)
Sahaflar
Çarşısı
ORDU CAD
Arch of Theodosius
KALAYCI ŞEVKİ S
BÜYÜK HAYDAR EFENDİ SOK
ABİHAYAT YENİDEVİR S
TİYATRO ARALIĞI SOK
YENİÇERİLER CAD
Beyazıt
KARŞIKAPI
⑧
BİLEÇİLER SOK
GÜVERCİLER PAZARI S
Column of
Constantine
NURUOSMANİYE CAD
Çemberlitaş
Hamamı
Tomb of Sultan Mahmut II
BABIALİ CAD
DİVAN YOLU CAD
Sultanahmet
Press Museum
Çemberlitaş
PEYKHANE SOK
ÇEŞME S
YAHYA PAŞA S
TATLI KUYU HAMAMI SOK
BEYAZIT KAYRAK SOK
BEYAZIT KABADAYI SOK
MİTHATPAŞA CAD
TİYATRO CAD
DİVAN-I ALİ SOK
Gazi Atik
Ali Paşa Camii
Fırat Kültür
Merkezi &
Şafak Cinema
GEDİK PAŞA CAMİ SOK
GEDİK
PAŞA CAMİ SOK
KARAKARRA TÜRBE SOK
EMİN SİNAN SOK
HAMAMI S
PERTEVPAŞA SOK
DİZDARİYE MEDRESESİ SOK
MEDRESESİ SOK
KATİP SİNAN CAMİ S
Museum of
Turkish &
Islamic Art
AHMEDİYE SOK
① YAHYA PAŞA S
Armenian
Protestant Church
Gedikpaşa
Hamamı
GEDİKPAŞA
PİYER LOTİ CAD
PİYER LOTİ CAD
SOGANAĞA CAMİ SOK
KATİP SİNAN MEKTEBİ SOK
TÜRBANİ SOK
TATLI KUYU HAMAMI SOK
SÜMBÜL
NUR SOK
SEMİH S
TÜLCÜ SOK
ÇAPHACI SOK
DEĞHAM SOK
HİPPODROME (ATMEYDANI)
Surp Hovhannes
GEDİKPAŞA CAD
TOKULU SOK
SARAYİÇİ
NEVİYE SOK
KADIRGA HAMAMI SOK
ÖZBEKLER SOK
KADIRGA LİMANI SOK
DİZDARİYEÇEŞMESİ SOK
TAVUKHANE SOK
Sokollu Mehmet
Paşa Camii
Armenian
Patriarchate
Panaya
Elpede
Surp
Asdvadzaszin
MOLLA TAŞI CAD
ŞAMSA SOK
ÇİFTE GELİNLER SOK
CİLVACI SOK
RALİPAŞA CAD
CAMİ SOK
TELLİ ODALAR SOK
BABAYİĞİT SOK
KUMKAPI HANI SOK
ŞAKİR EFENDİ ÇEŞME SOK
KUMKAPI
MEYDANI
ARAPZADE
AHMET SOK
KADIRGA LİMANI CAD
KADIRGA MEYDANI S
BEKRAM S
BEKRAM S
SEFERKETTİN SOK
KÜNKÜR SOK
KAPASLI SOK
ŞERAPNEL SOK
TAVŞOTAŞI ÇEŞMESİ S
OSDERİKÇİ BAKKALA SOK
Church of
St Sergius & Bacchus
AKSAKAL S
MARORFA MEDRESESİ S
CİNCİ MEYDANI SOK
DONUŞ SOK
TOSBİ S
YUSUF AŞÇI S
CÖMERTLER SOK
CÖMERTLER IŞIL S
SEHSUVARBEY SOK
NAKİLBENT SOK
KUMKAPI
KENNEDY CADDESİ (SAHİL YOLU)
Kumkapı
Harbour
N
SEA OF MARMARA

ACCOMMODATION
Niles   2
President   1

SHOPS
Armaggan   2
Horhor Antique Market   1
Şahaflar Çarşısı   3

EXPLORING THE BAZAAR

The **best time to visit** is during the week, as Saturday sees the bazaar and its surroundings crowded with local shoppers. Expect to get lost, as although all streets are marked their signs are often hidden beneath goods hung up on display. However, try finding Kavaflar Sokak for shoes, Terlikçiler Sokak for slippers, Kalpakçılar Başı and Kuyumcular *caddesi* for gold, and Tavuk Pazarı Sokak, Kürkçüler Sokak, Perdahçılar Caddesi and Bodrum Hanı for leather clothing. Carpet-sellers are just about everywhere, with more expensive collector's pieces on sale on Halıcılar Çarşısı, Takkeciler and Keseciler *caddesi*s, and cheaper ones in the İç Cebeci Hanı. Ceramics and leather and kilim bags can be found along Yağlıkçılar Caddesi, just off it in Çukur Han, and also along Keseciler Caddesi.

The **İç Bedesten**, located at the centre of the maze, was traditionally reserved for the most precious wares because it could be locked at night. You'll still find some silver and gold on sale, but these days it contains an eclectic mix of goods along with the jewellery. For a more authentic experience, check out **Kalcılar Han** where you will see silver being cast and worked with skills that have been handed down over the generations.

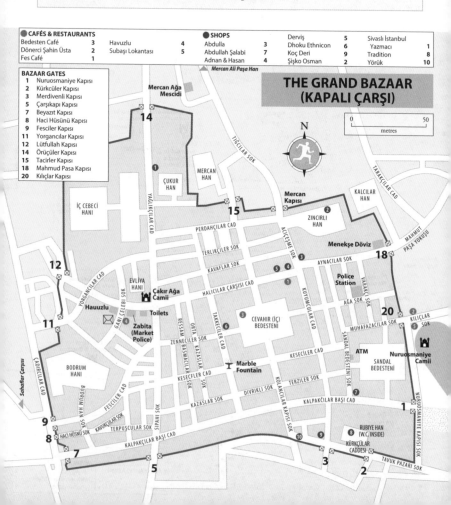

● CAFÉS & RESTAURANTS			
Bedesten Café	3	Havuzlu	4
Dönerci Şahin Üsta	2	Subaşı Lokantası	5
Fes Café	1		

● SHOPS		Derviş	5	Sivaslı İstanbul	
Abdulla	3	Dhoku Ethnicon	6	Yazmacı	1
Abdullah Şalabi	7	Koç Deri	9	Tradition	8
Adnan & Hasan	4	Şişko Osman	2	Yörük	10

BAZAAR GATES
1 Nuruosmaniye Kapısı
2 Kürkçüler Kapısı
3 Merdivenli Kapısı
4 Çarşıkapı Kapısı
7 Beyazıt Kapısı
8 Haci Hüsünü Kapısı
9 Fesciler Kapısı
11 Yorgancılar Kapısı
12 Lütfullah Kapısı
14 Örücüler Kapısı
15 Tacirler Kapısı
18 Mahmud Pasa Kapısı
20 Kılıçlar Kapısı

THE GRAND BAZAAR (KAPALI ÇARŞI)

Column of Constantine

Çemberlitaş • Divan Yolu

A short way southeast of the Grand Bazaar, where Vezirhanı Caddesi intersects with Divan Yolu, is the **Column of Constantine**, a burnt column of masonry, known in Turkish as the Çemberlitaş ("Hooped Stone"). It was erected by Constantine the Great in 330 AD, to commemorate the city's dedication as capital of the Roman Empire. The column consists of seven drums of porphyry and used to be surmounted by a statue of the emperor. The iron hoops from which it derives its Turkish name were bound around the joints in the porphyry after an earthquake in 416 damaged the column. The current scorched condition dates from the great fire of 1779, which destroyed much of the surrounding area. Opposite it to the east is the tourist-friendly Ottoman-era Çemberlitaş Hamamı (see p.228).

Tomb of Sultan Mahmut II

Divan Yolu 82, Sultanahmet • Daily 9am–5pm • Free

Just east of the Çemberlitaş T1 tram stop lies a walled **cemetery**, dominated by the 1838 **Tomb of Sultan Mahmut II**, a large, ornate *türbe* containing the coffins of Mahmut and his son (Sultan Abdülaziz) and grandson (Sultan Abdülhamit), as well as some of his female relatives. The well-tended cemetery contains dozens of graves of lesser statesmen, and includes that of **Ziya Gökalp**, the architect of Turkish nationalism, who died in 1924.

Press Museum

Divan Yolu 84 • Mon–Sat 10am–6pm • Free

The rather run-down **Press Museum** (Basın Müzesi) offers a fascinating insight into the world of the Turkish press, dating back to the sixteenth century. Exhibits include copies of newspapers from the early Republican era, including one from 1928 in both Arabic and Roman scripts (Arabic was banned in 1928 as part of Atatürk's modernization programme), which features a cartoon where anthropomorphized Arabic letters are being chained up and led away into oblivion. Upstairs is a room devoted to the (depressingly numerous) number of Turkish journalists slain in the course of their work – the most recent addition being that of the Istanbul Armenian Hrant Dink, assassinated by an ultranationalist youth in January 2007.

Nuruosmaniye Camii

Vezirhanı Caddesi, Beyazıt

From Divan Yolu, a north turn up Vezirhanı Caddesi leads to the **Nuruosmaniye Camii**, or Mosque of Sacred Light, opposite one of the main entries into the Grand Bazaar, the Çarşı Kapı. Begun by Mahmut I in 1748 and finished seven years later by Osman III, this mosque was the first and most impressive of the city's European-influenced, Baroque-style mosques, and set the fashion in Baroque and Rococo architecture for the following century. The square main prayer hall, dominated by a semicircular apse-like projection containing the *mihrab*, is surmounted by a lofty dome. The courtyard is of most architectural interest, however, as instead of the usual square or rectangle it is almost horseshoe-shaped. Neglected by most visitors, it is both attractive and, due to its proximity to the Grand Bazaar, always busy with worshippers.

Gazi Atık Ali Paşa Camii

Yeniçeriler Caddesi, the western extension of Divan Yolu

The **Gazi Atık Ali Paşa Camii** is one of the oldest mosques in the city. It was built in 1496 by Atık Ali Paşa, a eunuch who rose to the rank of grand vizier under Sultan

Beyazıt II. He was eventually deposed, but rose once again to high office before being killed in battle in 1511. The main dome over the prayer hall is a little over twelve metres in diameter, though the sense of space inside is heightened by the addition of a half-dome over the *mihrab* and smaller twin domes to either side. This design – essentially a rectangular room divided unequally by a huge arch – predates that of the city's larger, more famous mosques.

Süleymaniye Mosque Complex

Süleymaniye Külliyesi • Süleymaniye Mah, Fatih

Northwest of the Grand Bazaar, on the third hill of the old city, the **Süleymaniye Mosque Complex** (Sülemaniye Külliyesi), is a homogenous series of buildings including theological schools, a hospital, library, soup kitchen, caravanserai, shops and tombs. These buildings are clustered around the centrepiece of the entire agglomeration, a magnificent mosque, the Süleymaniye Camii. Built by the renowned architect **Mimar Sinan** (see box, p.82) in honour of his most illustrious patron, Süleyman the Magnificent, the mosque and its associated buildings are arguably his greatest achievement. The complex stands on the grounds of the first palace built in the city by the conquering Ottomans. When, in 1465, the imperial entourage moved to the new palace at Topkapı, the grounds of the old one were given over to the construction of the Süleymaniye, on a superb site overlooking the Golden Horn and its waterside parks and gardens. Begun in 1550, it took just seven years to complete, with Sinan and his family living on site during the entire process.

Many visitors first view the Süleymaniye from the Eminönü waterfront area, from where its slender minarets and curvaceous dome are seen to their best advantage. It is generally approached, however, from the southwest, via the aptly named Süleymaniye Caddesi, which joins the pedestrian street of Sıddık Samı Onal Caddesi right in front

---

MİMAR SİNAN: MASTER BUILDER

Many of the finest works of Ottoman civil and religious architecture are the product of a genius who had the good luck to come of age in a rich, expanding empire willing to put its considerable resources at his disposal. **Mimar Sinan** (1489–1588) served as court architect to three sultans – Süleyman the Magnificent, Selim II and Murat III – but principally to the first, who owed much of his reputation for "magnificence" to this gifted technician.

Sinan was born in a small village near Kayseri, the son of Christian parents. Conscripted into the janissaries in 1513, he served in all the major Ottoman campaigns of the early sixteenth century. Thus compelled to travel the length and breadth of southeastern Europe and the Middle East, Sinan become familiar with the best Islamic and Christian architecture and was immediately able to apply what he had learned in the role of military engineer, building bridges, siegeworks, harbours and even ships. This earned him the admiration of his superiors, including Sultan Süleyman, who in recognition of his abilities appointed him court architect in April 1536.

Sinan completed his first major religious commission, Istanbul's **Şehzade Camii** (see pp.84–85) in 1548, and shortly thereafter embarked on a rapid succession of ambitious projects in and around the capital, including the **Süleymaniye Camii** (see pp.82–84) and the waterworks leading from the Belgrade Forest. Sinan then turned his matured attention to the provinces, gracing Edirne with the **Selimiye Camii** between 1569 and 1575 (see pp.270–271), and a decade later fulfilling a long-standing wish as a devout Muslim by overseeing the restoration of the **Harem-i-Zerif mosque** in Mecca.

Unusually for his time, Sinan could make an objective assessment of his talents: he regarded most of his pre-1550 works as apprentice pieces, and posterity has generally agreed with the self-evaluations in his memoirs, the *Tezkeret-ül-Bünyan*. Despite temptations to luxury, he lived and died equally modestly, being buried in a simple tomb he made for himself in his garden in the grounds of the Süleymaniye Camii – the last of more than five hundred constructions by Sinan, large and small, throughout the empire.

of the mosque. Formerly known as **Tıryakı Çarşısı**, "market of the addicts", the name derives from the fact that the coffeehouses in this street, whose rents augmented the upkeep of the foundation, also served opium. Today the same street is lined with pleasant pavement-cafés selling traditional Turkish meals at reasonable prices, including the tasty beans at the *Erzincanlı Ali Baba* (see p.179) café.

Süleymaniye Camii

Visitors enter the **Süleymaniye Camii** through the main northwest portal, which opens onto the spacious, colonnaded courtyard. Once inside, the overwhelming impression is one of light and uncluttered space, with a central dome 47m high (twice its diameter), surmounting a perfect square of 26.5m. The sense of space is further emphasized by the addition of supporting semi-domes to the northwest and southeast of the dome, while the monumental arched spaces to the southwest and northeast are filled with great tympana walls, pierced by a series of windows through which the light pours. The four great rectangular piers supporting the dome have been cleverly masked on two sides by linking them in with the arched colonnade walls.

A rope prevents non-worshipping visitors from entering the main part of the prayer hall, but it's easy enough to admire the restrained arabesques and Koranic calligraphy adorning the interior, along with the simple Proconnesian marble *mihrab*. The tiles here, used sparingly for effect, are top-notch İznik-ware, fired with flower motifs in blue, red and turquoise on a white ground. The interior always feels cool, partly because a clever air-flow system was incorporated into the original design to direct soot from the candles and oil lamps to a single point – where it was collected and used for ink. The stained-glass windows here, the master work of one İbrahim the Sot, are extremely beautiful.

Tombs of Süleyman and Roxelana

Daily 5.30am–8pm • Free

In the **cemetery** outside the southeast prayer-wall of the mosque are the tombs of Süleyman the Magnificent and Haseki Hürrem, better known to the West as Roxelana, his powerful wife. Süleyman's tomb is particularly impressive: its doors are inlaid with ebony, ivory, silver and jade, and his turban is huge. Above, the spectacular inner dome has been faithfully restored in red, black and gold, inlaid with glittering ceramic stars. Both here, and in the neighbouring tomb of Roxelana, original tiles and some fine stained glass have survived the centuries.

Süleymaniye Library

Süleymaniye Külliyesi • Mon–Sat 8.30am–5pm

Behind the line of cafés on Sıddık Samı Onal Caddesi lies the **Süleymaniye Library**, housed in the Evvel and Sani *medrese*s (theological schools). These buildings, mirror images of each other, are situated around shady garden courtyards. Süleyman established the library in an effort to bring together collections of books scattered throughout the city: there are some eighty thousand manuscripts stored here, gathered from eleven palaces and dating from the reigns of six different sultans. In theory, the library is open to the public, though they don't seem too keen on visitors and you'll need to leave your passport at the gate and wear an identifier tag around your neck.

Ancillary buildings

A *mektep* (primary school) stands on the corner of Sıddık Samı Onal Caddesi and Süleymaniye Caddesi, and there are Koran schools and a language school, which taught the proper pronunciation of Arabic for reading the Koran. At the southwest corner of Sıddık Samı Onal Caddesi is the domed building of the *dar-üş-şifa* or hospital, under restoration at the time of writing. Around the corner, opposite the entrance to the courtyard of the Süleymaniye mosque is the *imaret* (soup kitchen), which, despite its ornate design, was constructed as a public kitchen supplying food for the local poor.

Fittingly, it now houses a reasonable restaurant, the *Darüzziyafe* (see p.187). Just beyond it and currently closed to the public is a *kervansaray* which, in the Ottoman era, provided accommodation for travellers.

Tomb of Mimar Sinan
Corner of Mimar Sinan Caddesi and Fetva Yokuşu

The **Tomb of Mimar Sinan**, at the northwest corner of the complex, just beyond the *kervansaray*, is in a triangular garden, which was the location of the architect's house during construction work. At the corner of the triangle is an attractive fountain. Perhaps there is no nicer way of being remembered than by providing the gift of water to passing strangers, but in Sinan's case it nearly caused his downfall. The fountain, as well as Sinan's house and garden, were liberally supplied with water, but when the mosques further down the pipeline began to run short, Sinan was charged with diverting the water supply for his household needs. The tomb itself has a magnificent carved turban, a measure of the architect's high rank – the eulogy written on the south wall of the garden picks out the bridge at Büyükçekmece as Sinan's greatest achievement.

Fetva Yokuşu, the road to the left of Sinan's tomb as you face it, leads down the hill to the Eminönü waterfront/Galata Bridge, and it makes for a fascinating twenty-minute stroll through a colourful bazaar neighbourhood. If you don't fancy the walk, pop into the *Ağa Kapısı* café (see p.179) for stunning views over the Golden Horn and the Bosphorus. Alternatively, Mimar Sinan Caddesi, the street running between the tomb and the terrace wall of the Süleymaniye Camii, runs past rows of shops that are still a part of the mosque complex and sell paraphernalia for prospective pilgrims to Mecca, to the beautifully restored **Süleymaniye Hamamı** (see p.228).

The Aqueduct of Valens
Runs at right angles to, and spans, Atatürk Bulvarı

The magnificent **Aqueduct of Valens** was originally built during the late fourth-century waterworks programme carried out by Emperor Valens, part of a distribution network that included reservoirs in the Belgrade Forest and various cisterns located around the city centre. It was in use right up to the end of the nineteenth century, having been kept in good repair by successive rulers, who maintained a constant supply of water to the city in the face of both drought and siege. More than six hundred of its original thousand metres are still standing, though the best single viewpoint is where the aqueduct crosses Atatürk Bulvarı – here it is two storeys high, reaching a height of 18.5m.

Column of Marcian
Kıztaşı Caddesi

The little-visited Column of Marcian (450–457 AD) stands a couple of hundred metres southwest of the Aqueduct of Valens, at the crossroads of Kıztaşı Caddesi and Dolap Sokak. Known to Turks as Kız Taşı (The Girl's Stone), it is one of only four surviving columns erected to honour Byzantine emperors in the city (the Column of Constantine is another; see p.81). Although the statue of the emperor has gone, the granite column still sports a Corinthian capital and an eagle-carved plinth, while at the base is an inscription and a relief-carved goddess of victory. It's now a traffic island at a quiet crossroads, but in many ways is more impressive than Constantine's column in Beyazıt.

Şehzade Camii
Şehzadebaşı Caddesi

Constructed in 1548, the **Şehzade Camii** stands in a pleasant park area southeast of the Aqueduct of Valens (see p.84). This "Mosque of the Prince" is so called because

Süleyman the Magnificent had it built (by the ubiquitous Sinan; see box, p.82) in honour of his son Mehmet, who died of the plague aged 21. It is neither as large nor as dramatically situated as the Sülemaniye Camii, and in terms of architectural innovation falls short of the master's greatest works. Unlike the Süleymaniye, here Sinan used four semi-domes to support the central dome; the massive piers needed to support this spoil the aesthetics of what is a rather plain interior. Outside, however, the architect let his imagination run free, especially on the twin minarets, which are ribbed and decorated with vertical bands of low-relief-carved geometric patterns.

The Kalenderhane Camii and around
Mart Şehitleri Cad 16

The **Kalenderhane Camii** is named after the Kalender dervishes who converted the thirteenth-century Byzantine Church of Kyriotissa into a *tekke* (dervish monastery) after the 1453 Conquest. The mosque still retains the cruciform ground plan of the Byzantine church it superseded, and much of the church's marble revetment and sculpture is still in place. In front of the mosque, excavations going down 38m for the Vezneciler station on the M2 metro line have revealed the remains of a Roman building, part of a Byzantine palace and an Ottoman *hamam*.

The area just north of the Kalenderhane, where one of the final arches of the Aqueduct of Valens (see p.84) spans Mart Şehitleri Cad 16, is now a bohemian student quarter, with a few cheap cafés. For a more traditional feel, follow the line of the aqueduct back west for a couple of hundred metres, to *Vefa Bozacısı* (see p.179). Established in 1876 and little changed since, this is the oldest surviving purveyor in the city of *boza*, a fermented millet drink once drunk throughout the Ottoman world. Atatürk (see pp.292–295) himself frequented the place, and the glass he drank from is proudly on display.

Beyazıt Meydanı

Just to the west of the Grand Bazaar, **Beyazıt Meydanı**, the main square of bustling Beyazıt, is the principal approach to Istanbul University. Just off the east of the square is the famous **Sahaflar Çarşısı**, the secondhand-booksellers' market (although most of the books on sale nowadays are new). The Ottoman book market dates back to the eighteenth century, but long before that there was a Byzantine book and paper market on the site. After the Conquest, it lost its original identity to the spoonmakers, though booksellers gradually moved back in once printing and publishing were legalized in the second half of the eighteenth century.

Heading west from Beyazıt, on the south side of the tram line opposite the southwest corner of the meydanı are a jumble of fallen marble columns decorated with curious tear-drop patterns. These formed part of the famed triumphal **Arch of Theodosius** which once marked the entrance to the Forum of Theodosius. Rebuilt on the site of the Forum Tauri in 393 by Emperor Theodosius I and thus renamed after him, it was the largest public space in Constantinople.

Beyazıt Camii
Beyazıt Meydanı

Beyazıt Camii, on the eastern side of Beyazıt Meydanı, was completed in 1506 and is the oldest surviving imperial mosque in the city. It has a sombre courtyard full of richly coloured marble, including twenty columns of verd antique, red granite and porphyry. Inside, the building is a perfect square of exactly the same proportions as the courtyard (although the aisles make it feel elongated). The sixteenth-century fittings, including the carvings of the balustrade, *mihrab* and *mimber*, are all highly crafted.

Istanbul University

Enter through the ornate gateway on the north side of Beyazıt Meydanı • Daily 9am–3pm

Istanbul University commands an impressive position at the crown of one of the city's seven hills; indeed, the **Beyazıt Kulesi**, a 50-metre-high fire tower, built in 1826 and located in the grounds, is a landmark all over the city. You need to go through a security check in the elaborate gateway to enter the university grounds, but bear in mind that the tower is not open to visitors.

The university occupies the site of the Old Palace of Mehmet the Conqueror, the imperial residence from 1453 until it burned to the ground in 1541, after which it was rebuilt to serve as a residence for concubines who had been retired after the accession of a new sultan. The present main university building was constructed by the French architect Bourgeois in 1866, to house the Ministry of War. The ministry moved to Ankara in 1923, along with the other departments of state, when the university (which until then had been scattered around the city in various *medrese*s of the imperial mosques) was relocated here.

3

Laleli and Aksaray

The noisy, ugly spaghetti junction where Atatürk Bulvarı crosses Ordu Caddesi is the main focus of the districts of **Aksaray** and **Laleli**. The atmosphere is distinctly different from anywhere else in Istanbul; though not immediately appealing, there are a number of worthwhile sights here that lie well off most visitors' radars.

Many of the people here are from Russia, Eastern Europe and the Turkic states of Central Asia. In the early years following the collapse of the Soviet Union, Aksaray and Laleli were the centre of the so-called "suitcase trade", as poor traders arrived with cases loaded with odds and sods to sell, bought up local goods and sold them back in their home country. It's not exactly a rich area today, but most people coming from the former Soviet states now are here to spend, spend, spend, and the shops are full of some of the most outrageously nouveau riche and designer (both fake and genuine) fashion items you're likely to see anywhere.

Turkish women avoid Aksaray and Laleli, as it still has a reputation (justly so) for prostitution, though this is now confined to the quarter southwest of the Atatürk Bulvarı/Ordu Caddesi crossroads, where shady clubs and importuners abound.

Istanbul University Faculty of Science and Literature

Ordu Caddesi

The imposing building housing the **Istanbul University Faculty of Science and Literature** was completed in 1944, and was designed according to the precepts of the Second National Architectural Movement, a nationalist style of architecture that took its inspiration from Fascist movements in Italy and Germany. Designed by two of the pioneering Turkish architects of the day, Sedad Hakki Eldem and Emin Haid Onat, it is essentially a modernist building that incorporates a few elements of traditional Turkish architecture. With its monumental but plain, almost brutal, facade it couldn't be more of a contrast to ornate Laleli Camii, just down the road (see below).

Laleli Camii

Ordu Caddesi • Laleli/Üniversite T1 tram stop

Built in the Ottoman Baroque tradition of Nuruosmaniye Camii (see p.81) and the Ayazma Camii in Üsküdar, the attractive **Laleli Camii** is perched above busy Ordu Caddesi. This mosque nonetheless owes more to traditional Ottoman architecture than ideas imported from Europe. It was founded by Mustafa III, whose octagonal tomb is located at the southeast gate. Selim III, who was assassinated by his janissaries, is also buried there.

The main Baroque elements in the mosque complex are the use of ramps (including one that the reigning sultan would have used to ride up to his loge), the grand staircases and the exquisite detail, noticeable in the window grilles of the tomb and in the carved eaves of the *sebil* (drinking fountain). Inside, a mass of pillars dominates, especially to the west, where the columns beneath the main dome seem to crowd those supporting the galleries into the walls. Back outside, the foundations of the mosque are used as a covered **market**, selling the cheapest of clothes and acting as an inducement for the local populace to worship at the mosque.

Istanbul Municipality Building
Şehzadebaşı Caddesi

The colossal **Istanbul Municipality Building**, designed by Nevzat Oral in 1953, was the first truly modernist, International Style building in the city. It's worth seeking out (you can hardly miss it even if you wanted to) as a contrast to the more venerable buildings of the old city. A rectangular structure with a grid facade, mounted on a columnar base, its austere form is leavened by the use of attractive blue mosaic tile cladding. It has a definite presence, though plans are afoot to sell off the building and turn it into a hotel.

3

Gedikpaşa and Kumkapı

The areas directly south of the Grand Bazaar, **Gedikpaşa** and **Kumkapı**, centred around three major streets – Gedikpaşa, Tiyatro and Mithatpaşa *caddesi*s – that run at steep angles down to the Sea of Marmara, lack any sights of real note but are great places in which to wander. In addition to a scattering of small mosques, there are a number of nineteenth-century Armenian Apostolic (orthodox) and Greek Orthodox **churches**, attesting to the districts' cosmopolitan past. A handful of Greeks still live around here, rather more Armenians, and you're almost as likely to hear Kurdish spoken as Turkish, as recent decades have seen a wave of migrant workers from the impoverished southeast of Turkey arrive to set up homes and businesses in these narrow streets.

Armenian Protestant Church
Gedikpaşa Caddesi

The handsome rendered-stone **Armenian Protestant Church** dates back to 1914, when it was rebuilt on the site of an earlier wooden church (1850) that suffered the same fate as so many wood structures in the old city – destroyed by fire. The church serves as a community centre for the mainly impoverished local Armenians, many of whom only arrived here from the former Soviet Armenia post-1990.

Surp Hovhannes
Sarayıçı Sokak

The Armenian Apostolic church of **Surp Hovhannes** (St John's) dates back to 1827, though the original wooden structure burnt down and was replaced by the current building in 1876. The door to the compound in which the church is set is usually open, an encouraging sign of increasing tolerance towards minority Armenians by the city's Muslim Turkish majority, though photography is forbidden inside the cradle-vaulted church.

FISH FRENZY

Cobbled Çapraz Sokak, which leads to the now-defunct suburban railway line running parallel to the sea, is a dense mass of **fish restaurants** (over forty of them), which erupt, especially on Friday and Saturday evening, into a frenzy of eating, drinking (mainly *rakı*), smoking, dancing (to *fasil* music) and more drinking. It's not exactly a local crowd (most of the area's inhabitants are too poor to dine out here) but largely Turks from elsewhere in the city out to party. It is an experience to eat here, but none of the restaurants stand out.

Panaya Elpeda
Gerdanlık Sokak

The substantial domed Greek Orthodox church of Kumkapı's **Panaya Elpeda**, with its gated entrance, dates back to the fifteenth century but has been rebuilt many times – the current, attractive Neoclassical structure belongs firmly in the nineteenth century. It contains one of the city's many *ayazma*s (sacred springs), but the caretakers aren't keen on letting visitors in.

Surp Asdvadzadzin
Şarapnel Sokak

If you have any interest at all in Istanbul's Christian minorities, the one unmissable site in Gedikpaşa/Kumkapı is the Armenian Apostolic church of **Surp Asdvadzadzin** (known in Turkish as the Meryem Ana Kilisesi or Church of the Virgin Mary), dating back to 1641 – though much of what you see today dates from a rebuilding in 1886. This is the one Armenian church where you're guaranteed to see a sizeable congregation at the Sunday service, as its position, opposite the Armenian Patriarchate, makes it the city's most important. With black-clad priests chanting in front of the gilt altar, shafts of light illuminating the nave, the smell of incense heavy in the air, and members of the soberly dressed congregation kneeling and genuflecting before taking their pew, it's a moving sight. Ironically given the ethnic cleansing of Armenians from Turkish soil in 1915 (see box, p.293), Armenians had been welcomed to the city with open arms after the 1453 Ottoman Turkish conquest as part of Mehmet the Conqueror's programme to rebuild and regenerate his new capital. Many of them eventually settled in this part of the old city.

The northwest quarter

Bounded by the major thoroughfare of Fevzi Paşa Caddesi to the west, the land walls of Theodosius to the north, the Golden Horn to the east, and the traffic-choked highway of Atatürk Bulvarı to the south, the northwest quarter is one of the least visited yet most interesting areas of old Istanbul. The magnificent Kariye Museum (once the Byzantine Church of St Saviour in Chora) aside, none of the sights here are major draws. For the most part, the only people you will see are locals going about their daily business – which is, of course, one of the area's greatest attractions. Remember that few people here speak a foreign language, mosques are often locked except at prayer times and most churches only open for services once a week.

This was once a very cosmopolitan area, with **Muslims, Christians, Jews** and gypsies living in close proximity to each other. Most (though not all) of the Christians and Jews have long since departed, and the Muslims that are left, particularly in Fatih, are noted for their orthodoxy. Men in skullcaps, voluminous *şalvar* trousers, long shirts and bushy beards are more redolent of Pakistan than Turkey, as are some of the women, draped head to toe in black *chadors*. Many of the area's inhabitants are migrants from impoverished rural areas in Anatolia and the Black Sea, and you may well hear Kurdish spoken in the streets.

ARRIVAL

THE NORTHWEST QUARTER

By ferry Perhaps the most pleasant way to reach the area is by ferry up the Golden Horn, from Eminönü or Karaköy to Ayvansaray (hourly 7.50am–7pm from Eminönü; hourly 7.45am–6.55pm from Karaköy).

By bus The #99 bus from Eminönü will drop you just beyond the Atatürk Bridge for Zeyrek, but it also continues up to Fener, Balat and Ayvansaray. The #38/E from Eminönü stops on Atatürk Bul, just below the Zeyrek Camii, before it

continues onto Edirnekapı (for the Kariye Museum; see pp.92–95) via Fatih Camii and the Yavuz Selim Camii. The #36/V and #37/Y from Vezneciler are both handy for the Fatih and Yavuz Selim mosques.

By tram If you find the buses off-putting, take the T1 tram to Aksaray and walk for ten minutes up to the Aqueduct of Valens, beyond which the "quarter" begins.

Zeyrek

Zeyrek, an attractive area notable for its steep, cobbled streets and ramshackle wooden houses interspersed with small mosques, has a couple of interesting sights. İtfaiye Caddesi, an important street abutting the Aqueduct of Valens, has been pedestrianized and re-branded Kadınlar Pazarı (The Women's Market) and is a lively area full of restaurants.

The Women's Market

Kadınlar Pazarı • Atatürk Bulvarı, running at right angles northwards from the Aqueduct of Valens (see p.84) • Daily 9am–10pm

If you're tired of the touristy food markets such as the Spice Bazaar it's worth heading out to the **Women's Market**, a bustling, elongated square in the shadow of the Aqueduct of Valens. All the shops ringing the square are owned by people from the southeast of Turkey, mainly Kurds, making it an atmospheric and cheap place to stock up on pistachio nuts (those labelled Siirt have quite a different flavour from those marked Antep), walnuts, almonds and dried fruits. There's an incredibly pungent array of goat's cheeses too, as well as the dried yoghurt, *tarhana*, used in soups – plus a large number of excellent, down-to-earth eating places, including *Siirt Şeref* (see p.188) and *Sur Ocakbaşı* (see p.188).

Zeyrek Camii

İbadethane Arkası Sok 6–8; reached by turning left off İtfaiye Caddesi

In the heart of Zeyrek nestles **Zeyrek Camii**, the former Church of the Pantocrator, built in the twelfth century and converted into a mosque at the time of the Conquest. A major restoration of the building should be completed by 2015, after which it will continue its function as a mosque. It originally consisted of two churches and a connecting chapel, built between 1118 and 1136 by John II Comnenus and Empress Irene. The chapel was built as a mausoleum for the Comnenus dynasty and continued to be used as such by the Paleologus dynasty. Empress Irene also founded a monastery nearby, which was to become one of the most renowned religious institutions in the empire and later the official residence of the Byzantine court, after the Great Palace had been reduced to ruins. No trace remains of the monastery, nor of its hospice, asylum or hospital.

Upper Fatih and Çarşamba

The reputation of **Fatih** ("the Conqueror") and **Çarşamba** as conservative Islamic areas is deserved, though they're not associated with intolerance towards visitors of different religious and cultural persuasions – it's still worth bearing in mind, however, that locals

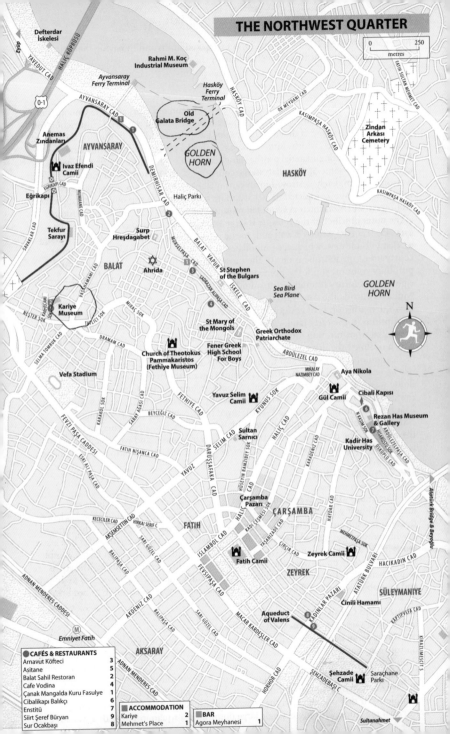

THE NORTHWEST QUARTER

0   250
metres

Defterdar
İskelesi

Eyüp

YAVEDUT CAD

HALIÇ KÖPRÜSÜ

Rahmi M. Koç
Industrial Museum

FATİH SULTAN MEHMET CAD

OK MEYDANI CAD

Ayvansaray
Ferry Terminal

Hasköy
Ferry
Terminal

KASIMPAŞA HASKÖY CAD

HASKÖY CAD

Zindan
Arkası
Cemetery

AYVANSARAY CAD

0-1

Old
Galata Bridge

KASIMPAŞA HASKÖY CAD

Anemas
Zındanları

AYVANSARAY

GOLDEN
HORN

HASKÖY

İvaz Efendi
Camii

DEMİRHİSAR CAD

EĞRİKAPI CAD

Eğrikapı

Haliç Parkı

Tekfur
Sarayı

MUHNNME CAD

Surp
Hreşdagabet

BALAT VAPUR İSK

MÜRSELPAŞA CAD

St Stephen
of the Bulgars

SAVAKLAR CAD

Ahrida

PAŞA HAMAMI CAD

BALAT

Sea Bird
Sea Plane

GOLDEN
HORN

Kariye
Museum

NEŞTER SOK

TAHTACI SOK

St Mary of
the Mongols

SADRAZAM ALİPAŞA CAD

İSKELE CAD

N

MİRAÇ SOK

DRAMAM CAD

Greek Orthodox
Patriarchate

SELMA TOMRUK CAD

Church of Theotokus
Pammakaristos
(Fethiye Museum)

Fener Greek
High School
For Boys

ABDÜLEZEL CAD

Vefa Stadium

KARAKOL SOK

SARAY AĞASI CAD

FETHİYE CAD

BEYCEĞIZ SOK

FEVZİ PAŞA CADDESİ

ESKİ ALİ PAŞA CAD

Yavuz Selim
Camii

KYUNUS SOK

MİRALAY
NAZIMBEY CAD

Aya Nikola

HALIÇ CAD

Cibali Kapısı

Gül Camii

Rezan Has Museum
& Gallery

SELİM CAD

FATİH NİŞANCA CAD

DARÜŞŞAFAKA CAD

YAVUZ

Sultan
Sarnıcı

KARADENİZ CAD

Kadir Has
University

ABDÜLEZEL PAŞA CAD

HÜSEYIN RAMİZBEY SOK

KÜÇÜKPU CAD

Atatürk Bridge & Beyoğlu

KECECİLER CAD

AKŞEMSETTİN CAD

HIRKAI ŞERİF C

SARI GÜZEL CAD

FATİH

Çarşamba
Pazarı

ÇARŞAMBA

KADI ÇEŞMESİ SOK

YAZARZADE CAD

HAYDAR CAD

MEHMETPAŞA SOK

Zeyrek Camii

Zeyrek Camii

HACIKADIN CAD

ADNAN MENDERES CADDESİ

BALIPAŞA CAD

İSLAMBOL CAD

HALIÇ CAD

Fatih Camii

ZEYREK

EĞRİÇIR CAD

ATATÜRK BULVARI

SÜLEYMANİYE

KAPTIVEFA CAD

Emniyet Fatih

M

AKDENIZ CAD

BALIPAŞA CAD

SARI GÜZEL CAD

FEYSİPAŞA CAD

MACAR KARDEŞLER CAD

KADINLAR PAZARI

Çinili Hamamı

KIRAZLIMESCİT S

ADNAN MENDERES CADDESİ

AKSARAY

HORHOR CAD

Aqueduct
of Valens

Şehzade
Camii

Saraçhane
Parkı

ŞEHZADEBAŞI C

Sultanahmet

---

here may be more likely to take exception to naked limbs and to having their picture taken without due warning than elsewhere in the city.

Fatih Camii
İslambol Caddesi • Tombs of Mehmet II Wed–Sun 9am–4.30pm • Free

Fatih Camii, the "Mosque of the Conqueror", was begun ten years after the Conquest of Istanbul, in 1463, making it the first purpose-built mosque in the city. Construction took place on the site of one of the most important Christian buildings in the city, the Church of the Holy Apostles, which until 1028 was the burial place of all Byzantine emperors. Much of the building material for the mosque complex came from the demolished church, such as some of the pillars in the courtyard of the mosque. Completed in 1470, it was almost completely destroyed in an earthquake as early as 1766. A major restoration of the mosque was completed in 2013, and it's well worth the trip out here to appreciate an historic and monumental Ottoman mosque that receives very few foreign visitors.

The **outer precinct** of the mosque is large enough to accommodate the tents of a caravan. It is enclosed by a wall and, to the north and south, by the *medrese* (theological academy) buildings, which accommodated the first Ottoman university. The **inner courtyard** of the mosque is one of the most beautiful in the city. Verd antique and porphyry columns support a domed portico with polychrome edges, while an eighteenth-century fountain is surrounded by four enormous poplar trees. Over the windows outside the courtyard in the west wall, the first verse of the Koran is inscribed in white marble on verd antique. At either end of the mosque portico there are inscriptions in the early İznik *cuerda seca* technique, whereby coloured glazes were prevented from running into each other by a dividing line of potassium permanganate, which outlined the design. The inscription over the mosque portal records the date and dedication of the mosque, and the name of the architect, **Atık Sinan**. According to one tale he was executed the year after its completion on the orders of Mehmet, because the dome wasn't as large as that of Haghia Sophia. In another, the Christian architect is rewarded for his fine work by having the nearby church at which he was a congregant, Mary of the Mongols (see pp.99–100), saved from conversion to a mosque.

The **tombs of Mehmet II** and of one of his wives, Gülbahar, are situated to the east of the mosque. The originals were destroyed in the earthquake, and while Gülbahar's tomb is probably a replica of the original, the *türbe* of the Conqueror is sumptuous Baroque.

The Çarşamba Pazarı
Çarşamba • Wednesday 9am–dusk

The **Çarşamba Pazarı** or **Wednesday Market** is the largest in the city. Its origins are uncertain, but it seems likely it was first established here in the Byzantine period, when this area was still rural. Eventually, as the city grew and engulfed the district, the entire neighbourhood was named Çarşamba after the market. The bazaar stretches for block after block in the streets to the northwest, southwest and southeast of the Fatih Camii complex, its awning, strung up between the narrow streets, providing welcome shade. The goods on display here range from the usual cheap-and-cheerful household implements to fresh fruit and vegetables, and from cheap (and often even cheaper looking) clothing to bed linen.

Yavuz Selim Camii
Yavuz Selim Caddesi, Fatih • Tomb of Selim the Grim Mon & Wed–Sun 9.30am–4.30pm • ₺1

The **Yavuz Selim Camii**, also called the Selimiye Camii, is one of the most attractive mosques in the city, and looks even more attractive after a long period of restoration. Built on a terrace on the crest of one of Istanbul's seven hills (the fifth, counting from Topkapı), it holds a commanding position over the surrounding suburbs. The mosque of Yavuz Selim, or Selim the Grim, was probably begun in the reign of Selim and completed in that of Süleyman the Magnificent. It is more basic than the other imperial mosques, with just a single large dome atop a square room with a walled courtyard in front of it. The *avlu* (courtyard) in front of the prayer hall is quite beautiful, with a central fountain surrounded by tall cypress trees, the floor of the portico paved with a floral design and the columns a variety of marbles and granites.

The interior of the mosque is stunning in its simplicity, the shallower-than-usual dome emphasizing the sense of space. Light floods in through a series of windows in the tympanum arches and from the twenty-four stained-glass windows piercing the dome. The interior falls well short of the austere, though, with gorgeous blue and white İznik tiles filling the lunettes above the lower windows and gilt work highlighting the beautiful geometry of the stalactite carving above the *mihrab*.

The **tomb of Selim the Grim**, beside the mosque, has lost its original interior decoration but retains two beautiful tiled panels on either side of the door. Other tombs in the complex include that of four of Süleyman's children, probably the work of Sinan. The views from the northeast of the complex, looking out over the Golden Horn, are glorious.

Viewed on the approach down Yavuz Selim Caddesi, the mosque presents one of the most impressive façades to be seen in the city, in part because of its position next to the **Cistern of Aspar**, one of three open cisterns built during the fifth and sixth centuries in Constantinople. For centuries, this space housed market gardens and a village, but these were cleared years ago and sections are now in use as an attractive park.

A MULTI-FAITH CITY

As recently as the early years of the twentieth century, the Ottoman lands that in 1923 became the new Republic of Turkey were home to a bewildering variety of **faiths** – Sunni Muslims, Alevis, Sufi dervish orders such as the Mevlevi and Nakşibendi, Jews, Yezidis, Greek, Syrian Orthodox and Armenian Apostolic Christians, Nestorians, plus converts from all these "native" branches of the Christian faith to Catholicism and Protestantism. During World War I and the War of Independence, however, all this was to change. Most Christians in Anatolia, seen as collaborators and potential fifth columnists by the Turkish Nationalists, either fled, were deported or killed. Non-Sunni Islam sects, also viewed with suspicion by the founders of the new, secular Turkish nation, were driven underground. Only in **Istanbul** did Christians remain in any numbers – over forty percent of the population – and despite the gradual emigration of most non-Muslims over the years since the formation of the Republic, Istanbul remains a multi-faith city.

In 1923, the **Greek Orthodox** population of the city was around 380,000. It has now declined to some 2000, but the Orthodox Patriarchate is based in Fener (see p.99) and continues to serve the needs of the local Greek population, remaining, by tradition at least, the spiritual centre of the entire Eastern Orthodox Christian world. The **Armenian Apostolic (orthodox) Christians** have fared rather better, with a population of around 70,000. The community is spread across the city, though their religious focus is firmly in the old city, at Kumkapı (see pp.87–88), where the Patriarchate building stands opposite a nineteenth-century church that attracts a full congregation every Sunday (see p.88). The Ottoman Empire was very welcoming to Sephardic Jews fleeing persecution in Spain in the fifteenth century and the community also prospered. Around 20,000 **Jews** now live in the city, with their most notable synagogues being in Balat (see p.100) and across the Golden Horn in Galata.

Of course, today's Istanbul is largely populated by **Sunni Muslims**. As elsewhere in the Islamic world, orthodoxy is finding a new voice – as you will discover if you wander the streets of neighbourhoods such as Fatih. Many Istanbulites, however, wear their religion very lightly (or take no heed at all), and for the average devout male, it's enough to attend the midday prayers on a Friday in one of the city's beautiful mosques and enjoy his Sunday off with his family. The Muslim population is not as homogenous as you might think, however. By some estimates, around twenty percent of Turkish citizens are **Alevi** – a curious (to the outsider) and mystical mix of Islam, shamanism and Shiism. While Sunni Islam is controlled by the state (religious officials such as *imam*s are paid by the government, and sermons centrally checked), Alevis have led an "underground" existence beyond state sanction, worshipping in simple halls or private rooms known as *cemevi*. By tradition, they are staunch supporters of the secular regime (to avoid religious bigotry), even though they are neither recognized by, nor receive funding from, the state.

Sultan Sarnıcı

Ali Naki Sokak

This recently restored covered Byzantine cistern, now known as the **Sultan Sarnıcı** (Sultan's Cistern), is around 29m by 19m. It has the usual brick-vaulted ceiling supported by 28 columns, some marble, others granite, each topped with beautifully carved Corinthian capitals. A few of the capitals bear the initials, in Greek, of the craftsmen who carved them, while others sport crosses. The cistern now serves as a function room, so don't be surprised to find the columns decked out with frills if there's a wedding celebration in the offing. There's neither official opening times nor an admission charge, but assuming there is no function on you're free to wander round and explore.

Church of Theotokos Pammakaristos

Fethiye Camii/Müzesi • Fethiye Caddesi, Katip Mustehattın Mah, Fatih • Mon, Tues & Thurs–Sun 9am–4.30pm • ₺5

A major, but little-visited, Byzantine gem, the **Church of Theotokos Pammakaristos**, is a medium-sized church, attractively set on a terrace overlooking the Golden Horn. Built in the twelfth century it conforms to the usual cross in a square design, its large central dome enhanced by four smaller, subsidiary domes. Despite the Ottoman conquest of Constantinople in 1453, it remained a Christian place of worship; indeed, between 1456 and 1587 it served as the seat of the **Greek Orthodox Patriarch** (now situated nearby, in the district of Fener). It was finally converted into a mosque in 1573, when it was renamed the Fethiye Camii or "Mosque of the Conquest". The main body of the building continues to function as a mosque and is usually only unlocked around prayer times. The southwest wing (originally a side chapel or parecclesion of the main church, added in 1310) was partitioned off during restoration work undertaken in 1949 and now serves as a **museum**. Helpful display boards in the entry to the chapel locate and give information on each of the mosaics, superb examples of the renaissance of Byzantine art, including, in the dome, Christ Pantocrator, encircled by the twelve prophets of the Old Testament. Other notable scenes show Christ with the Virgin Mary, the baptism of Christ and St John the Baptist.

The Kariye Museum

Kariye Müzesi • Kariye Mahallesi, Edirnekapı • Mon, Tues & Thurs–Sun 9am–6pm • ₺15 • ⓦ choramuseum.com

Perched on a hill high above the old Jewish quarter of Balat; a stone's throw from the land walls of Theodosius, is the **Kariye Museum** [Kariye Müzesi]. Formerly the **Church of St Saviour in Chora**, its interior is decorated with a superbly preserved series of **frescoes and mosaics**. Among the most evocative of all the city's Byzantine treasures, it is thought to have been built in the early twelfth century on the site of a much older church far from the centre: hence "in Chora", meaning "in the country".

Between 1316 and 1321, the polymath statesman, scholar, philosopher and patron of the arts Theodore Metochites rebuilt the central dome and added the narthexes, the parecclesion (funerary chapel) and the stunning mosaics and frescoes that adorn both them and the nave. The unfortunate Metochites was stripped of his court position in 1328 following one of the all too common dynastic upheavals, and then imprisoned. He was eventually freed, though, and on his death in 1331 was buried in the funerary chapel of his magnificent church.

Turned into a mosque following the Ottoman conquest, the mosaics and frescoes were whitewashed over until their restoration by the Byzantine Institute of America between 1948 (when it stopped functioning as a mosque) and its opening as a museum ten years later.

You should try to view the mosaics as they were originally intended by their (unknown) artists, as many of them fall into one of three narrative sequences, each telling a biblical story. This is not always easy as all the mosaics, bar the three in the nave, are spread confusingly over the walls, arches, pendentives and lunettes of the

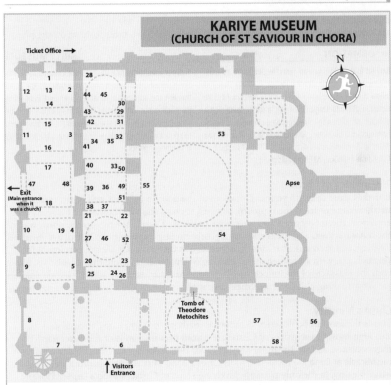

KARIYE MUSEUM
(CHURCH OF ST SAVIOUR IN CHORA)

Ticket Office →

N

Exit
(Main entrance when it was a church)

Apse

Tomb of Theodore Metochites

Visitors Entrance

4

THE INFANCY OF CHRIST
1 Joseph dreaming & the journey to Bethlehem
2 Enrolment for taxation
3 Nativity scene
4 The journey of the Magi & Magi appear before Herod
5 Herod enquires of the whereabouts of the new-born child
6 The flight into Egypt (partial)
7 Massacre of the innocents, ordered by Herod
8 Herod's soldiers continue slaying children
9 Mothers mourn their slain
10 Elizabeth flees with her baby son, John the Baptist
11 Joseph dreams of a return to Nazareth
12 Christ returns to Jerusalem

THE MINISTRY OF CHRIST
13 Christ with the doctors
14 John the Baptist bears witness to Christ
15 John the Baptist bears witness to Christ
16 Christ is tempted by the devil
17 Miracle at Cana, Christ turns water into wine
18 Multiplication of loaves
19 Christ healing a leper
20 Christ heals a blind and dumb man
21 The healing of two blind men
22 Christ healing St. Peter's mother-in-law
23 Christ heals the bleeding woman
24 Christ heals the withered hand
25 Christ heals a leper
26 Healing scene (inscription lost)
27 Christ heals assorted illnesses

THE LIFE OF THE VIRGIN MARY
28 Joachim has his offerings rejected
29 Joachim goes into the wilderness to pray
30 Anne's prayers are answered (Annunciation)
31 Meeting at the Golden Gate (Joachim and Anne)
32 Birth of the Virgin Mary
33 The first seven steps of the Virgin

THE LIFE OF THE VIRGIN MARY (CONTINUED)
34 Priests bless the Virgin
35 The Virgin caressed by her parents
36 The Virgin is presented to the temple, aged three
37 An Angel gives bread to the Virgin
38 Instruction of the Virgin
39 The Virgin is given purple wool to weave
40 Zacharias praying before the rods of the suitors
41 The Virgin is awarded to Joseph
42 The Annunciation of the Virgin
43 The Annunciation of the Virgin
44 Joseph goes away & returns to find Mary pregnant

THE GENEALOGY OF CHRIST
45 The Virgin and Child with Christ's ancestors
46 Christ Pantacrator with Christ's ancestors

THE DEDICATORY MOSAICS
47 The Virgin and Angels
48 Christ Pantactor
49 Enthroned Christ and donor
50 St Peter
51 St Paul
52 The Deesis

THE NAVE MOSAICS
53 Jesus with Bible
54 The Virgin Hodegetria
55 Dormition of the Virgin

THE FRESCOES
56 The resurrection (Anastasis)
57 The Second Coming
58 Souls of the damned

outer and inner narthexes. Use the plan (see p.95) to help you negotiate the museum and identify the scenes; numbers in the text below relate to their position on the plan.

INFORMATION   **KARİYE MUSEUM**

Arrival To reach the museum from the city centre, take the M1 metro from Aksaray to the Topkapı/Ulubatlı stop and follow the line of the land walls heading northeast before turning right onto Kariye Camii Sok, a street containing a number of picturesquely renovated wooden houses, painted in pastel colours. Alternatively, and dropping you closer to the museum at Edirnekapı, take bus #32, #36K or #38/E from Eminönü, #87 from Taksim.

Tickets and entrance The museum entrance is on the north side of the church; purchase your ticket before going through the automated turnstile. To enter the building itself follow the path (noting the prominent bulge of the apse, supported by buttresses) through the garden area to the door on the south side, which leads into the south bay of the inner narthex.

The Infancy of Christ

It makes sense to begin your explorations at the door in the west wall of the outer narthex, the exit from the museum, as when it was a church this was the main entrance. The Infancy of Christ narrative begins just north of here, on the north wall of the **outer narthex**, and the scenes are all conveniently located in the distinctive lunettes (semicircular recesses). Particularly impressive in this sequence are the **Enrolment for Taxation** (2), with an apprehensive-looking Mary standing before the tax officials, along with the **Massacre of the Innocents** (7). In this partially damaged scene, Herod's soldiers are shown taking children from their distraught mothers' arms, then butchering them.

Christ's Ministry

This is the most difficult series to follow as many of the scenes are damaged and, although most of the works of Christ are spread over the vaults of the outer narthex, they continue on into the inner narthex. Worth looking out for in the outer narthex is the **Miracle at Cana** (17) which depicts Christ, hand outstretched, turning water into wine. Nearby, in the only partially surviving scene of **Christ Healing a Leper** (19), the legs of the poor soul about to be healed are covered in almost comic-book spots. In an impressively complete scene in the inner narthex, **Christ Healing St Peter's Mother-in-Law** (22), St Peter is pictured alongside his bedridden mother-in-law, with Jesus taking the poor woman's outstretched hand.

The Life of the Virgin Mary

Located in the inner narthex, these mosaics are based on the apocryphal gospel of St James, which gives an account of the birth and life of the Virgin and was very popular in the Middle Ages. They are remarkably complete and beautifully executed. One of the most delightful is the **First Seven Steps of the Virgin** (33), which shows the infant Mary tottering between her mother, St Anne, and her father Joachim. Another warming family scene, the **Virgin Caressed by her Parents** (35), depicts the infant Mary cradled between her mother and father. In **Zacharias praying before the Rods of the Suitors** (40), the Virgin Mary makes her marriage choice by selecting from the twelve sticks left by her suitors – she picks the one that is sprouting.

The inner narthex domes

In the northern dome of the inner narthex is a medallion of the **Virgin and Child**. In the sixteen upper ribs the kings of the house of David are depicted, below them a further eleven ancestors (45). A similar medallion in the southern dome of the inner narthex shows **Christ Pantocrator** in a medallion, while below him are ranged 24 of Jesus' ancestors, ranging from Adam to Jacob (46).

The dedicatory mosaics

These six large mosaic panels, placed in both the outer and inner narthexes, portray the dedication of the church to both Christ and the Virgin Mary. Above the main doorway into the outer narthex is **The Virgin and Angels** (47) depicting Mary, hands outstretched, with the infant Christ, shown here symbolizing the universe, on her bosom. Opposite, above the door through to the inner narthex, is **Christ Pantocrator** (48) bearing the inscription "Jesus Christ, the Land of the Living". Moving through into the inner narthex, straight ahead above the door into the nave is the **Enthroned Christ and Donor** (49). Perhaps the single most interesting mosaic of all, it depicts Theodore Metochites offering a model of the building to a seated Christ. The turban-like hat he is wearing is called a *skiadon* (sunshade). **St Peter** (50), the keys to heaven in his left hand, is portrayed on the left of the door to the nave, **St Paul** (51) on the right. Finally, right of St Paul is a large scene, **The Deesis** (52), showing Christ with his mother and two benefactors, Isaac (who built the original church) and a female figure, described in the inscription as "Lady of the Mongols, Melanie (also known as Mary) the Nun", the illegitimate Byzantine princess after whom the nearby Church of Mary of the Mongols (see p.99) is named.

The nave mosaics

Partially covered with revetment marble panels, the nave contains three striking mosaic panels. To the left of the apse, **Jesus** (53) holds an open bible in his hand. To the right of the apse **The Virgin Hodegetria** (54) cradles the infant Christ, while on the west wall above the door to the outer narthex is the **Dormition of the Virgin** (55), showing Mary on her death bier, Christ behind her holding a swaddled infant representing her soul.

The funerary chapel

In the north wall of the **funerary chapel** is the **tomb of Metochites**, the donor of the church, although the inscription has been lost. There are three other tombs in the walls here, as well as some finely carved marble capitals, but the real glory is the frescoes. Contemporary with the work of the Italian painter Giotto, they seem to have much more in common with the early Renaissance than the stylized paintings of the earlier Byzantine period. There are over thirty different scenes depicted, all dealing, aptly for a funerary chapel, with death or resurrection.

The most spectacular is the **Resurrection** (56) also known as the Harrowing of Hell or, in Greek, the *anastasis*. This is a dramatic representation of Christ in action, trampling the gates of Hell underfoot and forcibly dragging Adam and Eve from their tombs. Satan lies among the broken fetters at his feet, bound at the ankles, wrists and neck, but still writhing around in a vital manner.

Along the Golden Horn

Most of the sights on the western bank of the Golden Horn lie more or less on the line of the old sea walls, which once ran right around the peninsula and linked into either end of the great land walls of Theodosius – and thus completely encircled and protected first the Byzantine and then the Ottoman imperial capitals.

The best starting point is the **Atatürk Bridge** (Unkapanı Köprüsü), accessible by any Fatih- or Eyüp-bound bus from Eminönü. As you head northwest along the bank of the Horn, the narrow streets and jumbled houses of Fatih, Fener and Balat tumble down from the hills above. Warm Sundays bring droves of picnicking families to the strip of park between the road and waterfront.

Rezan Has Museum & Gallery

Rezan Has Müzesi • Kadir Has Üniversitesi, Cibali • Daily 9am–6pm • Free • ☎ 0212 533 6532, ⓦ rhm.org.tr • Bus #99 from Eminönü

The intriguing **Rezan Has Museum & Gallery** is housed in the **Kadir Has University**, an imposing, late nineteenth-century former tobacco factory. The museum and exhibition space are located on the north (right as you face it) of the university building, attractively laid out in the bowels of the tobacco factory, itself built over a Byzantine cistern and Ottoman *hamam*. At the time of writing the original collection, a series of cases set out chronologically with top-drawer artefacts from the Neolithic through to the Selçuk Turkish era, had been replaced by an exhibition of Urartian jewellery, but it is likely the permanent collection will be reinstated late in 2015. An exhibition space adjacent to this marvellous private collection hosts an eclectic but well-regarded series of temporary exhibitions, which have included everything from contemporary art to the Ottoman fire service. Also here is *Enstitü*, the well-regarded restaurant of the Istanbul Culinary Institute (see box, p.192).

Greek Orthodox Patriarchate
Fener Rum Patrikhanesi • Mursel Paşa Caddesi • Daily 9am–5pm • Free

The **Greek Orthodox Patriarchate** (Fener Rum Patrikhanesi*)*, has been the spiritual centre of the Orthodox world since 1599 and remains so today – despite the fact that a Turkish court controversially ruled in 2007 that the spiritual authority of Patriarch Bartholomew I was confined solely to Turkey's few remaining Greek Orthodox Christians, rather than to the Orthodox Christian community worldwide. This appears to have little effect on the coachloads of tourists from Athens and elsewhere in Greece, who flock to the early eighteenth-century **Church of St George** (which stands in the compound of the Patriarchate) on Sunday mornings in the tourist season – especially for the Easter Sunday Mass – or bring their offspring here to be christened. The church was rebuilt after a fire in 1720 and was much renovated again in the nineteenth century. Unlike its Byzantine predecessors it has a pitched roof as, following the Conquest of 1453, churches in Constantinople (or indeed throughout the Ottoman Empire) were not permitted to have domes as this architectural feature was associated with mosques – an injunction not repealed until the Tanzimat reforms of the nineteenth century (see pp.289–290). Inside is an elaborate gilt iconstasis and, in the southeast corner, two fine eleventh-century portative mosaic icons. One, on the iconstasis itself, depicts John the Baptist, the other on the south wall the Virgin Hodegetria, "She who shows the way", so named as the Virgin Mary points towards the infant Christ she is cradling.

St Mary of the Mongols
Kanlı Kilise • Tevki Cafer Mektebi Sokak, Fener

The thirteenth-century **church of St Mary of the Mongols** (in Greek, the *Panaghia Mouchliotissa*) is known in Turkish as the **Kanlı Kilise** or "Bloody Church". It's difficult to find in the backstreets above and behind the Patriarchate. The best landmark is the monumental red-brick Victorian Gothic-style **Fener Greek School for Boys** (see p.100). Keep this to your left as you ascend the hill via the stepped street of Tevki Merdivenli Sokak until you reach the church. Rendered and painted an uninspiring red, this is the only Byzantine church in the city where Orthodox services have been carried out from before the Muslim conquest to the present day – the church contains a copy of the *firman* (decree) given by Mehmet the Conqueror that permitted worship to continue here. According to one story, the church was saved from conversion to a mosque because of the architect of the Fatih Camii, **Atık Sinan** (see p.92).

Ring the bell to gain admittance from the family who look after the church and live in the compound. They, like many such caretakers, are not Istanbul Greeks but Orthodox Christians of the Arab rite who hail from Antakya (Antioch) in the southeast of Turkey. The founder, or major renovator of the church, was Mary Palaeologina (Melanie the Nun), depicted in the Deesis mosaic in the Kariye Museum (see pp.94–98). The illegitimate daughter of Emperor Michael Palaeologus VIII, Mary was sent to Tabriz to be the bride of the Mongol khan Hulagu. En route, her proposed husband died and she ended up marrying his son, Abagu. After spending many years in distant Tabriz, on her husband's death she returned to Constantinople. When it was suggested she marry another khan she demurred and instead became a nun, spending her remaining days in the convent attached to the church named after her.

Fener Greek High School for Boys
Sancaktar Yokuşu Sok 36, Fener • Free

The massive **Fener Greek High School for Boys**, built with bricks especially imported from France, was completed in 1883, although there has been a school on the site since Byzantine times. An unmissable sight on the slopes of the old city's fifth hill, it is surmounted by a dome which houses an astronomical observatory. In many ways the school symbolizes the tragic decline of the Greek minority in the city, as in 2014 there were just 58 pupils rattling around in this huge building. Downhill from it is the much smaller Greek High School for Girls, closed since the 1980s but given a short lease of life as a venue during the 2013 Istanbul Biennial.

St Stephen of the Bulgars
Mürsel Paşa Cad 85–88, Fener • Daily 8am–5pm • Free

St Stephen of the Bulgars is a curious, neo-Gothic white-painted church, stranded on a massive traffic-island-cum-park area. Built in 1896, it is made entirely from iron, cast in Vienna and carted all the way to Istanbul. That the Bulgarian branch of the Orthodox Church had the temerity to erect their church so close to the Greek Orthodox Patriarchate shows just how much rivalry there was between ethnic Bulgarians and Greeks in the late nineteenth and early twentieth centuries – a rivalry encouraged by the Ottomans and that was to lead to much bloodshed in the eastern Balkans. Signs of rust betray the chosen building material and the church was undergoing major renovation at the time of writing, which may be complete by 2015. Assuming it has reopened by the time of your visit, the best time to attend is during one of the thrice-yearly services held on Easter Sunday, December 27 or January 6.

Ahrida Synagogue
Kürkçu Çeşme Sokak, Balat • Contact the Chief Rabbinate at least a couple of weeks in advance to arrange a visit; you'll need to email a completed Visitor Information Form (email address below) and a scanned copy of the photo page of your passport • ☎ 0212 243 5166, ✉ security@musevicemaati.com

The **Ahrida Synagogue** is tucked inconspicuously away in the backstreets of the old Jewish neighbourhood of Balat. Sephardic Jews, expelled from Spain, were given sanctuary in the Muslim Ottoman Empire from 1492 (see box, p.287), and many naturally gravitated towards its capital, Istanbul – with large numbers ending up in Balat. The Jewish population has long since moved on, but the synagogue receives a remarkable number of visitors despite its out-of-the-way location and the fact that visits must be arranged in advance. Dating from the fifteenth century, it was rebuilt after a fire in the Ottoman Baroque style in 1694. The deceptively large interior can hold a congregation of 350, and its curved *tevah* (pulpit) is said to represent Noah's Ark.

Surp Hreşdagabet
Kamış Sok 2, Balat

The massive stone walls of the compound of **Surp Hreşdagabet** (Church of the Holy Archangels) are marred with graffiti and its heavy doors usually locked. The best time to gain admittance is on Thursday or Sunday mornings when there is a service. Built as a Greek Orthodox church in the thirteenth century, it was later given to the local Armenian community following the conversion of their original church in Fatih into a mosque in 1627. The church's chief claim to fame today is the supposedly curative properties of its *ayazma* (holy spring) and the curious rite held on the second weekend of September each year, when hundreds of Christians and Muslims alike come to have their ailments miraculously cured, and animals are sacrificed and the meat distributed to the needy.

The land walls

If you enjoy history and exploring on foot, the walk alongside the six-and-a-half-kilometre-long land walls of Theodosius II is one of the most interesting day-long outings in the city. Despite the ravages of time and several earthquakes, most recently in 1999, they have survived remarkably well. Some sections have been completely rebuilt in newly dressed stone and cement bricks; although some critics doubt the historical accuracy of some of this restoration work, at least the casual visitor can gain a wonderful impression of defensive fortifications that were un-breached for more than a thousand years. A walk along the walls can take as little as two hours, though a full day will allow time to fully enjoy them and the adjacent sites.

THE LAND WALLS
AND AROUND

Ⓜ Light Railway/Hafif Metro

Eyüp

Ayvansaray
Ferry Terminal

AYVANSARAY CAD

HASKÖY CAD

KASIMPAŞA CAD

Zindan
Arkası
Cemetery

NISANCA

Anemas Zindanları

Panghia
Blachernae

Old
Galata
Bridge

HASKÖY

OF MEYDANI CAD

Ivaz Efendi
Camii

AYVANSARAY

Haliç
Parkı

Eğrikapı

Tekfur
Sarayı

Surp
Hreşdagabet

BALAT

SALAKLAR CAD

EDIRNE KAPI RAMI CAD

Edirne
Cemetery

Bayrampaşa

Otogar-Bus Terminal

O-1

Edirne Kapı

Edirne
Kapı
Bus Garage

Kariye Museum

Ahrida

BALAT YAHUR ISKELE CAD

BALAT YAHUR

Golden
Horn

Mihrimah
Camii

Church of
Theotokus
Pammakaristos
(Fethiye Museum)

Aya Nikola

EDİRNEKAPI

Topkapı
Cemetery

Vefa Stadium

MIRAS SOK

FETHIYE CAD

Yavuz Selim
Camii

KYUNIŞ SOK

HALIÇ CAD

Gül Camii

Kadir Has
University

ABDÜLEZELPAŞA CAD

ADNAN MENDERES CADDESI

Ulubatlı /
Topkapı

FEVZI PAŞA CADDESI

AKŞEMSETTIN CAD

DARÜŞŞAFAKA CAD

YAVUZ SELIM CAD

Eski İmaret
Camii

FATIH

Fatih Camii

Zeyrek Camii

ZEYREK

FEVZIPAŞA CAD

ATATÜRK BULVARI

Topkapı

SULUKULE

Topkapı

Pazartekke

Ahmet Paşa
Camii

Çapa Hospital

KOCA NIŞAN CAD

HALIÇ CAD

Aqueduct
of Valens

KADINLAR PAZARI

ŞEHZADEBAŞI CAD

Şehzade
Camii

Panorama
1453 Museum

Pazartekke

TATLIPINAR CAD

Çapa

Ⓜ Emniyet Fatih

ADNAN MENDERES CADDESI

HORHOR CAD

Istanbul
University

Mevlana Kapı

MEVLANAKAPI CAD

GÜNAYDIN SOK

BOSTER C.

MILLET CADDESI

Findıkzade

AKSARAY

Laleli Camii

SEHIT ADESI

AHMET VEFIKPAŞA CAD

KEZIK CAD

DUZTHAN CAD

Haseki

Aksaray

Ⓜ Aksaray

MUSTAFA KEMAL CAD

Balıklı
Cemetery

Çukur
Bostan

Haseki
Hospital

Haseki
Camii

HASEKI CAD

CERRAHPAŞA CAD

Yusufpaşa

Valide
Camii

HAYRIYE TÜCCARI CAD

Silivri
Kapı

KIZILELMA CADDESI

SILIVRIKAPI CAD

Hadım
İbrahim
Paşa Camii

Hekimoğlu
Ali Paşa Camii

Ramazan
Efendi Camii

KOCA MUSTAFAPAŞA CAD

Cerrahpaşa
Hospital

KÜÇÜK LANGA CAD

NAMIK KEMAL CAD

Yenikapı

Havaş
★ Airport
Bus Stop

Yenikapı
Waterfront
Parkı

KENNEDY CADDESI

Zoodochos Pege & Cemeteries

Land Walls of Theodosius II

Belgrat Kapı

Koca Mustafa
Paşa Camii

HOŞKADEM CAD

ORGENERAL NAZIF GÜRMAN CAD

SAMATYA CAD

KENNEDY CADDESI

İBB Türkmenistan
Parkı

Yenikapı
Ferry
Terminal

Aya Konstantino

İmrahor Camii

Samatya Kilisesi

Surp Hovannes

N

Yedikule Kapı

Yedikule
Museum

Kazlıcesme

Ⓜ

YEDİKULE

KENNEDY CADDESI

SEA OF MARMARA

0   500
metres

● CAFÉS & RESTAURANTS
Ali Haydar   8
Bağdatlım   6
Develi   7
Durak Köfte   1
Fatih Belediyesi
  Sosyal Tesisleri   3
Merkez Efendi Köftecisi
Özen Kardeşler   5
Safa Meyhanesi
Zinnet   2

Marble Tower

Yalova (İznik & Bursa) & Güzelyalı (Bursa)

Most of the inner wall and its 96 towers are still standing; access is restricted on some of the restored sections, though elsewhere there's the chance to scramble along the crumbling edifice. The walls were built from limestone with contrasting bands of thin red bricks. Mortar mixed with brick dust was used liberally to bind the masonry; the towers had two levels, separated by brick barrel-vaults.

The number of run-down **slum dwellings** along the city walls has been reduced dramatically, but the towers and other nooks and crannies of the walls still attract vagrants and worse, making it a potentially risky area after dark. If time is limited, the two best **sites** to visit are the Yedikule fortifications and the Mihrimah Camii, a beautifully restored mosque designed by Mimar Sinan. The Kariye Museum, a former Byzantine church containing some of the best-preserved mosaics and frescoes in the world, also lies close to the walls (see pp.94–98).

ARRIVAL   THE LAND WALLS

By bus Buses from Eminönü include the #84 to Topkapı and #28 and #336E to Edirnekapı, or the #37Y from Vezneciler to Edirnekapı. To reach the northern terminus of the walls by bus catch the #36CE, #44B or #99 bus from Eminönü to Ayvansaray; buses to the southern terminus of the wall at Yedikule include the #80 from Eminönü, the #80T from Taksim.

By dolmuş The Bakırköy dolmuş from the top of Tarlabaşı Bul near Taksim Square should drop you at the southern terminus of the walls.

By taxi From Taksim a taxi to Yedikule will cost around

₺24, from Sultanahmet around ₺18.

By tram and metro You can catch the T1 tram to the Pazarteke stop, or the M1 metro to Ulubatlı /Topkapı. To get to the southern start of the walls near Yedikule take the Marmaray metro from Sirkeci or Yenikapı (linked to the M2 metro from Taksim/Beyoğlu) to Kazlıçeşme and walk back west for 5min to the line of the walls.

By ferry The Haliç ferry from Karaköy or Eminönü to Ayvansaray İskelesi on the Golden Horn, just before the Haliç bridge, puts you right on the northern terminus of the walls, ideal to either start or, even better, end your walk.

Brief history

The walls were named after **Theodosius II**, even though he was only 12 years old when their construction was started in 413 AD. Stretching from the Sea of Marmara to Tekfur Sarayı, 2km further out than the previous walls of Constantine, the walls were planned by Anthemius, Prefect of the East, to accommodate the city's expanding population. Along with the sea walls, which they join to the north above the Golden Horn at the Tekfur Sarayı and to the south on the shore of the Sea of Marmara, they formed a near impregnable defence for the city. The land walls were almost completely destroyed by an earthquake in 447 and had to be rebuilt in haste, since Attila's forces were on the point of attack. An ancient edict was brought into effect whereby all citizens, regardless of rank, were required to help in the rebuilding. The Hippodrome factions of Blues and Greens (see box, p.64) provided sixteen thousand labourers and finished the project in just two months. The completed construction consisted of the original wall, 5m thick and 12m high, separated from an outer wall of 2m by 8.5m by a 20m strip of land, and a 20m wide moat. There were 96 towers of assorted shapes – square, round and polygonal – on the line of both the inner and outer walls, so many that a visiting Crusader remarked that a child could toss an apple from one to another with ease. It's little wonder that even Attila's Huns decided against a siege.

Yedikule

The **Yedikule** neighbourhood, at the southern end of the land walls, around 5km from Sultanahmet, is an attractive quarter. Whether you reach the neighbourhood by metro, bus, dolmuş or taxi (see pp.25–28), the natural starting point is the **Marble Tower** at the extreme southern end of the land walls. Here the land and sea walls joined; the tower itself was either a part of the defences or a small imperial pavilion. Heading north across the highway, avoid walking along the inside of the walls as there is a city dog-pound here that seems to have far more canines outside it than in. Instead, wind

5

through the pleasant park outside, exiting back onto the road, under the metro bridge and pass a cemetery. Enter the old city through Yedikule Kapı (Yedikule Gate) and veer right to find the entrance to Yedikule Museum.

Yedikule Museum

Kale Meydanı Caddesi • Tues–Sun 8.30am–6.30pm • ₺10

The **Yedikule Museum** comprises the substantial remains of fortifications added to the line of the Byzantine land walls by Mehmet the Conqueror in 1457–58, and with their twelve-metre-high curtain walls they form the castle-like structure that can be seen today. Despite its design, this was never actually used as a fort, instead serving as a prison, treasury and office for the collection of revenue of the *Vakıf* (pious foundation). The tower immediately to the left of the museum entrance was used as a prison and many of the inscriptions carved into the walls by prisoners (virtually impossible to find today) were by foreign ambassadors on some hapless errand. The only structure in the great courtyard inside the fortification itself is a crumbling Ottoman mosque.

The so-called **Golden Gate** was a triumphal arch built under Theodosius I in 390 and flanked by two marble towers, it originally stood alone and was used by important visitors of state and conquering emperors making a grand entrance into Constantinople. When Theodosius II built the new line of walls, the Golden Gate was incorporated into them (the section of land wall containing the gate was later incorporated into the Yedikule fortifications of Mehmet the Conqueror). The shape of the three arches is still visible on both sides of the wall, but it takes a degree of imagination to invest the structure with the glamour and dignity it must once have possessed. Michael Palaeologus was the last emperor to ride through in triumph, when the city was recaptured from occupying Crusaders (see pp.282–283). After the empire went into decline, the gold-plated doors were removed and the entrance bricked up.

It's possible to climb the left hand (as you face west) of the two towers. In the Ottoman period the ground-floor chamber supposedly doubled as an execution chamber and the "well of blood", into which heads would roll, can still be seen. The most famous victim of the execution chamber was Osman II, deposed and murdered in 1622 by his janissaries, and thus providing Ottoman history with its first case of regicide. Take care climbing the myriad steps as they are uneven and lighting inadequate – but the views from the top are superb.

The walls between the Yedikule and Mevlana gates

A right (north) turn from Yedikule Kapı will allow you to explore the walls running north from here, admiring the market gardens in the shadow of the ramparts, to **Belgrat Kapı** (Belgrade Gate). It was named for the captives who were settled in this area by Süleyman the Magnificent after his capture of Belgrade in 1521. Heading through the gate, you can ascend the renovated walls and walk north along the battlements for some three hundred metres, descending again opposite an all-weather football pitch. North from Belgrat Kapı to Silivri Kapı, the walls are largely untouched, though the sections around **Silivri Kapı** itself have been extensively renovated. Just inside the gate is a pretty Sinan (see p.82) mosque, the **Hadım İbrahim Paşa Camii**, named after the eunuch grand vizier who had it built. It has been beautifully restored and its intimate interior makes a refreshing change from the grand imperial mosques of the centre of the old city. There are handy toilets in the mosque compound.

WALL WALK EATS

A walk alongside the walls, and scrambles up the ramparts and towers, will give you a hearty appetite. Fortunately there are plenty of authentic neighbourhood places en route, where a substantial lunch will set you back less than a small beer in a Beyoğlu bar. Most of these eating establishments are set back a little from the line of walls - see p.181 and p.187 for details.

There is more restoration work at the **Mevlana Kapı**, and also some interesting inscriptions on the outer wall. The Theodosian walls reached completion at this gate, since it was here that the Greens, building from the Marmara, met the Blues (see box, p.64), who were working southwards from the direction of the Golden Horn. A Latin inscription to the left of the gate celebrates this fact: "By the command of Theodosius, Constantine erected these strong fortifications in less than two months. Scarcely could Pallas [Athena] herself have built so strong a citadel in so short a time."

Zoodochos Pege

Silivrikapı Seyıt Nizam Cad 3 • Daily 8.30am–4.30pm • Free • To get here, cross the dual carriageway via the pedestrian lights and walk a short way down Seyıt Nizam Caddesi; just past an Ottoman-era fountain, turn right onto Silivrikapı Caddesi and follow it around to reach Zoodochus Pege on your left

Known to the Turks as the *Balıklı Kilise* (Church with Fish), the shrine/church complex of **Zoodochos Pege** lies some 500m west of Silivri Kapı, in the midst of a sea of beautifully green and silent cemeteries. The well-kept shrine, dating back to the early Byzantine era, and the church built in 1833, are set in a walled compound dominated by a giant plane tree. The marble iconostasis resembles the facade of a classical temple, and the gloomy interior has maintained a certain sanctity. The focus, though, is very much on the *ayazma* (sacred spring) reached by steps leading down from the right of the church entrance. Fish swim lazily in a floodlit pool, and the row of taps above the basin, where pilgrims take the "holy" waters, are in the shape of crosses. According to legend, a hungry monk was frying some fish when he heard that Constantinople had fallen to the Turks. The disbelieving monk apparently said that was about as likely as the fish in his pan coming back to life, with which they leapt out of the pan and into the pool, where their descendants remain to this day. Visit on a Sunday, and the surrounding Muslim, Armenian and Greek Orthodox cemeteries are crowded with people paying their respects to the departed.

North along the walls to Topkapı

From Mevlana Kapı, follow the outside of the walls along a pleasant stretch of pavement that has been constructed on the line of the moat. Just south of Topkapı, the walls have been destroyed to make way for the enormous thoroughfare of Millet Caddesi. To cross (not easy, with the tramway running in the middle of a busy dual carriageway) the road, use the pedestrian crossing a little to the east of the walls. Before you reach the road, on the outside of the walls, across a stretch of urban park built above the busy road running beneath, is the dramatic **Panorama 1453 History Museum** (see below).

Continue walking on the inside of the walls until you reach the **Topkapı** ("Gate of the Cannonball"), named after the most powerful cannon of Mehmet the Conqueror, which in 1453 pounded the walls near here. This was one of the main entries into the city and was known in the Byzantine era as the Gate of St Romanus.

Panorama 1453 History Museum

Topkapı Kültür Parkı, Merkez Efendi Mahallesi • Daily 9am–6.30pm • ₺10 • ⓦ panoramikmuze.com • T1 tram from Sultanahmet to the Topkapı stop

Set in a pleasant park on the west side of the horrendously busy Topkapı/Edirnekapı Caddesi, the small **Panorama 1453 History Museum** pays homage to one of the landmark dates in Turkish history, the siege and capture of Constantinople by Sultan Mehmet (known after his historic victory as Fatih Sultan Mehmet or Mehmet the Conqueror). The centrepiece is a scene depicting the Ottoman army besieging the walls painted in a 360° sweep around the drum and shallow dome of the building, viewed from a central, circular platform. There are ten thousand painted human figures in the spectacular scene, with balls of Greek fire raining down on the besiegers, and the green banners of Islam held aloft by the attackers. Between the viewing platform and the

5

painted scene, the battlefield has been re-created with a realistic tableau of models and mannequins. The museum is cleverly lit and though serious historians may scoff at the overly dramatized scene, it's undeniably impressive, helping bring to life one of the most momentous events in world history. It's all the more powerful for being set in the shadow of the walls themselves, close to the point the Ottomans first breached them on May 29, 1453. Unfortunately, all the sign boards are in Turkish, and the audio guide (₺5) of little use.

Sulukule to the Golden Horn

Between Topkapı and Edirnekapı, there's a pronounced valley, formerly the route of the Lycus River, now taken by Adnan Menderes (Vatan) Caddesi. To cross the road use the underpass marked by the metro sign a little to the east of the line of the wall. At this point, the walls were at their least defensible, since the higher ground outside gave the advantage to attackers. The famed **Orban cannon** of Mehmet the Conqueror was trained on this part of the walls during the siege of 1453, hence their ruinous state. It was here, too, that Constantine XI was cut down on the siege's final day. **Sulukule** – the area inside the walls between Adnan Menderes Caddesi and Edirnekapı – was home to a gypsy community for close on a thousand years, but most of its traditional houses have already been bulldozed by the local municipality to make way for more upmarket residences, incurring a critical 2008 UNESCO report. The development means that once you have crossed Adnan Menderes Caddesi you need to head outside and continue north, past the new housing, before cutting inside again a couple of hundred metres south of the **Mihrimah Camii**.

Mihrimah Camii

Edirnekapı • Daily dawn to dusk

One of many early Sinan works commissioned by Mihrimah, the favourite daughter of Süleyman the Magnificent, and her husband Rüstem Paşa, the beautiful **Mihrimah Camii** is situated on the sixth and highest of Istanbul's seven hills (77m above sea level). Dating from somewhere around the middle of the sixteenth century, it has recently been restored to its former grandeur; this is one of Sinan's great works, perhaps because the architect was infatuated by the beautiful Mihrimah. Raised on a platform, it can be seen from all over the city, with the area beneath occupied by shops. The entry to the mosque today is from the north side, with the courtyard still under restoration at the time of writing. Although domed as per the standard Ottoman pattern the building is strikingly different in design to many of Sinan's other mosques, being very tall (37m) in comparison to the ground area it covers. It's also very light, as the four tympana walls are pierced by three rows of windows.

Edirnekapı to Eğrikapı

Edirnekapı is so named because the road through it leads to modern Edirne; in the Byzantine period it was the Gate of Charisius. Pass through the narrow gate from the city side and outside there's a plaque (in Turkish) proclaiming that this is where Mehmet the Conqueror made his triumphal entry into the city in 1453.

After crossing Fevzi Paşa Caddesi, continue north along the inner side of the walls for a couple of hundred metres to Kariye Bostancı Sokak (this street leads to the Kariye Museum; see pp.94–98). Opposite this, steps lead up to a renovated section of wall, from where precipitous ladder-style steps (only for those with a head for heights) lead steeply up to the wall-top proper and thence to a tower boasting superb views over the Golden Horn, the Bosphorus and the Sea of Marmara. A little further along is the **Tekfur Sarayı** or Palace of the Porphyrogenitus. Built in the thirteenth or fourteenth century, this was a residence of the Byzantine royal family as an annexe of the virtually vanished Blachernae Palace (see p.107). It has a fine facade, with contrasting bands of red brick and pale stone, pierced by arched windows. Apparently, it was later used as a zoo, then a brothel, and, in the nineteenth century, as a poorhouse for down-on-their-luck Jews. The structure was undergoing major renovation at the time of writing and will be an exhibition and convention centre on completion. Next to it is a weekend-only **pigeon market**, where tumbling pigeons (well-trained ones do somersaults when their owners clap their hands) can change hands for hundreds of dollars.

Just beyond the palace, the original Theodosian walls, now lost, probably continued straight north to the Golden Horn. The remaining sections of surviving wall are later additions, built in the seventh century to enclose the expanding suburb of **Blachernae**, which had been left outside the original walls. They were rebuilt and massively strengthened in the reign of Emperor Manuel Comnenus (1143–80) and later. The first gate in this newer section of walls is the narrow Eğrikapı, north of which are cobbled lanes winding through attractive cottage gardens and old houses.

Anemas Zindanları to the Golden Horn

Next to the prominent İvaz Efendi Camii is the **Anemas Zindanları** (closed for renovation at the time of writing), all that's left of the once magnificent Blachernae Palace, an imperial Byzantine palace of great importance from the twelfth century onwards. A few minutes down from here, reached from Dervişzade Sokak, is the unremarkable-looking **Greek Orthodox church of Panghia Blachernae**. The present structure dates only from 1867, but it was once one of Constantinople's most important churches, founded over a sacred spring (which still flows today) in the fifth century. The inhabitants believed that the robe and mantle of the Virgin Mary, brought here by pilgrims from Jerusalem, protected their city from harm. The church, which is usually open, also contained the Mandalyon, a piece of cloth bearing a miraculous imprint of Christ's face. This holy relic was looted by the Crusaders in the thirteenth century and the original church burnt to the ground in 1434.

From the church it is just a few minutes' walk down to the Golden Horn, from where you can get a bus or ferry from the Ayvansaray quay back to Eminönü.

Eyüp

Eyüp, around 1km north of the land walls and bordering the western bank of the Golden Horn, is one of the holiest places in Islam, its mosque being the site of the tomb of Eyüp Ensari, the Prophet Mohammed's standard-bearer. Muslims come here from all over the Islamic world on pilgrimage – try not to visit on Fridays, out of respect for conservative worshippers.

Eyüp Camii

Cami Kebir Sok 7 • Daily dawn to dusk

The **Eyüp Camii** was built by Mehmet the Conqueror in honour of Eyüp Ensari, one of the small group of companions of the Prophet who was killed during the first Arab siege of Constantinople (674–678); a condition of the peace treaty signed following the siege was that his tomb be preserved. Later, the mosque hosted the investiture ceremonies of the Ottoman sultans: indeed, mosque and tomb face each other across the courtyard that was used for the ceremony. The exact site is marked by a raised platform surrounded by railings, from which two plane trees grow.

The original mosque was destroyed in the eighteenth century, probably by the same earthquake that put paid to Fatih Camii (see p.92). The present Baroque replacement, filled with light, gold, pale stone and white marble, was completed in 1800. The **tomb of Eyüp Ensari** (Tues–Sun 9.30am–4.30pm; free) is far more compelling, however (footwear should be removed and women should cover their heads before entering). Its facade and vestibule are covered in tile panels from many different periods and, although the effect is a bit overwhelming, the panels constitute a beautiful and varied display of the art form; you could spend weeks visiting individual buildings to see as many different designs and styles.

By ferry and bus The mosque is most easily reached up the Golden Horn from Karaköy or Eminönü – it's the last ferry stop before the Horn peters out into two small streams. The mosque and tomb are about a ten-minute walk from the Eyüp ferry terminal on Camii Kebir Caddesi; alternatively, you can catch the #99, #36CE or #39/A bus from Eminönü.

Tombs of Sokollu Mehmet Paşa and Siyavus Paşa
Camii Kebir Caddesi • Tues–Sun 9.30am–4.30pm

Two of the best of the many tombs for Ottoman dignitaries in this area are those of **Sokollu Mehmet Paşa and Siyavus Paşa**, which stand opposite each other on either side of Camii Kebir Caddesi, five minutes' walk from Eyüp Camii towards the Golden Horn. Five years before his assassination, Sokollu Mehmet Paşa commissioned Mimar Sinan to build his tomb, an elegantly proportioned, octagonal building of around 1574, notable for its stained glass, some of which is original; connected to the tomb by an elegant three-arched colonnade is a former Koran school. Siyavus Paşa's tomb, on the other hand, was probably actually built by Sinan for the children of Siyavus Paşa, who had died young. It's decorated with İznik tiles.

Eyüp cemetery

Eyüp is still a popular burial place, and the hills above the mosque are covered in plain modern stones interspersed with beautiful Ottoman tombs. To the north of the mosque, off Silahtarağa Caddesi, Karyağdı Sokak leads up into the **Eyüp cemetery**. Following the signs up this lane through the graveyard – most beautiful at sunset with an arresting view of the Golden Horn – it takes about twenty minutes from Eyüp Camii to reach the romantic **Pierre Loti Café**.

If you've walked enough, there's a twin-cabin **cable car** (signed *Telefrik* in Turkish) linking the shores of the Golden Horn with the top of the hill (daily 8am–11pm; ₺4 each way, or use your Istanbulkart). The cable car lies some four hundred metres north of the Eyüp ferry terminal.

VIEW TOWARDS THE OLD CITY FROM THE GALATA TOWER

Galata and the waterfront districts

Galata lies across the curving inlet of the Golden Horn from the old city. In the late Byzantine period this district was a semi-independent Genoese colony and the great fortification-cum-lookout erected by the mercantile Italians, the Galata Tower, remains an Istanbul landmark. Today, the area is very much a part of vibrant, go-ahead Istanbul, as over the last decade or so the city's nightlife, shopping and arts scene, once centred on Beyoğlu's (see pp.118–127) busy İstiklal Caddesi has spilled down the steep hillside into Galata and Karaköy. Nomenclature hereabouts is a little confusing, as sometimes Galata is seen merely as a part of the much bigger and vaguely defined area of Beyoğlu, but more confusingly is officially known in Turkish as Karaköy (literally "Black Village").

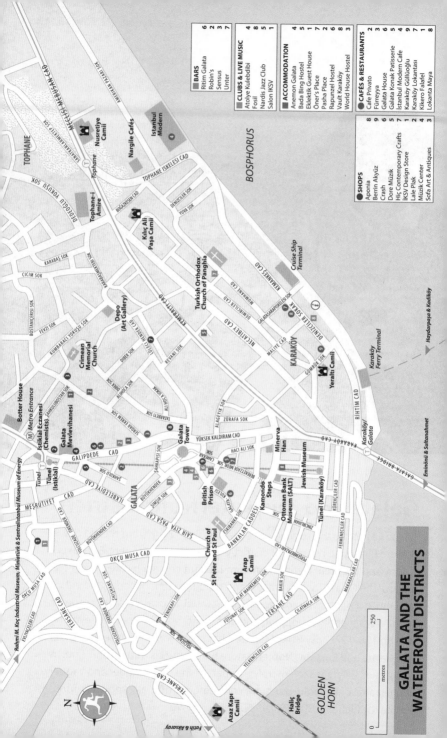

GALATA AND THE WATERFRONT DISTRICTS

SHOPS	
Aponia	8
Berrin Akyüz	9
Crash	6
Dore Müzik	5
Hiç Contemporary Crafts	7
İKSV Design Store	2
Lale Plak	1
Müzik Center	4
Sofa Art & Antiques	3

CAFÉS & RESTAURANTS	
Cafe Privato	2
Füreyya	3
Galata House	6
Galata Konak Patisserie	5
İstanbul Modern Cafe	4
Karaköy Güllüoğlu	9
Karaköy Lokantası	7
Kikero Falafel	1
Lokanta Maya	8

ACCOMMODATION	
Anemon Galata	4
Bada Bing Hostel	5
Eklektik Guest House	1
Oher's Place	7
Pasha Place	2
Rapunzel Hostel	6
Vault Karaköy	8
World House Hostel	3

CLUBS & LIVE MUSIC	
Atolye Kulebdibi	4
Fosil	8
Nardis Jazz Club	5
Salon İKSV	1

BARS	
Rıtım Galata	6
Robin's	2
Sensus	3
Unter	7

TOPHANE

BOSPHORUS

Nusretiye Camii

Nargile Cafés

İstanbul Modern

Tophane-i Amire

Kılıç Ali Paşa Camii

Cruise Ship Terminal

Turkish Orthodox Church of Panghia

KARAKÖY

Karaköy/ Galata Ferry Terminal

Yeraltı Camii

Haydarpaşa & Kadıköy

Depo (Art Gallery)

Crimean Memorial Church

Botter House

Metro Entrance

İstiklal Eczanesi (Chemists)

Galata Mevlevihanesi

Galata Tower

Minerva Han

Jewish Museum

British Prison

Kamondo Steps

Ottoman Bank Museum (SALT)

Church of St Peter and St Paul

Tünel (İstiklal)

Tünel (Karaköy)

GALATA

Arap Camii

Rahmi M. Koç Industrial Museum, Miniatürk & Santralİstanbul Museum of Energy

Haliç Bridge

Azaz Kapı Camii

GOLDEN HORN

Fatih & Aksaray

GALATA BRIDGE

Eminönü & Sultanahmet

N

0   250
metres

For the purposes of the description in this guide, the area comprising the waterfront between the Atatürk Bridge to the west and Kılıç Ali Paşa Camii to the east and bounded to the north by a line formed by Bankalar and Kemeraltı *caddes*is is Karaköy. North of this line, to the Tünel entrance at the southern end of İstiklal Caddesi, is Galata. The area around the **Galata Tower**, neglected and run-down for decades, is rapidly developing into a trendy, bohemian quarter, with a rash of arts and music venues, galleries, boutique hotels, cafés and bars springing up – plus a panoply of street art adorning shop-shutters and likely looking walls. It's worth strolling along the old banking street of Bankalar Caddesi, admiring the intriguing Art Nouveau-style **Kamondo Steps** and imposing nineteenth-century architecture. Down towards the waterfront is the **Arap Camii**, a large mosque converted from a fourteenth-century Catholic church, while up the hill you can watch the dervishes whirl at the **Galata Mevlevihanesi**.

6

Karaköy, which has morphed into one of the city's hippest neighbourhoods (see box, p.114), served as a port for both the Byzantines and the Ottomans, when it was enclosed within the walls of the Castle of Galata. The shipping industry has declined but massive cruise ships dock a few hundred metres east of the Galata Bridge, ferries ply across to Asia from the terminal a little nearer to the bridge, and a number of private ferries run from a dock just west of it. Apart from the fine nineteenth-century commercial buildings, look out for the **Jewish Museum**, once the Zülfaris Synagogue, and the **Yeraltı Camii**.

Northeast from Karaköy, parallel to the waterfront, is **Tophane**, a district that once housed an Ottoman cannon foundry. Two late Ottoman-era mosques, the **Kılıç Ali Paşa** and **Nusretiye**, are worth seeing, though the trendy **Istanbul Modern** gallery, superbly set on the Bosphorus waterfront, is the major draw.

Head west and north along the shore of the Golden Horn from Galata and things soon change, with run-down factories, off-limits military installations and neglected apartment blocks the order of the day. But even here urban regeneration is in full swing and there are three key sights spread along the Horn: the excellent **Rahmi M. Koç Industrial Museum**, with exhibits ranging from a penny farthing to a submarine; kids' favourite **Miniatürk**, with scale models of Turkey's most famous sites; and **Santralİstanbul**, an energy museum housed in a refurbished power station on the campus of Bilgi University.

ARRIVAL AND GETTING AROUND   GALATA AND THE WATERFRONT DISTRICTS

Arrival Visitors coming from the old city usually cross the Galata Bridge on foot (quite an experience) or ride the T1 tram across it and alight at the Karaköy stop. Another option is to walk from the Haliç stop of the M2 metro, right in the centre of the controversial metro bridge across the Golden Horn that opened in early 2014.

Getting around The area is compact enough to enjoy on foot, though if you're heading for the Istanbul Modern it's worth riding the tram one stop on to Tophane or, to avoid the steep hill, you can ride the historic funicular, Tünel (see p.29), to the top and walk down in a few minutes to the Galata Tower.

Brief history

During the early centuries of Ottoman rule, many Spanish Jews, Moorish traders, Greeks and Armenians settled in **Galata**, which became established as the city's **European quarter**. In time, foreign powers set up their embassies in the area, and it became a popular haunt of visiting merchants, traders, seamen and adventurers. The nightlife of the quarter was notoriously riotous even in the seventeenth century, when the Ottoman traveller Evliya Çelebi wrote "Whoever says Galata says taverns." Galata's development was hampered by the steep hill it is built on, and by the nineteenth century neighbouring Beyoğlu, on flatter land at the top of the hill, had superseded it as the location of choice for the city's European or Europeanized elite.

Galata

The fascinating district of **Galata** is dominated by the famous Galata Tower, but there's much else to see. Be prepared to explore it on foot though, as the narrow, steep streets are impractical for public transport (except for the underground funicular, Tünel). Bankalar Caddesi (shown by its old name of Voyvoda Caddesi on some maps), reached by walking up the hill from the north end of the Galata Bridge along Karaköy Caddesi, is lined with superb nineteenth-century buildings that once housed (as the name "Bankalar" suggests) the city's major banks. Occupying a corner plot at the end of this street is a beautifully restored building, the **Minerva Han** dating to 1911. The beige facade is enlivened by panels of pale-blue tiles, while a couple of Neoclassical stone statues, in the form of cherubs holding baskets of fruit, surmount the entrance. Formerly the Greek Bank of Athens, the building is now an annexe of the Sabancı University.

Ottoman Bank Museum and SALT gallery

Bankalar Cad 35, Karaköy • Tues–Sat noon–8pm, Sun 10.30am–6pm • Free • ⓦ obmuze.com

Voyvoda Caddesi, more commonly and appropriately known today as Bankalar Caddesi (Street of Banks), is home to the former head office of the Ottoman Bank, designed in 1890 by renowned architect Vallaury, also responsible for the *Pera Palace Hotel* (see p.123) and Archeology Museum (see pp.58–61). In late 2011 the building became a part of the Garanti Bank's **SALT** contemporary arts project, complete with a public library, rooms dedicated to research, and an exhibition space. It also contains the fascinating **Ottoman Bank Museum**, which relates the story of the bank's history through to the 1930s, as well as housing archive material from places as diverse as Beyoğlu's Italian Consulate and the nearby Church of St Peter and St Paul.

Around Bankalar Caddesi

Close to the museum and running up from Bankalar Caddesi towards the Galata Tower are the sculptural **Kamondo Steps**, dating to the 1860s. The gracefully curving twin staircases were commissioned and paid for by the wealthy Jewish Kamondo family, and photographed by Henri Cartier-Bresson in the 1960s.

A five-minute walk to the west is the **Arap Camii**. With its tall square tower and pyramidal roof this mosque was, under the Genoese, the largest church in Galata. It was later converted into a mosque to serve the needs of the Moorish community that settled here in the early sixteenth century following their expulsion from Spain. It stands on one side of an attractive closed courtyard, decorated with assorted pieces of ancient marble.

Further up the hill, on Galata Külesi Sokak, the Dominican **Church of St Peter and St Paul** dates back to the fifteenth century though the current building, designed by the Fossati brothers (who were also responsible for the restoration of the Haghia Sophia) only dates back to 1841. Mass is held every day at 7.30am and on Sundays at 11am.

British prison

Galata Külesi Sok 61

The stone-built **British prison**, dating back to 1904, is tucked away on a narrow street below the Galata Tower. Today it houses the *Galata House* restaurant-café (see p.189) and the friendly owners will happily show you graffiti left by former inmates, including a sketch of the Rock of Gibraltar and the poignant words, "An unfavourable wind has brought the ship of my life to this shore." Under the capitulations granted by the Ottomans, Western powers had the right to try their citizens under their own law, rather than the draconian Ottoman code, so consulates possessed their own courthouses and prisons.

The Galata Tower

Galata Külesi • Galata Meydan • Daily 9am–8pm • €6.50 or ₺12

Built in 1349 by the Genoese, the **Gelata Tower** (Galata Külesi) sits on the site of a former tower constructed by Justinian in 528. Originally known as the Tower of Christ, it stood at the apex of the several sets of fortifications that surrounded the Genoese city-state. It has had a number of functions over the centuries, including as a jail, a fire tower and even a springboard for early adventurers attempting to fly.

At 61m high, the tower's **viewing gallery** – an elevator goes almost to the top but there's one flight of steps to negotiate – offers magnificent panoramas of the city and views across the Sea of Marmara and the Golden Horn. The view of Eminönü is particularly spectacular from here: the boats that nudge in and out of the ferry terminal form a foreground to the skyline of Beyazıt and Sultanahmet, with the Yeni Camii directly below Nuruosmaniye, the Spice Bazaar beneath Beyazıt Camii and the Beyazıt fire tower rising above the Rüstem Paşa Camii. It's best to get here when it opens at 9am for the best morning light, or evening when the sun is at its lowest and the views most photogenic, though by mid-afternoon there are often long queues. There's also a café on the top floor offering predictably overpriced drinks and snacks. The area around the base of the tower has recently been refurbished and is now a pleasant plaza area.

The Galata Mevlevihanesi

Galipdede Caddesi · Mon & Wed–Sun 9.30am–5pm · ₺10 · *Sema* dances usually held May–Sept Sun 5pm; Oct–April twice-monthly 3pm · ₺40 · ⓦ galatamevlevihanesimuzesi.gov.tr

An unassuming doorway on Galipdede Caddesi leads to the courtyard of the **Galata Mevlevihanesi**. A former *tekke* (lodge) containing a *semahane* (ceremonial hall) of the whirling dervishes, the building now serves as a museum to the Mevlevi Sufi sect. Originally constructed in 1491, this is the oldest surviving dervish monastery in Istanbul, though much of what you see today dates from a post-fire rebuild in 1824.

The Mevlevi Sufi order is one of the many mystical sects of Islam once rife across Anatolia, and banned by Atatürk in 1925 because of their supposed reactionism. The founder of the sect, Mevlana, was an iconoclast who, in the thirteenth century, repudiated the strictures and hypocrisy of mainstream Sunni Islam. He preached love, charity and tolerance, and believed that union with God was possible through contemplation, meditation, dance and music, hence the "whirling" ceremonies the disciples engage in.

The courtyard of the loge is an oasis of peace in buzzing Galata, with benches where you can sit and admire the beautifully carved tombstones of the order's departed adherents. The ground floor of the main building has been carefully organized to illuminate various aspects of dervish culture. Here you can see the begging bowls and staffs of wandering ascetics, the musical instruments of the all-important ensembles who provide the haunting accompaniment to the ritual dervish dances and a map showing how the Mevlevi order is spread throughout Turkey, the Middle East and the Balkans. There's even a whirling dervish hologram.

The real treat, however, is the Baroque-style *semahane* upstairs, with its gorgeous painted ceiling, gilded woodwork and Neoclassical capitals. Tickets for the performances held by various Mevlevi lodges from across the city are usually sold outside the museum on the day of the performance. Doors open half an hour before the performance commences; if

---

A CLASH OF CYMBALS, NOT CULTURES

Istanbul is often stereotyped as a place where the Christian West conflicts with the Islamic East. But clashes of a very different nature frequently take place on the city's "**Music Alley**" (Galipdede Caddesi – those of eager would-be buyers crash-testing a pair of cymbals. **Zildjian**, one of the best-known cymbal manufacturers in the world, originated back in 1618 when Armenian alchemist Avedis Zildjian, while seeking a way to turn base metals into gold, discovered the perfect metal to produce the perfect sound – an alloy of copper, silver and tin. The business prospered in the Ottoman centuries, supplying cymbals to the military Mehter Band (see p.128). In 1928 a new factory was established in Massachusetts in the US, though the original Istanbul workshop continued until 1978. Still going concerns in the city, however, are Istanbul Agop (ⓦ Istanbulcymbals.com) and Istanbul Mehmet (ⓦ Istanbulmehmet.com.tr), both set up by former craftsmen from the Zildjian workshop. The handmade wares of these two companies predominate in the shops on "Music Alley". Ironically, the Zildjian cymbals stocked by a few shops here are imported from the US.

you don't get there early you'll end up with a restricted view. The performers are genuine dervishes, despite the fact that the sect remains technically illegal, but the audience are invariably tourists, many of whom view the entire proceeding through a camera lens.

Karaköy

The port area of **Karaköy** is rapidly morphing from a rough-and-ready port area to a hipsters' hangout (see box, p.114). Just west of the **Galata Bridge**, the vital link between the two sides of European Istanbul (see p.71), is a small dock from where Türyol ferries run across the Golden Horn to Eminönü and across the Bosphorus to Üsküdar, Haydarpaşa and Kadıköy.

Karaköy's **port**, a Byzantine, then Ottoman shipyard, was once enclosed within the city walls of Galata and, from 1446 until the fall of the Byzantine city to the Ottomans in 1453, was further protected by a great chain stretched across the mouth of the Horn to prevent enemy ships from entering (see box, p.72). The waterfront west of the Galata Bridge is generally a run-down area of ships' chandlers (where you can purchase anchors and chains) and a few basic restaurants specializing in grilled fish and *köfte*. The views across to Eminönü are impressive, though it's an area best avoided at night. Things get smarter on the east side of the bridge, with a mix of good and distinctly average waterfront restaurants. Front-of-house hustlers abound, as this is where the cruise-ship passengers disembark after docking at the modernist Karaköy terminal, recognizable by its distinctive airport-style conning tower.

GETTING AROUND   KARAKÖY

Funicular Just inland from Galata Bridge is the Tünel underground funicular (see p.29), which will whisk you up to İstiklal Caddesi; the Tünel entrance is on Tersane Caddesi, just to the left of the first road junction beyond the bridge.

Azaz Kapı Camii
Atatürk Köprüsü Yanı

The single most interesting sight in Karaköy is the **Azaz Kapı Camii**, situated below the level of traffic-choked Atatürk Bridge, a fine Sinan mosque, completed in 1578. Its style is reminiscent of the great Süleymaniye Camii, another Sinan masterpiece across the Golden Horn in the old city (see pp.82–84), but on a much smaller scale. At its entrance is an ornate marble *sebil* (fountain) built in the Baroque style in 1733 for Valide Sultan Saliha Hatun, mother of Sultan Mahmut I.

The Jewish Museum
500 Yıl Vakfı Türk Musevileri Müzesi • Perçemli Sokak • Mon–Thurs 10am–4pm, Fri & Sun 10am–2pm • ₺10 • ⓦ muze500.com

The Ottoman Empire was long a safe haven for Jews fleeing persecution, pogroms and massacres in Christian Europe. They formed a very sizeable minority in the city and many prospered, taking advantage of Muslim strictures against usury and the Ottoman

KARAKÖY: ISTANBUL'S HIPSTERVILLE

Since the Istanbul Modern (see pp.115–116) opened in 2004, and neighbouring Tophane became a focus for those interested in modern and contemporary art, the industrial port area of Karaköy has been undergoing an unlikely makeover. Here, Istanbul's young creatives sit in chic cafés engrossed in their Macs, sipping on a café cortado or virgin mojito, working on their latest design, while the inhabitants of the old Karaköy continue to get their hands dirty in the adjacent motorbike repair shops and hardware outlets. Despite the religious conservativeness of nearby Tophane, the old and new ways of life seem to co-exist here (possibly helped by the fact that only a couple of local joints (*Unter*, p.196 and *Fosil*, p.201) officially serve alcohol). Café hopping here is a nice way to pass time, and gives you an insight into the lifestyle of young Istanbulites. None of the many identikit cafés on Kılıç Ali Paşa Mescidi Sokak or Mumhane Caddesi would look out of place in the cooler districts of London or New York. Grab a seat and watch Istanbul change in front of your eyes.

gentlemen's disdain of trade and playing a significant role in bringing prosperity to Galata and its environs. The origins of the Zülfaris Synagogue on Meydanı Perçemli Sokak, which houses the **Jewish Museum**, can be traced back to 1671, though the present building was erected in the nineteenth century. It was founded to celebrate the 500th anniversary of the arrival of the Jews following their expulsion from Spain and contains a small but fascinating amount of material, much of it donated by local Jewish families such as the Kamondos.

Although the ethnography section of the museum is interesting enough, with the expected display of torah, menorah, traditional costume and the like, it is the collection of photographs (and accompanying storyboards) outlining the successful relationship between Jews and Turks over the centuries that commands attention. Unlike the Ottoman Christian minorities, the Jews never agitated for their own state, and in 1920 there were Jewish deputies in the fledgling Republic's National Assembly. In 1933, Atatürk invited Jewish academics from Nazi Germany to help his modernization programme, thus saving them from almost certain death.

Yeraltı Camii
Kemankeş Caddesi

Originally constructed around 580, the subterranean keep of the long-gone Castle of Galata is thought to be what is now the **Yeraltı Camii**, or the "Underground Mosque". Inside is a forest of thick columns, supporting a low, vaulted ceiling. Two tombs in one corner purport to be those of Muslim martyrs killed in the first Arab siege of Byzantium (674–678 AD).

Tophane

Approached from Karaköy along Kemeraltı Caddesi (a waterfront stroll may look an attractive option on a map but is, in practice, impossible) and a steep half-kilometre downhill from İstiklal Caddesi, **Tophane** is a mixed area of run-down dockland dotted with venerable Ottoman buildings.

Kılıç Ali Paşa Camii
Necatibey Caddesi

The most notable of Tophane's Ottoman buildings is the **Kılıç Ali Paşa Camii**, an attractive mosque dating from 1580, designed by the doyen of Ottoman architects, Sinan, towards the end of his life. Based on the Haghia Sophia (see pp.45–49), it was built to honour a former Italian slave who, when freed, became both an admiral and a Muslim and was the only Ottoman admiral to come up smelling of roses after their disastrous defeat in the Battle of Lepanto in 1571. Appropriately for a naval man, Kılıç Ali Paşa's mosque was placed on the banks of the Bosphorus. Though somewhat gloomy, the interior of the mosque is enlivened by a number of colourful stained-glass windows with arabesque designs. Originally part of a *külliye* complex, the octagonal tomb of the admiral stands in the small garden behind the mosque, while its *hamam* (see p.228) was reopened to bathers after a lengthy restoration in 2013.

Istanbul Modern
Meclis-i Mebusan Caddesi • Tues, Wed & Fri–Sun 10am–6pm, Thurs 10am–8pm • ₺17 • ⑩ Istanbulmodern.org • From Sultanahmet, take the T1 tramway to the Tophane stop just west of Nusretiye Camii, from where it's a three-minute walk

Tophane is home to the city's contemporary art collection, **Istanbul Modern**, set in a stylish revamped warehouse on the edge of the Bosphorus, just in front of the Nusretiye Camii and the *nargile* cafés (see box, p.116). The museum's interior is all big, blank white walls and an exposed ventilation system, with views across the Bosphorus to the Topkapı Palace. An exhibition in the main gallery, to the right of the entrance, outlines the development of modern Turkish art and places it in its historical and social context. Beginning with the adoption of Western styles in the Tanzimat (reform) period between 1839 and 1876

6

NARGILE: HUBBLE-BUBBLE BUT NO TOIL OR TROUBLE

To most Westerners, the smoking device known (among other names) as the water pipe, hubble-bubble or hookah is associated with the hashish-toking counterculture of the 1960s. Either that or images of indolent, turbaned Muslims puffing away in some Eastern bazaar conjured up by romantic Orientalist painters such as Delacroix. In today's Istanbul, however, the **nargile** (as the water pipe is known here) is part and parcel of everyday life for many Turks. After decades of declining popularity, *nargile* smoking is now popular again, mainly among the young, the affluent and students. *Nargile* cafés are booming, some decked out in faux-Ottoman style, others über-contemporary, and the largest concentration is in Tophane, behind the Nusretiye Camii and en route to the Istanbul Modern.

The *nargile* first became popular in Istanbul in the seventeenth century, having spread there from India via Iran and Arabia. The spoilsport sultan of the time, Murat IV, leant on by the religious authorities, prohibited its use, but to no avail – *nargile* smoking became a popular (though male-only) pursuit and really only began to lose its popularity with the advent of the Turkish Republic, when all things Ottoman were deemed old-fashioned and reactionary.

In Ottoman times, opium was often the smoker's preference; today, it is strictly tobacco – albeit the strong stuff – and arguments rage in Turkey over which is more harmful, cigarette or *nargile*. You may find it rather intimidating to try one for the first time surrounded by local "old hands" but don't be put off. The whole point of *nargile* cafés is for people to come together, loll around on floor cushions and smoke, chat and chill.

(mainly formal oils) it moves on to showcase the twin strands of art in the early Republic – state-sponsored "heroic realism" and the private artists influenced by modern Western art movements. A section entitled "War and Art" deals mainly with the emerging Republic's struggle with the West in the War of Independence, another showcases the abstract art that began to influence Turkish painters from the 1950s. Downstairs, there's a reference library, a cinema showing arts and independent films, plus plenty of space for the temporary and pop-up exhibitions – an intriguing range of photographic and installation art by mainly Turkish artists – and an outside sculpture garden.

Up the Golden Horn

North along the shore of the Golden Horn from Beyoğlu and Karaköy lies the poor neighbourhood of **Kasımpaşa**. This industrial dockland area has the dubious distinction of being the cheapest property on the Istanbul Monopoly board. It is also the birthplace of Tayip Erdoğan, a working-class boy made good and now the charismatic if controversial leader of the ruling AKP (see pp.298–301).

A couple of kilometres further up the Horn, **Hasköy** was for centuries a Jewish village, though most of Istanbul's approximately twenty thousand Jews have now moved further out of the city. It was also the location of an Ottoman naval shipyard and a royal park, which was cultivated as a fruit orchard throughout Ottoman rule and today is blessed with one unusual sight – the **Rahmi M. Koç Industrial Museum**.

Once a fetid stretch of virtually lifeless, polluted water, the upper reaches of the Golden Horn have now been cleaned up. Fishermen now try their luck from the (shadeless) stretches of promenade that run along the water's edge – you can follow this from the model mania that is **Miniatürk**, in the district of **Sütlüce**, to the **Santralİstanbul** energy museum, a twenty-minute walk away to the north.

Rahmi M. Koç Industrial Museum

Hasköy Cad 27 • April–Sept Tues–Fri 10am–5pm, Sat & Sun 10am–8pm; Oct–March Tues–Fri 10am–5pm, Sat & Sun 10am–6pm • ₺12.50 • ⓦ rmk-museum.org.tr • Catch bus #47 from Eminönü, on the opposite side of the Horn, or the #54/HT from Taksim; better, the Haliç ferry that runs between Eminönü/Karaköy and Eyüp stops at Hasköy ferry terminal, from where it is a short walk

Istanbul's only industrial museum, the **Rahmi M. Koç Müzesi** is a gem, and makes a welcome change from the standard Byzantine and Ottoman sights. Constructed in the eighteenth century as a factory for anchors and their chains, the museum's arching brickwork and spacious halls have been authentically restored. The work was completed by Rahmi M. Koç in 2001, one of Turkey's most famous – and wealthiest – industrialists, to house his private collection of models, machines, vehicles and toys, originating from all over Turkey and Europe but mainly from Britain. The best time to visit is Saturday afternoon, when there are special exhibitions based around a collection of slot machines, the old Kadiköy–Moda tram and the history of flight.

On the first floor, the starboard main engine of the *Kalender* steam ferry, made in Newcastle upon Tyne in 1911 and decommissioned in the 1980s, is the main exhibit – press a button and you can see its pistons move. On the ground floor are a number of old bikes, from penny farthings to an early Royal Enfield motorbike complete with basket chair for side carriage. The model railway is disappointing in terms of moving parts; far better is the ship's bridge, reconstructed from a number of Turkish and British vessels of the 1920s to 1940s. All the instruments are explained in English, with sound effects and working parts, including an echo sounder, an early dimmer switch and a very loud alarm bell. The museum's ongoing projects include raising the Australian navy's first submarine, sunk off Gallipoli in World War I.

The other section of the museum, across the main road by the Golden Horn, contains a moored submarine (₺7 entry) and a section of train track complete with a tiny old station. There's also a street of period shops, from a chemist's complete with a set of old jars labelled "poison" to a ship's chandler's. Boy racers will love the selection of carefully restored cars covering the sublime (a 1965 Rolls Royce Silver Cloud) to the ridiculous (a 1985 Trabant).

The museum hosts a number of temporary exhibitions, so it's worth checking their website before you visit.

Miniatürk

Imrahor Caddesi • May–Oct Mon–Fri 9am–7pm, Sat & Sun 9am–8pm; Nov–April daily 9am–9pm • ₺10 • ⓦ miniaturk.com.tr • Bus #47, #47/C or #47/E from Eminönü or the #54/HT from Taksim

On the north side of the monumental Haliç Bridge, in dull Sütlüce, is one of those attractions you'll either love or hate: **Miniatürk**. Although it's set more or less on the banks of the Golden Horn, you could be anywhere, as the attraction is entirely surrounded by a high fence. On display here are over a hundred 1:25 scale models of some of Turkey's most impressive sights, spaced out along a 1.8-kilometre signed route. Forty-five of them are of attractions in Istanbul – from the relatively obscure (Sirkeci Post Office) through to the most famous (the Blue Mosque) – another 45 cover sights in Anatolia, including the Library of Celsius at Ephesus and Atatürk's mausoleum, the Anıtkabir, in Ankara, and there are also fifteen from former Ottoman dominions. Not all of the well-detailed models are buildings – if you've ever wanted to see Cappadocia's fairy chimneys or the travertine cascades of Pamukkale in miniature, then this is the place to come. Miniatürk's **Zafer Müzesi** (Victory Museum) celebrates Atatürk's military successes at Gallipoli in 1915 (see p.292) and during the Turkish War of Independence. Of interest to youngsters will be the giant chess set, maze and play area to the right of the entrance.

Santrallstanbul Museum of Energy

Kazım Karabekir Cad 2 • Tues–Fri 10am–6pm, Sat & Sun 10am–8pm • ₺10 • ⓦ santrallstanbul.org • A free shuttle bus runs from Kabataş half-hourly from 8am until 8.30pm (20min), and the #47 runs between Eminönü and Santrallstanbul

Set in the attractively landscaped campus of Bilgi University and built on reclaimed industrial land, **Santrallstanbul Museum of Energy** is housed, appropriately enough, in an old power station (*santral* in Turkish). Between 1914 and its closure in 1983, this plant, the Silahtaraua, was the only electricity generating station in Istanbul. The interior is now a successful mix of the carefully preserved innards of the power plant and high-tech, interactive wizardry. Best of all is the gigantic control room with its banks of dials, gauges, switches and AEG metres, like the cockpit of some *Flash Gordon*-style 1930s spaceship.

Beyoğlu, Taksim and around

Vibrant Beyoğlu, across the Golden Horn from the old city, is centred on manic İstiklal Caddesi (Independence Street). Istanbulites come here in droves to shop, wine and dine, take in a film, club or gig, visit a gallery or the theatre, or simply promenade, and ever more visitors are basing themselves in this lively area to make the most of the nightlife and culture. Historic shopping arcades and apartment blocks with elegant Art Nouveau and Secessionist facades pepper the nineteenth-century streets, and nearby is an impressive museum-cum-gallery, the Pera Museum, and the grand nineteenth-century *Pera Palace Hotel*, once favoured by gentry arriving on the Orient Express.

İstiklal Caddesi runs for 1.5km from the **Tünel**, the historic underground funicular railway (see p.29), to **Taksim Square**, the focal point of the city and a symbol of the secular Turkish Republic. North of Taksim Square are the upmarket residential suburbs of **Nişantaşı** and **Teşvikiye**. Once the hunting grounds of the Ottoman nobility, the area was given over to residential development in the nineteenth century and became the preserve of the monied elite – including the family of Nobel Prize-winning novelist **Orhan Pamuk** (see box, p.126), who once lived in Nişantaşı. Apart from the impressive **Military Museum** in Harbiye, there are no obvious sights here, but it's a good place to shop for designer-label goods.

ARRIVAL AND GETTING AROUND

BEYOĞLU, TAKSİM AND AROUND

By tram From the old city you can reach Taksim by taking the T1 tram to Karaköy, followed by the Tünel to the southern end of İstiklal Cad and then rattling up to the monumental square on the antique tram. Alternatively, take the tram to Kabataş and the modern funicular up to Taksim.

Getting around Broad İstiklal Caddesi, which links Galata with Taksim Square, has a period tram running its entire length but both it, and the surrounding side streets, are best explored on foot. From Taksim Square there are frequent buses north to Harbiye and Nişantaşı, including the #43, or for Nişantaşı/Teşvikiye take the M2 Metro to the Osmanbey stop.

Beyoğlu

In the Ottoman era, **Beyoğlu**, then known as Pera (Greek for "beyond" or "across") was, along with Galata, the **European quarter** of the city. Home to merchants, businessmen and diplomats, its fine nineteenth-century, Parisian-style apartment blocks were a complete contrast to the wooden buildings in the largely Muslim quarters of the old city across the Golden Horn. The area was very popular with the city's non-Muslim minorities and the names of Armenian and Greek architects adorn the fronts of some of İstiklal Caddesi's grander buildings. Growth here was encouraged by the completion of the **Orient Express** railway in 1899, bringing tourists to the area and resulting in the construction of many grand hotels, including the *Pera Palace* (see p.123). Beyoğlu continued to prosper into the early years of the twentieth century, with music halls, opera houses, inns, cinemas and restaurants all packed to the rafters.

Although the Greek minority escaped the population exchange of 1923 (see p.293), many soon began to drift away, a situation exacerbated by the wealth tax imposed on Turkey's minorities in World War II, the pogroms of the 1950s and expulsions of the 1960s. Other minority groups such as the Armenians and Jews followed suit, and Beyoğlu began to lose both its cosmopolitanism and its prosperity. The revival of the area began in the late 1980s, and, in 1990, the pedestrianization of **İstiklal Caddesi** and the reinstallation of the old tramway heralded the transformation of the area. Today, Beyoğlu's cosmopolitan nature has reasserted itself; so many foreigners have snapped up the district's apartments that by 2010 the ten percent quota of properties that non-Turkish nationals could own had been reached.

İstiklal Caddesi and around

Known as the "Grand Rue de Pera" prior to the foundation of the Turkish Republic in 1923, **İstiklal Caddesi** (Independence Avenue) is the city's most exciting street. It was widened and straightened following a fire in 1870 that destroyed over three thousand buildings: to fully appreciate its unspoilt and (largely) late nineteenth- and early twentieth-century architectural delights, you need to keep your eyes up, above the level of the shops and places to eat.

Crimean Memorial Church

Serdar-ı Ekrem Sokak • Service Sun from 9am • ₺10 donation welcomed

The idea for the Anglican **Crimean Memorial Church**, also known as Christ Church, was first floated by the Society for the Propagation of the Gospel in Foreign Parts; in

BEYOĞLU, TAKSIM & AROUND

CAFÉS & RESTAURANTS

Antiochia	23
Canım Ciğerim	19
Çokçok Thai	12
Divan Brasserie	15
Dürümzade	4
Fıccın	14
Hacı Abdullah	5
Helvetia	22
İmroz	6
Kafe Ara	11
Kenan Üsta Ocakbaşı	3
Mandabatmaz	13
Meze by Lemon Tree	16
Mikla	17
Nizam Pide	7
Nizam Pide 2	8
Parsifal	1
Refik	21
Saray	9
Van Kahvaltı Evi	18
Yeni Lokanta	20
Yirmibir Kebap	10
Zencefil	2

BARS

360	24
5.Kat	27
Büyük Londra Oteli	22
Cafe Smyrna	35
Chianti	5
Çukurcuma 49	21
Fiyaka	28
Haspa Cafe & Bar	9
James Joyce Irish Pub	7
KV	37
Leb-i Derya	36
Limonlu Bahçe	32
Nu Pera	30
Ritim Bar	13
Rocinante	6
Rock n Rolla	1
Solera	31
Sugar & Spice	29
Urban	20

ACCOMMODATION

Büyük Londra	4
Cihangir	3
Devman	10
House Hotel Galatasaray	5
Marmara Pera	7
Mama Shelter	2
Pera Palace	8
Richmond	11
Tomtom Suites	9
Triada Residence	1
Villa Zurich	6

CLUBS & LIVE MUSIC

Bigudi	17
Bronx Pi	34
Feraye	18
Gizli Bahçe	12
Hayal Kahvesi	11
Indigo	23
Jolly Joker Balans	14
Kallavi Meyhane	2
Kassette	33
Mektup	3
Mini Muzikhol	26
Munzur	15
Nublu	4
Peyote	10
Pinokyo	8
Pixie Underground	25
Roxy	19
Tek Yön	16

SHOPS

A La Turca	6
Ambar	7
By Retro (Suriye Pasajı)	11
Demirören Mall	1
Denizler Kitabevi	9
Eren	12
Homer	5
Kontra Plak	3
Mavi	8
Mephisto	2
Paşabahçe	10
Roll	4

N

KURTULUŞ CAD

EBURIZA DERHAGI SOK

PIR HÜSAMETTIN SOK

KURTULUŞ DERESI CAD

SIRKET SOK

DILBAT SOK

FESLEĞAN SOK

KALYONCU KULLUĞU CAD

KÜRDELA SOK

AKKIRAZ SOK

ÖMER HAYYAM CAD

HARMAN SOK

BILGIN SOK

SIMITÇI SOK

ATAMAN SOK

TEKIR SOK

Sururi Parkı

KERAMET SOK

SAMANCI FERHAT CAD

EMIN CAMI SOK

BALLI SOK

AYNALI ÇEŞME CAD

REFIK SAYDAM CAD

HAMALBAŞI CAD

KAMER HATUN CAD

British Consulate

Avrupa Pasajı

Aznavur Pasajı

Hazzopulo Pasajı

Galerist

KARAYSI SOK

MEŞRUTIYET CAD

ACARA SOK

KALLAVI SOK

Mısır Apartment

St Antoine

Merkez Han

SALT Beyoğlu (Art Gallery)

Pera Museum

Gallerist (Gallery)

Beyoğlu Is Merkezi

TERKOZ CK

Palais de Hollande

Mudo

POSTA CILAR CAD

BALYOZ SOK

TEPEBAŞI CAD

Cité de Syrie (Suriye Pasajı)

ASMALI MESCIT

Pera Palace

GÖNDI SOK

Arter (Gallery)

Borusan Arts & Cultural Centre

ISTIKLAL CAD

Art Nouveau Façades

MINARE SOK

ŞEHBENDER SOK

St Mary Draperis

Patisserie Markiz (Art Nouveau Interior)

JURNAL SOK

SOFYALI SOK

Botter House

G YAZGAN SOK

M **Metro Entrance**

ŞAHKULUBOSTAN SOK

KUMBARACI

Tünel
T **Tünel (İstiklal)**

İstiklal Eczanesi (Chemists)

Galata Mevlevihanesi

Eminönü & Sultanahmet

Crimean Memorial Church

KASIMPAŞA

BÜLENT DEMIR CAD

GENERAL ASIM GÜNDÜZ CAD

ÇIVICI SOK

ASÜRLAR MEYDANI SOK

ÇAK SOK

TEPEBAŞI CAD

KASIM SOK

SIPAHI FIRINI SOK

TALI SOK

Kasımpaşa Stadium

TURABI BABA CAD

MELEZ SOK

HAVUZ KAPISI CAD

Hasanpaşa Parkı

SIFAHNE CAD

AMBARBAKASI SOK

HUZUR SOK

TALI SOK

Kasımpaşa İskelesi

TEPEBAŞIKARCA SOK

TEPEBAŞIAKARCA SOK

REFIK SAYDAM CAD

KUTLU SOK

MINARE SOK

EVLIYA ÇELEBI CAD

DEĞU MUSA CAD

MEŞRUTIYET CAD

ÇIVICI SOK

REFIK SAYDAM CAD

Golden Horn

7

DIPLOMATIC RESIDENCES

The Turkish capital Ankara is now home to the country's embassies, but in the late Ottoman period, when Istanbul was the empire's capital, most foreign diplomats were based in palatial embassies on and around İstiklal Caddesi. Most still function as consulates and are some of the most attractive buildings in the district. The recently restored **Palais de Hollande** at İstiklal Cad 393 was built in 1858 on the site of the home of Cornelis Haga, the first Dutch diplomat in Constantinople during the fifteenth century, and is still the Dutch Consulate. Further along İstiklal Caddesi and off to the right on Nuri Ziya Sokak is the imposing **French Palace**, with its large central courtyard and formally laid-out gardens, the residence of ambassadors and consuls from 1831. Below the palace, on Tomtom Kaptan Sokak, stands the **Italian Consulate**, originally the Palazzo di Venezia, built in the seventeenth century and the earliest surviving diplomatic building in Beyoğlu. Casanova stayed here in 1744 and, according to his memoirs, didn't make a single conquest, although one İsmail Efendi claims to have been seduced by him. The **British Consulate**, a hundred metres or so north of İstiklal Caddesi on Hamalbaşı Caddesi, is the most impressive of all the consular buildings in Beyoğlu. Completed in 1855, it is set, following the 2003 terrorist attack that killed the then British Consul Roger Short, in a well-protected walled compound. It is a striking Renaissance-style structure, designed by Charles Barry, architect of the Houses of Parliament in Westminster, London.

gratitude for Britain's support for Ottoman Turkey in the Crimean War of 1853–6 Sultan Abdülmecit granted the land on this steep site overlooking the Bosphorus for a church. Although the first stone was laid in 1858 it wasn't completed until 1868; the architect was G.E. Street, also responsible for the Royal Courts of Justice in London. This incongruous yet beautiful neo-Gothic church, complete with a fine bell-tower and organ imported from England in 1911, is set in an idyllic walled compound-garden of chestnut, fig, oleander and palm. The church closed in the 1970s but reopened in 1991 and is today home to an energetic Anglican chaplain. As well as serving both the local community and visitors, refugees from places as disparate as Nigeria and Sri Lanka have received sanctuary here, and they make up much of the congregation.

Botter House
İstiklal Cad 457–77

At the southern end of **İstiklal Caddesi** is **Botter House**, widely regarded as the finest building of its kind in the city. The apartment block boasts a stone facade decorated with stylized, relief-carved flowers and wrought-iron work executed in the "whiplash" style so typical of the curvilinear Art Nouveau movement. Commissioned in 1901 as a showroom, workshop and family house by Dutchman Jan Botter, tailor and couturier to Sultan Abdülhamit II, it is one of a number of structures around Istanbul designed by the Italian architect Raimondo D'Aronco. At the time of writing it was boarded up and being renovated as a hotel.

Asmalımescit Sokak

Buzzing **Asmalımescit Sokak** has long been known for its plethora of lively *meyhane*s while Sofyalı Sokak, which runs off it at right angles towards Tünel, has more recently become known as "shot" alley because of the number of bars offering cheap slugs of spirits. A clamp-down on tables set out on the streets by the local municipality in 2011 has robbed the area of some of its former vitality, though it's still very vibrant.

St Mary Draperis
İstiklal Cad 429 • Mon & Wed–Sat 10am–noon & 2–6pm, Tues & Sun 2–6pm • Mass Mon–Fri 8am, Sun 9am

The oldest church in the area, **St Mary Draperis** is set well below street level and reached by a steep flight of steps from İstiklal Caddesi. Its origins on this site (the church was founded in the fifteenth century across the Golden Horn in Sirkeci) go back to 1678, but several fires over the centuries mean that the current building, designed by the Italian architect Semprini, dates only to 1904.

Patisserie Markiz and around

İstiklal Cad 360–2

The **Patisserie Markiz**, opposite St Mary Draperis (see p.122), boasts a beautiful Art Nouveau interior. Pride of place is given to two faïence wall panels designed and executed in France, *Le Printemps* and *L'Automne*. The place is now the average *Yemek Külübü* fast-food restaurant, but the listed interior is unchanged. Heading north up İstiklal Caddesi, on the same side of the street as St Mary Draperis is **Arter** (see p.207), a major gallery.

Pera Palace Hotel

Meşrutiyet Cad 52 • ☎ 0212 377 4000, ⓦ perapalace.com

For many of its well-heeled passengers, the palatial **Pera Palace Hotel** signified the real end of the line for the famous Orient Express (see box, p.8). Designed in the flamboyant Rococo style by the Turkish-French architect Alexander Vallaury in 1892, this luxurious hotel ensured wealthy European visitors to the city enjoyed the levels of comfort they were accustomed to in London or Paris. Situated in the district of Pera (today's Beyoğlu), the European quarter of the city, the *Pera Palace* hosted an array of impressive and glamorous guests. The founder of the Turkish Republic, Kemal Atatürk, was a frequent visitor, and the room he used, 101, has been turned into a **museum** in his honour. Ernest Hemingway stayed here while reporting on the Turkish War of Independence in the early 1920s; actresses Zsa Zsa Gabor, Greta Garbo and Rita Hayworth brought a touch of Hollywood glamour, and the courtesan-turned-spy, Mata Hari, a frisson of decadent intrigue. Alfred Hitchcock checked into the *Pera Palace* when he was in Istanbul, while another master of suspense, Agatha Christie, was a regular guest and wrote part of *Murder on the Orient Express* in her favourite room, 411.

The hotel closed in 2006 and received a massive makeover before reopening in 2010 (see p.172); it has since rocketed in price and lost some of its raffish charm. For a cheaper indulgence, head to the hotel's elegant ground-floor tearoom for the ₺50 afternoon tea.

7

Pera Museum

Meşrutiyet Cad 25, Tepebaşı • Tues–Thurs & Sat 10am–7pm, Fri 10am–10pm & Sun noon–6pm • ₺15 • ⓦ peramuzesi.org

Refined Meşrutiyet Caddesi, running parallel with İstiklal Caddesi to the south, is home to one of the city's premier galleries, the **Pera Museum** (Pera Müzesi), housed in a beautifully restored, late nineteenth-century building, once the prestigious *Bristol Hotel*. The ground floor is home to a decent café and gift shop full of expensive but tasteful souvenirs. On the first floor is the surprisingly interesting Anatolian Weights and Measures Collection, an exhibition of period photographs of Istanbul and the Kütahya Tiles and Ceramics Collection. The latter is a comprehensive collection of eighteenth- to twentieth-century wares from a northwest Anatolian pottery town which produced (and indeed continues to produce) ceramics similar to its better known rival, İznik.

The most impressive of the permanent exhibits is on the next floor up, the Orientalist Painting Collection. Dating from the seventeenth to the nineteenth centuries, among the works of mainly European painters is one by the Ottoman dignitary responsible for setting up the city's Archeology Museum (see pp.58–61), Osman Hamdi, the *Tortoise Trainer*. In 2004 the museum paid US$3.5 million to acquire this celebrated work. The museum also hosts major temporary exhibitions on its upper floors and has featured work from artists including Joan Miró and Andy Warhol. Appropriately, art-house movies are screened at the in-house Pera Cinema (see website for details).

St Antoine and around

St Antoine İstiklal Caddesi • Daily 8am–7pm • Mass Sun 10am • **Research Centre for Anatolian Studies** İstiklal Cad 181 • Tues–Sat 10am–6.30pm, Sun noon–6.30pm • Free

The Franciscan **Church of St Antoine** is a fine example of red-brick neo-Gothic architecture. Originally founded in 1725, it was demolished to make way for a tramway at the beginning of the nineteenth century and rebuilt in 1913 by the Istanbul-born, Italian architect Mongeri. Just south of St Antoine is the **Research Centre for Anatolian Civilisations** at the Merkez Han. Look out for fascinating exhibitions with an archeological or historical theme in this street-level exhibition space run by the prestigious Koç University. Upstairs is an excellent library, and on the rooftop you'll find the posh *Divan Brasserie* (see p.189) with stunning views over the Bosphorus. More or less opposite is the excellent **SALT Beyoğlu** gallery (see p.208), while a shade further north from the church is the fine **Mısır Apartment**, built in 1910 by an Armenian architect, home to several art galleries (see p.208) and the trendy bar-restaurant *360* (see p.197).

Galatasaray Meydanı

The small square a little less than halfway along İstiklal Caddesi is known as **Galatasaray Meydanı** and is named after the famous school, the **Galatasaray Lycée**, set behind iron railings to the south of the square. The *lycée* was originally founded in the fifteenth century to complement the Palace School in the Topkapı Sarayı. The current school originated in 1868, when it was remodelled on French lines, though the building it is housed in dates back only to 1908. Many of Turkey's leading academics, politicians and civil servants were educated here. One of the by-products of the new, Western curriculum was sport, and in 1905 the nation's leading football team, **Galatasaray** (see pp.225–226), was born here.

Aya Triada

İstiklal Caddesi

At the very end of İstiklal Caddesi, as it runs into Taksim Square, is the monumental Greek Orthodox Church of **Aya Triada** (Church of the Holy Trinity).

HISTORIC ARCADES

Çiçek Pasajı (Flower Passage) is the most comprehensively restored of the many fine late nineteenth- and early twentieth-century arcades off İstiklal Caddesi. Originally known as the **Cité de Pera**, it takes its present name from the anti-Bolshevik Russian émigrés who set up flower shops in the arcade in the 1920s. Gradually, the flower shops were replaced by taverns, though the music and entertainment for these drinking dens was supplied courtesy of the same Russian émigrés. Today, it's home to a collection of attractive but rather overpriced and touristy restaurants.

In addition to Çiçek Pasajı, there are a number of other period arcades, which once housed primarily Armenian- and Greek-owned cafés, restaurants, shops and offices, dotted along the length of İstiklal Caddesi. The most southerly is **Suriye Pasajı**, once the Cité de Syrie, an arcade with a fine facade designed by the Greek architect Bassiladis in 1908. Inside is the cornucopia-like vintage-clothes outlet By Retro (see p.218). Further north, near Galatasary tram stop, is the **Hazzopulo Pasajı**, dating from 1871 and today well known for its cheap and cheerful tea garden; just beyond is the **Aznavur Pasajı** (1893), by the same Armenian architect responsible for the Mısır Apartment (see p.208). Reached from Sahne Sokak, just beyond Galatasaray Meydanı, the **Avrupa Pasajı** is one of the grandest arcades, with a barrel-vaulted roof and a line of Neoclassical statues; today, it's home to many gift shops. Just up from Çiçek Pasajı is **Halep (Aleppo) Pasajı**, housing a clutter of clothes and jewellery stores, the Ses 1185 theatre, Biletix ticket outlet (see p.195) and a cinema. More or less opposite is **Atlas Pasajı** (1877), a beautiful four-storey arcade containing a decent cinema (see p.209) and a host of alternative-clothing stores.

CLOCKWISE FROM TOP TAKSİM SQUARE (P.127); ÇIÇEK PASAJI (P.124); CHURCH OF ST ANTOINE (P.124)>

Designed in 1880 by Vasili Ionnidi, it was built to a cruciform plan, with the main body of the church surmounted by a colossal dome. The interior is beautifully decorated, with the marble and gilt iconostasis particularly impressive. It's difficult to gain entry beyond the narthex unless you coincide with a service, so Sunday mornings are the best bet.

Çukurcuma and Cihangir

Wander into the streets south and east of the most northerly section of İstiklal Caddesi and you immediately escape the hustle and bustle and enter a world of alternative-clothes stores and bric-a-brac shops. The best places to begin exlporing are the streets of **Turnacıbaşı Sokak** and **Faik Paşa Yokuşu**. The former is home to an historic baths, the **Galatasaray Hamamı**. This neighbourhood, **Çukurcuma**, is rapidly following the lead of adjoining **Cihangir**, a hip, arty district where well-heeled Istanbulites (and a sizeable foreign contingent dominated by Americans) gaze down on the Bosphorus from stylish pavement cafés.

Museum of Innocence

Masumiyet Müzesi • Çukurcuma Caddesi, Dalgıç Çıkmazı 2 • Tues, Wed & Fri–Sun 10am–6pm, Thurs 10am–9pm • ₺25 • ⓦ masumiyetmuzesi.org

The arty **Museum of Innocence**, opened in 2012, is the brainchild of Turkey's best-known author Orhan Pamuk (see box, p.126). Linked to his novel of the same name, the museum has boosted Çukurcuma's bohemian-chic reputation. Downstairs, a glass case contains the butts of the 4,213 cigarettes smoked by the main character of Pamuk's novel of the same name between 1976 and 1984, while engaged in a doomed affair with a woman of lower social status, Füsun. It helps to have the read the book before visiting – not least because if you present the book for stamping on the relevant page you get in free – but even if you haven't, lovers of nostalgia will enjoy the videos of period Turkish adverts and glass cases with collections of kitsch pot dogs, vintage costumes and the like. All the exhibits are things the novel's lovers wore, used, saw or experienced during their affair, artily laid out in a converted 1920s townhouse.

ORHAN PAMUK: UNLIKELY HERO OF CONSCIENCE

Few Turks know what to make of their nation's first Nobel Prize-winner, Nişantaşı-born novelist **Orhan Pamuk**. To the liberal left, he's a talented writer who dares to challenge the Kemalist, nationalist-orientated establishment – who in turn accuse him of betraying his country. Moderates bask in the success of one of their nation's sons without questioning his beliefs too closely; others condemn him while studiously avoiding reading his works.

The **controversy** surrounding Pamuk began in 2004, when the novelist was reported as saying in a Swiss newspaper "I am the only one willing to say that one million Armenians and thirty thousand Kurds were murdered in Turkey". He was accused of "insulting Turkishness", a crime under article 301 of the Turkish Constitution. Although the ensuing court case was subsequently dropped, in 2008 it emerged that Pamuk may have been the **assassination target** of an ultra-nationalist "deep-state" gang working within the establishment. As a result, he now spends most of his time abroad.

It's surprising that such a storm has broken over the head of this benign-looking, fifty-something intellectual. An urbane, cerebral author, his early works dealt with cultural and philosophical rather than political issues, and it wasn't until 2004's *Snow* that Pamuk engaged in major political discourse. Many Turkish critics, however, believe that by bringing up two of the nations "sacred cows" – the "so-called" **Armenian Genocide** and the "**Kurdish problem**" – in an interview with a European newspaper, he was deliberately courting what they saw as the anti-Turkish West in the hope of winning the Nobel Prize. Such machinations by Pamuk are unlikely, although his open **rejection of nationalism** in a country still in nation-building mode makes him an object of suspicion.

#DİRENGEZİ: TROUBLED TIMES IN TAKSİM

Taksim Square's central location and vast scale make it ideal for **mass gatherings** and subsequent expressions of public feeling. In February 1969, over thirty thousand leftists battled with right-wing agitators and two protestors were killed, 150 more wounded. On May 1, 1977 during a Labour Day demonstration attended by half a million people, 36 of the predominantly left-wing demonstrators were killed by alleged right-wing extremists shooting into the crowd from the roof of the Intercontinental (today *Marmara*) Hotel.

Trouble flared up once again in May 2013, when Gezi Park (see pp.299–300), a green space within Taksim Square, was threatened with destruction to make way for a shopping mall. Police dealt brutally with a peaceful environmental protest, which led to several weeks of nationwide anti-government demonstrations. Political parties and rights movements from across the board came together in Taksim's Gezi Park to protest; in the main, resistance was peaceful and good natured. Indeed, one of the central characteristics of the protests was the humour of the graffiti scrawled on every wall. Slogans such as "you shouldn't have banned that last beer" (in reference to newly introduced laws restricting alcohol sales) and "we're already emotional kids, no need for the tear gas" competed with the hashtag #direngezi ("resist, Gezi") used on social media. Mainstream media largely ignored the protests at first, and CNN Turk came under fierce criticism for showing a penguin documentary during the first violent clashes, prompting countless penguin parodies, and the slogan "Diren Antartika".

For two weeks, protesters "occupied" Gezi Park, camping on every last surface, creating a kind of utopian community where no money was exchanged. Donations of food, blankets and other essentials flooded in and were distributed efficiently. Makeshift hospitals, libraries, speaking platforms and stages (there was even a veterinary clinic) sprang up overnight. The nearby *Divan Hotel* won great praise from sympathizers for allowing doctors to set up a clinic to tend to the injured – until the police started tear-gassing the premises.

PM Recip Tayyip Erdoğan (against whom much of the frustration was directed) denounced the protestors as traitors, terrorists and *çapulcu* (looters or layabouts), a title the protestors quickly appropriated, proudly claiming "Every day I'm çapulling" (in reference to a popular song). It took over a month – and several brutal clearance operations – before protests began to die down. Since then, riot police have turned out in their tens of thousands at the first hint of a protest to prevent further demonstrations in iconic Taksim Square. The *Gezi Café*, in the southwest corner of the park, is a pleasant enough place to sit over a glass of tea and mull over events.

Taksim Square and around

Taksim Square takes its name from the low **stone reservoir** on its southwestern side, today a modest municipality-run art gallery in front of which Roma flower sellers set up their stalls. It was constructed in 1732 to distribute water brought from the Belgrade Forest by aqueduct ("Taksim" in Turkish means "distribution"). Opposite it is the **Cumhuriyet Anıtı** (Republic Monument) dating to 1928, with bronzes of Atatürk and other Turkish nationalist revolutionary leaders, symbol of the secular Turkish Republic. Ironically the artist was the Italian sculptor Canonica.

A grandiose scheme fostered by the AKP government to redevelop the area and rebuild the historic Ottoman-era Topçu Barracks as a shopping mall was put on hold by the Gezi Park protests which erupted here in the spring of 2013 (see box above). The monumental **Atatürk Cultural Centre** (Atatürk Kültür Merkezi or AKM), to the east of the square, was home to the State Opera and Ballet, the Symphony Orchestra and the State Theatre Company. Designed by architect Hayati Tabanioğlu in 1956 it has, like so many concrete international-modern buildings, attracted much criticism. At the time of writing it was closed, its future, like that of the whole of the square, uncertain.

Military Museum

Asker Müzesi • Valikonağı Caddesi, Harbiye • Wed–Sun 9am–5pm • ₺4 • To get there, walk north along Cumhuriyet Caddesi from Taksim Square for fifteen minutes, or take the M2 Metro to Osmanbey

The **Military Museum** (Asker Müzesi), housed in the military academy where Atatürk (see p.292) received some of his education, is well worth visiting. The first objects of

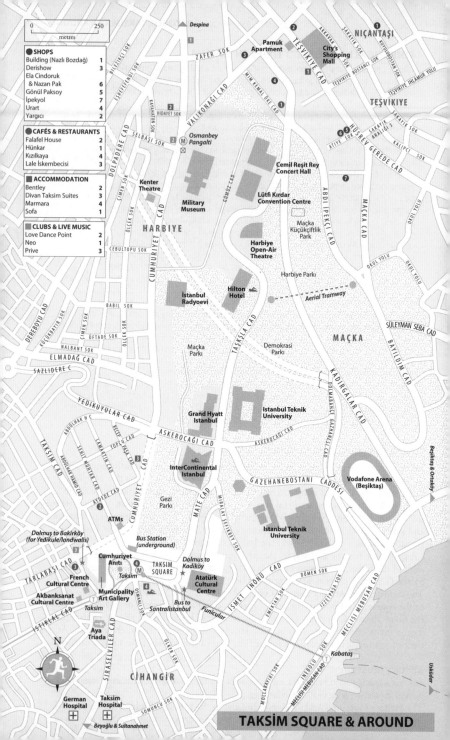

TAKSİM SQUARE & AROUND

	metres	
0		250

● SHOPS
Building (Nazlı Bozdağ)	1
Derishow	3
Ela Cindoruk & Nazan Pak	6
Gönül Paksoy	5
İpekyol	7
Urart	4
Yargıcı	2

● CAFÉS & RESTAURANTS
Falafel House	2
Hünkar	1
Kızılkaya	4
Lale İskembecisi	3

■ ACCOMMODATION
Bentley	2
Divan Taksim Suites	3
Marmara	4
Sofa	1

■ CLUBS & LIVE MUSIC
Love Dance Point	2
Neo	1
Prive	3

NİÇANTAŞI
TEŞVİKİYE
TEŞVİKİYE CAD
HÜSREV GEREDE CAD
SAKAYIK SOK
KALIPCI SOK
MAÇKA CAD
ATİYE SOK
City's Shopping Mall
TEŞVİKİYE BOSTANCI SOK
KUYUMCULAR SOK
SAKAYIK BOSTANCI SOK
TEŞVİKİYE İHLAMUR YOLU
SAKAYIK ARALIĞI S
Despina
Pamuk Apartment
ZAFER SOK
BİLEZİKCİ SOK
ESREFEFENDİ SOK
MİM KEMAL ÖKE CAD
KATAVANIN CAD
HİDAYET SOK
Osmanbey Pangalti
Cemil Reşit Rey Concert Hall
VALİKONAĞI CAD
SELBAŞI SOK
GÜMÜŞ CAD
Lütfi Kırdar Convention Centre
ABDİ İPEKÇİ CAD
Maçka Küçükçiftlik Park
DOLPADERE CAD
CUMHURİYET CAD
Kenter Theatre
Military Museum
Harbiye Open-Air Theatre
OKUL YOLU
OKUL YOLU
CİMEN SOK
ÖLCEK SOK
HARBİYE
Harbiye Parkı
MAÇKA
SÜLEYMAN SEBA CAD
CEBULTOPU SOK
İstanbul Radyoevi
Hilton Hotel
Aerial Tramway
BABİL SOK
CİMEN SOK
ÜFTADE SOK
ÖLCEK SOK
TAŞKIŞLA CAD
Maçka Parkı
Demokrasi Parkı
BAYILDIM CAD
DEREBOYU CAD
KÜÇÜKBAYIR SOK
NALBANT SOK
ELMADAĞ CAD
SAZLIDERE C
YEDİKUYULAR CAD
ABDULHAK H C
RECEP PAŞA CAD
TOPÇU CAD
Grand Hyatt İstanbul
İstanbul Teknik University
ASKEROCAĞI CAD
KADİRGALAR CAD
DOLMABAHÇE GAZHANESİ CAD
TAKSİM CAD
ABDULLAH RAMİZ SOK
ŞEHİT MUHTAR CAD
LAMARTİN CAD
ASKEROCAĞI CAD
InterContinental İstanbul
GAZEHANEBOSTANI CADDESİ
Vodafone Arena (Beşiktaş)
Beşiktaş & Ortaköy
AYDEDE SOK
Gezi Parkı
MATE CAD
MİRALAY ŞEFİK BEY SOK
İstanbul Teknik University
ATMs
Bus Station (underground)
Dolmuş to Bakırköy (for Yedikule/landwalls)
TARLABAŞI CAD
French Cultural Centre
Cumhuriyet Anıtı
TAKSİM SQUARE
Taksim
Dolmuş to Kadıköy
Atatürk Cultural Centre
İSMET İNÖNÜ CAD
DÜMEN SOK
EMEKTAR SOK
İZZETPAŞA SOK
MECLİSİ MEBUSAN CAD
Akbanksanat Cultural Centre
Municipality Art Gallery
Taksim
OSMANLI SOK
Bus to Santralistanbul
Funicular
İSTİKLAL CAD
Aya Triada
SİRASELVİLER CAD
ÜLKER SOK
CİHANGİR
Kabataş
Üsküdar
MOTTALAVASINI SOK
MECLİSİ MEBUSAN CAD
İNEBOLU SOK
German Hospital
Taksim Hospital
SOMUNCU SOK
Beyoğlu & Sultanahmet

N

interest, in the pleasant garden area, include a massive nineteenth-century Krupp cannon used in the Gallipoli campaign, a Russian T-26B tank, one of the first used by the Turkish military, and a 1962 Lockheed CF-104 jet. The Turks take intense pride in their military history and there's a huge amount to see here in the labyrinthine maze of corridors and rooms, much of it housed in old-fashioned dark wood, glass-fronted cabinets – and most exhibits are labelled in English as well as Turkish.

The first room traces the origins of the Turks in Central Asia, the second has a wonderfully heroic diorama of the great Selçuk Turkish victory over the Byzantines at Malazgirt in 1071, while the third is devoted to the rise of the Ottomans, and includes the standard raised at the crucial Battle of Kosovo in 1389. The capture of Constantinople in 1453 is covered in the "Conquest of Istanbul" room, with another striking diorama. Near here, in an untidy pile, is part of the great chain which the Byzantines used so successfully for centuries to bar enemy ships from entering the Golden Horn.

The first floor concentrates largely on World War I, particularly the 1915 Gallipoli (see pp.261–266) campaign which is seen by Turks, quite rightly, as crucial to their survival as a sovereign power. The usual paraphernalia of World War I battles can be seen here, from heavy machine guns to canteens, medals to map cases. Also on the first floor is the **Mehter Band** (see box, p.129), which performs for museum visitors from Wednesday to Sunday (3–4pm).

Originating in 1289, **Mehter Band** members were janissaries who accompanied the sultan into battle. The band became an institution, symbolizing the power and independence of the Ottoman Empire. During public performances, band members sang songs about their heroic ancestors and Ottoman battle victories. They had considerable influence in Europe, helping create new musical styles, such as the Spanish *a la turca*, and inspiring numerous composers (examples include Mozart's *Marcia Turca* and Beethoven's *Ruinen von Athens, Opus 113*). The kettledrum, *kös* in Turkish, was also introduced to the West as a result of interest in the Mehter Band. The band was abolished by Mahmut II in 1826, along with the janissary corps, and only re-established in 1914, when new instruments were added.

Nişantaşı and Teşvikiye

The area that today comprises the wealthy suburbs of **Nişantaşı** and **Teşvikiye**, a kilometre or so north of Taksim Square, was once the hunting grounds of the Ottoman nobility. The name Nişantaşı, or "target stone", derives from the custom of Ottoman soldiers setting up specially shaped stones to use for target practice here. The area began to be developed residentially in the nineteenth century and it soon became the preserve of the moneyed elite – including the family of Nobel Prize-winning novelist **Orhan Pamuk** (see box, p.126), who once lived in Nişantaşı. There are no obvious sights here, but the City's Mall (see p.222) has some of Istanbul's most elite stores under one air-conditioned roof, and around it are a number of pleasant streets lined with fine, early twentieth-century apartments whose ground-floor shops boast equally exclusive outlets.

BOYS SWIMMING IN THE BOSPHORUS NEAR MECİDİYE CAMİİ

Beşiktaş and Ortaköy

Beşiktaş and Ortaköy, the two suburbs fronting the Bosphorus between the tram terminus at Kabataş and the Bosphorus Bridge, are firmly part of the city, despite Ortaköy's former status as a village. Beşiktaş boasted its own royal palace, a hippodrome and an important church (all now long gone) in the Byzantine era and developed into a major port under Ottoman rule; it remains an important ferry terminal today and is the first stop on the famous Bosphorus Cruise (see box, p.147). The area's real draw though, is its clutch of late nineteenth-century palaces and pavilions overlooking the strait – ornate, European-style residences for the last sultans of the decaying Ottoman Empire.

Palaces aside, until recently it was a little run-down, much frequented by students (Beşiktaş has the highest number of universities per square kilometre in the country) and other impecunious types, but the area's character is changing, with a former tobacco warehouse having been converted into the luxury *Shangri-la* hotel and a row of nineteenth-century houses transformed into a designer shopping street. **Ortaköy**, or the "Middle Village", a little further up the Bosphorus, has a picturesque waterfront setting and is crammed with upmarket cafés and bars packed with affluent young Istanbulites. The "village" is sandwiched between the horribly busy main coast road and the pretty waterfront, itself dominated by a splendidly ornate Ottoman Baroque mosque and the gigantic, yet sleek, bulk of the Bosphorus suspension bridge.

Beşiktaş

Northeast of Taksim Square, along the Bosphorus, the busy suburb of **Beşiktaş** is one of the best-served transport hubs in the city. Concrete shopping centres and a sprawling fruit-and-vegetable market cluster around the main shore road and ferry terminal, in front of which stands the bus station. Most visitors are here to see the **Dolmabahçe Palace**, successor to Topkapı as the residence of the Ottoman sultans. Even if you don't visit the palace it's worth spending a few hours in the neighbourhood to visit the city's excellent **Naval Museum**, the unimaginatively titled but worthwhile **National Palaces Painting** and **Palace Collections** museums, as well as leafy **Yıldız Parkı** and the **Çırağan Palace**. It's also home to one of Istanbul's three major football teams (see p.226) and the upmarket **Akaretler** shopping area (see p.222).

8

GETTING THERE   BEŞIKTAŞ

By bus To get here by bus, take #25/T or #40 from Taksim.

By tram and funicular The T1 tram from Sultanahmet and Eminönü runs as far as Kabataş, as does the funicular down from Taksim Square, from where it's a little under 1km to the Dolmabahçe Palace.

By ferry Ferries run to and from the Asian side, to Kadıköy and Üsküdar (₺3).

Dolmabahçe Palace

Dolmabahçe Sarayı • Dolmabahçe Caddesi • Tues, Wed & Fri–Sun 9am–4pm; aim to arrive early to avoid the crowds that amass from 10am onwards • Selamlık/administrative section ₺30, Harem ₺20, combined ticket ₺40 (no combined tickets sold after 3pm) • You are obliged to join a tour of the administrative and/or Harem section (approx 2hr 30min for the combined tour; English-speaking tours run every 15min), with tours of the administrative section starting from the palace entrance; keep your entrance ticket handy as you'll need it to get into both • No cameras allowed inside • ⓦ millisaraylar.gov.tr

The **Dolmabahçe Palace** is the largest and most extravagant of all the palaces on the Bosphorus, with an impressive 600m-long waterside frontage. Flanked by symmetrical flower-lined gardens with a magnificent clover-shaped pond and fountain at its heart, the exterior of the palace is arguably more beautiful than the interior, although if ostentatious displays of wealth and fittings dripping with gold are to your taste you may disagree. Built in the mid-nineteenth century by Armenian architect Karabet Balian and his son Nikoğos, the palace's brazen riches suggest that good taste suffered along with the fortunes of the Ottoman Empire. The modern European stylings opt for flamboyance over flair, with crystal-lined staircases and chandeliers, dazzling upholstery and such profuse lashings of gold that the effect is a virtual assault on the senses. Indeed, critics see the palace's wholesale adoption of Western architectural forms as a last-ditch effort to muster some respect for a crumbling and defeated empire.

With groups of up to fifty people ushered through at a rapid pace, the tour experience (see p.133) is more akin to the herding of cattle, and the friendly, multilingual guides spend the majority of their time dealing with crowd control while dealing out choice snippets of information about the key rooms.

The first half of the tour consists of shuffling down corridors, sneaking a peek into the cordoned-off rooms and trundling single-file through exhibition rooms displaying

semi-interesting collections of delicate teacups and ornate household items. Thankfully, the second floor holds a few more impressive highlights – the **Sultan's reception room** is a Venetian-style boudoir with an outrageously decadent gold-plated ceiling; the antiquated **Abdülmecit Library** offers an intriguing glimpse into the past; and the *hamam* and bathing quarters feature possibly the world's most luxurious squat toilet, made of exquisite marble. In the **dining hall**, the handmade parquet floors – an intricate puzzle design carved from ebony, rosewood and mahogany – are an incongruously delicate masterpiece hidden beneath the fancy furnishings.

The 36-metre-high **ceremonial hall** (double the height of the rest of the rooms), its ceiling held up by 56 elaborate columns, is the crown jewel of the tour and its centrepiece, a 4.5-tonne crystal chandelier glittering with 664 bulbs, is one of the largest ever made – a lavish present from Queen Victoria. The grand dome and pillars are actually made of wood and painted to create a 3D illusion that gives the impression of sculpted marble, an effect employed across many of the palace's ceilings. The ceremonies conducted in this hall were accompanied by an orchestra playing European marches and watched by the women of the *harem* through the *kafes*, grilles behind which women were kept hidden even in the days of Westernization and reform.

The Harem section, reached along the waterfront, provides little stylistic deviation from the main building; its main attraction is Atatürk's bedroom, where the founder of the Turkish Republic died in 1938. The room itself, with its enormous Turkish flag adorning the bed, is a little disappointing, but it's nevertheless one of the most popular rooms in the palace for Atatürk-loving Turkish visitors. The clock in the room is still set at 9.05 – the time of his death.

8

INFORMATION   **THE DOLMABAHÇE PALACE**

Tickets and tours On entering the grounds the ticket booth is to the left of the main entrance, where you are obliged to join a tour of the administrative and/or *harem* section (approx 2hr 30min for the combined tour). Keep your entrance ticket handy as you'll need it to get into both. Aim to arrive early to avoid the crowds that amass from 10am onwards. Tours of the administrative section commence (follow the individual visitors signs) from the grand palace entrance, a looming feat of neo-Baroque architecture. English-speaking tours run every 15min so it's worth checking the times first before wandering the gardens.

National Palaces Painting Museum

Milli Saraylar Resim Müzesi • Barbaros Hayrettin Paşa İskelesi Sokak • Tues, Wed & Fri–Sun 9am–5pm • ₺10 • Enter from the Kaymakamlık Building, around 300m northeast along the main road from the Dolmabahçe Palace entrance (see p.131) • ⓦ millisaraylar.gov.tr

The **National Palaces Painting Museum** houses some fine, late nineteenth- and early twentieth-century works of art. The paintings are spread over two floors of a grandiose annexe of the Dolmabahçe Palace, which in the Sultan Abdülmecit period accommodated the crown princes. On the first floor the Ceremony Hall is dedicated to the romanticized oriental scenes of Russian painter Ivan Konstantinovich Ayvazovsky, another room displays pictures brought to the palace from Paris, yet another to paintings from the Orientalist school. Downstairs are works by Turkish painters including Osman Hamdi Bey (1842–1910) – the first Ottoman Muslim painter to have his work displayed abroad and whose most famous work is in the Pera Museum (see p.123). A wander around these palatial European-style rooms, all stucco ceilings, gilt and chandeliers, will give you an idea of the opulence of the adjoining palace without actually having to visit it.

Palace Collections Museum

Saray Koleksiyonları Müzesi • Entrance on Dolmabahçe Caddesi • Tues–Sun 9am–5pm • ₺5 • ⓦ millisaraylar.gov.tr

Housed in the former kitchens of the Dolmabahçe Palace, the **Palace Collections Museum** contains a staggering 42,000 different items, all of them from the palace. The mother-of-pearl-inlaid *hamam* slippers, Singer sewing machines, cast-iron AEG fans and delicate Limoges-ware tea sets are just some of the relatively mundane objects that help further our understanding of life in the palace during the late nineteenth and early twentieth centuries. The interior of the kitchens has been attractively restored and the objects are well displayed – look out for the stereoscope made in London's Pall Mall and the most contemporary item on display, the 1930s Ericsson telephone switchboard that was so essential for communication in the gargantuan palace.

Naval Museum

Deniz Müzesi • Barbaros Hayrettin Paşa İskelesi Sokak, off Beşiktaş Caddisi • Tues–Sun 9am–5pm (summer weekends 10am–6pm) • ₺6 • ⓦ denizmuzesi.tsk.tr

The revamped **Naval Museum** is housed in a well-designed building completed in 2013. On the entrance floor are a kids' play area, café and temporary exhibitions area. A huge room, lit by windows looking onto the strait, contains a magnificent collection of restored caïques, one complete with life-like mannequins. These elegant boats were once used to row the sultans to and from their homes along the Bosphorus; the oarsmen (*bostanci*) reputedly barked like dogs while they rowed so that they could not overhear the sultans talking. The largest of these caïques, dating from 1648, needed an incredible 144 oarsmen to power it. Downstairs is an exhibition devoted to woodcarving in the Ottoman navy, which has some superb ships' figureheads. Other rooms have exhibits and information on important milestones in Ottoman naval history, right up to the Çanakkale/Gallipoli campaigns (see p.261–266) of World War I.

Çırağan Palace

Çırağan Caddesi

The sumptuous **Çırağan Palace** has a long history dating back to the seventeenth century, but today's European-style palace was first constructed in 1855 when Sultan Abdülmecit decided to move his official residence from Dolmabahçe. It was finally completed in 1874 during the reign of his brother Abdülaziz, who added a more Eastern flavour with Arabic touches, such as the honeycomb stalactites decorating the windows. It was here in the palace that, in 1876, Abdülaziz was either murdered or committed suicide (the cause of death was never established), and where Murat V was later imprisoned, until his death in 1904, after being deposed by his brother.

Abandoned until 1908, Çırağan housed the Turkish parliament until 1910, when a fire reduced it to a blackened shell. It was restored in 1990, with reference to the original plans, to its present magnificence as one of Istanbul's most luxurious hotels, the *Çırağan Palace Kempinski* (see p.173) with a second renovation undertaken in 2006.

Visitors can enter the west side of the palace grounds to marvel at the ornate facade and take pictures, but entrance here is limited to guests of the imperial palace suites. The main hotel entrance is a good 200m further down Çırağan Caddesi; here non-guests may be admitted to eat or drink at one of the hotel's several swanky restaurants (see pp.190–191).

Yıldız Parkı

Yıldız Parkı, a vast wooded area opposite the Çırağan Palace (see above) and dotted with mansions, pavilions, lakes and gardens, was the centre of the Ottoman Empire for thirty years during the reign of Abdülhamit II. The buildings in and around the park constitute **Yıldız Palace**, a collection of structures in the old Ottoman style that are a total contrast to the Dolmabahçe Palace. Most of the pavilions date from the reign of Abdülaziz, but it was Abdülhamit – a reforming sultan whose downfall was brought about by his intense paranoia – who transformed Yıldız into a small city and power base.

Its superb hillside location makes the park one of the most popular places in Istanbul for city-dwellers thirsting for fresh air and open spaces, and on public holidays it's always crowded. Of the many buildings in the park, only the Yıldız Chalet Museum

(Şale Köşkü) is open to the public, though it's easy enough to wander around the outside of the other pavilions, each with marvellous terraces and panoramic views of the Bosphorus.

INFORMATION   YILDIZ PARKI

Arrival The palace buildings are a 15min walk up through the park from the southern entrance on Çırağan Caddesi. If you don't fancy the steep climb, you can take any bus or minibus from the main square in Beşiktaş by the ferry terminal and up Barbaros Bul. Get off just after the former British Council building (opposite the *Conrad Hotel*) and follow the signs to "Yıldız Üniversitesi" and "Şehir Müzesi" to the right.

Opening hours Daily 8am–11pm.

Eating A relaxing café, the *Kır Kahvesi* (9am–10pm) is a good spot for enjoying the shade provided by the towering chestnut, beech, linden and plane trees. Alternatively, the *Malta Köşkü*, built in 1870 and once used to imprison Sultan Abdülhamit's brother, Murat (on Abdülhamit's orders), is a reasonably priced restaurant-café (daily 9am–10pm).

Yıldız Chalet Museum

Şale Köşkü • Tues, Wed & Fri–Sun: March–Sept 9.30am–5pm; Oct–Feb till 4pm • ₺4

The most important surviving building in Yıldız Parkı is the **Chalet Museum**. Like the Dolmabahçe Palace (see pp.131–133), it was designed partly by the Armenian Balian brothers and partly by the Italian Raimondo Tommaso D'Aronco. The first of the pavilion's three separate sections was modelled on a Swiss chalet, while the other two were built to receive Kaiser Wilhelm II on his first and second state visits, in 1889 and 1898. The inside of the *köşk* belies its peeling exterior – the most impressive room, the **Ceremonial Hall**, takes up the greater part of the third section and has a Hereke carpet so big (approximately 400 square metres) that part of a wall was knocked down to install it. In the attractive dining room, at the top of the central stairway in the central section, the dining chairs were carved by the reclusive Abdülhamit himself, who lived here after deciding that the Bosphorus-front Dolmabahçe and Çırağan palaces were too open to potential assassins.

Yıldız Porcelain Factory

Yıldız Sarayı Porselen Fabrikası • Mon–Fri 9am–noon & 1–6pm • ₺5

Southeast of the Chalet museum is the **Yıldız Porcelain Factory** established here in 1890 to produce tableware for the palace. The pottery is still functioning, and the designs stick very closely to the ornate late nineteenth-century European styles favoured by the last Ottoman sultans. The gift shop stocks a range of the factory's produce, and there's an adjoining café with good views over the park.

Ortaköy

Once a tiny fishing village, **Ortaköy** is now home to a burgeoning art scene with clusters of chic restaurants and cafés, upmarket theme bars and a bustling crafts market. The suburb runs north under the looming, transcontinental **Bosphorus Bridge** (Boğaziçi Köprüsü), completed in 1973 to celebrate the Turkish Republic's fiftieth anniversary. Ortaköy retains its allure in spite of the heavy renovations, with its cobbled pathways and quaint riverside setting.

Heading north from the boardwalk area, just beyond the bridge, the neighbourhood plays host to some of the city's glitziest clubs (see p.202), where celebrity-spotting and cash-splashing takes place to a backdrop of the Bosphorus and a plethora of swanky restaurants.

ARRIVAL   ORTAKÖY

On foot Ortaköy is easily reached by foot from Beşiktaş – a pleasant 1km stroll down the road.

By bus You can take the #40 or #42/T bus from Taksim, or the #30 from Eminönü.

By tram and funicular Another possible route is to take the tram from Sultanahmet or the funicular from Taksim Square to Kabataş, then catch the #22, #22/RE or #25/E to Ortaköy.

Ortaköy waterfront

The charming waterfront in Ortaköy is the heart of the village, a lattice of paved streets on and around the Bosphorus, where debonair restaurants, tiny clothing boutiques and arty cafés have taken over even the tiniest of fishermen's cottages. The Sunday market is a popular if unexciting affair, with a wide array of colourful crafts on sale. A variety of cheap food stands offer everything from scrumptious fruit-filled waffles dripping with chocolate sauce to stuffed potatoes laden with cheese, yoghurt and olives. This is also the location of the distinctive Ottoman Baroque mosque **Büyük Mecidiye Camii**, completed in 1855. The architect was the Armenian Nikoğos Balian, also partly responsible for the Dolmabahçe Palace (see pp.131–133). Unremarkable inside, the mosque was built right on the edge of the strait and is a favourite photographers' subject with the Bosphorus Bridge in the background.

Running parallel to the Bosphorus, the main street, Muallim Naci Caddesi, boasts the attractive Greek Orthodox church of **Aya Fokas** (St Phocas), constructed in 1854, and the **Ezt Ahayim** synagogue; both are usually locked.

Surp Aszdvadzadzin

Ilhan Caddesi • Services on Sun, or the caretaker may let you in

Ortaköy was, and to some extent remains, a cosmopolitan and tolerant area of the city, embracing numerous different religions. Perched high above the waterfront is the Armenian church of **Surp Aszdvadzadzin**, built between 1661 and 1684. Plain on the exterior, the barrel-vaulted, Neoclassical interior is lavishly decorated, and the gold-gilded altar is monumental.

8

HAYDARPAŞA STATION

Asian Istanbul

With so much to see and do in the historic old city and in energetic Beyoğlu, most visitors put a trip across the Bosphorus to the Asian side of Istanbul well down their list of priorities. This is a shame, as even a quick visit will give you a more rounded feel of how this great metropolis ticks. Kadıköy has a good sprinkling of worthwhile sights and boasts a compact but lively shopping area, some decent nightlife and one of the city's best restaurants, *Çiya Sofrası*. Its northern neighbour, Haydarpaşa, is worth a wander for its impressive early twentieth-century station, the Crimean War Cemetery and the colossal Selimiye Barracks, home to the Florence Nightingale Museum.

The opening of the Bosphorus tunnel in late 2013 means that the European and Asian sides of the city are now linked by a metro line – the Marmaray (see p.27). The first station on the Asian side is by the waterfront in conservative **Üsküdar**, and was founded by the mercurial Athenian statesman-adventurer, Alcibiades, in 409 BC, and became known as Chrysopolis. The old city apart, there is nowhere else in Istanbul with such a concentration of fine **Ottoman mosques**, including a couple by the sixteenth-century master architect Sinan. The landmark **Maiden's Tower** (Kız Kulesi) lies just offshore, and you can eat at *Kanaat Lokantası*, another of Istanbul's gastronomic highlights. Despite appearances to the contrary, **Kadıköy** has similarly ancient origins: **Greek colonists** founded a city, Chalcedon, near present-day Kadıköy as early as 680 BC – some twenty years before the colony across the straits that became Byzantium, then Constantinople and finally Istanbul.

GETTING THERE   ASIAN ISTANBUL

By ferry Regular ferries run to Kadıköy from Eminönü (daily 7.30am–9pm), Karaköy (daily 6.30am–midnight) and Beşiktaş (daily 8.15am–9.45pm); to Haydarpaşa from Karaköy (daily 6.30am–midnight); and to Üsküdar from Eminönü (daily 6.30am–11pm) and Beşiktaş (daily 7am–9pm).

By metro Marmaray-line trains run from Sirkeci to Üsküdar daily 6am–midnight. For Kadıköy, continue past Üsküdar to Ayrılık Çeşmesi and change to the M4 metro; Kadıköy is one stop south.

Kadıköy

The suburb of **Kadıköy** makes for an enjoyable outing from the European side of the city. It's a lively place, with some great shops, restaurants, bars and cinemas. One of the area's charms is its "local" feel – hardly surprising as, unlike Sultanahmet or Beyoğlu, most of the people out and about here are residents. Towards the end of the nineteenth century, when the introduction of steam-driven ferries made commuting across the Bosphorus feasible, Kadıköy became a popular residential area for foreign business-people and wealthy Greeks and Armenians, whose most visible legacy is the **churches** southeast of the ferry terminal. There's a scattering of older constructions amid the concrete: look out for the tall, narrow curves of the cream, Art Deco-style **Kurukahveci Mehmet Efendi building**, headquarters of the famous Turkish coffee brand, and the beautifully restored **Süreyya Opera House** on Bahariye Caddesi (see p.206); completed in 1927, its ornate Neoclassical facade is adorned with relief-work pilasters, cherubs and Classical-style theatre masks.

Most things of interest in Kadıköy are to be found between the waterfront **Sahil Yolu** (coast road) and **Bahariye Caddesi**, a right turn off Söğütlüçeşme Caddesi, the steep, wide street leading uphill from the ferry terminal. The latter two streets have their own tram, a grittier version of İstiklal Caddesi's. Indeed, the area bounded by Söğütlüçeşme Caddesi to the north, Bahariye and Emin Bey *caddesi*s to the east and south and the Bosphorus waterfront to the west is something of a mini-Beyoğlu, with a similar mix of alternative-clothing stores, bookshops and bric-a-brac shops dotted among the cafés and restaurants spilling out onto jam-packed pedestrianized streets. It's also one of the best areas in the city for shopping – especially for spices, coffee, olives, dried fruit, nuts, Turkish delight and other goodies – in the colourful permanent market centred on **Güneşlibahçe Sokak**. A couple of nineteenth-century churches here attest to Kadıköy's non-Muslim past: the Greek Orthodox Aya Eufemia and the Armenian church of Surp Takavor, opposite each other on Muvakkithane Sokak.

Kadıköy is home to Turkey's wealthiest football club, **Fenerbahçe** (see p.226), who reached the quarter-finals of the UEFA Champions League in 2008 and the semis of the Europa League in 2013. Their impressive stadium, the Rüştü Saraçoğlu, lies at the foot of the hill 400m east of Bahariye Caddesi. Running along its eastern side is the main drag known as **Bağdat Caddesi**, once part of the old Silk Route from China. It's of little interest today except as a place to pose, and as a place to buy the clothes to pose in.

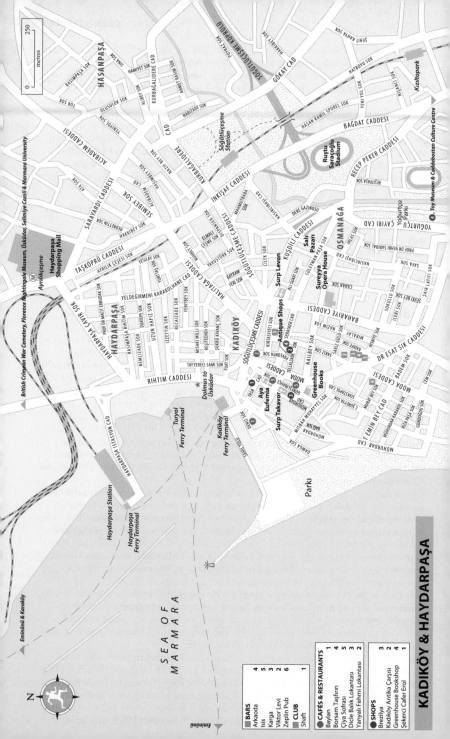

Toy Museum

Dr. Zeki Zeren Sokak, Göztepe • Tues–Sun 9.30am–6pm • ₺8 • Bus #GZ1, #GZ2, #10, #10/B or #10/S

Established in 2005 in a lovely nineteenth-century wooden villa – which, until the 1950s, housed one of the city's most famous toyshops – the **Toy Museum**, is the brainchild of contemporary poet Sunay Akin. It exhibits some four thousand toys on four floors, the oldest dating back two hundred years. Toys are presented according to theme, with rooms devoted to trains, space travel and soldiers; there are some century-old German-made porcelain dolls on display, and a Barbie in her first employment role as an air stewardess, among others. Much, but by no means all, of the collection is foreign, and there are examples of handmade dolls from Anatolia, a whirling-dervish puppet, and products of the Eyüp Sultan toy factory – legendary for its toy-making in the eighteenth century.

Haydarpaşa

North up the Bosphorus from Kadıköy, **Haydarpaşa** is dominated by the massive **Selimiye Barracks**. Built in the early nineteenth century, they housed the new, Western-style army created to bring the power of the corrupt janissary corps to an end; today, they are worth a visit for the **Florence Nightingale Museum**. Opposite, on Selimiye Camii Sokak, is the **Selimiye Camii**, the mosque constructed, along with the nearby *hamam*, for the use of the barracks' soldiers. Rivalling the barracks for sheer size is the main building of **Marmara University**, designed by Raimondo D'Aronco and notable for its quirky clock towers, though the **Karaca Ahmet Mezarlığı**, the largest Muslim graveyard in Istanbul, is a more accessible destination. Shaded by ancient cypress trees, it's a sprawling place thought to have been founded in the mid-fourteenth century and now holding an estimated one million graves. A ten-minute walk from the barracks on Tıbbiye Caddesi in the direction of Üsküdar, it can also be reached by any number of buses, including the useful #12 and #12/A.

Haydarpaşa station

The waterfront area is adorned by the imposing, Germanic bulk of **Haydarpaşa station**, fronted by the attractive ferry terminal building designed by Vedat Tak in 1913, the architect responsible for the Central Post Office building near Sirkeci station (see p.69). Haydarpaşa station itself was designed by the German architects Otto Ritter and Helmuth Cuno; the historic main line was completed in 1908 as part of Germany's grandiose plans for a Berlin-to-Baghdad railway and presented to Sultan Abdülhamit II as a present by Kaiser Wilhelm II. The palace-like building is an impressive sight as you cross from Europe to Asia by ferry: perched right on the edge of the Bosphorus, it was actually partially built on 1100 pillars sunk into the water.

One feature of the station is its multitude of beautiful stained-glass windows, which suffuse the cavernous interior with soft, pastel-coloured light. Germany's defeat in World War I ensured that the railway never served its intended purpose – linking Germany with the oil fields of the Persian Gulf and its African colonies. Haydarpaşa has been made defunct by the Marmaray project (see p.27) and it will likely become either a hotel or shopping centre.

British Crimean War Cemetery

Daily 7am–7pm • To get here, turn off Tıbbiye Caddesi into Burhan Felek Caddesi, between the university building and the emergency entrance to the GATA military hospital

Situated between the sea and Tıbbiye Caddesi, directly north of Haydarpaşa station, is the Marmara University and the **British Crimean War Cemetery**, a beautifully kept spot maintained by the Commonwealth War Graves Commission. Given as a gift to Britain by the Ottoman authorities at the time of the Crimean War, it is dotted

9

with cypress, plane and ornamental firs and shelters the dead of the Crimean and the two world wars. The largest monument here is an obelisk with four wreath-holding angels at each corner, "raised by Queen Victoria and her people in 1857". The cemetery is in two parts, with the obelisk and various inscribed gravestones in the first, smaller part, and a more extensive graveyard in the larger landscaped area beyond. The Crimean War, which caused the death of most of the soldiers and civilians interred here, was pointless: less than sixty years later, Britain was fighting against, rather than with, the Ottoman Turks and alongside Russia (at least until the Bolshevik Revolution); all of which makes the inscriptions on the gravestones and markers even more poignant.

Florence Nightingale Museum

Kavak Iskele Caddesi • By appointment only, Mon–Fri 9am–5pm • Free • Fax a photocopy of the identity page of your passport, plus your desired visiting date and time, and your telephone number, to the museum's military guardians, several weeks before your intended visit • ☎ 0216 553 1009 or ☎ 0216 310 7929

The imposing **Selimiye Barracks**, whose northwest wing was used as a hospital by the British during the Crimean War (1854–56), today houses the **Florence Nightingale Museum**. Florence Nightingale (see box below) lived and worked in the northern tower, where she reduced the death toll among patients from twenty percent to two percent, and established universally accepted principles of modern nursing. The museum contains two of her famous lamps, and you can see the rooms where she lived and worked. Whether you think it's worth the effort involved to gain access depends on your level of interest in the great woman, especially as you may now need to make your request to visit weeks in advance. Most visitors find the monumental barracks and the whole rigmarole of dealing with the Turkish military (who lead the tour) at least as fascinating as the museum itself.

FLORENCE NIGHTINGALE: THE LADY OF THE LAMP

The **Crimean War**, fought between Russia and the ailing Ottoman Empire and its allies (Britain and France) between 1854 and 1856 was a particularly gruelling one. When news reports reached Britain of the appalling suffering of British troops in the campaign – caused largely by poor living conditions and totally inadequate medical care – public indignation led to a team of nurses, headed by **Florence Nightingale**, being sent to the military hospital at the Selimiye Barracks (see above) in Scutari (modern Üsküdar) on the Asian side of the Bosphorus. Nightingale spotted the connection between bad hygiene and ill health and concentrated mainly on cleaning the wards and medical equipment (such as it was); nevertheless, over four thousand soldiers died in her first winter. Despite her best efforts – she is said to have walked 6km of hospital ward each evening, her famous lamp in hand – her ministrations could not prevent **typhus**, **cholera**, **typhoid** and **dysentery** ripping through the hospital. The following year, the sewers of the hospital were overhauled and better ventilation introduced – massively reducing infection rates. However, ten times more troops died from disease than battle wounds in the Crimean campaign.

A strict Unitarian, Nightingale saw herself as a God-given mission to alleviate suffering. Her dedication revolutionized health care and helped establish the universally accepted principles of modern nursing. She wrote a book on nursing, and in 1860 set up a training school for nurses at St Thomas's Hospital in London. She became a legend in Victorian Britain and was immortalized in Henry Longfellow's poem *Santa Filomena*:

Lo, in that hour of misery
A lady with a lamp I see
Pass through the shimmering gloom
And flit from room to room
Florence Nightingale

Üsküdar

Devout and conservative **Üsküdar** (a corruption of "Scutari" – the name used for what was a separate town in the late Byzantine era), has a completely different character to its rowdy near-neighbour Kadıköy. Since the 1950s, the area has been characterized by wholesale migration from the more Islamic regions of Anatolia and has long been a centre of Islamic mystical sects. There are some fine imperial mosques in and around this (relatively) quiet suburb, plus a lively covered market. Secondhand furniture and ornaments are on offer at the **Üsküdar Bit Pazarı** (flea market) in Büyük Hamam Sokak, and there are also some reasonable jewellery and clothes shops. South along the quayside, in an area known as **Salacak**, are some good pavement cafés and bars, offering fantastic views across to Topkapı Palace and old Istanbul.

Mihrimah Camii
Iskele Meydanı

The most dominant mosque in Üsküdar is **Mihrimah Camii** or **Iskele**, opposite the ferry terminal. It sits on a high platform, fronted by an immense covered porch. Designed by Mimar Sinan for Mihrimah, daughter of Süleyman the Magnificent, and built in 1543–44, this is the only Ottoman mosque with three semi-domes (rather than two or four), a result of the requirements of its problematic site against the hillside behind. It also has an unusual double portico, the first built by Sinan in the city. The mosque is usually open, and the inside is well worth a peek for its particularly light and airy interior, a result of the copious use of arch-shaped stained-glass windows by the architect – particularly apt as Mihrimah means "Sun and Moon" in Persian.

Yeni Valide Camii
Hakimiyet-i Milliye Caddesi

The **Yeni Valide Camii** was built between 1708 and 1710 by Ahmet III in honour of his mother. The mosque is most easily identified by the valide sultan's green, birdcage-like tomb, whose meshed roof was designed to keep birds out while allowing rain in to water the garden below (now rather untidily overgrown). There's an attractive *şadırvan* (ablutions fountain) in the courtyard; the grilles of its cistern are highly wrought, their complex geometric pattern echoed in the stone carvings above them. The mosque is generally left open.

Çinili Camii and around
Cavuşdere Caddesi • Both mosque and *hamam* are best reached by a taxi from the waterfront (around ₺8)

One of the most attractive mosques in Üsküdar is the **Çinili Camii**, or Tiled Mosque. Dating from 1640, it's set in a pleasant, tree-shaded courtyard, but you will need to find the caretaker to open up the mosque itself. The tiles are mainly blue and turquoise, but there's a rare shade of green to be found in the *mihrab*. Below the mosque, in the same street, is the beautifully restored **Çinili Hamamı** (see p.228), which retains its original central marble *göbek taşı* (literally "navel stone") where massages are performed against a backdrop of the original marble revetment panels covering the walls.

Atık Valide Külliyesi
Valide Külliyesi Sokak

Dating from 1583, the **Atık Valide Külliyesi** mosque is a work of the master architect Mimar Sinan (see box, p.82). Built for Nur Banu, wife of Selim II and mother of Murat III, its name means "Old Mosque of the Sultan's Mother". The mosque's courtyard, surrounding an attractive *şadırvan*, is a colonnaded gem, unusual in that it contains a (very popular) teahouse. Worth inspecting inside the mosque are the wooden galleries that run around three sides of the prayer hall's interior, which are beautifully painted, and the İznik tiles, from western Anatolia, covering the *mihrab*.

Şemsi Paşa Camii
Paşa Lima Caddesi

The **Şemsi Paşa Camii**, beautifully situated on the waterfront looking across the Bosphorus to the skyline of the old city, rivals Örtaköy's Mecidiye Camii (see p.137) as the mosque with the most picturesque situation in the city. Built in 1580 and designed by the great Sinan, it's considerably older than the Mecidiye. Its simple, domed structure looks glorious when seen from the water; it has been beautifully restored both inside and out. The mosque may be locked outside of prayer times but there is usually someone around to open it for visitors.

Maiden's Tower
Museum Tues–Sun noon–7pm • Free • **Restaurant** Daily 7.30pm–1am • **Tower** Boats from Salacak (on the main coast road between Üsküdar and Harem) daily 9am–6.45pm (₺20) • A private boat service operates for those who are eating and/or drinking at the tower from 8.30pm–12.30am; ⓦ kizkulesi.com.tr

To the south of Üsküdar, on an island in the Bosphorus, is the small, white **Maiden's Tower** (Kız Kulesi), also known as Leander's Tower. The first tower was built by the Athenian commander Alcibiades in the fifth century BC to help tax and control ships passing through the Bosphorus. In the Byzantine period, a chain was stretched between it and another tower on the historic peninsula, to better ensure passing ships paid their dues, and it wasn't until the Ottoman era that it began to be used as a lighthouse. Several myths are associated with it: in one, a princess, who was prophesied to die from a snake bite, came there to escape her fate, only to succumb to it when a serpent was delivered to her retreat in a basket of fruit. The tower also featured in the 1999 James Bond film, *The World Is Not Enough*. It's worth visiting on a good day for the panoramic views up and down the Bosphorus and across to both the European and Asian sides of the city from the tower. In the evening, the tower functions as an average but expensive restaurant – dining here is all about the location rather than the food.

RUMELİ HİSAR FORTRESS, ABOVE THE BOSPHORUS

The Bosphorus and the Black Sea resorts

One of the world's most eulogized stretches of water, the 31km-long Bosphorus Strait divides Europe from Asia and connects the Marmara and Black seas. The name derives from the Greek myth of Io, lover of the god Zeus, who transformed her into a cow to conceal her from his jealous wife Hera. She plunged into the strait to escape a gadfly – hence Bosphorus, or "Ford of the Cow". The strait's width varies from 698m to 4.7km, and its depth from 30m to 110m. Around 55,000 cargo ships, oil tankers and ocean liners pass through the strait each year; for residents and visitors alike, the Bosphorus remains Istanbul's most important transport artery.

The passenger ferries and sea buses that weave their way up and down from shore to shore provide one of Istanbul's real highlights: along the way are imperial palaces, waterside mansions known as *yalı*s (see box, p.149) and ancient fortresses interspersed with affluent waterfront suburbs, which become increasingly more like real villages the further north you head.

Further away from the city are the beach resorts on the **Black Sea**. The former Greek fishing village of **Kilyos**, on the European side of the Bosphorus, has been overdeveloped but boasts a thriving summer beach-bar-club scene. **Şile**, equally built-up, is more laidback and enjoys a cliff-top location and white sandy beaches.

10

ARRIVAL AND GETTING AROUND

By bus To get more of a feel for the suburbs and villages themselves, hop on one of the buses that run back and forth on either side of the strait.

By ferry You can tour the strait by catching one of the ferries that ply the waters from Eminönü as far up as Anadolu Kavağı (European side), or from Çengelköy up to İstinye (Asian side). Timetables (*vapur seferler*) are available from ferry terminals and tourist offices, though most visitors prefer the ease of the various Bosphorus cruises (see box below).

The European Shore

The **European Shore** is built up as far as Emirgan; the so-called Bosphorus villages of Kuruçeşme, Arnavutköy and Bebek are little more than suburbs of the city, whatever their predominantly wealthy residents may wish to believe. The former fishing villages of **Arnavutköy** and **Bebek** are still attractive, but the simple waterside *meyhane*s and cafés of old have been replaced by swanky fish restaurants and bistros catering to the elite. Further north is the spectacular Ottoman-era fortress of **Rumeli**

THE BOSPHORUS CRUISE

Taking a boat trip up the Bosphorus from the bustling quays of Eminönü to the quiet fishing village of Anadolu Kavağı is one of the most pleasant Istanbul experiences you could have. The **Bosphorus Cruise**, run by the Şehir Hatları company (see p.28), leaves from Eminönü's Boğaz ferry terminal just east of the Galata Bridge (daily 10.35am, May–Sept also at 1.35pm and in mid-summer also at noon; one way ₺15, round trip ₺25). The journey to the furthest point of the cruise, Anadolu Kavağı (Asia), takes just over an hour and a half, with **stops** en route at Beşiktaş, Kanlıca (Asia), Sarıyer and Rumeli Kavağı (both Europe). There is a near three-hour lunch and exploration stop at the inevitably tourist-thronged Anadolu Kavağı (see p.156). Boats return at 3pm year-round, stopping only at Beşiktaş; May to September, there's an additional boat at either 5 or 6pm. It's possible to leave the cruise at any landing to explore the waterfront or hinterland and return to the city centre by bus, though very few people do.

In summer, especially at weekends, the queues to buy **tickets** can be very long, so give yourself at least half an hour to make your purchase – or, better still, buy your ticket a day or two in advance. There are also often long queues to board, so latecomers will find themselves sat in the worst seats. The ferries are rather antiquated but comfortable enough, and you can buy snacks, sandwiches and drinks.

Running between mid-June and mid-September only, a Şehir Hatları **night-time cruise** (₺20) makes an alternative and attractive option, with the great suspension bridges lit up like Christmas trees and the lights of Asia and Europe twinkling on either side. The boat departs Eminönü's Boğaz ferry terminal at 7pm, reaching Anadolu Kavağı at 8.30pm, where it moors for dinner, before arriving back in Eminönü around midnight.

A **shorter cruise** is also available from Eminönü costing ₺10. The ferry goes as far as the second (Fatih) bridge, taking around two hours for the round trip. Ferries leave at 2.30pm (daily April–Oct; Sun & public holidays only Nov–March).

The Turyol company (see p.28) also runs short tours to the second bridge, with departures every hour on the hour Mon–Sat, more frequently on Sundays. Tickets cost ₺12 for the ninety-minute round trip.

Hisarı and, just south of it, the unusual **Borusan Contemporary** gallery. Continuing north past the second Bosphorus suspension bridge, **Emirgan** boasts the **Sakıp Sabancı Museum**, which hosts major touring exhibitions of world-class art, and beautiful **Emirgan Parkı**. Beyond this, the major attractions are **Sadberk Hanım Museum**; the fishing village of **Rumeli Kavağı**, the furthest point of the Bosphorus Cruise; and, west of Sariyer, **Belgrade Forest**, a weekend haven for Istanbulites escaping the bustling city.

GETTING AROUND   THE EUROPEAN SHORE

By metro You can also take the M2 Metro from Yenikapı (old city), Şişhane or Taksim to the Hacıosman Metro stop in Sariyer, then the #25/A bus to Rumeli Kavağı. The last

#25/A back to Sariyer leaves at 9.30pm, from where you can catch the M2 Metro or a bus back to Taksim/Şişhane.
By bus The #22 and #22/RE buses run from the T1 tram

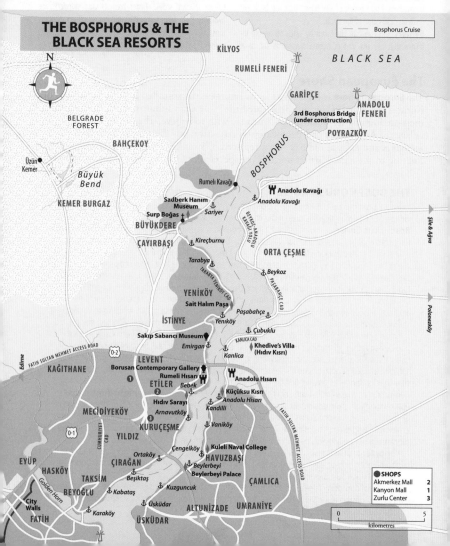

terminus at Kabataş as far as Emirgan, the #25/E onto Sariyer. From Taksim the #25/T, #40, #40/T and #42/T go to Sariyer, from where there are plenty of dolmuşes or the #25/A bus on to Rumeli Kavağı.

By ferry Şehir Hatları (see p.28) ferries run between some of the Bosphorus suburbs, both on the European and Asian shores, but making the right connections is tricky. Consult their timetables.

Kuruçeşme

From Ortaköy, the coast road runs north under the 1.5km Bosphorus Bridge, the first of two intercontinental bridges that span the strait. **Kuruçeşme** (Dry Spring) is home to the Türkcell Kuruçeşme Arena, a waterside music venue hosting major Turkish and foreign acts. The **Cemil Topuzlu Parkı**, slightly to the south, is a small but pleasantly landscaped waterfront park. Offshore is **Galatasaray Island**, a floating pontoon owned by the famous football club (see p.226); accessed by a free ferry service, it boasts an Olympic-sized swimming pool, cafés, restaurants, a nightclub and great Bosphorus views.

Arnavutköy

Merging into Kuruçeşme, **Arnavutköy** is one of the most beautiful of the Bosphorus suburbs, especially when seen from the water, and is famous for its line of *yalı*s, wooden waterfront mansions (see box below). In the pretty backstreets above the main drag are the ruins of a synagogue, while a little to the east is the imposing bulk of the nineteenth-century Greek Orthodox **Ayos Taksiarches** (Church of the Taxiarch), which hosts an *ayazma* (sacred spring) in a nearby chapel.

Bebek and around

Bebek (Turkish for "baby") is the beginning of real wealth on the Bosphorus, and the suburbs from here to Sariyer are home to some of the most impressive Bosphorus *yalı*s. The fifteen-minute walk from Arnavutköy follows an attractive park-fringed (but shadeless), waterfront promenade, popular with swimming children, fishermen and sunbathing pensioners. En route, before you reach the ferry terminal, you'll pass Bebek's most famous building, the Khedive Palace (**Hıdıv Sarayı**), an Art Nouveau-style mansion belonging to the Egyptian consulate, built in 1907.

YALIS

Istanbul's billionaire elite may choose to live in luxury penthouse apartments, but in Ottoman times the place to be – at least in summer – was a **yalı**, a wooden mansion, right on the shores of the Bosphorus. These sumptuous two- or three-storey villas boasted manicured lawns peppered with rose beds and trees planted to provide shade, sloping down to the water's edge. Caïques bringing residents and guests to the *yalı* were moored in an opening right under the house. Inside, the mansions were separated into the *haremlık*, used by women and family members only, and the *selamlık*, usually an all-male preserve where guests were entertained. There was also a *hamam*, a kitchen area and, of course, servants' quarters.

Most *yalı*s (from the Greek word for "coast") have not survived the vicissitudes of time, succumbing to fire, storm damage or wayward shipping. Those that remain are reminders of a less industrialized age when sailing boats rather than super-tankers drifted along the Bosphorus. There are some good examples on the European Shore in Arnavutköy and north of İstinye (look out for the palatial **Ahmet Atıf Paşa Yalı** near Yeniköy). But the best are on the Asian side, from slightly south of the Bosphorus Bridge right up to Beykoz; the dilapidated **Amcazade Hüseyin Paşa Yalısı**, just shy of the Fatih Bridge, is the oldest *yalı* on the Bosphorus. All are subject to preservation orders; and if you should be wealthy enough to think about buying one, be warned – the bureaucracy involved in restoration is positively (and perhaps appropriately) Byzantine.

10

Borusan Contemporary

Perili Köşk • Hisar Cad 5 • Sat & Sun 10am–8pm • ₺10 • ☎ 39352000, ⊛ borusancontemporary.com • Buses #40 and #40/T from Taksim, #22, #22/RE and #25/E from Kabataş

The cutting-edge contemporary arts centre **Borusan Contemporary** is intriguing for more than just its exhibits. On weekdays, the centre operates as the headquarters of Borusan Holdings, one of Turkey's wealthiest companies, its employees leaving their workplace uncannily tidy for weekend culture lovers. The building itself has an eerie history. Begun in 1910 as the Yusuf Ziya Paşa Köşkü, work on it stalled during World War I. Locals claimed to have heard weird noises emanating from the empty, ten-storey brick-built mansion and began to call it by the name it's still known by today, the Perili Köşk ("Haunted Mansion"). Permanent works on display include those by painter Jerry Zenluk, sculptor Keith Sonnier and photographer Robert Mapplethorpe. From the flat roof there are dramatic views over the Bosphorus, the Fatih suspension bridge and the fortress of Rumeli Hisarı.

Rumeli Hisarı

Yahya Kemal Caddesi, Rumeli Hisarı • Daily except Wed 9.30am–4.30pm • ₺3 • Buses #40 and #40/T from Taksim, #22, #22/RE and #25/E from Kabataş

The impressive fortress of **Rumeli Hisarı** is dramatically situated in the shadow of the first Bosphorus (Fatih) bridge. Grander than its counterpart, Anadolu Hisarı, across the strait (see p.154), this Ottoman fortress was constructed in four months in 1452. Its purpose was to prevent besieged Constantinople receiving military aid and supplies from the Black Sea – hence its original name of Boğaz-kesen or "the throat [strait] cutter". The two fortifications played an important role in the eventual fall of the city in May 1453 by cutting off the supply lines to the beleaguered Byzantine inhabitants.

Rumeli Hisarı is an extremely impressive fort, comprising three major and three smaller towers, linked by curtain walls, and is spectacularly sited on twin hilltops. It is said to have been constructed in the shape of the name of the prophet Muhammad. There's little to see inside but the views are grand – though take great care with children as there are no guard-rails on the steps or parapet walkways. Completed in 1988, the nearby Fatih Bridge, the second to be built across the strait, is among the world's longest suspension bridges (1090m), and spans the Bosphorus at the point where King Darius of Persia crossed the straits by pontoon bridge in 512 BC (see box, p.278).

Emirgan

Before the opening of the Sakıp Sabancı Museum (see below), the leafy suburb of Emirgan was best known for its beautiful park, the **Emirgan Parkı** (daily 8am–5pm). Its immaculately landscaped gardens make it the most appealing park in the city. Young kids will love its fairy-tale, Swiss chalet-style wooden *köşk*s (one painted pink, one white, the third yellow and white), artificial lake and waterfall, and playground; adults will appreciate the swathe of green grass and stands of mature trees for shade. The *köşk*s have decent cafés or, for a cheaper snack, buy a *gözleme* (a cheese or spiced-potato, *paratha*-style bread) from the stand at the entrance.

Sakıp Sabancı Museum

Sakıp Sabancı Cad 42, Emirgan • Tues, Fri, Sat & Sun 10am–6pm, Wed 10am–8pm • ₺15 • ⊛ muze.sabanciuniv.edu • Buses #40 and #40/T from Taksim, #22, #22/RE and #25/E from Kabataş

Set in gorgeous landscaped gardens just behind the waterfront, in a beautiful 1920s villa known as the Atlı Köşkü, **Sakıp Sabancı Museum** plays host to major international exhibitions, which have included artists as diverse as Picasso, Dalí and Anish Kapoor. Permanently on display are some exquisite examples of Ottoman calligraphy, including some beautiful Korans, while a modern glass-and-steel extension to the building features Turkish artists of the late nineteenth and early twentieth centuries. The Sakıp Sabancı is also the home of the stylish *Müzedechanga* (see p.191), the new incarnation of the now-closed *Changa* restaurant in Beyoğlu.

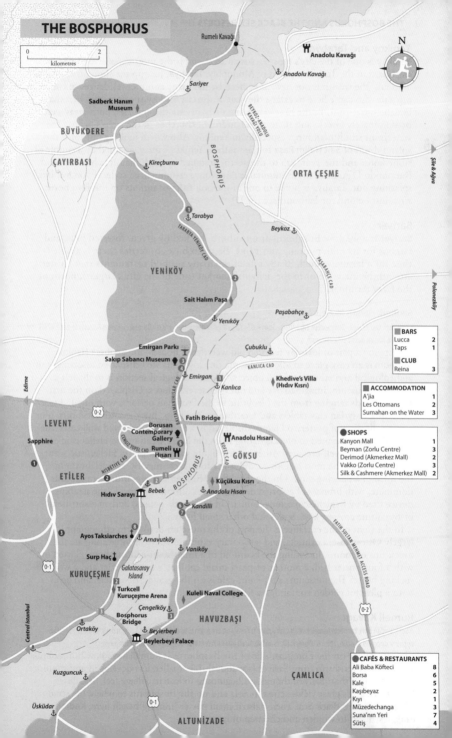

THE BOSPHORUS

0 ——— 2
kilometres

N

Rumeli Kavağı ⚓

♜ Anadolu Kavağı
⚓ Anadolu Kavağı

BEYKOZ-ANADOLU KAVAĞI YOLU

Sarıyer ⚓

Sadberk Hanım Museum ⚓

BÜYÜKDERE

ÇAYIRBAŞI

BOSPHORUS

ORTA ÇEŞME

Kireçburnu ⚓

Şile & Ağva ▶

Beykoz ⚓

TARABYA YENIKÖY CAD

Tarabya ⚓ 1

YENİKÖY

PAŞABAHÇE CAD

2

Sait Halım Paşa ♦

Paşabahçe ⚓

Polonezköy ▶

Yeniköy ⚓

BALTALİMANIHİSAR CAD

Çubuklu ⚓

KANLICA CAD

Emirgan Parkı ♦
Sakıp Sabancı Museum ♦ 3
4

Khedive's Villa (Hıdıv Kısrı)

Edirne

Emirgan ⚓ 1
⚓ Kanlıca

(0-2)

LEVENT

Borusan Contemporary Gallery ●
Rumeli Hısarı ♜ 5

CENGİZ TOPEL CAD

Fatih Bridge

♜ Anadolu Hısarı

GÖKSU

KOZ CAD

Sapphire ●
1

NİSBETİYE CAD

ETİLER

Küçüksu Kısrı ⚓

BOSPHORUS

2 1

Hıdıv Sarayı 🏛
Bebek ⚓

⚓ Anadolu Hısarı

FATİH SULTAN MEHMET ACCESS ROAD

6 ⚓ Kandilli
7

3 ●
Ayos Taksiarches ●
⚓ Arnavutköy

8

Surp Haç ♦

⚓ Vaniköy

Galatasaray Island

KURUÇEŞME

Kuleli Naval College

Turkcell Kuruçeşme Arena
Bosphorus Bridge

Çengelköy ⚓
3

Central İstanbul

HAVUZBAŞI

(0-2)

1
⚓ Ortaköy

♦ Beylerbeyi
🏛 Beylerbeyi Palace

Kuzguncuk ⚓

ÇAMLICA

(0-1)

Üsküdar ⚓

ALTUNİZADE

10

Yeniköy and Tarabya

Yeniköy is one of the city's most exclusive areas and is the most expensive square on the board in the Turkish version of Monopoly. **Tarabya**, just up the shore, is almost as affluent. The wealth is not new, as evinced by the many summer residences of consular officials who came here to escape the heat of the city and by the gorgeous *yalı*s that dot the waterfront. In the nineteenth and early twentieth centuries, both areas were predominately Greek, and there are a handful of **churches** in the streets behind the waterfront still functioning, especially in Yeniköy. Also worth looking out for is the splendid *yalı* of **Sait Halim Paşa** to the south of Yeniköy's quay, guarded by a couple of stone lions, and the Twin Yalı to the north, designed by Abdülhamit's chief architect, Raimondo D'Aranco, in his inimitable Art Nouveau-influenced style. If you feel like splashing out, Tarabya is home to one of the best **fish restaurants** on the Bosphorus, *Kıyı*, just behind the harbour (see p.191).

Sariyer

Sariyer is a wealthy Bosphorus-front suburb, backed by green, forested hills, and famous for its milk pudding and *börek*. Between buses or ferries there is ample time for a leisurely lunch in any one of the many seafood **restaurants** that cluster around the quayside or in the daily **fish market** (one of the city's largest), north of the ferry terminal.

Sadberk Hanım Museum

Büyükdere Cad 27–29 • Daily except Wed 10am–5pm • ₺7 • ⓦ sadberkhanimmuzesi.org.tr • Buses #25/E from Kabataş and the #25/T and #40 from Taksim pass by the museum

Occupying a pair of lovingly restored old waterfront houses, the **Sadberk Hanım Museum** is an easy place to idle away some time, with its well-displayed assortment of archeological and ethnographical objects. The archeological section is to the left as you enter the museum, imaginatively laid out over several floors. Displayed on the first floor are finds ranging from the Neolithic to the Phrygian periods, with highlights including Assyrian clay tablets and Urartian bronze belts, buckles and horse-bits, plus a fine collection of pottery oil lamps displayed in a vertically mounted wall case. The second floor is devoted to objects dating from the Mycenaean to the Hellenistic eras, including some well-executed Athenian red-figure vases and pretty Hellenistic scent bottles, though the most arresting exhibit is a fourth-century BC candelabrum in the form of a dancing satyr. On the third floor, Roman and Byzantine-era exhibits dominate, with bronzes of assorted deities, a fine collection of *strigil* (the scraping device used by hygiene-conscious Romans in their bath-houses) and an assortment of Byzantine crosses, keys, scales and other small finds.

To the right of the entrance is the part of the museum devoted to ethnographic, largely Ottoman-era exhibits, and temporary exhibitions. Most interesting are the mock-ups of rooms, including the bedroom of a nineteenth-century home, kitted out with a four-poster bed, a mother-of-pearl-inlaid cabinet, a brass brazier and a wooden rocking horse. The museum's shop-cum-café is on the ground floor here, and gives onto a pleasant garden containing a few pieces of statuary.

Rumeli Kavağı

A Şehir Hatları ferry connects Rumeli Kavağı with Anadolu Kavağı on the Asian side at 8.10am and 3.50pm daily, with ferries in the opposite direction at noon, 2pm, 6.05pm, 7.10pm and 8pm, all of which continue down the Bosphorus to Sariyer

The last village on the European side of the Bosphorus is **Rumeli Kavağı**, a 2km dolmuş ride or short ferry trip from Sariyer (see above). It's smaller, less developed and more down to earth than Sariyer, though it's beginning to lose its village feel. The quiet waterfront gives great views across to Asia and up the Bosphorus to where the strait merges with the Black Sea. There's also a small pay swimming **beach** here, **Kadınları Plajı**, restricted to women and children only.

Belgrade Forest

Most easily reached by car; by public transport, take #25/E bus from Kabataş to Büyükdere and then a dolmuş to the village of Bahçeköy, on the east side of the forest – from here it's a 1.5km walk to Büyük Bend reservoir

Several kilometres west of Büyükdere, an anonymous suburb astride the main road between Beşiktaş and Sariyer in the İstranca hills, lies **Belgrade Forest** (Belgrad Ormanı), originally a hunting preserve of the Ottomans. The pine, oak and beech forest is now a popular retreat from the rigours of the city.

A sophisticated system of dams, reservoirs, water towers and aqueducts is still in evidence around the forest, which supplied Istanbul with most of its fresh water during the Byzantine and Ottoman eras. The most impressive of the aqueducts is the *Uzun* or **Long Aqueduct**, a 1km walk south of Büyük Bend dam (one of seven dams in the forest). Its tiers of tall, pointed arches were built by Sinan for Süleyman the Magnificent in 1563. Close to the reservoir are the remains of Belgrade village, whose name came about after the capture of Belgrade in 1521, when a community of Serbian POWs were settled here to take over the upkeep of the water-supply system.

10

The Asian Shore

On the **Asian Shore**, a number of once-small villages have merged into a great suburb stretching all the way up from Üsküdar to the second Bosphorus bridge. Still quite attractive despite the urban sprawl, these former fishing villages hold a few surprises, from the waterfront nineteenth-century **Beylerbeyi Palace** and the Ottoman fortress **Anadolu Hisarı**, to the **Hıdıv Kısrı**, a beautiful nineteenth-century villa set in a pleasant park, and the shell of a **Byzantine fortress** at Anadolu Kavağı.

GETTING AROUND   **THE ASIAN SHORE**

By bus The #15 runs all along the Bosphorus shore from Üsküdar's main square as far as Beykoz. From Kadıköy to Beykoz, catch the #15/BK and #15/F; to reach Anadolu Kavağı from here, take the #15/A.

By ferry Şehir Hatları ferries (see p.28) run between some of the Bosphorus suburbs, both on the European and Asian shores, but making the right connections is tricky. Consult their timetables.

Beylerbeyi Palace

Abdullah Aga Caddesi • Tues, Wed & Fri–Sun 8.30am–5pm • ₺20 • Bus #15 or #15/B from Üsküdar

The main attraction of **Beylerbeyi**, on the north side of the Bosphorus Bridge, is the **Beylerbeyi Palace**, a nineteenth-century, white-marble summer residence and

---

A SECOND BOSPHORUS

In the spring of 2011, plans were announced for a grandiose scheme to build a new Bosphorus channel, **Canal Istanbul**, to the west of the metropolis. The work is to be completed by 2023 to coincide with the one hundredth anniversary of the foundation of the Turkish Republic. The advantages are obvious: the "original" Bosphorus would be freed from the dangerous tankers crowding the strait, leading to a safer city for residents and visitors alike, easing the city's over-burdened transport infrastructure and thus a boon to tourism. Critics, however, point out that the project will be unfeasibly expensive, especially as by the terms of the Montreux Convention of 1936 merchant and passenger ships can use the Bosphorus both freely and without a toll, meaning the new mega-canal will almost certainly have to provide free passage.

Construction of a controversial **third Bosphorus bridge** began in 2013 despite much opposition, suggesting the government may get their way with the canal project. The government claim it is necessary to reduce traffic congestion, while opponents are convinced it will not only lead to more traffic in the city, but will also destroy Istanbul's last major green area, as the forest and wetlands around the bridge will inevitably be developed for housing and industry. Even the name of the bridge, the Yavuz Sultan Selim, caused an outcry as the sultan after whom it is named was responsible for massacring tens of thousands of Anatolian Alevis in1514 (see box, p.93).

guesthouse of the Ottoman sultans. The palace was much admired by contemporary visitors from Europe – after her stay in 1869, Empress Eugénie had its windows copied in the Tuileries Palace in Paris. The interior decoration was designed by Sultan Abdülaziz himself, while some of the furniture, including the matching dining chairs in the *harem* and the *selamlık*, was carved by Sultan Abdülhamit II during his six years of imprisonment here, up to his death in 1918. The central staircase, with its fanciful twisting shape, is perhaps the highlight, but there are all kinds of details to savour, from the neo-Islamic patterns on the ceilings down to the beautiful Egyptian *hasır* (the reed matting on the floor). The pleasant café in the gardens is a very popular weekend breakfast spot.

Çengelköy
Bus #15 from Üsküdar

The pretty village suburb of **Çengelköy** is a short walk from Beylerbeyi. Its main landmark building, the **Kuleli Naval College**, once served as a hospital under the direction of Florence Nightingale in the Crimean War, though it's currently closed to the public. There's little of interest here apart from the boutique hotel *Sumahan on the Water* (see p.174), housed in an old *rakı* distillery, and its very stylish restaurant.

Küçüksu Kasrı
Tues, Wed & Fri–Sun 9.30am–4pm • ₺5 • Bus #15 from Çengelköy – after passing a boatyard to your left, cross a bridge over the Küçüksu Deresi; get off at the next stop, walk back to the sign saying "Küçük Saray Aile Bahçesi" and you'll find the palace at the end of a drive

Küçüksu Kasrı, sometimes known as Göksu Palace, takes both its names from the two nearby streams that empty into the Bosphorus. Built in 1857 by Nikoğos Balian, son of the architect of Dolmabahçe Palace, its exterior is highly ornate – the Rococo carving is best seen from the Bosphorus, the intended approach. The whole of the palace interior is decorated with lace and carpets from Hereke and lit by Bohemian crystal chandeliers. The floors are mahogany, inlaid with rose- and almond-wood and ebony; upstairs is an ebony table on which Sultan Abdülaziz was wont to arm-wrestle with visitors of state. The palace was constructed on the site of several earlier incarnations, and the fountain from one of these still stands, a fine example of Ottoman Baroque, built in 1796.

Anadolu Hisarı
Bus #15 from Üsküdar

The **Küçüksu Deresi** and the **Göksu** are the streams formerly known to Europeans as the "Sweet Waters of Asia", their banks once graced by picnicking parties of Ottoman nobility. On the north bank of the Göksu stands the Ottoman fortress of **Anadolu Hisarı** (open 24hr; free), beneath the towering Fatih Bridge. It was built by Beyazıt I in 1397, when the Ottoman forces first reached the strait separating Asia from Europe. Along with the more recent Rumeli Hisar fortress opposite (see p.150) the castle could effectively cut off the strait to unwanted shipping. Apart from its fine position, it's of little real interest except to castle-buffs.

Kanlıca
Bus #15 from Üsküdar

Backed by verdant forest, the attractive suburb of **Kanlıca** is famed for its **yoghurt**, which can be eaten at any of the little quayside restaurants – try the cheap and cheerful *Asırlık*, by the ferry landing, housed in an old wooden building with a veranda giving right onto the Bosphorus. Alternatively, the *A'jia* **hotel** (see p.173), in a delightful *yalı* at Çubuklu Cad 27 (see box, p.149), has a considerably more upmarket **restaurant**.

On the top of a hill, a twenty-minute walk behind the waterfront, is the wonderful **Khedive's Villa** (Hıdıv Kısrı) built for Abbas Hilmi Paşa, the last Khedive (the title given to governors of Egypt in Ottoman times), in 1900. It's an eclectic architectural mix, but look out for the Art Nouveau metalwork on the steam-powered lift and the gorgous stained-glass ceiling lights in the central tower. The building is now a restaurant and is surrounded by a beautifully maintained park with a café, both offering superb views over the Bosphorus.

10

Anadolu Kavağı

Bus #15 from Üsküdar to Beykoz; from there, take the #15/A

The last call on the Bosphorus Cruise from Eminönü (see box, p.147) is laidback **Anadolu Kavağı**. The village has a distinct, if dilapidated, charm – balconied houses with boat-mooring stations overlook the river, while the main street is lined with some reasonable **fish restaurants**. All offer fixed-menu meals aimed squarely at the Bosphorus cruisers, most of whom are captive prey for the three hours the boat docks here. A couple of decent options are the family-run *Ceneviz*, housed in an old building that once served as the village's *kahvehane* (teahouse), and the *Coskun Balıkçı*, set in an old wooden house, though neither are licensed for alcohol.

Sprawling across an overgrown hilltop above the town is the Byzantine **fortress** from which the village takes its name. With its typical Byzantine masonry of alternating bands of pale stone and red brick and D-shaped towers, it's an impressive sight and was once of supreme strategic importance as guardian of the strait. The views from the top over the Bosphorus are superb. To get to the fortress, follow Mirşah Hamam Sokak from the dock and walk uphill for half an hour.

The Black Sea resorts

The **Black Sea** is relatively accessible from Istanbul, and if you're staying in the city for any length of time over the summer, its seaside villages may exert a considerable pull. Bear in mind, however, that it takes up to two hours to reach Şile (not counting getting to the departure point, Üsküdar, on the Asian side of the Bosphorus), and not much less to reach Kilyos.

Kilyos

There's little of historical interest in **Kilyos**, the nearest resort to Istanbul on the European side of the Bosphorus. The former Greek fishing village has sadly succumbed to a tide of holiday-home development, the beach is crowded, and the area's most imposing monument, a medieval Genoese castle, is occupied by the Turkish army and off-limits. If beach sports are your thing, however, there are a couple of private **beaches**, which offer assorted entertainment as well as loungers and umbrellas (see below).

ARRIVAL   **KİLYOS**

By metro and bus From the city centre, take the M2 Metro from Şişhane or Taksim to the Haciosman Metro stop. From here, bus #151 runs to Kilyos and Demirciköy from 6am to 9.30pm, with the last bus returning weekdays at 10.40pm, weekends at 10.20pm. The journey takes around 45min.

BEACHES

Dalia 2km from Kilyos in the village of Demirciköy. ☎ 0212 204 0368, ⓦ clubdalia.com. The low-key Dalia is a more relaxing option than Solar Beach, though it still offers various watersports. Mon–Fri ₺25, Sat & Sun ₺40. June–Sept daily 8am–6pm.

Solar Beach ☎ 0212 201 2101, ⓦ solarbeach.com.tr. Offers activities ranging from beach volleyball tournaments and bungee jumping to skateboarding and hovercrafting; it also hosts the Electronica Festival every June. Mon–Fri ₺30, Sat & Sun ₺45. June–Sept daily 8am–7pm.

Şile

The construction of a major road linking **Şile** to the suburbs of Asian Istanbul has led to increased development; some live in Şile and commute into the city, others are Istanbulites who have a weekend summerhouse in the town. Out of season, it's easy to see Şile's attraction, perched on a clifftop overlooking a large bay and a tiny island, with white sandy **beaches** stretching off to the west, but it gets very crowded in the summer, especially at weekends when hordes of visitors pour in from stiflingly hot Istanbul. Beaches apart, there's little to occupy you here except to admire the pretty French-built black-and-white-striped **lighthouse** and the fourteenth-century **Genoese castle** on a nearby island – though neither is open to the public. To reach the seafront from the bus station, head down the attractively cobbled Üsküdar Caddesi, a street lined with cafés and bars. At the end of the street, with fine views over the harbour and pretty rock formations below, is the *Panorama Restaurant*, a good bet for a reasonably priced fish meal.

Şile's main historical claim to fame is that it was visited by Xenophon and his Ten Thousand, the army that was left leaderless when its officers were all slain by the Persians. They stayed in Şile, then known as Kalpe; in his memoirs, Xenophon noted how well the site suited the establishment of a city.

10

ARRIVAL   ŞILE

By bus Several buses depart daily for Şile from a stop behind the waterfront mosque Şemsih Paşa Camii in Üsküdar. The Şile Ekspres departs at 11.30am and 5.20pm, returning at 5.40pm and 7.20pm. The slower #139 has ten departures daily between 6.30am and 10pm, with the last bus back from Şile at 7pm. In summer, especially at weekends, seats are at a premium for late-afternoon/evening returns, so it's best to book your seat back on arrival; otherwise, you risk waiting around or even getting stranded overnight.

The Princes' Islands

The Princes' Islands, situated in the Sea of Marmara some fifteen kilometres southeast of the city and just a few kilometres off the Asian landmass, have always been a favourite retreat for Istanbulites. Four of the nine islands are easily accessible by ferry from Istanbul, the nearest taking only 35 minutes by sea bus. Predictably enough, this makes them very popular – the number of visitors has risen from six million per year in 2005 to a whopping ten million in 2010 – so they're hardly unspoilt island retreats. Head out around the coast or, even better, inland, and you'll soon escape the crowds.

Apart from the odd utility vehicle, no cars are allowed on the islands; their place is taken by four-person horse-drawn carriages known as phaetons (*fayton* in Turkish). Bicycling is very popular and an ideal way to get around these small islands, with rental bikes available at every ferry terminal – alternatively, as distances are generally short, you can explore on foot. There are plenty of (mainly pay) beaches, making them the city's best option for a day's sunbathing and swimming. The islands' are an easy day-trip from Istanbul – many come just to enjoy the bargain-priced boat and, once on the islands, do little more than mill around the cafés and restaurants at the ferry landing points. But to fully appreciate their laidback charm it's worth staying over (see p.174).

Brief history

The islands have been inhabited since Classical times, but their first claim to fame derived from the copper mines of **Chalkitis** – modern Heybeliada – long since exhausted (but still visible near Çam Limanı). In the Byzantine era, numerous convents and monasteries were built on the islands and these became favoured – because of their proximity to the capital and ease of surveillance – as **prisons** for banished emperors, empresses and princes. (They were often blinded first, both to prevent their escape and to ruin any future bids for power, as Byzantine custom dictated that an emperor must not be physically disfigured.) After the Conquest in 1453 (see pp.284–285), the islands were largely neglected by the Ottoman Turks and became a place of refuge for Greek, Armenian and Jewish communities.

In 1846, a ferry service was established and the islands became popular with Pera's wealthy merchants and bankers, mainly from the Christian and Jewish minorities, and it is their ornate wooden villas that give the islands their defining character. It wasn't until the early years of the Republic, however, that they became Istanbul's favourite **summer resort**. Mosques began to appear in the villages, and hotels and apartment buildings soon followed. A Turkish naval college was established on Heybeliada, and the islands received the rubber stamp of Republican respectability when Atatürk's huge private yacht, the *MV Savarona*, was moored here as a training ship for naval officers; it's still here and there are plans for it to be turned into a museum.

Sivriada, which is uninhabited and cannot be visited, gained public notoriety in 1911 when all the stray dogs in Istanbul were rounded up, shipped out there and left to starve; while Yassıada is best known for its history as a prison island, used by the Byzantines in the eleventh century for the detention of political dissenters. The trial of Prime Minister Adnan Menderes and two of his former ministers took place there in 1961, following a military coup, and he was hanged shortly afterwards (see p.296).

ARRIVAL

The Princes' Islands are easy to reach, but get to the ferry at least an hour before departure in summer, especially on Sundays, as the queues can be massive. Having a topped-up Istanbulkart (see box, p.25) will save you having to queue for a ticket but won't guarantee you a seat, so it's still best to arrive early.

By ferry Şehir Hatları ferries run from the Adalar ferry terminal in Kabataş (handily placed beyond Beşiktaş at the end of the tram line) to the main islands of Kınalıada, Burgazada, Heybeliada and, lastly, Büyükada (June 20–Sept 18, 15 daily 6.50am–midnight; Sept 21–June 19, 9 daily 6.50am–10.30pm; ₺5, ₺3.5 with an Istanbulkart). It takes around fifty min to reach Kınalıada, and about ninety to Büyükada. The last ferry back from Büyükada departs at 11.40pm weekdays, 9.50pm weekends. Ferry times do change – consult Şehir Hatları timetables (see p.28) before travelling. Several smaller private companies, such as Mavi Marmara and Dentur Avrasya, also operate boats from Kabataş to the islands. They use smaller boats than Şehir Hatları, with pleasantly open decks to catch the summer breezes, and charge ₺5 one way.

By sea bus The more expensive but much quicker sea bus (*deniz otobüs*) service also runs from Kabataş (June 20–Sept 18, Mon–Fri 8.15am–8.50pm, Sat & Sun 9am–8.50pm; Sept 21–June 19, Mon–Fri 1–2 daily; ₺10, ₺7.80 with an Istanbulkart), taking as little as 35min to Büyükada. Not all sea-bus departures visit all the islands – check before boarding. Also note that sea buses have no open deck, which is not so enjoyable on a warm summer's day.

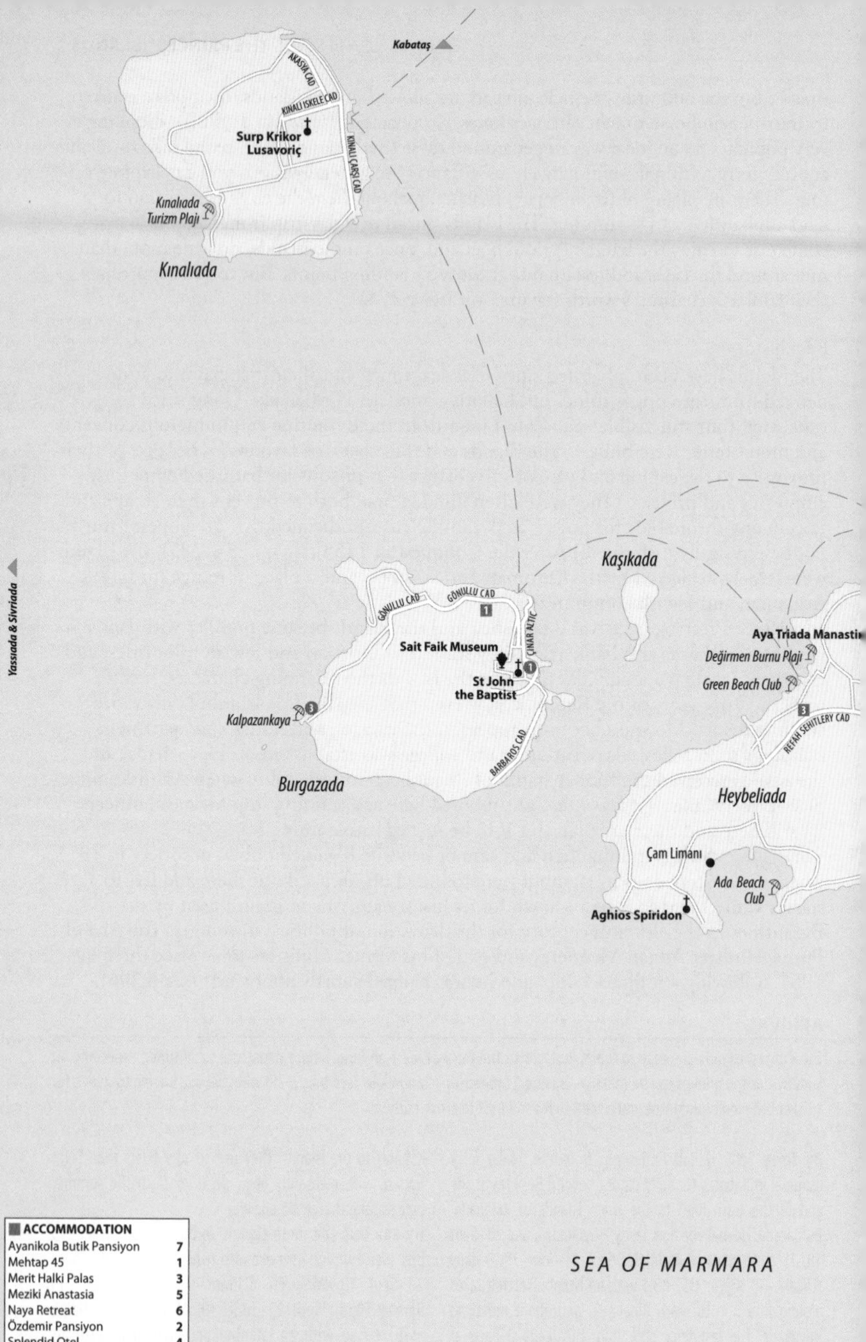

Kabataş

MASSİK CAD

KINALI İSKELE CAD

KINALI ÇARŞI CAD

Surp Krikor Lusavoriç

Kınalıada Turizm Plajı

Kınalıada

Yassıada & Sivriada

GÖNÜLLÜ CAD

GÖNÜLLÜ CAD

1

Kaşıkada

ÇINAR ALTIÇ

Sait Faik Museum

1

St John the Baptist

Aya Triada Manastiri

Değirmen Burnu Plajı

Green Beach Club

3

RESAN ŞEHİTLERY CAD

Kalpazankaya **3**

BARBAROS CAD

Burgazada

Heybeliada

Çam Limanı

Ada Beach Club

Aghios Spiridon

SEA OF MARMARA

■ **ACCOMMODATION**

Ayanikola Butik Pansiyon	**7**
Mehtap 45	**1**
Merit Halki Palas	**3**
Meziki Anastasia	**5**
Naya Retreat	**6**
Özdemir Pansiyon	**2**
Splendid Otel	**4**

THE PRINCES' ISLANDS

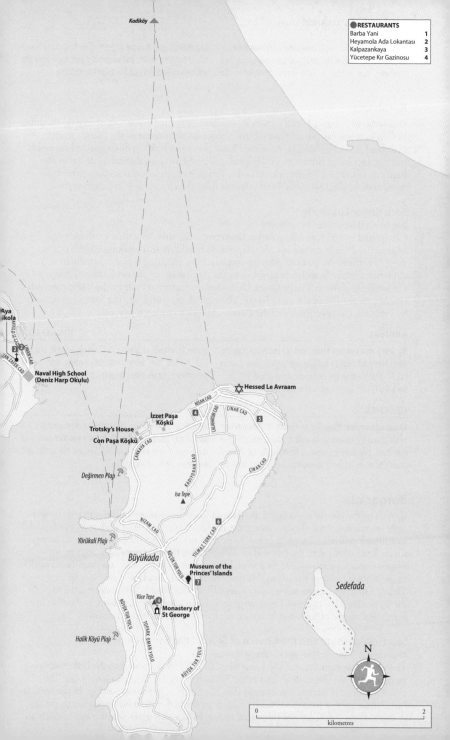

Kadiköy ▲

RESTAURANTS

Barba Yani	1
Heyamola Ada Lokantası	2
Kalpazankaya	3
Yücetepe Kır Gazinosu	4

Aya
ikola

Naval High School
(Deniz Harp Okulu)

✡ Hessed Le Avraam

İzzet Paşa
Köşkü

Trotsky's House
Con Paşa Köşkü

Değirmen Plajı

Isa Tepe ▲

Yörükali Plajı

Büyükada

Museum of the
Princes' Islands

Sedefada

Yüce Tepe
Monastery of
St George

Halik Köyü Plajı

N

0		2
	kilometres	

Island-hopping Getting between the main islands is easy, but check ferry times at the docks and don't rely simply on a timetable; the service is notoriously changeable. An Istanbulkart or a handful of *jetons* (see box, p.25) makes island-hopping easier, but remember that each ferry trip will set you back ₺5 (₺3.5 with an Istanbulkart).

Kınalıada

Kınalıada, or "Henna Island", takes its name from the red colouring of its eastern cliffs; in Greek, it was known as *Proti* ("First"), since it's the nearest of the islands to the mainland. Like Heybeliada, Kınalıada has a history of holding distinguished prisoners in exile, including Romanos IV Diogenes, deposed after his disastrous defeat at the Battle of Manzikert by the Selçuk Turks. Today, its population is seventy percent Armenian, swelled by friends and relatives from the city visiting in summer.

Surp Krikor Lusavoriç
Three streets back and uphill from the ferry terminal

Completed in 1857, the **Surp Krikor Lusavoriç** is the sole Armenian Orthodox (Apostolic) church on the islands. Step inside to admire this working church's most notable feature, the painted glass lunette windows depicting historic Armenian churches, mainly from lands now lost to the Armenians in distant Eastern Turkey. On a hilltop above is a large Greek Orthodox monastery, rebuilt in the late eighteenth century on the site of the early Byzantine original; it's worth visiting for its icons, sent by Peter the Great of Russia to the Greek Orthodox patriarch Jeremias in 1723.

ARRIVAL
KINALIADA

By ferry and sea bus Ferries and sea buses run from the Adalar ferry terminal in Kabataş (see p.159); they dock at the ferry terminal on the east coast of the island.
By bike Cycling is the best way to tour the island, and the entire circuit takes an hour or so. There are a couple of shops just behind the ferry terminal renting out poorly maintained but adequate bikes for ₺5 an hour.

BEACHES

Kınalıada Turizm Plajı This free beach on the southeast of the island is a forty-minute walk or fifteen-minute cycle ride from the ferry terminal. Like virtually all Princes' Islands' beaches, it's stony, so you'll probably want to cough up ₺10 for a sun lounger and umbrella. Next door to it is a posher pay beach (₺30) with its own outdoor pool, and there are a few more pay beaches on the north and northeast shores of the island.

Burgazada

Known to the Greeks as Antigoni, **Burgazada** lacks the quantity of late nineteenth- and early twentieth-century houses that make Büyükada (see p.164) so attractive. Fortunately its laidback charm and sophistication more than make up for this, along with its narrow streets lined with palm, fig, bay and oleander. This is the only one of the four major islands not completely ringed by a road, but you can cycle (or walk) up unsurfaced tracks to the highest point of the island, Hristos Tepesi or "Christ's Hill" for stunning views. There's also a late nineteenth-century Greek Orthodox church here, built on the site of the Byzantine Monastery of Theokoryphotos. It's in a locked compound, but visible in front are a couple of fine, deeply incised capitals from the original monastery.

Sait Faik Museum and the Church of St John the Baptist
Burgaz Çayırı Sok 15 • Tues–Fri 10am–noon & 2–5pm, Sat 10am–noon • Free

This small **museum**, beautifully refurbished in 2013, is dedicated to the bohemian novelist **Sait Faik** (often described as the Turkish Mark Twain), who lived here. The house has been so carefully preserved that you feel like you're trespassing. In the writer's bedroom, a pair of pyjamas is neatly folded on the bed, with a hot water bottle on top of them. Even if you are not interested in Sait Faik, a visit gives you the opportunity to see the elegant interior of an island house originally built for a wealthy Greek businessman. A useful locator for the museum is the imposing Greek Orthodox **Church of St John the Baptist**. Built in 1899 on the site of a much earlier church, its dome dominates the main settlement as you approach the island on the ferry.

ARRIVAL AND GETTING AROUND   BURGAZADA

By ferry and sea bus Ferries and sea buses run from the Adalar ferry terminal in Kabataş (see p.159); they dock at the ferry terminal on the east coast of the island.
By bike Bikes are available for ₺7.5 a day from Karagöz

Bisiklet, a couple of blocks from the ferry terminal.
By phaeton Phaetons congregate just north of the ferry terminal, offering long tours of the island for ₺45, or a shorter version for ₺35.

BEACHES

Kalpazankaya For cheap swimming (₺5), head to Kalpazankaya on the west coast of the island, a fifteen-minute bicycle or ₺30 phaeton ride from the ferry

terminal. The small, rocky swimming area has a fine restaurant of the same name in the pine trees above it (see p.193). Daily 10am–midnight.

11

Heybeliada

Heybeliada ("Island of the Saddlebag", due to its shape), was called Halki (Copper) by its original Greek inhabitants. The island has managed to retain much of its village identity, and it has a more down-to-earth, conservative feel than the other islands. Istanbul residents flock here in their thousands at weekends for the island's beaches. The family of the famous Istanbul writer Orhan Pamuk (see box, p.126) regularly spent the summer in one of the island's fine wooden Art Nouveau-style mansions.

One building you might come across during a stroll around the island is the **Naval High School** (Deniz Harp Okulu), on the east side of the island, along the coast road from the main jetty, which was originally the Naval War Academy, situated here since 1852. The Greek Orthodox **St Nicholas** (Aya Nikola) church is a prominent red-and-cream building with a curious clock tower, just behind the waterfront in the town centre. On the south side of the island, on a pine-forested promontory, is the wooden monastery of **Agios Spiridon**. It's run-down and seldom visited but the location, among trees overlooking the sea, is atmospheric.

Aya Triada Manastiri

Mon–Sat 10am–noon & 2–4pm • Free • By appointment only • ☎ 0216 351 8563

Heybeliada's main point of interest is the nineteenth-century **Aya Triada Manastiri**, the Greek Orthodox School of Theology, majestically situated on the peak of the island's northernmost hill. You'll need to provide scholarly credentials to view its library of 230,000 books, which includes an important collection of Byzantine manuscripts. The building is set in beautiful grounds, and encloses a pretty, eight-hundred-year-old church, with a stunning gilt iconostasis. It's a pleasant fifteen-minute walk through pine forest (or cycle or take a phaeton; see below). Until 1973, Orthodox priests were trained here and you can see the dusty classroom filled with age-blackened desks where the acolytes received instruction.

ARRIVAL AND GETTING AROUND   HEYBELİADA

By ferry and sea bus Ferries and sea buses run from the Adalar ferry terminal in Kabataş (see p.159); they dock at the ferry terminal on the main quayside of Rıhtım Caddesi, on the west coast of the island.
By bike Cycling is perhaps the best way to enjoy Heybeliada, its pine forests and hills making for scenic rides and rambles, with the added bonus of taking in one of the beaches. There's bike rental near the quayside at Imralı Sok

3, and several other outlets nearby; all charge ₺5/hour, ₺15 all day.
By phaeton Prices for phaetons from Ayyıldız Caddesi (which runs parallel to the front) to various destinations around the island are posted on a board in the street (eg Aya Triada ₺27); tours of the island are also available by phaeton (20min ₺58, 40min ₺45).

BEACHES

Ada Beach Club ⓦadabeachclub.com. Attractively situated in a large bay on the island's south coast, it has a free shuttle-boat service from the ferry terminal area. There's a rather scruffy "people's" beach next door, where for ₺10 you can rent a sun lounger. ₺30. Daily 9am–sunset.

Değirmen Burnu Plajı A good mid-range option, set in pretty pine forest on the south shore of a peninsula projecting from the northwest corner of the island. It's a small, shingly curve of beach at the foot of some small cliffs, and feels much wilder than the posher beach clubs. A half-hour walk from the ferry terminal, it is best reached by phaeton. Mon–Fri ₺13, Sat & Sun ₺15. Daily 9am–sunset.

Green Beach Club ⓦgreenbeachclub.com. The smartest beach on the island, on the opposite side of Heybeliada from the ferry terminal – a free boat departs from just north of the quay for beach-goers. There's thumping Turkish pop all day, but the on-site café is reasonably priced and the small, sandy, shallow-water beach is ideal for kids. Mon–Fri ₺30, Sat & Sun ₺40. Late April to Sept 8am–sunset.

Büyükada

11

Büyükada ("Great Island"), known to the Greeks as *Prinkipo* ("Princes' Island") is the largest of the islands and has long been inhabited by minorities. It has traditionally been a place of retreat or exile, and Leon Trotsky lived here from 1929 to 1933, when he began to write his *History of the Russian Revolution*. To reach Trotsky's house head southwest from the busy ferry-terminal area, along Çankaya Caddesi, the main road used by the phaetons, turn right after **Con Paşa Köşkü**, a beautifully restored *fin-de-siècle* mansion, and head down steep Hamlacı Sokak. Trotsky's former home is the last brick-built villa on the right-hand side of the street; today it's roofless.

The large mansions of Büyükada tend to have beautiful gardens full of magnolia, mimosa and jasmine, and in the surrounding pine forests myrtle, lilac and rock roses grow wild. The scents of the island on a summer's evening are one of its most memorable aspects, though often far stronger is the less desirable whiff of horse-dung.

Museum of the Princes' Islands (Adalar Müzesi)

Aya Nikola Mevkii • Tues–Sun 9am–6pm summer, 9am–5pm winter • ₺5

After decades of ill-advised development, the island is beginning to take its past seriously. The open-air **Museum of the Princes' Islands** (ⓦadalarmuzesi.org) on the east coast of the island tells the history of the archipelago through Ottoman archive material, period photographs and oral history resources, as well as giving information on their geology and flora and fauna. Everything is well labelled in English as well as Turkish and it really helps to bring the islands to life, with illuminating information on everything from the effect the anti-Greek pogroms of 1955 had on the islands' substantial Greek population to the founding by an English businessman of a macaroni factory in 1876.

Yüce Tepe and İsa Tepe

The island consists of two hills, both topped with monasteries. The southernmost, **Yüce Tepe**, is the location of the **Monastery of St George** (open daily 9am–4pm) which is thought to have been built on the site of a twelfth-century building. Close up, it consists of a series of chapels on three levels, with the oldest – containing an *ayazma* or sacred spring – on the lowest level. In Byzantine times, the monastery functioned as an asylum – the iron rings set into the floor of the chapels were used for restraining the inmates. To reach St George, take a phaeton to the small Luna Park on the saddle between the two main hills, where there are tacky souvenir stalls, parked phaetons and a café. From here it's a stiff fifteen-minute walk up a steep cobbled path to the monastery. Next to it is the welcome *Yücatepe Kır Gazinosu* restaurant (see p.193). The cycle ride from the town to the monastery is a worthwhile alternative: ride southwest from the central square behind the waterfront, past the *Splendid Palace* hotel and onto Çankaya Caddesi, with its succession of gorgeous wooden *fin-de-siècle* villas, before branching left and up into the forest; it takes around twenty minutes to ride to the saddle/Luna Park.

The huge but decrepit building on the northern hill, **İsa Tepe**, is a late nineteenth-century Greek orphanage, closed down in 1964. Said to be the second-largest wooden building in the world, it has long been the subject of wrangling between Turkey and its ethnic Greek Orthodox minority. In 2010, a Strasbourg court ruled that the building, appropriated by the Turkish authorities, should be returned to its original owners, the Fener Greek Patriarchate (see p.99). It's easy to reach from the Luna Park on foot or by bike, but you'll have to confine your explorations of the dangerously dilapidated wooden structure to gazing through the bars of the locked perimeter fence.

ARRIVAL AND GETTING AROUND   BÜYÜKADA

By ferry and sea bus Ferries and sea buses run from the Adalar ferry terminal in Kabataş (see p.159); they dock at two adjacent terminals on Büyük İskele Cad in Büyükada's main town, from where the main square and most of the hotels, restaurants and shops are just a short walk away.

By bike With motor vehicles banned, there are bike rental shops (₺5/hr, ₺15/day) everywhere. Recommended is Trek, on Nisan Cad 23, just behind the clock tower, which has new, well-maintained bikes. Wherever you rent from, however, make sure you check that the brakes and gears

work properly before setting off – if you're planning to cycle inland, you'll need them. You'll also need to leave some ID as a guarantee. With swimming breaks and ascents to the high points there's plenty of scope to spend the whole day on two wheels, though you can comfortably whizz right around the island in 90min.

By phaeton Horse-and-carriage tours (for up to four people; short tour ₺70, long tour ₺80) leave from the phaeton park off the main square on İsa Çelebi Sok, 50m southwest of the ferry terminal.

11

BEACHES

Değirmen Plajı Off Çankaya Caddesi, on the west coast. The cheapest (but tiniest) beach on the island, and the closest to the ferry terminal. ₺10. 10am–sunset.

Halik Köyü Plajı South from the ferry terminal lies the best of the islands' beaches, reached on a seven-minute stroll from the coast road, down a stepped path through typical Mediterranean trees and shrubs (or there's a free boat from the ferry terminal), with a cheap on-site café and showers. Although the beach itself is stony, looking not across the urban sprawl of Istanbul but south across the sea

to the green, southern shores of the Sea of Marmara, it's not hard here to imagine yourself on a remote Aegean or Mediterranean island. ₺15. Daily 8am–dusk.

Yörükali Plajı ⓦ yorukali.com. A little further south than Değirmen Plajı is this much bigger beach, dating back to 1935, which offers a free boat transfer from the ferry terminal. Sunbathing is accompanied by loud Turkish pop, but the beach is sandy and good for kids. ₺30 including lounger and umbrella. Mid-April to Sept 8am–sunset.

Accommodation

The number of visitors to Istanbul rises each year, so it's best to book as far in advance as possible. Every type of lodging is available, from multinational hotel chains and exclusive boutique establishments to basic city hotels and hostels. Apart from the most modest establishments (and even in many of these), en-suite bathrooms and breakfast are included in the price. Most also provide air conditioning for the hot, humid summers and double glazing and central heating to cope with the winter chills. All but a handful of the accommodation choices listed below provide free wi-fi access and most have a fixed terminal or two as well. Apartments have become very popular too, and can be better value than other forms of accommodation.

Budget and type of accommodation aside, the biggest decision you'll have to make is which part of the city to stay in. The **old city**, which includes Sultanahmet and other areas falling within the old Byzantine land walls, remains the most popular choice. The neighbourhoods across the Golden Horn, including trendy Galata and **Beyoğlu**, where the nightlife and contemporary culture are as important as historic sights, are fast catching up. It's here that you will find the greatest concentration of apartments for rent. If you have the money and hanker after exclusivity, the hotels fronting **the Bosphorus** may be an attractive alternative, for business or upmarket shopping Taksim and the suburbs north of it may be of interest. Spring and autumn are often busy and, particularly if you have your heart set on a special place, especially one of the more exclusive boutique hotels, it's advisable to book as far ahead as possible. Rooms with a sea view, or that look over landmark sites such as the Haghia Sophia or Blue Mosque, carry a premium. There are **hostels** in both the old city and on the other side of the Golden Horn in Galata/Beyoğlu.

ESSENTIALS

Rates In this guide (including the Out of the City chapters), accommodation prices are, unless stated otherwise, quoted as the lowest price per double room in high season, though for backpacker hostels the rate for dorms is per person. Many hotels now work on a yield management basis, which means that in slack periods prices can be very low, while in busy period rates climb steeply. An increasing number of places offer a discount for non-refundable fixed bookings and for booking through the hotel's own website. Almost all prices below are given in euros, reflecting how most hotels advertise their rates.

Seasons Peak season runs from mid-March to mid-November and Christmas and New Year, when prices are at their highest (though some establishments are a little cheaper in July and August). Most places offer discounts during the main low season, usually around fifteen to twenty percent.

12

SULTANAHMET

The majority of first-time visitors to the city tend to stay in **Sultanahmet**, among the major attractions of the Blue Mosque, Topkapı Palace and Haghia Sophia. The options around the **Hippodrome** are particularly good from a historical perspective, but the highest concentration of accommodation is to be found in and around **Akbıyık Caddesi**, an immensely popular backstreet with a package-resort atmosphere. There are plenty of quieter streets in nearby **Cankurtaran**, the area between Sultanahmet and the Sea of Marmara. The hotels off **Divan Yolu** have the advantage of being handy for the Topkapı–Eminönü–Kabataş tram.

AROUND THE HIPPODROME

★ **Cheers Lighthouse** Çayıroğlu Sok 18 ☎ 0212 458 2324; map p.46. An imaginative offshoot of the excellent *Cheers* hostel (see p.168) this cosy eighteen-bed, five-room hostel spread over three floors offers a wide range of accommodation for discerning visitors who appreciate the communal hostel vibe yet want plenty of privacy. The penthouse suite, on the top floor of the period townhouse, has one double and two single beds, a jacuzzi in the en-suite bathroom, plus Sea of Marmara views, while the six-bed Pomegranate dorm has views of the quiet street below. On the ground floor is a great lobby, bar and terrace with views over the now defunct suburban railway line to the sea, and the quality of food on offer in the attached restaurant is outstanding. Dorm €18, penthouse suite €120

Deniz Houses Çayıroğlu Sok 14 ☎ 0212 518 9595, ⊕ denizhouses.com; map p.46. This very friendly establishment is set in a couple of adjacent townhouses on an interesting side street. Rooms looking onto the street are smaller and cheaper than those with sea views (€65). The south-facing sea-view rooms are great, especially as they have tea- and coffee-making facilities, but in high summer the afternoon sun can be pretty fierce on the glass. The owners also run the Backpackers Travel Agency (see p.30), so are more helpful than most when it comes to organizing your stay. €45

★ **İbrahim Pasha** Terzihane Sok, 5 Adliye Yanı ☎ 0212 518 0394, ⊕ ibrahimpasha.com; map p.46. This lovingly converted pair of early twentieth-century townhouses forms arguably the most tasteful boutique hotel in Sultanahmet, successfully blending a stylish modern interior with Ottoman antiques. The 24 uncluttered rooms are very comfortable and, owing to the side street location, quiet. The views from the recently expanded roof terrace across the domes and minarets of Sultanahmet and down to the Sea of Marmara are superb, and the freshly prepared breakfast in the cosy and charming breakfast room is a delight. Very friendly and well run, with a useful guide to the city's best restaurants for all guests, and a superb lobby library full of books on both the city and Turkey in general. Ten percent discount for cash. €99

TOP FIVE PERIOD HOTELS

A'jia Bosphorus, see p.173
Empress Zoe Cankurtaran, see p.169
House Hotel Galatasaray İstiklal Caddesi
and around, see p.172
İbrahim Pasha Sultanahmet, see p.167
Pera Palace İstiklal Caddesi and around,
see p.172

Turkoman Asmalı Çeşme Sok, 2 Adliye Yanı ☎0212 516 2956, ⊛turkomanhotel.com; map p.46. Opened back when the term "boutique hotel" meant somewhere with period character and individuality, the friendly *Turkoman* continues to offer distinctive accommodation. Fashioned from a converted house done out in nineteenth-century Turkish style, right on the Hippodrome and opposite the Egyptian Obelisk, it boasts fine views of the Blue Mosque from the roof terrace. Each attractive room is named after one of the old Turkoman tribes, and has a brass bed and wooden floors. Ask for one of the front, Hippodrome-facing rooms. Free airport transfers. **€109**

AROUND TOPKAPI PALACE

Ayasofya Konakları Soğukçeşme Sok ☎0212 513 3660, ⊛ayasofyakonaklari.com; map p.46. Created from a series of ten nineteenth-century wooden houses on a cobbled street squeezed between the walls of the Topkapı Palace and the Haghia Sophia, this is, without a doubt, one of the most atmospheric hotels in the city. The choice of rooms is bewildering, ranging from roomy suites to compact doubles. Staying in one of the rooms in the imposing Konuk Evi, a detached wooden mansion in its own garden opposite the main hotel, is about as close to period living as you can get, with original brass beds, parquet flooring adorned with Turkish carpets, and painted wooden ceilings. **€170**

Cheers Zeynepsultan Cami Sok 21 ☎0212 526 0200, ⊛cheershostel.com; map p.46. This hostel, set in an old house on a quiet side street just off the tram line below the Haghia Sophia, makes a refreshing change from the old-city options clustered around Akbıyık Caddesi. There are several dorms of varying sizes, one of which is en suite, another female only. There are also doubles and twins available. Apart from the peaceful location, a real draw is the terrace bar, which looks over mature plane trees onto the west face of the Haghia Sophia, a view few visitors ever see. Dorm **€16**, double **€70**

AROUND DIVAN YOLU

Kybele Yerebatan Cad 35 ☎0212 511 7766, ⊛kybelehotel.com; map p.46. Established over twenty years ago, this is a good choice if you're looking for somewhere a little quirky and oozing with retro charm. A late nineteenth-century rendered brick building, handily situated just behind busy Divan Yolu, it boasts over four thousand multi-hued antique-style light fittings. The sixteen spacious rooms have old wood flooring and brass and iron bedsteads. A rich breakfast, including olive oil from the Aegean village home of the three friendly brothers who run it, is served in a shady courtyard full of candelabra, cushions, and retro knick-knacks, and there's a charming wooden outbuilding that serves as a lounge/library. **€110**

Nomade Ticarethane Sok 15 ☎0212 513 8172, ⊛hotelnomade.com; map p.46. Described as "ethnic trendy" by the French designer responsible for its chic interior, this hotel has white-floored rooms finished in bold colours, with rich coordinating fabrics and white furniture. Rooms are a little on the small side, and some of the furniture is showing signs of wear, but it has one of the very best roof terraces in the old city and the lavish breakfast includes the not always standard filter coffee. **€100**

Ottoman Hotel Imperial Caferiye Sok 6/1 ☎0212 513 6151, ⊛ottomanhotelimperial.com; map p.46. Hard to believe this wonderfully situated, lavishly refurbished hotel was once the *Yücelt Hostel*, springboard for India-bound overlanders in the 1970s. The best rooms (€240), have great views of the Haghia Sophia, baths and plasma TVs; standard rooms face the main (tram) road, and all have tea- and coffee-making facilities. Attached is the very well-regarded *Matbah* restaurant (see p.186). Good value for the location and level of comfort and style. **€125**

White House Çatalçeşme Sok ☎0212 526 0019, ⊛Istanbulwhitehouse.com; map p.46. Immaculately presented rooms make this a popular choice for those seeking a touch of Ottoman style with all the mod cons. Think cream and gilt cornices, grained and painted wood furniture and sumptuous bedspreads and patterned wallpaper. It may be a touch ostentatious for some, but the lavish breakfasts, real coffee and roof terrace with commanding views of Haghia Sophia, Haghia Eirene and the Bosphorus more than compensate. **€139**

CANKURTARAN

★**Agora Guest House and Hostel** Amiral Tafdil Sok 6 ☎0212 458 5547, ⊛agoraguesthouse.com; map p.46. Blurring the lines between hotel and guesthouse, this is an excellent budget choice right in the heart of the old city. The tastefully furnished communal breakfast/lounge area has a massive flat-screen TV, a funky terrace and a great atmosphere. There are ten well-appointed doubles, and dorms range from four to ten beds, all mixed bar one, ten-bed female-only dorm. Highly recommended, with the caveat that there aren't quite enough toilets when the hostel is full. Dorm **€17**, double **€80**

Alp Akbıyık Cad, Adliye Sok 4 ☎0212 517 9570, ⊛alpguesthouse.com; map p.46. Fine establishment,

12

with a dark wood exterior, situated down a quiet lane. The smallish rooms, accessed from a winding marble staircase, are immaculately furnished, some with four-poster beds. Rooms 403 and 404 command a sea view. The pretty, partially covered breakfast terrace gives great views over the old city and Sea of Marmara. €80

Big Apple Bayram Fırını Sok 12 ☎0212 517 7931, ⓦhostelbigapple.com; map p.46. This well-run hostel, located right in the heart of the old city, offers dorms with laminate floors and metal bunk beds with comfy mattresses. There are shared, clean, toilets and showers on each floor. There's also a female-only dorm. For a substantial price hike, double, triple and family rooms are available – though a couple of these are windowless. There's a decent covered terrace with a cushioned area for lounging and a small roof terrace – both boast good views over the Sea of Marmara and Princes' Islands, and are the venue for the reasonable Turkish-style breakfast and cheap night-time drinking. Dorm €22, double €85

★**Empress Zoe** Akbıyık Cad, Adliye Sok 10 ☎0212 518 2504, ⓦemzoe.com; map p.46. Comprised of several traditional townhouses, themselves built over the remains of an Ottoman bath-house, this is a friendly hotel with history. The 25 rooms are decorated throughout with the personal touch of American owner Ann Nevans. Most rooms are in dark wood with richly coloured textiles and attractive wall-paintings, all are individually decorated and furnished, and vary from standard doubles to a penthouse suite. You'll pay at least €20 more for one with a balcony, a sea view or private garden. Part of the basement walls belong to the remains of the Great Byzantine Palace, and the sun terrace has panoramic views of the Blue Mosque and Haghia Sophia. There's a lovely garden to one side, shaded by cypress, palm and bay trees where you can have breakfast or an evening aperitif. €140

Four Seasons Tevfikhane Sok 1 ☎0212 638 8200, ⓦfourseasons.com; map p.46. Until the early 1980s, this formidable Neoclassical building served as the Sultanahmet Prison before being completely renovated as one of the city's leading hotels. The watchtowers and exercise court are still evident beneath the flowers and vines, but the 54 beautiful high-ceilinged rooms are unrecognizable as former cells. The rooms are as sumptuous as you would expect, the courtyard grounds an oasis of tranquility. Excellent, attentive service, and a couple of great rooftop bars, but suite prices run into the thousands. €560

★**Hanedan** Akbıyık Cad, Adliye Sok 3 ☎0212 516 4869 or ☎0212 418 1564, ⓦhanedanhotel.com; map p.46. Tucked away on a quiet side street off Akbıyık Cad, this friendly hotel is great value for the quality of accommodation and service. The dark wood floors in the smallish rooms, all named after the various civilizations that have flourished in Anatolia, are offset by the plain,

pale walls, with the three facing the quiet side street having three beds – ideal for families. There's a roof terrace with stunning views over the Haghia Sophia and the Sea of Marmara, and a great spread for breakfast which includes filter coffee. Discount for long stays. €60

★**Peninsula** Adliye Sok 6 ☎0212 458 6850, ⓦhotelpeninsula.com; map p.46. Comfortable budget accommodation on a quiet side street, with the same owner as the *Hanedan* opposite. The eleven simply furnished rooms (laminate floors and plain pastel walls) boast a/c, central heating and double glazing as well as flat-screen TVs. The smallest doubles are cheaper than doubles in many of the hostels, and the place is spotlessly clean and well managed. Rooms and bathrooms are on the small side, but at these prices that's to be expected; there's also a roof terrace with great views. €45

Side Hotel & Pension Utangaç Sok 20 ☎0212 517 2282, ⓦsidehotel.com; map p.46. Established back in 1989 and owned by three charismatic brothers, this bright, spacious and friendly hotel-cum-pension offers immaculate service and traditional comfort for a reasonable price. The rooms on the hotel side are en suite and have a/c; those facing the rear have a small balcony. In the pension, six of the rooms on the upper floor share spotless bathrooms in the hall and have fans. There's a shared breakfast terrace that has great views of the Princes' Islands. Pension €40, hotel €80

Sultan Hostel Akbıyık Cad 21 ☎0212 516 9260, ⓦsultanhostel.com; map p.46. This large, well-established 160-bed hostel is very popular because of its convenient location, spotless rooms, comfy beds sporting gleaming white linen, and regularly cleaned, shared bathrooms. Dorm prices vary according to the number of beds per room, ranging from the 26-bed basement "Harem" room to more pricey six-bed dorms (€16); some have en-suite showers and toilets. Doubles are also available, though bathrooms are shared. The staff are very friendly and the restaurant (ten percent discount for guests), which spills out onto the street, is incredibly popular with both guests and passers-by. Dorm €12, double €46

★**Uyan** Utangaç Sok 25 ☎0212 518 9255, ⓦuyanhotel.com; map p.46. Atmospheric 29-room hotel set in a beautifully renovated, late 1920s corner-plot building in the heart of the old city. The cheaper

12

TOP FIVE BUDGET STAYS
Agora Sultanahmet, see p.168
Büyük Londra İstiklal Caddesi and around, see p.171
Cheers Sultanahmet, see p.168
Peninsula Sultanahmet, see p.169
Rapunzel Galata, see p.171

ground-floor rooms are a little gloomy, but other rooms are lovely and airy, with light wood, oriental-rug-scattered floors, white walls and white bed linen. There are different sized rooms to choose from, from small doubles to a honeymoon suite. "Blue Mosque", room 405, has great views over the Blue Mosque and Haghia Sophia, as well as Scandinavian-style furniture and a jacuzzi. An added bonus is the breathtaking view from the roof terrace. **€99**

SİRKECİ

The area of Sirkeci between the southern fringes of Gülhane Park and the old Orient Express station close to the mouth of the Golden Horn has become hotel central over the last few years, but is still less touristy than around the Haghia Sophia. The essential T1 tram line runs right through the district.

★Neorion Orhaniye Cad 14 ☎0212 527 9090, ⓦneorionhotel.com; map p.70. Fairly ordinary looking from the outside, this excellent 53-room hotel goes the extra mile to keep its guests happy. There's a basement pool, jacuzzi, sauna and Turkish bath, all free, as well as a superb roof terrace with fine views to the confluence of the Golden Horn and Bosphorus, where the management offer a free drink and *meze* nightly between 7 and 8pm. Rooms are immaculate, with a nod to Ottoman decor in the wood floors, dark wood furniture and nineteenth-century prints, as well as mod cons like a/c and LCD TVs. Bathrooms are reasonably proportioned by Turkish standards, and gleam with chrome and white porcelain fittings. **€196**

Sirkeci Mansion Taya Hatun Cad 5 ☎0212 528 4344, ⓦsirkecimansion.com; map p.70. This hotel was originally a nineteenth-century Ottoman *konak* (mansion), situated right next to the walls of Gülhane Parkı. Neither hip nor trendy, it is very professionally run and offers good old-fashioned comfort. There are tea- and coffee-making facilities in the rooms, palatial en-suite bathrooms and comfy beds. There's a fitness centre and small pool in the basement, and a decent fish restaurant on the roof terrace, which has commanding views over the park and Topkapı Palace. In addition, complimentary cooking classes, walks and afternoon tea are on offer – plus a free welcome dinner for stays of four days or more and a ten percent discount for bookings made through the hotel's website. **€196**

THE GRAND BAZAAR AND AROUND

The streets running down the hill to the Sea of Marmara south of the Grand Bazaar and Çemberlitaş remain workmanlike, with wholesale footwear outlets and leather workshops making a refreshing change from the touristy streets of Cankurtaran. The main sights are still within easy walking distance and the tram stops Beyazıt and Çemberlitaş are very convenient.

Niles Dibekli Cami Sok 13 ☎0212 517 3239, ⓦhotelniles.com; map pp.78–79. Well-established hotel offering better value than nearby Sultanahmet. Standard rooms are well appointed, with small but immaculate shower-bathrooms, while the suites (€180) are more elaborately decorated, in faux-Ottoman style, boasting marble, Turkish-bath-style bathrooms. There's a pretty ground-floor courtyard garden and a roof terrace with panoramic views over busy Yenikapı Harbour. Decent value, especially as there is a ten percent discount for booking through the website. **€105**

President (Best Western) Tiyatro Cad 25, Beyazıt ☎0212 515 6980, ⓦthepresidenthotel.com; map pp.78–79. Centrally located hotel away from the crowds and hawkers of Sultanahmet – a mere 100 yards from the Beyazıt tram stop and a five-minute amble to the Grand Bazaar. The hotel earns its four-star rating with a stylish rooftop pool bar and terrace restaurant offering stunning panoramic views of the Marmara sea, Blue Mosque and the old town; there's also a chic British-style pub and a gym and spa on site. The standard rooms are modest yet elegant and the price includes a decadent buffet breakfast (Turkish and Continental) served on the rooftop. Free airport pick-up available for direct bookings. **€130**

THE NORTHWEST QUARTER

There is only one hotel worth considering in this far-flung quarter of the old city, out by the Byzantine land walls, but it is a good-value gem.

Kariye Kariye Camii Sok 6, Edirne Kapı ☎0212 534 8414, ⓦkariyeotel.com; map p.91. Right next door to arguably the finest Byzantine site in the city (the Kariye Museum; see p.94) and a stone's throw from the Theodosian land walls, this nineteenth-century mansion has been restored with style and restraint. The rooms are done out in soft pastel colours, much of the furniture is ornate late nineteenth-century in style, and the polished honey-coloured parquet floor is enlivened by the odd tasteful kilim. There are ceiling fans rather than a/c, which is quite sufficient in this elevated, tree-shaded location. The reasonable prices reflect the rather small, shower-only bathrooms and the chipped paintwork. **€70**

12

GALATA, BEYOĞLU AND AROUND

Galata (also known as Kartaköy) is a bohemian quarter of period houses lining narrow streets tumbling down to the Golden Horn waterfront. The heart of Beyoğlu, the former European quarter, is undoubtedly **İstiklal Caddesi**, home to the city's densest concentration of restaurants, bars and clubs. **Tepebaşı**, a mixed commercial/tourist district just west of İstiklal Caddesi's southern end, is home to a few trendy rooftop bars and restaurants and the impressive Pera Museum. **Cihangir**, on the northern side of Sıraselviler Caddesi, is an affluent yet bohemian backwater with splendid views of the Bosphorus, while **Taksim**, the city's major business and shopping district, has a wide range of hotels aimed largely at business travellers and tour groups. To the north of Taksim Square, the posh neighbourhoods of **Harbiye** and, in particular, **Nişantaşı**, offer great shopping and a scattering of trendy places to eat and drink.

GALATA/KARAKÖY

Anemon Galata Büyükhendek Cad 11 ☎0212 293 2343, ⓦanemonhotels.com; map p.110. The sumptuous rooms in this rebuilt nineteenth-century townhouse near the Galata Tower aim squarely for comfort over style. Neo-Art Nouveau-style statuettes grace the lobby, stairs and bedside tables, while dark curtains, carpets and furniture contrast aesthetically with pastel and cream walls. The sizeable bathrooms have baths as well as showers, and the views from the incongruously designer-chic roof restaurant-bar are superb. €130

★**Bada Bing Hostel** Serçe Sok 6, Karaköy ☎0212 249 4111, ⓦbadabinghostel.com; map p.110. There's no shortage of trendy cafés, clubs and art galleries on the doorstep of this welcome addition to the Istanbul hostel scene, situated in the heart of an old dockland area. The a/c dorm rooms range from four to ten bed, with an eight-bed female-only option. There are stylishly decorated private rooms as well, plus a massive lounge area and roof-top terrace complete with bean-bags for lounging and cool beers for sipping. Owners Volkan and Bülent are mines of information on the city and keep the place spotless – for the moment at least it's arguably the best value hostel in town. Dorm €12, double €50

Noble House Galata Kadribey Çıkmaz 4 ☎0212 243 7446, ⓦnoblehousegalata.com; map p.110. The half-Turkish, half-Italian owner, Can Petruzzeli, is a real character and has made this hotel quite different to anything else the city can offer. It's gay friendly for a start, and the (smallish) rooms of this fine nineteenth-century townhouse are all decorated in a quirky manner, from faux-Ottoman to the "does exactly what it says on the tin" Black Room, making it a great choice if you're looking for something out of the ordinary. The situation, on a tiny dead-end alley just off ultra-fashionable Serdar-ı Ekrem Cad, is great, too, as is the cool little café next door. €110

★**Rapunzel Guesthouse** Bereketzade Camii Sok 3 ☎0212 292 5034, ⓦrapunzelistanbul.com; map p.110. This quirky hostel has bags of character with its original nineteenth-century stone walls, artistically scattered curiosities and colourful artwork. A little pricier than other backpackers' in the area, it's the small things here that make the difference – the roomy six-bed dorms with sparkling clean en suites, individual reading lights,

hairdryers, a hearty breakfast and on-tap potable water. The team of young, attentive staff are keen to mingle with guests and always on hand with tips and recommendations for the area. Look out for the black-and-pink sign, as this place is easy to miss, and ring the doorbell. Dorm €20, double €70

Vault Karaköy Bankalar Cad 5, Karaköy ☎0212 244 3400, ⓦthehousehotel.com; map p.110. The latest addition to the upmarket House brand, the *Vault* occupies an imposing building dating back to 1863 that was once the HQ of the prestigious Credit General Ottoman Bank. Many of the south-facing rooms (carrying a substantial premium) have great views across the Golden Horn to the old city, all have high ceilings, period furniture, large LCD TVs, iPod docks, work stations and chic bathrooms with Carrera marble floors. The German-made vaults in the basement have been preserved and are used to store the wine for the in-house restaurant; the original granite floors and Neoclassical pillars add character to the public areas. Noted architect Sinan Kafadar has done a sterling conversion job here. €175

World House Hostel Galipdede Cad 85 ☎0212 293 5520, ⓦworldhouseistanbul.com; map p.110. This colourful ninety-bed hostel ticks all the boxes for a budget traveller – clean, modern and in a great location. Bright, high-ceilinged rooms, coded security locks and friendly, enthusiastic staff lift this place a notch above the Sultanahmet hostel scene. Dorms sleep between four and fourteen, and there are double, triple and quad private rooms. Despite the nearby 24hr entertainment, it's quiet too – bar the prayer call from the adjacent mosque. The hostel also rents out short- and long-term apartments – check the website for details. Dorm €14, double €68

İSTIKLAL CADDESİ AND AROUND

★**Büyük Londra Oteli** Meşrutiyet Cad 117, Tepebaşı ☎0212 249 1025, ⓦlondrahotel.net; map pp.120–121. This palatial, mid-nineteenth-century building has a beautiful facade boasting caryatids and elaborate relief-carvings. The budget rooms are small, time-worn and cluttered with battered period furniture. The more expensive rooms at the front, some with views of the Golden Horn and old city, have been given a makeover but haven't quite lost their raffishness. Ernest Hemingway

12

stayed here in 1922 when he was a journalist covering the Turkish War of Independence, as did Alexander Hacke when shooting the definitive film of the city's music scene, *Istanbul: Crossing the Bridge*. The lobby bar is a study in nostalgia, all gilt, heavy drapes, dark wood and a caged grey parrot in the corner, plus a trendy but sensibly priced roof-bar with great views (see p.197). Ongoing construction on one side may make things noisy in the daytime. **€50**

Devman Asmalımescit Sok 52 ☎0212 245 6212, ⓦdevmanhotel.com; map pp.120–121. Modern, modest and well-run hotel at the bottom end of one of the city's liveliest night-time haunts. It is good value – all rooms are a/c and include a basic buffet breakfast. The street outside is a hive of activity until the early hours, especially at weekends, so it's not a great option for light sleepers. With its shiny bedspreads and multi-hued carpets it's not going to win any design awards, but the rooms are spacious, clean and the blue-tiled bathrooms are spotless. **€60**

★**House Hotel Galatasaray** Bostanbaşı Cad 19 ☎0212 252 0422, ⓦhousehotel.com; map pp.120–121. Having sewn up the city's chic international café market (see p.183), the House group have successfully branched out into hotels. This is their most subtle, tucked away on a quiet side street below heaving İstiklal Cad. The elegant 1870 facade has been left as it was, the name of its original owner, Zenovitch, still prominent above the entrance, a testament to the area's cosmopolitan past. Rooms are an almost perfect blend of nineteenth-century charm – think high ceilings, plaster relief work, wooden floors and heavy, panelled doors – with the thoroughly modern, including free-standing chrome shower stalls in the bedrooms, gleaming espresso machines and stylish low sofas in the living area (all rooms are suites). There's a lush breakfast on offer in the top-floor dining area, with great views towards the Galata Tower. **€155**

Mama Shelter İstiklal Cad 50–54 ☎0212 252 0100, ⓦmamashelter.com; map pp.120–121. Situated on the top floor of the Demirören shopping mall, this French-Turkish (the original is in Paris) concept hotel has definitely brought something new to the city's hotel scene. Rooms are reached by rather gloomy corridors, but once you open the door things brighten up immensely, with bright white walls, bed linen and curtains. It's not all modernist minimalism though, as the fun animal cartoon masks draped over the bedside lamps attest. Downstairs is a very hip bar and restaurant run by a Michelin-starred Turkish chef, which attracts hip locals as well as guests, especially on the DJ set nights (Thurs–Sun). There's even a touch-screen concierge service. **€83**

Marmara Pera Meşrutiyet Cad 21 ☎0212 251 4646, ⓦthemarmarahotels.com; map pp.120–121. Opulent yet stylish hotel housing the cool *Mikla* restaurant (see p.190), the *Marmara* claims to meld 1930s nostalgia with 1970s romanticism. A great feature of summer visits is the

elegant rooftop pool and bar, with glorious vistas over the city. The rooms feature modish modular furniture, crisp white linen and flat-screen TVs, and the views from those on the upper storeys are stunning. **€145**

Pera Palace Meşrutiyet Cad 52, Tepebaşı ☎0212 377 4000, ⓦjumeirah.com; map pp.120–121. A contender for the most atmospheric hotel in Istanbul (see box, p.123), the *Pera* was built in the nineteenth century to accommodate Orient Express passengers – its rooms are marked with the names of famous occupants such as Agatha Christie and Graham Greene. It reopened in 2010 following a lengthy restoration and has managed to maintain much of its character, though inevitably prices shot up. Even so, go for the most basic room with no Golden Horn view and rates are surprisingly agreeable for such a prestigious hotel. **€230**

Richmond Hotel İstiklal Cad 445 ☎0212 252 5460, ⓦrichmondint.com.tr; map pp.120–121. Nowhere near as trendy as you might think given its central location on buzzing İstiklal Cad and the presence of one of Beyoğlu's coolest rooftop bars, *Leb-i Derya Richmond*. The standard rooms are plain and attractively simple, with white walls and muted brown soft-furnishings, but do come with music systems. It's perennially popular with businessmen and travellers alike – and if you can stretch to a suite, they're considerably more stylish. Top-floor rooms at the back have Bosphorus views and a hefty €40 supplement. **€148**

★**TomTom Suites** Boğazkesen Cad, Tomtom Kaptan Sok 18 ☎0212 292 4949, ⓦtomtomsuites.com; map pp.120–121. A designer hotel fashioned from an early nineteenth-century Franciscan nunnery, virtually opposite the ornate and historic Italian Consulate (see box, p.122). The suites are spacious and soothingly decorated in soft whites and muted browns; bathrooms have underfloor heating, a jacuzzi and rain showers. Tucked away on the slope below bustling İstiklal Cad this is, by Beyoğlu standards, an extremely quiet location. **€189**

Triada Residence İstiklal Cad, Meşelik Sok 4 ☎0212 251 0101, ⓦtriada.com.tr; map pp.120–121. There are just eleven stylish rooms in this lovely turn-of-the-century townhouse on a quiet side street opposite Aya Triada church. All have boldly grained wood laminate floors and furniture, plain, pale walls adorned with tasteful prints, tea and coffee machines and large LCD TVs. One of the few genuine boutique-style hotels in this part of town, there are fabulous views from the penthouse suite over the domes of the Greek Orthodox church, a collection of vintage radios in the downstairs foyer-cum-breakfast room and a shared sauna. **€120**

CİHANGİR

Cihangir Arslan Yatağı Sok 33 ☎0212 251 5317, ⓦen .cihangirhotel.com; map pp.120–121. Old-fashioned comfort on a quiet backstreet in the affluent, rather arty suburb of Cihangir. The hotel underwent a major facelift in 2013 and the new, bold carpets won't be to everyone's taste but the rest of the decor is soothingly pale and simple. Service is excellent, and a huge buffet breakfast is served on a commanding terrace. You'll pay an €10 supplement for a room with a Bosphorus view but there's a 25 percent discount for bookings made at least 21 days in advance on the hotel's website. €110

Villa Zurich Akarsu Yokuşu Cad 44–46 ☎0212 293 0604, ⓦhotelvillazurich.com; map pp.120–121. Delightful, good-value hotel situated on a trendy street in Cihangir, where well-heeled but slightly alternative locals mingle with a sizeable foreign community. It offers large, well-equipped doubles – some with stunning panoramas of the Bosphorus – and a baby-sitting service is available. The rooftop terrace has the best views of all, serving as the breakfast salon and, in the evening, the well-regarded *Sur Balık* fish restaurant. €96

TAKSİM SQUARE, HARBİYE AND NİŞANTAŞI

Bentley Halaskargazı Cad 75, Harbiye ☎0212 291 7730, ⓦbentley-hotel.com; map p.128. One of the first wave of retro-modernist hotels in the city, the Italian-designed *Bentley* offers minimalist urban chic in a convenient location between Taksim Square and upmarket Nişantaşı. White, beige and black are the tones of choice in the appealing rooms, each kitted out with flat-screen TV and workstation. There's also a gym and a sleek restaurant. €220

Marmara Taksim Square ☎0212 251 4696, ⓦthemarmara.com.tr; map p.128. This premier five-star, twenty-storey hotel, right on Taksim Square, is one of Istanbul's landmark buildings. The spacious and luxurious rooms all have great views over Beyoğlu and mix functional chic with old-fashioned, faux-Ottoman flourishes. Facilities include a swimming pool, gym, Turkish bath and spa. Rooms on the upper floor were undergoing upgrades in summer 2014. €209

Sofa Teşvikiye Cad 123 ☎0212 368 1818, ⓦthesofahotel.com; map p.128. Housed in an attractive turn-of-the-nineteenth-century block, the *Sofa* is one of those designer hotels that offer minimalist charm for maximum prices. That said, it's well located in the heart of chic Nişantaşı, the 82 rooms are spacious, with natural-wood floors and restrained furnishings, the en-suite bathrooms feature rainshowers and herbal soaps, and there's a small fitness room and spa. It's also home to the fashionable rooftop *Frankie* restaurant, which melds Turkish and Mediterranean cuisines. €220

BEŞİKTAŞ AND ORTAKÖY

There are no budget options in Beşiktaş or Ortaköy – you pay a massive premium for the waterfront locations here, but they're worth considering if you are looking for distinctive Bosphorus-front accommodation close to the city centre and major sights.

Çırağan Palace Kempinski Çırağan Cad 32 ☎0212 326 4646, ⓦkempinski.com; map p.132. Unashamedly luxurious hotel, housed in an elaborately restored Ottoman palace right on the waterfront. Every possible extravagance is on offer here, from a selection of gourmet restaurants, an enormous outdoor pool and spa, an indoor art gallery, designer boutiques and even optional airport pick-up by helicopter. €420

Four Seasons Istanbul at the Bosphorus Çırağan Cad 28 ☎0212 381 4000, ⓦfourseasons.com/bosphorus; map p.132. Set in a sprawling nineteenth-century palace on the Bosphorus and offering all the luxuries you'd expect of a *Four Seasons* hotel – high-end cuisine, innovative spa menu, lavish furnishings and high prices. €590

W Hotel Süleyman Seba Cad 22 ☎0212 381 2121, ⓦwistanbul.com.tr; map p.132. Super-sleek boutique hotel that feels more like a nightclub than a hotel with its purple and green lighting, glittering pillars and mirrored ceilings. This place is all about the show so dress to impress and look important whether frequenting the indoor pool and spa or sipping a custom-made cocktail in the flashy lounge bar. Showy rooms feature iPod docks, state-of-the-art TVs and fulsome minibars; the most expensive suite has its own DJ deck and wet bar. €198

THE BOSPHORUS AND BLACK SEA RESORTS

★**A'jia** Çubuklu Cad 27, Kanlıca ☎0216 413 9300, ⓦajiahotel.com; map p.151. This sixteen-room hotel, converted from the beautiful Ahmet Rasim Paşa *yalı* (traditional wooden waterfront mansion) has managed to retain its period elegance despite having received a full minimalist-style makeover. The rooms on the top floor, built into the roof space, have delightful balconies with simply stunning Bosphorus views – and also offer the best value. Books up very quickly in season as it is relatively good value for a prime Bosphorus-front location. €180

Les Ottomans Muallim Naci Cad 68 ☎0212 359 1500, ⓦlesottomans.com; map p.151. The lovingly restored Muhsinzade Mehmet Pasha Mansion, famed for its magnificent Ottoman architecture, now houses one of Istanbul's most exclusive hotels. If you can make it past the indulgent display of celebrity guest photographs lining the entrance foyer, the hotel offers such delights as a private

12

cinema and its own fleet of boats waiting to whisk guests down the Bosphorus. **€800**

★Sumahan on the Water Kuleli Cad 51, Çengelköy ☎0216 422 8000, ⓦsumahan.com; map p.151. A late-Ottoman distillery converted into a wonderful hotel right on the Bosphorus in the pretty suburb of Çengelköy, this is

one of the city's best boutique hotels, winning a number of prestigious awards. There's a range of stylishly decorated rooms blending the contemporary and the traditional, all with great views and some with fireplaces for those cool evenings. Like the *A'jia*, it has a modest number of rooms so book well in advance. **€295**

THE PRINCES' ISLANDS

Island accommodation is at a premium on weekends – you may have to pay up to fifty percent more than the prices given below for Friday and Saturday night stays. This does not prevent rooms filling up, so advance booking is definitely recommended. Accommodation on **Büyükada** is uniformly expensive, though the chance to stay in a grand restored mansion or boutique sea-front hotel may be appealing; accommodation is cheaper and more down to earth on neighbouring **Heybeliada**.

BURGAZADA

Mehtap 45 On the northeast coast of the island ☎0216 381 2660; map pp.160–161. Though it's got all the mod cons, this is fairly spartan for a boutique hotel and might not seem incredibly good value, but the rooms are comfortable enough, the views northwest to the metropolis superb, and owner Abbas will proudly tell you how much England football legend Bobby Charlton enjoyed his four-day stay here. The island itself offers the best combination of beauty and peace. **€90**

HEYBELIADA

Merit Halki Palas Refah Şehitler Cad 88 ☎0216 351 0025, ⓦmerithotels.com; map pp.160–161. A nineteenth-century villa, restored in dubious taste by the Merit hotel group, this is the only five-star hotel on the islands, incorporating a gym, jacuzzi and outdoor pool. Rooms are plainly decorated, enlivened with floral-pattern bedspreads and many have good views of either pine forest or the sea. **€150**

Özdemir Pansiyon Ayyıldız Cad 41 ☎0216 351 1866; map pp.160–161. The cheapest option on the island, offering tiny chalet-type en-suite rooms with a shower over squat toilets, plus larger rooms in the main block with ceiling fans and decent bathrooms. Front rooms get some street noise and light. No breakfast. **₺100**

BÜYÜKADA

★Ayanikola Butik Pansiyon Aya Nikola Mevki 104 ☎0126 382 4143, ⓦayanikolabutikpansiyon.com; map pp.160–161. Right on the waterfront in the former vineyard of the nearby Aya Nikola monastery, on the east coast of the island, this eleven-room boutique hotel is a

gem. Each room has a sea view and is individually furnished with antique furniture and fittings, which contrast wonderfully with the plain white walls, stripped floors and exposed brickwork. The "special" rooms have a bed right next to the picture-window giving stunning views over to Asia. **₺330**

Meziki Anastasia Malül Gazi Cad 24 ☎0216 382 3444, ⓦmezikihotel.com; map pp.160–161. A gorgeous mansion on the eastern outskirts of the main settlement, not far from the ferry terminal, the *Meziki* is housed in an Italian-designed, *fin-de-siècle* villa liberally adorned with neo-Renaissance murals. Rooms are large, high-ceilinged and furnished with antique furniture, with those on the front boasting sea views. For period charm, it's hard to beat but note that there are shared bathrooms on the landings. **₺340**

Naya Retreat Maden, Yılmaz Türk Cad 96 ☎0216 382 4598, ⓦnayalstanbul.com; map pp.160–161. A fine 105-year-old wooden mansion set in lush gardens on the island's east coast, the unusual *Naya* is a hybrid yoga/alternative therapy/meditation centre-cum-semi-rural retreat. It is run by the well-travelled and laidback Ludwig, who offers rooms furnished in an upmarket ethnic-hippie style, in the house, or tents in the rambling garden. **€110**

★Splendid Palace Nisan Cad 23 ☎0216 382 6950, ⓦsplendidhotel.net; map pp.160–161. A few minutes west of the ferry terminal, the *Splendid*, dating from 1908, was once host to Edward VIII and Mrs Simpson. It has serious *fin-de-siècle* grandeur, with cupolas, balconies, a good restaurant, excellent service and a garden with a decent-sized swimming pool out back. Rooms underwent a major upgrade in 2013, with new wooden floors and subtle muslin drapes at the windows enhancing their high-ceilinged grandeur. Closed Nov–March. **US$145**

APARTMENTS

Apartments are a good choice for many visitors, particularly if you are staying for a while or if you are a group or family. Even booked on a night-by-night basis, the price of a small apartment is often less than you'd pay for a room in a hotel of a similar standard and for stays of a week or more the cost can drop substantially. The number of companies offering apartments for rent across the city has rocketed in recent years, with stiff competition offered by **Airbnb** (ⓦairbnb.com), which enables private individuals to let their rooms, apartments or houses through a safe booking system. A selection of

Istanbul's apartment-rental companies are listed below, followed by a number of recommended properties (prices shown are per night).

LETTING COMPANIES

Arsu Living Istanbul Apartments Beyoğlu ☎+90 531 2217156, ⊚ living-Istanbul.com. A German-Turkish couple offering five well-priced, nicely fitted out apartments in and around Beyoğlu.

Istanbul Apartments Tel Sok 27, Beyoğlu ☎0212 249 5065, ⊚ Istanbul.com. Professionally run Turkish operation with a good choice of apartments on İstiklal Cad and in Cihangir.

Istanbul!place apartments ☎+44 7729 251676, ⊚ Istanbulplace. Run by a friendly Anglo-Turkish couple, Tarkan and Julia, Istanbul!place offer fifteen beautifully restored apartments, all housed in fine late nineteenth-century houses in and around the trendy Galata district.

Manzara Istanbul Tatarbeyi Sok 26b, Galata ☎0212 252 4600, ⊚ manzara-Istanbul.com A reliable organization run by a German-born Turkish architect, with around forty carefully chosen properties, mainly in Galata and Beyoğlu.

RECOMMENDED PROPERTIES

Divan Taksim Suites Cumhuriyet Cad 31, Taksim ☎0212 254 7777, ⊚ taksimsuites.com.tr; map p.128. White blinds, white rugs, white furnishings, blonde-wood floors: this is Scandinavian-style minimalism in the heart of Taksim. The suites all work on an open-plan scheme, with well-kitted-out kitchens off a spacious sleeping/dining/sitting area. The 110m-square Bosphorus penthouse suite offers great views over the waterway and as much light as you can handle through its roof windows. All suites have large work stations and wi-fi, plus music system and TV. **€190**

★**Istanbul Suite Home** Dizdariye Çeşmesi Sok 51, Sultanahmet ☎0212 458 5255, ⊚ Istanbulsuitehome .com; map p.46. Situated a little way from the main tourist haunts, in a tall, narrow townhouse on a quiet backstreet south of Divan Yolu, the five apartments here are extremely stylish and very good value. Modish without being minimalist, all pale wood and white, three apartments have two bedrooms, two a single bedroom. All have a spacious dining area with attached kitchen. The appliances

are all top quality and there's a shared roof terrace with views over the Sea of Marmara. Affable owner Yuksel also has a property in arty Cihangir. **€125**

★**Mehmet's Place** Ayvansaray Cad, Balat, ⊚ airbnb .com/rooms/1091681; map p.91. Situated in the atmospheric and historic neighbourhood of Balat, this is a brilliant location for anyone wanting to escape the tourist fleshpots of Sultanahmet and Galata/Beyoğlu. Essentially it's an open-plan living/sleeping and kitchen affair, with an en-suite w.c. and shower. But the real plus is the private roof terrace with great views to the Golden Horn just a stone's throw away. Mehmet's mum lives below and is very helpful (particularly with the washing as there's no machine in the flat), though she doesn't speak much English. Plenty of buses ply the road outside to Taksim/Beyoğlu and Eminönü (for Sultanahmet) but best is the Ayvansaray ferry pier, a two-minute walk away, for a leisurely boat ride to Karaköy and Eminönü. **£37**

Öner's Place Bereketzade Medresesi Sok, Galata ⊚ airbnb.co.uk/rooms/3382936; map p.110. Fabulously located just below the landmark Galata Tower, the best thing about this apartment is the private terrace with panoramic views to the old city, Golden Horn and Bosphorus. Owner Öner is friendly and reliable and the place is superbly located for the local nightlife. Sleeps four, with one bedroom and a sofa bed in the sitting room. **£73**

★**Pasha Place** Serdar-I Ekrem Cad, Galata ⊚ Istanbulplace.com; map p.110. *Pasha*, the flagship apartment of Istanbul!place apartments, is located on the third floor of one of this fashionable street's most attractive nineteenth-century apartments. Facing south, the sitting room and main bedroom have fantastic views across rooftops and the Golden Horn to the old city skyline, and over the confluence of the Horn and Bosphorus to Asia. High ceilings, white walls, original wooden or antique tile flooring make this a perfect blend of period elegance and contemporary styling, especially when flooded with light on bright days. There are three bedrooms (two doubles, one twin), a well-equipped and stylish kitchen, and separate shower room and w.c. **€300**

12

NİZAM PİDE

Eating

Gourmets rank Turkish food, along with French and Chinese, as one of the three classic cuisines. This is great news for visitors to the nation's cultural capital, as the very best of it can be found here in Istanbul. The city's rich and varied cuisine derives from its multi-ethnic Ottoman heritage, when it was capital of an empire stretching from the Middle East to the Balkans and the Caucasus to North Africa. Istanbulites, like all Turks, are demanding when it comes to food, and want the freshest ingredients, the best service and, if possible, a little something extra. Everyone you speak to will have an opinion on where to find the best dishes; whether it's a (seemingly simple) bean stew or an elaborate contemporary offering.

Fortunately for them, Turkey, with so many climatic zones and an important rural economy, produces a stunning array of **fresh fruit and vegetables** – the best of which find their way to the markets and shops of the metropolis. Fresh **fish** comes in from the nearby Black Sea, Sea of Marmara and Aegean, and the Anatolian **lamb** is as succulent and the **yoghurt** as thick, creamy and delicious as you'd expect from a people who trace their origins back to Central Asian nomadic pastoralism.

Istanbul has eating places to suit every budget, though **prices** have risen across the board in recent years. A breakfast portion of the flaky, crumbly cheese-pie *peynirli böreği* will cost around ₺4, a sesame-seed-coated bread ring or *simit* a quarter of that from a street vendor. A few lira will get you a tasty takeaway chicken-filled *döner* wrap in parts less frequented by tourists, three more a hearty vegetable or pulse stew from a basic restaurant; fresh, oven-baked *pide* (Turkish-style pizza) will set you back around ₺10 depending on the location of the restaurant. By way of contrast, a latte will burn at least a ₺7 hole in your pocket, while a meal with drinks at a chic fusion-style joint in Beyoğlu or one of the upmarket Bosphorus fish restaurants will cost in excess of ₺100 a head.

Once there was a fairly firm line drawn between different kinds of eating establishments in Turkey, but this has broken down recently, particularly in Istanbul.

TRADITIONAL EATING PLACES

There are plenty of places to find good-value meals in the city, though these are often unlicensed. Nowadays it's quite common to find establishments that combine elements of everything, often concentrating on *hazır yemek* (pre-prepared food) for the lunchtime trade and knocking out kebabs and *pide* in the evening. These kinds of eating places can be found all over the city, though they are at a premium in Sultanahmet. Street-cart vendors fill the culinary gaps.

Börekçi dish up different kinds of pastries, both savoury and sweet, and are particularly popular at breakfast time.

Büfe contrary to what the name suggests, these are not open buffets but instead late-night (often 24-hour) joints that serve up fast food such as *tost* (cheese toastie), *ıslak* hamburger (burger steamed in its bun in a tomato and garlic sauce) and *döner* kebab.

Çorbacı specialize in various kinds of soup, popular for breakfast in winter, for lunch or after a night out on the town.

Esnaf Lokantası are, traditionally, restaurants emphasizing *ev yemeği* (home-style food) and *hazır yemek* (also known as *sulu yemek* meaning "watery food") – pre-cooked dishes kept warm in a steamtray, especially stews. The food at the best *esnaf lokantası*s can be the most delicious you'll have in the city.

Kebapçı and **köfteci** specialize in the preparation of kebabs and meatballs respectively, with a limited number of side dishes – usually just an array of salad, yoghurt and desserts. They vary enormously in quality but the best will make you realize why Turks are so passionate about grilled meat.

Meyhane (taverns) have a long history in this city and are more popular now than ever, with hordes of Istanbulites going out on the town, especially at weekends, to eat their way through reams of *meze* (starters) and fish or meat mains, downing copious amounts of *rakı* before singing and dancing along to roving bands of Roma musicians.

Ocakbaşı A twist on the kebab restaurant, where kebabs and other meats are grilled over charcoal in front of their hungry customers – the more fortunate get to cosy right up to the grill. The vast majority serve alcohol and at their best the food is exquisite.

Pastane the Turkish take on the patisserie serves up all kinds of *baklava*, milk-based puddings and more familiar sweets such as chocolate eclairs and profiteroles.

Pideci concentrate on flat-breads topped with cheese, meat, vegetables and various combinations of them all, baked to perfection in wood-fired ovens.

Restoran are less boisterous than *meyhane*. The simpler serve little more than grilled meats, salads and an array of *meze* to accompany the alcohol, while the more upmarket ones specialize in dishes with their origins in the finest Ottoman cuisine, or reflect the changing times and serve fine Mediterranean or Asian-influenced cuisine.

13

The demarcation made here between the various eating places (and, indeed, the bars listed in "Nightlife") is far from precise, with many cafés serving full meals as well as snacks – by and large, if it's listed under restaurants, it's the kind of place where you'd sit down to an evening meal.

ESSENTIALS

Alcohol is forbidden in Islam so, even in a secularized Muslim country like Turkey, many restaurants do not serve it. Of the traditional eating establishments, you will only find *içki* (alcoholic drinks) in *meyhane*, *restoran* or *ocakbaşı* (see box, p.177), but there are plenty of modern cafés, fusion and international-style restaurants that are licensed, and more than a few kebab places also serve alcohol. We have indicated in the listings which places are unlicensed.

CAFÉS, PATISSERIES AND CHEAP EATS

Café society in Istanbul is as wide ranging as in any other European capital, with everything from traditional male-only teahouses to stylish (and expensive) café-bars – and an ever increasing number of multinational coffee chains. Most of the trendy café-bars are to be found in Beyoğlu, though there are a few passable options in the tourist heartland of Sultanahmet.

SULTANAHMET

Çiğdem Pastanesi Divan Yolu Cad 62 ☎0212 526 8859, ⓦcigdempastanesi.com; map p.46. For over fifty years, *Çiğdem* has been offering a good selection of both Turkish and non-Turkish pastries and sweets. Try the crisp on the outside, chewy on the inside *acı badem*, a traditional almond-flavoured biscuit, or the reliable *baklava* (₺6 a portion). Also does a decent range of coffees, from Turkish to lattes, and of course tea. Unlicensed. Daily 8am–11pm.

Doy Doy Sıfa Hamamı Sok 13 ☎0212 517 1588, ⓦdoydoy-restaurant.com; map p.46. A backpacker's favourite, with a well-deserved reputation for cheap and well-prepared kebabs and *pide* from ₺11, and *sulu yemek* from ₺5. There are a few choices for vegetarians. Dining is on four floors, including a roof terrace with great views of the Sea of Marmara and, at night, the illuminated Blue Mosque. Unlicensed. Daily 8am–11pm.

Edebiyat Kıraathanesi Divan Yolu Cad 14 ☎0212 526 1615, map p.46. Handily located next to the Sultanahmet tram stop, this cavernous place is run by the Turkish Society for Literature and, appropriately, is a peaceful and comfy place to sit down, linger over a glass of tea or a latte (₺7) and sample one of a mouthwatering array of cakes and puddings while reading the latest Pamuk or Shafak novel. Daily 9am–10pm.

Pudding Shop (Lale Restaurant) Divan Yolu Cad 6 ☎0212 522 2970, ⓦpuddingshop.com; map p.46. This Sultanahmet institution first opened its doors in 1957, and in the late 1960s became *the* meeting place for hippies and other travellers travelling overland to India (see box, p.62). *The Pudding Shop* is still dishing up its signature rice pudding (₺7) along with a wide array of traditional Turkish dishes. Service is canteen-style, but the food's good, it's right near the major sights and serves alcohol. Daily 7am–11pm.

Tarihi Sultanahmet Köftecisi Divan Yolu Cad ☎0212 511 3960, ⓦsultanahmetkoftesi.com; map p.46. The longest established of three *köfte* specialists at this end of Divan Yolu, and frequented by Turkish celebrities (check out the framed newspaper clippings and thank-you letters on the tiled walls). A plate of tasty meatballs, pickled peppers, fresh bread and a spicy tomato-sauce dip costs ₺14. Windows in the upstairs salons boast views across to the Haghia Sophia and Blue Mosque. Unlicensed. Daily 11am–11pm.

EMİNÖNÜ AND SİRKECİ

Lezzet-i Şark Hasırcılar Cad 52, Eminönü ☎0212 514 2763; map p.70. Located on the road running between the Spice Bazaar and the Rüstem Paşa mosque, this casual joint is popular with local shopkeepers for its specialties from the Gaziantep region. Particularly tasty are the *içli köfte* (nut-studded crumbly meatballs encased in a crispy bulgur shell; ₺4) and the *künefe* (cheese wrapped in shredded pastry and soaked in syrup; ₺8) which sizzles over open coals. Unlicensed. Daily 8am–7.30pm.

Şehzade Çağ Kebabı Hocapaşa Sok 3/a ☎0212 520 3361; map p.70. Like all the best local eating places in Istanbul, *Şehzade Çağ Kebabı* specializes in just one thing and concentrates on doing it right. *Çağ Kebabı* (from the mountainous Erzurum region) is said to be the forerunner of the more ubiquitous *döner*, but cooked on a horizontal

TOP FIVE SOUTHEAST TURKISH CUISINE

rather than vertical spit. Order slices of the grilled meat as a portion or in a *dürüm* (wrap) for ₺14. The only other options on the menu are meant to be eaten as condiments; spicy tomato paste, salad, and buffalo yoghurt. Unlicensed. Mon–Sat 11.30am–8pm.

Set Üstü Çay Bahçesi Gülhane Parkı, Sirkeci ☎0212 513 9610; map p.70. This open-air café, tucked away at the southern end of the park near the Goth's Column, with great views over the Bosphorus and back up to the walls of the Topkapı Palace, does excellent samovar-style Turkish tea and is a great place to rest up after sightseeing. Also has a simple snack-menu with toasted sandwiches for ₺5. Unlicensed. Daily 9am–10pm.

AROUND THE GRAND BAZAAR

★**Ağa Kapısı** Nazir Izzet Efendi Sok 11 ☎0212 519 5176; map pp.78–79. Tucked away on a dead-end street just below the Süleymaniye Camii and frequented mainly by local traders, conservative students and their lecturers, the three-storey *Ağa Kapısı* has picture windows beyond compare, giving stunning panoramic views down over the Galata Bridge, the mouth of the Golden Horn and the Bosphorus beyond. The food is simple and cheap – try the *gözleme* (a kind of *paratha* stuffed with goat's cheese, ₺6) and a glass of tea, traditional Turkish style, or indulge in one of their Ottoman-style sherbet drinks (₺6) or a *melengiç* (wild pistachio) "coffee" (₺6). Smokers may opt to simply puff away on a flavoured *nargile* (₺15) on the roof terrace. Unlicensed. Daily 8am–midnight.

Erenler Çay Bahçesi Çorlulu Ali Paşa Medrese, Yeniçeriler Cad 36–38 ☎0212 528 3785; map pp.78–79. In the courtyard of the 300-year-old *medrese* (religious school) of Çorulu Ali Paşa, *Erenler Çay Bahçesi* is a cheap-and-cheerful bazaar-worker-oriented *nargile* café with waterpipes for ₺12, tea for a lira and snacks like toasted sandwiches (₺5) on offer. Unlicensed. Daily: April–Oct 7am–3am; Nov–March 7am–midnight.

Fes Café Ali Baba Türbe Sok 25/7a, off Nuruosmaniye Cad, Kapalı Çarşı ☎0212 526 3071; map p.80. A trendy mix of traditional and new, with designer tables spilling out onto a quiet cobbled street. There's a big flat-screen TV, mellow piped music and, despite its location, the majority of the clientele are mainly well-heeled Turks. Sandwiches are wholesome and filling and reasonable value at ₺13, and there's also a good selection of home-made cakes. A hole-in-the-wall branch can be found in the Grand Bazaar on Hacılar Cad 62, which keeps bazaar opening hours. Unlicensed. Daily 8am–9pm.

★**Tarihi Kuru Fasulye Süleymaniye Erzincanlı Ali Baba** Siddik Samı Onar Cad 11 ☎0212 513 6219; map pp.78–79. In the gorgeous Süleymaniye Camii complex, with tables set out on the precinct between the mosque and *medrese* behind, this simple place serves up some of the tastiest beans in town (and they're not out of a can) for a bargain ₺5 – though beware of the hot chilli pepper draped innocently atop your steaming bowl of buttery, tomato-sauce-drenched pulses. Unlicensed. Daily 9am–7pm.

Vefa Bozacısı Katip Çelebi Cad 104/1 ☎0212 519 4922, ⓦvefa.com.tr; map pp.78–79. Worth a look just to see the interior: old tiled floor, dark wood shelves, ornate Victorian-style mirrors, 1920s light-fittings, and bottles of vinegar with label designs unchanged for decades (Atatürk was here in 1937). The *boza* (₺3), a custard-like, viscous drink made by fermenting millet or bulgur wheat with sugar and water (best drunk in the winter months), is an acquired taste but very healthy. Unlicensed. Daily 7am–midnight.

IN THE GRAND BAZAAR

★**Bedesten Café** Cevahir Bedesteni 143–151, Kapalı Çarşı ☎0212 520 2250; map p.80. An oasis of peace and tranquillity in the Grand Bazaar, decorated with two giant *alem* – the brass crescent- and star-topped finials that adorn mosque domes and minarets – and an even bigger portrait of Atatürk. The food is prepared using quality ingredients with delicacies such as the scrambled tomato and pepper omelette *menemen* or a full Turkish breakfast for ₺12. Lunch mains include Turkish ravioli (*mantı*) in garlic and yoghurt sauce (₺18), and there's a great selection of cakes. It even has its own toilets, a rarity among bazaar establishments. Unlicensed. Mon–Sat 8.30am–6.30pm.

★**Dönerci Şahin Usta** Nuruosmaniye Kılıçlar Sok 7 ☎0212 526 5297; map p.80. One of the best places in the city to try a real *döner* kebab, conveniently situated right outside the Nuruosmaniye Gate of the Grand Bazaar. Succulent lamb freshly layered on the vertical spit each morning is dished up with sliced tomatoes, onions smothered in sumac, green peppers and an oven-fresh mini-*pide* bread. It's a hole-in-the-wall place with no seats, and the long queues attest to its loyal clientele; this is the real deal (cheaper kebab joints use fatty meat and frozen, pre-prepared *döners*). ₺9 for a kebab, best washed down with the frothy salted yoghurt drink *ayran* (₺2). Unlicensed. Mon–Sat 10am–3pm.

Havuzlu Ganı Çelebi Sok 3, Kapalı Çarşı ☎0212 527 3346; map p.80. Appealing Grand Bazaar restaurant, with

---

TOP FIVE FISH RESTAURANTS
Balıkçı Sabahattin Sultanahmet, see p.186
Giritli Sultanahmet, see p.186
İmroz İstiklal Caddesi and around, see p.189
Kıyı Bosphorus, see p.191
Suna'nın Yeri, see p.192

AN A–Z OF TURKISH CUISINE

Appetizers (meze) Turkey is justly famous for its *meze*, in many ways the heart of the nation's cuisine. The best and most common include: *patlıcan salatası* (aubergine mash), *semizotu* (purslane weed, usually in yoghurt), *mücver* (courgette fritters), *sigara böreği* (tightly rolled cheese pastries), fava (broad bean paste), *imam bayıldı* (cold baked aubergine with onion and tomato) and *dolma* (stuffed vegetables).

Baklava and pastry-based desserts There are a variety of different *baklava*-related desserts, all permutations of a sugar, flour, nut and butter mix. The best is *antep fıstıklı sarması* (pistachio-filled *baklava*); *cevizli* (walnut-filled) *baklava* is usually a little cheaper. Also worth trying is *künefe*, another southeastern Turkish treat made from mild goat's cheese, wrapped in shredded wheat soaked in syrup, and baked in the oven.

Bread (ekmek) The standard Turkish loaf, sold from glass-fronted cabinets outside grocery stores across the city, is good fresh but soon goes stale. Flat, semi-leavened *pide* bread is served with soup, at *kebapçıs* and during Ramadan. Unleavened *lavaş*, like a tortilla, is the wrap of choice in *döner* joints. Occasionally found is *Mısır ekmeği* (corn bread), a Black Sea staple.

Cheese (peynir) *Beyaz peynir*, which is virtually Identical to Greek Feta, is not Turkey's only cheese. *Dil peynir* ("tongue" cheese), a hard, salty cheese that breaks up into chewy strands, and plaited *oğru peynir*, can both be grilled or fried like Cypriot *halloúmi*. *Tulum peynir* is a strong, salty, goat's cheese cured in a goatskin. *Otlu peynir* is cured with herbs and eaten at breakfast; cow's-milk *kaşar*, especially *eski* (aged) *kaşar*, is also highly esteemed, and is similar to cheddar.

Fish (balık) Budget mainstays include *sardalya* (sardines – grilled fresh), *hamsi* (anchovies – usually fried) and *istavrit* (horse mackerel). *Mercan* (red bream), *lüfer* (bluefish), *kılıç* (swordfish) and *orfoz* (giant grouper) are highly prized and expensive. *Çipura* (gilt-head bream) and *levrek* (sea bass) are usually farmed and consequently good value – if less tasty. Fish is generally served grilled.

Grilled meats (ızgara) Kebabs include the spicy *Adana*, with its sprinkling of purple sumac herb betraying Arab influence; *İskender kebap*, best sampled in the city of Bursa (see p.251), is heavy on the tomato sauce and yoghurt. *Köfte* (meatballs), *şiş* (meat chunks, usually mutton or beef) and *çöp* (bits of fatty lamb or offal) are other options. Chicken (*piliç* or *tavuk*) is widely available, usually either as a skewer-cooked *şiş* or a breast fillet. In some places, you can ask for a *dürüm*, when the meat and garnish are served in a flat-bread wrap. *Pirzola*, tiny lamb chops, are usually only available in more upmarket restaurants.

Ottoman-style decor and white tablecloths on dark wood tables laid out beneath a barrel-vaulted ceiling. Offers a good range of kebabs (the *İskender* is recommended) and *hazır yemek* dishes. Brisk service, tasty food and reasonable prices (kebabs around ₺12). Unlicensed. Mon–Sat 10am–5pm.

Subaşı Lokantası Nuruosmaniye Cad 48, Çarşı Kapı ☎ 0212 522 4762; map p.80. Behind Nuruosmaniye Camii, just outside the main entrance of the Grand Bazaar, this traditional *lokanta* serves excellent lunchtime food to the market traders. Highly rated by many Turkish newspapers (their restaurant reviews adorn the walls), you should go early (noon–1pm), as it gets packed and food may run out. Mains cost upwards of ₺10 a portion, with meat dishes costing more – try the stuffed peppers or delicious *karnıyarık* (mince-filled aubergine). Unlicensed. Mon–Sat 11am–5pm.

THE NORTHWEST QUARTER

Arnavut Köfteci Mursel Paşa Cad 149; map p.91. Although not quite so long established as the late

nineteenth-century Greek building in which it's housed, this one-room café has been around for fifty years or more – the owner a fair bit longer. The motley array of vintage Formica-topped tables, each a different pastel hue, are usually packed with down-to-earth locals, though a crop of trendy media types turns up from time to time. The *köfte* (₺8) are delicious, especially when washed down with a glass of *ayran*. Unlicensed. Mon–Sat 4.30am–6.30pm.

Café Vodina Vodina Cad 39, Balat ☎ 0212 531 0057; map p.91. Located inside the Balat Cultural Centre, this makes an excellent spot for lunch. Its serves a daily changing menu of good wholesome food, like stuffed vine leaves and *mantı* (meat-filled dumplings in a yoghurt sauce), similar to those you would find in a Turkish home, with prices around ₺10–15/dish. The café has a cosy feel and there is a small garden out the back. You may stumble upon one of their regular events, from flea markets to jam-making workshops. Unlicensed. Daily 10am–8pm.

Çanak Mangalda Kuru Fasulye Ayvansaray Cad 25 ☎ 0212 621 5835; map p.91. This local favourite serves up

13

Ice cream (dondurma) The genuine *Maraşlı döşme dondurma* (whipped in the Kahraman Maraş tradition – a bit like Italian *gelato*) is the ice cream of choice in Istanbul. The chewy texture comes from the addition of mastic and *salep* (wild orchid root powder).

Meat dishes (et yemekleri) *Karnıyarık*, aubergine halves stuffed with a rich mince-filling, is a delicious staple, as is *güveç*, a clay-pot casserole. *Hünkar beğendi* (beef stew on a bed of puréed eggplant and cheese) has its origins in Ottoman times and is a must-try. *Saray kebap* (beef stew topped with bechamel sauce, and oven-browned), *macar kebap* (Hungarian-style stewed meat and vegetables topped with mashed potato and cheese, then baked) are both standards.

Milk-based puddings (muhallebi) *Süpangile* ("süp" for short, a corruption of *soupe d'Anglais*) is a rich chocolate pudding with sponge or a biscuit inside. More modest are *keşkül* (a vanilla and nut-crumble custard) and *sütlaç* (rice pudding). The most unusual dish is *tavukgöğsü*, a cinnamon-topped morsel made from boiled and strained chicken breast, semolina starch and milk. *Kazandibi* (literally "bottom of the pot") is *tavukgöğsü* residue with a dark crust on the bottom.

Offal (sakatat) *Böbrek* (kidney), *yürek* (heart), *ciğer* (liver) are found in some *ocakbaşıs*; far more common is *kokoreç*, seasoned lamb's intestines often cooked on a charcoal grill and available from street vendors.

Salad (salata) *Çoban* (shepherd's) *salatası* is the generic term for the widespread cucumber, tomato, onion, pepper and parsley salad; *yeşil* (green) salad, usually just some *marul* (lettuce), is only seasonally available. *Mevsim salatası* or seasonal salad – perhaps tomato slices, watercress, red cabbage and lettuce hearts, sprinkled with cheese and drenched in dressing, often accompanies a kebab meal.

Soup (çorba) Commonest are *mercimek* (lentil), *ezo gelin* (bulgur and tomato broth). *Kelle paça* (head and trotters) or *işkembe* (tripe) soup laced liberally with garlic oil, vinegar and red pepper flakes, are esteemed hangover cures.

Steamtray dishes (hazır or sulu yemek) Dishes such as *kuru fasulye* (bean stew – rather like baked beans in tomato sauce), *taze fasulye* (French beans), *sebze turlu* (vegetable stew) and *nohut* (chickpeas) are usually found in *esnaf lokantası*s (see box, p.177). Meaty favourites include *sebzeli köfte* (meatballs stewed with vegetables) and various types of chicken stew.

Turkish Delight (lokum) In its basic form, *lokum* is just solidified sugar and pectin, most commonly flavoured with rosewater and dusted with sugar. More expensive versions are nut filled, usually either walnuts or pistachios. It's not traditionally found in restaurants or even *pastanes*, but is for sale in virtually every souvenir shop and the Grand and Spice bazaars (see p.77 and p.72, respectively).

---

hearty bowls of *kuru fasulye* (tomato-based white bean stew) with either cured beef or chunks of lamb for ₺10, along with buttery *pilav* (rice) for ₺5.50, and thick creamy yogurt for ₺6. It's a no-frills joint and a little pricier than the competition but is a reliable stop for a quick fill. Unlicensed. Daily 11am–9pm.

THE LAND WALLS

Bağdatlım Silivri Kapı Cad 77 ☎0212 589 7788; map p.102. This worker's café, less than five minutes' walk west of Silivri Kapı, is excellent for charcoal-grilled kebabs, especially those in a *dürüm* (wrap), starting from ₺5. Eat on low stools in the open porch area at the front of the café and watch the street life outside. Daily 10am–10pm.

Durak Köfte Mihrimah Sultan Camii Altı ☎0212 532 5581; map p.102. Handily located in front of the Mihrimah Camii, this tiny tradesman's café does most of its business with mosque regulars and the minibus drivers from the garage opposite. It is justly famed for its Rumeli

(Macedonian)-style grilled meatballs (₺8) but also does excellent lentil soup. Daily 9pm–8pm.

Fatih Belediyesi Sosyal Tesisleri Topkapı ☎0212 523 0898; map p.102. This municipality-run restaurant, handily placed midway along the length of the land walls of Theodosius, has tables outside set right against a well-restored section of them, with well-priced grills (from ₺15) and snacks like toasted sandwiches (₺6) and the scrambled egg and pepper dish, *menemen* (₺10). Daily 9am–10pm.

Merkez Efendi Köftecisi Mevlana Kapı Cad 39 ☎0212 587 9868; map p.102. Noted for its delicious grilled meatballs (₺9), this simple café has a handful of tables and some low stools on the street outside. Like *Özen Kardeşler* more or less opposite, it's just a few minutes' walk west from Mevlana Kapı. Daily 9am–9pm.

Özen Kardeşler Mevlana Kapı Cad; map p.102. Excellent for all kinds of *sulu yemek* dishes, such as *nohut* (chickpeas in tomato sauce) and Turkish-style mousakka (similar to the Greek version but lacking the cheese-sauce

13

topping). Locals eat early at lunchtime so the choice of dishes narrows dramatically after 1pm. Stews from ₺5. Daily 8am–10pm.

GALATA AND THE WATERFRONT DISTRICTS

★**Café Privato** Tımarcı Sok 3b, Galata ☎0212 293 2055, ⓦprivatocafe.com; map p.110. The breakfast here, served up until mid-afternoon most days, is commonly regarded as one of the best in town. Cosy and quaint, the tables are bestowed with a staggering array of dishes: home-made organic jams, mini Georgian pancakes, five types of cheese, dressed olives and more. Though not cheap at ₺30/serving, one full breakfast is usually enough for two people. Non-breakfast goodies include home-made meatballs, *mantı* and a good-value mixed *meze* plate. Daily 9am–midnight.

Galata Konak Patisserie Hacı Ali Sok 2, Galata ☎0212 252 5346, ⓦgalatakonakcafe.com; map p.110. Just down from the Galata Tower, this stylish café dishes up delicious lattes (with amaretto biscuits) as well as a range of tempting cakes and desserts from ₺8.50. For something a little more substantial, head up the lantern-lit stairwell or take the antique lift to the rooftop restaurant for a range of Turkish and European dishes and an expansive view over the Golden Horn. Popular with locals and tourists alike, it always seems to be packed. Unlicensed. Daily 9am–9pm.

Istanbul Modern Café Meclis-i-Mebusan Cad Antrepo 4, Tophane ☎0212 292 2612; map p.110. A chic, fashion-conscious place, as you would expect from a café attached to the city's leading contemporary arts gallery (see p.208), with a spacious terrace overlooking the Bosphorus. A blend of international and Turkish food (mains from ₺24) but with the snail's-pace service it's probably better to just opt for a latte – it's worth the ₺10 to sit on the terrace and watch the ships go by. Daily 10am–midnight.

★**Karaköy Güllüoğlu** Rıhtım Cad 17, off İskelesi Cad 10–12, Karaköy ☎0212 293 0910, ⓦkarakoygulluoglu .com; map p.110. Buttery, nut-filled *baklava*, often eaten with a generous dollop of ice cream, takes pride of place here and draws in sweet-toothed families from across the city. A *karışık tabağı* (mixed plate) costs ₺9 – make sure to get a dollop of the chewy Maraş ice cream for an extra ₺1.50. This branch is the original of a popular countrywide chain, founded in 1949 by the Güllüoğlu family, *baklava* connoisseurs from Gaziantep, the nation's pistachio and *baklava* capital. Daily 10am–midnight.

Kikero Falafel Yörük Çıkmazı 5, Galata ☎0212 243 5070; map p.110. Tucked down a small side street just off Galipdede Cad, aka "Music Alley", this tiny place only has a few stools, so is not the place for a lengthy meal, but makes a great stop for a vegetarian lunch on the go. The friendly staff serve up delicious hot, crunchy falafels in a choice of

wraps, sandwiches, portions or salads (₺5–10). Unlicensed. Daily 9am–9pm.

İSTİKLAL CADDESI AND AROUND

Canım Ciğerim Minare Sok 1, Beyoğlu ☎0212 252 6060; map pp.120–121. Just off buzzing Asmalımescit Cad, this is a low-key restaurant that's very popular with locals. Take a seat on one of the tiny stools and order chicken, lamb or liver *şiş* skewers, served with fresh flat *lavaş* bread and four varieties of salad, plus grilled vegetables (₺20). For a lighter bite, a pre-prepared *dürüm* wrap costs ₺10. Daily noon–1am.

Dürümzade Kamer Hatun Cad 26/a ☎0212 249 0147; map pp.120–121. On a busy side street, this tiny corner joint has become something of an institution. They serve up various *dürüms* (wraps) with perfectly char-grilled meats for an excellent value ₺5–10. The secret here is the chewy flatbread they use which is rubbed with spice mix before being toasted on the grill. Daily 8am–4am.

Helvetia General Yazgan Sok 12, Asmalımescit ☎0212 245 8780; map pp.120–121. There's no sign above the door here, instead look out for the faint words written on the wall of this corner building. The hidden theme continues inside where there are no menus, just a steam counter displaying the day's offerings. There's a vegetarian focus but meat and chicken dishes are sometimes available. This is healthy Turkish home cooking at its best, and affordable too with a mixed plate of up to five choices costing just ₺11. Unlicensed. Daily noon–midnight.

Kafe Ara Tosbağa Sok 8/a, off Yeniçarşı Cad, Beyoğlu ☎0212 245 4105, ⓦkafeara.com; map pp.120–121. A great place, tucked away just off Galatasaray Meydanı, with a raft of tables out in the alley and a lovely dark wood bistro-style interior lined with black-and-white images by Ara Güler (see box, p.206). Choose from big bowls of salad from ₺16 or more expensive dishes like steak cooked with a basil sauce for ₺30. The clientele are generally prosperous, but it's not overly posh and is the perfect spot to rest your feet after the rigours of shopping on İstiklal Cad. Unlicensed. Mon–Thurs 7.30am–midnight, Fri 7.30am–1am, Sat & Sun 10.30am–midnight.

★**Mandabatmaz** Olivia Geçidi off İstiklal Cad; map pp.120–121. This tiny Turkish coffee joint is more of an institution than a café. Open since 1967, you get the impression it hasn't changed a jot, impressive in the face of the rampant development of the surrounding area. Pull up a stool in the cramped interior or on the street outside and, for ₺3, enjoy one of the best Turkish coffees in Istanbul – thick, velvety and chocolate like – the result of its custom-roasted coffee beans. Unlicensed. Daily 9am–midnight.

Nizam Pide Büyükparmakkapı Sok 13, off İstiklal Cad, Beyoğlu ☎0212 249 7918, ⓦnizampide.com; map pp.120–121. Excellent *pide* (₺11 and up), from the traditional *kuşbaşı pide*, topped with diced meat, to a more exotic mushroom-topped variety. Also serves great soups and beans in a rich tomato sauce. There's a second branch – *Nizam Pide 2* – on Kalyoncu Kulluk Cad, behind Nevizade Sok in the Fish Market, and both are regularly rated among the top ten *pide* outlets in Turkey. Unlicensed. Open 24hr.

★ **Saray** İstiklal Cad 107, Beyoğlu ☎0212 292 3434, ⓦsaraymuhallebicisi.com; map pp.120–121. Best value of Istanbul's upmarket patisseries (sweets range between ₺5–10). Established in 1935, the emphasis is on classic Turkish desserts such as *fırın sütlaç* (baked rice pudding), *irmik helvası* (semolina with nuts) and *baklava*-type sweets, including wonderful *fıstık sarma* (pistachios packed in a syrup-drenched pastry roll), though it also serves good savoury Turkish food. Daily 6am–11pm.

Van Kahvaltı Evi Defterdar Yokuşu 52/a, Cihangir ☎0212 293 6437; map pp.120–121. Among the many identikit trendy cafés in Cihangir, this stands out for its regional cuisine. Specializing in breakfast (the type that can actually be eaten all day in Turkey) from the Van region in Eastern Turkey with dishes such as *kavut* (roasted wheat flour blended with honey and walnuts), *jaji* (yoghurt and cottage cheese), and aubergine pancakes. Expect to wait for a table on weekends. Daily 8am–7pm.

TAKSİM SQUARE AND AROUND

Falafel House Şehit Muhtar Cad 19 ☎0212 253 7730, ⓦfalafelhouse.net; map p.128. Run by a Palestinian father and son, the falafel here are as tasty, and the hummus as rich, smooth and creamy, as you'd expect from such a partnership. A set falafel, hummus and salad meal costs ₺15. Expect Arab neighbours while you eat at the street tables or inside the fluorescent-lit galley-like interior. Unlicensed. Daily 10am–1am.

Kızılkaya Sıraselviler Cad 2 ☎0212 251 1357; map p.128. The very first in a line of Turkish fast-food joints at the entrance to İstiklal Cad from Taksim Square. It is immensely popular with the late night crowd who come to snaffle *ıslak* hamburgers (burgers steamed in their bun and smothered in a tomato and garlic sauce), for just ₺2.50, and whose deliciousness rises in direct proportion to the number of beers consumed. Unlicensed. Open 24hr.

Lale İşkembecisi Tarlabaşı Bul 3 ☎0212 252 6969; map p.128. Turks swear by *işkembe çorbası* (tripe soup) as a cure for hangovers, and there's plenty of need for that remedy in hedonistic Beyoğlu. This famous Taksim institution, established in 1960 and housed in a smart but historic building, specializes in the bits others disdain and if you fancy tripe (₺11), lamb's head, brain or trotter soup, this is the place to head for (or you can play safe with a lentil soup). Be wary, though, Tarlabaşı Bul has a dodgy reputation at night for crime (see p.128). Unlicensed. Open 24hr.

BEŞİKTAŞ & ORTAKÖY

House Café Salhane Sok 1 ☎0212 227 2699, ⓦthehousecafé.com; map p.132. With ten branches scattered around Istanbul and a spanking-new boutique hotel opened up next door, this chain of modern café-restaurants is a hit with the young and affluent. Putting a posh spin on western classics, menu staples range from burgers and pizzas to a scrumptious Sunday brunch

---

FIVE STREET-FOOD FAVES

One of the most enjoyable ways of tasting the best Istanbul has to offer is to work your way around the city snacking on the incredible street food, sold from carts and trays at street corners and other likely spots. This can be as simple as raw almonds on ice, but there are far more elaborate and substantial dishes available.

Çiğ Köfte These patties of kneaded bulgur wheat, stained orange by the hot pepper paste that is one of their chief constituents, are served wrapped in a flat bread with salad, pomegranate concentrate and spicy sauce for around ₺3.

Kokoreç Not for the squeamish, this carnivorous treat is actually sheep's intestines wrapped around other bits of offal, before being grilled over charcoals that are wheeled around the backstreets of Taksim. It is then finely chopped, and mixed with spices and salad before being served in bread (around ₺5).

Midye Dolması These mussels that have been cooked and stuffed with an aromatic spiced rice mixture are a favourite of many on their way home after too many drinks. They cost around ₺1 each and the vendor will continue to serve them to you until you say stop, before counting the shells to tot up the bill (note that *midye* are best avoided during the hot summer months).

Simit This typical Turkish breakfast food is sold on practically every street corner. Similar to a bagel, but covered in sesame seeds, it's particularly good with white cheese (₺1.40).

Tavuklu Pilavı Served from glass containers on wheelable carts, this delicious buttery rice, studded with chickpeas, comes with or without shredded chicken and usually served with a sprinkling of black pepper and a glass of *ayran* for ₺2–3.

13

(₺35). Elegant white-and-gold decor and a beautiful terrace showcase why this place is so popular. Daily 8am–1am.

Karadeniz Pide ve Döner Salonu Mumcu Bakkal Sok 6, Beşiktaş ☎ 0212 261 7693; map p.132. This little hole in the wall has to be one of the most popular *döner* kebab joints in the city, and often has a long line snaking down the road. Don't be put off though because the queue moves quickly and it's definitely worth the wait. Served with sumac-smothered onions in a folded *pide* (chewy flatbread) for ₺6. Unlicensed. Mon–Sat 11am–5pm.

Pando Kaymakçı Mumcu Bakkal Sok 5, Beşiktaş ☎ 0212 258 2616; map p.132. A dilapidated hut that can't have changed much since it opened in the early 1900s, this place is one of the neighbourhood's most popular breakfast haunts, with a spread of sumptuous *kaymak* (clotted cream made from buffalo milk) and fresh honey, eggs, tomatoes, olives and cheese coming to around ₺15. With an understated facade it's easy to miss, so head for the Beşiktaş fish market and ask one of the locals to point you in the right direction – the owner and namesake, now pushing 90, is something of a local institution. Daily 7am–6pm.

ASIAN ISTANBUL

Baylan Muvakkithane Cad 19, Kadıköy ☎ 0216 336 2881; map p.140. This famous patisserie is a must for nostalgia buffs, with its 1950s dark wood and chrome frontage. The trellis-shaded garden area is popular with mums and their offspring, many of whom tuck into traditional ice creams or plates of pastel-coloured macaroons for ₺8. Evidence of the Christian Armenian origins of the café can be seen in liqueur chocolates on sale here. Unlicensed. Daily 10am–10pm.

Borsam Taşfırın Güneşli Bahçe Sok 32, Kadıköy ☎ 0216 337 0504; map p.140. Located on the same street

of the more famous *Çiya*, this corner joint knocks out crispy *lahmacun* (spicy minced-meat-topped flatbreads) from its wood-fired oven for just ₺3 (although one is never enough). Fill it with a sprinkling of fresh parsley and a squeeze of lemon, then roll it up and eat it with your hands. For the authentic experience, wash it down with a cold, salty *ayran*. Unlicensed. Daily 10am–10pm.

THE BOSPHORUS

Ali Baba Köfteci Arnavutköy Bebek Cad 69, Arnavutköy ☎ 0212 265 3612; map p.151. Cheap-and-cheerful pine-clad place specializing in generous portions of *köfte* and *piyaz* (haricot beans topped with sliced onion) for around ₺18. Many famous visitors have given their seal of approval to this modest Arnavutköy institution – just check out the signed photos of footballers, politicians and pop stars on the walls. Unlicensed. Daily 11am–11pm.

Kale Yahya Kemal Cad 16, Rumelihisarı ☎ 0212 265 0097; map p.151. One of a run of brunch spots close to both Rumeli Hisarı and Borusan Contemporary. Cheaper than many of its rivals, it is a firm favourite with locals, often resulting in a queue for weekend brunch. This bustling place is great for people watching; a full breakfast costs ₺25 and try a lighter spinach-stuffed *gözleme* for just ₺7.50. Unlicensed. Daily 6am–9pm.

Sütiş Sakıp Sabancı Cad 1/3, Emirgan ☎ 0212 323 5030, ⊛ sutis.com.tr; map p.151. Conveniently situated next to the Sakıp Sabancı Museum, this popular spot offers a Bosphorus view and a large seating area (both indoor and outdoor). Priding itself on using local produce, it serves up excellent *su böreği* (layers of soft pastry filled with crumbly cheese) as well as breakfast options, *döner* wraps (₺14.50) and delicious sweets such as *ayva tatlısı* (caramelized quince) for ₺6. Unlicensed. Daily 6am–2am.

RESTAURANTS

The restaurant scene in Istanbul is, as to be expected in such a huge and fast developing city, very varied. There are countless places offering **international cuisine**, and an increasing number of Istanbulites appear as fond of pasta, burgers, pizzas et al as they do their native cuisine. The liveliest restaurants and *meyhanes* (see box, p.177), catering largely to young Istanbulites heading out on the town, are in **Beyoğlu** and **Taksim**, especially on Nevizade and Asmalımescit sokaks. **Kumkapı**, southwest of Sultanahmet and almost on the shores of the Sea of Marmara, has over fifty *meyhanes* (see box, p.87) but the area has become a little tacky in recent years and many locals prefer the less frantic atmosphere of Samatya. Many *meyhanes* offer fixed menu deals, with either a couple of home-produced drinks included or, more expensive, as many (local) drinks as you wish. Wandering gypsy musicians and the drunken carousing of hordes of Istanbulite revellers make for a fun meal out in these areas. The more upmarket **Ortaköy**, fronting the Bosphorus, is another option – especially if you're heading for one of the nearby waterfront clubs (see p.202). The eating places in **Sultanahmet** cannot compare in terms of quality or entertainment to those across the Golden Horn, but if you're looking for somewhere convenient after a heavy day's sightseeing, there are a few honourable exceptions. The well-heeled can combine dinner with an evening sea-taxi (see p.29) ride north along the Bosphorus to a fancy fish restaurant. Alternatively, cheap ferries run across the Bosphorus to the Asian suburb of **Üsküdar**, which has a couple of decent options, and to **Kadıköy**, with its lively bars, fish market and one of the city's most popular restaurants.

CLOCKWISE FROM TOP LEFT STUFFED-MUSSEL VENDOR, BEYOĞLU; *MEYHANE* OFF İSTIKLAL CADDESI; TYPICAL TURKISH KEBAB; *DARÜZZIYAFE* RESTAURANT, SÜLEYMANIYE CAMİİ (PP.82–84)>

13

VEGETARIAN FOOD

Given the quality and quantity of fresh fruit and vegetables (not to mention pulses) produced in Turkey, things should be pretty good for **vegetarians**. Unfortunately, those tasty-looking vegetable dishes on offer in the steamtrays in most *lokantas* are usually made with lamb- or chicken-based broth; even bulgur and rice may be cooked in meat stock, as can lentil soups. To check, ask "*İçinde et suyu var mı?*" ("Does it contain meat stock?"). In traditional restaurants, strict vegetarians should confine themselves to *meze*, salads, omelettes, *börek* and the cheese-topped varieties of *pide*.

SULTANAHMET

Albura Kathisma Akbıyık Cad 26 ☎0212 518 9710, ⓦalburakathisma.com; map p.46. Quite a few restaurants in the area now serve regional Anatolian-style dishes, but *Albura* was among the first and remains one of the best. It also declares itself a "hassle-free zone", a welcome relief after too much time in Sultanahmet. Try the special Kathisma Palace, a lamb casserole with figs and almonds (₺58 for two people). The dining room is a cavernous but stylish bare-brick affair, and there are plenty of outside tables on this bustling tourist street. Daily 10am–midnight.

★**Amedros** Hoca Rüstem Sok 7, Divan Yolu ☎0212 522 8356; map p.46. A sophisticated café-restaurant that's a world away in ambience to the tourist dives that dominate Sultanahmet's dining scene. It's best in summer, when the action moves to the white-clothed tables in the narrow pedestrian street. The interior manages to be both stylish and homely, and the food is good, too – a mixture of European (steaks, pastas, salads) and traditional Anatolian (the *testi* kebab, a succulent lamb and vegetable stew slow-cooked in a sealed clay pot, is a good bet). The service is attentive without being obsequious and the whole place is very professionally run. Mains from ₺25. Daily 11am–1am.

★**Balıkçı Sabahattin** Seyit Hasan Koyu Sok 1, Cankurtan ☎0212 458 1824; map p.46. A fish restaurant in the refreshingly down-to-earth streets beside Cankurtaran station, just a five-minute walk from touristy Sultanahmet. It's not cheap (it's the in-place for moneyed locals), but is about as atmospheric as you can get, with vine-shaded tables set out in a narrow alley (in summer) and a wood-floored dining room in an old wooden house (winter). Starters begin at ₺10, mains from ₺30, with seasonal, locally caught fish on the menu. Daily 11am–1am.

Dubb İncili Çavuş Sok ☎0212 513 7308, ⓦdubbindian .com; map p.46. A funky spot serving up authentic Indian dishes in a chic, "ethnic" setting. The rooms, spread over several floors, are small, and there's a roof terrace and tables on the street. Delicious *samosas* and *pakoras* cost ₺14, and vegetarian or meat curries range from ₺16–40. Reservations advised at weekends. Nearby in Cankurtaran, on Amiral Taftil Sok 25, *Dubb Ethnic*

(☎0212 517 6828), is run by the same people and offers a selection of Indian, Japanese, Korean, Turkish and Thai dishes. Daily noon–midnight.

Giritli Keresteci Hakkı Sok, Ahırkapı ☎0212 458 2270, ⓦgiritlirestoran.com; map p.46. Atmospheric fish restaurant set in a historic building near the *Armada Hotel*, specializing in Cretan dishes (the owner/chef's great-grandfather was an immigrant from Crete). For a no-holds-barred evening out go for the fixed menu at ₺136, and enjoy a seafood pilaf, 23 *meze* morsels and three hot starters, followed by a choice of four or five fish – and as much beer, wine or *rakı* as you can drink. Daily noon–midnight.

Khorasani Ticarethane Sok 39/41, Divan Yolu ☎0212 519 5959, ⓦkhorasanirestaurant.com; map p.46. If you are staying in Sultanahmet, this is the nearest place to sample authentic southeastern Turkish cuisine, including hummus and the spicy walnut and pepper dip, *muhamara* (₺13 and ₺14 respectively). The wonderful kebabs are prepared *ocakbaşı* style over a charcoal grill – try the pistachio version (₺34). There are tables on the cobbled pedestrian street, and a stylish mezzanine-floored dining room for colder weather. Watch out for the ten percent service charge. Daily noon–1am.

Matbah Caferiye Sok 6/1 ☎0212 514 6151, ⓦmatbahrestaurant.com; map p.46. Attached to the *Ottoman Imperial Hotel*, all dishes served here are based on those prepared in the Topkapı Palace kitchen in Ottoman times. The menus, which took chef Necati a year and a half to prepare, are seasonal – if you're curious about the type of food favoured by the Ottoman sultans, give it a try. Garlicky lamb trotter served on rye bread (₺22), or goose baked with rice in a delicate pastry cover (₺38) are just a couple of dishes on offer. Great views over the Caferiye Medresesi, too. Daily 11am–midnight.

Seasons Four Seasons Hotel Sultanahmet, Tevkifhane Sok 1 ☎0212 402 3000; map p.46. If you feel like treating yourself and fancy a change from the standard Turkish offerings, this is good fine dining choice. Set in a glass pavilion (with both indoor and outdoor seating available), inside an atmospheric hotel that was formerly a jail, dishes range from a club sandwich (₺35) to grilled lamb fillet served with ricotta- and spinach-stuffed aubergine (₺62); it's pricey, but worth a splurge. Daily 11.30am–midnight.

13

EMİNÖNÜ AND SİRKECİ

Hamdi Et Lokantası Kalçin Sok 17 Tahmis Cad, Eminönü ☎0212 528 0390; map p.70. The uninspiring facade of this five-storey joint fronting the square in Eminönü belies the quality and value of the food on offer inside. The best bet is to sit is the terrace, which offers great views over the Golden Horn, Galata and the Bosphorus beyond. Tender, charcoal-grilled kebabs of various kinds form the mainstay of the menu, but it's also a good place to try another southeastern Turkish speciality, *lahmacun*, a thin *chapati*-type bread smeared with spicy minced meat. The *baklava* desserts are also top-notch. It's not cheap though, with kebabs starting at ₺23. There is also a branch in the *Radisson Blu Pera* hotel on the opposite side of the Golden Horn. Daily 11am–midnight.

Orient Express Sirkeci Gar, Eminönü ☎0212 522 2280; map p.70. Although undoubtedly trying to cash in on its atmospheric location in the waiting room of the former terminus station of the famed Orient Express, this place does have more character than many of the old city's tourist-orientated eating places. The original stained-glass windows are still *in situ*, the tables are set with period-style cloths, napkins et al, and the waiters look like they might have stepped right from the dining car of the Orient Express itself. The menu is distinctly Turkish, though, with kebabs from ₺18. Licensed. Daily 11am–midnight.

Pandeli's Mısır Çarşısı 51, Hamidiye Cad ☎0212 527 3909; map p.70. Over seventy years old, decorated throughout with blue and white tiling and run by Greek and Turkish owners, this is an atmospheric setting but sadly the food (and service) can be a little hit and miss. To get here, head through the main, waterfront-facing entrance of the Spice Bazaar; and on your left is a staircase leading up to the restaurant. Mon–Sat 11.30am–4pm.

★Paşazade Sirkeci İbn-I Kemal Cad 13 ☎0212 513 3757, ⓦpasazade.com; map p.70. Well-run faux-Ottoman place, one of a number of restaurants in the little streets to the west of Gülhane Parkı, all offering quite a different feel to the tourist places around Akbıyık Cad. The interior may verge on twee, but the service is good and the food (try the lamb shank with quince) tasty and reasonably priced (mains from ₺20). It's traditional Turkish cuisine with a twist, there's plenty of choice for vegetarians, and in warm weather the outside tables make for great people-watching. Daily noon–1am.

Surplus Zindan Han, Ragıp Gümüş Pala Cad 54 ☎0212 520 1002, ⓦsurplus.com.tr; map p.70. The latest restaurant of Turkish culinary heavyweight, Vedat Başaran opened early in 2014. Set on the top floor of a bright pink jewellery *han* close to the Galata Bridge, this classy restaurant offers staggering views of many of Istanbul's best sights. The food is an ultra-contemporary take on some Ottoman classics, such as pomegranate-glazed quail on a bed of cured beef and bulgur. With a good Turkish wine

menu and mains from ₺45–66 this makes a great option if you want to treat yourself to something a little out of the ordinary. Daily noon–11pm.

AROUND THE GRAND BAZAAR

★Akdeniz Hatay Sofrası Ahmediye Cad 44/a, Aksaray ☎0212 531 3333, ⓦakdenizhataysofrasi.com.tr; map pp.78–79. This cavernous, brightly lit and spotless place may not suit those in search of a romantic dinner, but it serves some of the very best southeastern Turkish food in the city. There's a strong Arab influence to the mind-bogglingly extensive menu (the Turkish province of Hatay, on the southeastern Mediterranean seaboard, is still claimed by Syria as its own). The creamy hummus is served warm and liberally sprinkled with pistachios, and the *bakla*, a broad bean purée drenched in tahini sauce, is delicious; the whole chicken roasted in salt (*tuzda tavuk*; ₺54), needs to be ordered a couple of hours ahead. There's even a range of home-made delicacies to take away from the small in-store shop. Unlicensed. Daily 8am–midnight.

Darüzziyafe Sifahane Sok 6, Beyazıt ☎0212 511 8414, ⓦdaruzziyafe.com.tr; map pp.78–79. The most distinctive choice if you're looking for a sit-down lunch while exploring the Süleymaniye mosque and its environs – this was once the kitchen that formed part of the Süleymaniye mosque complex. The long, narrow dining hall, with its domed roof, is a very atmospheric environment in which to tuck into traditional Ottoman-style Turkish cuisine. Try the hearty *tencere külbastı*, a stewed beef kebab with carrots and onions. It's not too pricy considering the surroundings, with cold *meze* dishes from ₺8 and mains from ₺17. Unlicensed. Daily noon–11pm.

Nar Lokanta Armaggan, Nuruosmaniye Cad 65 ☎0212 522 2800, ⓦnarlokantasi.com; map pp. 78–79. On the fifth floor of the Armaggan luxury goods store, this restaurant is the first venture of the NAR Gourmet brand, known for their high-quality, organic local produce. Specializing in regional Turkish cuisine that you might not find elsewhere, it's a little pricier than other places, though the quality makes it worth it, especially the lunchtime buffet of cold *meze* (individual dishes start from ₺5). Main courses range from ₺16–60. Mon–Sat 8.30am–10pm.

THE NORTHWEST QUARTER

Asitane Kariye Hotel, Kariye Camii Sok 18 ☎0212 534 8414, ⓦasitanerestaurant.com; map p.91. Garden restaurant next door to the Kariye Museum; it's expensive, but the combination of good food and service in a peaceful garden location make it a worthwhile splurge. The menu offers Ottoman cuisine created using authentic recipes – try the quince or melon stuffed with minced meat and aromatic rice (₺38). Meals are served on a lovely chestnut-shaded terrace accompanied by classical Turkish music. Daily 11.30am–11.00pm.

13

★**Balat Sahil Restoran** Mürselpaşa Cad 245, Balat ☎0212 525 6185; map p.91. This is a rough around the edges but charming little old school *meyhane* located on the Golden Horn coastal road. Choose your *meze* (₺7–15) from the daily changing offerings on the counter – the stuffed onions and the braised artichoke are particularly delicious. For mains, there is the catch of the day, paid for by the kilo – a fraction of the price you'd pay at any of the Bosphorus restaurants. *Rakı* is the drink of choice here and there are always several old boys here consuming great quantities of it. Mon–Sat 1pm–1am.

Cibalikapı Balıkçı Kadir Has Cad 5 ☎0212 533 2846, ⓦcibalikapibalikcisi.com; map p.91. This nostalgic *meyhane* gives you a taste of the Istanbul of yesteryear as well as some delicious dishes. Choose your *meze*, many with a seafood emphasis, from the tray bought to your table (₺4–17) and complete the meal with the catch of the day, grilled to perfection. Alternatively, opt for their taster menu (₺150), though the price doesn't include drinks. Reservations recommended on weekends. Daily 1pm–1am.

Enstitü Kadir Has Üniversitesi Kadir Has Cad, Cibalikapı ☎0212 251 2214, ⓦIstanbulculinary.com.tr; map p.91. Creative food at affordable prices is dished up by Istanbul's star chefs of the future in this restaurant that serves as a training for recently qualified graduates from the attached Istanbul Culinary Institute (see p.192). The menu changes each month but includes unusual pairings such as slow-cooked beef with fresh sour cherries and aubergine purée (₺18). Located within the Kadir Has university (see p.98), the restaurant has a modern decor and light, airy feel. Mon–Sat 7am–6pm.

★**Siirt Şeref Büryan** İtfaye Cad 4, Fatih ☎0212 635 8085; map p.91. Located in the shadow of the towering late-Roman Aqueduct of Valens, this great establishment has been dishing up regional dishes from the Arab/Kurdish southeast of Turkey for decades. Best is the *perde pilav*, a tasty concoction of rice, shredded chicken, almonds, pine-nuts and various herbs cooked in a pot until the outside "burns" to a tasty crust (₺12). *Büryan* is spring lamb cooked in a deep clay *tandır* (tandoori) oven and served chopped on a bed of soft *pide* bread. The street on which it stands is a colourful area full of (mainly Kurdish) immigrants from the southeast. Unlicensed. Daily 10am–midnight.

Sur Ocakbaşı, İtfaye Cad 27, Fatih ☎0212 533 8088, ⓦsurocakbası.com; map p.91. Overlooking an atmospheric pedestrianized square known as the "Women's Market" (see p.90), this down-to-earth *ocakbaşı* has dished up to food to luminaries as varied as TV chef and food personality Anthony Bourdain and legendary Turkish folk singer Orhan Gençbey. Try the *saç tava*, a fried meat and vegetable stew served in the shallow wok-like pan it was prepared in (₺22), stuffed intestines (*bumbar*), kebab or *lahmacun*. Daily 10am–midnight.

LAND WALLS AND AROUND

★**Ali Haydar** Gümüş Yüzük Sok 6, Samatya Meydan ☎0212 584 2162; map p.102. Also known as *İkinci Bahar* (Second Spring) after the popular Turkish TV series that was set here (pictures of which decorate its walls). The charming decor is matched by some delicious culinary offerings that belie the southeastern roots of its proprietor. *Çig köfte* is still made using raw meat and the kebabs are tender and juicy (try the pistachio-studded variety, ₺23), but make sure to save room for the mouthwatering *katmer* dessert. This folded dough delight, packed with clotted cream and pistachios and then baked, is well worth the ₺20 price tag. Daily 11am–midnight.

★**Develi** Gumuş Yüzük Sok 7, Samatya ☎0212 529 0833, ⓦdevelikebap.com; map p.102. Established in 1912, this famous place is noted for its excellent kebabs, cooked Gaziantep style, and a range of southeastern Turkish speciality starters including hummus. A great attraction here is the traditional square the restaurant overlooks, the sea views from the terrace and the fact that it's licensed. Kebabs start from ₺18. Great *baklava* for the sweet-toothed, too (₺8). Daily noon–midnight.

Safa Meyhanesi İlyasbey Cad 12, Yedikule ☎0212 585 5594, ⓦsafameyhanesi.com; map p.102. The chandelier taking centre stage of the long, narrow dining room sets the tone of this old school establishment; that and the copious *rakı* bottles lined up behind glass cabinets. This is probably the most atmospheric *meyhane* in town, with a nostalgic 1940s feel. The food here is standard *meyhane* fare but reasonably priced (*meze* are ₺7–15), but it's well worth a trip to this very untouristy neighbourhood to sit amongst the local intelligentsia and soak up the charm. Daily noon–midnight.

Zinnet Türk Dünyası Kültür Evleri 6, Topkapı Kültür Parkı ☎0212 567 1077; map p.102. *Zinnet*, situated close to the Panorama 1453 museum (see p.105), is set in the "Turkish World" centre, with its curious selection of ethnographic exhibits from the Turkic region of Central Asia. Likewise, the menu here offers Kyrgyz, Kazakh, Uzbek, Turkmen, Uighur, Tatar, and Azeri dishes. Service is friendly although little English is spoken. *Göşnan* (meat-filled pie) and *acılı legmen kavurması* (spicy thick home-made noodles) are particularly delicious. Mains from ₺12. Unlicensed. Daily 9am–10pm.

GALATA AND THE WATERFRONT DISTRICTS

Fürreyya Serdar-ı Ekrem Sok 2b, Galata ☎0212 252 4853, ⓦfurreyyagalata.com; map p.110. This tiny establishment, just a stone's throw from Galata tower, is conveniently located at the entrance to chic, boutique-filled Serdar-ı Ekrem Sok. A little gem of a fish restaurant, it's rather unusual in that it's not adjacent to the water. *Fürreyya* serves up perfectly cooked seafood with a few modern touches, at very reasonable prices. The fish wrap (₺10), prawn casserole (₺22) and fishcakes with basil sauce (₺19) all come highly recommended. Daily noon–11pm.

Galata House Galata Külesi Sok 61 ☎0212 245 1861, ⓦthegalatahouse.com; map p.110. This restaurant offers all the comfort of eating in your own living room with small, cosy rooms, an outdoor terrace lit by fairy-lights and a menu of hearty Russian, Tartar and Georgian cuisine (mains around ₺25) – try the house speciality *Hingali* (Georgian meat-filled dumplings in a tomato sauce). English-speaking host Mete and his wife Nadire, converted the former British Prison into this restaurant eleven years ago and are happy to show you around and entertain you with their many stories of the area and times past. History buffs can ogle the original prison fittings and try to decipher graffiti etched into the wall by prisoners. With only fifty seats, it's best to book ahead. Tues–Sun 2pm–midnight.

Karaköy Lokantası Kemankeş Cad 37a, Karaköy ☎0212 292 4455; map p.110. The striking turquoise tiles and wrought-iron spiral staircase are enough to draw you into this culinary cornerstone. The quality dishes such as grilled octopus (₺20) and artichoke hearts (₺12) will make you come back. This fine establishment has two distinct characters; an *esnaf lokantası* by day and *meyhane* by night (see p.177 for the distinction), so choose your dining time accordingly. Mon–Sat noon–4pm 6pm–midnight.

Lokanta Maya Kemankeş Cad 35/a, Karaköy ☎0212 252 6884, ⓦlokantamaya.com; map p.110. A modern and very stylish twist on a traditional *lokanta*, *Maya* is run by a Turkish woman, Didem, who studied at the French Culinary Institute in New York. On the daily changing menu, soups such as cauliflower with cured beef croutons start at ₺12, a wonderful array of *meze* from just a little more. It's a block back from the waterfront hustle (and there's plenty here as this is where the behemoth cruise ships dock) in a comparatively peaceful location. Reservations a must. Mon–Sat noon–5pm, 7–11pm.

İSTİKLAL CADDESİ AND AROUND

Antiochia General Yazgan Sok 3, Asmalımescit ☎0212 292 1100, ⓦantiochiaconcept.com; map pp.120–121. One of the best options for enjoying tasty southeastern Turkish cuisine in the Beyoğlu area. Try the *zahter* (a tangy wild thyme salad) or the spicy walnut and pepper *muammara* dip – better yet, get a mixed *meze* plate for ₺25 – followed by a marinated kebab served with paper-thin *lavaş* bread (kebabs from ₺17). One of the owners, Jale Balcı, has written a book about Antakya (ancient Antioch) cuisine, available here. Mon–Sat 11am–2am.

Çokçok Thai Meşrutiyet Cad 51 ☎0212 292 6496, ⓦcokcok.com.tr; map pp.120–121. Designer Thai restaurant with a well-deserved reputation for both style and quality. Relax in the cocktail lounge before your meal and try one of the unusual concoctions on offer – Rain Odaiba is flavoured with ginger and coriander. Ingredients are brought in from Thailand and the chef is Thai, so this is the real deal. The lunchtime special set menu (noon–6pm) costs ₺49 (for soup, spring roll, fishcake, main with jasmine rice and tea) and in the evenings, mains cost from ₺27. Tues–Sun noon–midnight.

Divan Brasserie Beyoğlu Merkezhan İstiklal Cad 181 ☎0212 243 2481; map pp.120–121. Located on the top floor of a renovated *han* containing the Köç Research Center for Anatolian Civilizations on the ground floor, this upmarket French-style brasserie belongs to the hotel group of the same name. The views out across the Bosphorus and entrance to the Golden Horn are staggering, especially towards sundown. The menu is a Mediterranean affair and on the pricey side with mains from ₺35, a small beer for ₺18, but it makes a welcome break from the chaos of İstiklal Cad below. Daily noon–midnight.

★**Fıccın** İstiklal Cad, Kallavı Sok 13 ☎0212 293 3786, ⓦficcin.com; map pp.120–121. Unpretentious and great-value place on this quiet (by Beyoğlu standards) side street offering some unusual and substantial dishes. Try the eponymous *fıccın*, a kind of hearty, Caucasian meat pie, or the *çerkez mantısı*, a ravioli-style dish where the pasta is stuffed with tomato and served in a yoghurt sauce (mains from ₺8). Soups include a tasty rocket-based one, wine and beer are both reasonably priced, and there's plenty of choice for vegetarians. Tues–Sat 8am–10pm.

Hacı Abdullah İstiklal Cad, Sakızağacı Cad 17 ☎0212 293 8561; map pp.120–121. An Istanbul institution, this is one of the oldest traditional restaurants in the city (established in 1888). Though it's a little overpriced, and the food quality wavers, it remains an experience for its old world ambience and smart service. Most main courses are around ₺25 – try the *hünkar beğendili kebap* (beef stew on a bed of aubergine and cheese purée) and follow with the *ayva tatlı* (stewed quince with clotted cream) for ₺9. Unlicensed. Daily 11am–10pm.

★**İmroz** Nevizade Sok 24; map pp.120–121. This Greek-owned Istanbul legend has been dishing up reasonably priced fish dishes (mains from ₺16) since 1941. Spread over three floors and both sides of the busy pedestrian thoroughfare, it is perhaps the liveliest of the fish restaurants in the Balık Pazarı area. You can choose from a bewildering array of *meze* brought around on a tray. Despite the excellence of the food, most locals come here to drink and talk, and volume levels rise alarmingly as the *rakı* kicks in, so don't bother if you're looking for a quiet tête-à-tête with a loved one. Daily 11am–2am.

★**Kenan Üsta Ocakbaşı** Kurabiye Sok 18 ☎0212 293 5619; map pp.120–121. Master grillsman Kenan has been preparing succulent meat on this street for forty

13

years, the last eight of them as owner of his own place. Watch him cook *lavaş* (tortilla-style bread) over his basement charcoal grill, smear it with olive oil, sprinkle it with pepper flakes, thyme and salt, then pop it back on the grill to finish. This bread is used as the "plate" to serve an astonishing array of kebabs and grilled meat to a loyal and virtually one hundred percent Turkish clientele. All the *meze* (so often laid out ready-made in chiller cabinets), salads and kebabs are prepared fresh. Choose from a selection of *rakı*s and enjoy a superb Turkish meal. Starters are ₺5, kebabs ₺25, and a double *rakı* ₺15. Daily noon–2am.

Meze By Lemon Tree Meşrutiyet Cad 83/b ☎0212 252 8302; ⓦmezze.com.tr; map pp.120–121. A contemporary take on the *meyhane* concept by two innovative chefs who have created a playful menu that changes with the season. The *meze* themselves are exquisitely presented and cost ₺11. Mains such as the sea bass fillet cooked in paper with almonds and apricots cost ₺43. This is a popular choice with wealthy young Istanbulites, who fill the air with buzzing conversation as the night goes on, so best to make reservations in advance. Daily 6pm–midnight.

Mikla Marmara Pera Hotel, Meşrutiyet Cad 167/185 ☎0212 293 5656; map pp.120–121. The food served here is as simple and elegant as the venue's Scandinavian-inspired interior (fittingly so, as the chef is Turkish/Swedish in origin). The food is a Turkish/Mediterranean fusion – try the succulent lamb shank with summer vegetables. The three-course à la carte menu costs ₺150 and the tasting menu is ₺240. Dress "casually upscale" as their website advises, if only to ensure you don't encounter problems passing through the ground-floor hotel security. Daily 6–11.30pm.

Parsifal Kurabiye Sok 13 ☎0212 245 2588, ⓦparsifalde.com; map pp.120–121. A sophisticated, inexpensive menu blending Turkish and international influences, with an imaginative range of non-meat dishes, such as leek and soya burgers, and a mouthwatering spinach pie. It's been around since 1996, and proprietor Ayfer Oğulları knows her business, and has created a homely, bistro-style atmosphere from the long, narrow dining area. Daily 11am–11pm.

Refik Sofyalı Sok 10–12, Tünel ☎0212 245 7879; map pp.120–121. Modest *rakı*-infused Turkish joint, a meeting point for local intellectuals, that specializes in Black Sea cuisine. *Kara lahana dolması* is a traditional stuffed cabbage dish, popular with the locals. Refik Baba, the good-natured owner, likes to chat in numerous languages, though he doesn't speak much of any. Set menu ₺90, including as many local alcoholic drinks as you desire. Mon–Sat noon–midnight, Sun 6.30pm–midnight.

★**Yeni Lokanta** Kumbaracı Yokuşu 66 ☎0212 292 2550; map pp.120–121. Heralded as Istanbul's best new restaurant, the owner/chef Çivan Er made his name as head chef at the highly regarded but now defunct Changa restaurant before opening here. Known for given traditional Anatolian and southeastern Turkish dishes a contemporary twist, the results are well worth the price tag (mains ₺29–55), and both the cocktail and wine list are appealing. Advance reservations essential, especially for dinner. Mon–Sat 11.30am–midnight.

Yirmibir Kebap Hazzo Pulo Pasajı, off İstiklal Cad ☎0212 244 3873; map pp.120–121. To find this charming restaurant, enter the narrow passage close to Galatasaray Meydanı. Tucked behind the throngs of students and shopkeepers drinking tea and smoking *nargile* is a little kebab joint run by the same team as the café next door. Despite its chic-but-cosy decor, the food here is very authentic southeastern Turkish with delicious fresh *meze*, including olive oil-braised chard (₺7) and aubergine kebab (₺25) cooked over the open grill. Daily noon–3am.

Zencefil Kurabiye Sok 8 ☎0212 244 4082; map pp.120–121. Long-standing, homely place with an ever-changing menu that includes vegetarian versions of various Turkish dishes, and Western-style meals such as vegetarian lasagne and quiche (from as little as ₺13), plus great salads, home-made breads, herbal teas, mint lemonade and local wines. The courtyard area is a particularly enticing place to relax and enjoy your food. Mon–Sat 9am–midnight.

TAKSİM SQUARE AND AROUND

Hünkar Mim Kemal Öke Cad 21, Nişantaşı ☎0212 225 4665, ⓦhunkar1950.com; map p.128. Classic Ottoman/Turkish cuisine at its best. Originally opened in 1950 in ultra-orthodox Fatih, across the Golden Horn in the old city, it (wisely, given Nişantaşı's prosperity) moved to its present location in 2000. The trademark dish is *hünkar beğendi* (₺29) – literally "admired by the sultan" – with tender lamb served on a bed of smoky, mashed aubergine. The *irmik helvası*, a deliciously sweet semolina and almond dessert, is done particularly well here. There's also a decent wine list; evening reservations are recommended. Daily noon–midnight.

BEŞİKTAŞ

Banyan Muallim Nacı Cad Salhane Sok 3 ☎0212 259 9060, ⓦbanyanrestaurant.com; map p.132. Inventive Asian fusion cuisine featuring jazzed-up versions of all the usual suspects – dim sum, tempura, wok-fried noodles – and throwing in a few surprises too. Everything from Vietnamese to Indian gets a nod, with a wide range of vegetarian options. The terrace views of Ortaköy mosque and the Bosphorus Bridge are stunning, but they'll cost you, with mains starting around ₺40. Daily noon–midnight.

Tuğra Çırağan Palace Kempinski Hotel, Çıragan Cad 32 ☎0212 326 4646; map p.132. Set on the first floor of the

13

Çırağan Palace, this Ottoman-inspired restaurant offers candlelit terrace seating, imperial court recipes, live classical Turkish music and spectacular vistas over the Bosphorus. Try the *testi kebap* (₺69), cooked in a specially designed pottery urn that you crack open with a small hammer, but be sure to save some room, as the laden dessert trolley will soon catch your eye. Dress smart and bring your credit card – this is one of the city's priciest options. Daily 7pm–midnight.

ASIAN ISTANBUL

★**Çiya Sofrası & Kebapçı** Güneşlibahçe Sok 43, Kadıköy ☎0216 330 3190, ⓦciya.com.tr; map p.140. A very well-regarded place on a pleasant pedestrianized street. "*Çiya*" means "mountain" in Kurdish, though the inspiration for the food here comes from many different corners of this vast country – and beyond to the Middle East and the Balkans. There are actually three restaurants, the two on the right as you approach along Güneşlibahçe street are kebab-orientated (the house *Çiya* kebab is tender meat coated with crushed pistachio and walnut, rolled in a thin unleavened bread and then baked – delicious), the one on the left focuses on salads, *meze* and stews. Choose your own selection of *meze* and salads and have your plate weighed to learn the price (around ₺15 for a substantial lunch). An institution with Istanbulites, expats and visitors alike, not to be missed. Daily 10am–midnight.

Dicle Balık Lokantası Muvakkithane Cad 31/a, Kadıköy ☎0216 233 8474, ⓦdiclebalikrestaurant.com; map p.140. Most people ship across to Kadıköy for the wonderful *Çiya Sofrası*, but this bustling, spotless fish restaurant in the heart of the suburb's busy fish market makes a great alternative. *Meze* range between ₺6 and ₺15, there's a tasty fish *pilaf*, a hearty fish soup cooked in a clay pot and a whole range of fresh fish (the owners have the most-esteemed stall in the market). Wine by the glass is reasonably priced, and there's also terrace above the busy street offering a window to the Bosphorus. Daily 11am–1am.

Kanaat Lokantası Selmanipak Cad 25, Üsküdar ☎0216 341 5444, ⓦkanaatlokantasi.com.tr; map p.144. Established in 1931, this is one of the city's more famous *lokantas*, featuring copies of İznik-tile panels from the Selimiye Camii in Edirne and a copper chimneypiece. This huge, spotless and bustling place is excellent value and offers a vast range of cold starters for ₺8–12 and the same number of hot for a little more – the *Çerkez tavuğu* (Circassian chicken in walnut sauce) is divine. Mains start from a bargain ₺13 and include some of the best *pirzola* (lamb chops) you'll find anywhere. The desserts are equally magnificent and include fruits such as fig, quince or apricot stuffed with nuts and topped with cream (₺9). Unlicensed. Daily 6am–11pm.

Yanyalı Fehmi Lokantası Yağlıka İsmail Sok 1, off Soğütlüçeşme Cad, Kadıköy ☎0216 336 3333; map p.140. Established back in 1919 by refugees from Greece, this well-run place serves up some of the best food on the Asian side of the Bosphorus with twenty types of soup alone, including non-standards such as okra or spinach. The *çömlek* kebab – meat, aubergine, beans, peppers, onion and garlic oven-cooked in a clay pot – is delicious (₺19). Or try the Persian-style chicken, including a *pilaf* containing parsley, nuts and egg. Desserts include *kabak tatlası* (candied courgette), delicious when, as here, it's done well. Unlicensed. Daily 9.30am–10.30pm.

THE BOSPHORUS

Borsa Adile Sultan Sarayı Vaniköy Cad 12, Kandilli ☎0216 460 0304, ⓦborsarestaurants.com; map p.151. One of Istanbul's longest-established restaurants, *Borsa* has been serving up Turkish classics since 1924. There are three branches across the city; this one is set in a former royal residence of an Ottoman princess. Combined with a Bosphorus view, it is a great place to taste authentic Turkish cuisine, although with main courses at around ₺45 you pay for the privilege. Daily noon–midnight.

Kaşıbeyaz Köybaşı Cad 10, Yenikapı ☎0212 299 5000 ⓦkasibeyaz.com.tr; map p.151. One of a small chain of kebab restaurants specializing in food from Gaziantep, a city in southeastern Turkey renowned for its cuisine, with a glitzy interior and a spacious terrace. Unusually for Istanbul's upmarket Bosphorus-facing restaurants, *Kaşıbeyaz* focuses on the produce of the land, rather than the sea. Try the *Ali Nazik* (char-grilled kebab meat on a bed of garlicky yoghurt and smoked aubergine) for ₺35 and the *gavurdağı* salad (made with walnuts, tomatoes, chillis and pomegranate syrup) for ₺12. Daily noon–midnight.

★**Kıyı** Kefeliköy Cad 126, Tarabya ☎02162 262 0002, ⓦkiyi.com.tr; map p.151. This is one of the very best fish restaurants in the city, patronized by a well-heeled but slightly bohemian crowd. The decor is a restrained mix of the old (wood-panelling) and the new (exposed ventilation system), enhanced with superb prints by Ara Güler (see box, p.206) and examples of contemporary Turkish art. Expect to pay at least ₺150 a head for a full fish meal with alcohol. Daily noon–2am.

★**Müzedechanga** Sakip Sabancı Cad 22, Emirgan ☎0212 323 0901; map p.151. Designed by the Autobahn group, this funky restaurant is located inside the Sakip Sabancı Museum. They serve up Turkish/Mediterranean-fusion cuisine such as white grouper on borlotti bean purée with a mint and green chilli salsa in a stylish but unstuffy environment – goatskin-covered bar stools mix easily with stripped-wood floors and retro 1950s-esque light fittings. There's a nice terrace with the inevitable Bosphorus views. Mains around ₺70, plus a good wine list. July–Sept Tues–Sun 10.30am–1am.

13

COOK LIKE A LOCAL, EAT LIKE A LOCAL

Istanbul is fast becoming as popular a destination for foodies as it is for history buffs. If you want to do more than just scratch the surface of the food scene here, a cookery class or a food tour make great introductions to the city's culinary diversity.

Cooking Alaturka Akbıyık Cad 72/a ☏0212 458 5919, ⓦ cookingalaturka.com. A great place to start, Cooking Alaturka runs fun and informative Turkish cookery classes right in the centre of Sultanahmet. The courses are the brainchild of Dutch Istanbul-resident Eveline Zoutendijk, who opened the city's first cookery school back in 2003. For €65 per head, you can learn how to prepare a four-course Turkish meal, for either lunch or dinner, with Eveline and chef Feyzi Yıldırım – and then eat it. Once you've learned how to stuff an aubergine without scooping out its tasty innards first, there's no looking back. For ₺55 a head you can eat a fixed-menu four-course meal here without the hassle of cooking it yourself.

Istanbul Culinary Institute ☏0212 251 2214, ⓦ istanbulculinary.com.tr. For a lesson in a professional culinary school environment, this is the best option. Check their website for their monthly programme of evening amateur workshops, which cost between ₺80 and ₺110. Programmes are themed, with "Aegean Flavours" and "Mezes" among the many options. The three-hour classes end with dining on the results, accompanied by Turkish wine.

Istanbul Eats ⓦ istanbuleats.com. To get to grips with Istanbul's vibrant food scene in a very different way, Istanbul Eats run backstreet culinary adventures for small groups (2–6 people) of foodies who want to avoid the usual tourist haunts. There are different options available (US$75–125), so you can choose between Hidden Beyoğlu, Kebab Crawl, Culinary Secrets of the old city and more. As well as trying a whole range of traditional Turkish fare, there's the chance to buy Turkish herbs, spices and deli-style favourites at the same prices the locals do. They also offer a Shop/Cook/Feast adventure ($110) that takes visitors food shopping in a more residential area before doing just what it says on the tin: preparing regional specialities and washing it down with a glass or *rakı*. They also do a handy guide to the city's lesser-known places to eat entitled *Istanbul Eats: Exploring the Culinary Backstreets* (available from most museum and book shops in the city).

Turkish Flavours ☏0532 218 0653, ⓦ turkishflavours.com. Selin Rozanes is a colourful character with years of experience in the tourism and culinary industry. She offers food-tasting walks around the Spice Bazaar and Kadıköy market, stopping at Çiya for lunch, for US$145, or a cooking class that begins with a tasting session at the Spice Bazaar before heading to her home on the Asian side to cook up a storm (US$125). The latter offers the chance to see the inside of a Turkish home, and learn some of the distinctive Sephardic Jewish dishes that reflect Selin's own background.

Suna'nın Yeri Iskele Cad 2/a, Kandilli 0216 332 3241; map p.151. Located right next to the Kandilli ferry port, this low-key affair is one of the locals' best kept secrets. Choose from a limited range of daily prepared *meze* (a surprisingly welcome change from those with a bewilderingly wide range to choose from), followed by delicious fried or grilled calamari, anchovies or fresh fish. There's no menu here, and alcohol is only served on the quiet in this unlicensed place. The wooden tables next to the water are about as close to the Bosphorus as you can get, and the prices are modest, with grilled fish mains from ₺18. Daily noon–10pm.

PRINCES' ISLANDS

The restaurants on Heybeliada cater to locals all year round, and consequently there are plenty to choose from – generally simple and cheap, offering standard fish, *lokanta*, kebab and *pide* fare; most are situated on Ayyıldız Cad. In Büyükada, there are lots of so-so fish restaurants along the seafront to the left of the ferry terminal. One street back from the shore road, İskele Cad has a selection of cheaper cafés, selling all the usual Turkish dishes.

Barba Yani Yalı Cad 6, Burgazada ☏0216 381 2404; map pp.160–161. Some 50m to the left of the jetty as you land, this Greek-run restaurant serves reasonably priced fish dishes and *meze* (expect to pay around ₺60 per person, including an alcoholic drink). With its natty checked tablecloths and harbour front location, it's an atmospheric spot to while away the time waiting for the next ferry back to the city.

Heyamola Ada Lokantası Yalı Cad, Heybeliada (opposite Mavi Marmara ferry port) ☏0216 351 1111, ⓦ heyamolaadalokantasi.com; map pp.160–161. In a strip of outdoor restaurants facing the water, this stands out with its colourful, chintzy decor. The food here is also a cut above the rest. The *meze* have a distinctly Aegean leaning with some unusual creations and are priced reasonably at ₺8 and up – try the delicious *cevizli kabak* (walnuts with courgettes). The wine list also offers some excellent lesser-known names with surprisingly low prices. Mon–Fri 10am–midnight, Sat–Sun 8am–midnight.

★**Kalpazankaya** Mevkii 26, Burgazada ☎0216 381 1111; map pp.160–161. Superbly situated on a headland overlooking a tiny beach on the west shore of the island, this casual place dishes up over thirty different delicious *meze* (₺5–25), fifteen different hot starters (₺6–35) and seasonal fish sold by the kilo. It's the ideal place for a quiet lunch, with the sound of the waves on the rocks and the breeze brushing through the canopy of olive trees, or for a more lively, *rakı*-downing evening. It's well worth making the effort to walk or cycle out here from the ferry pier, or if you're feeling lazy catch a *fayton* for around ₺20, as it's a world away from the usual touristy island restaurants. Daily noon–midnight.

Yücetepe Kır Gazinosu Aya Yorgi, Yüce Tepe, Büyükada; map pp.160–161. Simple but excellent restaurant right on Yüce Tepe, the hilltop crowned by the Monastery of St George, offering superb views across the island and the Sea of Marmara. The food is basic but freshly prepared and hearty, with *paçanga böreği* (a deep-fried pastry filled with cheese and savoury salami; ₺10) being one of the highlights. The home-made chips are delicious, as is the yoghurt-drenched aubergine starter (all ₺6). Big beers are a reasonable ₺10. Daily 9am–11pm.

LEB-I DERYA, BEYOĞLU

Nightlife

The vast majority of Istanbul's best bars, clubs and live music venues are concentrated in and around Beyoğlu, particularly on bustling İstiklal Caddesi, where the gamut runs from student bars with tables on the pavement to chic clubs perched on roof terraces. The Bosphorus waterfront in Ortaköy and Kuruçeşme boasts some of the glitziest clubs around, places where you'll rub shoulders with the city's nouveau-riche and wannabe celebrities, dance to the "best" Euro and Turkish pop and stagger back to your hotel with a massive hole in your trip's budget. Across the water, in the more unassuming Asian suburb of Kadıköy, lurk more down-to-earth venues, but the last ferry back to Europe leaves just as the action is hotting up.

A night out in Istanbul can **cost** as much as in London or New York, particularly if you head up to exclusive rooftop joints or down to the Bosphorus waterfront clubs. Alcohol is taxed at an exorbitant rate, and a large beer in even a modest bar here is likely to be at least ₺8, a small one double that in one of the upmarket clubs, and cocktails, imported spirits and the like are even more prohibitively priced. Probably the best-value night out is at a **meyhane** (tavern), where you can listen to a Turkish *fasıl* band and enjoy a multi-course meal, or a **Türkü bar**, where the beer is still a little over the odds but there's no charge. However, Istanbul offer's every kind of night, from sweaty rock gigs to all-night clubbing in underground clubs.

While there's an increasing amount of foreigners in trendy Beyoğlu, once you're out of Sultanahmet the vast majority of the people you'll be talking to, drinking with and dancing alongside will be Istanbulites. Usually a friendly, outgoing and gregarious lot, part of the fun of a night on the town is discovering more about them and their city – not as difficult as you might think, as many speak excellent English.

Istanbul is also becoming an increasingly important destination on the international pop music circuit, attracting some top acts – particularly in the summer months when outdoor shows are feasible. Check Biletix for what's on where (see box below).

BARS

Istanbul is far from dry; away from conservative Islamic areas such as Fatih, **bars** range from the downright seedy to the achingly chic. In Sultanahmet the bars are tourist-oriented and other drinkers tend to be either fellow visitors or locals who work in the tourist trade. The liveliest places to drink here are Akbıyık Caddesi (which resembles the main drag of a Mediterranean resort on summer evenings) and Divan Yolu. Across the Golden Horn, however, lies buzzing Beyoğlu, which is where you should head for a real night out: a variety of bars – including many of the rooftop drinking establishments that have become so popular of late – line the lively streets and alleys leading off İstiklal Caddesi. **Kadıköy**, on the Asian side of the Bosphorus, has several atmospheric drinking holes on its popular "bar street". The line between Istanbul's bars and cafés is blurred, so many of the places listed below also serve food and coffee, often until late.

SULTANAHMET

Cozy Pub Divan Yolu Cad 66 ☎0212 520 0990, ⓦcozypub.com; map p.46. Situated on a prominent corner plot, this pleasant dark wood bar has tables out on the street in the warmer months – great for people-watching on hectic Divan Yolu. A large beer is ₺11, not bad for the location, a glass of local wine ₺15. There's a very Western-slanted food menu, with salads, pastas for ₺20, and a big mixed *meze* plate, ample for two, for ₺27. Daily 10am–2am.

Just Bar Akbıyık Cad 26 ☎0532 387 5729; map p.46. A lively bar popular with hostel residents, this is not the place for a quiet drink. Beers are reasonably priced (₺10) and served in ice-cold glasses, and the fun-loving bartenders will happily attempt your favourite cocktail. There's a small dancefloor space on weekend nights. Daily 10am–2am.

Pierre Loti Roof-Pub Piyer Loti Cad 5, Divan Yolu ☎0212 518 5700, ⓦpierrelotihotel.com; map p.46. There are plenty of hotel roof-bars with views in the old city, but this has to be one of the best. Reached by the hotel elevator to the fourth floor, then up a couple of flights of stairs, it's the perfect place to watch the sun go down over the domes, minarets and waterways – a virtually uninterrupted 360-degree view. A glass of wine costs ₺15, large beer ₺12, and drinks are served with a bowl of *çerez* (mixed nuts and roasted salted pulses). Daily 11am–midnight.

TICKETS AND LISTINGS

Tickets for many events, sporting as well as music, are available from specialist booking agency **Biletix** (☎0216 454 1555, ⓦbiletix.com), either online or from outlets across the city. Bigger venues such as *Babylon* have both an online and venue-based booking service; otherwise, buy your tickets at the door.

For **magazine listings**, pick up a copy of *Time Out Istanbul* (₺6) or *The Guide Istanbul* (₺10). Or check out their websites; ⓦtimeoutistanbul.com and ⓦtheguideistanbul.com respectively. Otherwise, check the posters and flyers on and around İstiklal Caddesi. *Cornucopia*, a glossy bimonthly covering the Ottoman arts scene, auctions, galleries and exhibitions, is available from bookshops that stock foreign-language newspapers and publications (see p.31).

14

Terrace Istanbul Arcadia Blue Hotel, Dr Imran Oktem Cad 1, Sultanahmet ☎0212 516 6118, ⊚hotelarcadiablue.com; map p.46. The terrace bar on the ninth floor of the sleek *Arcadia Blue* hotel is one of the best viewpoints in the old city, taking in the distant Bosphorus and the Asian shore while, in the foreground, are the Topkapı Palace, Haghia Sophia, Baths of Roxelana, Blue Mosque, Hippodrome and Sea of Marmara. Not hugely atmospheric – and a beer is a pricey ₺18 – but it's worth it for the views, especially at sunset. Daily 10am–midnight.

SİRKECİ

Port Shield Pub Ebusuud Cad 2 ☎0212 527 0931; map p.70. Situated right opposite the Gülhane tram stop and just a short step downhill from the Haghia Sophia, this mock-English pub, part of a chain, is usually packed with sports addicts taking in big-screen football, rugby and cricket matches from around the world. Drinks are expensive (beers ₺15), but there's a decent pub-grub menu if you're craving a taste of home. Daily 11.30am–1.30am.

GRAND BAZAAR AND AROUND

Murat Bira Evi Gedikpaşa Cad 77/a ☎0212 517 8228; map pp.78–79. The mainly male clientele here sit at high tables and work their way through cheap Efes beer. There's a tiny menu of fried *hamsi* (anchovies), or stuffed mussels for under ₺10. It's not pretty, but it's a real working-class drinking den – and handy after a stressful shopping bout in the bazaar. Not really suitable for unaccompanied women. Daily 10am–midnight.

THE NORTHWEST QUARTER

Agora Meyhanesi Vodina Cad 128, Balat ☎0212 635 4891, ⊚balatagorameyhanesi.com; map p.91. If you've been exploring the colourful old neighbourhood of Balat and are in need of a stiff drink, the *Agora*, housed in a charming nineteenth-century building, is one of the few options. This traditional place has featured in more than one *dizi* (Turkish soap) and several famous Turkish singers have strutted their stuff here in between courses. Following a refurbishment, it's smartened up its act and now features a miniature *rakı* museum and a detailed timeline of the place. Daily noon–midnight.

GALATA AND KARAKÖY

Ritim Galata Galata Kulesi Sok 3/c ☎0212 292 4926, ⊚ritimgalata.com; map p.110. Just up from *Nardis Jazz Club* and down from the Galata Tower, this mellow bar attracts a more sophisticated crowd than many of the places up in Beyoğlu. In summer a few tables spill out onto the street, and the cosy interior, with its exposed-brick walls and black-and-white photography, is very stylish. Large beers cost ₺12, there are soothing sounds from the DJ, and a Turkish-fusion food menu. Daily 11am–midnight.

Robin's Galip Dede Cad 56, Galata ☎0212 245 9443, ⊚robins.com.tr; map p.110. This rooftop bar-restaurant is located inside the *Duo Hotel*. The international menu is overpriced and the drinks aren't cheap either. However, the views of the Galata Tower and across the Golden Horn to the old city make it an attractive choice for an upmarket sunset drink. Daily 8am–midnight.

Sensus Büyükhendek Cad 5, Galata ☎0212 245 5657, ⊚sensuswine.com; map p.110. Just a stone's throw from the tower (down a little side street and on the right), this self-described "wine and cheese boutique" has the feel of an old wine cellar. Service is chaotic at best, but the range of wines (from ₺9 a glass) and the atmosphere make it a pleasant stopoff (though best avoided weekend evenings). Daily 10am–11pm.

Unter Kara Ali Kaptan Sok 4, Karaköy ☎0212 244 5151, ⊚unter.com.tr. map p.110. The hipster magnet of Karaköy is known for its cool cafés; however, there are a few options for evening drinks and this is the most popular.

TURKISH BEER

Local brewery **Efes Pilsen** has a stranglehold on the Turkish beer (*bira*) market, so it's fortunate they produce a generally well-regarded pilsner-type brew. In most cafés and restaurants this comes in bottles, either 33cl in the more upmarket places, or 50cl in more down-to-earth joints; bars and clubs often have it on draught (*fıçı*). **Efes Dark** is a sweeter, stronger stout-style beer, while **Efes-Xtra** is eight percent proof, though neither is widely available in bars or restaurants. The Efes group also produce Bomonti, named after Turkey's first modern brewery, founded in Istanbul in 1894. A little lighter than Efes, there's not much difference in taste. Efes Malt has much more (malty) favour and is many visitors' beer of choice, though it's slightly dearer.

Tuborg, of Danish origins, is the other major home-grown beer. It is less widely available than Efes, though some people swear by it. Their red-label beer is stronger than the standard green. Foreign beers are now widely available in Istanbul, but you'll pay at least a third more for the dubious privilege of drinking Corona, Fosters, Heineken or Becks. If you're craving something a little different, there are two decent brewpubs in Istanbul, though neither are very conveniently located; *Taps Bebek* (see p.200, ⊚tapsbebek.com) and *Bosphorus Brewing Company* (⊚bosphorus-brewing.com) in Gayrettepe – the latter opened by a British family in 2012.

RAKI IS THE ANSWER

The Turkish national aperitif is **rakı**, an anise-flavoured spirit, found (under different names) throughout many of the former provinces of the Ottoman Empire. *Rakı* is usually drunk over ice and turns a milky white when topped up, as it should be, with water – giving the drink its Turkish nickname Aslan Süt (Lion's Milk). The most ubiquitous brand is **Yeni**, but connoisseurs claim Burgaz, Efe and Tekirdağ are better. Between 45 and 48 percent proof, it's the favourite tipple for Turkish men (and many women) in *meyhane*s (see p.177) and is the ideal accompaniment to plates of *meze* and fish, slipping down very easily. Expect to pay between ₺8 and 20 for a double, according to the salubriousness of your surroundings. A cheesy slogan on Istanbul T-shirts "*Rakı* is the answer: I don't remember the question" gives fair warning to those who overdo it.

14

Limited space (sometimes taken up by a DJ) inside means cool young Istanbulites spill out into the street. Tues–Sun 10am–midnight, Fri & Sat till 2am.

BEYOĞLU

5.Kat Soğancı Sok 7, off Sıraselviler Cad ☎ 0212 293 3774, ⓦ 5kat.com; map pp.120–121. In fashionable Cihangir, this is a sumptuous bar/restaurant/club with great views over the Bosphorus via the floor-to-ceiling windows or from the rooftop terrace bar. The owner, Yasemin Alkaya, was a noted film actress and runs the place with her mother. A slightly offbeat joint, its special evenings feature everything from world-cuisine tasting to after-dinner monologues by celebrity guests. Dining gives way to dancing as the evening progresses. Daily 10am–2am, Sat & Sun till–3am.

360 Mısır Apartmanı 311, İstiklal Cad ☎ 0212 251 1042, ⓦ 360istanbul.com; map pp.120–121. Located within one of İstiklal Cad's most attractive nineteenth-century apartment blocks, with a stunning interior of plate glass and bare brick, this rooftop bar/café/restaurant with panoramic views over the city has commanded a fair share of attention. It is the venue of choice for cash-rich Istanbulites and foreigners alike. DJs spin tunes on weekends and wine by the glass costs upwards of ₺25, salads around ₺30. If they don't like the look of you, you won't get in. Another branch, *360 East*, lies across the Bosphorus in Moda. Daily noon–2am, Fri & Sat till 4am.

Büyük Londra Meşrutiyet Cad 117 ☎ 0212 245 0670, londrahotel.net; map pp.120–121. The bar of this unspoilt hotel has avoided the modernization that ruined the interiors of so many of Beyoğlu's *fin-de-siècle* buildings in the 1970s and 80s, long before retro was cool in this part of the world. While many of them attempt to recreate the feel of distant times, the *Büyük Londra* doesn't have to – it's still all ornate wood and velvet drapes. You wouldn't want to spend all evening here, but it's worth popping in for an early drink or two and absorbing the atmosphere before heading off to livelier places. In the summer, make your way to the rooftop bar (one of the cheapest around) for a view out over the Golden Horn. Daily noon–11pm.

Café Smyrna Akarsu Cad 29, Cihangir ☎ 0212 244 2466; map pp.120–121. This street is home to an ever-increasing number of café bars whose clientele are a trendy, well-heeled set. There's a laidback feel in the long, narrow interior with its motley array of mirrors and retro collectibles. In summer, there are a few tables on the street. Like many of the city's café-bars, you'll feel equally at home here nursing a coffee or sinking a beer – plus there's some decent food on offer. Wine from ₺14 a glass, beers from ₺10. Daily 9am–2am.

Çukurcuma 49 Turnacıbaşı Sok 49, Cihangir ☎ 0212 249 0048; map pp.120–121. This laidback café-bar is popular with hip young locals and expats. Exposed brick walls and mismatched wooden furniture lend it a homely feel. Glass floors reveal a wine cellar, and the menu offers good pizzas (around ₺25) and salads. Beer costs ₺10, but most of the clientele drink their "Desperate House Wine" for ₺12. Daily 9.30am–midnight.

James Joyce Irish Pub Irish Centre, Balo Sok 26 ☎ 0212 224 2013; map pp.120–121. Housed in a wonderfully ornate and rambling nineteenth-century apartment block is the Irish Centre's lively pub, which also has a bar with a big-screen TV that gets very crowded for sporting events. Live bands play most nights of the week and an Irish breakfast is served all day. Drinks are pricier than in the low-key Turkish bars around it. Daily 1pm–2am, Fri & Sat till 4am.

KV Tünel Geçidi 6, off İstiklal Cad ☎ 0212 251 4338, ⓦ kv.com.tr; map pp.120–121. There's a distinctly Edwardian feel to this delightful café-bar: the interior's subtle lighting illuminates a clutter of antiques and bric-a-brac, quite a contrast to the clean, minimalist lines of many of the city's fashionable cafés. In summer, there are tables outside in the lovely old passageway it fronts, and you'd never know bustling İstiklal Cad was just a stone's throw away. Daily 8.30am–2am.

★ **Leb-i Derya** Kumbaracı Yokuşu 57/6 ☎ 0212 293 4989; map pp.120–121. Funkier, with a younger clientele than its sister venue in the *Richmond Hotel* (see p.172), the bar boasts a picture-windowed lounge, balcony and small roof terrace, all of which look out onto where the Golden

Horn meets the Bosphorus. It's a fabulous (if pricey) place for an early or late evening drink – a glass of wine is upwards of ₺19. Also has an elaborate menu if you're in the mood to eat. Daily 11am–4am.

★**Limonlu Bahçe** Yeniçarşı Cad 98, Galatasaray ☎0212 252 1094, ⓦlimonlubahce.com; map pp.120–121. Just a 5min walk from İstiklal Cad, the "Lemon Garden" is a calm oasis providing a welcome retreat from the chaos of Beyoğlu. Reached by an impossibly long maze of corridors, this leafy space is usually bustling with a young professional crowd. It's a little pricey (beers ₺12, mojitos ₺25), but worth it if you need an escape from the bustle outside. Also has an extensive food and soft drinks menu. Daily 9am–1am.

Nu Pera Meşrutiyet Cad 149 ☎0212 245 6070, ⓦnupera.com.tr; map pp.120–121. This restaurant/club complex, housed in a 200-year-old building, is popular with a young, well-off crowd. Two ground-floor restaurants, *Auf* and *Kauf*, offer drinks and dining, Pop (winter months) is a club within a bar that plays R&B, and *Nu Teras* (summer months) is a roof terrace with a view over the Golden Horn and the old city beyond, where DJs spin laidback tunes until the early hours. Daily 6pm–4am.

Ritim Bar Sahane Sok 20, Balık Pazarı ☎0212 24 90252, ⓦritimbar.com; map pp.120–121. Run by the owner of the *World House Hostel* (see p.172), this down-to-earth multi-storey bar is packed at weekends (and other nights as well) with a real mixture of locals, foreign students and guests from the hostel, attracted by the well-priced beer (₺6 midweek) and an eclectic mix of DJ-spun sounds on the roof terrace. Daily 10am–2am.

Rock n Rolla Kurabiye Sok 17 ☎0532 571 6902, ⓦrocknrollabar.com; map pp.120–121. One of several dive bars in a row that spill out onto the street outside, it's popular with English teachers and students. With a strictly rock and blues music policy, it attracts an alternative crowd. Has a decent selection of foreign beers as well as the usual domestic suspects, and serves up pub grub. Daily noon–6am.

★**Solera** Yeniçarşı Cad 44, Galatasaray ☎0212 252 2719; map pp.120–121. This tiny wine bar may be small, but it's perfectly formed. Stocking over 1000 different Turkish and international wines, ranging from ₺8/glass/₺34 a bottle up, it's also one of the cheapest places to get a decent wine in the city. Tasty snacks and *meze* are served, and owner Suleyman Er is always on hand to give advice. Daily 10am–1am.

Urban Kartal Sok 6 ☎0212 252 1325, ⓦurbanbeyoglu.com; map pp.120–121. This laidback café-bar is on a tiny street parallel to İstiklal Cad but with none of its crowds. Sit outside under the vines and admire the street art that covers the walls here. Popular with young professionals and expats, you can also sit in the chic interior. Salads, sandwiches and grilled foods are on the menu, and you can get a surprisingly decent glass of wine for just ₺10. Daily 9am–2am.

BEŞİKTAŞ AND ORTAKÖY

Kafe Pi Ortaköy Osmanzade Sok 16 ☎0212 259 4381, ⓦkafepi.com; map p.132. One of a trendy chain of bars across the city attracting a mainly young, professional clientele. The prominent position of this branch (right

---

BAR STREET

Just a short walk from the Kadıköy ferry pier is the buzzing centre of the Asian side's nightlife. Kadife Sokak aka Barlar Sokak (literally "Bar Street") is lined with bars, which all spill out onto the street at weekends, creating a knitted throng of alternative young locals and foreign students. To return to the European side after the ferries stop running, take a dolmuş (shared taxi) to Taksim from close to the ferry port for ₺5. Many of these bars are similar in prices and vibe, but a few stand out:

Arkaoda Kadife Sok 18 ☎0216 418 0277, ⓦarkaoda.com; map p.140. This has become the hipster destination of choice on the Asian side, due to its eclectic music policy, vintage furniture and exciting programme of events. Also has a small garden in the back. Daily noon–2am.

Isis Kadife Sok 26, Caferağa Mah, Kadıköy ☎0216 349 7381; map p.140. Three-storey townhouse that's a café by day and bar-club at night. Cutting-edge alternative music and good food, plus a garden shaded by chestnut and fig trees,

open during the summer months. A large beer will set you back ₺10. Daily 11am–2am.

Karga Kadife Sok 16, Kadıköy ☎0216 449 1725; map p.140. Self-consciously cool venue, this grungy/arty place is set in a tall, narrow nineteenth-century townhouse. Inside, it's all wood and wall, with plenty of gloomy nooks for young lovers. Part pub (the lower floors) and part art gallery (top floor), it also has a large, pleasant garden out back. Beer is a reasonable ₺10 for a large Efes, and there's a snack-type menu. Daily 11am–2am.

14

across from the waterfront in Ortaköy Meydanı) makes this a good option for those seeking to get nicely oiled before heading to one of the more expensive neighbourhood nightclubs (see p.202). Daily 8am–2am, Fri–Sat until 4am.

BOSPHORUS

Lucca Cevdet Paşa Cad 51/b, Bebek ☎ 0212 257 1255, ⓦ luccastyle.com; map p.151. This may be a casual café-bar but that's upmarket Bebek "casual", and unless you're fashionably dressed you may feel uncomfortable. That said, the interior's a fun mix of the genuinely old (check out the nineteenth-century ceiling reliefs), the retro (1950s-style prints) and the ethnic (African masks). On weekend evenings DJs get the crowd on their feet, and sometimes on the tables. Daily noon–2am.

Taps Cevdet Paşa Cad 119, Bebek ☎ 0212 263 8700, ⓦ tapsbebek.com; map p.151. Istanbul's first brewpub occupies a prime Bosphorus-facing location in the fancy Bebek neighbourhood. Spread over two floors with a few tables on the pavement outside, this is a chance to taste some of the best beer in Istanbul, with Kölsch, Munich Ale and Vienna Lager just some of the Germanic offerings

available. Pilsner from ₺15 and up. Alternatively, get a sampler and try them all. Daily 11am–11pm.

ASIAN ISTANBUL

Viktor Levi Damacı Sok 4, Caferağa Mah, Kadıköy ☎ 0216 449 9329; map p.140. If you're over in Kadıköy looking for something less arty and grungy than Barlak Sok this historic bar-restaurant may just fit the bill. It's housed in a rambling nineteenth-century house, with a massive shady courtyard garden out back, and serves its own wines, which it has been producing since 1914 and sells for upwards of ₺32 a bottle. There's a massive menu too, with *meze* starting from ₺5, grills from ₺18. Daily 11am–2am.

Zeplin Pub Moda Cad 11, Moda ☎ 0216 700 2002, ⓦ zeplinpub.com; map p.140. One of Istanbul's most sought-after areas, Moda is fast becoming an alternative for young professionals who have tired of Beyoğlu. There's a booming café and bar industry, with several good places to choose from. Decked out like a smart London pub, *Zeplin* focuses on its range of international beers, one of the widest in the city (₺9–23). Daily 11am–1am.

CLUBS AND LIVE MUSIC VENUES

Istanbul is a relatively dynamic **clubbing scene** – reflecting the rapid pace of modernization, rising living standards of living and the sheer number of young people around – half of Turkey's population is under 29. Most urban Turks stay up late so don't expect the real action until well after midnight. Unless you look the part, you might not make it past the bouncers, particularly in the flashy Bosphorus-front clubs; Beyoğlu clubs are less exclusive. Some establishments shut down for the summer (anywhere from mid-June to mid-Sept) and relocate to out-of-town venues – check listings for details. **Live music venues** vary widely. Many have "house" bands that play one or more regular nights per week, with the best bands/ artists (and highest entry fees – around ₺30, which may include a free drink, though the Bosphorus-front clubs are more expensive) reserved for weekends. This is especially true of the rock-style venues, where bands play either Turkish **rock** or sing covers in English. **Jazz** has a hardcore following; the people who do like it are, by and large, affluent and influential, and this has enabled a number of clubs to flourish and attract the biggest names from the international scene. There are plenty of talented jazz musicians from Istanbul who have made the international stage, including Okay Temiz and İlhan Erşahin, but they still play locally as well.

TURKISH WINES

The third largest producer of grapes in the world, Turkey should be a major-league player in the wine business, and there are vineyards scattered across western Anatolia between Cappadocia, the Euphrates Valley, Thrace and the Aegean. As yet though, **Turkish wine** (*şarap*) is little known outside the country, and expensive within it because the government levies an eighty percent tax on alcoholic beverages. It has, however, become the drink of choice for the middle classes, especially "modern" women. A drinkable wine bought from a supermarket starts from around ₺15. Expect to pay at least three times that for the same bottle with a meal in even a modest restaurant. A glass of wine in a cheaper café-bar will set you back upwards of ₺9. The cheapest palatable bets are the wines manufactured by Doluca (try the Villa or more expensive Antik), Pammukale and Kavaklıdere (Angora and Çankaya). Imported wines are affordable at supermarkets but prohibitively priced in restaurants. If you want to get to know Turkish wines better, visit one of the several wine bars that have sprung up in the city such as *Sensus* (p.196), and *Solera* (p.198) in Beyoğlu.

BEYOĞLU

Bronx Pi Terkoz Çıkmazı 8/1, off İstiklal Cad ☎0532 384 8080, ⓦbronxpisahne.com; map pp.120–121. Intimate and trendy club staging alternative and indie live acts, both local and international. Very popular with university students and twenty-somethings because of its reasonable drink charges. Entry varies according to act, free when there's no live music. Mon–Sat 8pm–4am.

Gizli Bahçe Nevizade Sok 27, off İstiklal Cad ☎0212 249 2192; map pp.120–121. The ideal place to extend your evening after the full-on *meyhane* experience of Nevizade Sok is this chilled bar-club, spread over the second and third floors of an Ottoman townhouse – with sofas to lounge on, and a balcony to escape to. The eclectic music – everything from jazz and blues to rock and house – is loud but there are quiet nooks to continue conversation. Daily 9pm–2am.

Hayal Kahvesi Büyükparmakkapı Sok 19 ☎0212 244 2558, ⓦhayalkahvesi.com.tr; map pp.120–121. Attractive brick-and-wood joint with blues, rock and indie every night from 10pm. Mostly decent local bands, but also book the occasional big name. Has a sister branch, *Çubuklu Hayal Kahvesi* in Burunbahçe on the Asian side of the Bosphorus (☎0216 413 6880). There's a free boat service from İstinye across the strait. Admission varies. Daily 5pm–4am.

Indigo Akarsu Sok 1/2, off İstiklal Cad ☎0212 244 8567, ⓦindigo-istanbul.com; map pp.120–121. This cavernous venue (with a capacity for 600) remains the venue of choice for underground electronic music lovers. With a Funktion-One soundsystem and a setup that sees the DJ play in the centre of the club, it's a forward-thinking venue that hosts international names from the house and techno scenes. After 5am it becomes *Koma* – an after-party club for ravers who keep going until 10am. Fri & Sat 11pm–5am.

★Jolly Joker Balans Balo Sok 22 ☎0212 251 7020, ⓦjjistanbul.com; map pp.120–121. Sprawling venue with good, on-site microbrewed German-style beer available in the adjoining bar. The main performance hall is impressive, seating up to 1500, and many of the shows are by mainstream Turkish pop and rock stars. Mon–Thurs 10pm–2am, Fri & Sat 10pm–4am.

Kasette Korsan Çıkmazı 6, off İstiklal Cad ☎0536 415 8018; map pp.120–121. This "club" is in fact the closed-off end of a cul de sac, which transforms after dark into a lively bar-club. Free entry means its gets incredibly busy with a younger crowd, but unaccompanied men won't get in. DJs from Turkey and German play house music, but there's no space for dancing. Daily 10pm–4am.

MiniMüzikhol Soğancı Sok 7, off Sıraselviler Cad ☎0212 245 1996, ⓦminimuzikhol.com; map pp.120–121. In the same building as *5.Kat* (see p.197), this intimate club is a favourite with the city's late-night hipsters and features both local and international DJs playing house, techno, hip-hop and dubstep. Cover charge is around ₺20 on weekends. Wed–Sat 10pm–4am.

TOP FIVE DRINKS WITH A VIEW

360 Beyoğlu, see p.197
Terrace Istanbul, see p.196
Leb-i Derya Beyoğlu, see p.197
Nu Teras (above Nu Pera) Beyoğlu, see p.198
Pierre Loti Hotel roof-Pub, see p.195

14

★Peyote Kameriye Sok 4, Balık Pazarı ☎0212 251 4398, ⓦpeyote.com.tr; map pp.120–121. One of the best places for alternative/indie types looking for an underground scene. The owners are in a band themselves, and they give stage space to upcoming rivals from across the metropolis. There's a lively roof terrace with an eclectic mix of music, live bands play on the second floor, while the first floor is given over to electronic music. Beers are a reasonable ₺8 and the (variable) entry charges start from ₺10 (although usually just to watch the live bands). Daily 10pm–4am.

Pixie Underground Toşbaşağa Sok 12; map pp.120–121. This small venue is musically one of the most cutting-edge clubs in Beyoğlu. Istanbul's only bass music club, the emphasis is on dubstep, drum'n'bass and jungle, and it's a chance to see some of Istanbul's up-and-coming producers. Beers are a respectable price and entry is either free or ₺10 for bigger name DJ's. Daily 2pm–4am.

Roxy Arslan Yatağı Sok 113, off Sıraselviler Cad ☎0212 249 1283, ⓦroxy.com.tr; map pp.120–121. Popular club established back in 1994, attracting a wide range of good-time punters happy to part with the ₺15–30 entrance fee. Music ranges from dance to blues and hip-hop to jazz, and there are live acts – see the website for details. Closed July and Aug. Fri & Sat 10pm–4am.

GALATA AND WATERFRONT DISTRICTS

Atölye Kuledibi Galata Kulesi Sok 4 ☎0212 243 7656, ⓦatolyekuledibi.com; map p.110. Stylish café-bar run by a group of local artists, musicians and actors, punctuated with a rotating wall of local artwork and photography. An odd mix of international dishes grace the menu, cooked up in an open kitchen and served alongside a wide array of creative cocktails. With low-key daily performances of live jazz, this innovative venue with no cover charge is a reliable bohemian option. Mon, Tues & Thurs noon–midnight, Wed, Fri & Sat noon–2am.

Fosil Kemankeş Cad 34c, 3rd Floor, Karaköy ☎0507 812 8531, ⓦfosil.com.tr; map p.110. This indie bar-club rocks to an urban cool aesthetic, enhanced by exposed piping, brickwork and rows of bare hanging light bulbs. Accessed via a black-curtained passageway on the main drag in Karaköy's waterfront district, the mysterious entrance makes the magnificent Bosphorus view even more impressive. Gets very busy on weekend

14

nights despite the steep prices. Daily noon–midnight, Wed–Sat till 4am.

★**Nardis Jazz Club** Kuledibi Sok 14, Galata ☎0212 244 6327, ⓦnardisjazz.com; map p.110. Run by local jazz musicians, this small, intimate venue offers a great introduction to the local jazz scene and is a popular haunt among the local middle classes. A blend of mainstream and modern jazz takes centre stage, with a little fusion and ethnic jazz thrown in for good measure. Bands are mostly Turkish but international solo artists are regularly invited to perform alongside them. ₺40 entrance fee, ensures only serious jazz fans enter (no talking during acts!). Mon–Sat 9.30pm–1am.

★**Salon İKSV** Sadi Konuralp Cad 5, Şişhane ☎0212 334 0752, ⓦsaloniksv.com; map p.110. Trendy multi-purpose venue backed by the Istanbul Foundation for Culture and Arts (IKSV), hosting contemporary ambient, electronic, jazz and indie concerts, plus some theatrical performances. Tickets are available from Biletix (see box, p.95), or commission-free from the venue. Opening hours vary according to the act.

ORTAKÖY

Anjelique Salhane Sok 5, off Muallim Naci Cad ☎0212 327 2844, ⓦanjelique.com.tr; map p.132. One of Istanbul's most popular, mainstream clubs, in the heart of buzzing Ortaköy. Spread over three floors in a Bosphorus-facing mansion, reimagined by design company Autobahn. Each floor plays a different type of music from Turkish pop to house so you can choose according either to your mood or pick the floor with the best crowd. No cover charge, but expensive drinks and you'll need to dress to impress if you want to get in. Daily 6pm–4am.

Kiki Osmanzade Sok 8 ☎0212 258 5524, ⓦkiki.com.tr; map p.132. Situated right in Ortaköy square, this is one of the least flashy clubs in the district – it's still very trendy but attracts a younger, less showy clientele, who come for

the deep house DJs. Spread over three floors, the best action takes place on the roof terrace in the summer months. Entrance is usually free, but like all clubs drinks aren't cheap – a small beer costs ₺14. Has a smaller branch on Siraselviler Cad, Cihangir. Wed–Sat 8pm–4am.

Reina Muallim Naci Cad 44 ☎0212 259 5919, ⓦreina .com.tr; map p.132. This exclusive joint has been running for nine years now and has clocked up a fair few celebrity guests in its time – Oprah Winfrey, Sting, Uma Thurman, Paris Hilton, to name a few. With its waterfront location, several dancefloors blasting Euro-pop and selection of themed restaurants (6–11pm), this is where the city's bright young things come to splash their cash. Entry is ₺70 at weekends, but usually free weeknights. Drinks are also exorbitant and if you don't have a chauffeur-driven car to collect you in the small hours, you'll probably feel out of place. Daily 6pm–4am.

Supper Club Muallim Naci Cad 65 ☎0212 261 1988, ⓦsupperclub.com; map p.132. This rather over-the-top venue is part of an Amsterdam-based group with branches around the world. Whether you view it as free-spirited hedonism or downright pretentious, this place aims to tickle the five senses with a roster of art, performance, video, dance and music. Thurs & Sun free, Fri & Sat ₺50 including a free drink. Thurs–Sun 9pm–2am.

ASIAN ISTANBUL

Shaft Osmancık Sok 13, Kadıköy ☎0216 349 9956, ⓦshaftclub.com; map p.140. Situated on a lively street, this is one of the few late-night options on the Asian side of the Bosphorus. Entry is a reasonable ₺25 on Fri & Sat (including one free drink), with sets from the (mainly) rock acts starting from 10.30pm. Midweek entry is free, and there's blues and jazz as well as rock on occasion. Daily 2pm–4am.

TRADITIONAL TURKISH MUSIC

There are many different types of Turkish music and all may, initially at least, sound incongruous, off-key even, to the Western ear – largely because of the copious use of quarter-tones. If you really want to scratch beneath the surface of what makes this city tick, it's worth searching out a **traditional music** venue. The *Türkü* bar, where traditional Anatolian folk

BABYLON: TURNING ISTANBUL ON

Responsible for revolutionizing the live-music scene in Istanbul, this iconic venue has brought some of the biggest names in music to the city. Run by Turkey's best event promotions company, Pozitif Live, it features a varied programme of local and foreign groups playing jazz, reggae, world, indie and electronic music. To get a flavour of *Babylon*'s sounds, tune into its online radio station, ⓦradyobabylon.com. At the time of writing, plans were well underway to open a second, larger *Babylon* in the historic Bomonti Beer Factory in Feriköy. Ticket prices, which vary wildly according to the act, can be bought in advance from ⓦbiletix.com; performances usually start around 10pm. In summer, *Babylon* moves to the Çeşme peninsula on the Aegean coast. The original *Babylon* is at Şehbender Sok 3, Asmalımescit ☎0212 292 7368, ⓦbabylon.com.tr, the new one at Bomonti Bira Fabrikası, Silahşör Caddesi, Feriköy. Days and hours depend on what's on.

songs are played, tends to be drinking and music-orientated, though most serve food as well. The *meyhane* (see box, p.178) experience is as much about the endless courses of food served as it is about the *fasıl* music (see p.303) that is played. In the **Türkü bar**, the focus is on the *bağlama*, a kind of long-necked lute played with amazing dexterity by experts. On a typical evening, expect to sit around, beer in hand, listening to its plaintive sounds. As the evening progresses, the *bağlama* player, perhaps accompanied by fellow musicians playing the *deblek* (a kind of bongo-drum) and a *ney* (a type of flute) raises the tempo and the audience gets to their feet, links fingers and dances the *halay*, the country's national dance. It's great fun and very popular among young Istanbulites – the latest global club sounds and traditional Anatolian folk music are not mutually exclusive in this city of paradoxes. *Fasıl* music is quite different and played mainly by Roma (gypsy) bands. Visit virtually any **meyhane** (such as those on Nevizade Sokak or Asmalımescit) and you won't be able to escape it even if you wanted to, as the musicians serenade each and every table in search of tips.

14

BEYOĞLU

Feraye Balo Sok 1 First Floor, off İstiklal Cad ☎0212 244 74 72, ⓦferaye.net; map pp.120–121. This smart *meyhane* is a favourite with local Turkish music lovers who come for the live performances on weekends. Inevitably the whole restaurant is on their feet by the end of the night. Prices are a little higher than elsewhere (fixed menu including drinks at ₺100), but the atmosphere makes it an experience. Daily noon–4am.

Kallavi Meyhane Kurabiye Sok 16, off İstiklal Cad ☎0212 245 1213, ⓦkallavi20.net; map pp.120–121. A small, traditional restaurant. The fixed menu (₺90) includes ten starters, four mains, a dessert and fruit, plus unlimited local drinks. With live *fasıl* music every night, it's very popular with the locals, so best to book ahead. There's another branch at Şefikbey Sok in Kadıköy. Mon–Sat 11am–2am.

★ **Mektup** İmam Adnan Sok 20, off İstiklal Cad ☎0212 251 0110, ⓦmektupbar.com; map pp.120–121. The food on offer here is limited in range but perfectly passable. More importantly, the *Türkü* music is of a very high standards – it has seen sets by notable artists such as Ebru Destan and Tuğbay Özay. Voted the best *Türkü* bar in the country by the *Hürriyet* newspaper, so booking is advisable – especially at weekends. Daily noon–4am.

Munzur Hasnün Galip Sok 21/a, off İstiklal Cad ☎0212 245 4669; map pp.120–121. The Munzur mountains, away to the east in the heartland of Turkey's Kurdish Alevî population (the Alevî have spawned the nation's best *bağlama* players), are the inspiration for this no-frills but lively *Türkü* bar. The food is okay, the drinks not too pricey, and when things get going there are plenty of linked bodies dancing around the tables. Daily 6pm–4am.

Nublu Sıraselviler Cad 55, Beyoğlu ☎0212 249 7712, ⓦnubluistanbul.net; map p.110. A cool split-level, low-lit joint featuring a leafy terrace and several cocktail bars. With its origins in New York, it has a jazz focus but also hosts bands and DJs from across the musical spectrum. Cover charge varies. Wed–Sat 10pm–4am.

NORTH OF TAKSIM

Despina Açıkyol Sok 9 ☎0212 232 6720. Out in the wilderness of the business district of Şişli, the sub-district of Kurtuluş was once home to a wealthy Armenian and Greek community. The *meyhane*'s Armenian founder, Madame Despina, died in 2006, but the spirit of the place lives on. Its *fasıl* band is renowned and people come out of their way to enjoy both the music and the Armenian-style *meyhane* food on offer. Daily noon–midnight.

TRADITIONAL DANCE AND CULTURAL SHOWS

Folk dancing to traditional music has managed to survive into the modern day, as have the rituals of religious orders such as the sufi Mevlevi (see p.113). The easiest way for visitors to sample some of the action is to attend a show. Those performed in the two places below are generally well regarded, though inevitably the entire audience will be fellow visitors.

★ **Hodja Paşa Culture Centre** Hodjapaşa Hamam Sok 3/b, Sirkeci ☎0212 511 4626, ⓦhodjapasha.com. Housed in a beautifully restored Ottoman *hamam*, with the dance area and seats atmospherically set beneath an exposed brick dome, a seventy-minute show introduces the visitor to music and dances from all parts of the Ottoman Empire for ₺70, including an interval drink. There's also a more specialist whirling dervish ceremony

put on by sufis from the Galata Mevlevihanesi.

Turkish Cultural Dance Theatre Fırat Culture Centre, Divan Yolu, Sultanahmet ☎0554 797 2646, ⓦdancesofcolours.com. Presents a whirling dervish music and dance show in a restored house that once belonged to a distinguished *dede* (leader). This is purely theatre, with no dinner or the other trappings of a club. ₺50. Mon, Thurs & Sat.

ISTANBUL MODERN

The arts

Vibrant Istanbul is the cultural hub of Turkey, and hosts an ever-increasing
number of arts and cultural festivals, matching most other European cities
for the breadth of its arts scene. In 2010 it was chosen as a European Capital
of Culture, which provided a real boost to the city's arts. However, state
funding remains relatively low, meaning that most of the city's arts facilities
are funded by wealthy investment groups or banks. However, the number of
galleries has increased substantially over the past decade or so; Istanbul is
fast becoming a new centre for contemporary art.

Istanbul's more prosperous citizens have embraced the European love of classical music, opera, ballet and theatre, and there are now numerous venues spread across the city. Central to this development is the Istanbul Culture and Arts Foundation (IKSV). Founded in 1973 under the leadership of Dr Nejat F. Eczacıbaşı, it organizes international cultural events in every field, and continues to expand its activities. Some of their most popular events include the Istanbul Music, Jazz, Film and Theatre festivals, as well as the Istanbul Biennial, and the Istanbul Design Biennial. If you happen to be in town when any of these events are taking place they offer an excellent opportunity to witness some of the best acts from around the world, often collaborating with Turkish artists to create some truly unique performances. However, keep your eyes open for posters advertising the many smaller, independent festivals that take place across the city throughout the year.

ESSENTIALS

Information on all music and theatre events, and on the various cultural festivals, is available from the Istanbul Foundation for Culture and Arts (IKSV), Sadı Konuralp Cad 5, Şişhane, Beyoğlu (☎0212 334 0700, ⌨iksv.org).
Tickets for most events and performances can be purchased online from Biletix (⌨biletix.com), whose website is in both Turkish and English; there are several Biletix outlets around the city. Otherwise, you can buy tickets from the relevant venue, either online or from their box office. For what's on, check *The Guide Istanbul* (⌨theguideistanbul.com*)* or *Time Out Istanbul* (⌨timeoutistanbul.com).

CLASSICAL MUSIC AND THE PERFORMING ARTS

As part of his great push to westernize the fledgling Turkish Republic and break from the Ottoman past, Atatürk tried to inculcate new values among the population, among them a love for Western **classical music**, **opera**, **ballet and theatre**. He was partially successful, and today most educated, middle- and upper-class Turks have at least a passing interest in Western cultural forms. The Istanbul State Symphony Orchestra and Istanbul State Opera and Ballet Company are funded by the government, but there are several privately funded orchestras, including the renowned Borusan Philharmonic. The season runs from November to May, but in summer, historic buildings such as the former Byzantine church of Haghia Eirene and the Galata Mevlevihanesi provide prestigious venues for the **Istanbul Music Festival** (see p.33). Istanbul also has a thriving **theatre** scene, with venues in districts as diverse as ultra-orthodox Fatih and upmarket Harbiye, but most foreign productions are performed in Turkish, giving them limited appeal to most visitors. The best opportunity to see productions in English is during the **International Istanbul Theatre Festival** (see p.33), when many foreign companies hit town; ultra-cool Garaj Istanbul draws in international as well as home-grown artists, while the Kenter and Tiyatro Pera theatres stage occasional performances in English.

Akbank Culture and Arts Centre (Akbank Sanat) İstiklal Cad 8/a, Beyoğlu ☎0212 252 3500, ⌨akbanksanat.com. Multimedia centre including a café, art gallery, dance studio, music room, library and theatre. The centre also hosts film festivals and organizes the annual Akbank Jazz Festival (see p.34). Tues–Sat 10.30am–7.30pm.

Borusan Arts and Cultural Centre İstiklal Cad 213, Beyoğlu ☎0212 336 3280, ⌨borusansanat.com; map p.121. An arts complex that incorporates the Borusan Music House performance venue, which is home to the Borusan Philharmonic Orchestra, one of Turkey's most successful private orchestras, as well as one of the country's most extensive CD libraries and a decent art gallery.

Cemil Reşit Rey (CRR) Darülbedayi Cad 1, Harbiye ☎0212 232 9830, ⌨crrkonsersalonu.org. The middle-class Istanbulite's venue of choice, this purpose-built concert hall features chamber, classical, jazz and Turkish music, plus regular performances by visiting international orchestras. It also has its own well-regarded symphony orchestra and hosts the annual CRR Jazz February festival. Daily performances in season (Oct–May).

Cemil Topuzlu Open Air Theatre Taşkışla Cad ☎0212 232 1652; map p.128. Istanbul's biggest contemporary amphitheatre, just a ten-minute walk from Taksim Square, can seat up to 4500, making it a popular choice for summer concerts and events when many of Istanbul's most popular venues shut down.

Garaj Istanbul Kaymakan Reşit Bey Sok 11, off Yeniciler Cad, Beyoğlu ☎0212 244 4499, ⌨garajistanbul.org; map pp.120–121. Trendy, stripped-down performing arts venue in a former underground car park just off Galatasaray Meydanı, reached from Kaymakan Sok. This is as cutting-edge as it gets in Istanbul, with workshops, films and art projects associated with modern dance, theatre, music and other performances. Its own company performs at the venue and

15

ISTANBUL THROUGH THE LENS

With its unique continent-straddling topography and incredible Byzantine and Ottoman history, the teeming metropolis of Istanbul is a photographer's dream. It's little wonder that so many talented snappers have found their muse in such an iconic city. Born in 1928, **Ara Güler** began his career in photojournalism in Istanbul in 1950. The Armenian photographer later worked for *Time-Life*, *Paris-Match* and *Der Sturm* and, after making friends with Henri Cartier-Bresson, he joined the renowned Paris-based Magnum Agency. Although Güler has taken pictures all around the world and interviewed and photographed luminaries such as Churchill, Picasso and Dalí, he'll almost certainly be best remembered for the startling **black-and-white images** of his native city. It is no surprise that Istanbul's most famous literary son, Nobel Prize-winner Orhan Pamuk (see box, p.126) used a selection of Güler's photographs to illustrate his 2005 memoir *Istanbul: Memories of a City*. Pamuk's melancholic text is enhanced by Güler's gritty images – ferries on the Golden Horn belching black smoke, washing strung across dank, narrow streets in the poor neighbourhood of Balat, or a ragged street urchin peeping out from behind an Ottoman tombstone in Eyüp. The small size and poor-quality reproduction of the photos used in Pamuk's book do not do his images justice: for an idea of Güler's mastery of his craft, check out the book *Ara Güler's Istanbul: 40 Years of Photographs* (2009); or sip a coffee while admiring the images adorning his appropriately named *Kafe Ara* (see p.182); or look at his website ⓦaraguler.com.tr. He is an artist who has done as much, if not more, for Istanbul as Cartier-Bresson did for Paris.

One contemporary photographer who shares Güler's keen eye for a striking image is the online sensation **Mustafa Seven**. Born in 1974 in the eastern Anatolian town of Sivas, Seven takes great pictures of his adopted home, Istanbul, and has gained a huge international and domestic following with his shots of the city uploaded to Instagram. Like Güler, he sees great beauty in Istanbul's more downtrodden neighbourhoods and characters, from burnt-out cars to pigeon-fanciers, beached and broken boats to working-class fisherman on the Galata Bridge. The results he achieves with his iPhone and camera are impressive. To see for yourself visit ⓦinstagram.com/mustafaseven or ⓦmustafaseven.com.

---

tours abroad, and it attracts quality performing artists from around the world. With seating limited to 250, it's worth booking for most things. Closed July & Aug.

Haghia Eirene Topkapı Palace, Sultanahmet; map p.46. An atmospheric venue in the cavernous interior of the Byzantine Church of the Divine Peace. Staging classical music concerts at irregular intervals, usually in aid of charity, it features prominently in June's annual Istanbul International Music Festival. The seating may be reminiscent of a school assembly and the acoustics are not brilliant, but this remains a special place.

İş Arts Centre İş Sanat Kültür Merkezi, İş Kuleleri, Kule 17, Levent ☎0212 316 1083, ⓦissanat.com.tr. Out in the business district of Levent and best reached from the M2 Levent Metro stop, this multi-purpose venue, with an eight-hundred-capacity main auditorium, is housed in a tower block. Classical music performances, jazz and world-music concerts are held here, as well as theatre, and there's an art gallery attached.

Kenter Theatre Halaskargazi Cad 9, Harbiye ☎0212 246 3589, ⓦkentertiyatrosu.org. Founded by the famous Turkish actress Yıldız Kenter, who appears in many of the plays, this theatre presents some English-language performances of playwrights such as Shakespeare and Chekhov. It's also the venue for the Turkish Shadow Play,

the traditional puppet show performed on most weekend mornings. Season runs Oct–April.

Lütfi Kırdar Congress and Exhibition Centre Gümüs Cad 4, Harbiye ☎0212 373 1100, ⓦicec.org. With a conference auditorium seating some 3500 and a performance hall, the Anadolu Auditorium, for over 2000, this is one of the city's premier spots for classical music and ballet – and for the best in traditional Turkish music. It also holds major events including the Contemporary Istanbul art fair (Nov), in a new state-of-the-art exhibition hall.

Ortaoyuncular İstiklal Cad 140, Beyoğlu ☎0212 251 186, ⓦortaoyuncular.com; map pp.120–121. Set up in 1980 by the multi-talented director and playwright Ferhan Sensoy, this beautiful old theatre stages an eclectic mix of Turkish plays. Season runs Oct–May.

Süreyya Opera Bahariye Cad 29, Kadıköy ☎0216 346 1531, ⓦsureyyaoperasi.org; tickets ⓦwww.dobgm .gov.tr; map p.40. A gorgeous, beautifully restored opera house built in 1924, this is a delightfully intimate place to watch opera, ballet and classical music and a rare oasis of culture on the Asian side of the Bosphorus. Season runs Oct–May.

Türker İnanoğlu Maslak Show Centre Büyükdere Cad, Derbent Mevki, Maslak ☎0212 286 6686,

ⓦ timshowcenter.com. Located out in distant Maslak, and best reached by bus #25/T (Taksim–Sariyer), this is a populist venue, with everything from gypsy orchestras and Chinese acrobatic teams to ballet and Broadway shows. It's big, it's brash, and it's a long way from the old city – both in distance (15km from Taksim) and atmosphere – but it's certainly Istanbul as it is today.

Zorlu Center PSM Zorlu Center, Zincirlikuyu ☎ 0850 222 6776, ⓦ zorlucenterpsm.com; map p.151. Reached by taking the M2 Metro to Gayrettepe, then following the signs underground, this glitzy state-of-the-art theatre may be inside a shopping mall but has become the new venue of choice for many of the city's biggest performances including orchestras, musicals, ballet and more.

GALLERIES AND EXHIBITION SPACES

The visual arts scene in Istanbul is burgeoning, with new galleries opening with dizzying regularity. The inaugural **International Istanbul Biennial** (see box, p.209), held in 1987, kick-started the current boom by giving a platform to both foreign and local artists. Corporate sponsors, particularly banks, have filled the void left by state funding and opened up a number of multi-purpose **exhibition venues** – mostly around Beyoğlu, but with a few other destinations worth visiting for contemporary art enthusiasts. There are also several art fairs that create a buzz around the city and attract both international galleries and collectors: the most prominent are Art International (Sep) and Contemporary Istanbul (Nov) – see p.33 for more information. For a guided tour of Istanbul's galleries check out ⓦ artwalkIstanbul.com, whose knowledgeable guides offer a variety of routes to view the city's various art collections. Alternatively consult ⓦ theguideIstanbul.com for what's on. Alongside contemporary movements, traditional art forms remain a strong attraction in Istanbul, and many of the best examples can be found in the city's museums. Check out the excellent Calligraphy Collection at Sakıp Sabancı Museum (p.150), the Kütahya Tiles and Ceramics Collection at the Pera Museum (p.123) or the Orientalist paintings at the Palace Paintings Museum (p.133).

15

Arter İstiklal Cad 211, Beyoğlu ☎ 0212 243 7667, ⓦ arter .org.tr; map pp.120–121. Four storeys of exhibition space for local and international contemporary artists, backed by the wealthy Vehbi Koç Foundation. Installations, performance art and more take centre stage in this prominently located gallery. Tues–Thurs 11am–7pm, Fri–Sun noon–8pm.

Borusan Contemporary Perili Köşk Baltalımanı Hısar Cad 5, Rumelihisarı ☎ 0212 393 5200 ⓦ borusan contemporary.com; map p.151. This unusual exhibition space is actually the headquarters of the logistics company, Borusan Holding. Housed in a red-brick "haunted mansion" beside the second Bosphorus bridge, the office staff dutifully clear their desks every Friday, and it opens to the public each weekend with a varied array of exhibitions, spread over nine floors and roof terrace. See p.150 for more information. Entry ₺10. Sat–Sun 10am–8pm.

DEPO Lüleci Hendek Cad 12, Tophane ☎ 0212 292 3956, ⓦ depolstanbul.net; map p.110. Housed in a former tobacco warehouse and spread over four floors, DEPO hosts exhibitions, talks and screenings with a distinct sociopolitical focus, often dealing with controversial issues such as urban transformation, minority rights and the relationship between art and politics.

Galerist Meşrutiyet Cad 67/1, Tepebaşı ☎ 0212 252 1896, ⓦ galerist.com.tr; map pp.120–121. Commercial gallery of considerable repute, showcasing some of the very best contemporary Turkish artists as well as international stars. On the first floor of a beautifully restored eighteenth-century building whose original features contrast strikingly with the contemporary works on display, just a few doors down from the Pera Museum. Tues–Sat 11am–7pm.

OTHER CONTEMPORARY ART DESTINATIONS

While the backstreets of Beyoğlu are where most of the contemporary art galleries can be found, there are several other pockets where Istanbul's art scene flourishes:

Akaretlar Süleyman Seba and Şair Nedim Caddesi; map p.132. The elegant rows of houses that make up Akaretlar were built to provide accommodation to the royal staff of the nearby Dolmabahçe Palace (see pp.131–133). Since the area was rejuvenated in 2008, it has become home to some of Istanbul's fanciest boutiques, cafés and art galleries, including Rampa (ⓦ rampaistanbul.com), C.A.M. (ⓦ camgaleri .com), Art350 (ⓦ art350.com), Kuad (ⓦ kuadgallery .com) and ArtON (ⓦ artonistanbul.com).

Teşvikiye Vali Konağı and Abdi İpekçi Caddesis and around; map p.128. Known more as a luxury shopping destination, the inevitable injection of money into upmarket area of town Teşvikiye, and in the Nişantaşı quarters has now spawned a number of respected contemporary art galleries including x-ist (ⓦ artxist.com), Ilayda (ⓦ galleryilayda.com), Kare (ⓦ kareartgallery.com), Merkur (ⓦ galerimerkur.com), and Dirimart (ⓦ dirimart.org).

Istanbul Modern Meclis-I Mebusan Cad, Liman İşletmeleri Sahası Antrepo 4, Karaköy ☎0212 334 7300, ⓦistanbulmodern.org; map p.110. Istanbul's answer to Tate Modern in London, with regularly changing exhibits by contemporary Turkish and foreign artists, plus a cinema showing art-house movies, workshops (including ones for kids), a library, photography gallery and a chic café-restaurant. Admission ₺17 (see p.115 for more information). Tues–Sun 10am–6pm, Thurs until 8pm.

Mısır Apartment Mısır Apartmanı, İstiklal Cad 163; map 120–121. This landmark Art Nouveau building close to Galatasaray Meydanı, was built in 1910 by Hovsep Aznavur, an Armenian architect, to be the residence for the last Khedive of Egypt (Mısır means "Egypt" in Turkish). It now houses a changing number of contemporary art galleries that include: Galeri Zilberman (ⓦgalerizilberman.com), Galeri Nev (ⓦgalerinevIstanbul.com), the Nesrin Esirtgen Collection (ⓦnesrinesirtgencollection.com), and Pi Artworks (ⓦpiartworks.com). You can see some of the best of the city's emerging and established artists while snooping around this grand building. Tues–Sat 11am–6.30pm.

Pera Museum Meşrutiyet Cad 141, Tepebaşı ☎0212 334 9900, ⓦperamuzesi.org.tr; map 120–121. The top three floors of a grand, wonderfully restored, nineteenth-century building display Ottoman painting and artefacts alongside big names from the contemporary art world. See p.123 for more information. Entry ₺15. Tues–Sat 10am–7pm, Sun noon–6pm.

Sakıp Sabancı Museum İstinye Cad 22, Emirgan ☎0212 277 2200, ⓦmuze.sabanciuniv.edu; map p.151. Housed in a 1920s villa known as the Atlı Köşk, and owned by one of Turkey's wealthiest families, the Sabancıs, this welcome addition to the Istanbul arts scene has held major exhibitions by the likes of Picasso, Dali, and Monet. See p.150 for more information. Entry ₺15. Tues–Sun 10am–6pm, Wed until 8pm.

SALT Beyoğlu İstiklal Cad 136 ☎0212 377 4200, ⓦsaltonline.org; map p.110. Owned by the Garantı Bank, this not-for-profit institution (which includes an exhibition space, a walk-in cinema and a research centre) displays works and organizes events with a strong sociopolitical commitment. Has a second branch in a renovated nineteenth-century Ottoman bank building in Karaköy (see p.112). Tues–Sat noon–8pm, Sun noon–6pm.

CINEMA

The Turkish **film industry** is booming, with internationally acclaimed directors such as **Nuri Bilge Ceylan**, **Fatih Akın** and **Ferzan Özpetek** leading the way (see pp.307–308). As a result, an increasing amount of screen time is being taken up by home-grown films – until quite recently, Hollywood releases, with Turkish subtitles, dominated Istanbul's cinemas. The problem for the non-Turkish-speaking visitor is that, unless you catch a movie at one of the film festivals (see p.33), it will be in Turkish with no subtitles. If you're thinking of taking your kids to a film while you're here (tempting, given the paucity of child-orientated sights in the city), bear in mind that this is also true of the imported films aimed at youngsters – they are dubbed into Turkish. Many of the modern multi-screen **cinemas** are situated in large shopping malls; a few old-style screens hang on in Beyoğlu, once the centre of domestic film production. Most cinemas still retain a fifteen-minute coffee-and-cigarette interval. Tickets cost from ₺8 to ₺20, depending on the cinema, though most offer midweek Halk Günü (People's Day) discount nights. The annual **International Film Festival** (mid-April to May) and the excellent ten-day **!f International Independent Film Festival** in February take place mainly at cinemas in Beyoğlu. Keep your eyes open for posters for the many other small film festivals that happen throughout the year.

Beyoğlu Sineması Halep Pasajı, off İstiklal Cad, Beyoğlu ☎0212 251 3240, ⓦbeyoglusinemasi.com.tr; map pp.120–121. A slightly downtrodden cinema inside historic Halep Pasajı, showing the usual Turkish and international suspects at reasonable prices most of the year, but it also features prominently during film festivals.

THE WRITING'S ON THE WALLS

Istanbul's street art scene is on the rise, and in plain view for anyone walking in the streets around İstiklal Caddesi and down into Karaköy. Keep your eyes peeled and you may catch a glimpse of the detailed animal stencils of No More Lies, the robotic designs of Turbo, or the fantastical cartoon-like scenes of Cins. The scene has been given a boost by both the Istanbul Street Art Festival (Sep, ⓦstreetartIstanbul.com) and Mural Istanbul Festival, which have witnessed entire sides of buildings in Maltepe (on the Asian side) transformed into stunning works of public art. You can download the Street Art Istanbul App (ⓦstreetart-Istanbul.com) and let your phone lead you to some great on-wall art, or take a guided tour with Istanbul Tour Studio (ⓦIstanbultourstudio.com).

ISTANBUL BIENNIAL

Organized by İKSV, the **Istanbul Biennial** is a major showcase of contemporary art. From relatively humble beginnings back in 1987, it has grown incrementally and now rivals Venice, São Paulo and Sydney. Held on odd-numbered years, the biennials usually run September through November, are themed and use different venues across the city, from historic buildings such as the Topkapı Palace to urban-chic industrial warehouses. In 2013, the focus was on public space as a political forum, but organizers chose to withdraw from its planned activities in spaces around the city due to the Gezi Park protests (see p.127).

The İKSV also organizes a Design Biennial, which started in the autumn of 2012 (and occurs in even years). It features a wide range of designs from across many fields, with a governing theme such as "Imperfection" or "The Future is Not What it Used to Be". For more information on both, check out ⓦiksv.org.

Cinemaximum Fitaş İstiklal Cad 24–26, Beyoğlu ☎0212 251 2020, ⓦcinemaximum.com.tr; map pp.120–121. A popular ten-screen cinema not far from Taksim Square, showing the newest films, with bowling downstairs and an open-air club on the roof. The smartest of the cinemas in Beyoğlu, but not the most atmospheric.

Atlas İstiklal Cad 209, Atlas Pasajı ☎0212 252 8576; map pp.120–121. A three-screen cinema set above the shops of this historic arcade, showing the usual programme of Hollywood and home-grown products – with the occasional, more arty film from time to time.

Feriye Çirağan Cad 124, Ortaköy ☎0212 236 2864, ⓦumutsanat.com.tr; map p.132. Three-screen cinema with a well-regarded café and seats either in the auditorium or (for a supplement) balcony. Handy if you're looking to kill some time before heading out to the bars and clubs in Ortaköy; most of its screenings are mainstream despite it being situated in a cultural complex.

Istanbul Modern Meclis-I Mebusan Cad, Liman İşletmeleri Sahası Antrepo 4, Karaköy ☎0212 334 7300, ⓦistanbulmodern.org; map p.110. The best place for art-house, alternative and documentary films in the city, located on the lower floor of the art gallery (see p.115). Programme changes monthly.

Levent Cinimaximum Kanyon Mall, Büyükdere Cad 185, Levent ☎0212 353 0853, ⓦcinemaximum.com.tr. Unsurprisingly, given its location in this ultramodern shopping mall, the ticket prices are above average, but they are worth it if you're looking for comfy seats and high sound quality.

Şafak Yeniçeriler Cad, Çemberlitaş ☎0212 516 2660, ⓦozenfilm.com.tr; map pp.78–79. The closest cinema to Sultanahmet, buried in the bowels of the Fırat Kültür Merkezi shopping mall, with seven screens showing the latest international and Turkish releases.

Yeşilçam İmam Adnan Sok 10 ☎0212 249 6800, ⓦyesilcamsinemasi.com; map pp.120–121. This retro, bohemian, single-screen basement cinema is the best place to see Turkish and foreign art-house movies, and is the cheapest in the area, too. The walls of the gloomy café/foyer are papered with old cinema posters, and there's an antique projector on display. Unfortunately, they don't run the film if only a few people turn up – which happens quite regularly.

Gay and lesbian Istanbul

Istanbul is the gay capital of Turkey, with the scene centred around Beyoğlu and Taksim, where most of the places reviewed in this section can be found. Although transvestite and transsexual singers and entertainers have been held in high esteem in Turkey since Ottoman times, and consensual acts between 18-year-olds and over are legal, homosexuality remains a societal taboo. Turkish law contains ambiguous legal prohibitions on "public exhibitionism", citing "offences against public morality" regarding homosexuality. Lambda, Turkey's foremost gay-liberation group was closed for a time by the courts for "moral impropriety". But every June, tens of thousands of people march down İstiklal Caddesi in a colourful and joyous celebration of LGBTI Pride Week, making it the largest gay march held in any predominantly Muslim country.

The country as a whole, even the cultural capital of Istanbul, remains very **conservative**. Affection between males is part and parcel of society – straight males linking arms in public or resting their hand on a friend's thigh while chatting are common sights – homosexual Turkish people usually feel obliged to keep their sexual orientation well under wraps. It's only in the moderately hedonistic atmosphere of the clubs of liberal Taksim that they feel free to express themselves – perhaps not surprisingly, as it's still technically possible to be arrested for cruising. Having said this, you'd be very unlucky to run into problems with the authorities, or experience anything akin to gay-bashing, even though the word "*ibne*" (passive partner in a homosexual relationship) is considered a very bad insult here.

WEBSITES AND MEDIA

Lambda maintain the premier gay website ⓦ lambdaistanbul.org but it's in Turkish only, so the best introduction to the Istanbul gay scene (in English) are websites such as ⓦ gaysofturkey.com, ⓦ istanbulgay.com and ⓦ istanbulgaybar.com. They give a rundown of the best gay bars, clubs and gay-friendly hotels; review the sauna cruising scene; and have a section on lesbian Istanbul. Another good site in English is the commercial site ⓦ hipsultan.com – gay tourism is their business but even if you're not interested in their services, they have some good tips. Alternatively, **TimeOut Istanbul** (see p.31) reviews gay and lesbian venues and has regular features on the city's gay scene. For accommodation, ⓦ turkey -gay-travel.com will help you find gay-friendly places to stay. Many gay bars and clubs have Facebook pages and Twitter feeds that are more up to date than their websites; it's well worth doing some social-media research in planning your night out.

BARS AND CLUBS

Bigudi Mis Sok 5, Terrace Floor, off İstiklal Cad, Beyoğlu ☎ 0535 509 0922; map pp.120–121. The only dedicated lesbian venue in town, situated on the roof terrace of an apartment building. Check their Facebook page (Bigudi-Club) for up-to-date event listings. Free. Fri & Sat 8pm–5am.

Chianti Café-Bar Balo Sok 31, off İstiklal Cad, Beyoğlu; map pp.120–121. This gay-exclusive bar offers a chance to enjoy some live traditional Turkish music (Wed–Sun). Functions as a café during the day and gets busy in the evenings. Daily 4pm–2am.

Fiyaka Yeni Çarşı Cad 38, Galatasaray; map pp.120–121. Located above *45'Lik Bar*, this small mixed bar hosts regular themed nights. Entrance price depends on what's

on, so check their Facebook page for the latest. Wed, Fri & Sat 10pm–4am.

Haspa Café & Bar Küçük Parmakkapı, İpek Sok 18/2, off İstiklal Cad, Beyoğlu ☎ 0212 243 8601 map pp.120–121. A local pre-club haunt favourite popular with a fun young crowd. With live music and entertainment some nights and reasonably priced drinks, this has become a favourite for many. Daily 6pm–3.30am.

Love Dance Point Cumhuriyet Cad 349, Harbiye ☎ 0212 296 3358, ⓦ lovedp.net; map p.128. Glitzy, high-tech and spacious club opposite the Military Museum. For over a decade, DJs here have spun a wide range of sounds, from techno to Turkish pop. Its motto is "Love's here, where are you?" Cover charge depends on who's

16

BÜLENT ERSOY: THE NATION'S FAVOURITE DIVA

The rounded, smiling and heavily made-up face of **Bülent Ersoy** is a common sight on Turkey's TV screens and in the country's gossip magazines. Born in 1952, Ersoy became a popular singer before undergoing a sex change in 1981 – though she kept her male first name. Seen by the authorities, if not many of the general public, as a social deviant in a hard-line state still reeling from the effects of the 1980 military coup, she was banned from performing in public. After a period of exile in Germany, Ersoy returned to Turkey following a change in the law that allowed her to become a "legal" female. She went on to become even more popular than before, her public apparently adoring her flamboyant behaviour and outrageous dress sense as well as her singing and acting abilities. Despite the scandal caused when she married a man some twenty years her junior, Ersoy went on to co-host one of the nation's most popular TV shows, **Popstar Alaturca**. In 2008, she was in trouble again, when she publicly declared that were she a mother she would not send her son to fight in Iraq, where the Turkish military were conducting operations against the Kurdish Workers Party (PKK) – daring words in a country where it's forbidden to call conscription into question.

GRINDR: AN APP TOO FAR

The battle for gay rights in Turkey flared up again in September 2013, when the popular gay dating app/website Grindr was banned by the Istanbul Anatolia 14th Criminal Court of Peace. The court upheld an anonymous complaint that Grindr "features prostitution and obscenity" and access to Grindr was blocked. Cited as a "protection measure", many saw the ban as another infringement on social freedoms, indicative of an increasingly conservative government. Local gay-rights and campaigning groups quickly teamed up with Grindr's creators to appeal the court decision, but the ban remained in force in late 2014, with no likelihood of Turkey's 125,000 Grindr users – the biggest number of any Middle Eastern country – getting back online in the near future.

DJing, but usually around ₺25, which includes one drink. Fri & Sat 11.30pm–5am.

Neo Halaskargazi Cad 113, Osmanbey ☎0212 231 4653, ⓦneoistanbul.co; map p.128. The people behind the ever-popular *Love Dance Point* opened *Neo* as a glamorous alternative, featuring drag shows, gogo boys and other entertainment. ₺25 (free before 1.30am). Fri–Sat midnight–5am.

Pinokyo Café & Bar Büyükparmakkapı Sok 26 off İstiklal Cad, Beyoğlu; map pp.120–121. Daily shows featuring gogo boys and girls, male belly dancers, and drag queens provide the draw here. Daily 5pm–4am.

Prive Tarlabası Bul 28, Taksim ☎0212 235 7999; map p.128. Gay-only dance club, with a devoted following due to its reputation as a pick-up place. The city's oldest gay club, it has more recently combined with a trans club called *No Name*. This street has a bad reputation in the city for muggings and petty theft, so take care if you decide to venture out here. Sun–Thurs free, Fri & Sat ₺25, including

a drink. Daily 11pm–4am.

Rocinante Café Bar Oğut Sok 6/2, Sakızağcı Sok Cad, Beyoğlu ☎0212 244 8219; map pp.120–121. Behind the prominent Ağa Camii (mosque) on İstiklal Cad is this popular lesbian-friendly café-cum-meeting point. Daily 2pm–2am.

Sugar and Spice Sakalsalim Çıkmazı 3/a, off İstiklal Cad, Beyoğlu ☎0212 245 0096, ⓦsugar-cafe.com; map pp.120–121. Low-key meeting and hangout joint off the busy main drag; somewhere to grab a coffee or a beer and decide what you're going to do later on, with food on offer from 1pm–10pm. Daily 11am–1am.

Tek Yön Siraselviler Cad 63/1 Beyoğlu ☎0212 233 0654, ⓦwww.clubtekyon.com; map pp.120–121. Probably the most popular, long-standing mainstream gay club. The friendly staff perform occasional drag shows, and there's a garden out back to escape the noise. Daily 11pm–4am.

16

SHOPPING IN BEYOĞLU

Shopping

Whether trawling through an Ottoman-era bazaar for carpets, sizing
up T-shirts in a retro-clothing shop, or mixing with the middle classes in
one of the city's myriad shopping malls, Istanbul has more than enough
opportunities to keep the most dedicated shopaholic busy – there's even
an annual forty-day shopping festival to entice buyers to the city with the
lure of discounted prices. The Grand Bazaar may be a tourist trap, but it's
nonetheless an unmissable experience. Known in Turkish as the Kapalı
Çarşı, this hive of over four thousand shops has, for centuries, been
performing the same function as modern shopping malls – putting a
host of different traders selling a welter of different goods under the
same roof.

17

More manageable – and the place to head for spices and sweets such as the ubiquitous *lokum* (Turkish delight) – is the **Mısır Çarşısı**, or Spice Bazaar, on the Golden Horn waterfront in Eminönü. You can also try the Arasta Bazaar for a slimmed-down Grand Bazaar experience. In addition, there are dozens of street markets across the city, selling everything from fruit and vegetables to cheap household utensils and fake designer clothing; best is the Çarşamba Pazarı, held in the conservative Fatih district every Wednesday.

İstiklal Caddesi in Beyoğlu is Istanbul's main shopping thoroughfare, and is traffic-free, save for an antique tram and service vehicles. Many major Turkish and international chains can be found along here, as well as the city's best bookshops. A number of arcades or **pasaj**, some dating to the nineteenth century, run off İstiklal Caddesi, selling a mix of alternative and bargain secondhand clothing, interesting jewellery, retro cinema posters and quirky household items. Scattered around the city are a number of other shopping districts. Upmarket **Nişantaşı** and **Teşvikiye** are the places to head for international and Turkish designer fashion and accessories, with Cartier, Armani, Gucci et al displaying their wares in appropriately expensive shops – particularly on Abdi İpekçi and in the City's Mall. For foodstuffs, bric-a-brac and bargain clothing, the pedestrian streets behind the ferry terminal in **Kadıköy**, on the Asian side of the city, form a compact and atmospheric place to shop.

Malls are mushrooming across the city, with almost ninety up and running in 2014 and more in the offing. Many are situated in awkward-to-reach suburbs but some, such as Kanyon and Zorlu Center, can be accessed quickly by the metro system. One advantage of mall shopping is that prices are all marked up so you don't have to bargain.

ESSENTIALS

Opening hours Most shops are open Monday to Saturday from 9am to 7pm, though malls typically open daily from 10am until 10pm. Supermarkets and hypermarkets open daily from 9am to 10pm but smaller food shops close much earlier. The Grand Bazaar is open Monday to Saturday from 9am to 7pm and is credit-card friendly, as are most shops bar the smallest of grocers (*bakkals*) or kiosks.

JEWELLERY

Dressing up and looking good is part and parcel of life for many Istanbulites, and is often taken to extremes by the well-heeled "ladies who lunch" in wealthy residential districts such as Nişantaşı and Bebek. **Jewellery** is big business in Turkey, with gold and silver items sold by the gram. Traditionally, gold bangles and the like were purchased as hedges against inflation (earning interest is forbidden in Islam) and given as part of the "bride price" in traditional marriages. The Grand Bazaar and nearby Nuruosmaniye Caddesi are two good places to look for traditional and antique jewellery, Beyoğlu, Nişantaşı and the malls for modern designs.

Ela Cindoruk & Nazan Pak Atiye Sok 14/5, Teşvikiye ☎ 0212 232 2664, ⓦ elacindoruknazanpak.com; map p.128. A small and exclusive gallery-cum-shop run by a talented duo, one of whom studied jewellery design at Parsons School of Design in New York, the other under a master atelier in the Grand Bazaar. As well as their own designs, they also stock items by internationally renowned designers. Mon 2–7pm, Tues–Sat 10.30am–7pm.

Özlem Tuna Nemlizade Han 23 (Floor 5), Ankara Cad 65, Sirkeci ☎ 0212 527 9285, ⓦ ozlemtuna.com; map p.70. A showroom that features the work of Tuna: a world-renowned contemporary jewellery designer who makes chunky statement pieces at prices that won't (completely) break the bank. Mon–Fri 9am–6pm.

Urart Abdi İpekçi Cad 18/1, Nişantaşı ☎ 0212 246 7194, ⓦ urart.com.tr; map p.128. This place has been going for well over thirty years, selling very upmarket jewellery, based on ancient Anatolian and Central Asian designs. They charge big bucks for their finely wrought stuff but at least pump some of it back into the arts in Turkey through sponsorship of events such as the Golden Orange Film Festival. Mon–Sat 9am–7pm.

ANTIQUES AND BRIC-A-BRAC

If you're expecting to find a real bargain, you'll probably be disappointed – a city of over fifteen million ensures a buoyant price for the **antiques** available. Bear in mind that you're supposed to have clearance from the Museums Directorate to take anything out of the country that's over one hundred years old: in theory, the seller should already

CARPETS AND KILIMS

Turkish **carpets** and **kilims** are world-famous, and with the best selection to be found in Istanbul, it's not surprising that buying one is high on many visitors' lists. Be warned, though, that they are no longer necessarily cheaper in Turkey than overseas. It's also worth knowing that if you are introduced to a carpet dealer by a tout (and there are plenty of those hanging around Sultanahmet and the Grand Bazaar) or tour operator, a hefty commission will be added. It's very easy to be drawn into buying something you don't really want at a price you can barely afford once you've been smooth-talked and given copious quantities of apple tea. That said, it's still possible to get a good purchase here, and enjoy the process, providing you heed the following tips:

- Do some research, preferably before you leave home (check out some of the books reviewed in the "Crafts" section of "Contexts").
- Avoid buying in the first shop you visit, and look around several. You can always go back – preferably the next day, when you've had time to think about it.
- Don't be embarrassed at how many carpets the dealer is laying out for you – that's his (or usually his lowly assistant's) job.
- Ask as many questions about the pieces that interest you as you can – this will test the dealer's worth, and could give you some interesting historical background should you make a purchase.
- Check the pieces for flaws, marks, density of weave, etc – this way, the dealer will know you're serious.
- Even in the most reputable shop, bargaining is essential. Whatever you do, don't engage in the process if you've no intention of buying.
- You'll probably get a better deal for cash.
- Most important of all, only buy the piece if you really like it and are sure it'll look the part back home – any other considerations such as future appreciation are mere distractions.

CARPET OR KILIM?

A **kilim** is a pile-less, flat-woven wool rug. The better-quality ones are double-sided (that is, the pattern should look much the same top or bottom). A *cicim* is a kilim with additional, raised designs stitched onto it; while the *sumak* technique, confined in Turkey to saddlebags, involves wrapping extra threads around the warp. By and large, kilims, traditionally woven by nomadic Anatolian tribal groupings, are generally cheaper and more affordable than carpets. Turkish **carpets** are single-sided, with a pile, and can be wool, silk or a mixture of both; the higher the silk content, the more expensive the rug.

DEALERS

The following are all based in the Grand Bazaar (Mon–Sat 9am–7pm).

Adnan & Hasan Halıcılar Cad 89–92 ☎ 0212 527 9887, ⓦ adnanandhasan.com; map p.80. A wide range of modern and antique kilims and carpets from a reputable dealership, established in 1978, with Ushak and Hereke carpets vying for shop space with Anatolian and Caucasian kilims.

Dhoku Takkeciler Sok 58–60 ☎ 0212 527 6841, ⓦ dhoku.com; map p.80. Fixed prices for kilims made in the traditional way (with natural dyes and no child labour) but with contemporary (often large, geometric blocks of colour) styling.

Şişko Osman Zincirli Han ☎ 0212 528 3548, ⓦ siskoosman.com; map p.80. Arguably the most knowledgeable dealer in the Grand Bazaar, the reputable Şişko ("Fat") Osman has family origins in the east of Turkey, but he has been flogging top-quality rugs here for many years. Over sixty percent of his clients are Turks, which gives some idea of the quality of the

(mainly) dowry pieces on offer here. His kilims range from €400 to €2500 and carpets €500 to €2500 – excluding the more expensive period pieces, some dating back to the eighteenth century, stocked in one of his four adjacent shops.

Tradition Rubiye Han 11/12, Kürkçüler Sok ☎ 0212 520 7907, ⓦ tradition-carpet.com; map p.80. Opened in 1988 and co-run by Frenchwoman Florence Heilbron, this fine establishment has a very good reputation, lots of repeat customers (including a whole coterie of French diplomats and politicians) and sells pieces from €50 to €10,000.

Yörük Kürkçüler Cad 17 ☎ 0212 527 3211; map p.80. Run by Ersoy, whose family came to the city from the Caucasus in 1864 via the Central Anatolian town of Kayseri. The stock runs from chemical-dyed pieces for as little as €80 to vintage dowry pieces up to €5000. Very reliable.

17

have an authorization certificate for the goods from the directorate; if not, don't buy. Nobody is going to worry about a nineteenth-century biscuit tin, but a seventeenth-century Ottoman sword is a different matter. The best place for twentieth-century items (up to 1980s stuff) is the streets leading down from İstiklal Caddesi in Çukurcuma, or the Horhor Flea Market (see below).

A La Turca Faik Paşa Yokuşu 4 ☎0212 245 2933, ⓦalaturcahouse.com; map pp.120–121. Located in charming Çukurcuma, this chic antique store run by the welcoming Erkal Aksoy attracts international attention for its unique atmosphere and stunning collection. Mon–Sat 10.30am–8pm.

Abdullah Şalabi Sandal Bedestan 6, Grand Bazaar ☎0212 522 8171; map p.80. Established in 1880 and run by the fluent-English-speaking Pol Şalabi, this small shop stocks a treasure-trove of icons, jewellery from 1800 to the 1950s and much else besides. Mon–Sat 9am–7pm.

Horhor Antique Market Yorum Kırık Tulumba Sok 13/22, Aksaray ☎0212 525 9977; map pp.78–79. Over two hundred bric-a-brac and antique shops in a multi-storey building in the drab suburb of Aksaray, a fifteen-minute walk from the Aksaray Metro station; there are

bargains to be found. Daily 10am–8pm.

Kadıköy Antiques Street Antika Çarşısı, Tellalzade Sok, Çakıroğlu İş Han, Kadıköy; map p.40. Tellalzade Sok has a number of small shops selling all kinds of retro and bric-a-brac items, plus some genuine antiques and an excursion here fits in well with food or souvenir shopping and the wonderful *Çiya Sofrası* restaurant (see p.191).

Sofa Art and Antiques Nuruosmaniye Cad 53a, Nuruosmaniye and Serdar-ı Ekrem Sok 47, Galata ☎0212 292 3977, ⓦkashifsofa.com; map p.110. With one store located just outside the Grand Bazaar, and one in trendy Galata, husband-and-wife team Kaşif and Dilek have all the bases covered – and are some of the most friendly and knowledgeable old hands in the business. Their shops are treasure-troves of Ottoman and European finds. Mon–Sat 9am–7pm.

BOOKS

There are some good stockists of English-language **books** around the city, and it's also rewarding to browse through the secondhand-book markets and shops. The best known is the Sahaflar Çarşısı (Old Book Market) at Beyazit, though it also sells new titles. Numerous secondhand bookshops cluster in Beyoğlu, especially in the backstreets off the east side of İstiklal Caddesi and down towards the Çukurcuma antique district. The annual **Istanbul Book Fair** (ⓦistanbulbookfair.com), held in late October or early November, is held in the Istanbul Sergi Sarayı on Meşrutiyet Caddesi, near the *Pera Palas Hotel*.

Denizler Kitabevi İstiklal Cad 395, Beyoğlu ☎0212 249 8893; map pp.120–121. Specialists in nautical books and charts, plus an extensive range of collectors' books on Turkey and the Ottomans. Mon–Sat 9.30am–7.30pm.

Eren Sofyala Sok 34, Tünel, Beyoğlu ☎0212 251 2858, ⓦeren.com.tr; map pp.120–121. Art and history books, old maps and miniatures, with a website in English for ordering specialist books. Mon–Sat 10am–6.30pm.

Galeri Kayseri Divan Yolu 58, Sultanahmet

☎0212 512 0456, ⓦgalerikayseri.com; map p.46. The biggest distributor of English-language books in Turkey, with a vast range of texts on Ottoman history and all other imaginable Turkish – and particularly Istanbul-related – topics. Daily 9am–8.30pm.

Greenhouse Bookshop Café Moda Cad 28, Kadıköy ☎0216 550 4961. Managed by an Englishwoman, it stocks an excellent range of books in English, with an extensive children's department. Mon & Wed–Sat 10am–6.30pm.

SUPERMARKETS AND CORNER SHOPS

If the thought of shopping for food at a street market sounds like too much hassle, Istanbul has plenty of **supermarkets**. Although their fruit and vegetables are generally inferior in quality and much more expensive, it's easier to buy smaller quantities in them, and there's invariably a deli-type counter with a great array of different local cheeses, olives, pickles, salami-style meats and, sometimes, ready-prepared *meze*. The upmarket Macrocenter supermarkets at Abdi İpekçi Cad 24 in Nişantaşı, Kanyon Shopping Mall and on Muallimnacı Caddesi down by the Bosphorus in Kuruçeşme are good bets; alternatively, all the malls listed have a supermarket (see pp.222–223) – look out for the names Migros, Real, Tansaş and Corona. There are also smaller outlets, known as *market* or *bakkal*, all over the city, which are basically **corner shops** selling a limited range of fruit and vegetables, soft drinks (and sometimes alcoholic beverages – if you're looking for a shop selling booze, ask for a *tekel*), cheese, olives, packaged food, bread and the like. They're pricier than the supermarkets but often much more convenient.

Homer Yeni Çarşı Cad 28, Beyoğlu ☎0212 249 5902, ⓦhomerbooks.com; map pp.120–121. Arguably the best bookshop in the city, with a wonderful selection of everything archeological, historical and cultural written on Turkey. There's a good selection of English children's books, and the staff are very helpful. Mon–Sat 10am–7.30pm.

Sahaflar Çarşısı Sahaflar Sok, Beyazıt; map pp.78–79. Between the Grand Bazaar and the Beyazıt Camii, this historic collection of small bookshops (dating back to the early Ottoman period) now concentrates on textbooks for students from the nearby university, but also has a reasonable selection of guides and other books about the city. Mon–Sat 9am–7pm.

FOOD AND SPICES

Turkey is a major producer and consumer of **herbs** and **spices**, and Istanbul is a great place to stock up on them, most obviously in the atmospheric **Mısır Çarşısı** (Spice Bazaar). Look out in particular for red *pul biber* (chilli flakes), *isot* (extra-hot chilli flakes, virtually black in colour), *sumac* (ground berries with a citric flavour that are good on salads), *kekik* (thyme), *nane* (mint) and *kimyon* (cumin). They're more than just a novelty, but the strings of dried peppers, aubergines and okra that Turks use over the winter, when the fresh product is not available, do work well as colourful kitchen decorations. *Nar ekşisi*, the viscous pomegranate **syrup** used so liberally in many Turkish salads, is cheaper and will be much better here than in your home country. A more unusual product is *pekmez*, a natural fruit molasses usually made from either grapes or mulberries – it makes a sweet but healthy topping for yoghurt. Turkish **coffee** (*Türk kahvesi*) is as traditional a Turkish product as you can get, though you'll need a *cezve* pan to make it properly back home. Dried **fruits** are both great value and delicious – especially *kayısı* (apricots), *dut* (mulberries) and *incir* (figs) – as are pistachios (usually known as *Antep fıstığı*, after the town in southeast Turkey where they're grown), *fındık* (hazelnuts), which come from the Black Sea region, *ceviz* (walnuts) and *badem* (almonds). Then of course, in all its gelatinous splendour, there is *lokum*; known in the west as **Turkish delight**, there are in fact many varieties of this traditional favourite.

Ali Muhidin Hacı Bekir Hamidiye Cad 83, Eminönü ☎0212 522 0666, ⓦhacibekir.com.tr; map p.70. Founded in 1777, this is a reliable place to buy top-quality Turkish delight (choose from over twenty varieties) and more unusual delicacies such as *fındıklı ezmesi* (hazelnut marzipan). The interior is a delight, with an eye-catching array of sugary treats displayed on vintage wooden shelves and in glass-fronted cabinets. It's tricky to find, hidden in the bustling narrow streets near the Spice Bazaar, but well worth the effort. Or try the Kadıköy branch, opposite *Baylan* (see p.184) on Muvakkithane Cad. Mon–Sat 8am–9pm, Sun 9am–9pm.

Brezilya Güneşlibahçe Sok 42, Kadıköy ☎0216 337 6317; map p.40. This place has been roasting and grinding coffee since 1920, but also stocks a good line of mulberry, grape, apricot and plum *pestil* (sheets of solidified molasses) and *cevizli sucuk* (a walnut-filled sausage of chewy molasses). Daily 9am–8pm.

Karaköy Güllüoğlu Mumhane Cad 171, Karaköy ☎0212 293 0910, ⓦkaraköygulluoglu.com; map p.110. Arguably the finest, and certainly the best-known, *baklava* in the city: delicious, buttery and nut-filled. If you're looking to take some home, this is a great place to buy it, though you pay for the quality. Daily 10am–midnight.

Kurukahveci Mehmet Efendi Tamis Sok 66, Eminönü ☎0212 511 4262, ⓦmehmetefendi.com; map p.70. There are always big queues outside this wonderful paean to the aromatic coffee bean, housed in an impressive Art Deco building to the west of the Spice Bazaar. Sells beans and grounds for Turkish and filter coffees, plus *sahlep*, the ground-orchid-root drink so popular in Istanbul in the winter. There's another branch across in Kadıköy, a few minutes' walk back from the ferry terminal. Mon–Sat 9am–7pm.

Mısır Çarşısı Eminönü ⓦmisircarsisi.org; map p.70. To choose between the myriad purveyors of different spices, herbs, herbal teas, Turkish delight, nuts and dried fruit inside the historic Mısır Çarşısı (Spice Bazaar) would be meaningless. A number of stalls back onto the outside of the walls, selling fresh cheese, olives, dried fruits and nuts: here (and in the surrounding streets) prices are actually cheaper than in the Mısır Çarşısı itself. Daily 9am–7pm.

Şekerci Cafer Erol Yasa Cad 19, Kadıköy ☎0216 337 1103, ⓦsekercicafererol; map p.40. A family confectionery business that began back in 1807; the Kadıköy branch, opened in 1945, is a work of art. Antique shop fittings, jars full of traditional *akide* (boiled sweets), Turkish delight, *baklava* and, a real visual treat, exquisite *badem ezmesi* (marzipan) fruits. It's not cheap, but it is top quality. Daily 9am–9pm.

Tatlıcı Safa Hasırcılar Cad 10, Eminönü ☎0212 527 2277, ⓦtatlicisafa.com; map p.70. A small outlet in a fascinating street just west of the Spice Bazaar, offering a quality range of *baklava* and other nut-filled filo-pastry desserts for considerably less than more famous rivals. Well worth seeking out. Daily 9am–7pm.

HIGH-STREET, DESIGNER AND ALTERNATIVE FASHION

You'll find all the usual **high-street fashion shops** in Istanbul, as well as more upmarket names such as Armani and Versace. **Turkish shops** (with multiple branches) to watch out for include: Beymen, Damat Tween, Homestore, Mavi,

17

Mudo, Silk and Cashmere, and Yargıcı. Vakko is one of the oldest and best-known fashion chains in Istanbul; Vakkorama is its youth-market offshoot. For **shoes**, look for Desa, Hotiç and Vetrina. **Designer clothing** outlets are mainly located in the shopping malls (see pp.222–223) or in the streets around the districts of Nişantaşı and Teşvikiye (take the metro to Osmanbey and walk down Rumeli Caddesi). Many of the shops listed below also have branches in the shopping malls. **Turkish fashion** is beginning to compete on the catwalks, thanks to names such as to Rıfat Özbek and Hussein Chalayan. Other names to watch out for in Turkish haute couture are Gönül Paksoy, Dıce Kayek, Ferruh Karakadli, and Bora Aksu, all of whom are working with the best Turkish fabrics: leather so fine that it is now processed for the Italian market, Bursa silk, and the universally famous Angora wool.

Aponia Store Galipdede Cad 101/a ⓦaponiastore .com; map p.110. A quirky design store-cum-coffee shop where you can find original T-shirts, bags, hoodies and posters that make affordable souvenirs. Daily 10am–10pm.

Beyman Zorlu Center, Zincirlikuyu ☎0212 306 3300, ⓦbeymen.com; map p.151. Quality chain shop for tailored men's and women's suits, dress shirts, silk ties and scarves, and other accessories. Daily 10am–10pm.

Crash Galipdede Cad 35, Galata ☎0212 252 7743; map p.110. A small, alternative outlet in up-and-coming Galata, with a good range of individually designed T-shirts, hoodies and shorts – plus some secondhand retro stuff as well. Mon–Sat 10am–9pm.

Gönül Paksoy Atiye Sok 6a, Teşvikiye ☎0212 216 9081; map p.128. A one-of-a-kind designer, Gönül's clothing and accessories are mostly based on traditional Ottoman designs and motifs, using naturally woven and hand-dyed material. Mon–Sat 10am–7pm.

İpekyol Bronz Sok 65/7, off Abdi İpekçi Cad, Nişantaşı ☎0212 225 98 51, ⓦipekyol.com.tr; map p.128. This classy chain of stores, found all over Istanbul, is a good option if you're searching for some quality evening wear that won't bankrupt you. Mon–Sat 10am–7pm, Sun noon–6pm.

Mavi İstiklal Cad 195, Beyoğlu ☎0212 244 6255, ⓦeu .mavi.com; map pp.120–121. Gap-inspired jeans label,

selling good-quality denim wear, T-shirts, sweatshirts and funky bags – plus some trendy Istanbul T-shirts that make a welcome alternative to the usual tourist tat. Mon–Sat 10am–10pm, Sun 11am–10pm.

Roll Turnacıbaşı Sok 13/1, off İstiklal Cad, Beyoğlu ☎0212 244 9656; map pp.120–121. A good option for indie types, where owner Hüseyin puts a defiantly Turkish twist on our obsession with the recent past, producing a range of tongue-in-cheek T-shirts emblazoned with "legendary" Turkish cars such as the Murat 124 and the Anadol, as well as favourite comic-book and film characters. Mon–Sat 10am–10pm, Sun noon–9.30pm.

Silk & Cashmere Akmerkez Mall, Nisbetiye Cad, Etiler ☎0212 282 0235; map p.128. Quality scarves, hats, gloves, sweaters and shirts, using imported fabrics from China. Daily 10am–10pm.

Vakko Zorlu Center, Zincirlikuyu ☎0212 708 3333, ⓦvakko.com.tr; map p.151. Classy 50-year-old Turkish fashion label renowned for its sense of style and use of fine fabrics. The clothes don't come cheap though, and you have to dress up a bit if you want to feel comfortable. Daily 10am–10pm.

Yargıcı Vali Konağı Cad 30, Nişantaşı ☎0212 225 2912, ⓦyargici.com.tr; map p.128. Well-made and reasonably priced quality clothing in mostly pastel shades, from work suits and floral dresses to sportswear and underwear. Mon–Sat 9.30am–7.30pm, Sun 1–6pm.

BUDGET AND SECONDHAND FASHION

Many Western high-street stores produce their clothes in Turkey, and a number of stalls and markets across the city specialize in seconds, production overruns and samples at bargain prices (₺10 and up for T-shirts and tops, ₺25–50 for jeans and trousers). Fakes abound, however, and manufacturers often insist labels are cut out, so it's not always easy to find a genuine bargain. The most convenient places to look for these items are the various arcades (some of them of historic interest; see box, p.124) off İstiklal Caddesi.

Atlas Pasajı Off İstiklal Cad 209, Beyoğlu; map pp.120–121. This historic arcade behind the Atlas Cinema, with its barrel-vaulted roof and Neoclassical columns, is youth-orientated, with alternative/street-style clothes outlets, cheap-and-cheerful jewellery shops, piercing places and CD/DVD shops, plus an amazing selection of original film posters in a couple of the basement shops. Daily 9.30am–11pm.

Beyoğlu İş Merkezi İstiklal Cad 187, Beyoğlu; map pp.120–121. Three floors of end-of-line and seconds clothing, especially T-shirts, sweatshirts and jeans, with the occasional genuine bargain for the persistent. Daily 10am–10pm.

By Retro Suriye Pasajı, İstiklal Cad, Beyoğlu ☎0212 245 6420, ⓦbyretro.com; map pp.120–121. In the basement of this historic arcade is Europe's largest

secondhand-clothing shop (so it claims). Owner Hakan Vardar scours Europe for vintage clothes and there are rails and rails of it here. Daily 10am–10.30pm.

Terkoz Çıkmaz İş Merkezi Beyoğlu; map pp.120–121. A side street off İstiklal Cad, down towards Tünel, crammed with stalls of badly organized overruns bearing Western high-street names such as Next, River Island and Gap. Go right to the end and down the stairs for a more organized bargain-bin action. Daily 10am–10pm.

MARKETS

If you want to see the real commerce of Istanbul, as it used to be, step out of the malls, leave the over-touristy bazaars and head to the backstreets to find one of the weekly markets. You're unlikely to come across any other tourists here, just savvy expats and throngs of locals – mostly women who wouldn't dream of going anywhere else to stock up their larders. Although they mostly deal in seasonal fruits and vegetables, olives, pickles, cheeses and similar mouthwatering produce, many also have kitchenware and clothing sections too. Prices are usually displayed and it's almost unheard of to be overcharged here; you're more likely to leave thinking you should have paid more.

Beşiktaş Pazarı Beşiktaş; map p.132. Despite being held in a car park, this is one of the more upmarket markets, reflecting the relative wealth of nearby Akaretler. Good for buying delicious *meze* and ready-to-eat food as well as cooking ingredients. Sat 6am–6pm.

Çarşamba Pazarı Fatih. Occupying the narrow streets close to Fatih Camii, this is the most atmospheric of the city's markets, but better for fruit, vegetables and the like than bargain clothing. There are a few homespun souvenirs like handmade wooden spoons, rolling pins and breadboards. Wed 6am–8pm.

Tarlabaşı Pazarı map pp.120–121. One of the most colourful and lively of all the markets, with the local immigrant population – Iraqi, African, Roma and Kurdish – giving it a more diverse feel. Sun 10am–6pm.

Salı Pazarı Kadıköy; map p.40. A short taxi ride from the ferry port lies this huge market, as good for bargain clothing as it is for fresh produce. Tues 8am–6pm.

HANDICRAFTS AND GIFTS

You don't have to splash big money on a carpet or kilim to have something tangible and authentic to remember your visit by. Traditional **ceramics** from the western Anatolian town of Kütahya, including tiles, vases and plates, can be good purchases, as can embroidered tablecloths, cushion covers and towels. Meerschaum pipes, often carved into the shape of Ottoman dignitaries, make an unusual souvenir, as do *peştemals*, the cotton-wraps worn in the city's steamy *hamams*. **Copperware**, still spun (and traditionally tin-plated) in bazaars in far-away Turkish towns such as Gaziantep, is good value, as are the mother-of-pearl-inlaid backgammon sets and other **wood** items from the same town. In their own way just as authentic as the traditional Ottoman crafts are the modern twists on old designs sold in upmarket household goods shops such as Paşabahçe – especially **glassware**.

Armaggan Nuruosmaniye Cad 65 ☎0212 522 4433, ⓦarmaggan.com; map pp.78–79. A slightly ostentatious store spread over four floors that specializes in luxury goods but with an emphasis on natural materials and traditional manufacturing methods. Combine shopping with a trip to the excellent *NAR* restaurant on the fifth floor (see p.187). Mon–Sat 8.30am–10pm.

Ambar Kallavi Sok 12, off İstiklal Cad, Beyoğlu ☎0212 292 9277; map pp.120–121. This small, family-run shop sells a great range of organic and natural products from food to soap. Mon–Sat 9am–7.30pm, Sun 12.30–7.30pm.

Caferağa Medresesi Caferiye Sok, Soğukkuyu Çıkmazı 1 ☎0212 513 3601, ⓦcaferagamedresi.com; map p.46. Built by the great Ottoman architect Sinan in the sixteenth century, this beautiful courtyard *medrese* is now an artists' workshop-cum-traditional handicrafts shopping centre. It's a charitable foundation and a rare low-key shopping opportunity in Sultanahmet, with traditional wares for sale, plus workshops where visitors can join in and learn about painting miniatures, marbling, calligraphy and other Turkish arts. Mon–Sat 8.30am–7pm.

Chez Galip At Meydan 78, Sultanahmet ☎0212 638 5180, ⓦchezgalip.com; map p.46. The pottery on sale at this prominent boutique overlooking the Hippodrome is made by hand in the Central Anatolian town of Avanos. Some of the pottery is based on traditional Ottoman wares, but more interesting is the range derived from Hittite and other ancient Anatolian peoples. It's not cheap, but the quality is excellent. Daily 9am–8pm.

Cocoon Küçük Ayasofya Cad 15 ☎0212 638 6271, ⓦcocoonchic.com; map p.46. Four floors showcasing gorgeously hued and patterned felt hats, bags, animals and even jewellery, plus a wide range of traditional Central Asian textiles, carpets and kilims. It's all very tastefully done and the prices not too unreasonable. There's a smaller shop in the Arasta Bazaar (same hours). Daily 9am–7pm.

Hammam Kule Çıkmazı 1/c, opposite the Galata Tower ☎0212 245 7075, ⓦhammam.com.tr; map p.110.

Charmingly presented handmade soaps, essential oils, loofahs and lotions line the shelves here, providing everything necessary for an indulgent *hamam* experience. The ornate soap bowls and traditional Turkish towels would make great gifts, as would the beautiful hand-painted wooden soap-boxes. Daily 11am–7pm.

Hiç Contemporary Crafts Lüleci Hendek Sok 35, Karaköy ☎ 0212 251 9973, ⊕ hiccrafts.com; map p.110. A small shop on an up-and-coming street that sells tasteful furniture and accessories by local designers with a contemporary ethnic feel, along with gorgeous Central Asian *ikat* and *suzani* fabrics. Mon–Sat 11am–7pm.

Istanbul Handicrafts Center Kabasakal Cad 5, Sultanahmet ☎ 0212 517 6748, ⊕ istanbulhandicraftcenter.com; map p.46. Similar to but less laidback than the Caferağa Medresesi (see p.220), this is another former *medrese* where today artists and craftsmen keep alive traditional skills such as *ebru* marbling, calligraphy, lace-making and embroidery. Daily 9am–8pm.

İKSV Design Store Sadi Konuralp Cad 5, Şişhane 0212 334 0830, ⊕ iksvtasarim; map p.110. If contemporary design is more your thing, this showroom of the Istanbul Culture and Arts Foundation, is a great destination for picking up some truly unique homeware and accessories that blend the old and the new. Mon–Sat 11am–9pm, Sun noon–6pm.

İznik Classics Arasta Çarşısı 119, Sultanahmet ☎ 0212 517 1705, ⊕ iznikclassics.com; map p.46. Some of the best examples of İznik tiles you'll see anywhere, beautifully displayed in this small shop in the Arasta Bazaar (there are other outlets in the Grand Bazaar and on nearby Utangaç Sok). The tiles are handmade by different artists, and all reflect the high quality of the finest period of İznik pottery; they are consequently expensive, with prices from ₺120 and up. Daily: summer 9am–9pm; winter 9am–7pm.

Paşabahçe İstiklal Cad 314, Beyoğlu ☎ 0212 244 0544, ⊕ pasabahce.com.tr; map pp.120–121. Sells a range of well-designed items that add the finishing touches to the homes of many middle- and upper-class Istanbulites – from cruet sets to juicers, dinner services to clocks. Some of its glass products, made from the Beykoz factory up the Bosphorus, are worth looking out for. Mon–Sat 10am–8pm, Sun 11am–7pm.

Yörük Collection Yerebatan Cad 35, Sultanahmet ☎ 0212 511 7766, ⊕ yorukcollection.com; map p.46. Run by the same team responsible for the charmingly eccentric *Kybele Hotel* (see p.46), this well-laid-out shop sells everything from beautiful silver and turquoise jewellery and contemporary-style kilims to cushion covers to framed Ottoman miniatures. Throw in hand-dyed silk scarves and Üzbek embroidery and the eclectic nature of this fine shop becomes apparent. Daily 9am–8pm.

TEXTILES AND FABRICS

Turkey is famous for its textiles and fabrics – as well as producing reams of mass-produced cotton for Western and Turkish clothing manufacturers, it also has a small number of small-scale businesses and individuals who produce *peştemal*s (*hamam* wraps), towels, tablecloths, runners and rolls of fabric.

Abdulla Halıcılar Cad 53, Grand Bazaar ☎ 0212 527 3684; map p.80. Restrained design is the key to this chic shop selling bath wraps (*peştemal*), bed linen, fluffy towels and the like – it tweaks traditional products to fit the tastes of the city's new elite and Western visitors alike. Also does a tasteful range of mohair rugs and handmade olive-oil-based soaps. Beautiful displays, helpful staff and fixed prices make it an oasis of peaceful browsing in the sometimes overwhelming Grand Bazaar. Mon–Sat 9am–7pm.

Derviş Keseciler Cad 51, Grand Bazaar ☎ 0212 528 7883, ⊕ dervis.com; map p.80. Another Grand Bazaar outlet stocking a lovely range of traditional handicrafts, including *peştemal*s and towels. It also does a nice line in vintage kaftans imported from the Turkic republics of Central Asia, along with silk scarves. Mon–Sat 9am–7pm.

Jennifer's Hamam Arasta Bazaar, Sultanahmet ☎ 0212 518 0648, ⊕ jennifershamam.com; map p.46. All the textiles here are made from organic cotton, linen or silk and woven by hand on traditional looms. Prices are a little above average because of this, but the product is top-notch, with a fabulous range of *peştemal*s, fluffy towels and scarves on offer. The owner is a knowledgeable Canadian. Daily 9am–8pm.

Sivaslı Istanbul Yazmacı (Necdat Danış) Yağlıkçılar Sok, Grand Bazaar ☎ 0212 526 7748; map p.80. This place has been selling hand-woven textiles for over forty years, and has an excellent reputation for its keen prices and wide range of scarves, *peştemal*s, tablecloths and reams of gorgeous fabrics. They supplied the textiles used in the Hollywood film *Troy*. Mon–Sat 9am–7pm.

LEATHER

Leather is big business in Turkey; if you are after a belt, bag or jacket, it's worth hunting around. Prices aren't as low as they once were, except for the poor-quality items, and unless you know your stuff it's easy to get ripped off. Overall, it's probably better to buy from one of the outlets listed below.

17

Derimod Akmerkez Mall, Nisbetiye Cad, Etiler ☎ 0212 282 0668; map p.151. Excellent top-quality leather goods including coats, jackets, bags and shoes. Classic rather than cutting-edge, but then most people don't want to make a short-lived fashion mistake at these prices. Daily 10am–10pm.

Derishow Valikonağı Cad 20/1, Nişantaşı ☎ 0212 248 4639, ⓦ derishow.com.tr; map p.128. This branch of a small chain, is located in the wealthiest shopping district, and offers one-of-a-kind modern designs. Daily 10am–7pm.

Koç Deri Kürküçüler Cad 22/46, Grand Bazaar ☎ 0212 527 5533, ⓦ kocderi.com; map p.80. Established in 1960, this specialist leather shop in the Grand Bazaar runs up stuff for the likes of Armani and Dolce & Gabbana. Needless to say it's not cheap, but it does have a good reputation. Mon–Sat 9am–7pm.

Nazlı Bozdağ Building, Hacı Emin Efendi Sok 23/a, Tesvikiye ☎ 0212 293 8259, ⓦ nazlibozdag.net; map p.128. The works of one of Istanbul's most cutting-edge young designers, working exclusively with leather to create contemporary statement pieces are available at Building, a trendy boutique. Mon–Sat 10am–7.30pm.

MUSIC AND MUSICAL INSTRUMENTS

Turkish **music** aside, you'll find a good general selection of world music, classical, pop and jazz in the music shops listed below and in the many outlets on İstiklal Caddesi and in the shopping malls. International CDs are often pricier than elsewhere in Europe, as there's no real discounting, but Turkish CDs are considerably cheaper. For **musical instruments**, traditional and otherwise, there's a myriad of instrument shops on and around Galipdede Caddesi (aka Music Alley), near the upper Tünel station in Beyoğlu. Drummers take note: many specialize in, or at least stock, top-quality home-produced cymbals (see box, p.113).

D & R Kanyon Mall ☎ 0212 353 0870, ⓦ dr.com.tr; map p.151. Chain that stocks a decent range of traditional and contemporary Turkish sounds, as well as foreign CDs, DVDs, computer accessories, books, magazines and games. There are other branches across the city.

Dore Müzik Şahdeğirmeni Sok 3/b, just off Galipdede Cad, Tünel ☎ 0212 236 5713, ⓦ doremuzik.com.tr; map p.110. One of several shops selling the famed Turkish Zildjian cymbals (sadly now made in, and imported from, the USA), alongside various major drum brands and some traditional Turkish percussion items. Daily 10am–7pm.

Kontra Plak Yeni Çarşı Cad 60/a, Galatasary ☎ 0212 243 8680, ⓦ kontrarecords.com; map pp.120–121. One of a new breed of hip record shops in Beyoğlu, this basement store has a cool feel and stocks an impressive range of records and CDs of all genres from Turkey and beyond. Daily 9am–10pm.

Lale Plak Galipdede Cad 1, Tünel, Beyoğlu ☎ 0212 293 7739; map p.110. A funky, old-style music shop, the best place for traditional Turkish music CDs but even more so for jazz. The staff know their stuff – as you'd expect at a business that's been going for nigh-on fifty years. Daily 9am–7pm.

Mephisto İstiklal Cad 197, Beyoğlu ☎ 0212 249 0687, ⓦ mephisto.com.tr; map pp.120–121. A modern book and music store on the main shopping street, with a good stock of Turkish CDs, a laidback vibe and a nice café to take a break in. Daily 9am–midnight.

Müzik Center Galipdede Cad 19, Tünel, Beyoğlu ☎ 0212 244 5885, ⓦ istanbulmusic.net; map p.110. This shop is one of many on a street jammed with musical instrument shops, but stands out thanks to its wide range of Turkish folklore instruments. There's a mixture of cheaper beginner instruments and top-quality handmade items, all made in Turkey, plus some antique pieces on sale too. Music enthusiasts can purchase a *darbuka* (a goblet-shaped hand drum) for anywhere between ₺30 and ₺600 or a *bağlama* (a long-necked seven-string lute typically played with a plectrum) for upwards of ₺150 and can then take part in one of the shop's many music workshops. Daily 9.30am–7pm.

SHOPPING MALLS

Although it's easy to view the US-style mall culture sweeping the city as a body-blow to the traditional Turkish way of life, a mall is in many ways just a modern version of a bazaar.

Akaretler Şair Nadim Bey Cad 11, Akaretler, Beşiktaş; map p.151. Not a shopping mall, but a series of nineteenth-century houses once home to the workers at the nearby Dolmabahçe Palace, now given over to exclusive shops selling everything from luxury towels to international designer clothes by the likes of Jimmy Choo. It's near the trendy *W* hotel (see p.173) and makes an alternative to Nişantası for upmarket shopping opportunities. Daily 10am–7pm.

Akmerkez Nisbetiye Cad, Etiler ☎ 0212 282 0170; map p.151. One of the first of the new Western-style shopping centres, with restaurants and a cinema, and shops carrying most top Turkish brands, plus quality European and American outlets. Daily 10am–10pm.

City's Mall Teşvikiye Cad 162, Nişantaşı ☎ 0212 373 3333, ⓦ citysnisantasi.com; map p.128. An upmarket addition to the city's mall scene, well designed, with sleek Art Deco lines. It's exclusive and mainly fashion-orientated

– think Louis Vuitton, Dolce & Gabbana, Gaultier and the like. There's an attached luxury multi-screen cinema and a few posh places to eat. Daily 10am–10pm.

Demirören İstiklal Cad, Beyoğlu ☎ 0212 249 9999, ⓦ demırorenistiklal.com; map pp.120–121. Opened to great fanfare in 2011 by Real Madrid and Portugal legend Cristiano Ronaldo, this mall is controversial (İstiklal Cad is lined with historic buildings) but likely to be the most convenient for the majority of visitors, and includes a Virgin Megastore, Mothercare and Gap among many other shops, as well as a cinema. Daily 10am–10pm.

Kanyon Büyükdere Cad 185, Levent ☎ 0212 353 5300, ⓦ kanyon.com.tr; map p.151. A canyon-shaped, four-storey, state-of-the-art shopping mall featuring most popular Western consumer chains for clothes, food, gifts et al, with an extremely plush cinema to boot. Daily 10am–10pm.

Zorlu Center Zincirlikuyu ☎ 0212 336 9160, ⓦ zorlucenter.com; map p.151. An impressive mixed-use centre containing a shopping mall, hotel, residences and a performing-arts facility (see p.207). Since opening in 2013, it has taken over from Kanyon as the city's most exclusive designer haven and also features international restaurant chains, such as Jamie's Italian and Tom's Kitchen. Daily 10am–10pm.

FENERBAHÇE FOOTBALL STADIUM, KADIKÖY

Sports and activities

The most popular spectator sport in the country is football, and the heart
of the game in Turkey is very much the metropolis of Istanbul. The city's
so-called Big Three clubs – Beşiktaş, Fenerbahçe and Galatasaray – have
massive support, not only in Istanbul but also throughout Anatolia.
Basketball, a major component of the national sports curriculum in
schools, is next favourite, its main league again dominated by teams from
Istanbul. The majority of adult Turks confine their passion for sport to
watching football and basketball matches on TV, or gambling on the
outcome of games.

Keeping fit is an alien concept for many in a city where most people simply work too long or just can't afford to regularly attend the gym. It's hardly surprising, then, that Turkey won only five medals in the 2012 Olympics. One of those was for wrestling, and the traditional sport of **oil wrestling** remains popular in rural Turkey – the place to see it is at the Kırkpınar Festival near Edirne (see p.271).

BASKETBALL

Basketball's roots in Turkey lie in prestigious Robert College, a school founded in Istanbul in 1863 by an American philanthropist. The first basketball match in Turkey was played there in 1904, and the sport's still going strong. The predominantly young and vociferous fan-base of the professional clubs has its roots at high-school level, where basketball has great popularity and inter-school rivalry is fierce. Many club sides are affiliated with the big football teams, and this – combined with the sponsorship lifeblood of the sport– throws up team names such as Beşiktaş İntegral Forex, Galatasaray Liv Hospital, and Fenerbahçe Ülker. The seasons of 2012–2014 saw a win apiece for each of the above in the sixteen-strong Turkish Basketball League (TBL). The national team, known as the "Twelve Giant Men", took second place in both the FIBA EuroBasket and FIBA World Cup in 2014. A few Turkish players have transferred to the NBA, though far more US players have come the other way, and many TBL teams have American, Russian and European players in their ranks. For further information on venues, matches and **tickets**, see ⓦ tbf.org.tr. Tickets for many matches (₺20 and up) are available from ⓦ biletix.com.

Beşiktaş İntegral Forex BJK Akatlar Spor ve Kültür Kompleksi, Gazeticiler Sitesi, Beşiktaş ☎ 0212 283 6600, ⓦ bjk.com.tr.

Fenerbahçe Ülker Fenerbahçe Spor Kulübü Lefter Küçükandonyadis Tesisleri, Münir Nurettin Selçuk Cad, Kızıltoprak ☎ 0216 347 8438, ⓦ fenerbahce.org.

Galatasaray Liv Hospital Abdi İpekçi Arena 100 Yıl Cad, Zeytinburnu ☎ 0212 679 7420, ⓦ galatasaray.org.

FOOTBALL

One of the whipping boys of **international football** in the 1980s, today Turkey is a side to be taken seriously. In 2002 they reached the semi-finals of the World Cup and in 2008 they reached the semi-finals of the 2008 European Championship, though they failed to qualify for the 2014 World Cup. Several Turkish players now play in the best leagues in the world, and there are a number of world-class Turkish-German players including Mesut Özil, who plays for Arsenal and was part of the winning 2014 World Cup German squad. When in Istanbul, the national team usually play in one of the Big Three's stadiums. The domestic league is dominated by Istanbul's **Beşiktaş**, **Fenerbahçe** and **Galatasaray**, but teams from Anatolia have begun to challenge their metropolitan rivals, with Bursaspor and Trabzonspor being ones to watch. The season runs from August to May, with a winter break from mid-December to mid-January. Despite supporters' fanaticism, only the derby matches sell out quickly, and tickets for other games are usually easy to come by. The celebrations following derby match or national team victories are a sight to behold, with carloads of cheering fans hanging out of windows, waving flags and blaring horns. **Tickets** for most major matches can be purchased from Biletix (ⓦ biletix.com) or from the ground on match day; remember that ticket prices increase substantially for derby and other big games; expect to pay upwards of ₺45.

THE WORST AND BEST OF ISTANBUL FOOTBALL FANS

Football violence is a problem in Turkey and every week in the season sees incidents somewhere in the country. Opposition supporters' coaches are regularly pelted with stones, seats ripped up and objects thrown onto the pitch. In September 2013, a derby match between Galatasary and Beşiktaş was called off because of a violent pitch invasion in the 92nd minute. In 2011 the Turkish Football Federation penalized the Fenerbahçe club by banning their supporters for two matches. At the last minute, they relented slightly, allowing under-12s and women only, free of charge. Fanatical Fenerbahçe supporters seized on this unexpected offer with relish, and around 43,000 women and kids roared on their favourites.

During the Gezi Park protests (see p.127), one of the strongest symbols of unity among the protesters was the sight of fans from rival teams standing side by side, or even tying the scarves of opposing teams together. Beşiktaş' fan group, Çarşı, played a key role in mobilizing support, their experience of protesting bringing some organization to an unplanned movement. Before then Çarşı were best known for their left-leaning persuasion with their catchphrase "Çarşı, her şeye karşı" (Çarsı is against everything) summing up their anti-racist, anti-fascist, anti-sexist character.

18

Beşiktaş Vodafone Arena, Dolmabahçe Cad, Beşiktaş ☎0212 310 1000, ⓦbjk.com.tr. Completed in 2014 for an estimated $80 million to replace the İnönü Stadium, it is the most convenient of the city's stadia, seating nearly 42,000 and set into the hillside just above the Bosphorus, near the Dolmabahçe Palace. Beşiktaş, known as the Kara Kartal or Black Eagles, traditionally play in black-and-white-striped kit. They have a more working-class fanbase than their rivals and are the least successful, with an appalling record in Europe. Constant changes of manager have not helped their cause but in Çarşı, their supporters' organization known for its leftist and anti-authoritarian leanings, they have the most effective and politicized fan-group in the city. According to Beşiktaş fans, "real men don't support teams playing in coloured strips" – a reference to the red and yellow of Galatasaray and the blue and yellow of Fenerbahçe.

Fenerbahçe Şükrü Saraçoğlu Stadium, Kadiköy ☎0216 449 5667, ⓦfenerbahce.org. The wealthiest club side in the country, nicknamed the *Sarı Kanarya* or Yellow Canaries, Fenerbahçe reached the quarter-finals of the Champions League in 2008 and the semi-finals of the Europa League in 2013. Their stadium has a 50,500 capacity

and is the best appointed in the city, nestled in a valley some twenty minutes' walk from the waterfront in Kadıköy, in Asian Istanbul. Despite the club's origins in the district's expat (mainly British) and Christian minorities at the start of the twentieth century, it was the favourite of the nationalist Atatürk. Today's big-name supporters include Nobel Prize-winning author Orhan Pamuk and former Prime Minister Recep Tayyip Erdoğan.

Galatasaray Türk Telecom Arena ☎0212 305 1925, ⓦgalatasaray.org. Despite winning the league title in 2008 and achieving Turkey's only international success at club level by lifting the UEFA cup in 2000, Galatasaray's star has been somewhat eclipsed of late by Fenerbahçe. The club was formed by a group of Muslim students from Beyoğlu's Galatasaray Lycée (see p.124) in 1905. In seemingly perpetual financial turmoil, they moved to the cavernous Atatürk Olympic Stadium for the 2003/4 season, then back to the Ali Samı Yen, but since 2010 have settled in the purpose-built Turk Telekom Arena, a 53,000-seat stadium in Şişli. Previous managers include the Scotsman Graeme Souness, who caused an uproar when he planted a Galatasaray banner in the centre circle of Fenerbahçe's pitch, following a cup-final victory there in 1996.

SWIMMING POOLS

Few Turks swim either seriously or well, which is hardly surprising given the paucity of public pools nationwide, even in booming Istanbul. If you're desperate for a dip, the big hotels such as the *Hilton*, *Marmara Taksim* and *Ceylan InterContinental* are the best option, though they are uniformly expensive with prices upwards of ₺100 per person per day.

WATERSPORTS

As you would expect for a city surrounded by water, there are a number of ways to get off the land and enjoy the city from the sea, strait or estuary.

Kitesurfing There are several options for adrenaline-seekers around the Black Sea resort of Kilyos, notably Burç Beach and Dalia Beach. The water is choppy so it's not ideal for complete novices, but it's a great place to get the hang of the kite itself. Visit ⓦkiteboardIstanbul.com for more details.

Rowing Istanbul Tour Studio (ⓦIstanbultourstudio.com) offers visitors a chance to see the city before it wakes up, with early morning rowing classes on the Golden Horn (suitable for complete beginners).

Sailing The best time for sail enthusiasts to visit is during the Bosphorus Sailing Fest (ⓦbmwsailingfest. com) which sees the wealthy neighbourhood of Bebek come alive with nautical festivities. Otherwise, companies such as Istanbul Lite (ⓦIstanbulite.com) offer private tours to the Princes' Islands.

Windsurfing For a memorable experience, try riding the breeze on the Marmara with an expansive view of Istanbul in the background: lessons and rentals are available at the Suadiye Windsurf Club (ⓦsuadiyewindsurfclub.com).

"WILD" SWIMMING

The famous Bosphorus strait is both polluted and notorious for its treacherous currents, but that doesn't stop the annual cross-Bosphorus swim, an event dating back to 1969. It's usually held in late July, attracts some 1500 participants and begins in Kanlıcı on the Asian shore, ending in Kuruçeşme in Europe. The 6.5km-long swim is organized by the Turkish Olympic Committee; for details see ⓦbogazici.olimpiyat.org.tr. For a more regular dip in safer, cleaner seas, head out to the Princes' Islands (see pp.158–165), or the Black Sea resorts of Kiliyos or Şile (see pp.156–157) or, closer by, Florya (see p.231).

FOR GROWN-UP KIDS

Turkey's "first and only escape room", known as **istrapped**, tests participants' logic skills. After being locked into a room with your friends, you are given one hour to try to escape, solving clues and strategically using real-world objects to open doors and solve problems. Conveniently located in the nightlife district of Asmalımescit (see p.122), this makes for a fun pre-dinner activity or an offbeat rainy-day idea. Suitable for between two (₺100) and five people (₺150). See ⓦ istrapped.com.

18

RUNNING

An increasing minority of Istanbulites have taken to **running**, though the crowded and often semi-obstructed pavements, horrendous traffic and air pollution are just some of the disincentives. Best bet, if you are staying in Sultanahmet, is the concrete **promenade** running along the shores of the Sea of Marmara, though it's tough on the feet. Other options include the pedestrianized path along the Bosphorus around Bebek or the **Yıldız** or **Emirgan** parks (see p.134 & p.150) but dedicated runners in need of a fix should head out to the **Belgrade Forest** (see p.153), where there's a 6.5km dedicated trail, or the motorized-traffic-free **Princes' Islands** (see pp.158–165) for a 14km jog around Büyükada, the biggest island. By far the best time to run in the city is early on a Sunday, with the streets much quieter than at any other time in the week. For serious runners, the **Istanbul Marathon** (ⓦ Istanbulmarathon.org) gives entrants the opportunity to run from Asia to Europe and there are shorter alternatives and a fun-run for the less committed. It's now held every November and gives the twenty-thousand-or-so competitors the unique chance to cross the Bosphorus Bridge on foot. The **Istanbul Half Marathon** (ⓦ Istanbulyarimaratonu.org), held every April, has 21km and 10km options.

CYCLING

Things are difficult for would-be **cyclists**, as the traffic is dense, ill-disciplined and generally regards cyclists as annoyances to be forced out of the way. However, things are changing and in recent years more and more young middle-class Turks have been buying bicycles and taking up cycling as more than just a Sunday leisure pursuit. There are several bicycle rental shops around the city, along with cycling organizations including the internationally popular monthly city ride, Critical Mass. What's more, several companies are now offering guided bicycle tours of the city. Istanbul On Bike (ⓦ Istanbulonbike.com) currently offers four different routes around the Golden Horn, old city, Bosphorus and Asian Istanbul. They also offer bicycles for rent, although taking to the streets of Istanbul is only recommended for very experienced city riders, who may enjoy cycling up the Bosphorus on the European side, or following the path around the Golden Horn. For less experienced cyclists, there's a waterfront cycle lane in Kadıköy on the Asian side of the Bosphorus (which gets rather clogged with pedestrians at weekends); otherwise any of the Princes' Islands makes a very appealing cycling destination (see pp.158–165).

HAMAMS

The **hamam** (Turkish bath) once played a pivotal role in hygiene, social discourse and religious life (they were usually part of a mosque complex, and cleanliness is part and parcel of Islam) in Turkey, but as the standard of living has increased, its importance (and the number of establishments) has drastically declined. As an exercise in nostalgia, however, it's well worth visiting one, particularly as the historic *hamam*s of Istanbul, Bursa and Edirne are architectural gems. Lounging around on warm marble slabs, your fellow bathers lost in the steam and light streaming in from tiny bottle-glass windows set in an ancient dome, is an experience few people can resist. The historic *hamam*s of the old city promote themselves remorselessly, and their brochures decorate the foyers of most Istanbul pensions and hotels. If you're out wandering and fancy an impromptu session in one of the smaller, neighbourhood baths, they are usually signposted – if in doubt look for the distinctive roof domes.

Ayasofya Hürrem Sultan Hamamı Bab ı Humayan Cad 1, Sultanahmet ☎ 0212 517 3535, ⓦ ayasofya hamami.com; map p.46. The Rolls Royce of the city's *hamam* scene, which opened in 2011 following years of restoration. Built by Mimar Sinan in 1556, it replaced the Byzantine baths of Zeuxippus on the same site and was named in honour of Süleyman's wife, Roxelana (known as Haseki Hürrem to Turks). The building is exquisite, with most of the original features having been preserved – even the marble squat toilets. There are separate men's and women's sections and all staff are highly trained masseurs. It's expensive, but considering the building's historical significance and the quality of service this is to be expected. Bath packages from €85. Daily 7am–midnight.

Çağaloğlu Hamamı Prof Kazim İsmail Gürkhan Cad 34, Çağaloğlu ☎ 0212 522 2424, ⓦ cagalogluhamami .com.tr; map p.46. The most popular baths this side of town, famous for their beautiful *hararet*s (steam rooms)

18

HAMAM PRACTICALITIES

*Hamam*s are usually either for men or women, or sexually **segregated** on a schedule, though a few offer mixed-sex bathing. Bring soap and shampoo or buy it in the foyer (most tourist-frequented *hamam*s have a shop and café). Men are supplied with a *peştemal*, a thin, wraparound sarong, women generally enter in knickers but not bra; both sexes get *takunya*, awkward wooden clogs (or more prosaic plastic slippers), and later a *havlu* (towel). Leave your clothes in the changing cubicle (*camekan* in Turkish), where there are generally lockers for valuables.

The *hararet* or **main bath chamber** ranges from plain to ornate, though any decent *hamam* will be marble-clad, at least up to chest height. Two or more *halvets* – semi-private corner rooms with two or three *kurnas* (basins) each – lead off from the main chamber. The internal temperature varies from tryingly hot to barely lukewarm, depending on how good the *hamam* is. Unless you're with a friend, it's one customer to a set of taps and basin; refrain from making a big soapy mess in the basin, which is meant for mixing pure water to ideal temperature. Use the scoop-dishes provided to sluice yourself.

At the heart of the *hamam* is the *göbek taşı* or "navel stone", a raised platform positioned over the furnaces that heat the premises. It will be piping hot and covered with prostrate patrons absorbing the heat. It's also usually the venue for the (very) vigorous **massages** from the *tellak* (masseur). A simple *kese* (abrasive mitt) session, in which dead skin and grime are scrubbed away, will probably suit more people. Terms for the *tellaks'* services should be displayed in the foyer. Few *hamam*s have a female masseur; if you would feel uncomfortable with a male masseur do check In advance.

Rates vary enormously depending on the location, history and architectural merit of the *hamam*, with those in the historic old city generally far pricier than those in outlying districts. Scrubs and massages cost extra, so make sure you know what you'll be paying in advance.

– open cruciform chambers with windowed domes supported on a circle of columns. The baths were built in 1741 by Mahmut I to pay for the upkeep of his library in Haghia Sophia, and the arches, basins and taps of the hot room, as well as the entries to the private cubicles, are all magnificently Baroque. Florence Nightingale is said to have bathed here and the *hamam* has appeared in several movies, including *Indiana Jones and the Temple of Doom*. €30 for self-service bath, €50 includes a scrub and massage. Daily 8am–10pm.

Çemberlitaş Vezirhan Cad 8, Çemberlitaş ☎ 0212 522 7974, ⓦ cemberlitashamami.com.tr; map pp.78–79. Across Vezirhanı Cad from the Çemberlitaş Column is the celebrated four-hundred-year-old Çemberlitaş Hamamı, founded in the sixteenth century by Nur Banu, one of the most powerful of the valide sultans (mothers of the sultans). Its central location means that the masseurs are used to foreigners, making it a good, if expensive, place to be initiated into the rites of the Turkish bath. ₺90 includes a scrub and bubble wash, ₺153 also includes an oil massage. Daily 7.30am–midnight.

Çinili Hamamı Çavuşdere Cad 204, Üsküdar ☎ 0216 553 1593, ⓦ cinilihamam.com; map p.44. Set in the Asian suburb of Üsküdar (see pp.143–145) this is one of the best-value *hamam*s in the city. It's clean, housed in a historic domed building dating back to 1684 and is about as authentic an experience as you can get, with few foreign

visitors having the determination to get here or to cope with the non-English-speaking staff. ₺25 for just the *hamam*, ₺37 for a scrub and bubble massage. Daily: men 7am–10pm; women 8am–7.30pm.

★**Kılıç Ali Paşa Hamamı** Hamam Sok 1, Tophane ☎ 0212 393 8010, ⓦ kilicalipasahamami.com; map p.110. This luxurious sixteenth-century *hamam* forms part of the Kılıç Ali Paşa mosque complex, on the Beyoğlu side of Galata bridge. It opened in 2013 after a seven-year restoration process and although it is one of Mimar Sinan's stunning works, it doesn't attract the crowds of Sultanahmet's historic baths. Offers an excellent opportunity for real relaxation and is also ideal for first-timers, as visitors are walked through every step. ₺130 includes scrub and bubble massage and an oil massage costs an extra ₺80. Daily 8am–4pm (women); 4.30pm–midnight (men).

★**Süleymaniye Hamamı** Mimar Sinan Cad 20 ☎ 0212 519 5569, ⓦ suleymaniyehamami.com.tr; map pp.78–79. Built by Sinan in 1557, legend has it that the great architect took all his baths here from 1557 to 1588, but today it doesn't accept single males or females, only couples and families; the bathing is mixed-gender. It has been beautifully restored and is atmospherically located near the incomparable mosque of the same name. Good value: €35 for bath, scrub and massage. Daily 10am–11pm, last entry 9pm.

MİNİATÜRK MINIATURE PARK

Kids' Istanbul

Turks adore children, in a very uninhibited Mediterranean manner. Younger kids may sometimes receive rather more attention than either they or their parents expect, especially if they are blonde. It's common practice to pinch chubby kiddie cheeks as a sign of affection, an act often accompanied by the word *maşallah*, which serves both to praise your offspring and ward off the evil eye. Turkish families tend to take their children with them wherever they go and think nothing of letting them run around restaurants until the early hours. In this sense, Istanbul is a great place to visit with kids.

19

Being dragged around the Haghia Sophia and Topkapı Palace for hours on end is unlikely to appeal to children, and the sheer number of bodies at the Eminönü waterfront, İstiklal Caddesi or the Grand Bazaar may be stressful. Be prepared to take a break from the city-centre hassle from time to time. Gülhane Parkı in Sultanahmet (see p.58) is a handy wide-open space for kids to let off steam and there are more (and better) parks beside the Bosphorus. Alternatively, take a boat trip up the strait, across to Asia or out to the Princes' Islands (see pp.158–165), or visit one of the handful of child-orientated attractions scattered around the city and its environs. A ride on either the modern tram or the period tram rattling along İstiklal Caddesi is fun, and the underground Tünel funicular is also fascinating for kids (see p.29), as is the cable car from the Golden Horn up to the *Pierre Loti* café in Eyüp (see p.108).

Turkish **food** is sure to appeal to children – *köfte* is essentially just a tasty type of burger, *pide* a pizza without the tomato paste, and *gözleme* a stuffed pancake – and there are plenty of familiar fast-food outlets dotted around the city. Maraş ice cream is just as delicious as Italian *gelato* and comes in myriad flavours, while Turkish chocolate is as good as you'll taste anywhere. In general, restaurants are relaxed and very welcoming to families – just don't expect highchairs or changing facilities in the toilets.

Toys sold in markets and stores tend to be more expensive than the same thing would be back home. Nappies are widely available from all the supermarkets, most *eczane* (chemists) and many *bakkals* (general stores), and there are Mothercare branches across the city.

MUSEUMS, ATTRACTIONS AND GALLERIES

Archeology Museum (see pp.58–61). Has a Children's Museum, with a miniature wooden Trojan horse and replica Neolithic dwellings among other exhibits. Kids are just as likely to be enthralled by the museum's wonderful sarcophagi and other intriguing artefacts. Free for under-12s.

Istanbul Modern (see p.115). Runs summer art workshops for children aged 7–12 years, in Turkish. Free for under-2s.

Military Museum (see pp.127–128). Tanks, Ottoman-era weaponry and colourful dioramas will appeal to many children. Free for children and students.

Miniatürk (see p.117). Bound to engage interest with over 100 pint-sized models of some of Istanbul's (and Turkey's) most impressive monuments and sights, from Atatürk International airport to the Haghia Sophia.

Panorama 1453 Museum (see p.105). Built in sight of the walls besieged in 1453, this museum gives a stunning 360-degree artist's impression of the action.

Pera Museum (see p.123). This art-focused private museum runs regular children's workshops in parallel to its exhibitions and events.

Rahmi M. Koç Industrial Museum (see pp.116–117). Far more to keep them entertained than, for instance, the Archeology Museum, with a submarine moored in the Golden Horn to explore, a cute railway station and length of track, a cornucopia of vintage cars, motorbikes and planes, plus regular special exhibitions and events aimed specifically at children.

Sakıp Sabancı Museum (see p.150). Usually has a child-friendly art and design workshop running alongside its latest exhibition. Free for under-14s.

Santrallstanbul Energy Museum (see p.117). Although not well maintained, it allows kids to ride an electricity-producing bike, see the world through a snake's eyes and watch lightning bolts in a plasma globe. There are also summer art-based workshops here – though they're in Turkish.

Toy Museum (see p.141). Though inconveniently located out in Göztepe, this is as much for adults as kids, with its collection of toys, dolls and the like dating back to the nineteenth century. There are special activities at weekends, including a puppet show.

PARKS

To escape the urban hustle and bustle, head for one of the city's parks – although providing little in the way of play equipment, there are normally plenty of grassy areas, trees for shade and, in the first three listed below, fabulous views down over the Bosphorus.

FREEBIES

All the state-run museums are free for children under 12. This includes the Haghia Sophia, Kariye Museum, Archeological Museum, Topkapı Palace, Mosaic Museum, and Museum of Turkish and Islamic Arts – all of which hold varying degrees of interest for the little ones. On all public transport, kids under 7 travel free.

Emirgan Parkı Emirgan (see p.150). This park in the posh Bosphorus suburb of Emirgan makes a great day's outing with kids, especially when combined with a trip to the Sakıp Sabancı Museum (see p.150) and lunch at *Sütis*, or one of the park's cafés. There's some decent play equipment for little ones, a delightful ornamental lake complete with waterfall and ducks, and the late-Ottoman wooden pavilions are like something out of *Heidi*. Daily 7am–10.30pm.

Gülhane Parkı Sirkeci (see p.58). The opening hours of this park are not set in stone, so if there's no one else around you may be turfed out earlier. There's a meagre amount of play equipment, but plenty of space to run around, and a nice tea garden, the *Set Üstü* (see p.179) for snacks. Summer 7am–11pm, winter 9am–dusk.

Yıldız Parkı Çırağan Cad, Beşiktaş (see p.134). A lovely landscaped park full of mature trees for shade on hot summer days. There's a paltry amount of play equipment (for younger kids only), but it's a great place to run around in. There's a café or two, fine Bosphorus views, and the guided tour of the opulent Şale Köşkü is not too demanding for older kids. The park is set on a steep slope, so if you're pushing a buggy: beware. Summer 9am–6pm, winter 9am–5.30pm.

ACTIVITIES

Aqua Club Dolphin Cemal Paşa Cad, Su Oyunları Merkezi, Bahçeşehir ☎0212 672 6161, ⓦaquaclubdolphin.com. Impressive waterpark with all the usual slides, twister bowls and floatrides in well-landscaped gardens, plus dolphin shows (for an extra fee). Free shuttle buses depart from outside the (defunct) Atatürk Kültür Merkezi on Taksim Square between 8.30am and 9.30am; alternatively, take bus #76/D or #76/E from Taksim. Women ₺30; men ₺40 (Mon–Sat) & ₺45 (Sun), children (5–12) ₺20, under-5s free. May to mid-Sept 9am–6pm.

Istanbul Aquarium Yeşilköy Halkalı Cad 93, Florya ☎0212 574 2130, ⓦIstanbulakvaryum.com. Aimed primarily at children, this large centre dedicated to all things aquatic is arranged by sea or ocean and will keep them entertained for a few hours. Adults ₺35, children (3–16) ₺25. Daily 10am–8pm.

Turkuazoo Forum Mall, Paşa Cad, Bayrampaşa ☎0212 443 1350, ⓦforumIstanbul.com.tr. Has all the aquatic draws you'd expect, from piranhas and sharks to stingrays and reef fish, drifting around in 29 tanks and an 80m-long acrylic tunnel. It's in Europe's largest mall, so there's lots more to do here, including a ten-screen cinema. To get here, take Metro 1 to Kocatepe. Adults ₺34, children (3–16) ₺25. Daily 10am–8pm.

Sapphire Büyükdere Cad, Levent; Metro 4, Levent, ⓦIstanbulsapphire.com. This graceful, award-winning 54-floor, 261-metre-high tower, completed in 2011, is Istanbul's tallest building and was the tallest building in Europe when it was built. The views from the top are stunning, while older children will enjoy Sky Ride, a helicopter flight simulation that provides a thrilling virtual air-tour of Istanbul. ₺18 or ₺28 with Sky Ride. Daily 10am–10pm.

Vialand Yeşilpınar Bölge Park İçi Yolu, Yeşilpınar ☎0850210 85 63, ⓦvialand.com.tr. Open since 2013, this huge theme park is the biggest of its kind in Istanbul. As well as the rides and historical re-enactments, there is a shopping mall, cinema and bowling alley. ₺70 (Mon–Fri), ₺65 (Sat & Sun); children (5–14) ₺50 (Mon–Fri), ₺55 (Sat & Sun). Mon–Fri 10am–6pm Sat–Sun 10am–8pm.

BEACHES AND DAY-TRIPS

While swimming in the Bosphorus or the Golden Horn is out of the question, both the Marmara and the Black Sea offer a few opportunities for a day at the beach.

Black Sea resorts A trip to Kilyos or Şile (see p.156 and p.157) is another possibility, though it entails a long bus journey (up to 2hr each way depending on traffic) and there are dangerous currents; the beaches are fine, if very crowded in midsummer.

Bosphorus Cruises Most kids like boats and the Bosphorus Cruises (see p.139) are great fun and reasonably good value. There are two impressive suspension bridges to cruise under, a medley of seaborne traffic of all shapes and sizes to gawp at, and an endless stream of vendors with refreshments ranging from fresh orange juice to yoghurt dusted with icing sugar.

Florya The closest seaside option to the city centre is located in the wealthy neighbourhood of Florya, close to Atatürk Airport. Providing a very welcome break when the weather gets too sticky, Güneş Plajı (sunshine beach) is open to the public during the summer months only (entrance ₺15). There are sunloungers, cafés and a shallow sea for splashing around in. Best reached by taking a dolmuş (shared taxi) from the top of Tarlabaşı Bul (just off Taksim Square).

Princes' Islands A trip to these islands in the Sea of Marmara (see pp.158–165) provides a welcome break from the heat of the city. You can take a ride in a horse-drawn carriage, rent a bike or splash about in the sea from one of the (mainly) pay beaches. Bear in mind that both these trips can get very crowded, especially at weekends, so get there early to bag seats for everyone.

19

AYA SOFYA CAMII (HAGHIA SOPHIA)

İznik and Termal-Kaplıcılar

The laidback lakeside retreat of İznik, surrounded by rich agricultural land and forested hills, is easily reached from Istanbul by high-speed ferry across the Sea of Marmara, followed by an hour's bus ride southeast. Encircled by impressive city walls, it was known as Nicaea in ancient times and played a key role in the development of Christianity. Long on history and short on crowds, it makes a great introduction to rural Turkey. Even closer to Istanbul lies the delightful and aptly named thermal-spa resort Termal-Kaplıcılar, oozing *fin-de-siècle* charm amid the lush, wooded hills that surround it.

İznik

It's hard to believe that **İznik**, a somnolent farming community at the east end of the lake of the same name, was once the seat of empires and the scene of desperate battles. But looking around the fertile olive-grove-mantled valley, you can understand its attraction for imperial powers needing a fortified base near the sea-lanes of the Marmara. Today, İznik is a backwater, slumbering away among its orchards, with tourism playing a distinct second fiddle to agriculture. The town's famous sixteenth-century ceramics, among the best ever produced in Turkey, are now all but absent from İznik's museums and mosques. But the art has been revived and numerous shops specializing in İznik pottery dot the town's streets. It's possible to visit İznik as a long day-trip from Istanbul and have sufficient time to sample its monuments, but you'd be rushed and would end up seeing the sites (in summer at least) in the heat and glare of the midday sun. Worse, you'd have no time to absorb the atmosphere of this out-of-the-way place, which is as far removed from the big city as you can imagine. The lake itself, backed by low, wooded mountains, is quite beautiful, with reed-fringed shores and snow-white egrets fishing in the shallows.

With its grid-plan streets, İznik is easy to navigate. The main north–south boulevard **Atatürk Caddesi** and its east–west counterpart **Kılıçaslan Caddesi** link four of the seven ancient gates, dividing the town into unequal quadrants. Only enthusiasts will want to walk the entire perimeter of the double **walls**, now missing most of their hundred original watchtowers, but three of the gates are worth your time. Heavy traffic has been rerouted through modern breaches in the fortifications to prevent vibration damage to the original openings, which are only accessible to pedestrians and service vehicles. The **lake** is swimmable in summer, but the town beaches are scrappy and weed, algae and litter often foul the lake edges; you really need a car to reach the more attractive spots. Both roads out of town, along the shore of the lake, stay close to the water and offer swimming possibilities at various tiny beaches along the way.

20

Brief history

Founded by Antigonus, Alexander the Great's general, in 316 BC, the city was seized and enlarged fifteen years later by his rival Lysimachus, who named it **Nicaea** after his late wife. He also gave Nicaea its first set of walls and the grid plan typical of Hellenistic towns; both are still evident. The Bithynian kingdom took over Lysimachus' rule and Nicaea alternated with nearby Nicomedia (modern İzmit) as its capital until it was bequeathed to Rome in 74 BC. Under the Roman emperors, the city prospered as capital of the province, and it continued to flourish during the Byzantine era.

THE FIRST COUNCIL OF NICAEA – A DEFINING MOMENT IN CHRISTIANITY

In 325 AD, when Christianity was still very much in its infancy, the Emperor Constantine invited bishops from all over the empire to his lakeside palace in Nicaea to discuss the hot topic of the day – the **nature of Christ**. Was he of "like nature" but basically made of lesser stuff than God, as the followers of the presbyter Arius of Alexandria were claiming? Or was he, as a majority of believers thought, divine? This was not just some arcane theological question; it was a controversy that threatened the very fabric of the empire. Across the Near East, rabble-rousing rival bishops were spouting their rhetoric, their followers scrawling pro- or anti-Arian graffiti on city walls and inflamed mobs of both persuasions were rioting in the streets.

At Nicaea, Constantine managed to persuade a majority of the bishops present to vote for his compromise, which was that God and Christ were "consubstantial" (that's to say, Christ was both divine and human). Christ (the Son) was now officially accepted as divine and a co-equal part of the Holy Trinity, along with the Father and the Holy Spirit. The **Nicaean Creed**, as it became known, is still central to Christian belief today.

Nicaea played a pivotal role in early Christianity, by virtue of hosting two important **ecumenical councils**. The first, convened by Constantine the Great in 325 AD, resulted in the condemnation of the Arian heresy (see box, p.233). The seventh council (the second to be held here) was presided over by Empress Irene in 787 AD; this time, the Iconoclast controversy was settled by the pronouncement, widely misunderstood in the West, that icons had their proper place in the church so long as they were revered but not worshipped.

Nicaea's much-repaired walls seldom repelled invaders, and in 1081 the Selçuks took the city, only to be evicted by a combined force of Byzantines and Crusaders sixteen years later. The fall of Constantinople to the Fourth Crusade in 1204 propelled Nicaea into the spotlight once more, when the Byzantine heir Theodore Lascaris retreated here and made this the base of the improbably successful **Nicaean Empire**. The Lascarid dynasty added a second circuit of walls before returning to Constantinople in 1261, but these again failed to deter the besieging Ottomans, who, led by Orhan Gazi, the victor of Bursa, broke through in March 1331.

Renamed İznik, the city experienced a golden age of sorts, interrupted briefly by the pillaging of the Mongol warlord Tamerlane in 1402. Virtually all of the surviving monuments predate the Mongol sacking, but the most enduring contribution to art and architecture – the celebrated **İznik tiles and pottery** – first appeared during the reign of Çelebi Mehmet I, who brought skilled potters from Persia to begin the local industry. This received another boost in 1514 when Selim the Grim took Tabriz and sent more craftsmen west as war booty; by the end of the sixteenth century, ceramic production in İznik was at its height, with more than three hundred functioning kilns. It was to be a brief flowering, since within another hundred years war and politics had scattered most of the artisans. By the mid-eighteenth century, the local industry had packed up completely, with products from nearby Kütahya serving as inferior substitutes. İznik began a long, steady decline, hastened by near-total devastation during the War of Independence (see p.292).

The southeast quadrant

The town's southeast quadrant is home to a number of interesting buildings. Chief among these is the **Süleyman Paşa Medresesi** on Gündem Caddesi. Built in 1332, it is the oldest such Ottoman structure in Turkey and the first example in Anatolia of a school with an open courtyard, surrounded by eleven chambers and nineteen domes. Three blocks south of the *medresesi*, on Yakup Sokak, is the **Yakub Çelebi Zaviyesi**, a fourteenth-century *zaviye* (dervish lodge) that was converted into a mosque, founded by the luckless prince Yakub Çelebi, who was slain by his brother Beyazıt I at Kosovo in 1389. A block to the east, nothing but foundations remain of the **Kimisis Kilisesi** (Church of the Assumption), the presumed burial place of Theodore Lascaris, which was destroyed in 1922.

Haghia Sophia (Aya Sofya Camii)
Atatürk Caddesi

The Byzantine Haghia Sophia (Church of Holy Wisdom) founded by Justinian, is today the Aya Sofya Camii, set in pleasant gardens full of white- and pink-blooming oleander and palms. The current structure was built after an earthquake in 1065 and, as the cathedral of the provisional Byzantine capital, hosted the coronations of the four Nicaean emperors. The Ottomans converted it to a mosque on taking the city and the architect Mimar Sinan (see box, p.233) restored it, but the premises were already half-ruined when reduced to their present sorry condition following the War of Independence. There is little to see inside, bar an impressive synthronon (the semicircular tier of seating for clergy) in the apse, some fragments of mosaic flooring, and a faint **fresco** of Christ, John and Mary, found at ground level behind a glass panel to the left as you enter. After serving for years as a museum, it was controversially converted back to a mosque in 2012, a move that symbolized the resurgence of Islam

İZNİK TILES TODAY

The best tiles made in İznik today, both at the İznik Vakıf and various other workshops around town, are composed primarily of locally quarried, finely ground quartz. They have good acoustic properties, which make them especially suitable for use in mosques.

The tiles, beautiful and expensive, are redolent of the golden age of the Ottoman imperial past, and as such are much sought after to adorn high-profile Turkish company headquarters. In Istanbul you can see them decorating the stations on the Metro line from Taksim to Levant, in the newly refurbished Tünel and at the new terminal buildings of Atatürk International Airport. They can also be seen on display in the Montréal Peace Park (also known as the Turkish Peace Park) in Canada.

in a country with ten years of pro-Islamic AKP (see pp.298–301) governance behind it. Turkey's secularists and Orthodox Christians worldwide fear the church of the same name in Istanbul (see pp.45–49) may well go the same way.

İznik Vakıf

Halı Saha Arkası • Daily: Sept–June 8am–6pm; July & Aug 6–11am • Free • ☎ 0224 757 6025, Ⓦ iznik.com

The **İznik Vakıf**, or İznik Foundation, clearly signposted in the southwest quadrant, was established in 1995 with the dual intentions of researching the early techniques used to produce İznik tiles and restarting production using traditional methods. Today, tiles of extremely high quality are manufactured and sold on site, though prices are high, and exact replicas of original designs are not reproduced for fear of them being passed off as genuine. During a visit, you'll see different production stages and receive a brief history of the İznik *œuvre*.

The northeast quadrant

Just north of Kılıçaslan Caddesi squats the **Hacı Özbek Camii**, the earliest known Ottoman mosque, built in 1333 but much adulterated. Walk further along the road and you'll soon reach a vast landscaped park to the north, dotted with İznik's most famous monuments.

Yeşil Cami

Yeşil Camii Sokak

The **Yeşil Camii**, or Green Mosque, was erected towards the end of the fourteenth century and takes its name from the green İznik tiles that once adorned its minaret. Disappointingly, they've long since been replaced by examples of tri-coloured, mediocre Kütahya tile-work. However, it is a small gem of a building nonetheless. Tufted with a stubby minaret that harks back to Selçuk architectural models, its highlight is the fantastic marble relief on the portico.

İznik Museum and Nilüfer Hatun İmareti

Tues–Sun 9am–noon & 1.30–5pm • ₺3

The **İznik Museum** is housed in the **Nilüfer Hatun İmareti**, a building with a T-shaped ground-plan that served originally as the meeting place of the Ahi brotherhood, a guild drawn from the ranks of skilled craftsmen that also acted as a benevolent society. It was commissioned by Murat I in 1388 in honour of his mother, Nilüfer. Daughter of a Byzantine noble, Nilüfer Hatun was married off to Orhan Gazi to consolidate a Byzantine–Ottoman alliance. Her abilities as a ruler were soon recognized by Orhan, who appointed her regent during his frequent absences.

Although the museum houses painstakingly restored pieces of fourteenth-century İznik tiles, which were excavated from the town's kilns, they are all incomplete and there are few of the beautiful sixteenth-century mosque ornaments and massive plates that are commonplace in the museums of Istanbul and abroad. More interesting is an exhibition of **Selçuk tile fragments** found in the area around the Roman theatre and in local kilns. Whether these earlier tiles were produced locally or imported is uncertain, though some evidence suggests that İznik ware is in part descended from that of the Selçuk Turks.

The museum also has a good selection of finds, dating back to 6000 BC, from excavations at a nearby *hüyük* (settlement mound) called Ilıpınar – including pottery, bone tools and a fine Bronze Age clay burial sarcophagus. There are plenty of Roman-era relics on display, including a bronze dancing Pan, some Byzantine gold jewellery and, standing out among the nondescript marble clutter, a sarcophagus in near-mint condition. The garden area boasts a couple of very impressive Roman-era sarcophagi, along with stelae, giant pithoi (urns) and Ottoman headstones, complete with carved turbans or fezzes.

The walls and beyond

The eastern **Lefke Kapısı**, the closest gate to the Yeşil Camii, is a three-ply affair including a triumphal arch dedicated to Hadrian between the two courses of walls. Just outside is a stretch of the ancient **aqueduct** that until recently supplied the town; it's possible to get up on the ramparts here for a stroll. You can do the same at the northerly **Istanbul Kapısı**, the best preserved of the gates, the outer part of which was constructed as a triumphal triple arch to celebrate the visit of the Roman Emperor Hadrian in 124. The inner gate is decorated by two stone-carved **masks**, which were probably taken from the nearby Roman theatre. The wall area to the east of this gate is packed with small workshops manufacturing wooden crates for the local fruit industry.

Other traces of Roman Nicaea are evident in the southwestern quarter: a section of **ancient wall** delimits the Senatus Court, extending from the surviving tower next to the **Saray Kapısı**. The sadly neglected, graffitied **Roman theatre** lies just inside this gate, and has lost most of its seating, but on the exterior retaining wall of the seating area you'll find a slab carved with a round shield and sword – a gladiator symbol. The area between the town and the lake here is a mass of orchards, with olives, figs, apple, medlar, walnut and mulberry growing in profusion, along with cypress, linden and plane trees.

ARRIVAL AND DEPARTURE   İZNİK

By sea bus The best way to reach İznik from Istanbul is to take the IDO sea bus (ⓦido.com.tr) from Yenikapı to Yalova (70min; ₺9), from where regular dolmuşes run to İznik (1hr; ₺9). The first sea bus departs Yenikapı at 8am, the last back leaves Yalova at 9.45pm.

By bus There's one daily bus to Istanbul, leaving the *otogar*

(bus station) in the southeast quadrant at 7.45am, arriving first at the Harem (see p.24) and then the Esenler (see p.24) terminals in Istanbul. If you're heading on to Bursa (see pp.240–253), minibuses depart from the *otogar* between 5.30am and 9pm.

INFORMATION

Tourist office Located on Kılıçaslan Cad, just east of the Aya Sofya, in the *Belediye* (municipality) building. There's

also an information kiosk on Atatürk Cad, next to the Aya Sofya Camii, but it is open infrequently.

ACCOMMODATION

Rooms, singles in particular, are at a premium in İznik and reservations are recommended between mid-June and mid-September – especially at the weekends.

Çamlık Motel Sahili Cad 11 ☏0224 757 1631, ⓦiznik-camlikmotel.com. This spotless, well-run hotel has small but comfortable rooms with balconies overlooking the lake, and is surrounded on three sides by olive groves and mulberry trees; there's also an excellent attached restaurant (see below). ₺135

★ **Cem Otel** Göl Sahili 34 ☏0224 757 1687, ⓦcemotel.com. Set back slightly from the foreshore, the *Cem* is a long-established and well-run place. Rooms are plain but soothingly toned, spotless and equipped with flat-screen TVs. Rear rooms make up for the lack of a lake view with baths; front rooms have showers. There's a handy roof

terrace and a decent restaurant (which doubles as the breakfast room) downstairs. ₺150

Kaynarca Pansiyon Gündem Sok 1 ☏0224 757 1753, ⓦkaynarca.s5.com. The most appealing budget option, run by English-speaking Ali and his charming family, offering dorm beds as well as en-suite singles, doubles and triples. All rooms have satellite TV, though there's neither a/c nor fans. Breakfast (₺7.5) is served on the rooftop terrace, and there's a kitchen for guests' use. There are no advance bookings possible, and payment is by cash only, but the owner guarantees to find you a bed somewhere in town in the event they are full. Dorm ₺25, double ₺70

EATING AND DRINKING

Eating by the lakeshore, where some of the restaurants are licensed, is particularly popular with visitors; it's worth trying grilled or fried *yayın*, the excellent local catfish. For snacks or dessert, there are plenty of tea gardens, cafés and ice-cream parlours overlooking the lake. The town centre has a number of decent places for an (unlicensed) meal.

Artı Göl Sahili Yolu. A lake-view bar with tables set out in a pleasant garden. Attracts a fairly young crowd, drawn by the cheap beer (₺6) and the chance to strum their guitars in the open air. Daily 11am–midnight.

Çamlık Motel Sahili Cad 11 ☏0224 757 1362, ⓦiznik-camlikmotel.com. The nicest of the waterside restaurants has a lovely shady setting and dishes up *meze* and kebabs,

including their speciality fish kebab, for around ₺35 a head with beer.

Karadeniz Pide Salon Kılıçaslan Cad ☏0224 757 0143. This tiny cafeteria in a characterful 1930s building serves fresh and cheap *pides* washed down with *ayran* – you can watch the food being pulled into shape in the kitchen at the back. Daily 9am–11pm.

20

★**Köfteci Yusuf** İznik Lisesi Karşısı, ☎ 444 6162, ⓦ kofteciyusuf.com.tr. A smart, new glass palace of a place, with friendly black-and-orange-suited waiters, serving up *köfte* as delicious as anywhere in Turkey. The large portions come accompanied by a spicy tomato dip and grilled pepper and tomato – all for ₺12. They do a range of kebabs and other grills as well. Daily 8am–11pm.

DIRECTORY

Banks The banks and ATMs are on Atatürk Cad, close to the Aya Sofya Camii.

Hamam Both men and women can use the İkinci Murat Hamamı (daily: women 8am–2pm; men 4–10pm; ₺18)

just southeast of İznik's central roundabout and the Aya Sofya Müzesi.

Internet Get online "next" door to the *Kaynarca Pansiyon* on Gündem Sok.

Termal-Kaplıcılar

The famous hot springs at **Termal-Kaplıcılar** lie in pleasantly forested hills 12km to the southwest of the scruffy port town of Yalova, on the southern shore of the Sea of Marmara, southeast of Istanbul. Taking the waters in the *fin-de-siècle* splendour of one of the bath-houses built around these springs, a little higher up in the hills than the town of Termal itself, is a real wind-down after the hectic pace of life in the city – perhaps preceded by a stroll along some of the forest trails. Although visited by Byzantine and Roman emperors, Termal's springs only became fashionable again at the turn of the twentieth century, and most of the Ottoman buildings date from that era.

20

Atatürk Müzesi

Baltacı Çiftliği • Tues–Sun 8.30am–noon & 1–5pm • ₺3

Atatürk had a house built for him in Kaplıcılar, now open as **Atatürk Müzesi**. Designed in the modernist style by one of the leading architects of the new Republic (see pp.294–295), Sedad Hakki Eldem, it was built in 1929 and took a mere 38 days to complete – in time to host the visiting Shah of Iran. The house is still furnished pretty much as it was in Atatürk's day and gives a real insight into the man and his times. The bedroom of his adopted daughter, Sabiha Gökçen (who was also the nation's first female pilot), is kitted out with typically curvaceous Art Deco furniture. The RCA radio that the great man was glued to, night after night, is on display, as is a German-made piano and a sideboard hand-carved by a reminder of the pre-Republican era, Sultan Abdülhamit. Atatürk visited the house each summer until his death in 1938.

Kurşunlu Hamamı

Daily 8am–11pm • Mon–Fri ₺20, Sat–Sun ₺25

The biggest single draw in Kaplıcılar is the outdoor pool of the Art Nouveau **Kurşunlu Hamamı**, a complex of *hamam*s with a swirling roof and bits of Roman relief-carving set into the walls. Here you can wallow in the hot waters and admire the architecture and sun-dappled forest canopy around you. Water temperatures reach 65°C, so the best time to visit is in winter, when the hot water provides a haven from the seasonal chill. In summer, you'll find yourself jumping out to sunbathe in order to cool off. Several **hamams** here – popular for their beneficial effect on rheumatism and skin diseases – offer communal pools with separate chambers for tour groups.

ARRIVAL AND DEPARTURE	TERMAL- KAPLICILAR

By sea bus and bus Take the IDO sea bus (ⓦ ido.com.tr) from Istanbul's Yenikapı terminal to Yalova (₺9), from where there are frequent dolmuşes from the bus station next to the ferry terminal for the half-hour run to Kaplıcılar, beyond Termal (₺3). The first sea bus departs Yenikapı at 8am, the last back leaves Yalova at 9.45pm, so a day-trip is

very feasible. Don't make the mistake of getting off in the actual town of Termal, with its rash of pensions, hotels and basic restaurants; instead, continue on to Kaplıcılar, where the major baths (including Kurşunlu) are located. There are also frequent buses to Yalova from İznik.

ACCOMMODATION

Çınar Otel Kaplıcı, Termal ☎0226 675 7400, ⓦyalovatermal.com. This luxury hotel dates back to the late nineteenth century, though it was substantially reconstructed in the early 1980s. The rooms are plain, with white walls offset by dark wood trim and small balconies overlooking a courtyard shaded by a giant plane tree. ₺260

Dinana Otel Üvezpınar Kaplıcı, Termal ☎0226 675 7668, ⓕ0226 675 7293. On one of the hills surrounding Termal sits this family-run, clean hotel, with twenty pleasant rooms that all have balconies overlooking the forested mountains, and a restaurant serving simple meals. The hotel is in the village of Üvezpınar, 2km up the road from Termal. Several of the dolmuşes from Yalova run right up to the village. ₺85

20

YEŞİL TÜRBE

Bursa and Uludağ

As the crow flies, the historic and beautifully situated city of Bursa is less than a hundred kilometres from Istanbul. It's a good city for walking around, whether through the hive of bazaars, the sprawling parks of the Hisar district or the anachronistic peacefulness of the Muradiye quarter. Snow-addicts may be more interested in the resort of Uludağ, perched high above the city, Turkey's longest-established ski resort. It's possible to take in Bursa on an intense day-trip from Istanbul, but to make the most of it you should spend at least one night here – several if you want to ski on Uludağ.

Bursa

21

Draped ribbon-like along the leafy lower slopes of Mount Uludağ (Great Mountain), which towers more than 2000m above it, the city of **Bursa** overlooks the fertile plain of the Nilüfer Çayı. It manages to do more justice to its setting than any other Turkish city, with the possible exception of Istanbul. The Ottoman Empire's first capital, it contains some of the finest early Ottoman monuments in the Balkans, nestled within (mostly) appealing neighbourhoods.

Industrialization over the last four decades and a population fast approaching three million mean that the city has lost some of its former elegance. Silk and textile manufacture, plus patronage of the area's thermal baths by the elite, were for centuries the most important enterprises. Today manufacturing takes precedence, with Tofaş (Fiat), Renault and Bosch all having major plants here, supplemented by canneries and bottlers processing the rich harvest of the plain. Following the upheavals of the late nineteenth and early twentieth centuries, Bursa was flooded with immigrants from former Balkan possessions of the Ottoman Empire. The vast numbers of more recent migrants, however, attracted by job opportunities at the various factories, hail from rural, poverty-stricken eastern Anatolia.

Uludağ University also makes its presence felt; students provide a necessary leavening in what might otherwise be a uniformly conservative community. Some of this atmosphere derives from Bursa's historic role as first capital of the Ottoman Empire: it is the burial place of the first six sultans and their authority emanates from the mosques, tombs and social-welfare foundations built at their command. Relatively few Westerners visit Bursa but Arabs come here in droves, attracted by the city's Islamic sights, the bath-houses clustered round the hot springs and the green cool of Uludağ.

Some history

Although the area had been settled at least a millennium previously, the first city here was founded early in the second century BC by Prusias I. A king of ancient Bithynia, he named the town **Proussa** after himself, in typically Hellenistic fashion. Legend claims that Hannibal helped him pick the location of the acropolis, today's Hisar.

Overshadowed by nearby Nicomedia (modern İzmit) and Nicaea (İznik), the city stagnated until the **Romans**, attracted by its natural hot springs, began spending lavish amounts on public baths and made it capital of their province of Mysia. Justinian introduced sericulture (rearing silkworms to produce silk), and Byzantine Proussa flourished until the Arab raids of the seventh and eighth centuries, and the subsequent tug-of-war for sovereignty between the Selçuks and the Greeks, precipitated its decline. During – and after – the Latin interlude in Constantinople (1204–61), the Byzantines reconsolidated their hold on Proussa, but not for long.

The start of the fourteenth century saw a small band of nomadic Turks, led by one **Osman Gazi**, camped outside the walls of Proussa. The city capitulated in 1326, following a ten-year siege, to Osman's son, Orhan, and the **Ottomans** ceased to be a wandering tribe of marauders. Orhan marked the acquisition of a capital and the organization of an infant state by styling himself sultan, giving the city its present name and striking coinage. Bursa began to enjoy a second golden age: the silk industry was expanded and the city, outgrowing the confines of the original settlement, clustered around a citadel, was adorned with monuments.

In the years following Orhan's death in 1362, the imperial capital was gradually moved to Edirne, but Bursa's place in history, and in the hearts of the Ottomans, was ensured; succeeding sultans continued to add buildings and to be laid to rest here for another hundred years. Disastrous fires and earthquakes in the mid-nineteenth century, and the War of Independence, only slightly diminished the city's splendour.

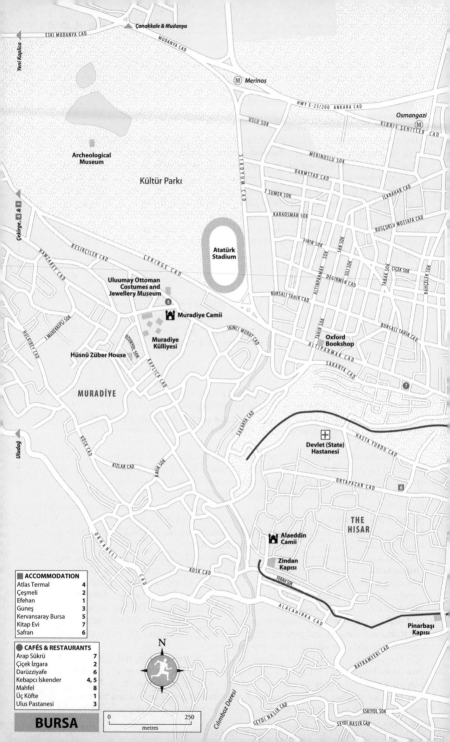

ESKI MUDANYA CAD

Çanakkale & Mudanya

MUDANYA CAD

Yeni Kaplıca

M Merinos

HWY E-23/200 ANKARA CAD

USLU SOK

Osmangazi

KIBRIS ŞEHİTLER CAD

M

MERINOSLU SOK

Archeological
Museum

Kültür Parkı

DARMSTAD CAD

STADYUM CAD

İLKBAHAR CAD

J SUMER SOK

KARAOSMAN SOK

RUŞÇUKLU MUSTAFA CAD

Çekirge, 4 & 5

FIRIN SOK

SAN SOK

BEŞİKÇİLER CAD

ÇEKİRGE CAD

Atatürk
Stadium

ALTIPARMAK SOK

DEĞİRMEN CAD

SİLİ SOK

TABAK SOK

ÇİÇEK SOK

BAHÇELER SOK

HAMZABEY CAD

Uluumay Ottoman
Costumes and
Jewellery Museum

6

BURSALI TAHİR CAD

İ MÜDENEKY SOK

Muradiye Camii

BURSALI TAHİR CAD

HİLKREST CAD

Muradiye
Külliyesi

İKİNCİ MURAT CAD

TAHİR SOK

Oxford
Bookshop

Hüsnü Züber House

MEDNYOL SOK

ALTIPARMAK CAD

SAKARYA CAD

7

MURADİYE

KAPILCA CAD

Uludağ

KÖŞK CAD

BAHÇE SOK

SAKARYA CAD

Devlet (State)
Hastanesi

NASTA YURDU CAD

KIZLAR CAD

ORTAPAZAR CAD

6

THE
HISAR

ORHANELİ CAD

Alaeddin
Camii

KÖŞK CAD

Zindan
Kapısı

FERAH SOK

ALACAHIRKA CAD

Pınarbaşı
Kapısı

BAYRAMYERİ CAD

SEYDİ NASIR CAD

Cilimboz Deresi

ESKIYOL SOK

SEYDİ NASIR CAD

N

ACCOMMODATION

Atlas Termal	4
Çeşmeli	2
Efehan	1
Guneş	3
Kervansaray Bursa	5
Kitap Evi	7
Safran	6

CAFÉS & RESTAURANTS

Arap Sükrü	7
Çiçek İzgara	2
Darüzziyafe	6
Kebapcı İskender	4, 5
Mahfel	8
Üç Köfte	1
Ulus Pastanesi	3

0   250
metres

BURSA

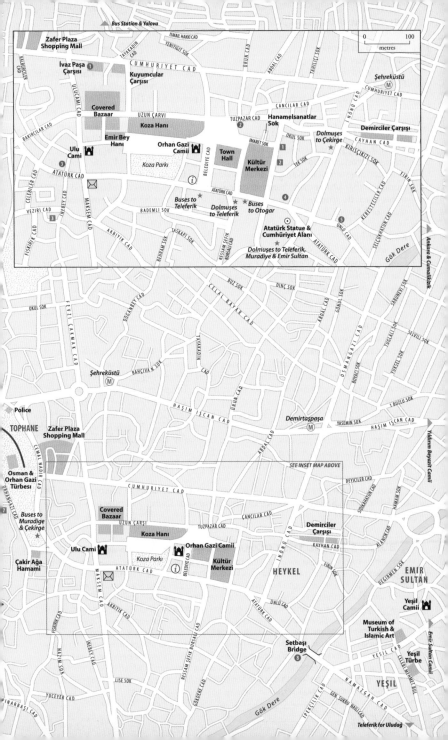

Bus Station & Yalova

Zafer Plaza
Shopping Mall

İSMAİL HAKKI CAD

İvaz Paşa
Çarşısı

KUYUMCULAR
Çarşısı

CUMHURİYET CAD

Şehreküstü
CUMHURİYET CAD

Covered
Bazaar

UZUN ÇARVİ

Koza Hanı

Emir Bey
Hanı

Ulu
Cami

Orhan Gazi
Camii

Town
Hall

Kültür
Merkezi

Hanamelsanatlar
Sok

Dolmuşes
to Çekirge

Demirciler Çarşısı

CAYHAN CAD

ATATÜRK CAD

Koza Parkı

BADEMLİ SOK

Buses to
Teleferik

Dolmuşes to
Teleferik

Buses
to Otogar

ATATÜRK CAD

AKBIYIK CAD

TAŞKAPI SOK

Atatürk Statue &
Cumhuriyet Alanı

Dolmuşes to Teleferik,
Muradiye & Emir Sultan

Ankara & Cumalıkızık

Gök Dere

0   100
metres

BUZ SOK

DİNÇ SOK

CELAL BAYAR CAD

DOĞANBEY CAD

FEVZİ ÇAKMAK CAD

OKUL SOK

Şehreküstü

BAHÇİVAN SOK

TAYAKADIN CAD

URUN CAD

ABDAL CAD

OSMANGAZİ CAD

HAŞİM İŞCAN CAD

Demirtaşpaşa

YASEMİN SOK

HAŞİM İŞCAN CAD

Yıldırım Beyazıt Camii

Police

TOPHANE

Zafer Plaza
Shopping Mall

CEMAL NADİR CAD

Osman &
Orhan Gazi
Türbesi

Buses to
Muradiye
& Çekirge

Çakır Ağa
Hamamı

ORHANGAZİ CAD

SEE INSET MAP ABOVE

Covered
Bazaar

UZUN ÇARŞI

CUMHURİYET CAD

Koza Hanı

TUZPAZAR CAD

ÇANCILAR CAD

Demirciler
Çarşısı

Ulu Cami

Orhan Gazi Camii

KAYHAN CAD

Koza Parkı

Kültür
Merkezi

BELEDİYE CAD

İMNÜ CAD

FIRIN SOK

HEYKEL

EMİR
SULTAN

ATATÜRK CAD

MAKSEM CAD

AKBIYIK CAD

FİSKİRLİ CAD

İNEBEY CAD

RESSAM ŞEFİK BURSALI CAD

GÖZDERE CAD

ÜNLÜ CAD

DEYİCİLER CAD

SÜLEYMANİYE CAD

NAMAZ SOK

ALİNCCAD

DEĞİRMEN SOK

Yeşil
Camii

Museum of
Turkish &
Islamic Art

Yeşil
Türbe

Setbaşı
Bridge

Emir Sultan Camii

YEŞİL

NAMAZGAH CAD

GÖZDERE CAD

LİSE SOK

NAZIM SOK

YÜCEYER CAD

PINARBAŞI CAD

İPEKÇİLİK CAD

GEN SUKRU NAİLCAD

Gök Dere

ÇELEBİ MEHMET BUL

YEŞİL

YEŞİL CAD

Teleferik for Uludağ

21

Orhan Gazi Camii
Orhan Gazi Meydanı

The 1336 foundation of the **Orhan Gazi Camii** makes it Bursa's second-oldest mosque. Originally built as a *zaviye* for itinerant dervishes, this is the earliest example of the T-form mosque, with *eyvans* flanking the main prayer hall. The large central dome boasts eight windows which let light flood into the interior. The single minaret was not part of the original design, and wasn't erected until 1846, when the mosque was restored by the French architect Léon Parvillée. **Karagöz puppets**, the painted camel-leather props used in the Turkish national shadow-play, are supposed to represent workers who were involved in building the Orhan Gazi Camii. According to legend, the antics of Karagöz and his sidekick Hacıvat so distracted their fellow workmen that Orhan had them beheaded. Later, missing the comedians and repenting of his deed, he arranged to immortalize the pair in the art form that now bears the name of Karagöz.

Koza Parkı
Between Atatürk and Uzun Çarşısı Caddesis

Compact, paved **Koza Parkı**, with its fountains, benches and street-level cafés, is the real heart of Bursa. It's very busy throughout the day and early evening, but the plaza empties soon after dusk and the walkways are deserted by 11pm – no doubt owing much to the fact that none of the places to eat around here are licensed.

Ulu Cami
Corner of Atatürk and Ulu Cami Caddesis

On the far side of Koza Parkı looms the tawny limestone **Ulu Cami**, built between 1396 and 1399 by Yıldırım Beyazıt I, from the proceeds of booty won from the Crusaders at Macedonian Nicopolis. Before the battle, Yıldırım (meaning "Thunderbolt") had vowed to construct twenty mosques if victorious. The present building of twenty domes supported by twelve free-standing pillars was his rather loose interpretation of this promise, but it was still the largest and most ambitious Ottoman mosque of its time. The interior is dominated by a huge *şadırvan* pool in the centre, whose skylight was once open to the elements, and an intricate walnut *mimber* (pulpit) pieced together, it's claimed, without nails or glue. Its glass central dome allows light to flood in, illuminating the hordes of local and foreign Muslim pilgrims as they pray or sit and relax in the peaceful interior.

From the north porch of the mosque, you can descend stairs to the two-storey **Emir Bey Hanı**, originally a dependency of the Orhan Gazi Camii and now home to various offices and shops.

BURSA SILK AND THE COCOON AUCTION

The highlight of the year in Bursa is the **cocoon auction** of late June and early July, when silkworm breeders from around the province gather to hawk their valuable produce. At this time, Bursa's Koza Hanı becomes a mass of white torpedoes, each one about the size of a songbird's egg; the moth, when it hatches, is a beautiful, otherworldly creature with giant onyx eyes and feathery antennae. As long as you're careful, the merchants don't mind you walking the floor; alternatively you can watch the melee from the upper arcades.

After being sent into a tailspin by French and Italian competition two hundred years ago, the Bursa silk trade has recently experienced a tentative revival of sorts. However, the quality of contemporary fabric cannot compare to museum pieces from the early Ottoman heyday and most of the better designs are made up in imported material, which is, however, still better quality than the Turkish. If you're buying silk in Bursa make sure the label says *ipek* (silk) and not *ithal ipek* (artificial silk).

The bazaar quarter
Around Uzun Çarşısı Caddesi

As you would expect of a prominent settlement astride one of the many branches of the ancient silk route, trade and commerce have long been mainstays of the local economy. From the Ottoman period onwards, the heart of this commercial activity was a **complex of bazaars** to the north and east of Bursa's main mosque, the Ulu Cami (see p.244).

Koza Hanı
North side of Koza Parkı • Daily 8am–8pm

The centrepiece of the bazaar quarter is the **Koza Hanı**, or "Silk-Cocoon Hall" (see box opposite), flanking Koza Parkı close to the Orhan Gazi Camii (see opposite). Built in 1491, when Bursa was the final stop on the Silk Route from China, it's still filled with silk and brocade merchants (plus a few jewellery stores), and prices are generally far cheaper than in Istanbul. On the lower level, in the middle of a cobbled courtyard, a miniscule *mescit* (small mosque) perches directly over its *şadırvan*, while a subsidiary court bulges asymmetrically to the east; there are teahouses and public benches in both.

Covered Bazaar and Bedesten
North of Uzun Çarşısı • Mon–Sat 9am–7pm

The assorted galleries and lesser halls that comprise the covered bazaar are a delight for shoppers hunting for ready-to-wear clothing, silk goods, towels and bolts of cloth and furniture. The nearby *bedesten* is given over to the sale and warehousing of jewellery and precious metals.

Demirciler Çarşısı and beyond
Around İnönü Caddesi • Mon–Sat 9am–7pm

Despite quake and blaze, the **Demirciler Çarşısı**, or Ironmongers' Market, has kept its traditions intact. This market is on the east side of İnönü Caddesi, best crossed by the pedestrian underpass at Okcular Caddesi. Stall upon stall of blacksmiths and braziers attract photographers, but be advised that some expect a tip for posing. From here, you can easily continue past a small mosque and some cabinet-makers' workshops to **Fırın Sokak**, which is lined with some of the finest old dwellings in town. At the end of this, the Irgandı Sanat Köprüsü bridge spans the **Gök Dere**, one of two streams that tumble through Bursa, forming an approximate eastern boundary for the centre. The bridge, an ill-advised copy of Florence's Ponte Vecchio, is lined with small shops and cafés, all struggling for business.

Yeşil Cami and Yeşil Türbe
Yeşil Caddesi • Yeşil Türbe opens daily 8am–noon & 1–5pm • Free

A few minutes' walk east of the city centre, across the Gök Dere stream, the neighbourhood of Yeşil is built around its namesake mosque and tombs. Designed by the architect Hacı Ivaz, the **Yeşil Camii** sits atop a slight rise and was begun in 1413 by Çelebi Mehmet I, victor of the civil war caused by the death of Beyazıt I. The mosque is unfinished; work ceased in 1424, three years after Mehmet himself died, and it has endured severe damage from two nineteenth-century earth tremors. But it's easily the most spectacular of Bursa's imperial mosques, well deserving of the restoration work it underwent in 2014.

The incomplete entrance, faced in a light marble, is all the more easy to examine for the lack of a portico; above the stalactite vaulting and relief calligraphy you can see the supports for arches never built. A foyer supported by pilfered Byzantine columns leads to the **interior**, a variation on the T-plan usually reserved for dervish *zaviyes*. A fine *şadırvan* occupies the centre of the "T", but your eye is monopolized by the hundreds of polychrome **tiles** that line the *mihrab* and, indeed, every available vertical surface up to five metres in height, particularly two recesses flanking the entryway.

21

Green and blue pigments matching the carpets predominate, and praying amid this dimly lit majesty must feel something akin to worshipping inside a leaf. Tucked above the foyer, and usually closed to visitors, is the **imperial loge**, the most extravagantly decorated chamber of all. Several artisans from Tabriz participated in the tiling of Yeşil Camii but the loge is attributed to Al-Majnun, whose name translates as "intoxicated on hashish".

On the same knoll as the mosque, and immediately across the pedestrian precinct separating them, the **Yeşil Türbe** contains the sarcophagus of Çelebi Mehmet I and his assorted offspring. Inside, the walls and Mehmet's tomb glisten with the glorious original Tabriz material.

Museum of Turkish and Islamic Arts
Türk ve İslam Eserleri Müzesi • Yeşil Caddesi • Tues–Sun 8am–noon & 1–5pm • Free

The *medrese* (theology academy) just east of the Yeşil Camii now houses Bursa's Museum of Turkish and Islamic Arts, built around a pleasant courtyard with a fountain, trees and picnic tables. If the museum is short-staffed, certain rooms may be closed, but in theory you can view İznik ware, Çanakkale ceramics, kitchen utensils, inlaid wooden articles, weapons and a mock-up of an Ottoman *sünnet odası* (circumcision chamber). There's also a case containing some fine Karagöz shadow-puppets, for which the city is famous.

Emir Sultan Camii
Doyran Caddesi

The **Emir Sultan Camii**, a 300m-walk east of Yeşil, can be found among extensive graveyards where every religious Bursan hopes to be buried. The mosque was originally endowed to three sultans by a Bokharan dervish and trusted adviser, beginning with Beyazıt I. But it has just been restored again after enduring an Ottoman Baroque overhaul early last century, so you can only guess as to what's left of the original essence. The pious, however, seem to harbour no doubts, coming in strength to worship at the tombs of the saint and his family.

Yıldırım Beyazıt Camii
3km northeast of the city centre

Perched on a small hillock at the northeastern edge of the city, the **Yıldırım Beyazıt Camii** is a substantial hike from downtown – take a dolmuş (marked "Heykel–Beyazıt Yıldırım" or the more common "Heykel–Fakülte") from the dolmuş terminus behind the Atatürk statue on Cumhüriyet Alanı, which passes 200m below the mosque. Completed by Beyazıt I between 1390 and 1395, the Beyazıt Camii features a handsome, five-arched portico defined by square columns. The interior is unremarkable except for a gravity-defying arch bisecting the prayer hall, its lower supports tapering away to end in stalactite moulding. The only other note of whimsy in this spare building is the use of elaborate niches out on the porch.

The associated **medrese**, exceptionally long and narrow because of its sloping site, huddles just downhill; today, it's used as a medical clinic. The **türbe** (tomb) of the luckless Beyazıt, kept in an iron cage by the rampaging Tamerlane until his death in 1403, is usually locked. Perhaps the mosque custodians fear a revival of the Ottoman inclination to abuse the tomb of the most ignominiously defeated sultan.

The Hisar

The **Hisar**, the citadel area that was Bursa's original nucleus, nowadays retains just a few clusters of dilapidated Ottoman housing within its warren of narrow lanes and some courses of medieval wall along its perimeter. From where Atatürk Caddesi becomes Cemal Nadir Caddesi, just short of the distinctive glass pyramid marking the **Zafer Plaza** mall, it's possible to clamber up the pedestrian walkways to the summit of Hisar.

The view from the cliff-top **park** at the summit, sprawling around the tombs and clock tower, is impressive, with reasonable cafés at the head of the walkways leading down to Cemal Nadir and Altıparmak *caddesi*s. From either of these streets you can follow signs west to Muradiye (see below), along the most direct route, or by veering inland for a walk around the neighbourhood. At the southernmost extreme of the citadel, you exit at the **Pınarbaşı Kapısı**, the lowest point in the circuit of walls and the spot where Orhan's forces finally entered the city in 1326. From there you can stroll parallel to the walls, re-entering at the **Zindan Kapısı**, inside of which is the simple **Alaeddin Camii**, erected within a decade of the Conquest and therefore the oldest mosque in Bursa.

A more straightforward route follows Hasta Yurdu Caddesi until another generous swathe of park studded with teahouses opens out opposite the public hospital. The furthest teahouses have fine views of the Muradiye district and, from the final café and section of wall, easy-to-find stairs descend to the **Cılımboz Deresi**, the second major stream to furrow the city.

Muradiye

Dolmuşes regularly depart from the stand behind Heykel (the Atatürk statue on Cumhüriyet Alanı) in Bursa's city centre; buses #2/A and #6/F2 leave from the stop at the southern end of Cemal Nadir Caddesi

Across Cılımboz Deresi from the Hisar lies medieval **Muradiye**, a green and pleasant suburb where Bursa's best-preserved Ottoman-era dwellings line quiet streets that spring into life for the Tuesday **street market**. The centrepiece of this tranquil district is the **Muradiye Külliyesi**, a mosque complex begun in 1424 by Murat II. It was the last imperial foundation in Bursa, though the tombs for which the mosque complex is famous were added piecemeal over the next century or so.

Muradiye Külliyesi Türbesi

Daily: May–Sept 8am–noon & 1–5pm; Oct–April 8am–5pm • Free

The ten royal tombs, **Muradiye Külliyesi Türbesi**, are set in tranquil gardens shaded by towering pine and plane trees. Should any of the entrances to the tombs be locked, there are custodians on site who will open up for you. The first tomb is that of **Şehzade Ahmet** and his brother Şehinşah, both murdered in 1513 by their cousin Selim I to preclude any succession disputes. The opulence of the İznik tiles within contrasts sharply with the adjacent austerity of **Murat II's tomb**, where Roman columns inside and a wooden awning out front are the only extravagances. Murat, as much contemplative mystic as warrior-sultan, was the only Ottoman ruler ever to abdicate voluntarily, though pressures of state forced him to leave the company of his dervishes and return to the throne after just two years. He was the last sultan to be interred at Bursa and one of the few lying here who died in his bed; in accordance with his wishes, both the coffin and the dome were originally open to the sky "so that the rain of heaven might wash my face like any pauper's".

Next along is the tomb of **Şehzade Mustafa**, Süleyman the Magnificent's murdered heir; perhaps a sign of his father's remorse, the tomb is done up in extravagantly floral İznik tiles, with a top border of calligraphy. Nearby stands the tomb of **Cem Sultan**, his elder brother Mustafa and two of Beyazıt II's sons, decorated with a riot of abstract, botanical and calligraphic paint strokes up to the dome. Cem, the cultured and favourite son of Mehmet the Conqueror, was one of the Ottoman Empire's most interesting might-have-beens. Following the death of his father in 1481, he lost a brief dynastic struggle with the successful claimant, his brother Beyazıt II, and fled abroad. For fourteen years he wandered, seeking sponsorship of his cause from Christian benefactors who in all cases became his jailers: first the Knights of St John at Rhodes and Bodrum, later the papacy. At one point, it seemed that he would command a Crusader army organized to retake Istanbul, but all such plans came to grief for the simple reason that Beyazıt anticipated his opponents' moves and each time bribed them

21

handsomely to desist, making Cem a lucrative prisoner indeed. His usefulness as a pawn exhausted, Cem was probably poisoned in Italy by the pope in 1495, leaving nothing but reams of poems aching with nostalgia and homesickness.

Hüsnü Züber House

Uzunyol Sok 3 • Tues–Sun 10am–noon & 1–5pm • ₺3

The **Hüsnü Züber House**, a former Ottoman guesthouse built in 1836, sports a typically Ottoman overhanging upper storey, wooden roof and beams and a garden courtyard. It now houses a collection of carved wooden musical instruments, spoons and farming utensils, many of which were made by the artist and pyrographer Hüsnü Züber himself, the present owner, who lives there. The main exhibit, however, is the house itself, one of the few of its era to have been faithfully, meticulously restored and opened to the public.

Uluumay Ottoman Costumes and Jewellery Museum

Murat Cad 2 • Daily 9am–6pm • ₺5

Housed in the cells of the former theological college of Dair Ahmet Paşa Medresesi, the **Uluumay Ottoman Costumes and Jewellery Museum** displays a range of original traditional costumes from all over the former Ottoman domains – from Kosovo and Bursa to Bosnia and Zonguldak on Turkey's Black Sea. The mannequins the costumes are displayed on revolve in their glass cases when you enter the room and give a vivid impression of the ethnic hodge-podge that was the Ottoman Empire. There's a pleasant garden-café out back where local musicians sometimes hang out and play the flute and the *saz*, a long-necked lute-like instrument favoured by Turkish folk musicians.

Kültür Parkı

Token admission charge when entry booths are staffed

Sprawling **Kültür Parkı**, a kilometre or so from the city centre, is best reached from Çekirge Caddesi, through the southeast gate. Inside the park, there's a popular tea garden, a small boating lake, a mini-zoo, and a number of restaurants and *gazino*-style nightclubs. As you stroll, however, it quickly becomes obvious that there's no potential for solitude – though courting couples try their best – and no wild spots among the regimented plantations and too-broad driveways.

Archeology Museum

Arkeoloji Müzesi • Tues–Sun 8am–12.30pm & 1.30–5pm • ₺5

At the west end of Kültür Parkı, just below Çekirge Caddesi, is the Archeological Museum. Exhibits in the Stone Room vary from the macabre (a Byzantine ossuary with a skull peeking out) to the homely (a Roman cavalryman figurine), but the adjacent hall featuring metal jewellery from all over Anatolia – watch chains, breastplates, belts, buckles, bracelets, anklets, chokers – steals the show. The west wing houses a modest coin gallery and miscellaneous small, ancient objects, the best of which are the Roman glass items and Byzantine and Roman bronzes. Oil lamps, pottery, a token amount of gold and far too many ceramic figurines complete these poorly labelled exhibits; while a garden of sarcophagi, stelae and other statuary fragments surrounds the building.

Çekirge

Buses (including the #2/A), as well as dolmuşes, shuttle to and from the dolmuş stand near the tourist office on Atatürk Caddesi

The thermal centre of **Çekirge** (meaning "Grasshopper" and presumably a reference to the natural soundtrack of a summer evening) lies two kilometres northwest of the city centre. Most visitors come here to experience the Çekirge hot springs, which flow out of Uludağ's mountainside and are tapped into by the various hotels and bath-houses.

Yeni Kaplıca

Daily 7am–11pm • ₺17; scrub ₺17, soap massage ₺22, oil massage ₺35

The male-only **Yeni Kaplıca** ("New Baths") are accessible by a steep driveway beginning opposite the *Çelik Palas Oteli*, lying just beyond the Kültür Parkı (see p.248). In their present form, the baths date from the mid-sixteenth century. According to legend, Süleyman the Magnificent was cured of gout after a dip in the Byzantine baths here and he ordered his vizier Rüstem Paşa to completely overhaul the building. Fragments of mosaic paving stud the floor, and the walls are lined with once exquisite but now blurred İznik tiles.

Eski Kaplıca

Daily 7am–10.30pm • Men ₺28, women ₺24; scrub ₺18, soap massage ₺28

The wonderful **Eski Kaplıca** (Old Baths), huddled at the far end of Çekirge Caddesi, next to the *Kervansaray Bursa Hotel*, are Bursa's most ancient baths (and much the nicest public bath for women). Byzantine rulers Justinian and Theodora first improved a Roman spa on the site, and Murat I in turn had a go at the structure in the late fourteenth century. Huge but shallow keyhole-shaped pools dominate the *hararetler*, or hot rooms, of the men's and women's sections, whose domes are supported by eight Byzantine columns. Scalding (45°C) water pours into the notch of the keyhole, the temperature still so taxing in the main basin that you'll soon be gasping out into the cool room, seeking relief at the fountain in the middle.

Hüdavendigar (Birinci) Murat Camii

On a hillock just west of the Çekirge thermal centre stands the **Hüdavendigar (Birinci) Murat Camii**, which, with its five-arched portico and alternating bands of brick and stone, seems more like a church teleported from Ravenna or Macedonia than a mosque. Indeed, tradition asserts that the architect and builders were Christians, who dallied twenty years at the task because Murat I, whose pompous epithet literally means "Creator of the Universe", was continually off at war and unable to supervise the work. The interior plan, consisting of a first-floor *medrese* above a highly modified, T-type *zaviye* at ground level, is unique in Islam. The upper storey, wrapped around the courtyard that's the heart of the place, is unfortunately rarely open to visitors.

Murat himself lies, embalmed, in the much-modified **türbe** across the street – complete apart from his entrails, which were removed by the embalmers before the body began its long journey back from Serbia in 1389. In June of that year, Murat was in the process of winning his greatest triumph over the Serbian king Lazarus and his allies at the **Battle of Kosovo**, in the former Yugoslavia, when he was stabbed to death in his tent by Milod Obiliç, a Serbian noble who had feigned desertion. Murat's son Beyazıt, later better known as Yıldırım, immediately had his brother Yakub strangled and, once in sole command, decimated the Christian armies. Beyazıt's acts had two far-reaching consequences: the Balkans remained under Ottoman control until early in the twentieth century, and a gruesome precedent of blood-spilling was established for most subsequent Ottoman coronations.

ARRIVAL AND DEPARTURE
BURSA

By bus Regular buses (from ₺23) depart from Istanbul's Harem and Esenler stations (see p.24), taking 3hr from Harem, 4hr from Esenler depending on traffic. Buses arrive and depart from the bus station (☎ 0224 261 5400) 10km north of Bursa; to get there, catch the #38 opposite the town hall on Atatürk Cad. Çağlar, Kamil Koç, Pamukkale and several other companies run between Istanbul and Bursa and vice versa (with ferry transfer).

By sea bus The high-speed sea bus (ⓦ ido.com.tr) takes 70min (from ₺11) from Yenikapı ferry terminal to Yalova, from where buses and dolmuşes (₺10–15, depending on the company) run to Bursa (around 50min). Either way, you'll arrive at Bursa's bus station, 10km north of town on the Yalova road. To get to the city centre, take a yellow #38 bus; buy a ticket (₺3) from the kiosk before boarding. Alternatively, catch one of the (less frequent) crossings

21

from Yenikapı to Güzelyalı (90min) and then a bus or dolmuş to the start of Bursa's metro system, at Organize Sanayı (30min). Once on the metro, travel to the Dehreküstü stop, from where it's a 15min walk south to the city centre.

By sea plane A novel, if more expensive, way to reach

Bursa from Istanbul is with Seabird (⊕ seabird.com). Sea planes take off from Istanbul's Golden Horn (Haliç), giving passengers great views of the old city from the air, with prices from ₺125 one way. Planes land at Gemlik, from where the #101 bus runs every 10min to Gemlik centre; frequent buses to Bursa take around 25min.

INFORMATION

Tourist information The tourist office can be found in Koza Parkı, opposite Orhan Gazi Camii, in a row of shops

under the north side of Atatürk Cad (Mon–Fri 8am–noon & 1–5pm; ☎ 0224 220 1848).

GETTING AROUND

Bursa's position at the foot of the mountain has dictated its elongated layout, with most of the major boulevards running from east to west, changing their names several times as they go. Though Bursa is narrow, with many points of interest bunched together, it's sufficiently long enough for you to want to consider **public transport** to reach the outlying attractions.

By bus Only the #2/A (connecting Emir Sultan in the east of town with Çekirge to the west) and the #3/A (linking Heykel with the Uludağ *teleferik*) are the most useful, and you need to buy tickets for them at the kiosks, which are handily located next to most central stops.

By dolmuş Dolmuşes are much simpler to use than the buses (fares start at ₺1.5); appearing in various colours, they all bear destination signs on their roofs, start from fixed points around the city, and pick up and let down passengers at places clearly marked with a large "D".

By metro The new and extensive metro system (daily; 6am–midnight) is not as useful for visitors as it could be, as it doesn't connect the major points of interest, but is handy for travelling to and from the ferry terminal at Güzelyalı (see pp.249–250).

Car rental There are a number of car rental firms in town, including Aktif (Çekirge Cad 139; ☎ 0224 233 0444); Avis (Çekirge Cad 143; ☎ 0224 236 5133); Budget (Çekirge Cad 39/1; ☎ 0224 223 4204); and Europcar (Çekirge Cad 41; ☎ 0224 223 2321).

ACCOMMODATION

Rooms in **reasonably priced hotels** are plentiful in Bursa, as it's a little off the backpackers' trail and often treated as a day-trip from Istanbul. Rich foreigners, particularly Arabs, gravitate toward the **luxury spa-hotels** in the western suburb of Çekirge (see pp.248–249), 4km out of the centre, but there's also a cluster of modest establishments out here, around the **Birinci Murat Camii**. If you're interested in seeing monumental Bursa, then staying centrally, around Atatürk Caddesi, makes more sense.

CENTRAL BURSA

Çeşmeli Gümüşçeken Cad 6 ☎ & ☎ 0224 224 1511, ⊕ cesmelihotel.com. Named after the *çeşme* (fountain) incorporated into the wall to the right of the front door, and much nicer than it looks from the outside, this immaculate, extremely welcoming hotel is run entirely by women. Rooms have minibars, TVs and fans, and a decent buffet breakfast is included. A real home from home. ₺130

Efehan Gümüşçeken Cad 34 ☎ 0224 225 2260, ⊕ efehan.com.tr. Pleasant, three-star comfort in a modern (yet old-looking), centrally located hotel. Extras include minibar and satellite TV. Ask for one of the top rooms for mountain views. ₺120

Guneş İnebey Cad 75 ☎ 0224 222 1404, ☎ otelgunes @yahoo.com. Cheap, clean and friendly, in a much-restored old house with centrally heated rooms; showers and squat toilets are located on the landings. The singles (₺35) are tiny but good value. The backpackers' choice in Bursa, it is

often full of Korean and Japanese travellers. ₺70

★ **Kitap Evi** Burç Üstü 21 ☎ 0224 225 4160, ⊕ kitapevi .com.tr. For those in search of something different, this boutique hotel on the citadel may well suit. There is a mixture of suites and standard doubles on offer, though all are individually furnished and decorated. Front rooms have fine views over Bursa but those facing the rear garden area are quieter. €83

Safran Arka Sok 4, off Ortapazar Cad ☎ 0224 224 7216, ⊕ safranotel.com. A beautifully restored wooden house in the old part of town, up on the Hisar. The nine rooms are modern, with a/c, minibar and TV, and are extremely comfortable. If you want a good-value boutique hotel in a quiet, atmospheric location, this is the place. ₺120

ÇEKIRGE

Atlas Termal Hamamlar Cad 35 ☎ 0224 234 4100, ⊕ atlasotel.com.tr. The full thermal experience for a fraction of the usual price. The *Atlas* has two shiny marble *hamams* set in a mock Art Nouveau interior, as well as a reasonable restaurant, garden courtyard and terrace. The bedrooms are fussily traditional but have flat-screen TVs and boast excellent modern bathrooms. ₺140

Kervansaray Bursa Çekirge Meydanı ☎0224 233

9300, ⓦkervansarayhotels.com. A gargantuan and sumptuous hotel, next to the Eski Kaplıca (see p.249), with an assortment of Turkish baths, saunas and swimming pools (the outdoor one is large enough for a vigorous swim). There are five pricey restaurants and a baby-sitting service. €94

EATING AND DRINKING

Bursa's cuisine is solidly meat-oriented and served in a largely alcohol-free environment, reflecting the city's conservative nature. The best street to get a drink with your meal (or just a drink), is pedestrianized **Sakarya Caddesi**, between Altıparmak Caddesi and the walls of the Hisar above. This former fish market and the main street of the old Jewish quarter has been reborn as an atmospheric place for an outdoor fish dinner or a drink on a summer's evening.

CAFÉS

Mahfel Namazgah Cad 2, Setbaşı Bridge, Heykel. Very popular café in a shady location above the river, dishing up Western- and Turkish-style snacks to a predominantly young set. Desserts from ₺7. Live music weekend evenings. Daily 9am–11pm.

Ulus Pastanesi Öztat Apt 92, Atatürk Cad, Heykel; ⓦuluspastanesi.com. This tiny, old-fashioned shop/café has been going since 1920 and claims to be the oldest producer of *kestane şekeri* (chestnuts boiled and soaked in sugar) in Turkey; it uses no artificial ingredients whatsoever. It also does a mean chocolate cake (₺8); wonderful Turkish coffee; speciality candied figs and orange peel served with a dollop of cream; and a health-giving mulberry syrup (₺5).

RESTAURANTS

★**Arap Sükrü** Kuruçeşme Mah, Sakarya Cad 6 & 29, Tophane. There are actually two rival establishments housed here, owing to fraternal disputes: *Çetin* and *Ahmet*. There's little to choose between them: fish in all shapes and sizes (mains from ₺20, starters from ₺5), with beer, wine or *rakı* to wash it down, are served at tables on both sides of the cobbled street.

★**Çiçek İzgara** Belediye Cad 5, Heykel ⓦcicekizgara .com. The best value centrally for lunch and dinner is this popular place on the upper floor of a period house behind

the Belediye (Town Hall). Flawless service, white-tablecloth elegance and extremely reasonable prices – the house special and award-winning *İzgara köfte* is ₺12, a cheese-stuffed version is ₺13. Great rice pudding, too. Unlicensed. Mon–Sat 10am–11pm.

Darüzziyafe İkinci Murat Cad 36, Muradiye; ⓦdaruzziyafe.com.tr. Housed in the beautifully restored *imaret* (kitchen) of the Muradiye Camii, you couldn't ask for more atmospheric surroundings to try *hünkar beğendi* (lamb stew served on a bed of mashed aubergine) or *mantarlı çoban kavurma* (sautéed meat, mushrooms, peppers and onions). Mains start from ₺12; for dessert try the delicate *keskülü fukara*, a kind of walnut and pistachio fool served with Maraş ice cream. Unlicensed. Daily noon–10pm.

Kebapcı İskender Atatürk Cad 60, Heykel; ⓦiskender .com.tr. If you're in Bursa, you're beholden to sample *İskender* (see box below) – and this is the place to do it. The characterful 1930s building sees a steady stream of locals tucking into the only meal on offer – *İskender*. It's not cheap at ₺22 but the meat is tender, the rich tomato sauce delicious, and the waiters even come around and drizzle melted butter on top to enrich it further. There's another branch on Unlu Cad 7.

Üç Köfte İvaz Paşa Çarşısı 3. The name means "Three Meatballs", which is what you get for ₺12, served up one at a time so the food on your plate is always piping hot. Unlicensed. Mon–Sat 11am–3pm.

BURSA SPECIALITIES

There are two famous dishes particular to Bursa. One is *İskender kebap*. Essentially *döner kebap* soaked in a rich butter, tomato and yoghurt sauce, it was named after its supposed inventor, İskender (Alexander) Usta, a Bursan chef. The other is *İnegöl köftesi*: rich little pellets of mince often laced with cheese (when they're known as *kadarlı köfte*), introduced by Balkan immigrants in the 1930s. *İskender kebap* is rich and extremely filling – think twice before going for the "*bir buçuk porsiyon*" (one-and-a-half portion) on offer in most places. The city is also famous for its *kestane şekeri* (candied chestnuts) which are on sale everywhere – the chocolate-covered ones usually appeal most to the Western palette and make a great alternative to Turkish delight as a gift for friends or family.

21

ENTERTAINMENT

Bursa has relatively few nocturnal or weekend events, and the student contingent is responsible for any concerts that do occur. The **Kültür Merkezi** or Cultural Centre, on Atatürk Caddesi (☎ 0224 223 4461), hosts ever-changing art exhibitions and occasional concerts. The **open-air theatre** in the Kültür Parkı is the main venue for the touristy musical performances and folkloric presentations that form a big part of the annual **Bursa Festival** (June & July; ⊛ bursafestival.org). In early July there's the **Altın Kargöz** international folk-dance competition (⊛ bursa.bel.tr), held in the open-air theatre. It lasts a weekend and brings in teams of colourfully dressed troupes from Georgia and Greece to Taiwan and Mexico.

DIRECTORY

Banks and exchange There are plenty of banks with ATMs on Atatürk Cad, and exchange offices (Mon–Sat 8am–8pm) in the covered bazaar and on Altıparmak Cad.

Bookshop Adım Kitapçılık, Altıparmak Cad 50.

Consulate UK (honorary consulate), Resam Şefik Bursalı Sok, off Başak Cad ☎ 0224 220 0436.

Hamams Head out to Çekirge for Eski Kaplıca (see p.249).

Hospitals Devlet (State) Hastanesi, Hasta Yurdu Cad, Hisar

(☎ 0224 220 0020); Üniversite Hastanesi, P. Tezok Cad, Hastane Sok, Çekirge (☎ 0224 442 8400).

Internet access Bursa is well endowed with internet cafés – a reliable option is Bara Internet on Kocaoğlu Sok.

Left luggage At the bus station (daily 24hr).

Police Cemal Nadir Cad.

Post office Corner of Atatürk and Maksem Cads.

Uludağ

Presiding over Bursa, the 2543-metre-high **Uludağ** is a dramatic, often cloud-cloaked massif, its northern reaches dropping dizzyingly into the city. In ancient times, it was known as the Olympos of Mysia, one of nearly twenty peaks around the Aegean with the name (Olympos being possibly a generic Phoenician or Doric word for "mountain"), and it has a place in mythology as the seat from which the gods watched the battle of Troy (see pp.259–261). Early in the Christian era, the mountain range became a refuge for monks and hermits, who were replaced after the Ottoman conquest by Muslim dervishes.

These days, the scent of grilling meat has displaced the atmosphere of sanctity, since Bursa's natives cram the alpine campsites and picnic grounds on holidays and weekends. Getting there is definitely half the fun if you opt for the **cable car** (*teleferik*; see p.253) which stops at Kadı Yayla pastures (1231m), where shepherds still graze their flocks in a forest clearance. You can get off and wander around here before continuing up to the last stop at the **Sarıalan** picnic grounds (1635m), where a cluster of cafés and trinket shops await. Despite the weekend and holiday-period hordes, it's a pretty spot, with curious rock-outcrops, forest all around and the distant ridge-line being a marked contrast to the concrete of Bursa below.

Much of the dense middle-altitude forest has been designated a **national park**, and there are several marked hiking trails from Sarıalan. In fact, the best part of the mountain lies outside the park to the east, where a few hours' walking will bring you to some glacial **lakes** in a wild, rocky setting just below the highest summit. The prime months for a visit are May and June, when the wild flowers are blooming, or September and October, when the mist is less dense. However, due to its proximity to the Sea of Marmara, the high ridges trap moist marine air, and whiteouts or violent storms can blow up during many months of the year.

SKIING ON ULUDAĞ

Skiing is possible on Uludağ from December to March (though it's better earlier in the season than later). There's a dense cluster of hotels, some with their own ski lift, at **Oteller** (1800m), where you can rent skis and ski clothes. There are thirteen different skiing areas around Oteller (around ₺50/day for a lift pass), which are served by eight chairlifts and seven T-bars. Prices and lift queues rise dramatically at weekends and during public holidays, especially in the New Year and the school mid-winter break (usually the last week in Jan and the first in Feb).

ARRIVAL AND DEPARTURE

ULUDAĞ

By cable car To reach the lower cable-car terminus from Bursa, take a dolmuş labelled "Teleferik" from the semi-underground rank behind the Atatürk statue (just south of Atatürk Cad). The wobbly *teleferik* gondolas (daily: every 10–40min; outward 8am–10pm; return 7.50am–10.20pm; ₺20 return) stop first at Kadı Yayla before continuing up to Sarıalan every 10min or so in peak periods, but do not run in high winds. Long queues are the norm at weekends and in the summer school holidays (mid-June to mid-Sept). Sarıalan, at the top, has an army of dolmuşes waiting to take you to Oteller.

By dolmuş The alternative is to take a dolmuş all the way to Oteller (₺9), which winds the 32km of paved road up from Bursa's Orhangazi Cad, though it can

occasionally be difficult to muster the necessary number of passengers (six).

By car It's possible to follow the same route as the dolmuşes in your own vehicle, the road veering off above Çekirge and climbing rapidly through successive vegetation zones. Staff at the Karabelen National Park gate, 20km into the park, charge ₺5/car when they're in the mood and sometimes have information to hand out. The final stretch of road, from just below the gate to the hotels at Oteller, is very rough cobblestone, designed to prevent drivers from skidding – or speeding – so allow an hour for the trip. In bad weather, you'll be advised to put chains on your wheels – and you may not be allowed to make the journey without them.

ACCOMMODATION

There's little difference between the four- and five-star resort **hotels** at the road's end in Oteller. By far the best option is to check ⓦturkeyskihotels.com or ⓦskiingturkey.com for vacancies, rates and possible package deals. In the skiing season, you'll find rates of over ₺350/night with full board – and no shortage of people prepared to pay – though out-of-season prices at the hotels that remain open can drop to half that.

STATUE COMMEMORATING THE GALLIPOLI BATTLES

Çanakkale, Troy and Gallipoli

Two of history's bloodiest campaigns – one legendary, one all too real – were
played out near the mouth of the Dardanelles, the narrow strait connecting
the Aegean with the Sea of Marmara, some 310km southwest of Istanbul.
The ancient city of Troy, scene of the epic conflict between heroes such as
Achilles and Hector and immortalized by the father of Western literature,
Homer, has long gripped the imaginations of people around the world. A
much more recent conflict, the Allied forces' disastrous attempt to take the
Dardanelles by force during World War I, also has great significance,
particularly for Australians, New Zealanders and the Turks themselves, who
all see it as marking the beginning of their "birth" as independent nations.

The obvious base from which to visit either or both of these sites is the modern town of **Çanakkale**, on the southern, Asian side of the Dardanelles; the World War I landing sites at **Gallipoli** (Gelibolu in Turkish) on the European side of the Dardanelles are a short ferry ride away, and Troy lies just 30km to the south. For the pilgrimage to Gallipoli, some people chose **Eceabat**, at the southern end of the Gelibolu peninsula and opposite Çanakkale, as their base. Its only significance is as the major ferry terminal for the straits, but it's the nearest town to the battlefield and landing sites and takes on a character of its own around ANZAC Day (April 25).

22

Çanakkale

It's the **Dardanelles** (Çanakkale Boğazı) that have defined **Çanakkale**'s history and its place in myth. The area's Classical name, **Hellespont**, is owed to one Helle, who, while escaping from her wicked stepmother on the back of a winged ram, fell into the swift-moving channel and drowned. From Abydos, just northeast of modern Çanakkale, the youth Leander used to swim to Sestos on the European shore for trysts with his lover Hero, until one night he too perished in the currents; in despair, Hero drowned herself as well. Lord Byron narrowly escaped being added to this list of casualties on his swim in the opposite direction in 1810.

The name Çanakkale means "Pottery Castle", after the garish Çanakkale pottery that finds its way into the ethnographic section of every Turkish museum. An appealingly compact waterfront town, Çanakkale is enlivened by the presence of some thirty thousand students at the local university.

North of the ferry terminal, a broad, café-lined esplanade leads to the huge wooden horse model that featured in the 2004 Hollywood film *Troy*. The main focus of interest, however, lies in the cobbled streets running south of the ferry terminal. Here lies the ornate, late nineteenth-century clock tower and the surviving European-style warehouses and houses, a reminder that before the horrors of World War I and the 1923 population exchanges (see p.293) this was a cosmopolitan town, with foreign consulates and Greeks, Jews and Armenians, as well as Turks, making up the local populace. Today, there's a string of lively bars and cafés in these narrow streets.

Brief history

In 480 BC, **Xerxes**' Persian hordes crossed the waters on their way to Greece; and in 411 and 405 BC, the last two naval battles of the **Peloponnesian War** took place in these straits, the final engagement ending in decisive defeat for the Athenian fleet. Twenty centuries later, **Mehmet the Conqueror** constructed the elaborate fortress of Kilitbahir directly opposite the Çimenlik Kale in Çanakkale (which he also built), to tighten the stranglehold being applied to doomed Constantinople. In March 1915, an **Allied** fleet attempting to force the Dardanelles and attack Istanbul was repulsed, with severe losses, by Turkish shore batteries, prompting the even bloodier land campaign usually known as Gallipoli. These days, the straits are still heavily militarized, and modern Çanakkale is very much a navy town.

Naval Museum

Deniz Müzesi • Çimenlik Park • Tues, Wed, Fri–Sun 9am–noon & 1.30–5pm • ₺4

Situated in the pleasant Çimenlik Park, itself adorned with assorted field guns, torpedoes and other vintage weaponry, is the town's Naval Museum. It is housed in the **Çimenlik fortress**, which dates back to 1461, constructed during the reign of Sultan Mehmet the Conqueror. Along with the fortress at Kilitbahir, clearly visible on the other side of the Dardanelles narrows, its purpose was to control the crucial straits. Much paraphernalia from the Gallipoli campaign is on show, including an unexploded 38cm shell fired from the British navy's premier battleship, the *Queen Elizabeth*. North of the fortress and moored to the quay is a replica of the mine-layer **Nusrat** (same hours and ticket as museum), which stymied the Allied fleet by, during the night, re-mining the zones that the French and British had swept clean by day.

Archeology Museum

Arkeoloji Müzesi • Yüzüncü Yıl Caddesi, 2km from the centre of town • Tues, Wed, Fri–Sun 8.30am–noon & 1–5.30pm • ₺5 • Flag down any dolmuş along Atatürk Caddesi signed "Kepez" or "Güzelyalı"; get off at the museum

An hour should be enough to take in the Archeological Museum – the collection is poorly labelled and the interior very gloomy, but some of the exhibits are quite stunning. Most impressive is the Polyxena Sarcophogus, the earliest relief-carved sarcophogus found in Asia Minor, dating back to the sixth century BC. One of the many ornate scenes carved on the side of the funerary monument depicts the sacrifice of Polyxena, a daughter of King Priam of Troy, by Achilles' son, Neoptolemus. Quite different but equally striking is a cabinet of terracotta figurines from ancient Assos. Dating from the fourth century BC, the quality of these grave goods, mainly depicting musicians, is superb. Also look out for the case of gold wreaths and diadems, and a lovely figurine of the goddess Aphrodite. The large garden area is littered with architectural and ceremonial remnants from the Classical-era sarcophagi – including columns, capitals, votive stelae and huge earthenware storage jars.

ARRIVAL AND DEPARTURE — ÇANAKKALE

By bus Regular buses, run by Çanakkale Truva, Metro and Kamil Koç companies, make the 310-kilometre trip to Çanakkale from Istanbul's Esenler bus station (5hr 30min; from ₺50). The bus will drop you near the ferry terminal in the town centre, close to all the listed accommodation, before heading onto the new, out-of-town *otogar* (inter-city bus station). To return the same way, buy your ticket from the bus companies on the south side of Cumhüriyet Meydanı near the tourist office, and along the western end of Cumhüriyet Bul. You can either board near the ferry terminal

VISITING GALLIPOLI AND TROY

The **World War I battlefields and Allied cemeteries** scattered along the Gelibolu (Gallipoli) peninsula are a moving sight, the past violence made all the more poignant by the present beauty of the landscape. The whole area is now either fertile rolling country, or cloaked in thick scrub and pine forest alive with birds, making it difficult to imagine the carnage of 1915. **Troy** lies in an equally haunting landscape, and it's even harder to picture the legendary warlike deeds of Achilles, Agamemnon and Odysseus taking place here. A guided tour of either of these sites can enhance your visit significantly, particularly the World War I battlefields, as there's little public transport and the sites are so widely spread out. The plethora of explanatory panels at Troy, and the convenient local minibuses to the adjacent village of Tevfikiye, make it the easier of the two to visit independently.

GUIDED TOURS

Hassle Free Tours (Cumhuriyet Meydanı 61, ⓣ 0286 213 5969, ⓦ anzachouse.com) operates from the ground floor of the *Anzac House Hostel*. They offer a three-hour Troy tour (daily 8.30am; €32), which returns in time to join their Gallipoli tour, departing around 11.30am (7hr; €40); this includes lunch and a boat trip off the ANZAC landing beaches. Over in Eceabat, *TJ's Hostel* (ⓣ 0286 814 3121, ⓦ anzacgallipolitours.com) offers the same tours a little cheaper, as does the *Crowded House* hostel's travel agency (see p.266). If there are a few of you, it might be worth hiring a car and your own guide for Gallipoli – TJ at *TJ's Hostel* is a mine of information, with an easy-going Aussie/Turkish demeanour, and Kenan Çelik (ⓣ 0532 738 6675, ⓦ kcelik.com) is also renowned. Down at Troy, the local-born expert is Mustafa Aşkin (ⓣ 09 542 243 9359, ⓦ thetroyguide.com), who speaks excellent English and has an engaging personality. Car rental is available in Çanakkale from Delta Rent a Car, Cumhuriyet Meydanı 21/1 (ⓣ 0286 814 1218).

Alternatively, you can book a **tour from Istanbul**. Hassle Free have a branch at Yeni Akbıyık Cad 10 in Sultanahmet (ⓣ 0212 458 5500, ⓦ anzachouse.com) and run gruelling (6.30am–midnight), one-day guided tours visiting the battlefield sites for €99. Again *TJ's* and *Crowded House* offer very similar day-trip deals.

or take the free bus service to the *otogar* and board there.

By sea bus Sea buses depart Yenikapı ferry terminal in Istanbul for Bandırma (2hr; from ₺25), from where frequent buses head on to Çanakkale (2hr 30min; ₺25).

By plane; Anadolu Jet flies from Sabiha Gökçen to Çanakkale airport, from where shuttle buses and taxis make the 7km journey into town.

To Troy and Gallipoli If you don't want to take a tour (see box opposite), catch a dolmuş to Troy from the minibus garage from just under the bridge on Atatürk Cad (daily 9.30am–8.00pm; April–Oct every 30min, Nov–March hourly; ₺6); but you'll need your own transport to reach the battlefield sites in Gallipoli.

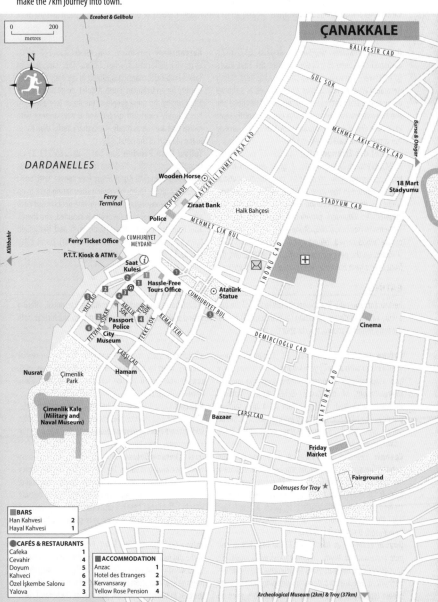

ÇANAKKALE

INFORMATION

Tourist information On Cumhuriyet Meydanı, next to the main dock (May–Sept Mon–Fri 8.30am–7.30pm, Sat & Sun 10.30am–6pm; Oct–April Mon–Fri 8.30am–5.30pm; ☎ 0286 217 1187, ✉ canakkaletourism@hotmail.com).

ACCOMMODATION

Other than around ANZAC Day (April 25), you'll have little trouble finding a room. Just south of the tourist office, the Saat Kulesi (clock tower) signals the entrance to a warren of alleys – Fetvane Sokak, Aralık Sokak, Yeni Sokak – that is home to various inexpensive hotels and *pansiyons*. Moving across Demircioğlu Caddesi, or closer to the water, you'll find the more upmarket hotels.

Anzac Saat Kulesi Meydanı 8 ☎ 0286 217 7777, ⓦ anzachotel.com. Practically opposite the Saat Kulesi (clock tower), this well-run two-star place has neat, plainly decorated en-suite rooms, plus a bath as well as a shower in the immaculate bathrooms. The owners of this hotel and the *Kervansaray* (see opposite) also run the slightly more expensive *Grand Anzac* (ⓦ grandanzachotel.com), around the corner on Kemal Yeri Sok. **₺120**

★ **Hotel des Etrangers** Yalı Cad 25–27 ☎ 0286 214 2424, ⓦ yabancilarioteli.com. A great addition to the local accommodation scene, this eight-room boutique hotel is housed in the same building, and uses the same name, as its 1870 precursor. French-built and run, the original *Des Etrangers* provided lodgings for Heinrich Schliemann (see box, p.260). Stone walls, wooden shutters, ornate wood-carved ceilings and wooden floors help summon up the past without sacrificing comfort, and the front rooms have balconies with partial sea views. **€90**

Kervansaray Fetvahane Sok 13 ☎ 0286 217 8192, ⓦ canakkalekervansarayhotel.com. This unusual (for Turkey) red-brick mansion was built in the early twentieth century for an Ottoman judge. A quiet, polite and friendly affair run by the same people as the *Anzac* (see above), it has a lovely courtyard garden and a new annexe with rooms that are just as comfy, if less characterful than those in the old part of the hotel. **€60**

Yellow Rose Pension Yeni Sok 5 ☎ 0286 217 3343, ⓦ yellowrose.4mg.com. More relaxed and less business orientated than rival *Anzac House* (see above), with basic – but en-suite – rooms of varying sizes dating back to an early 1980s conversion. The two private doubles out back are particularly popular. Breakfast is included, and there's also laundry service, video room, wi-fi and battlefield tours (arranged through *TJ's* over in Eceabat). Dorm **₺30**, double **₺70**

EATING

Restaurants and cafés line almost the full length of the quayside, both north and south of the main ferry terminal, offering a wide variety of dishes, including (as you'd expect) plenty of fish and seafood. As a simple rule of thumb, the further from the ferry terminal you go, the cheaper the prices.

Caféka Cumhuriyet Meydanı 28. Çanakkale's most stylish bistro with a funky yet elegant indoor dining space and a surprisingly affordable menu, including modern interpretations of traditional dishes such as spiced meatballs with herb yoghurt, chilli salsa and sautéed potatoes. The big salad bowls and assorted pasta dishes on offer are good value. Mains **₺10–20**. Daily 10am–midnight.

Cevahir Fetvane Sok 15/a. A very popular and good-value spot serving home-cooked food. Choose a medium or large plate (**₺8** and **₺10** respectively) and have it filled up with anything from chickpea stew to stewed okra, then help yourself to salad. A few tables dot the square outside in the warmer months. Unlicensed. Daily 10am–10pm.

Doyum Cumhuriyet Meydanı 13. The best kebab and *pide* restaurant in town, always packed with locals. It's spotlessly clean, the waitresses are attentive and the dishes well priced. The *kaşarlı pide* comes dripping with its tasty cheese topping, and the kebabs are tender. They even do

içli köfte, a spicy meatball wrapped in a bulgur-wheat coating. You'd be hard-pushed to spend more than **₺20**, considerably less if you go for *lahmacun* or *pide*. Daily 8am–midnight.

Kahcevi Çarşı Cad 14. The best place in town for latte, filter coffee and the like, this trendy little place has tables laid out on a quiet pedestrianized street just down from the Yalı mosque. Daily 10am–11pm.

Özel İşkembe Salonu Saat Kulesi Meydanı. A busy place specializing in soups. Try the delicious *ezogelin* (spicy lentil and tomato) or the hangover-curing tripe soup. There's even a brain soup, which is hard to find outside Istanbul. The bread here is a rarity too, a dense brown, and *ayran* is served in little bottles. Very popular with locals. Daily 8am–midnight.

Yalova Eski Gümrükhane Sok 7. Established in the 1930s in the old fish market, *Yalova* has a lovely old tiled floor in the downstairs eating area, a stylish roof terrace with views over the sea, and offers a wide range of fish and seafood – the best in town. Farmed fish (sea bass or sea bream) costs around ₺20 a portion; their "wild" brethren are sold per kilo and work out at much more expensive. Starters range from ₺5 for vegetable-based dishes to ₺20 for seafood *meze*. Daily 11am–midnight.

NIGHTLIFE

While nightlife for many locals tends to involve nothing more strenuous than a promenade and a meal along the front, the presence in town of a large student population means there's a burgeoning and surprisingly lively bar scene. Indeed, Fetvane Sokak, a narrow lane lined with some of the town's more attractive buildings, is now known locally as Barlar Sokak ("Bar Street"). Needless to say, things get even livelier around ANZAC Day, when Australians and New Zealanders make their presence felt. Several of the venues have **live music**, usually in an upstairs room, with a modest cover charge that includes a local drink.

22

★**Kahvesi** Fetvane Sok. Set in the restored *Yalı Han*, an Ottoman-era tradesman's hall with a courtyard, this is a favoured tea, coffee and *nargile* joint by day, while evenings see live music and much beer drinking from the local student population, especially at weekends. Daily 10am–midnight.

Hayal Kahvesi Fetvane Sok. An offshoot of Istanbul's famous *Hayal Kahvesi* club (see p.201), this is a cavernous bar inside a period building, with a courtyard café and live music upstairs most evenings. A 50cl beer will set you back ₺8, less in Happy Hour (6–7pm). To see the band (usually rock covers) there's often a cover charge, especially at weekends. Sun–Thurs noon–Fri & Sat noon–2am.

DIRECTORY

Banks and exchange A number of banks (Mon–Fri 9am–12.30pm & 1.30–5pm) can be found on Cumhuriyet Bul and, parallel to it, Kemal Yeri. ATMs can be found on these streets and next to the ferry terminal, and there's an exchange office next door to *Anzac House Hostel*.

Cinema The cinema below the Gima shopping centre, next door to the bus station, shows mainstream releases in English with Turkish subtitles.

Internet access Maxi Internet Café, Fetvane Sok. The Belediye Iş Merkezi also has many smaller internet cafés, and you can get online at most of the hotels and hostels, though these tend to be overpriced.

Hospital Hasan Mevsuf Sok (☎0286 217 1098).

Police Kayserili Ahmet Paşa Cad, just north of the ferry terminal.

Post office İnönü Cad (Mon–Sat 8am–11pm).

Troy

Daily: May–Sept 8am–7pm; Oct–April 8am–5pm • ₺15

Although by no means the most spectacular archeological site in Turkey, **Troy**, thanks to Homer, is a household name around the world. Known as Truva in Turkish, the remains of the ancient city lie around 37km south of Çanakkale, a few kilometres west of the main road. If you're expecting something on the scale of the city as re-created for the 2004 Brad Pitt epic *Troy* you are bound to be disappointed, as archeological excavations have revealed that the Troy of Homer (circa 1200 BC) would only have had a population of between five and ten thousand. The ruins are nonetheless impressive in the detail if not in scale, and modern scientific methods have managed to fill the gaps left by earlier excavations. Explanatory panels now dot the site, allowing laypeople to grasp the basic layout and gain a knowledge of the different settlement periods uncovered.

Brief history

Until 1871, Troy was generally thought to have existed in legend only. The Troad plain, where the ruins lie, was known to be associated with the Troy that Homer wrote about in the *Iliad*, but all traces of the city had vanished completely. In 1868, **Heinrich Schliemann** (1822–90), a German businessman who had made his fortune in America (see box below), obtained permission from the Ottoman government to start digging on a hill known to the Turks as Hisarlık, where earlier excavators had already found the remains of a Classical temple and signs of further, older ruins.

Schliemann's sloppy trenching work resulted in a certain amount of damage to the site, only rectified by the first professional archeologist to work at Troy, the respected Carl William Blegen, whose excavations began in 1932. Schliemann was also accountable for removing the so-called **Treasure of Priam** (see p.261), a large cache of beautiful jewellery that was taken back to Berlin and subsequently displayed there until 1941, when it was squirrelled away for safety under the city's Zoo Station. The hoard disappeared during the Red Army's sacking of the city in May 1945; long suspected of having been spirited back to the USSR, it resurfaced spectacularly in Moscow in August 1993 and is now on display in the Pushkin Museum there. A legal tussle between Germany and the Russian Federation to determine ownership is now in progress – as well as careful forensic examination of the precious items to answer allegations that Schliemann fraudulently assembled the treasure from scattered sites in Asia Minor.

Whatever Schliemann's shortcomings, his initial, unsystematic excavations did uncover nine layers of remains, representing distinct and consecutive city developments that span four millennia. The oldest, **Troy I**, dates back to about 3600 BC and was followed by four similar settlements. Either Troy VI or VII is thought to have been **the city described by Homer**: the former is known to have been destroyed by an earthquake in about 1275 BC, while the latter shows signs of having been wiped out by fire about a quarter of a century later, around the time historians generally estimate the Trojan War to have taken place. **Troy VIII**, which thrived from 700 to 300 BC, was a Greek foundation, while much of the final layer of development, **Troy IX** (300 BC to 300 AD), was built during the heyday of the Roman Empire.

Although there's no way of being absolutely sure that the **Trojan War** did take place, there's a fair amount of circumstantial evidence suggesting that the city was the scene of some kind of armed conflict, even if it wasn't the ten-year struggle described in the *Iliad*. It's possible that Homer's epic is based on a number of wars fought between the Mycenaean Greeks and the inhabitants of Troy, who, it seems, were alternately trading partners and commercial rivals. Homer's version of events, however, dispensed with these pedestrian possibilities, turning the war into a full-scale heroic drama, complete with bit parts for the ancient Greek gods.

The site

Just right of the official entrance stands a 1970s sculpture of the giant **wooden horse**; you can climb a ladder into the horse's belly and look out of windows cut into its flanks. The adjacent **excavation house** has a scale model of the site (when it's not out on loan) and an excellent video explaining the history of Troy and the excavations. Just beyond is the ruined city itself, on a small outcrop overlooking the Troad plain, which extends about 8km to the sea. The circular trail takes you around the site; the twenty or so panels enlisting the help of schematic diagrams are extremely helpful in bringing the ruins to life. Standing on what's left of the ramparts and looking across the plain that stretches out at your feet, it's not too difficult to imagine a besieging army, legendary or otherwise, camped below.

Most impressive of the extant remains are the **east wall and gate** (Panel 2) from Troy VI (1700–1275 BC), of which 330m remain, curving around the eastern and southern flanks of the city. The inward-leaning stone walls, 6m high and over 4m thick, would

---

HEINRICH SCHLIEMANN

German entrepreneur and archeologist **Heinrich Schliemann** was born into a poor Mecklenburg family in 1822. As a child he became obsessed with the myths of ancient Greece, a passion that would stay with him the rest of his life. Unable to pursue the interest professionally (although he did teach himself ancient Greek, in addition to several modern languages), he amassed a considerable fortune during the Californian Gold Rush of 1849, speculating on the stock market and as an arms contractor during the Crimean War. Always a larger-than-life character, he forsook commerce at the age of 46, then divorced his long-standing wife to marry a beautiful, seventeen-year-old Greek girl, Sophia, before going on to become the world's most celebrated and successful amateur archeologist.

have been surmounted by a further three metres or so of mud-brick walling. The most important monument of Troy IX (or Ilium), probably erected in the reign of Augustus (31 BC–14 AD), is the **Temple of Athena** (Panel 4). According to the Greek historian Strabo, an earlier temple on the same site was erected by one of Alexander the Great's generals, Lysimachus, after Alexander himself had visited the site and left his armour as a gift. Remains found by Schliemann proved the temple to be of the Doric order of ancient Greek architecture, and fragments of its coffered ceiling can still be seen dotted around.

The partially reconstructed **Megaron Building** (Panel 5b; protected beneath a giant sail-shaped canopy, the top of which marks the height and shape of the mound under which the remains lay before Schliemann started his excavations) dates back to 2300 BC. The mud-brick masonry was turned a bright red when Troy II was destroyed by fire. Schliemann, erroneously as it turned out, used the evidence of this fire to draw the conclusion that this had been Homer's Troy. The burnt bricks you see today are re-creations – the originals lie underneath. From this panel you can also see the massive trench Schliemann drove through the mound in the hope of finding Homer's Troy. A little further on is a ramp (Panel 8), paved with flat stones from Troy II (2500–2300 BC), which would have led to the citadel entrance. Just to the left of this is where Schliemann claimed he found the hoard of gold generally known as the Treasure of Priam, some of which his wife Sophia (see box opposite) was photographed wearing, making the Schliemanns famous around the world.

Many doubts have subsequently been cast on the provenance of it. Schliemann said that his wife Sophia helped him unearth the cache although she wasn't even in Turkey at the time of the find. The self-made archeologist also stands accused of collecting together precious objects found scattered across the dig site and putting them into a single cache – or even worse buying the precious items from elsewhere and planting them at Troy. What is certain is that the "treasure" could not have been Priam's, as the hoard dates from a considerably earlier period than that generally accepted for the Trojan War.

There's little left standing of the **South Gate** (Panel 12) of Troy VI, but the stretch of paving leading through it is impressive. What interests most visitors here, however, is the possibility that this could be Homer's Scaean Gate, scene of much of the dramatic action in the *Iliad* and portal through which the unwitting Trojans pulled the legendary wooden horse.

ARRIVAL AND DEPARTURE
TROY

By dolmuş From Çanakkale, dolmuşes depart from the minibus garage just under the bridge on Atatürk Cad (daily 9.30am–8.00pm; April–Oct every 30min, Nov–March hourly).

Tours A number of companies offer tours from Çanakkale (see box, p.256).

INFORMATION

Entrance The site is signposted by the ticket office – marked "Gişe" – just opposite the drop-off point where passengers from the dolmuş from Çanakkale alight.

Books There are a few small shops here where you can pick up a copy of the *Troia/Wilusa Guidebook* by Dr Manfred Korfmann, the archeologist who, between 1988 and his death in 2005, oversaw the site's excavation.

The book is copiously illustrated and really helps bring Troy to life, containing a map that will guide you around and pages of information corresponding to numbers on the signs at the site.

Eating There's a reasonable self-service cafeteria that makes most of its profits serving hungry coach parties.

Gallipoli (Gelibolu)

Burdened with a grim military history, but endowed with some fine scenery and beaches, the slender **Gelibolu (Gallipoli) peninsula** – roughly 60km in length and ranging between 4km and 18km wide – forms the northwest side of the **Dardanelles**, the narrow strait connecting the Aegean with the Sea of Marmara. Whether you approach the peninsula from Şarköy or (more likely) Keşan, the road there is pretty, swooping down in long arcs past the Saros gulf.

Site of the 1915 **Gallipoli landings** by the Allied troops, the peninsula contains a mind-numbing series of battlefields and cemeteries that tell of the tragic defeat by the Turkish forces. For Turks, the region also holds a great deal of significance, as the Gallipoli campaign made famous a previously unknown lieutenant-colonel, Mustafa Kemal, who later became Atatürk (see p.264). There's no public transport here so your best bet is a tour (see box, p.256) or to rent a car in Çanakkale.

Brief history

Soon after the start of World War I it became obvious to the Allies that Russia could not be supplied by sea, nor a Balkan front opened against the Central Powers, unless Ottoman Turkey was eliminated. **Winston Churchill**, in his earliest important post as First Lord of the Admiralty, reasoned that the quickest way to accomplish this would be to storm the Dardanelles with a fleet and bombard Istanbul into submission. A combined Anglo-French armada made several attempts on the straits during November 1914, which were repulsed, but they returned in earnest on March 18, 1915. This time they managed to penetrate less than 10km up the waterway before striking numerous Turkish mines, losing half a dozen vessels and hundreds of men. The Allies retreated and command squabbles erupted over allocation of troops to the campaign. The generals saw the Western Front as paramount, whereas politicians – foremost among them, Churchill – wanted to knock Turkey out of the war first in order to weaken Germany, while at the same time exciting anti-Turkish feelings in Bulgaria and bringing it, too, into the war.

Having regrouped at Mudros harbour on the Greek island of Limnos, the joint expeditionary forces took several months to prepare an amphibious assault on the Turkish positions along the peninsula. During this time, the British had no way of knowing that Turkish forces defending the straits were cripplingly under-supplied. Had they attempted it, another naval push down the Dardanelles might have succeeded, but instead the delay gave the Turks the chance to strengthen their own defences.

The plan eventually formulated by the British and French commanders called for an Anglo-French landing at Cape Helles, Seddülbahir and Morto Bay at the mouth of the straits, and a simultaneous **ANZAC** (Australia-New Zealand Army Corps) assault at Kabatepe beach 13km north. The two forces were to drive towards each other, link up and neutralize the Turkish shore batteries controlling the Dardanelles.

The landings

The Australians landed first at dawn on April 25, 1915, with the British and French making shore around an hour afterwards, followed by the New Zealanders later in the day. The rather harebrained scheme ran into trouble from the start. Anglo-French brigades at the southernmost cape were pinned down by accurate Turkish fire, and the French contingent was virtually annihilated; after two days, they had only managed to penetrate 6.5km inland – and never managed to move any further. The fate of the ANZAC landing was even more horrific: owing to a drifting signal buoy, the Aussies and Kiwis disembarked not on the wide, flat sands of Kabatepe, but at a cramped and Turkish-dominated cove next to Arıburnu, 2km north. Despite heavy casualties (around two thousand on the first day alone), the ANZACs advanced inland in staggered parties, as the Turks initially retreated. The next day, goaded by their commanders, they managed to threaten the Turkish strongpoint of Çonkbayırı above. It was here that one Mustafa Kemal, a previously unknown lieutenant-colonel, rushed in reinforcements, telling his poorly equipped troops, "I do not order you to fight, I order you to die." Amazingly, it worked: the ANZAC force never made it further than 800m inland, despite a supplementary British landing at Cape Suvla to the north. With the exception of ferocious battles for the summit in early August, both sides settled into long-term trench warfare. Finally, around Christmas 1915, the Allies gave up, with the last troops leaving Seddülbahir on January 8, 1916. Churchill's career went into temporary eclipse, while that of Mustafa Kemal was only just beginning.

From carnage to nationhood

The reasons for the **Allied defeat** are many. In addition to the chanciness of the basic strategy, the callousness and incompetence of the Allied commanders – who often

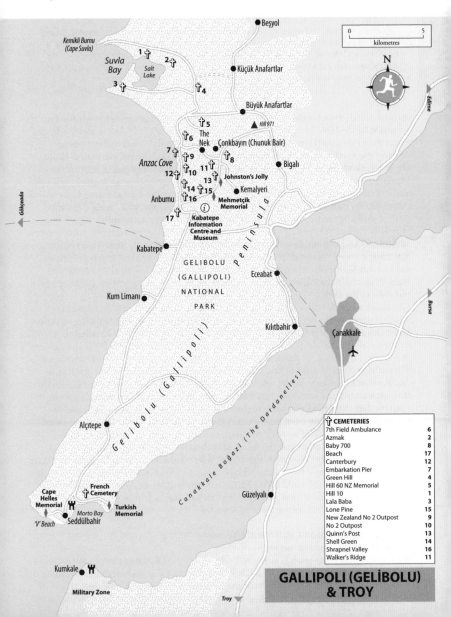

✝ CEMETERIES	
7th Field Ambulance	6
Azmak	2
Baby 700	8
Beach	17
Canterbury	12
Embarkation Pier	7
Green Hill	4
Hill 60 NZ Memorial	5
Hill 10	1
Lala Baba	3
Lone Pine	15
New Zealand No 2 Outpost	9
No 2 Outpost	10
Quinn's Post	13
Shell Green	14
Shrapnel Valley	16
Walker's Ridge	11

GALLIPOLI (GELİBOLU) & TROY

22

> ## ANZAC DAY
>
> **ANZAC Day**, April 25, is the busiest day of the year for Gallipoli, as thousands of Australians and New Zealanders arrive to honour the dead of the Allied defeat. The day begins with the **Dawn Service** at 5.30am at ANZAC Cove, though most people arrive much earlier to camp out, as the police close all the roads around the grave sites to traffic from 3am. The service used to be a somewhat informal ceremony, but in recent years thousands have attended, and it now features official speeches, prayers and a representative from the Australian or New Zealand forces playing a poignant "Last Post" as the sun rises over ANZAC Cove. An hour's breakfast break follows before the rest of the morning's ceremonies resume – **wreath laying** at the British, French and Turkish memorials, and more services at the Australian memorial at Lone Pine and the New Zealand memorial at Chunuk Bair. Future ceremonies look set to be less relaxed as in 2014 the status of the Gallipoli Peninsula was changed from a national park to a special historic area; alcohol cannot be sold or consumed in the latter.

countermanded each other's orders or failed to press advantages with reinforcements – cannot be underestimated. With hindsight, you cannot help but wonder why the Allies didn't concentrate more on Cape Suvla and the flat, wide valley behind, skirting the fortified Ottoman heights to reach the Dardanelles' northwest shore. On the **Turkish side**, much of the credit for the successful resistance must go to Mustafa Kemal, then relatively obscure, but later better known as **Atatürk**. His role in the Turkish victory at Çonkbayırı is legendary. Mustafa Kemal seemed to enjoy a charmed life, narrowly escaping death on several occasions, and, aside from his tactical skills, is credited with various other extraordinary accomplishments, but primarily that of rekindling morale, by threats, persuasion or example, among often outgunned and outnumbered Ottoman infantrymen. Indeed, most Turks believe that their nation, salvaged from the crumbling wreckage of the Ottoman Empire, was born at Gallipoli, when they found the man (Atatürk) with the bravery and acumen to resist the Allies, and the Turkish soldier proved he was every bit as brave and able as his foes.

At various times, half a million men were deployed by defenders and attackers alike; of these, well over fifty percent were **killed, wounded or** went missing in action. Allied deaths numbered around 52,000, while incomplete records have led to estimates of Turkish dead to be anywhere between 50,000 and 200,000. The carnage among the ANZACs, in particular, was especially severe relative to their countries' populations. Yet it would in fact be dwarfed by the number of ANZACs killed on the Western Front later in the war – around 10,600 lost their lives in the Gallipoli campaign compared with some 60,000 for the entire war. Claims voiced in some quarters that the Allied top brass regarded the "colonials" as expendable cannon-fodder have never fully been borne out; indeed, more British and Irish troops died at Gallipoli than ANZACs, with two Irish battalions suffering over fifty percent casualties on the first day and the 42nd Manchester Division being almost completely wiped out. However, this baptism by blood had several long-term effects: a sense of Australia and New Zealand having come of age as sovereign countries; the designation of April 25 as ANZAC Day, a solemn holiday in Australia and New Zealand (see box above); and a healthy antipodean scepticism in the face of blandishments to join international adventures.

Kabatepe Information Centre and Museum

9km northwest of Eceabat • Daily 8.30am–5pm • ₺3

The first stop on most tours is at the recently refurbished **Kabatepe Information Centre and Museum**, which contains a well-labelled selection of war memorabilia, including touching letters home, photographs of the trenches, weapons and uniforms. The only sour note is the rather grisly inclusion of some human, presumably Allied, remains.

The cemeteries, landing points and battlefields

The first points encountered along the coast road north of the centre are the **Beach**, **Shrapnel Valley** and **Shell Green** cemeteries – the latter 300m inland up a steep track, unsuitable for all but four-wheel-drive vehicles, and consequently missed out by most tours. These are followed by **ANZAC Cove** and **Arıburnu**, site of the first, bungled ANZAC landing and location of the dawn service on ANZAC Day. At ANZAC Cove, a memorial bears Atatürk's famous quotation concerning the Allied dead, which, translated into English, begins: "Those heroes that shed their blood and lost their lives … you are now lying in the soil of a friendly country." Looking inland, you'll see the fatal badlands that gave the defenders such an advantage. Beyond Arıburnu, the terrain flattens out and the four other **cemeteries** (Canterbury, No. 2 Outpost, New Zealand No. 2 Outpost and Embarkation Pier) are more dispersed.

A couple of kilometres north of Arıburnu are the beaches and salt lake at **Cape Suvla**, today renamed Kemikli Burnu ("The Bone-strewn Headland"), location of another six **cemeteries**: Hill 10, Azmak, 7th Field Ambulance, Green Hill, Lala Bala and Hill 60 (with its memorial to the New Zealand forces). All contain mainly English, Scottish, Welsh and Irish dead, with ANZAC graves also in Hill 10 and 7th Field Ambulance. The roads up here are little more than dirt tracks, and most tours don't make it this far.

From ANZAC Cove, tours go uphill along the road northeast that roughly follows what was the front line, to the strong points (now cemeteries) scattered around **Çonkbayırı** hill. To the left of this road is **Shrapnel Valley** – the single, perilous supply line that ran up-valley from the present location of Beach Cemetery to the trenches. First up is **Lone Pine** (Kanlı Sırt), lowest strategic position on the ridge and the largest graveyard-cum-memorial to those buried unmarked or at sea. Action here was considered a sideshow to the main August offensive further up Çonkbayırı; a total of 28,000 men died in four days at both points. Just up from Lone Pine is the **Mehmetçik Memorial** to the Turkish soldiers who perished, and at **Johnston's Jolly** (named after an officer who liked to "jolly the Turks up" with his gun) is a heavily eroded section of **trench**, peaceful now beneath the pine trees. **Quinn's Post**, the scene of some of the fiercest fighting of the entire campaign, is now the resting place of 473 of the fallen, 294 of them unidentified.

From here the road forks: to the left is **The Nek** – where much of the action of Peter Weir's film *Gallipoli* takes place – and **Walker's Ridge** cemetery; to the right, the road continues uphill to **Baby 700** cemetery – the high-water mark of the Allied advance on April 25 – and to the massive New Zealand memorial obelisk and the five-monolith Turkish memorial on the crest of **Çonkbayırı** hill (Chunuk Bair). On the Turkish memorial are Atatürk's words and deeds – chief among the latter being his organization of successful resistance to the Allied attacks of August 6–10. The spot where the Turkish leader's pocket watch stopped a fragment of shrapnel is highlighted, as is the grave of a Turkish soldier discovered in 1990 when the trenches were reconstructed. On this part of the front, the trenches of the opposing forces lay within a few metres of each other, and the modern road corresponds to the no-man's-land.

To the southern cape

The harbour of **Kabatepe** village lies 2km south of the Kabatepe Information Centre. There's a good beach to the north of town – the intended site of the ANZAC landing – but if you're after a swim, wait until you reach **Kum Limanı**, another 3km further south, where an even better strand fringes a warm, clean, calm sea, unusual this far north. There's been little development of this beautiful setting, but you probably won't be alone: a number of tour companies bring their clients here for a dip after battlefield sightseeing.

The British **Cape Helles Memorial** obelisk adorns the Turkish equivalent of Land's End, 16km beyond Kum Limanı and just past the village of Seddülbahir. From Cape Helles itself, the views south to Bozcaada (Tenedos), west to Gökçeada (Imvros) and

22

east to Asia are magnificent, and abundant **Ottoman fortifications** hint at the age-old importance of the place. Tucked between the medieval bulwarks is an excellent beach, the **V Beach** of the Allied expedition, behind which is a **campsite** – and the biggest of five **British cemeteries** in the area. A turning just before Seddülbahir leads to the **French Cemetery** above Morto Bay, one of the most striking of all the memorials, with its serried rows of named black crosses, and to the nearby **Turkish Memorial**, resembling a stark, tetrahedral footstool. Locally organized tours rarely venture this far, so if you're intent on seeing these two, you'll have to make your own arrangements (see box, p.256).

Eceabat

Eceabat, smaller than Çanakkale (see pp.255–257), is the closest base for visiting the battlefield sites, whether by yourself or on a tour. There is nothing much of interest – historical or otherwise – in the village itself and the only real reason to choose it over Çanakkale across the strait is to avoid the short ferry-hop.

ARRIVAL AND INFORMATION   ECEABAT

By bus and ferry Buses from Istanbul drop you near the ferry jetty, from where car ferries run across the Dardanelles to Çanakkale hourly (24hr; passengers ₺2.5, cars ₺29). The bus-company ticket offices are right in front of the jetty at Cumhuriyet Meydanı.

Information There's a PTT (post office) booth by the jetty, which can change money, and an ATM nearby.

ACCOMMODATION

Accommodation is plentiful, but you'll need to book well ahead if you want to stay in town for ANZAC Day.

Crowded House Hüseyin Avni Sok 4 ☎0286 814 1565, ⓦ crowdedhousegallipoli.com. A little way inland, more or less opposite the ferry terminal, this popular and well-run hostel has six-bed dorm rooms, doubles and a café. Also the home of the Crowded House Travel Agency (see box, p.256) and has a reader-friendly book-swap service. Dorm €8 double €30

★**Gallipoli Houses** Kocadere village, 7km northwest of Eceabat ☎0286 814 2650, ⓦ thegallipolihouses .com. This interesting addition to the Gallipoli accommodation scene has only ten rooms, spread over a series of clusters of lovingly restored village houses. Rooms are simple but well designed, with mod cons like a/c,

underfloor heating and free wi-fi. The well-regarded evening meals are a compulsory surcharge Mon–Fri, as there's nowhere else to eat in the village (€15 extra per person). Open March 15–Nov 15. Rooms from €70

TJ's To the right of the ferry terminal, looking inland from the waterfront ☎0286 814 3121, ⓦ anzacgallipolitours.com. This Turkish-Australian-run place was upgraded in 2012 and is now more hotel than hostel in standard, with LCD TVs and a/c in all the bright and cheery private rooms, though there are also six-bed dorms. There's also a good roof bar that gets busy in season. Dorm ₺30, doubles ₺70

OIL-WRESTLING FESTIVAL

Edirne

Out on the Thracian plain, some 230km northwest of Istanbul and only a short distance from the Greek and Bulgarian frontiers, lies the beautifully preserved Ottoman city of Edirne. Although tiny in comparison to Istanbul, with a population of around 150,000, Edirne once reigned as the capital city of the Ottoman Empire and has a clutch of impressive buildings to prove it. One of these, the Selimiye Camii, is arguably Turkey's finest Ottoman mosque, the crowning achievement of the imperial architect Mimar Sinan (see box, p.82). A delightfully relaxed and charming town, Edirne entertains a steady stream of day-tripping tourists, border-hoppers and students from the town's university. The town's annual Kırkpınar oil-wrestling festival (see box, p.271) attracts huge crowds and is the most important in the country.

Brief history

For all its humble beauty, Edirne is a town with a turbulent history – its strategic military position has led to its repeated conquest over the centuries. Founded as Orestias (if you believe the Greek mythology), Edirne has undergone numerous name changes throughout its varied history, first becoming the Thracian settlement of Uscudama and later, **Hadrianopolis**, designated the main centre of Roman Thrace by Emperor Hadrian.

Under the Byzantines it retained its importance as a pit stop for attempts on the capital or the Balkans, and time after time unsuccessful besiegers of Constantinople vented their frustrations on Hadrianopolis as they retreated. A fair few emperors met their ends here in pitched battles with Thracian "barbarians" of one sort or another.

By the mid-fourteenth century, the **Ottomans** had joined forces with the Byzantines in a web of mutual defence treaties and marriage links and in 1361 Hadrianopolis was surrendered to the besieging Murat I, making it the provisional Ottoman capital. It wasn't until 1458 that the Ottoman court was completely moved to the Bosphorus; a century later, Mehmet the Conqueror still trained troops and tested artillery here in preparation for the march on Constantinople.

Thanks to its excellent opportunities for hunting and falconry, Edirne, as the Turks renamed it, remained a favourite haunt of numerous sultans for three more centuries, earning the title *Der-I Saadet* or "Happiness Gate". It's said that there were enough victory celebrations, circumcision ceremonies and marriages held in Edirne to make even Constantinople jealous.

Decline set in during the eighteenth century, prompted largely by an **earthquake** in 1751. During each of the **Russo-Turkish wars** of 1829 and 1878–79, the city was occupied and pillaged by Tsarist troops; far worse were the Bulgarians, who in 1913 presided over a four-month spree of atrocities. The Greeks, as one of the victorious World War I Allies, **annexed Edirne** along with the rest of Turkish Thrace from 1920 to 1922, and Turkish sovereignty over the city was only confirmed by the 1923 Treaty of Lausanne.

Eski Cami

Talat Paşa Caddesi

The logical starting point for exploring Edirne is **Eski Cami**, the oldest mosque in town. This boxy structure, topped by nine vaults, is a more elaborate version of Bursa's Ulu Cami (see p.244). Emir Süleyman, son of the luckless Beyazıt I, began it in 1403, but it was his younger brother Mehmet I – the only one of three brothers left alive after a bloody succession struggle – who completed it eleven years later. The mosque is famous for its giant works of **calligraphy**, the most celebrated being the large Arabic inscriptions on either side of the front door, one in the name of Allah, the other of Mohammed. It is usually unlocked and open to visitors from early morning to early evening.

The Bedesten

Mimar Sinan Caddesi · Mon–Sat 9am–7pm

The **Bedesten**, Edirne's first covered market, was constructed by Mehmet I; a portion of its revenue went to the nearby Eski Cami (see above). The barn-like building, with its fourteen vaulted chambers – indebted to a Bursa prototype, as with Eski Cami – has been restored in the past decade, but modern shops and poor paintwork make the interior drab and unimpressive.

Semiz Ali Paşa Çarşısı

Corner of Londra Asfaltı and Saraçlar Caddesis · Mon–Sat 9am–7pm

The **Semiz Ali Paşa** bazaar was established by Mimar Sinan in 1568 at the behest of Semiz Ali, one of the most able and congenial of the Ottoman grand viziers. A massive

EDİRNE

Kırkpınar ←

Bulgaria & Kapıkule (18 km) ←

0 — 500 — metres

N

Bus Station, Train Station & Istanbul →

Tunca River

Tunca River

Meriç River

Meriç River

Karaağaç

Train Station

Muradiye Camii

Sarayiçi Wrestling Stadium, Saray Bridge & Fatih Bridge ←

İkinci Beyazıt Külliyesi

Beyazıt Bridge

HOROZLU BAYIR CAD

Edirne Museum

Museum of Turkish & Islamic Arts

Ruins of Hamam of Janissaries

Selimiye Camii

Kavaflar Arasta (Bazaar)

Bulgarian Consulate

TALAT PAŞA CAD

Buses to Kırkpınar & Bus Station

Dilaver Bey Parkı

KIYIK CAD

Eski Camii

Volkan Bus Office

Minibuses to border

ESKİ İSTANBUL CAD

Belediye

Police

Üç Şerefeli Camii

Hürriyet Meydanı

Bedesten

Döviz

Etur El Sanatlık Mağazası

Edirne 25 Kasım Stadium

PEŞTEMALCI CAD

SARAÇLAR CAD

Yeni Bridge

Meriç Bridge

HÜKÜMET CAD

Sokullu Paşa Hamamı

Semiz Ali Paşa Çarşısı

Kule Kapısı

Great Synagogue

MAARİF CAD

ORTAKAPI CAD

BALIKPAZARI CAD

CUMHURİYET CAD

KALEİÇİ

LONDRA ASFALTI

Gazi Mihal Bridge

Gazi Mihal Camii

fire in 1992 burned out many of its 130 shops, but renovations have been administered with care – particularly impressive is the beautiful multi-domed ceiling. Gold and silver jewellery and clothing are just some of the goods on offer here.

Üç Şerefeli Camii

Hürriyet Meydanı

Open from dawn until dusk, the **Üç Şerefeli Camii** replaced the Eski Cami as Edirne's Friday mosque in 1447. Ten years in the making, its conceptual design represented the pinnacle of Ottoman religious architecture until overshadowed by the Selimiye Camii (see below) a short time later.

The mosque's name ("Three-balconied") derives from the presence of three galleries for the muezzin on the tallest of the four **minarets**, all of which are decorated with a different pattern – checked, spiral, zigzag and fluted. Each of the three balconies is reached by a separate stairway within the minaret. The **courtyard**, too, was an innovation, centred on a *şadırvan* (ritual ablutions fountain) and ringed by porphyry and marble columns pilfered from Roman buildings. The experimental nature of the mosque is further confirmed by its **interior**, much wider than it is deep and covered by a dome 24m in diameter. It was the largest that the Turks had built at the time and, to impart a sense of space, the architect relied on just two free-standing columns, with the other four recessed into front and back walls to form a hexagon.

Seray Hamamı

Selimiye Camii Arkası 1 • Daily 9am–11pm (men), 9am–11pm (women) • ₺20

Located just behind the towering Selimiye Camii, this fourteenth-century Turkish bath was refurbished and reopened in 2012. It is now one of the most attractive *hamam*s in town and a bargain when compared to the famous baths in Istanbul. There are separate wings for men and women; they are accessed from opposite sides of the building.

Selimiye Camii

Meydan, Babademirtaş Mah

The masterly **Selimiye Camii**, arguably Turkey's finest mosque, was designed by the 80-year-old Mimar Sinan (see box, p.82) in 1569 at the command of Selim II. The work of a confident craftsman at the height of his powers, it's visible from some distance away on the Thracian plain and is virtually the municipal symbol, reproduced on the sides of Edirne's buses, postcards and tourist brochures.

You can approach the Selimiye across Edirne's central park, Dilaver Bey, then through the **Kavaflar Arasta** (Cobbler's Arcade; Mon–Sat 9am–7pm), which was built by Sinan's pupil Davut and is still used as a covered market. Every day, under the market's prayer dome, the shopkeepers promise that they will do their business honestly. At the end of the market, a flight of stone steps will take you to the mosque **courtyard**, a stunning spectacle with its surrounding portico made up of multiple domes, held up by ancient columns. At the centre of the courtyard, the delicately fashioned *şadırvan* (ablutions fountain) is the finest in the city. Each of the four identical, slender minarets has three balconies – Sinan's nod to his predecessors – and at 71m are the tallest in the world after those in Mecca. The detailed carved portal once graced the Ulu Cami in Birgi and was transported here in pieces, then reassembled.

It's the celestial **interior**, specifically the dome, which impresses most. Planned expressly to surpass that of Haghia Sophia in Istanbul (see pp.45–49), it just manages it – at 31.5m in diameter – by a few centimetres, and Sinan thus achieved a lifetime's ambition. Supported by eight mammoth twelve-sided pillars, the cupola floats 44m above the floor, inscribed with calligraphy proclaiming the glory of Allah. Immediately below the dome, the muezzin's platform, supported on twelve columns, is an ideal place from which to contemplate the proportions of the mosque. The delicate painting on the platform's underside is a faithful restoration of the original and gives some idea of how the mosque dome must once have looked. The water of the small marble drinking fountain beneath symbolizes life, under the dome of eternity. The most ornate stone carving is reserved for the *mihrab* and *mimber*, backed by fine İznik faïence illuminated by sunlight streaming in through the many windows.

Museum of Turkish and Islamic Arts

Tues–Sun 8am–6pm • ₺5

An associated *medrese*, at the northeastern corner of the Selimiye Camii, is now the Museum of Turkish and Islamic Arts (Türk ve Islam Eserleri Müzesi), housing assorted wooden, ceramic and martial knick-knacks from the province. There are fifteen rooms including one dedicated to oil wrestling (see box below), with a portrait gallery of its stars, a pair of oil-wrestler's leather trousers and blow-ups of miniatures depicting this six-hundred-year-old sport through the ages.

23

OIL WRESTLING AND THE KIRKPINAR FESTIVAL

Oil wrestling (*yağlı güreş*) is popular throughout Turkey but reaches the pinnacle of its acclaim at the doyen of tournaments, the annual **Kırkpınar Festival**, staged early each summer on the Saray İçi islet outside Edirne. The preferred date is the first week of July, but the three-day event is moved back into June if it coincides with Ramadan or either of the two major *bayrams* (religious holidays) following it.

The wrestling matches have been held annually (except in times of war or Edirne's occupation) for over six centuries and, despite the rather sterile environment of the stadium that now hosts the wrestling, traditional routines still permeate the event. The contestants – up to a thousand per year – dress only in short leather trousers called *kisbet* and are slicked from head to toe in diluted olive oil. Wrestlers are classed by height, not by weight, from five-year-olds up to the *pehlivan* (full-size) category. Warm-up exercises, the *peşrev*, are accompanied by the *davul* (deep-toned drum) and *zurna* (single-reed Islamic oboe), the music provided by the local Romany population. The competitors and the actual matches are solemnly introduced by the *cazgır* (master of ceremonies), usually himself a former champion.

The bouts, several of which take place simultaneously, can last anything from a few minutes to a couple of hours, until one competitor collapses or has his back pinned to the grass. Referees keep a lookout for the limited number of illegal moves or holds and victors advance more or less immediately to the next round until, after the second or third day, only the *başpehlivan* (champion) remains. Despite the small prize purse, donated by the Kırkpınar Ağaları – the local worthies who put on the whole show – a champion is usually well set up in terms of appearance and endorsement fees and should derive ample benefit from the furious on- and off-site betting. On the whole, gladiators tend to be villagers from all over Turkey who have won regional titles, starry-eyed with the prospect of fame.

FESTIVAL PRACTICALITIES

The wrestling itself spreads over three days, with the opening ceremony and children's bouts taking place from mid-afternoon Friday (free). Saturday's action lasts from midday until around 7pm, with the final bouts and award/closing ceremonies between midday and 7pm on the Sunday. The best way to get tickets is through booking agent Biletix (see box, p.195) which cost upwards of ₺55 on the Saturday and ₺77 on the Sunday in 2014.

The stadium is located just 1.5km from Selimiye Camii and makes a pleasant walk through the sleepy backstreets. However, local buses head to the stadium every half-hour from the centre of Edirne, and are clearly marked with Kırkpınar or take a taxi for no more than ₺10. The Edirne municipality invariably organizes a series of ancillary events that prolong the festivities for another three days and include free Turkish music concerts outside the arena and in the park below the Selimiye Camii at 9pm each evening. For more information, see Ⓦ kirkpinar.com.

Edirne Museum

Edirne Müzesi • Tues–Sun 9am–7pm • ₺5

Edirne Museum, a modern building just northeast of the Selimiye Camii precincts, contains a predictable assortment of Greco-Roman fragments. Its ethnographic section focuses on carpet weaving and other local crafts, including colourful village bridal-wear, which preceded the bland white dresses that have been adopted from the West.

Muradiye Camii

Mimar Sinan Caddesi • Admission only at prayer times

Northeast of the centre, the **Muradiye Camii** is an easy ten-minute, down-then-up, walk along Mimar Sinan Caddesi from the Selimiye Camii. According to legend, Celaleddin Rumi, founder of the Mevlevi dervish order, appeared in a dream to the pious Murat II in 1435, urging him to build a sanctuary for the Mevlevis in Edirne. The result is this pleasing, T-shaped *zaviye* (dervish convent) crouched on a hill looking north over vegetable patches and the Tunca River; the grassy entry court lends a final bucolic touch. The interior is distinguished by the best İznik tiles outside Bursa; the *mihrab* and walls up to eye level are solid with them. Higher surfaces once bore calligraphic frescoes, but these have probably been missing since the catastrophic earthquake of 1751. The dervishes initially congregated in the *eyvans* (transepts), which form the ends of the T's cross-stroke; Murat later housed them in a separate *tekke* (gathering place) in the garden.

The Great Synagogue

Maarif Caddesi

Edirne, along with Istanbul, İzmir and Salonica, was a major place of refuge for Jews fleeing persecution in sixteenth-century Europe – particularly Spain. The **synagogue** here, built in 1906, has twin stair-towers and a fine Neoclassical facade. It was once the largest in the Balkans, serving a population of some 22,000. Although its scheduled completion date was the end of 2012, it was still undergoing reconstruction works at the time of writing. Nevertheless, it is still worth strolling south down Maarif Caddesi from the city centre to have a look at it.

Along the Tunca River

At Edirne, the **Tunca River** is crossed by the greatest concentration of historic bridges in Thrace, most of them now restored. The best way to see them is to take a stroll along the river parallel to the dykes and water meadows of the Tunca's right bank. Despite the litter, and the odd down-and-out who frequents the riverbanks in the evening, stretches of the river are charming – storks wade in the sluggish brown waters, frogs croak in the reeds and willows and poplars line the banks. A good place to start is at the pair of bridges furthest upstream, the fifteenth-century **Saray (Süleyman)** and **Fatih** bridges, which join the respective left and right banks of the Tunca with the river island of **Saray İçi**. The island once supported the **Edirne Sarayı**, a royal palace founded by Murat II, which was blown to bits by the Turks in 1877 to prevent the munitions stored inside from falling into Russian hands. It is now located next to the modern concrete stadium, venue for the Kırkpınar wrestling matches (see box, p.271).

Following the riverbank west and downstream for half an hour brings you to the double-staged **Beyazıt bridge**, which crosses another small island in the Tunca River. This seventeenth-century bridge is more commonly known as the Tek Gözü Köprüsü ("One-Eyed Bridge"). Across the bridge, on the left bank, is the **İkinci Beyazıt Külliyesi** (see opposite).

Another twenty minutes' walk south along the river will bring you to the **Gazi Mihal bridge**, an Ottoman refurbishment of a thirteenth-century Byzantine span and hence the oldest around Edirne. Gazi Mihal was a Christian nobleman who became an enthusiastic convert to Islam – hence the epithet *Gazi*, "Warrior for the Faith". His namesake mosque is at the western end of the bridge, from where it's an easy 500m stroll back into town.

İkinci Beyazıt Külleyesi and Museum of Health

On the left bank of the river near the Tek Gözü Köprüsü bridge (see opposite) is the **İkinci Beyazıt Külliyesi**, built between 1484 and 1488 by Hayrettin, court architect to Beyazıt II. This is the largest Ottoman spiritual and physical-welfare complex ever constructed. Within a single irregular boundary wall and beneath a hundred-dome silhouette, are assembled a mosque, food storehouse, bakery, *imaret* (soup kitchen), dervish hostel, medical school and insane asylum. Except for its handsome courtyard and the sultan's loge inside, the **mosque** itself is disappointing, and more interesting is the **medical school** in the furthest northwest corner of the complex. This was conveniently linked to the *timarhane*, or madhouse, built around an open garden, leading to the magnificent **darüşşifa** (therapy centre). This hexagonal, domed structure consists of a circular central space with six *eyvan*s (side-chambers) opening onto it; the inmates were brought here regularly, where musicians would play to soothe the more intractable cases. Strange five-sided rooms with fireplaces open off three of the *eyvan*s. The *darüşşifa* is now home to the well-intentioned but fairly dull **Trakya University Museum of Health** (Tues–Sun 9am–5.30pm; ₺10), boasting a collection of old medical equipment and photographs.

23

ARRIVAL AND INFORMATION

By bus Regular buses from Istanbul's Büyük Otogar (approx every 20min; 5am–midnight; 2hr 30min; ₺30) arrive at Edirne's bus station (☎0284 225 1979), just over 2km southeast of the centre. A free minibus service runs into town, stopping opposite the Belediye (town hall). This is the easiest place to buy your return ticket, with Volkan, Metro, Ulusoy and Nilüfer offices dotted around the bus stop. All companies run buses to Istanbul approximately every hour from 8am till 8pm, with free minibus shuttles to the station leaving town 30min before departure.

Tourist office Londra Asfaltı 76 (Mon–Fri 9am–5pm; ☎0284 225 5260).

GETTING AROUND

On foot You can tour the main sights of Edirne **on foot**, but as the Ottoman monuments are widely scattered you'll need a full day to do it. Walking, you can follow the willow-shaded banks of the Tunca River for some distance, but midsummer is hot and humid and what starts out pleasurably can end up gruelling.

By phaeton You can also hire a **phaeton** (horse-drawn carriage; *fayton* in Turkish) from the bottom of Saraçlar Cad (₺30–50 for a city tour, but prices can be bargained down).

By bike Alternatively, rent a bicycle from the hire centre at the bottom of Saraçlar Cad, just before the railway bridge, for ₺3/hour or ₺20/day. With flat contours and little traffic, cycling is a much more popular activity here than in Istanbul, with cycle lanes on many of the major roads, also giving you a chance to explore the pretty riverside and surrounding areas.

ACCOMMODATION

Although there are several accommodation options in Edirne, advance bookings are recommended during the main Turkish holidays and the Kırkpınar festival. If you're travelling in low season be sure to negotiate as the prices displayed in hotel lobbies can often be reduced up to a third.

Aksaray Alipaşa Ortakapı Cad 8 ☎0284 212 6035, ☎0284 225 6806. One of the best budget options around, this no-frills hotel housed in a nineteenth-century wood-built mansion is as minimal as it gets. The cheapest rooms, with shared bathrooms, offer little more than a cramped room with a bed, but are definitely a bargain. Despite the lacklustre decor, rooms are clean and light, there's free wi-fi and the affable, English-speaking staff add a homely vibe. Breakfast isn't included. ₺75

Antik Maarif Cad 6 ☎0284 225 1555, ⊚edirneantikhotel.com. From the gold-painted door frames to the ornate, mock-antique furniture, this place aims for lavish but falls slightly short thanks to its chintz linens and jarring hotel-logo carpet. The large rooms are

23

comfortable, with high ceilings and moulded plasterwork, though the spacious bathrooms could do with a revamp. An acquired taste, perhaps, but there's nowhere else quite like it in town. ₺130

Efe Maarif Cad 13 ☎0284 213 6080, ⓦefehotel.com. Spirited, family-run hotel brimming with charm, *Efe* is nothing if not unique. It's the eccentric details that bring this place to life – vibrant photography collections throughout the hallways and traditional folk instruments dotted around reception. The stylish rooms are modern yet homely, there's an English-style pub (summer only) downstairs and a funky adjoining restaurant, *Patio*. ₺140

Grand Altunhan Saraçlar Cad, PTT Yanı ☎0284 213 2200, ⓦaltunhanhotel.com. Teetering between retro cool and slightly passé, this glitzy abode offers good value for money, with sizeable, airy rooms equipped with flat-screen TVs, a/c and big, comfortable beds. Don't be put off by the bright lights of the disco-themed bar adjacent to the foyer, as the rest of the joint is decidedly more restrained. ₺125

Rüstem Paşa Kervansaray Hotel İki Kapalı Han Cad 57 ☎0284 212 6119, ⓦedirnekervansarayhotel .com. One of the most atmospheric choices in town, this is an authentic *caravanserai* designed by the famed architect Sinan and built in 1561. Rooms are arranged around a large courtyard and are basic but comfortable. €60

Taşodalar Selimiye Camii Arkası 3 ☎0284 212 3529, ⓦtasodalar.com.tr. Built in the Ottoman Palace mansion where Mehmet the Conqueror was born, this ten-room boutique hotel lives up to its history with luxurious interiors. Each room is named after a famous historical figure from Edirne and oozes style, with carefully selected mock-Ottoman furnishings, chandeliers and four-poster beds. Spotless en suites add a modern touch and the exquisite tea garden and restaurant offer a magnificent view over the Selimiye Mosque. €80–200

Tuna Maarif Cad 17 ☎0284 214 3340, ⓦedirne tunahotel.com. Cheap wooden furnishings, rug-strewn floors and unsightly patterned linens make you feel like you're back in the 1980s, but this unassuming hotel is still good value for money and they may well accept a lower offer. The identical, medium-sized rooms are neat and cosy, and the friendly staff liven up an otherwise uninspiring building. ₺110

EATING AND DRINKING

Not one for the vegetarians, Edirne's speciality is *ciğer tava*, slices of calf's liver coated in flour and deep fried, typically served with a hot chilli garnish and raw onions; it is good enough to convert even the most reluctant liver eater. Many of Edirne's restaurants are unremarkable, with most of the more elegant fare confined to tourist-geared hotel restaurants and a smattering of lively cafés on Saraçlar Cad. Licensed places are scarce in the centre, while some of those along the river are as much about drinking (usually *rakı* or beer) as eating.

RESTAURANTS

Asmaaltı Ocakbaşı Saraçlar Cad 147 ☎0284 212 8712. This licensed meat-grill is a popular haunt among locals. Dark wood creates a rather heavy atmosphere downstairs, whereas the terrace is lightened by hanging vines and overlooks the local football team's ground. Mains are around the ₺20 mark and favourites include Ali Nazik and aubergine kebab. Daily 5.30pm–1am.

Balkan Piliç Saraçlar Cad 14. This nondescript little restaurant – look out for the chickens spit-roasting in the window – might not look up to much but it's packed with locals for good reason. There's plenty of wholesome *lokanta* fare on offer here, with a range of vegetable options and a hearty lamb roast. A plateful of various dishes will set you back around ₺15. Unlicensed. Daily 11am–10pm.

Ciğerci Kemal Usta Ortakapı Cad 3. Every local has their own favourite spot to enjoy the Edirne speciality, *ciğar tava* – strips of fried liver, best eaten with dried, fried red peppers and a bowl of *cacık* (yoghurt and garlic). On a street with several good options, this humble restaurant is always packed with locals. Vegetarians should steer clear though, as there's nothing else on the menu. A portion costs ₺12 but you can always ask for *az porsiyon* for ₺7 if you just want to try it. Unlicensed. Daily 9am–10pm.

Gazi Baba Meyhanesi Zındanaltı Cad 139 ☎0284 214 5050, ⓦgazibabameyhanesi.com. This classic Turkish tavern has been going since 1967 and offers a chance to enjoy an authentic *meyhane* experience, complete with *meze* (₺3–10), *rakı* and a lively atmosphere, sometimes enhanced by live *fasıl* music. Daily noon–midnight.

Köfteci Osman Kuyumcular Sok 2 ☎0284 212 7725, ⓦedirnelikofteciosman.com. As well as liver, Edirne is also known for its *köfte* (meatballs), which are large, juicy and come served with a spicy condiment. Part of a local chain that has been around since 1988, this is the largest of three branches, with a bustling open space and speedy service. A plate of meatballs will set you back just ₺12. Unlicensed. Daily 11am–midnight.

Melek Anne Kayseri Mantısı Maarif Cad 18. Friendly, female-run establishment serving up a rotating lunch menu of home-cooked specialities with prices costing around ₺10 for a fully loaded plate. Try the delicious *karnıyarık* (meat-stuffed aubergine) or *gözleme* (a cheese-, potato- or mince-stuffed flatbread). A quiet, tree-shaded garden and free wi-fi add to the appeal. Daily 8am–9pm.

Zindanaltı Meyhanesi Saraçlar Cad 127 ☎0284 212 2149. Decked out like an old drinking tavern with aged wooden panelling, dim lighting and a collection of curious antiquities hanging from the walls, there's also a peaceful rooftop terrace equipped with a gurgling water fountain for those preferring to eat in daylight. The *meze* selection (prepared by a former oil-wrestling champion) changes daily and is displayed in the counter at the entrance. Mains include classic Turkish options such as *köfte*, grilled chicken or lamb chops for around ₺20. Daily 10am–midnight.

BARS & CAFÉS

Figüran Café/Bar Ortakapı Cad 6 ☎0284 225 5588, ⓦfigurancafe.com. Located among some of the city's best liver restaurants, there's an old film theme running through this cosy bar. The wood-panelled walls are adorned with old film posters of everything from Turkish Yeşilçam (1950–70s) flicks to old school Hollywood classics. Consisting of a maze of tiny rooms, you are likely to get a space just to yourself. Cocktails are surprisingly good, but the music policy is a mixed bag of 80s and 90s hits. Daily midday–2am.

Limon Café & Restaurant Karaağaç Yolu Üzeri Lozan Cad 32/1 ☎0284 223 1314, ⓦlimonedirne.com. This family-friendly restaurant is 3km south of town, on the leafy road that runs adjacent to the Meriç River. The menu offers a mixture of Turkish and international fare with a wide selection of pasta, salads and burgers. With its rather kitsch decor, it makes an equally pleasant spot to enjoy a Turkish breakfast or sip on an ice-cold beer. To get here, take the Karaağaç-bound minibus from in front of the PTT, or any red city bus heading south along Saraçlar Cad. Daily 8am–1.30am.

SHOPPING

There are a few covered bazaars in Edirne, of which the **Semiz Ali Paşa Çarşısı** (entrances on Londra Asfaltı or Saraçlar Cad; daily 9am–7pm) is arguably the most interesting, selling everything from pottery and souvenirs to cheap clothing, shoes, jewellery and household goods. Look out for Yaren Müsik and Müsik Aleteri, traditional music shops selling hand-crafted *baglamas* and zithers. The **Kavaflar Arasta** (Cobbler's Arcade; Mon–Sat 9am–7pm) near the Selimiye Camii is a good place to buy Edirne's traditional fruit-shaped soaps although there's little else on display here. One local speciality is *badem ezmesi* (marzipan), and there's a tiny but delightfully old-fashioned shop, Ezmecioğlu (Semiz Ali Paşa Çarşısı 1), that sells the stuff for a fraction of the price you'll pay in the upmarket outlets in Istanbul's suburbs. You can also find the delicious pistachio- (*kavala*) and almond- (*kallavi*) studded biscuits in the row of shops below the Selimye Camii. Also look out for some of the best cheese in Turkey, *Edirne peyniri*, which has a firmer texture and more delicate flavour than the standard white Turkish goat's cheese.

DIRECTORY

Banks and exchange There are several banks with ATMs along Londra Asfaltı and Saraçlar Cad, as well as a number of *döviz* (exchange) offices on and around Hürriyet Cad, plus one at the entrance to the Semiz Ali Paşa Çarşısı.

Hospital İç Yol 22, behind the Bulgarian Consulate.
Police Karanfiloğlu Cad, behind Şerefeli Camii.
Post office Saraçlar Cad 19 (8am–8pm for letters, 9am–5.30pm for full postal services, closed Sundays).

23

استانبولی
فتح ایدن غازی سلطان
محمد خان

OTTOMAN-ERA MINIATURE

Contexts

History

It may no longer be a capital, but Istanbul – the hub of two of history's greatest empires, the Byzantine and Ottoman – is one of the world's truly great cities. Given its long, glorious past, it is impossible to separate the history of the city from that of the lands it ruled, a territory which, at the height of the city's power, stretched from the Balkans to the Middle East and from the Russian steppes to the deserts of North Africa.

Prehistory

Until recently we knew very little about the prehistory of the area on which the modern metropolis of Istanbul now stands. In 2008, however, the excavation of the Yenikapı Metro station uncovered a **Neolithic burial site**, dating back to around 6500 BC. The skeletons and pottery grave-goods, taken for safekeeping to the Archeology Museum in nearby Sultanahmet (see pp.44–67), may have been buried beneath the homes of the deceased, or formed part of a necropolis on the edge of a Neolithic settlement. This made the site at Yenikapı one of the earliest "villages" in Europe – part of a wider process whereby a sedentary, agricultural way of life spread from its source in Mesopotamia through Anatolia and across the Bosphorus into Europe. A few finds from the **Chalcolithic period** (4500–3000 BC) have been made in the area around the Hippodrome, in the heart of Sultanahmet, along with some from the **Early Bronze Age** (3000–2000 BC) suggesting that settlement of the peninsula (the area that would be enclosed much later by the Byzantine land walls) was continuous since its **Neolithic** beginnings.

The city of the blind

What we know of the Bronze Age, Dark Age and early Greek Archaic periods comes from **myth** and **legend** rather than archeological or source evidence. The story of Jason and the Argonauts, in which the hero Jason sets off to the land of Colchis (in the eastern Black Sea) in search of the Golden Fleece, almost certainly derives from a **major historical movement** – Greek colonization. From the mid-eighth century BC onwards, Greeks sailed north and east from the Aegean, through the Hellespont, the Sea of Marmara and Bosphorus (probably the site of the so-called "clashing rocks" which almost crushed Jason's ship, the *Argo*) and up into the Black Sea, where they founded numerous colonies. The **Bosphorus**, a narrow, twenty-two-mile-long strait, became a crucial conduit linking the city-states of ancient Greece with their newly established colonies in the Black Sea, and a settlement was eventually founded in the early seventh century BC on the shores of the Bosphorus, controlling the trade route between the Black and Mediterranean seas.

The founders, seafarers from Megara, near Athens, built their settlement, known as **Chalcedon**, on the Asian side of the strait, on the site of the modern Istanbul suburb of

6500 BC	800 BC	676 BC
The first traces of human settlement on the site of today's Istanbul	Greek colonists sail through the Bosphorus from the Aegean to the Black Sea	Seafarers from Megara in Greece establish a settlement in Chalcedon, today's Kadıköy (see p.139)

> ## THE FIRST BOSPHORUS BRIDGE
>
> In the late sixth century BC, the Persian king **Darius** ordered a bridge of boats to be built across the Bosphorus in order to facilitate troop movements and protect his supply lines in a campaign against the Scythians to the west and north of the Black Sea. According to the (probably highly exaggerated) figures of the ancient Greek historian Herodotus, some 700,000 Persian troops marched across this, the first Bosphorus bridge. Darius's expedition, which reached as far west as the Danube, is seen as the **first historic attack** by Asia on Europe, and was successful in stopping Scythian raids on the territory of the Persian Empire, which at that time spread from the banks of the Indus to the Bosphorus. Remarkably, the feat was not to be repeated until 1974, with the opening of the first Bosphorus suspension bridge.

Kadıköy. Some twenty years later, according to Greek tradition, an adventurer called Byzas, anxious to found a new city, consulted the Delphic Oracle.

The priestess told him, in cryptic fashion, to build his new city "opposite the land of the blind", and Byzas set out for the Black Sea having no idea what was meant. However, when he reached the Bosphorus he realized that the founders of Chalcedon had been "blind" not to notice that the peninsula opposite them, in Europe, was strategically a far better place for a settlement. Built on the top of a hill at the tip of the naturally defensible triangular peninsula, **Byzantium** commanded the passage both up and across the Bosphorus, had a natural deep-water harbour and defence in the inlet now known as the **Golden Horn** to the north, and only a narrow neck of land to defend against any possible enemy approaching from the west.

This location was coveted by the great powers of the day, and King Darius of **Persia** eventually absorbed Byzantium into his empire towards the end of the sixth century BC as part of his campaigns against the Scythians and the Greeks (see box above).

The classical era

By the end of the sixth century BC, the Greek cities of Asia Minor and the Hellespont region had become part of the Persian Empire. Usually they installed tyrants to keep control and this, allied with heavy taxation, caused increasing resentment among the independently minded inhabitants. When the powerful city-state of **Athens** was drawn into aiding the Greek cities of Asia Minor in their revolt against Persian rule at the beginning of the fifth century, the incensed Darius was determined to conquer mainland Greece. But following his vanquishing at Marathon in 490 BC and his successor Xerxes' defeats at Thermopylae and Salamis in 480 BC, then Plataea in 479 BC, the Persians abandoned efforts to push west. The **Spartan** general Pausanias, who had led the victorious Greeks at Plataea, was put in charge of a Greek fleet and in 478 BC captured Byzantium from the Persians.

Athens, Sparta and Alexander the Great

The inhabitants of the city, now free from the Persian yoke, were soon caught up in the conflict between the two superpowers of the Classical Greek world, **Athens** and **Sparta**. Byzantium soon became part of Athens' Delian League, its prosperity highlighted by the high tributes it paid to the league's coffers, a wealth based largely on its control of

667 BC	513 BC	478 BC
The foundation of Byzantium (Istanbul) by Greek colonists from Megara, led by Byzas	Darius, King of Persia, captures Byzantium	The Spartan leader Pausanias liberates the city from Persian rule and it becomes a part of Athens' Delian League

the grain trade from the Black Sea to the Mediterranean. Towards the end of the fifth century BC the city switched sides, cutting off the grain supply to Athens and helping ensure Sparta's victory in the long-running **Peloponnesian War**.

Opportunist Byzantium switched sides again in the fourth century BC, before rebelling in 356 BC and gaining its **independence**. In 340 BC, with Athens' star on the wane, newly emerging Macedonia threatened from the west. According to legend, the besieged city was saved when the forces of King Philip II of Macedon, attempting a night attack, were illuminated by a miraculous waxing of the moon. The superstitious inhabitants praised the moon goddess **Hecate** for their salvation and began using her symbol, the star and crescent moon, on their **coinage** – a symbol adopted by Christian Byzantium many centuries later. When Philip's successor, **Alexander**, marched east to take on the mighty Persian Empire in 334 BC, rather than risk valuable men besieging Byzantium, he bypassed it and crossed the Hellespont (modern Dardanelles) into Asia. Following his victory against the Persians at the battle of Granicus, Byzantium threw open its gates. As a reward it was allowed to keep its independence, though it was compelled to acknowledge Macedonian overlordship.

The advent of Rome

During the early Hellenistic period the city suffered repeated **Scythian attacks** and, desperately needing to fund its war chest, raised the levy it charged on ships passing through the Bosphorus. In 220 BC this provoked a war with Rhodes, which Byzantium lost. Then, as the Romans moved eastward in the second century BC, first into Greece and then Asia Minor, the city negotiated terms with the Roman Republic, keeping its **autonomy** in return for payment of an annual tribute. By AD 79, the republic had become an **empire**, and Byzantium lost its privileges. Then, following the murder of the Emperor Pertinax in AD 193, a power struggle broke out between Pescennius Niger and Septimius Severus as to who would succeed him. Byzantium backed the loser and the victorious Severus laid siege to the city. After three years' resistance, Byzantium fell and a vengeful Severus razed the city to the ground, putting most of its inhabitants to the sword.

The site of Byzantium was too strategically and commercially valuable to leave vacant and, within a few years, Severus ordered the city to be rebuilt. The new land walls followed a line west of the original, doubling the area of land occupied by the old Byzantium. Severus renamed the new city **Antoninia** and ordered the construction of three glorious temples to Apollo, Artemis and Aphrodite on the hilltop around where the Haghia Sophia and Topkapı Palace now stand.

The new Byzantium prospered quietly, but during the early part of the fourth century it was thrust into the limelight. In AD 284 the Emperor **Diocletian**, in an effort to sort out the administrative problems of running a huge and unwieldy domain, divided the empire into two parts, each ruled by an emperor (or *Augustus*) and a junior ruler (or *Caesar*). This so-called **tetrarchy** was unworkable from the start, the idea of dynastic succession clashing with the merit-based system envisaged by Diocletian, and **civil war** ensued. The ruler of the western part of the empire, **Constantine**, defeated his rival **Licinius**, the emperor of the east, near Chrysopolis, on the Asian side of the Bosphorus in 324. Constantine, now sole ruler of the whole Roman Empire, was impressed with the superb location of Byzantium, just across the strait from the scene of the final battle, and commemorated his victory by founding it as his new imperial **capital**.

340 BC	**334 BC**	**195 AD**
Philip of Macedon's night-time raid on the city fails	Byzantium surrenders to Philip of Macedon's son, Alexander the Great	Roman emperor Septimius Severus razes the city to the ground, only to rebuild it a few years later

From New Rome to Constantinople

Much work needed to be done to make the old city a worthy imperial capital. The **rebuilding** began in 326, with the city walls moved further westward yet again, enclosing an area some five times larger than the Antoninia of Septimius Severus. Work continued for four years, during which time the **Hippodrome** (an arena used for games and court ceremonies) and Forum were enlarged, an imperial palace and large public baths were built. Constantine followed **tradition** and ordered works of art from around the empire to be brought to glorify the new capital, including the Serpentine Column from the Temple of Apollo at Delphi, now in the **Hippodrome**. Then, in May 330, during a grand ceremony in the Hippodrome, Constantine named the old Byzantium Nova Roma or the "New Rome", though it soon came to be known as Constantinopolis (Constantinople) or "The City of Constantine".

The Byzantine Empire

Under Constantine, Christianity moved from persecuted faith to official religion (see box opposite). In 392, Emperor **Theodosius I** banned **paganism** and ordered the demolition of all pagan temples, a move effectively making the whole Roman Empire a Christian one. In 395, following the death of Theodosius I, the empire was divided by his two sons, with **Honorius** ruling the west from Rome and **Arcadius** the east from Constantinople. While the western part of the empire struggled to survive the invasion of the **Vandals** and **Goths**, Constantinople and the eastern half generally prospered. In 413, during the reign of Emperor Theodosius II, the land walls of the city were rebuilt a couple of kilometres further west again than those of Constantine. On a pragmatic level, the walls were needed to contain the growing population of the city and to withstand the threat of Attila the Hun; on a symbolic one they meant the city now incorporated seven hills, just like Rome. Although an **earthquake** caused the walls to tumble in 447, they were quickly rebuilt along the same lines. Theodosius II also ordered the construction of a monumental new church, the Haghia Sophia.

In 476, Rome fell to the Goths, and **Constantinople** became the sole capital of a much-reduced empire. The collapse of the western part of the empire also marked a significant change in the nature of the eastern half, which developed an ever more distinct Greek and Christian – or Byzantine – character.

Imperial expansion, artistic expression

Six emperors ruled between the death of Theodosius in 450 and the accession of the greatest of all Byzantine emperors, **Justinian** (527–65) – a period that saw increased tension between Rome and Constantinople over papal supremacy. Justinian's prospects were rather dim initially. The Sassanid Persians threatened the eastern borders of the empire and Justinian's great general, Belisarius, after some initial success, suffered an ignominious reversal in 531, after which the Byzantines were forced to pay a heavy tribute to ensure **peace**. Then, in 532, events at the heart of the empire almost led to disaster. Supporters of the two factions at the Hippodrome, the **Blues** and the **Greens**, named after the strip the rival charioteers wore, rioted in the streets of the capital. When Justinian ordered the execution of the ringleaders, the enraged mob turned its wrath on the emperor himself. Fortunately for him, the brilliant Belisarius was in the

324	330	337
Emperor Constantine declares the city will be the site of a new imperial capital and building commences	Constantine names the newly rebuilt city Nova Roma or the "New Rome", though it soon becomes known as Constantinople	Constantine is baptized as a Christian

CONSTANTINE AND CHRISTIANITY

Scholars still debate the date that Constantine fully embraced **Christianity**. In the **Edict of Milan**, issued in 313, he and his then co-ruler Licinius announced that this hitherto much persecuted faith was to be tolerated. His mother Helena, a devout Christian herself, no doubt exerted great influence over her son's beliefs and he was certainly attracted to the religion, though it seems he wasn't baptized until near his death in 337. Constantine had previously established his control of the Christian Church at the ecumenical **Council of Nicaea** in 325, when he ensured that the emperor was both head of state and head of the Church. Christianity, officially sanctioned and state-controlled, became the dominant faith of the Roman Empire, and many churches were built within the confines of the new city walls.

capital and not on campaign and he soon restored order, butchering thirty thousand rioters in the process.

The damage caused by the **Nika riots** gave Justinian a good excuse to glorify both himself and his imperial capital and, in the massive building spree that followed, the most magnificent structure erected was a third incarnation of the **Haghia Sophia**, the Church of the Holy Wisdom, since converted into a mosque and the name Turkicized to Aya Sofya (see pp.45–49). Other ecclesiastical buildings included the exquisite **Church of Sergius and Bacchus** (today's Küçük Aya Sofya; see p.66) and the **Haghia Eirene** (Aya İrini; see p.51), along with the rather more practical **Basilica Cistern** (Yerebatan Sarnıcı; see pp.61–62), which helped secure the capital's water supply.

Constantinople was now one of the greatest cities in the world. It sat at the centre of a revived empire, with Belisarius leading campaigns resulting in the re-conquest of much of its western part, including Italy, southern Spain and North Africa. The magnificence of Justinian's reign did not prevent his court historian, **Procopius**, from dishing up plenty of dirt on the emperor and his wife, a former prostitute who Procopius claimed danced publicly in the nude and encouraged geese to peck bread from her pubic hair.

Barbarians at the gate

In the centuries following the **death** of Justinian, the citizens of Constantinople had much cause to thank their city's natural defences and mighty walls. From the north came the Slavs and Avars, while the Serbs and Bulgars pressed from the northwest. The danger from the Sassanid Persians was even greater. Having taken Syria, Palestine, Egypt and much of North Africa from the Byzantines early in the reign of the Emperor **Heraclius** (610–641), they soon swept across Anatolia to reach the shores of the Bosphorus at Chalcedon, opposite Constantinople. Fortunately Heraclius was made of stern stuff and, taking command of a Byzantine army (the first emperor to do so since Theodosius I), he marched east and decisively defeated the Sassanians.

His work was soon undone. The armies of the new religion of **Islam** swept out of Arabia around 637 and all that Heraclius had won was lost to the Muslims. By 674, the **Arab armies** were at the gates of Constantinople, only to be repulsed by a formidable new weapon invented by the **Byzantines** and whose exact constitution is unknown to this day – Greek Fire. This lethal substance, a mixture of flammable oils, could burn on water and was used to great effect by the Byzantines, especially in naval

392	447	532
Paganism is banned by the Emperor Theodosius and the Roman Empire becomes an overtly Christian entity	The land walls are rebuilt and strengthened following a massive earthquake	Thirty thousand rioters, seeking to depose Emperor Justinian, are butchered in the Hippodrome

---

ICONOCLASM

Theological debate was very much a concern of the Byzantine Empire and in the eighth century a dispute arose over the use of images and icons. The **iconoclasts**, possibly influenced by similar prohibitions in Judaism and Islam, believed that figurative images, particularly of Christ and the saints, should not be venerated. Emperor **Leo III** (717–41) gave the movement official sanction when, in 726, he ordered the removal of a large gold icon of Christ from one of the doors of Justinian's palace. Opponents of the movement **rioted** in the streets, but this did not stop the iconoclasts, who ransacked churches and monasteries across the empire. Many wonderful works of religious art were destroyed during this period and Byzantine society was riven apart. The **Council of Nicaea** (see box, p.233) held in 787, ruled that icon worship was now permissible, but the dispute continued on until 847, further weakening an empire now beset by a new and more tangible threat, the Bulgars.

---

battles. The Arab armies, however, kept coming and it wasn't until they were repulsed from the city in 718 that the threat finally ended.

Having saved themselves from the Muslim Arabs, the Christian inhabitants of the empire did their best to destroy themselves. Debates over **icon worship** (see box above) resulted in vandalism and riots and destabilized Church and State for over a century. Yet despite all these problems, the Byzantine Empire endured. The Bulgars were repulsed twice by the land walls of Theodosius in the ninth and tenth centuries and, within the walls, the capital enjoyed a brief **artistic revival**. In 1014, Emperor Basil II (976–1025), the "Bulgar Slayer", finally put an end to the **Bulgar menace** and incorporated their lands into the empire. In 1054 the long-running disputes between Rome and Constantinople, stemming from doctrinal differences and competing claims as to who had authority over the Greek churches of southern Italy, resulted in a final schism between the **Catholic** and **Orthodox** churches. The Patriarch of Constantinople, despite being declared a heretic by the **pope**, was now more powerful than ever in the east.

The coming of the Turks

Having already lost land in the northwest to the Bulgars and much territory in the east to the Arabs, a new **Muslim** threat to the Byzantine Empire, the Turks, emerged in Anatolia. Originating from Central Asia, from the eighth century onwards these nomadic tribal peoples moved westwards in search of new pastures. Originally shamanists, by the end of the ninth century many had **converted** to Islam following their encounters with the Arabs. In 1071 one branch of these Turkic tribes, the **Selçuks**, met and decisively defeated the Byzantine army of Emperor Romanos IV Diogenes (1067–71) at Manzikert, near **Lake Van** in eastern Anatolia. Diogenes was captured and the victors swept into Anatolia, finally establishing their capital at Konya in **Central Anatolia**. Although the Byzantines did manage to recapture some lost territory, the empire was much reduced.

The crusades

Luckily for the Byzantines, the Muslim Selçuk Turks seemed happy enough to leave Constantinople alone. Instead it was fellow Christians, the **Crusaders**, who brought the city to its knees. The First Crusade passed through Anatolia en route to the Holy Land

537	674	726
A magnificent new cathedral, the Haghia Sophia is completed on the site of the one burnt in the riots of 532	The defenders of Constantinople use lethal Istanbul (flammable oils) against besieging Arab forces	Emperor Leo III declares icon veneration idolatry and many icons are destroyed, triggering rioting across the empire

in 1097 without any problem, but in 1175, during the Second Crusade, Frederick Barbarossa encouraged the Selçuks to launch an attack against the Byzantines. The two armies met at **Myriokephalo** in 1176, with the Selçuks decisive victors. It was a disastrous defeat, quickly followed by the Balkan states, fed up with ever-increasing taxation, seceding from the Byzantine Empire. More alarmingly, in 1185 the **Normans** captured and sacked the empire's second city, **Salonica**. The writing was on the wall for Constantinople, despite the fact that the Normans were defeated before they reached the capital. On the Third Crusade in 1187, the invaders took Adrianople (modern Edirne), some 300km east of Constantinople, causing great alarm in the city.

Emperor **Alexius III** (1195–1203) came to power by deposing his brother, **Isaac II** (1185–95). Isaac's son Alexius sought aid from the West to reinstate his father – a pretext that power-hungry Crusaders were only too happy to seize upon. The Fourth Crusade started in 1201, with the aim of capturing Constantinople – a plan backed by the **Doge of Venice**, who hoped to increase his city's trade by eliminating its eastern rival. In 1203 the Crusaders took **Galata**, on the north side of the Golden Horn. They now held a strategic position from which to attack the city without having to penetrate the near impregnable land walls. Alexius III fled the capital, taking the imperial treasury with him, and **Isaac II** regained the throne, though, because he had been blinded on his deposing by Alexius III, Isaac's son and co-emperor **Alexius IV** (1203–04) was the effective ruler. He was less than popular though, as his overtures to the West had resulted in the Crusaders turning their attention to **Constantinople** and, in January 1204 the populace revolted and deposed him.

The new emperor, **Alexius V** (1204), was left to face the Crusaders. On April 13, the besieging forces penetrated the less-formidable sea walls running along the south shore of the Golden Horn and poured into the capital. The Latin Crusaders had long coveted both the Byzantines' wealth (accrued from their extensive domains) and culture (derived from a fusion of the glories of ancient Greece and Rome and the precepts of Christianity). Motivated by resentment and greed, they ransacked the city. The artistic treasures and religious relics that had been amassed over the centuries were shipped west or destroyed and Alexius V was forced to jump to his death from atop the **column of Arcadius**.

Rule of what was left of the imperial capital was shared between **Count Baldwin** of Flanders and Dandolo, the **Doge of Venice**. The Byzantine Empire was not yet ready to fold, though. A new capital arose in **Nicaea** (modern İznik) on the south side of the Sea of Marmara. In 1261, its then emperor, **Michael VIII Palaeologos** (1261–82), took Constantinople from the Latins and was crowned for a second time in the church of Haghia Sophia – effectively restoring the Byzantine Empire.

With the Latins no longer threatening from the west, and the Selçuk Turks' ambitions to expand westward thwarted by rampaging Mongol armies, the Byzantine Empire, despite its much-reduced size and status, underwent a mini-renaissance. This is seen most obviously in the wonderful early fourteenth-century frescoes and mosaics in the Church of **St Saviour** in Chora (now the Kariye Museum; see pp.94–98).

The rise of the Ottomans

The **Ottomans**, like their **Selçuk** kin, hailed originally from Central Asia and were Muslim. By the late thirteenth century this semi-nomadic, Turkish tribal grouping had

1054	1071	1097
The Orthodox and Catholic churches split over doctrinal and other disputes	The first Turks, the Selçuks, appear in Anatolia and defeat Emperor Romanos IV Diogenes at Manzikert	The First Crusade passes through Constantinople en route to the Holy Land

settled in Phrygia, in northwest **Anatolia**. Their leader was Osman, and his followers were known as Osmanlı, later westernized into "Ottoman". Within a few years, Gazi ("warrior of the faith") Osman had extended the boundaries of his territory both to the east and the north. In 1326 his son and successor, Orhan, captured the important Byzantine city of Proussa (modern Bursa). Orhan took the title **sultan** and made Bursa capital of his mini-empire, marking the transition of the Ottomans from semi-nomadic pastoralists to a settled people with a state of their own. Orhan continued Ottoman expansion, largely at the expense of the Byzantines, taking Nicaea (İznik), Nicomedia (İzmit) and then Chrysopolis (Üsküdar), right opposite Constantinople on the Asian side of the Bosphorus.

The next sultan, **Murat I** (1360–89), captured Adrianople (Edirne) in 1361. Later he took Ottoman arms into the heart of the Balkans, conquering Thrace, Macedonia, Bulgaria and Serbia. The Ottomans also battled with their Muslim and Turkish kin and, in a campaign against the Muslim Karaman dynasty in western Asia Minor, actually used Christian mercenaries in their army. By the time of Murat I's successor **Beyazıt I** (1389–1403), the Byzantine Empire was little more than a rump state. Beyazıt, known as Yıldırım or "Lightning" for the speed of his military campaigns, besieged Constantinople in 1394 but, thanks to its walls, it survived. The inhabitants of the city could not, however, prevent the Ottomans building the fortress of **Anadolu Hisarı** on the Asian banks of the Bosphorus, just a few kilometres north of the city, in 1397, giving them control of trade through the strait. The Ottoman conquest of the city had an air of inevitability about it, but the arrival in Anatolia of the Mongol warlord Tamerlane, who routed Beyazıt's army at the Battle of Ankara in 1402, gave the **Byzantine Empire** a fifty-year reprieve. Beyazıt was caged for a year before meeting his end and to make matters worse his four sons warred over the accession. Fortunately for the Ottomans, Tamerlane died in 1405 and **Mongol** power waned. The Ottoman Empire, reunited by **Mehmet I** (1413–21), resumed its expansion in the reign of his successor, **Murat II** (1421–51).

The fall of Constantinople

Weakened by the continual loss of territory and numerous sieges, the fall of **Constantinople**, known by the Byzantine Empire and many beyond simply as "The Polis" (City) – as if there were no other – was inevitable. Constantinople, both symbolically and strategically, was too important not to be brought under Ottoman control. **Mehmet II** (1451–81) planned the siege meticulously. First he ordered the construction of the **Rumeli Hisarı**, a fortress on the European side of the Bosphorus directly opposite the Anadolu Hisarı fortress. The Ottomans now controlled traffic through the Bosphorus and blocked access to the city from the Black Sea. As the city was surrounded on three sides by water, he enlarged and outfitted a substantial fleet, which he placed in the Sea of Marmara to block access to the enemy from the south. Well aware of the number of times past sieges had foundered on the mighty land walls, Mehmet employed artillery and ballistics experts from Europe and then massed his land forces against the walls.

The defenders of Constantinople, led by the Emperor **Constantine XI** (1449–53), mobilized as best they could for the defence of their beleaguered city, manning the walls with troops, including their Italian allies, and stretching a huge chain across the

1204	1261	1316
Encouraged by the Doge of Venice, the army of the Fourth Crusade captures Constantinople and loots many of its treasures	Michael VIII Palaeologus recaptures the city from the Latins and the Byzantine Empire is restored	The Church of St Saviour in Chora is embellished with wonderful mosaics, commissioned by statesman Theodore Metochites

THE BYZANTINE LEGACY

For over a millennium this cosmopolitan, polyglot Christian empire kept the armies of Islam from Western Europe. The **Byzantine legacy** is a considerable one. Educated and civilized, its scholars and scribes copied and preserved Classical texts that might otherwise have been lost, arguably paving the way for the **Renaissance**. In terms of art and architecture its achievements were remarkable, particularly in the ecclesiastical field, with the innovative **Haghia Sophia** the inspiration for countless churches across the Orthodox world. Despite the various theological disputes that threatened to bring the empire to its knees on occasion, its capital, Constantinople, was a beacon of Christianity, and even today the city is the spiritual centre of Orthodox Christianity.

mouth of the Golden Horn to prevent the entry of Ottoman ships. When the siege began, in April 1453, Mehmet II outsmarted the defenders by building a trail over the hills of **Galata** and rolling his ships down into the Golden Horn above the chain. Batteries of Ottoman artillery, including what was then the largest cannon ever built, designed by the inventor **Orban**, pounded the land walls mercilessly. For seven long weeks the seven thousand defenders held out against some sixty thousand Ottoman troops, but in vain. On May 29, Ottoman cannon breached the land walls between the Topkapı and Edirnekapı gates and the attackers poured in. Constantine XI, the last Byzantine emperor, perished in hand-to-hand combat on the walls, though his body remained unidentified among the slain. The Turks raced through the streets of the fallen city to the Haghia Sophia. Here, according to legend, the Patriarch, celebrating Mass, disappeared into the church walls and will not reappear until the city is back in **Greek hands**.

The Ottoman Empire

Sultan Mehmet was determined to make the city a worthy new hub for his already far-flung empire, though the city did not actually usurp **Edirne** as capital until the reign of **Selim I** (1512–20). Now entitled Fatih, or "Conqueror" Mehmet, he boosted the shattered population of the city by bringing in both Muslims and Christians (mainly Greeks and Armenians) from around the empire and instituting the long-lasting millet or "nation" system (see box, p.287). He then restored what had been neglected during the Byzantine Empire's years of decline, and rebuilt that which had been destroyed in the siege and subsequent sack of the city, especially the roads, the sewers and the water system. The **Topkapı Palace** (see pp.50–55) was completed in 1465, just to the south of the Haghia Sophia, which of course, was itself turned into a mosque, the **Aya Sofya**. The magnificent Fatih Camii or "Mosque of the Conqueror", with its associated hospital, theological school and soup kitchens, was typical of the many mosque complexes built across the city, where worship and philanthropy went hand in hand. The city walls were rebuilt, and the massive fortification of **Yedikule** added to them. The Genoese, pardoned by Fatih Mehmet for helping in the defence of Constantinople, were compelled to remove the walls surrounding their enclave in **Galata**.

1326	1361	1397
A Turkish tribal leader, Orhan Gazi, captures Proussa (today's Bursa) and makes it his capital	Murat I captures Adrianople (today's Edirne) from the Byzantines	The Ottomans build the fortress of Anadolu Hısar on the Asian side of the Bosphorus: part of the plan to capture Constantinople

Expansion

Mehmet was not content with rebuilding the city. The loyal janissary corps (see box opposite), ably supplemented by regular forces made up of conscripts rewarded with grants of land at the end of their service, made the Ottoman **military machine** the envy of the age. The empire expanded at a faster rate than ever, with the addition of most of what is now Greece, Albania, the majority of Serbia and Bosnia-Herzegovina in the west, the southern Black Sea coast to the northeast and Rhodes in the Aegean. **Toleration** of the customs and faiths of its subjects helped prevent rebellion, and effective **administration** meant the empire ran relatively smoothly, with the sultan's domains divided into a number of easily regulated districts, trade and industry encouraged (to the extent of granting trading rights to potential rivals such as the Venetians and Genoese) and taxes levied efficiently.

Beyazıt II (1481–1512) improved the Ottoman fleet to such an extent that it was able to overtake Venice as the leading naval power in the Mediterranean, but was forced to abdicate by his own son, **Selim I** (1512–20). An orthodox Sunni Muslim, Selim's immediate concern was his Shi'ite neighbour **Shah İsmail** of Persia. Islam had split into these two competing groups following a dispute over who was the rightful successor to the Prophet Mohammed, with the majority (later known as Sunnis) convinced the successor should be chosen from the community of Muslims, a minority (who became known as Shi'ites) believing he must come from Mohammed's family. İsmail was starting to promote Shi'ism both within and without his empire, encouraging the Shi'ite population of Anatolia to question Selim's rule. The sultan took no chances and butchered forty thousand Shi'ites in Anatolia before heading east to defeat the Shah in the battle of **Çaldıran** in 1514, a victory which sealed the eastern border of the Ottoman Empire – and still forms, more or less, the modern frontier between Turkey and Iran. Selim then turned south and conquered **Mesopotamia**, **Syria** and **Egypt**. Crucially, Mecca and Medina now fell under Ottoman control, as did the spiritual leader of the Islamic world, the **caliph**. From now on, Ottoman rulers saw themselves as both sultan and caliph and were able to promote themselves and their causes on both a temporal and a spiritual plane.

Selim I, known in the West as Selim "the Grim" for his severe manner and bigotry, was succeeded in 1520 by his son **Süleyman** (1520–66), a ruler with the rather more impressive sobriquet "the Magnificent". Under his rule, the empire pushed its boundaries far into Europe. In 1529 the Turks caused the continent to quake by reaching the gates of **Vienna**, and until the failure of the siege of **Malta** in 1565 the Mediterranean was virtually an Ottoman lake. Arguably the leading world power of the sixteenth century, the Ottomans used the revenue raised from their military successes

---

ISTANBUL OR CONSTANTINOPLE?

The Ottomans were quite happy to keep the city's old name, **Constantinople**, albeit in the Turkicized form of "Konstantiniyye". This was, however, used alongside a new name, **Istanbul**, itself a corruption of the Greek *eis tin polin* or "to the city". The city was also known as **Islamboul** or "Full of Islam", a pious pun on the name Istanbul and, more rarely, **Dersaadet** or "Abode of Felicity". The name of the city wasn't changed officially until 1930, when the new Republic deemed "Constantinople" reactionary and imperialist.

1452	**1453**	**1453**
Mehmet II constructs Rumeli Hisarı on the European side of the Bosphorus, opposite Anadolu Hisarı, to control the strait	The two-month siege of the city ends with victory for the Ottomans and Mehmet II enters the city in triumph	The cathedral of Haghia Sophia becomes a mosque

INFIDELS IN THE EMPIRE

The Ottoman army had included **janissaries** in its ranks since the fourteenth century. This elite body was made up of Christian boys taken from their families, converted to Islam, and given the best military training. Other **non-Muslims** were barred from military service.

Indeed, the strict distinctions in the Ottoman world meant infidels were officially second-class citizens, known as "**rayah**" or cattle. This **millet** or "nation" system allowed the non-Muslim inhabitants of the empire (largely Armenian, Greek and Slav Christians and Jews), a fair degree of autonomy in return for paying their taxes. In spite of its apparent iniquities the system worked, with non-Muslim communities given a great deal of autonomy, and compared with the treatment of the Jews in Europe at the time, for example, the non-Muslim population of the empire was well off. Indeed, towards the end of the fifteenth century, the Ottomans sent "**mercy ships**" to the Iberian peninsula to collect and bring back to the empire the Jews persecuted and finally expelled by Spain and Portugal – many of whom eventually made their way to Istanbul and contributed greatly to the city's economic success. The Ottoman Empire may have been ruled by Muslims, but it was multi-ethnic, multi-faith and, for the period, very tolerant.

to glorify their great capital, **Istanbul**. Süleyman was blessed in having at his disposal the greatest architect of the Ottoman era, **Sinan**, who was equally fortunate to be living and working at a time when the empire's coffers were overflowing. His Istanbul masterpiece, rivalled only by his **Selimiye Camii** (see pp.270–271) in the former Ottoman capital of Edirne, was the **Süleymaniye** mosque complex (see pp.82–84), which still dominates the skyline of the city.

The rot sets in

Süleyman's reign is rightly seen as a **golden age** – especially when compared to a Western Europe of small kingdoms engaged in petty squabbles. The empire stretched from the Balkans in the west to the Persian border in the east and from the steppes of Russia south into Lower Egypt, had an imperial treasury capable of funding magnificent works of architecture and was governed by an able administrator and legislator. Yet the seeds of decline were already taking root.

Although earlier sultans had married, often expediently to princesses from neighbouring Muslim or Christian dynasties, **Süleyman** broke Ottoman precedent by wedding his favourite concubine, **Roxelana**, the daughter of a Ukrainian priest. The ambitious Roxelana ensured the succession of her first-born son, the weak and ineffectual **Selim II** (1566–74), and persuaded Süleyman to move the *harem* from the old palace grounds in Beyazıt into the Topkapı Palace. Under Selim II, Topkapı became a pleasure palace and the sultan was happy to indulge himself – becoming known in the West as "Selim the Sot".

Selim II's rule set a precedent that successive sultans were to follow, and they became increasingly **detached** from the reality of ruling the empire. Isolated in the palace, manipulated by unscrupulous grand viziers and the mothers of sultans or favourite concubines, successive sultans seemed to lack the mental strength to efficiently manage the empire. The introduction of the **Kafes** or "Cage" under **Ahmet I** (1603–17), in which the heirs apparent were incarcerated in a suite of rooms in the Harem until it was their turn to take the throne (see box, p.54), may have been less brutal than the

1459	1481	1492
Construction of the Topkapı Palace, the nerve-centre of the Ottoman Empire, begins	Beyazıt II becomes Sultan, later named "the Just" for his tolerant rule	Beyazıt sends an Ottoman fleet to Spain to save the expelled Jews

earlier custom of fratricide (**Murat III** had his five brothers put to death on his accession to the throne in 1574), but underlined the sultans' isolation.

Ahmet I was responsible for Istanbul's famous Blue Mosque (see p.64), but elsewhere the empire was stagnating. The **janissary corps** was becoming bloated, rising from some 12,000 under Mehmet II to 200,000 by the mid-seventeenth century. Rather than being an elite recruited from the empire's Christian population, membership was now handed down from father to son, effectively making the corps Muslim. Further easing of restrictions on membership allowed Muslims from outside the ranks of the janissaries to join the corps. Most had no military background – their only interest was to collect their pay and extort cash from the defenceless peasantry, or even from the sultans themselves.

This corruption and nepotism was compounded by external pressures, with a Europe revitalized by the **Renaissance** now looking hungrily at Ottoman domains. In 1536 the **French** signed a treaty with the empire involving various trading advantages but, more worryingly, giving French nationals **exemption** from Ottoman taxes and the right to be judged by their own consuls under foreign law. The privileges offered to the French, and then to other European nations and even companies, became known as the **Capitulations**. They helped undermine Ottoman sovereignty and increased Muslim resentment against the empire's Christians, many of whom became employees of the European traders and were given the same rights and privileges as their foreign employers.

In 1571, a Christian force led by **Don John** of Austria, put together under the pope's auspices to reduce Ottoman power in the Mediterranean, defeated the Ottoman fleet at Lepanto. The battle proved that the Ottomans were not invincible and put paid to further expansion in Europe for some time. The late sixteenth and early seventeenth centuries saw the Ottomans battling the **Persians** on their eastern frontier, ending with the loss of Baghdad to Shah Abbas I in 1624. **Murat IV** (1623–40) proved more able than his predecessors and was the first ruler since Süleyman the Magnificent to personally lead his troops to war, culminating in the retaking of Baghdad in 1638. But Murat died at the age of 30 and the rate of decline began to accelerate. In 1656 the janissaries staged a major **rebellion**, hanging a number of leading officials outside the Blue Mosque in their anger at receiving their pay in copper, while in eastern Anatolia local warlords challenged Ottoman authority. The population of the empire more than doubled (from around 12 million to 25 or 30 million between 1525 and 1600) and landless **peasants** streamed into Istanbul and other urban centres, putting more pressure on the system.

Efforts to **expand** into Europe proved disastrous. Following several defeats at the hands of the Austrians, the Turks suffered a humiliating defeat while attempting to take Vienna in 1683. The empire lost Hungary and other territory in Eastern Europe, though the treaties of Carlowitz (1699) and Passarowitz (1718) did stabilize the **Balkan frontier**.

An era of reform

At the turn of the eighteenth century, the Ottoman Empire did what all empires do once they stop expanding – declined. Yet **Istanbul**, far from the troublesome frontiers and with a stranglehold over the empire's finances, remained a city of splendour. **Sultan**

1514	1517	1529
Selim I, known to the west as "the Grim", wins a crucial victory over the Persian Shah	Selim I captures Medina and takes the title of Caliph	The Ottomans reach the gates of Vienna under Süleyman the Magnificent

Ahmet III (1703–30) and his able Grand Vizier İbrahim Paşa, both much influenced by European (especially French) arts and culture, oversaw something of a **renaissance** in the capital during the so-called **Tulip Period**. The Fountain of Sultan Ahmet III, outside the Topkapı Palace (see pp.50–55), is a good example of Baroque influence on Ottoman architecture in this period. More importantly, Ahmet set up the first press to print **books** in Ottoman Turkish. He also imported thousands of **tulip** bulbs from Holland and Persia, planting them in the palace gardens and illuminating them at night by roving tortoises with candles fixed to their shells.

Outside the capital, life was less frivolous. **Russia** had its eyes fixed firmly on Ottoman territory, especially the Bosphorus, control of which would give them crucial access from the Black Sea to the Mediterranean. The Ottomans suffered several reversals, notably off the **Aegean island** of Chios in 1771, and in 1779 they lost the **Crimea**. Russian interference in Ottoman affairs, often under the pretext of protecting the rights of the sultan's Greek Orthodox Christian subjects, would run until the Bolshevik Revolution of 1917 put a temporary end to Russian imperialism.

A much earlier **revolution**, that of France in 1789, was to have an enormous impact on the ailing Ottoman Empire. **Selim III** (1789–1807) came to the throne in the same year, and set out to reform the empire on Western lines. His efforts to reform the military were resisted by the janissaries, who forced him to dissolve a new force before rebelling and finally **murdering** the sultan. His successor, **Mahmut II** (1808–39), realized he would have to take things more slowly if he were to succeed in reforming the near-moribund institutions of the Ottoman state. He had a lucky break in 1812, when Napoleon's invasion of Russia compelled the **Tsar** to sign a **peace treaty** favourable to the Ottomans; he was less lucky in 1821 when a full-scale **rebellion** broke out in Greece. The revolt, which ended in 1830 with the formation of an independent Greek state, marked the beginning of the end for the cosmopolitan Ottoman world, as ethnic groupings from the Balkans to the Middle East sought to break away from the empire – including **Egypt**, which seceded in 1838.

In the capital, Mahmut II fared rather better. Like Selim III, he founded a new, **Western-style army**, but unlike his predecessor he managed to suppress the inevitable janissary revolt in 1826. Appropriately, it was the new, professionally trained troops who crushed the ill-disciplined janissaries, bombarding their barracks and leaving the Hippodrome piled high with their dead. Not content with quelling the revolt, Mahmut disbanded the old elite corps and banned their supporters, the reactionary Bektaşi dervish order. Prussian and Austrian advisers were brought in to train his new army, and a military academy and medical school founded, with French as the language of instruction. In further westernizing reforms, Mahmut introduced formal **civil and foreign services**, insisted that all but clerics must wear Western-style clothing and replaced the "oriental" turban with the **fez**.

The sick man of Europe

Sultan Abdülmecit (1839–61) was quick to build on the modernization programme of his predecessor, heralding an era of change known as the **Tanzimat** (Reorganization or Reform in Turkish). The Tanzimat Fermanı (Reform Decree) set out the changes needed to revitalize the moribund empire. These included devolving some of the sultan's powers to advisers, attempts to end taxation irregularities and the

1558	1571	1616
Completion of the Süleymaniye Camii, the masterpiece of the finest Ottoman architect, Sinan	A Christian fleet led by Don John of Austria defeats the Ottoman navy at Lepanto	The monumental Blue Mosque (Sultanahmet Camii) is completed after eight years

reorganization of the finance system and Civil and Military code on the French model. More Important and far more controversial was the declaration of full **equality** between the empire's Muslim and non-Muslim inhabitants, including Turks, Kurds, Armenians, Greeks, Jews and Circassians. The sultan further distanced himself from the past by moving his abode across the Golden Horn, from the Topkapı Palace to the grandiose European-style **Dolmabaçhe Palace** (see pp.131–133).

The empire also began to experience an **economic revival** that continued through the nineteenth century and manifested itself in the capital by a wide variety of civic and commercial projects. Heading these was the formation of the Ottoman Steamship Company in 1851, the construction of the Tünel underground funicular railway in Galata, the setting up of the British-funded Ottoman Bank, the construction of a bridge across the Golden Horn and the introduction of a postal service. Pera and Galata (today's Beyoğlu), inhabited mainly by foreigners and the city's Christian and Jewish minorities, underwent a **building boom**. European-style apartment blocks, music halls, cafés, bars and restaurants lined the streets, especially the Grande Rue de Pera (today's İstiklal Caddesi). Modern hotels, notably the *Pera Palace* (see p.123), sprang up in what is now Beyoğlu, catering to the influx of tourists from Europe, a stream that became a flood when the **Orient Express** began disgorging its affluent passengers at newly built Sirkeci Station in 1888.

Unfortunately, Abdülmecit's extravagance plunged the Ottoman state into **debt**, and traditional bazaar craftsmen were decimated by industrially produced goods from Western Europe. The Tanzimat reforms also alienated many Muslims, who resented the new-found equality of the Christians and Jews, especially as the European traders had favoured the Greek, Armenian and Jewish minorities over the Muslim majority since the Capitulations introduced in the sixteenth century. Even worse for the Muslims, the empire's Christian minorities now had the right and the funds to build places of worship, and shiny new **churches**, largely Armenian Apostolic and Greek Orthodox, sprang up across the capital.

Had the Ottoman Empire been left alone to sort out its internal problems, things might have turned out differently. As it was, the empire became embroiled in the machinations of **Britain**, **France** and **Russia**. In 1853 **Tsar Nicholas I** said of the ailing empire "We have a sick man on our hands – a man gravely ill. It will be a grave misfortune if one of these days he slips through our hands", a clear indication of Russian designs on Ottoman territory. The **Crimean War** of 1853–56 began with an argument between Russia and France over the protection to be extended by each to, respectively, the Orthodox and Catholic churches in Ottoman **Palestine**. In the end Russia demanded the right to "protect" all the Ottoman Empire's Orthodox Christian subjects. Determined to prevent Russia getting its hands on Ottoman territory, Britain and France backed the sultan. The war ended, more or less, in a stalemate, though one side-effect was to bring **Florence Nightingale** to the massive Selimiye Barracks on the Asian side of the Bosphorus in Üsküdar (see box, p.142).

Young Ottomans to Young Turks

Emboldened by the Tanzimat reforms, a new, liberal elite, the **Society of Young Ottomans**, sprang up in the reign of **Abdülaziz** (1861–76). Educated at the secular schools introduced in the reign of Abdülmecit and influenced by Western European

1683	1729	1779
An Ottoman army is humiliatingly defeated while attempting to capture Vienna	Sultan Ahmet I sets up the Ottoman Empire's first printing press	The Ottomans lose the Crimea to Russia, who will remain a thorn in their side until 1917

political thought, this elite sought a constitutional monarchy. Less liberal than his predecessor, Abdülaziz was not amused and exiled the ringleaders. He proved a weak and ineffectual ruler, however. The genie of ethnic-nationalism, heralded by Greece's declaration of independence, was now well and truly out of the bottle, with revolts in Lebanon, Crete, Bosnia-Herzegovina, Montenegro and then Bulgaria to contend with. Abdülaziz's brutal suppression of these rebellions turned the European powers against the empire and, with the economy in freefall, the Young Ottomans, led by one Mithat Paşa, deposed the sultan.

The short-lived reign of Abdülaziz's nephew **Murat** gave way almost immediately to that of **Abdülhamit** (1876–1909) who, a few months into his rule, signed off a new **constitution**. In theory this was a real step forward, confirming the equality of all Ottoman citizens, reducing the power of the grand vizier, introducing secular courts and establishing a parliamentary structure. The sultan, though, was confirmed as both head of state and caliph of the Islamic world, and was able to use his position to subvert the new constitution.

The empire soon came under pressure from all sides. In 1877, the **Russians** attacked from the Caucasus and the Balkans, resulting in great territorial losses and ending with the enemy forces a stone's throw from Istanbul. **Britain**, alarmed at the Russian advance, intervened and forced their withdrawal. As a reward Britain was given the right to govern **Cyprus** (to protect the sea link to India via Suez) in return for guaranteeing to defend the Ottomans if Russia attacked again. It also extracted a promise from the sultan to look after the empire's Christian minorities. Under the terms of the 1878 Conference of Berlin, the empire saw Romania, Montenegro and Serbia given **independence**, Bosnia-Herzegovina come under Austrian control, and Bulgaria gain autonomy.

In 1878, **Abdülhamit** dropped any pretence of consulting his ministers, and dissolved the chamber of deputies. He became increasingly paranoid, closeting himself away in a new palace, the **Yıldız Sarayı**, censoring the press and sending spies out across the empire. He began to emphasize the Islamic nature of the empire, seeing this as a bulwark against the designs of the Western powers, resulting in pogroms against the Christian Armenians in the east of **Anatolia** in 1895–96. At the same time, he cultivated Germany, which was then playing catch-up with the leading colonial powers, resulting in the construction of the **Berlin–Baghdad railway**, which ran through Istanbul. He also oversaw the introduction of an extensive **telegraph system** and tried to modernize the infrastructure of the state and to service its debts.

But, in 1889, a new movement arose to challenge the authority of the sultan. **The Committee for Union and Progress** (CUP) had its heart in the cosmopolitan city of Salonica in Macedonia, especially among the officers of the Third Army. Seeing the empire falling apart as various ethnic groups broke away to form states of their own, the CUP, nicknamed the Young Turks, began to see Turkish nationalism (as opposed to Pan-Islam or cosmopolitan Ottomanism) as a cure for the empire's ills. In July 1908 they demanded the **restoration** of the constitution of 1876 and, with feelings running high among the populace, the sultan acceded.

In 1909 **Abdülhamit** was deposed for supporting a rebellion against the CUP and was replaced by a figurehead Sultan **Mehmet V** (1909–18), who promised to respect the nation's will. Real power now lay with key officers within CUP and in 1913, enraged

1830	1839	1853
After a nine-year war, Greece breaks free of Ottoman control and becomes an independent state	The accession of Sultan Abdülmecit brings increased zeal to reform the empire along European lines	Tsar Nicholas I of Russia declares the Ottoman Empire the "sick man of Europe"

by what they saw as incompetence and cowardice in the war against an encroaching combined Bulgarian, Montenegran, Serbian and Greek army, the officers staged a coup and established a **military junta**. The unlikely alliance of Balkan states soon fell apart, allowing the Ottomans to retake parts of Thrace. This minor success was enough to make heroes of the junta, now effectively down to a triumvirate of Cemal Paşa, Talat Paşa and Enver Paşa.

World War I

The CUP was now firmly Turkish-nationalist, secular and technocrat in ideology, and authoritarian by nature. Ignoring public opinion and the counsel of other CUP members alike, the triumvirate signed an alliance with **Germany** on August 2, 1914. By November the country was at war with the Allied powers, getting off to a spectacularly bad start when Enver Paşa lost an entire army on the eastern front against Russia in 1914–15. On the southeast frontier the Arabs, with British support, rebelled and eventually gained their independence. The only bright spot was the successful resistance to Britain's attempts to force the Dardanelles, which guarded the sea approaches to the Bosphorus and Istanbul. The victory at **Gallipoli** (see pp.261–266) made a hero of **Mustafa Kemal**, later Atatürk, a young officer and CUP member, whose reward from an envious Enver was to be shunted off to various obscure fronts until the end of the war.

Following the 1917 Bolshevik Revolution, the Russians withdrew from the war and the Turks were able to secure their northeastern frontier. Despite this the Ottoman Empire, its cause hopeless from the outset of the war, surrendered to the Allies on October 30, 1918 and, on November 13, a British fleet sailed through the **Dardanelles** into the Bosphorus and occupied **Istanbul**.

An independent Turkey

At the end of World War I, Anatolia, the heartland of the Ottoman Empire, was shattered, its population drastically reduced by war, starvation and deportations. The victorious Allies immediately began their long-planned carve-up of the "sick man of Europe". The French occupied much of southeast Anatolia, the Italians parts of the Mediterranean and Aegean coast, the British Istanbul and Thrace, and the Greeks claimed İzmir, on the Aegean coast. Emboldened by the Ottoman Empire's humiliation and the backing of the Allies, particularly Britain, the Greeks were intent on reviving the idea of a **Greater Greece**, to include not only the Greek state that had emerged in 1830, but also much of the Aegean and Black Sea coastline of Anatolia, where millions of Greeks still lived. The sultan's abject capitulation to the Allies' demands, and the thought of the Ottoman Empire being totally dismembered and **Muslims** being made into second-class citizens, was too much for many Turks, who were now every bit as **nationalistic** as their former Balkan subjects.

The War of Independence

Mustafa Kemal, hero of Gallipoli, proved the catalyst for what would become known as the **War of Independence**. Foolishly commissioned by the collaborationist War Ministry to travel across Anatolia and halt the various bands of Turkish patriots who were refusing to lay down their arms, he set sail from Istanbul and landed at the Black Sea

1854	1856	1888
Florence Nightingale arrives in Istanbul to tend the wounded of the Crimean War	Abdülmecit abandons the Topkapı Palace and takes residence in the European-style Dolmabahçe Palace	Visitors from Europe arrive at newly built Sirkeci Station aboard the Orient Express

THE ARMENIAN QUESTION

World War I proved an unmitigated disaster for the empire's **Christian Armenians**. The traditional homeland of this ancient people was originally in what is now the far east of Turkey, but for many centuries they had lived in towns and cities right across Anatolia, with a huge population in **Istanbul**. At the start of the war, with Russia pressing from the east, they were seen by the Turkish authorities as the enemy within. Although some Armenians in the northeast border region did join the Russians following Enver's humiliating defeat at Sarıkamış in January 1915, most did not. The ethnic cleansing of the Armenian population actually began in Istanbul on April 24th 1915, with the round-up, deportation and killing of some 250 prominent Istanbul Armenians. Then, between May and October 1915, virtually the entire Armenian population of Anatolia was deported to the Syrian desert. Most did not make it and somewhere between 800,000 and 1.5 million Armenians perished in forced marches or were slain in massacres. Ironically, after the initial deportations, Istanbul's Armenian population were largely left alone, mainly due to the presence of so many foreign eyes in what was then the capital city of the Ottoman Empire.

The issue is still very much alive today, with Armenians claiming their losses amounted to genocide, and the Turkish state denying any systematic slaughter. The Armenian lobby in the US continually presses the administration to recognize the massacres of World War I as **genocide**. The pressure has been resisted, largely because Turkey remains a vital US ally in the Middle East. While running for the presidency, Barack Obama confirmed his support for the Congressional passage of the Armenian Genocide Resolution, though once elected in 2009 he failed to fulfill his promise. France, however, with an Armenian community of some 300,000, passed a bill recognizing the genocide in 1998, while in Switzerland it is a criminal offence to deny it. The land border between Turkey and Armenia has been closed since 1992 following the Armenian occupation of Nagorno-Karabagh, territory belonging to Turkey's Turkic ally, Azerbaijan.

port of **Samsun** on May 19, 1919. Kemal succeeded in lighting the torch of revolt across Anatolia and soon the Turks were fighting the French in the southeast, the Italians in the southwest, the Armenians in the northeast, and the Greeks in the west. In 1920, the Nationalists claimed to be the rightful government and established a parliament in the dusty Central Anatolian town of **Ankara**. In the same year the **Treaty of Sèvres**, imposed on Sultan Mehmet VI (1918–22) by the Allies and promising, among other things, İzmir and Thrace to Greece, independence to Armenia and autonomy to Kurdistan, only served to fuel the determination of the Nationalists. In 1922 they routed the Greeks at the battle of Dumlupınar and the humiliated remnants of the Greek army were evacuated from İzmir.

The **Nationalists** were now in control, and in November 1922 they abolished the sultanate, forcing Mehmet VI to slip away from Istanbul on a British warship, bound for exile in Italy. The war-weary Allies were forced to come to terms with the new Turkish state, and the **Treaty of Lausanne**, signed on July 24, 1923, recognized the frontiers won in the War of Independence. In the internationally mediated population exchange of 1923, nearly all the Greek Orthodox Christians left in Turkey (some 1.3 million) were sent to Greece, and the Muslim Turkish population of Greece were sent to Turkey. Although the Greek Orthodox population of Istanbul was exempted, along with the Muslims of western Thrace, it marked a sorry end for Ottoman cosmopolitanism and the ascendancy of virulent **ethnic nationalism**.

1889	1909	1914
Foundation of The Committee for Union and Progress (CUP), better known in the West as the Young Turks	Sultan Abdülhamit is deposed by the CUP	Ottoman Turkey signs an alliance with Germany and enters World War I

THE KURDS: FROM THE MOUNTAINS TO THE CITY

An ancient people of Indo-European origin and language (unlike the Turks), the **Kurds** are a people without a country. Scattered over the mountainous lands where Turkey, Iraq, Iran and Syria meet, they form a minority in each. By far the largest number live in Turkey – somewhere between 12 and 25 million – but Turkey does not officially accept Kurds as a minority group and, as such, exact numbers are hard to estimate. Kurds are, by tradition, transhumant pastoralists, and the rural-to-urban migration characterizing Turkey's development over the last sixty or so years has hit them hard. Not least because conflict between the **Kurdish Workers Party** (PKK) and the Turkish security forces, especially during the 1980s and 1990s, resulted in hundreds of thousands heading west as their villages were burned and pastures put off-limits by the state.

Today the largest Kurdish city in the world is neither Diyarbakır, the biggest Kurdish-dominated city in Turkey's southeast, nor Erbil, capital of the autonomous Kurdish enclave in northern Iraq, but Istanbul, with up to three million residents of Kurdish origin. Ironically, despite having spent decades opposing any form of independent Kurdish state emerging in the Middle East, a peace process between the ruling AKP government and the PKK was well underway in 2014. Even more incredibly, the virtually independent Kurdish state in northern Iraq had emerged as one of Turkey's major allies in this turbulent region. Paradoxically, however, proto-Kurdish state emerging across Turkey's borders in Northern Syria, with its links to the PKK, was being seen as every bit as bad as the new "Caliphate" being set up by the ultra-fundamentalist ISIS (Islamic State of Iraq and Syria) organization.

The Republic

The Turks, under the leadership of the charismatic **Mustafa Kemal**, had plucked victory from the jaws of defeat. A new, secular **Republic of Turkey** was declared on October 29, 1923. The old imperial capital of Istanbul was deliberately passed over in favour of the provincial town of Ankara, seat of the resistance in the War of Independence, and a new parliament created. **Istanbul**, shorn of its political role, had to rely on its business and commercial acumen. Yet it recovered from the war more quickly than the rest of the country because its influential Christian minorities – forcibly ejected elsewhere – were permitted to stay in the former capital.

The new Republic, under Kemal's watchful eye, set about a drastic programme of **reforms**. The caliphate was abolished, religious schools (*medrese*) and dervish orders closed, and Islam brought under state control. The fez, seen as progressive when it replaced the turban in the Tanzimat reforms, was outlawed as reactionary. The Gregorian calendar replaced the Islamic lunar one, alcohol was legalized, streets were numbered and the Western Sunday, rather than the Islamic Friday, became the official day of rest. **Women** won greater rights, with divorce now a matter for civil rather than religious courts, polygamy was banned, and eventually full voting rights were established. A team of language experts was set up to purge Turkish of its many Arabic and Persian loan words and the **Arabic alphabet** was replaced by a Latin one. In 1934 the entire population was forced to adopt surnames (this was when Mustafa Kemal became "Atatürk" or "Father of the Turks"). The name Constantinople, which had been used in Ottoman times alongside Istanbul, was also banned (see box, p.286).

The reforms were radical and inevitably there was some opposition, notably in the **Kurdish revolts** of 1925, 1930 and 1938, as well as **assassination** attempts on the great

1915	1918	1919
Turkish troops, under Mustafa Kemal (later Atatürk) defeat the Allied landing forces at Gallipoli	Britain begins its occupation of Istanbul after the Allied forces' victory in World War I	Mustafa Kemal lands at Samsun on the Black Sea, triggering the Turkish War of Independence

man himself. These put a dampener on the development of real democracy, and attempts to go beyond the one-party rule of the founding **Republican People's Party** (CHP) quickly foundered. In 1926 **Sedad Hakki Eldem**, the young Republic's leading architect and a great admirer of Atatürk and his revolution, while standing in line to meet his hero in Bursa, commented "He (Atatürk) was born to be ruler and that is how they treat him. I don't like that kind of behaviour but it seems to be in our blood."

Understandably suspicious of the Western powers that had so recently attempted to carve up what was left of the Ottoman Empire, the Republic was determined to be self-sufficient, setting up its own banks and instituting a series of five-year plans to boost **agriculture**. State-controlled industries like mining, steel and cement did provide a certain amount of independence, but they were heavily subsidized and grossly inefficient.

Atatürk, his liver ravaged by a lifetime's devotion to the fiery aniseed drink *rakı*, died on November 10, 1938, aged 59. Ironically for a man so determined to excise his people's Ottoman past, he passed away in that symbol of late nineteenth-century royal excess, the **Dolmabahçe Palace**, in the old imperial capital, Istanbul.

World War II and beyond

Atatürk was succeeded as **president** by former right-hand man and architect of Turkey's diplomatic success at Lausanne, **İsmet İnönü** (1884–1973). Keen to avoid the mistakes of World War I, İnönü steered a skilful diplomatic course when World War II became inevitable, signing neutrality pacts with Britain and France in 1939 and a treaty of non-aggression with **Nazi Germany** in 1941. İnönü kept Turkey out of the war, but he couldn't stop the conflict affecting his country, and a **black market** economy developed; there were shortages of basic commodities, profiteering, and massive government budget deficits. To compensate, the state introduced the Varlık Vergisi, or "**Wealth Tax**", applied in a discriminatory fashion to extort money from the remaining Armenian, Greek and Jewish population – most of whom lived in Istanbul. Defaulters had their property confiscated and/or were sent to **labour camps** in Anatolia, where many died. The country finally entered the war on the Allied side in early 1945, in order to qualify for **UN membership**.

Postwar democracy and two military coups

With Russia demanding territory in eastern Anatolia and joint control of the entrance to the Bosphorus, and the US promising aid to states threatened by communism, it was inevitable that Turkey would ally itself with the **Western powers**. The newly aligned Turkey, benefiting from **Marshall Plan aid**, was now under pressure to democratize. In the 1950 elections, a breakaway cell of the RPP, the **Democrat Party** (DP), led by **Adnan Menderes** (1899–1961), swept to victory. Flush with aid and loans, Menderes presided over an economic boom that saw the countryside flooded with shiny new imported tractors, and a new road system in **Istanbul** filled with equally shiny new cars and trucks.

Of farming stock himself, Menderes was worshipped by the conservative **rural population** (one of his first acts was to rescind Atatürk's ban on using Arabic in the call to prayer) but distrusted by the bureaucratic and commercial elite in the cities, especially Istanbul and, crucially, also the staunchly secular military. When the

1922	1923	1936
The Nationalists, led by Mustafa Kemal, abolish the Sultanate	The official establishment of the Republic of Turkey	Haghia Sophia, first a church, then a mosque, becomes a museum

economy began to falter in 1953, with a soaring **national debt**, huge trade deficit, and a massively over-valued lira, the DP became increasingly autocratic. Looking for a distraction from the country's economic woes, Menderes quickly found a suitable scapegoat, the Istanbul **Greek minority** population. In 1955, with tensions high over **Cyprus**, the DP-sponsored **demonstrations** soon got out of hand, with mobs ransacking Greek property. The police, apparently under orders not to intervene, stood and watched the mayhem. It was the beginning of the end for the city's **Greek Orthodox Christian minority**, many of whom left in the immediate aftermath of the riots.

With the country saved from bankruptcy only by an **International Monetary Fund loan**, an increasingly insecure Menderes became yet more authoritarian. Finally the military snapped, their pay and social status diminished, and staged a coup on May 27, 1960. Menderes and two of his right-hand men were hanged for **treason** and many other ministers were jailed. A new constitution was unveiled, and in 1961 İsmet İnönü became prime minister of a coalition government with a leading general, Cemal Güreş, as president. The paradox of a **democracy** being "saved" by military intervention was born.

The coup only served to further polarize and fragment the nation. During the 1960s, the number of political parties proliferated, with the mantle of the banned DP being taken up by the **Justice Party**. Istanbul's surviving minority Greek population suffered another blow in 1964, again against the backdrop of communal violence on Cyprus. Under the terms of a 1930 convention some 10,000 minority Greeks not holding Turkish passports were permitted to stay in the country. Turkey revoked this right and over 6000 (mostly Istanbulites) were forced to leave and had their properties confiscated. The RPP became an increasingly elitist party, drawing its support from the military, civil servants and business people owing their wealth to lucrative state contracts, and extremist parties emerged on both the left and right. **Street battles** between leftists and rightists, and violence on university campuses eventually led the military to intervene again on March 12, 1971.

The 1980 military coup

After a few years of relative calm, the 1970s were to prove even more divisive for Turkey. Street fighting erupted once again between radicalized groups, pitching left against right and Alevî (see box, p.93) against Sunni – alongside a renewed national consciousness among the country's largest minority population, the **Kurds**, and the rise of an openly Islamic political party, the National Salvation Party. Right-wing gunmen opened fire on protestors attending a May Day rally in Taksim Square on May 1, 1977, resulting in 39 deaths. By 1980 there were, at one stage, over twenty tit-for-tat politically orientated murders a day in Istanbul, where followers of a particular group could be told apart by the shape of their moustache or what clothes they were wearing. A military takeover was inevitable and on September 12, 1980, the nation underwent a third **coup** – much to the relief of ordinary Turks fed up with the escalating violence.

Rule by the new **military junta**, the National Security Council (NSC) lasted three years, with Istanbul and the rest of the country under **martial law**. Political parties were closed down, **trade unions** banned and their officials put on trial, universities purged of "radicals", and "seditious" literature burned. The new **constitution**, promulgated in 1982, was extremely restrictive in nature – banning, for example, the use of the Kurdish language – and hampered the development of democracy.

1938	**1939**	**1955**
Atatürk dies at Dolmabahçe Palace	During most of World War II, Turkey remains neutral	A weekend of rioting leads to the destruction of many Greek-minority-owned properties on İstiklal Caddesi

Turkey reborn

The junta's restoration of civilian rule in 1983 marked a new beginning for Turkey, with the rise of a different breed of politician, less shackled to the restraints of the Kemalist revolution. Whether they were **US-educated technocrats** such as Turgut Özal and Tansu Çiller or fiery **pro-Islamists** like Necmettin Erbakan and Tayyip Erdoğan, they began to see their country as part of, rather than isolated from, the world at large.

The Motherland Party and the Kurdish backlash

The first party to benefit from restored civilian rule was the newly formed **Motherland Party**, led by the charismatic half-Kurdish **Turgut Özal** (1927–93), which swept to power in the general elections (much to the chagrin of the military). Özal, a great orator and contradictory mix of pious Muslim and bon vivant, was in the mould of a **Thatcher** or **Reagan**, at least when it came to the country's finances, and he introduced sweeping reforms bringing Turkey in line with the **international economy**. This had mixed results, with a **tourism** boom boosting the nation's foreign currency reserves and spending on imported luxury goods decimating them. He angered the military-bureaucratic elite by easing restrictions on Islam, giving extra funding to the Department of Religious Affairs and allowing schools where religious instruction was a key component of the curriculum, inadvertently helping sow the seeds of **Islamic fundamentalism**.

Despite Özal's apparent liberalism, **human rights** abuses, which had peaked in the aftermath of the 1980 coup, continued. In the ethnically Kurdish southeast of the country, the military was engaged in a war of attrition with the **Kurdish Workers Party** (PKK). At a loss as to how deal with a people who refused to be assimilated, security forces sometimes resorted to less than legal methods to suppress the movement, further fuelling resentment in the economically backward southeast.

Özal died of a heart attack in 1993, depriving the country of a vigorous and reform-minded leader. Under Özal's successor and Turkey's first **female prime minister**, **Tansu Çiller** (b.1946), the early 1990s were dominated by corruption scandals, massive inflation and spiralling war in the southeast. This conflict drove hundreds of thousands of villagers from their land, exacerbating a rural–urban migration that had been under way since the 1950s, and which had accelerated following Özal's market-orientated reforms. The **migrants**, bringing with them a different culture, settled in shantytowns on the outskirts of the big cities, particularly **Istanbul**, where a population of a little under three million in 1980 had risen fourfold by 2003.

The advent of political Islam

The loosening of restrictions on Islam by the secular **Kemalist** state, begun under Menderes and reaching new levels under Özal, began to have a real effect in the political arena in the early 1990s. In the 1994 municipal elections, the overtly Islamic **Refah party** took Istanbul and many other cities across the land, including the capital, Ankara. Istanbul's Refah mayor was Tayyip Erdoğan, who proved himself to be efficient, pragmatic and honest – rare attributes in the Turkish political scene. He addressed many of the most pressing problems plaguing the **metropolis**, laying on extra buses, improving the waste-collection system, reducing pollution and providing facilities for the disabled. Secularist concerns that areas full of bars, clubs and

1960	1964	1971
Turkey's first military coup	6000 Greeks, most from Istanbul, have their property seized and are expelled from Turkey	Turkey's second military coup

restaurants such as Beyoğlu would be turned, overnight, into pious "dry" zones proved unfounded, and life went on much as before.

Following **Refah**'s success in the 1996 general elections, fears that the country would soon be subject to Iranian-style **Shariah rule** also proved groundless as Refah signed a **military treaty** with Israel, allowed the US continued use of airbases on Turkish soil, and party leader **Erbakan** laid a wreath at the mausoleum of that scourge of Islam, Atatürk. Despite this, in 1997 the nation's ultimate arbiters of power, the **National Security Council** (comprising Turkey's five top military commanders, the president, prime minister and three leading ministers) forced Erbakan to step down, in a "silent coup", and Refah was dissolved.

In 1998 **Erdoğan**, then mayor of Istanbul for the newly formed pro-Islamic **Fazilet party**, was jailed for four months for "inciting armed fundamentalist rebellion" in a speech he gave in the southeast of the country. Ironically, the words he was prosecuted for ("the mosques are our barracks, the minarets our bayonets, the domes our helmets") were written by Ziya Gökalp, a leading idealogue of Turkish secular nationalism. In 1999 a massive quake rocked the environs of the city, with some twenty thousand lives lost, mainly as a result of shoddy building. Both the government and, by inference, previous governments, were widely criticized for the decades of cronyism and indifference to flagrant breaches of building and planning regulations which led to the disaster. In 2001, a major financial crisis saw the lira halve in value against the dollar and inflation rocket – another sign of poor governance. It's not surprising, then, that the nation was ready for a change of direction – though few would have guessed at the time just how popular the next party to seize power would turn out to be.

The rise and rise of the Justice and Development Party

Following the banning of Fazilet for anti-secular activities, its replacement, the **Justice and Development party** (AKP), swept to power in 2002 with 34 percent of the vote. The first majority government for fifteen years, the election of a party composed of, and supported largely by, **conservative Muslims** sent shock waves through the secular establishment. Five years later the same establishment was rocked even more severely. Objecting to the nomination of one of its own party, **Abdullah Gül**, as president (particularly as Gül's wife wore the traditional Muslim **headscarf**, seen as a symbol of political Islam) the military posted a warning on their website. The threatened coup, or "e coup" as it has become known, forced early elections in July 2007. The **AKP** got a whopping 47 percent of the vote nationwide – the first time for fifty years that a party had won a **second term** in office with an increased majority and Gül was duly elected president. Then, in June 2011, for the first time in the history of the Turkish Republic, a party was elected for a **third consecutive term** with almost 50 percent of the vote.

Throughout this period the AKP's opposition, comprised of the military, the civil service, powerful media groups, academia and the party set up by Atatürk back in 1923 (the Republican People's Party or CHP), believed the secular nature of the state was under threat – as did many foreign observers. Indeed, many secular Turks, increasingly alarmed by the wave of popular support for the AKP, were convinced the government were preparing the way for an **Islamic theocracy**, pointing to everything from the government's resolve to repeal the law forbidding women wearing the **headscarf** from working in state offices or entering university to the inordinately high taxes on **alcohol**.

1977	1980	1983
39 demonstrators shot by extremists at a May Day rally in Taksim Square	Turkey's third military coup	Charismatic Turgut Özal sweeps to power as leader of the Motherland Party

Turkey's long-held ambition to be accepted as part of Europe had been boosted under the AKP in 2005, when accession talks formally opened, but by 2011 the process was mired in domestic indifference and outright hostility from EU member states France and Germany. Instead, the government embarked on a "**zero problems with neighbours**" policy that saw Turkey and Syria (arch enemies back in the 1990s) begin a massive mine-clearing project along their long mutual frontier (2008) and the introduction of visa-free border crossings.

One of the chief reasons for the AKP's repeated electoral success was that Turkey had begun a period of sustained economic growth. In part this was because the AKP were prepared to do business with everyone, from pariah regimes such as Syria and Libya through to Saudi Arabia, Russia and China. Foreign capital flowed into the country, particularly from the rich Arab states – and nowhere more so than to Istanbul, where property prices skyrocketed as a result.

The "**Arab Spring**" of 2011 brought a more realistic appraisal of AKP's grandiose foreign policy, with PM Erdoğan condemning Syria's leader Assad as ten thousand refugees flooded over the border into Turkey, and acting quickly to evacuate thousands of Turks from Libya, where they were working in the drilling and construction industries. Relations with Israel, already damaged in 2009 when Erdoğan stormed out of a meeting with president Peres in Davos, plummeted after Israeli commandoes stormed a Turkish ship taking aid to Gaza in 2010, killing nine Turkish citizens. Actions like these made the tough yet pious Erdoğan a well-known and popular figure to the Arab man in the street. Cynics at home, however, saw his moves as cheap populism at best and dangerous neo-Ottomanism – an attempt to regain influence in lands once under Ottoman control – at worst.

Gezi Park and a new authoritarianism

Even more worryingly the AKP, boosted by its third electoral success and the lack of a viable opposition, began to act in an increasingly authoritarian manner at home. Nowhere was this more evident than in the government's heavy-handed reaction to protests against the planned re-development of **Gezi Park** in Istanbul's iconic Taksim Square (see box, p.127). What started in May 2013 as a small-scale sit-in – a few protestors attempting to prevent trees being cleared to make way for a government-backed shopping mall – erupted into an "Occupy Wall Street"-style protest. Scenes of Taksim Square and adjoining streets filled with baton-wielding riot police beating protestors, and water cannon knocking them off their feet, were broadcast around the world. Clouds of tear-gas billowed over the square and down the city's major shopping and entertainment thoroughfare, İstiklal Caddesi.

Talk of a "**Turkish Spring**" among the international media proved far-fetched, but were used by Erdoğan to back claims that "foreign enemies" were behind the riots, always a sure-fire winner with a sometimes xenophobic Turkish public. A large proportion of the protestors were a new voice in Turkey. Young, urban, educated and media-savvy (social media such as Twitter played a huge part in coordinating, disseminating and publicizing the protests) they had benefited from the AKP's economic "miracle" but felt excluded from its vision of a more conservative and pious Turkey. Inevitably many other groups who felt estranged from the new Turkey joined

1993	1994	1997
Özal dies, leaving a political vacuum	The pro-Islamic Refah party win Istanbul in municipal elections and Recep Tayyip Erdoğan becomes mayor	The Refah party is dissolved by the military in the "silent coup"

in, including Alevîs (see box, p.93), Kurds, members of the LGBT community, supporters of Istanbul's "big three" football clubs and many more well-meaning protestors, as well as a few radical leftists and anarchists. Protests spread to many cities across the country and the government's disproportionate response – 11 people died around 8000 were injured – drew condemnation at home and abroad

Taksim Square was eventually cleared of protestors but the profound divisions in Turkish society seemed deeper than ever. Rumours that **Haghia Sophia** (Aya Sofya; see pp.45–49) would become a mosque again, new restrictions on the sale of alcohol and a tightening of abortion laws hardly helped dispel fears of creeping Islamism by the near fifty percent of the populace who didn't vote for the AKP, nor did carefully orchestrated pro-government rallies held in the wake of Gezi Park. As 2013 drew to a close the government became mired in a major corruption scandal, with several AKP ministers and their offspring, including Erdoğan's own son, implicated in the bribery accusations. The PM put the blame for the scandal on the powerful Turkish Islamic scholar-cum-community-leader **Fetullah Gülen**, and as 2013 segued into 2014 the government set about purging the police and judiciary of Gülen's supporters. Erdoğan accused Gülen and his secretive organization, former allies of the AKP, of trying to set up a "parallel state" within the country.

Despite this Islamist in-fighting the March 2014 local elections saw the AKP win 42 percent of the vote; the largest opposition group only 26 percent. Buoyed by yet another electoral success Erdoğan continued with his heavy-handed approach to governance. Protests coinciding with the first anniversary of the Gezi Park protests were summarily dealt with. More worryingly, the PM was defiant in the face of protests following the loss of 301 workers in the country's biggest-ever mining disaster at Soma in May 2014. The PM reacted angrily to accusations of government negligence, more or less stating that "these things happen in mining". That Turkey has the worst work-safety record in Europe is one thing; that it has the third worst in the world is a scandal. Tellingly, a 2013 OECD (Organisation for Economic Cooperation and Development) "happiness" report revealed that Turkey came bottom out of 36 industrialized countries in terms of life satisfaction, with Turks working the longest hours and receiving the lowest pay of the countries under consideration. Despite this, Erdoğan's stranglehold on power in Turkey was reaffirmed when he became the country's **new president** in August 2014. For the first time in Turkey's history a president had been elected by popular vote, with Erdoğan receiving the support of almost 52 percent of the electorate.

The present day

There is no doubt that Turkey has been transformed economically under the AKP. Major new highways lace the mountainous Anatolian interior, high-speed trains link major cities, domestic air travel is booming. Istanbul's transport infrastructure has been revolutionized too, with a metro linking the old and new cities via a bridge across the Golden Horn (opened early 2014), a metro tunnel under the Bosphorus (opened late 2013) joining Europe with Asia, and work on a third bridge across the strait commenced in 2013. A ground-breaking ceremony for a third airport, northeast of the centre, took place in spring 2014, and there's a possibility the grandiose plans to build a **mega-canal** linking the Sea of Marmara with the Black Sea (see box, p.153) to relieve the dangerously congested Bosphorus will reach fruition.

2002	2005	2007
The pro-Islamic AKP, led by Tayyip Erdoğan, sweep to power in the general elections	Accession talks for Turkey's membership of the EU formally open	The AKP wins the general elections with an increased majority

Along with Brazil, Russia, India and China, Turkey has become a major emerging economy, and gross national income has risen from $8,630 in 2002 to $18,390 in 2012. In 2013 Turkey had the seventeenth largest economy in the world. Strolling down Istanbul's major shopping street, İstiklal Caddesi, or around one of the swish suburban malls, visitors soon realize just how much disposable income there is in this vibrant city. And with over ten million visitors in 2013, Istanbul became the world's sixth most-visited city.

On a national level the Kurdish question remains a dangerous obstacle to Turkey's progress and future peace and much depends upon whether the AKP can reconcile Kurdish demands for "democratic autonomy" with an often virulent Turkish nationalism. Despite its faults the AKP has tried, unlike its predecessors, to negotiate with its Kurdish minority. The election of Erdoğan as president, however, is a development many regard as potentially dangerous, fearing that the fiery leader will change the constitution to give the largely ceremonial office of presidency more concrete powers. Unrest in Turkey's unenviable international neighbourhood is also potentially destabilizing. In 2014, ISIS controlled territory in Iraq and Syria on Turkey's southeastern frontier; Iran remained a wild card to the east; war between Turkey's Turkic ally Azerbaijan and Armenia was threatened in the Caucasus; and, across the Black Sea, Russia and Ukraine were virtually at war. That Turkey is a more overtly **Islamic country** after more than twelve years of AKP leadership is hard to argue against – the question is how this will affect the nature of the state and its relations with the wider world.

Istanbul itself faces many problems: its wondrous heritage is under threat from unbridled development (in 2010 it was close to being named and shamed on the **UNESCO Endangered Heritage** list), with the municipal authorities struggling to juggle the needs of the population with the preservation of its historic buildings. It continues to grow alarmingly quickly, with any improvements to infrastructure generally being only temporary – the population was reckoned at twelve million according to the 2007 census, but in 2011 believed to be closer to seventeen million. The ongoing war in Syria has also added to the population and to social pressures in the city, most visibly in the form of Syrian families begging on the streets. With up to two million refugees in Turkey in 2014, and only around a tenth of those in the camps set up to house them on the Syrian–Turkish border, tensions seem likely to rise.

Yet the city is sure to prosper. Looking both East and West, blessed with a location both stunningly beautiful and strategically crucial, this will always be, as one inhabitant wrote of the city when it was Constantinople, a "city of the world's desire".

2011	2013	2014
The AKP wins a record third term in office, capturing almost fifty percent of the vote in general elections	Protests against the redevelopment of Taksim Square's Gezi Park, brutally suppressed by police, turn into anti-government riots	Recep Tayyip Erdoğan becomes the first Turkish president elected by popular vote

Ottoman art and architecture

Istanbul was at least two millennia old when it fell to the Ottomans in 1453 (see p.284), but in the centuries that followed the former Byzantine capital was built anew. The cascading domes and soaring minarets of the imperial mosque complexes constructed under successive sultans still dominate the old city, but while religious buildings form the Ottomans' main architectural legacy, their palaces – and even the simple houses of ordinary citizens – are worthy reminders of a once-vibrant empire. Carpet-weaving, pottery, calligraphy and miniature painting also flourished under Ottoman tutelage.

Religious architecture

The Ottoman Empire was Islamic, and Istanbul's imperial **mosques** and associated structures, known collectively as *külliye*, were given lavish treatment. The complexes usually included a *medrese* (school), a *hamam*, an *imaret* (soup kitchen), a hospital, accommodation for travellers and a cemetery. The ultimate *külliye*, magnificently positioned on the crest of Istanbul's third hill, is the **Süleymaniye** (see pp.83–84), whose buildings are arranged with almost geometric precision around the mosque itself. Its architect, the incomparable Sinan (see box, p.82) is buried within its grounds. His finest achievement, however, is Edirne's **Selimiye Camii** (see p.270), where the mighty dome, cleverly supported by eight unobtrusive pillars, seems to float over the worshippers below.

Mosque features

Although there is no Islamic injunction for a mosque to have a **minaret**, most have at least one and many boast more; the Süleymaniye Camii (see p.83), atop Istanbul's third hill, has four, the Sultanahmet Camii, better known as the Blue Mosque (see p.64), boasts six. From the balconies of the minarets, pre-loudspeaker muezzins called believers to prayer. Their origin is ascribed variously to the fire watchtowers of pre-Islamic cities and early Christian ascetics, the Stylites, who dwelt atop pillars to bring them closer to God. While early Arab mosques derived from the simple, flat-roofed courtyard house of the prophet Mohammed, the later Ottoman style was based around domes and slender, cylindrical minarets.

Most mosques have a **courtyard** centred around the *şadırvan* or ritual-ablutions fountain, which worshippers use before prayer. A multi-domed **portico** on the northwest side of the mosque provides an "overspill" prayer area for busy times. Inside, the focus is the southeast, Mecca-facing **kıble** wall, punctured by a **mihrab** or prayer niche. Right of this is the **mimber**, a pulpit, from which the *imam* leads Friday prayers. As Islam forbids representation of the human form, Ottoman mosque interiors are enlivened by stylized geometric patterns and flowing Arabic calligraphy.

Secular buildings

The city's fifteenth-century conqueror, Sultan Mehmet II (see p.284), found its palaces already in ruins. Within five years a new palace, the **Topkapı** (see pp.50–55), rose on the splendid promontory overlooking the Bosphorus and Sea of Marmara. Following Islamic precepts, originating in the tented camps of nomadic warriors, Topkapı was a collection of low buildings set around a series of courtyards and gardens. By the nineteenth century the Ottoman Empire was busy reforming itself on European lines and the **Dolmabahçe Palace** (see pp.131–133), built in 1853, was inspired by European royal dwellings such as Versailles, and revelled in its ostentatiousness and gorgeous waterfront setting. By contrast, ordinary Ottoman citizens lived in humble wood, lath and plaster houses, crammed along narrow, atmospheric streets, their *cumbas* (projecting upper floors) often just a couple of metres from the home opposite. These dwellings coped much better with the earthquakes which are an ever-present fact of life for a city so close to a major fault line, but were subject to frequent fires, which is why so few remain today. The best places to see these homes are around Cankurtaran, Kumkapı and the northwest quarter (see pp.89–100).

Carpets and pottery

Whether providing comfort for the prostrated faithful or adding opulence to palaces or the *konak* (mansion) of a wealthy merchant, Ottoman-era Turkish **carpets** are real works of art. The best places to see examples – without getting smooth-talked in the Grand Bazaar – are the Carpet Museum (see p.49) and the Museum of Turkish and Islamic Art (see p.65).

The fourteenth-century arrival of blue-and-white Chinese porcelain inspired the Ottoman **potters**. The very best wares were produced in pretty, lakeside İznik (see pp.232–239), with the form reaching its apogee in the late sixteenth century, when craftsmen added a rich, tomato-red raised relief to a palette that already included blue, turquoise, magenta, green and grey – best seen in the sumptuously tiled interior of the Rustem Paşa Camii (see p.75). Many other mosques throughout the old city are graced by İznik tiles, however, including the Blue and Sokollu Mehmet Paşa mosques.

Calligraphy

Arabic is the language of the Koran, and to Muslims **calligraphy** is the highest art form as it represents the word of God – you'll see quotations from the Koran and the *hadith*s (sayings of the Prophet) adorning the interior of any Istanbul mosque. The Ottomans also produced exquisite manuscript Korans, prayer books, framed artworks (*levha*) and decorative books of calligraphic exercises, not to mention the sultan's delightfully ornate imperial monogram, all visible at the Sakıp Sabancı Museum (see p.150).

Miniatures

Miniature paintings were as much a part of illuminated Ottoman manuscripts as calligraphy, and a painting academy was established in the Topkapı Palace as early as the fifteenth century. As Ottoman power increased, so did the standard of the paintings, especially following the arrival of artists from Persia, Mesopotamia and Central Asia. Islamic convention was frequently ignored, with human figures, often the sultans themselves, figuring prominently, along with scenes from court ceremonies, legends and historical events such as the 1588 Siege of Vienna. Good examples can be seen at the Museum of Turkish and Islamic Art (see p.65) and the Sakıp Sabancı Museum (see p.150).

Music

Istanbul, following years of rural–urban migration, is now home to people from every part of Anatolia, and their musical heritage lives on. Traditional Turkish music, its roots stretching back millennia to the different cultures and civilizations that have flourished here, is complex and vibrant. It has managed to maintain both its creativity and popularity – even with the younger generation – though this has not prevented the rise of a lively, Western-influenced rock, pop, electronic and hip-hop scene.

Traditional Turkish music

Traditional sounds have more than held their own in this fast-changing country. Channel-surf Turkish TV any evening and you're bound to hit upon a show or two devoted to native Turkish music, with the sight of a moustachioed bard coaxing a melancholic folk song from his *bağlama* (lute) or an orchestra of tuxedoed men and sombrely clad women solemnly accompanying a warbling *sanatçı* (singer of Turkish classical music). **Arabesk**, an Arab/Egyptian-influenced style of music invariably charting the singer's wretched lot in life, remains extremely popular, especially among the poor and dispossessed. Its most famous proponent, İbrahim Tatlıses, is a national institution, who has survived three assassination attempts. *Türkü* bars (see p.203) are devoted to the various lovelorn strands of **halk müziği** (best translated as people's or folk music) and are very popular with the younger generation.

Played mainly by Roma (gypsy) bands, **fasıl**, a curious but lively hybrid of Ottoman classical and folk, with violins, clarinets, *darbuka* drums and powerful, emotive vocals to the fore, is the genre of Istanbul's vibrant **meyhane** scene (see p.177). The hypnotic, spiritual strains of **Sufi** music, most often associated with the Mevlevi or "whirling" dervish order, is very much a minority interest in its home country, though it can be heard in several places in the city, including the Galata Mevlevihanesi (see p.113).

Turkish classical or **sanat** music is the most inaccessible home-grown style to foreign ears – and the least popular domestically despite the undoubted virtuosity of its leading musicians. Originating in the Ottoman court, this subtle, partly improvisational but often gloomy sounding music is performed by chamber orchestras using a combination of traditional Turkish wind and string instruments backed by drums.

Music documentaries

The best introduction to a whole range of traditional Turkish music is Nezih Ezen's 2008 documentary, **Lost Songs of Anatolia** (ⓦlostsongsofanatolia.com). A talented musician himself, Ezen's unsentimental but sensitive film is a labour of love some five years in the making. Travelling across Turkey's vast landscape, recording and filming in obscure towns and remote villages, he vividly captures the musical heritage of modern Turkey – one deeply rooted in the many ethnic and cultural identities that make up the nation.

Although much of Fatih Akın's documentary **Crossing the Bridge** concentrates on contemporary music in Istanbul, there is plenty to keep traditional music buffs happy. The superb vocals and even better *saz* playing of Orhan Gençbay, a legend rivalled only by İbrahim Tatlıses in Arabesk music, are featured, as is the heart-rending voice of the young Kurdish singer Aynur Doğan. The haunting sounds of Mercan Dede, a fusion of Sufi and modern electronica, get an airing, alongside the Balkan influences of Selim Sesler, playing with an unlikely (but very talented) singer of traditional Turkish songs, Canadian Brenna MacCrimmon.

Contemporary music

Pop has a surprisingly long history in Turkey, from the tango stars of the 1930s through to Elvis Presley imitators in the 1950s. It wasn't until the late 1960s, though, that **rock** really took root, with the rise of the Anadolu (Anatolian) rock movement. Today, Western-style contemporary music is part and parcel of the diverse Turkish music scene – most of all in cosmopolitan Istanbul. The vast majority of these bands and singers perform in Turkish – which undermines their chances of achieving international success. But the best of them are worth a listen – and a sound-clash of genres is unavoidable if you venture out into the city's labyrinthine **nightlife** scene.

Rock

Duman are among the most accessible of the current crop of rock bands. Erroneously labelled punk in their early days, the Istanbul-based group are in fact a straightforward rock band, mixing up-tempo anthems with lighter ballads and traditional Turkish folk songs. *Bu akşam* ("This evening") and *Belki alışmam lazım* ("Maybe I'd better get used to it") are great songs by any standards.

Fellow "Stamboul" boys **Mor ve Ötesi** formed in 1995 and have built up a huge following in Turkey – in 2003 the indie four-piece played in front of 100,000 anti-Iraq war demonstrators in Ankara. Surprisingly, given their reputation for protest, they were chosen to represent Turkey in the 2008 **Eurovision Song Contest**, with *Deli* ("Crazy"), coming in seventh. In Turkey the Eurovision Song Contest is not seen as the laughably kitsch endeavour it is across parts of Europe – in this most patriotic of nations it is taken very seriously indeed.

Another band that features in Akın's *Crossing the Bridge* is **Replikas** – prog-rockers who take extended, experimental soloing to extremes but are talented musicians with a loyal following. Far more popular is **Şebnem Ferah**. Born in Yalova, near Bursa, she is of Balkan (Macedonian) ancestry. Her goth-metal looks, powerful voice and the helping hand of that doyenne of the Turkish music scene, **Sezen Aksu** (see p.306), have helped secure her fame – though her brand of soft rock and power ballads will not be to everyone's taste.

Istanbul-born Armenian **Hayko Çepkin** mixes Anatolian rock with scream-metal and a lively stage act. More radical are the long-established punk rockers **Rashit**, who have played with the likes of the Dead Kennedys and the Offspring and had their 2005 album *Herşeyin Bir Bedeli Var* released on Sony. In recent years, Balkan and gypsy music has gained popularity in Istanbul, and local bands like **Luxus**, who play smaller alternative venues across the city, incorporate this sound into their music.

Hip-hop

The roots of the rap scene in Turkey lie among the Turkish community in Germany. Invariably urban, often poor, disenfranchised and discriminated against, they found a natural outlet for their anger and frustration in hip-hop. The movement was kick-started by the controversial **Cartel** in the mid-1990s. Their debut album was banned in

---

PSYCHEDELIC ISTANBUL

Turkish music has a long tradition of psychedelia, a form that has influenced some of its most popular movements, beginning with the Anadolu Rock of **Erkin Koray** and kaftan-wearing **Barış Manço** in the 1970s. Playing Turkish folk melodies with electric guitars they created a truly different psychedelic sound that is one of the key elements of Anadolu rock. **Moğollar**, one of the biggest bands of that time, are still performing over forty years on. Today, the psychedelic flame is kept alight by a number of bands, including **BaBa Zula**, whose "Istanbul psychedelia" or "oriental-dub" blends traditional instruments with electronic production techniques. They gig regularly, and with their 60s hippie throwback looks and belly-dancer they make an entertaining live act. Psychedelia also lives on in the underground clubs, with acts such as **Barış K** and **FOC Edits** reworking old classics for discerning young crowds.

Turkey and the group split soon after. The scene in Istanbul really got going with another star of *Crossing the Bridge* (see p.304), the city's very own Eminem – **Ceza**. Worshipped by multitudes of the city's disaffected youth, he was born on the Asian side of the Bosphorus in Üsküdar, taking his stage name (*ceza* means punishment) from one of his early jobs – handing out fines to people who failed to pay their electricity bills. Ceza's success has bred envy, and in 2007 he was accused of lifting his beats straight from Eminem by rival Istanbul rapper **Ege Çubukçu**. Other names to look out for are **Sagopa Kajmer** and Ceza's sister, **Ayben**. Turkish vocals apart, what marks this home-grown hip-hop out from its US inspiration is the sampling of *arabesk* and other forms of traditional Turkish music rather than Western pop.

Electronic Music

Although rock remains the genre of choice for a large segment of the Turkish youth, electronic music has become the soundtrack of Istanbul's hipster scene. Clubs including *İndigo* (p.201), *Wake Up Call*, *MiniMüzikhol* (p.201), *Kasette* (p.201) and *Topless* all book a steady stream of international and Turkish house and techno DJs. Local acts to watch out for include **Kaan Düzarat**, who blends Turkish psychedelic influences into a mellow but distinctly danceable sound and **Murat Uncuoğlu**, manager of *İndigo*. A stalwart of the underground house music scene since the late 80s, he remains one of Istanbul's busiest DJs. Although bass music has never won mass appeal in Turkey, a number of dedicated dubstep producers play at the hip club *Pixie Underground* (p.201). The most successful is **Gantz**, who blends traditional Arabesk sounds into contemporary releases, capturing the spirit of modern Istanbul – in particular check out his enchanting work with Algerian-born **El Mahdy Jr.**

Pop

Pop music is huge in Turkey. It's also incredibly varied – though you might not think so on a first listen. Once a teen idol, now a housewives' favourite, **Tarkan** swivels his hips and belts out dance-orientated pop with apparent abandon, singing at the 2008 opening of the Istanbul Grand Prix. He's a big star in Germany as well as Turkey, and has produced one album in English.

Pop rockers/balladeers **Mustafa Sandal** and **Teoman** are firm fixtures on the TV music channels (see box above), as is the chanteuse **Yıldız Tilbe**. The multi-talented queen of the Turkish pop scene, **Sezen Aksu**, has helped to preserve and build upon the best of traditional Turkish urban music, both through skilfully updated covers of old songs and with new material incorporating their best elements. Nor is she afraid of controversy, tackling feminism, human rights and ethnic cleansing in Bosnia, and singing in Ladino (the language of Turkey's Jewish population) and Kurdish as well as her native Turkish. Her albums vary enormously in style but 1995's *Işık Doğudan Yükselir* ("The Light Rises from the East") is a good starting point. Another queen of the scene is the incredibly well-preserved, Istanbul-schooled **Ajda Pekkan**: born in 1946 and still touring, she has sold some thirty million albums worldwide and is a national icon. A more recent addition to the scene is **Can Bonomo**, a Sephardic Jewish indie-pop singer from İzmir who won seventh place in the 2012 Eurovision concert and has won praise from mainstream and alternative audiences.

Turkish cinema

Turkey has had a moderately successful film industry since the 1950s, when corny rural-boy-meets-rural-girl melodramas provided escapism for Anatolian villagers. The outside world took little notice until the 1970s, when a few maverick filmmakers took Turkish cinema in a more radical direction.

1971–99: Early successes

Yılmaz Güney, a popular actor turned director, was imprisoned several times for his leftist leanings. He nonetheless produced a series of hard-hitting films during the 1970s and 80s – the years surrounding the coups of 1971 and 1980. The best were *Sürü* ("The Herd"), which follows a Kurdish shepherd and his family taking their flock to sell in distant Ankara, and *Yol* ("The Road"). Written from the confines of his prison cell, with the outside directorial assistance of **Derif Gören**, *Yol* takes an allegorical look at the state of the nation (then still under martial law) by following the fortunes of five prisoners who have been allowed a week's parole. The film was banned in Turkey, which only served to bring it to the notice of the international community, and in 1981 *Yol* was joint-winner of the Palme d'Or. The film finally made it onto the country's cinema screens in 1999, when it played to packed houses. Güney died of cancer in 1984, aged 46, the year after the release of his last film, *Duvar* ("Wall"), an unrelentingly gloomy critique of the country's overcrowded and brutal prison system.

With the exception of Erden Kıral's 1983 movie *Hakkâri'de Bir Mevsim* ("A Season in Hakkâri"), a visually stunning film examining the experiences of a young teacher sent to a remote Kurdish village to staff the local school, Turkish films in the 1980s made little impact on the outside world. Despite a lack of financial backing, the 1990s proved kinder, and in 1994 **Erden Kıral**'s *Mavi Sürgün* ("The Blue Exile") was nominated for an Academy Award. In 1995, **Mustafa Altıoklar**'s *Istanbul Kanatlarımın Altında* ("Istanbul Beneath My Wings"), set in the seventeenth century during the reign of tyrant **Murat IV**, drew critical acclaim and was a box-office hit. **Hamam**, made in 1998 by Istanbul-born **Ferzan Özpetek**, told the story of an Italian star who inherits a run-down Turkish bath in Istanbul. Through his efforts to restore it, he discovers his own sexuality, making this one of the few Turkish films dealing with gay relationships to have gone on general release.

2000 to the present: critical accolades

The new millennium has seen Turkish cinema hit new heights. Leading the way is **Nuri Bilgi Ceylan**. Ceylan came to prominence with *Uzak* ("Distant") in 2002, a beautifully crafted, Istanbul-set film of urban alienation which won the Grand Prix at Cannes. In

TURKISH CINEMA – DOMESTIC REALITY

As in every country, what the critics adore, the vast majority of the public ignore. Nuri Bilge Ceylan's arty **Uzak** attracted some 20,000 cinema-goers within Turkey, whereas 2008's **Recep İvedik**, director Şahan Gökbakar's tale of an uneducated burping, farting and spitting taxi driver let loose in a five-star hotel grossed $24 million domestically. Equally successful was 2006's ultra-nationalistic **Kurtlar Vadisi – Irak** ("Valley of the Wolves – Iraq") a huge box-office action-thriller hit, in which the Turks get their fictional revenge for the real-life arrest of some of their military boys by the Americans in northern Iraq in 2003. Both films have spawned equally popular formulaic sequels, with *Recep Ivedik 4* hitting cinemas in 2014.

2006 the critically acclaimed but rather self-indulgent *İklimler* ("Climates") was released, an existentialist tale of a failing relationship starring Ceylan and his wife Ebru. The director returned to form in 2008 with *Üç Maymun* ("Three Monkeys"). Telling a familiar story of how power corrupts, the film won the prestigious Best Director Award at Cannes; its plot concerns a powerful politician involved in a hit-and-run incident, who escapes justice by sending his driver to prison in his place – and then sexually abuses the driver's wife. Ceylan cemented his reputation in 2011 with the epic *Bir Zamanlar Anadolu'da* ("Once Upon a Time in Anatolia"), a powerful thriller set on the austere Anatolian plateau. With nods to sources as diverse as Chekhov and Sergio Leone, the film was co-winner of the Grand Prix at Cannes.

In 2014 Ceylan went one better with *Kış Uykusu* ("Winter Sleep"), scooping the coveted Palme d'Or for an atmospheric tale of an ex-actor turned hotelier in remote Central Anatolia. Signalling his disquiet about Turkey's increasingly authoritarian government, Ceylan dedicated his award to those who had died in the Gezi Park protests of 2013 (see p.127). Fittingly, he received the Palme d'Or on the 100th anniversary of Turkish cinema.

Fatih Akın, a German-born and -bred Turk, had both Turkey and Germany claiming his 2004 Golden Bear winner, *Duvara Karşı* ("Head On"), as their own. Personalities and cultures clash in this sometimes brutal tale of ill-matched Turkish–German lovers. **Akın**'s 2005 documentary *Crossing the Bridge: The Sound of Istanbul*, made with **Alexander Hacke**, has won many recent plaudits and is an unparalleled introduction to this great city's music scene (see p.304). *Yaşamın Kıyısında* ("Edge of Heaven"), from 2007, won the Best Screenplay Award at Cannes and five awards at Turkey's equivalent of the Oscars, Antalya's Golden Orange festival. Shot in Germany, Istanbul and the eastern Black Sea city of Trabzon, it traces the interconnecting lives of four Turks and two Germans, touching on issues of cultural estrangement, family relationships, lesbianism and political activism. *Aşkı Ruhunu Kat* ("Soul Kitchen"), released in 2009, a comedy-drama set in a Greek-run Hamburg taverna, was a deliberate move to "lighten-up", but in 2012 Akın got back down to the serious business with a well-received documentary charting the struggles of a Black Sea town against a municipality landfill site, *Cenneti Kirletmek* ("Polluting Paradise").

A number of other Turkish films have taken their share of critical accolades since the advent of the third millennium. **Reha Erdem**'s 2006 *Beş Vakit* ("Times and Winds") portrays the often grim realities of growing up in an idyllic-looking Turkish village and makes moving use both of the breathtakingly beautiful location of the village and the fresh-faced innocence of its child actors. 2007's *Yumurta* ("Egg"), the first part of a trilogy directed by **Semih Kaplanoğlu**, won a fistful of awards at the Golden Orange. This typically Turkish tale traces the life of Yusuf, a struggling Istanbul poet who returns to his hometown when his mother dies. Second in the trilogy, *Süt* ("Milk"), rewinds to Yusuf's youth in his hometown, where he struggles to balance the family's milk business with writing poetry. 2010's *Bal* ("Honey"), last in the trilogy, won a Golden Bear at the Berlin International Film Festival and is set in the wild mountains of the eastern Black Sea.

Problems facing Kurdish Turks have surfaced in Turkish cinema of the twenty-first century. A two-man directorial team, Orhan Eskiköy and Özgür Doğan, directed 2008's *İki Dil Bir Bavul* ("On the Way to School"), a heart-warming documentary about the trials and tribulations of a middle-class Turkish teacher sent to a dirt-poor village school in the ethnically Kurdish southeast of the country. It won the pair the Best First Film award at Antalya's Golden Orange Film Festival. Based on a true story, 2008's *Gitmek* ("My Marlon, My Brando"), **Hüseyin Karabey**'s first feature is a gripping story of a Turkish woman's search for her Kurdish lover, trapped in northern Iraq following the American invasion of 2003.

Books

Many of the books reviewed below are, inevitably, general works on the Byzantine and Ottoman periods that include, rather than focus specifically on, Istanbul. For information on the latest books available, try I.B. Tauris (ⓦibtauris.co.uk) or Saqi Books (ⓦwww.saqibooks.com). In the UK, it's possible to track down many of the books listed here through Turkey specialists Daunt Books, 83 Marylebone High St, London W1M 4DE (ⓣ020 7224 2295, ⓦdauntbooks.co.uk). Most of the bookshops in Istanbul (see p.216) have a wide selection of books on Turkey, and much locally produced material (in English), which is hard to come by outside the city.

Note that "o/p" means **out of print**. Retail websites such as ⓦabebooks.com or ⓦbookfinder.com are excellent places to check for hard-to-find or out-of-print items; almost every book in this bibliography can be found secondhand or on a print-on-demand/special-order basis through these sources.

HISTORY

★**Roger Crowley** *Constantinople: The Last Great Siege: 1453.* Brilliantly written account of the fall of the Byzantine city to the Ottoman Turks by an ex-Istanbul resident passionate about his chosen subject. If you're only going to read one history book on the city, make it this one.

★**Caroline Finkel** *Osman's Dream.* A scholarly and meticulously researched yet thoroughly engaging history of the Ottoman Empire, from its origins in the twelfth century through to its early twentieth-century collapse. For a single-volume work on such a vast topic it does a very commendable job.

★**Jason Goodwin** *Lords of the Horizons.* A very readable account of the Ottoman Empire. Sceptics may decry its headlong pace and thematic approach, but if you've little or no prior knowledge of the Ottoman world, Goodwin's book helps bring a complex chunk of history to life.

Jonathan Harris *Constantinople: Capital of Byzantium* This very accessible book concentrates on Constantinople circa 1200, but its scope is inevitably much broader, making it a great introduction to the history and culture of the city in the Byzantine period.

Judith Herrin *Byzantium: The Surprising Life of a Medieval Empire* A delightful introduction to the subject, this book was initially sparked by a couple of hard-hatted builders working outside the professor's King's College study, who stopped work one day to ask her "What is Byzantine history?".

Michael Hickey *Gallipoli.* The best single-volume history of the campaign.

Halil İnalcık *The Ottoman Empire: The Classical Age, 1300–1600.* Just what the title says it is; this is the standard work, not superseded since its first 1973 appearance.

Patrick Balfour Kinross *The Ottoman Centuries.* Readable and balanced summary of Ottoman history, from the fourteenth to the twentieth century.

I. Metin Kunt & Christine Woodhead *Süleyman the Magnificent and His Age.* Concise summary of the reign of the greatest Ottoman sultan, and of the cultural renaissance over which he presided.

★**Philip Mansel** *Constantinople: City of the World's Desire, 1453–1924.* Nostalgic popular history, faintly anti-Turkish Republic, and focusing on the imperial capital. The best read on the city's Ottoman past, it's organized topically as well as chronologically.

Philip Mansel *Sultans in Splendour – the Last Years of the Ottoman World* (o/p). The illustrations – a collection of rare photos depicting unbelievable characters from the end of the Ottoman Empire – make this book. Well written, it contains much information not available elsewhere.

★**John Julius Norwich** *Byzantium: The Early Centuries, The Apogee and The Decline.* An astonishingly detailed, well-informed and readable trilogy. Norwich later compressed his great work into a single volume, the thorough and erudite *A Short History of Byzantium.*

Procopius *The Secret History.* An often raunchy account of the murkier side of the reigns of Justinian and his ex-courtesan empress, Theodora, from no less an authority than the imperial general Belisarius's official war historian.

★**Barry Rubin** *Istanbul Intrigues.* Unputdownable account of Allied forces/Axis powers activities in neutral Turkey during World War II, and their attempts to drag it into the conflict. Surprising revelations about the extent of Turkish aid for Britain, the US and the Greek resistance, and a wealth of detailed anecdote.

David Traill *Schliemann of Troy: Treasure and Deceit.* The man versus the myth: if you're intending to visit the ruins of ancient Troy, this volume, testing the crumbling edifice of Schliemann's reputation as an archeologist, will help bring the old Trojan walls to life.

Michael Wood *In Search of the Trojan War.* A very readable examination of the reality behind the legend that is Troy by

Britain's best-known populist archeologist, and a companion to the BBC series of the same name.

★**Erik J. Zürcher** *Turkey, A Modern History.* If you have time for only one volume covering the post-1800 period, make it this one; it's well written and lets in some revisionist fresh air over received truths. Also contains an opinionated, annotated bibliography.

BIOGRAPHIES

İpek Çalışlar *Madame Atatürk: The First Lady of Modern Turkey.* This brave book was condemned by many in Turkey for portraying the realities of life for a remarkably modern woman married, for a short time, to the founder of the Turkish Republic.

Saime Göksu & Edward Timms *Romantic Communist: The Life and Works of Nazım Hikmet.* Turkey's most controversial modern poet, banned and imprisoned for seventeen years at home, Hikmet spent much of his life in the Soviet bloc and died in Moscow.

★**M. Şükrü Hanioğlu** *Atatürk, an Intellectual Biography.* In exploring the ideas, ideologies and philosophies that

influenced Atatürk, this relatively slim volume goes a long way to explaining why modern Turkey is the contradictory country it is.

★**Patrick Balfour Kinross** *Atatürk, the Rebirth of a Nation.* Long considered the definitive English biography – as opposed to hagiography – of the father of the Republic and still preferred by some to the newer Mango text (see below).

Andrew Mango *Atatürk.* Despite massive press acclaim, this does not supersede Kinross's more readable tome as the best biography of the man, but merely complements it. Thorough and authoritative, but also steeped in military and conspiratorial minutiae.

MINORITIES AND RELIGION

★**Taner Akçam** *From Empire to Republic: Turkish Nationalism and the Armenian Genocide.* Brilliant study by a Turkish academic resident in the US, which shows how the ethnic cleansing of the Armenian population from 1895 to 1923, and the subsequent suppression of any memory of these events, was crucial to incipient Turkish nationalism – and remains at the root of the Republic's modern problems.

Peter Balakian *The Burning Tigris: A History of the Armenian Genocide.* As partisan as one would expect from an Armenian-American, it is, nonetheless, a compelling and thorough analysis of the background to, and execution of, the massacres of the Armenians on Ottoman soil during

the late nineteenth and early twentieth centuries.

★**Bruce Clark** *Twice a Stranger; How Mass Expulsion Forged Modern Greece and Turkey.* The Greeks of Istanbul initially avoided the fate of their kin elsewhere in Anatolia, but the forced population exchanges of 1923 made their eventual departure inevitable. A very readable study of a cataclysmic event.

Speros Vryonis *The Mechanism of Catastrophe.* Definitive study of the state-condoned and orchestrated anti-Greek riots of 1955, which left Istanbul's İstiklal Caddesi and Greek properties across the city in ruins and marked the start of the end for the city's Greek community.

VIEWS OF CONTEMPORARY TURKEY

★**Andrew Finkel** *Turkey: What Everyone Needs To Know.* Admirably succinct, well-written guide to the country by long-term Istanbul resident and journalist Finkel. It covers everything from the role and significance of Islam in society to Turkey's position in the world – and much else besides. Does exactly what the title claims it will.

★**Stephen Kinzer** *Crescent and Star: Turkey between two Worlds.* Engaging account of modern Turkey from the Istanbul-based correspondent of the *New York Times.* Whether *rakı*-drinking and *nargile*-toking with ordinary Turks, interviewing leading political figures, swimming across the Bosphorus or broadcasting the blues on his own show on Turkish radio, Kinzer has a gift for bringing the country to life.

Chris Morris *The New Turkey: The Quiet Revolution on the Edge of Europe.* More up to date than Mango's book, Morris (BBC correspondent in Turkey for four years) writes in a very readable manner on the usual topics, from political Islam to

the Greeks and Armenians, and from the Kurdish question to Turkey's EU accession quest.

★**Nicole & Hugh Pope** *Turkey Unveiled: A History of Modern Turkey.* A series of interlinked essays by two foreign correspondents who, after more than two decades in the country, understand Turkey better than most outsiders.

★**Alev Scott** *Turkish Awakening: A Personal Discovery of Modern Turkey* Scott's youth (under 30 at the time she wrote the book) and Anglo-Turkish origins give her a different perspective on contemporary Turkey, and especially on Istanbul. At times overly chatty, anecdotal and starry-eyed about Turkey (she describes the state-sanctioned violence against Istanbul's substantial Greek minority in 1955 as merely "race riots") it's still a great introduction to both city and nation.

★**Witold Szablowski** *The Assassin from Apricot City* The tale that gives this gripping selection of reportage its title deals with the Turk who almost killed the pope, but other sections slice revealingly through the underbelly of modern Istanbul, from prostitution to honour killings, from the Turkish male's sexual psyche to the Gezi Park protests.

TRAVEL AND MEMOIRS

Edmondo De Amicis *Constantinople* Lively and colourful account of the adventurous author's extended stay in the city in the 1880s. A lot may have changed in the intervening period, but it's amazing how much has stayed the same. The Foreword is by Umberto Eco.

Shirin Devrim *A Turkish Tapestry: The Shakirs of Istanbul.* Turbulent chronicle of an eccentric, dysfunctional and talented aristocratic Ottoman family whose exploits, if anything, became even more colourful after 1923.

Laurence Kelly (ed) *Istanbul: A Traveller's Companion.* Well-selected compendium of historical writing and fascinating eyewitness accounts of historical events such as the Crusaders' sack of Constantinople.

★**Geert Mak** *The Bridge.* Brilliant travelogue weaving the compelling tales of the petty traders, hustlers, pickpockets and fishermen who crowd Istanbul's iconic Galata Bridge with a wonderfully succinct and evocative history of one of the world's great cities.

Mary Wortley Montagu *The Turkish Embassy Letters.* Impressions of an eccentric but perceptive traveller, resident in Istanbul during 1716–18, whose disregard for convention and popular prejudice gave her the edge over contemporary historians.

★**İrfan Orga** *Portrait of a Turkish Family.* Heartbreaking story following the Orga family from an idyllic existence in late Ottoman Istanbul through grim survival in the early Republican era.

★**Orhan Pamuk** *Istanbul: Memories of a City.* A thoughtful and sometimes moving memoir by Turkey's most famous novelist, reflecting on the author's troubled relationship with himself, his parents and the city he was born and raised in. The book's overriding theme is melancholy and decline from imperial greatness – reinforced by the copious black-and-white illustrations by Turkey's leading photographer, Ara Güler.

ARCHITECTURE AND ARTS

Metin And *Turkish Miniature Painting – the Ottoman Period* (o/p). Attractive, interesting account of the most important Ottoman art form. Loads of colour plates and well laid out.

Diana Barillari & Ezio Godoli *Istanbul 1900: Art Nouveau Architecture and Interiors.* Superbly researched and illustrated account of the city's rich but neglected legacy of Art Nouveau architecture, in particular the works of Italian architect and Istanbul resident Raimondo D'Aronco. A nice corrective to the axiom that the city consists only of palaces, concrete towerblocks and crumbled wood terraces.

John Freely *John Freely's Istanbul.* Freely is the doyen of modern writers on the city. In this copiously illustrated book he combines descriptions of many of its monuments, much of its history and a wealth of personal musings on a lifetime's wandering through its streets to great effect.

★**Godfrey Goodwin** *A History of Ottoman Architecture.* The most comprehensive guide to Ottoman architecture, covering the whole of Turkey and providing a sound historical and ethnogeographical context for any Ottoman construction you care to name. Far too heavy to cart around though. Goodwin's *Sinan: Ottoman Architecture and Its Values Today* provides fascinating insights into the architect, his life and influences.

★**Murat Gül & Trevor Howells** *Istanbul: Architecture.* From the Watermark Architecture series, this well-illustrated volume covers all the city's major buildings, from Byzantine churches and Ottoman mosques through to lesser-known gems of the nineteenth and twentieth centuries, as well as the skyscrapers and malls of the modern city.

Richard Krautheimer *Early Christian and Byzantine Architecture.* An excellent survey from the Pelican "History of Art" series.

R.J. Mainstone *Hagia Sophia: Architecture, Structure and Liturgy of Justinian's Great Church* (o/p). A detailed study of one of the world's most important structures. A little technical, and the illustrations are only black and white, but it's about as exhaustive as you can get on the subject.

★**David Talbot Rice** *Art of the Byzantine Era.* A copiously illustrated general account of Byzantine art from the age of Justinian to the fall of Constantinople, with a lengthy chapter on the latter. An excellent introduction to the wonders of Byzantine architecture, frescoes, mosaics and other works of art.

J.M. Rogers *Sinan (Makers of Islamic Civilisation).* An eminently readable and well-illustrated introduction to the greatest architect of the Ottoman period.

Steven Runciman *Byzantine Style and Civilisation* (o/p). Excellent introduction to the world of Byzantium. His *The Fall of Constantinople, 1453* remains a classic study of the event, vying with the reader's attention from the equally well-written book by Crowley (see p.309).

★**Hilary Sumner-Boyd & John Freely** *Strolling through Istanbul.* First published in 1972 and indispensable if you love history and even more so if you like to conduct your researches on foot. The authors' knowledge and love of this incredible city shine through on every page. Copious sketch-maps and ground plans of monuments complement the informative text. Definitive.

Jane Taylor *Imperial Istanbul*. Excellent, stone-by-stone guide, complete with site plans, of the major Ottoman monuments in Bursa and Edirne as well as Istanbul.

CRAFTS

Alastair Hull *Kilims: The Complete Guide*. Comprehensive and thoroughly illustrated survey of Turkish kilims. His *Living with Kilims* is an excellent manual on how to use and care for (as opposed to museum-ize) kilims in interior-decoration situations.

James Opie *Tribal Rugs*. Contains examples of Turkish and Kurdish rugs as part of a general Central Asian survey.

Kurt Zipper & Claudia Fritzsche *Oriental Rugs: Turkish*. Extensive discussions of weaving techniques, symbols, rug categories and the weavers themselves, along with a regional survey of distinctive patterns.

TURKISH FICTION IN TRANSLATION

Yaşar Kemal Until the advent of Orhan Pamuk (see below), Kemal was the best-known Turkish novelist in the West. Early works such as *Mehmed My Hawk*, are set in the foothills of the Toros mountains, but some of his later (and better) novels, are set in and around Istanbul, including *The Sea-Crossed Fishermen*, a psychological drama set against the background of an Istanbul sea-fishing village.

Orhan Pamuk Internationally acclaimed, Istanbul-born writer and Turkey's first-ever Nobel Prize winner. His first work, *The White Castle*, is an excellent historical meditation in which a seventeenth-century Italian scholar is enslaved in the service of an Ottoman astronomer. Pamuk's 1998 novel *The New Life*, with nearly 750,000 copies sold, became Turkey's best-selling book ever, and had foreign critics in raptures. His subsequent *My Name is Red*, a late sixteenth-century Ottoman-set murder whodunnit, is marred by poor characterization and clunky translation. 2004's ★ *Snow*, Pamuk's most controversial and political novel, is arguably his best. Set in the bleak, lonely northeastern outpost of Kars, it examines once-taboo topics such as political Islam and Kurdish culture. 2010's *Museum of Innocence* is an Istanbul-set magnum opus, chronicling the life of a wealthy young man obsessed by an impoverished shop girl. Addicts can visit Pamuk's "real" Museum of Innocence in the backstreets of Istanbul's trendy Çukurcuma district (see p.126).

Elif Shafak Of Turkish origin but born in Strasbourg, Shafak was raised in Spain and now lives in Istanbul. Her novel *The Flea Palace* was an engaging account, in the mould of Armistead Maupin, of the interwoven, tragicomic lives of the residents of a once-grand Istanbul apartment block. She found herself, like Pamuk, drawing the ire of the establishment for her 2007 novel ★ *The Bastard of Istanbul*. In the book an exuberant, if dysfunctional, Turkish family play host to an Armenian-American girl in search of her identity. Well-drawn female characters drive a narrative which inevitably delves into the dirty linen basket of pre-Republican Turkey. Şafak's 2010 *Forty Rules of Love* deals with a subject dear to heart of the author, the Sufi mysticism of the Mevlana, while 2012's *Honour* is back on controversial ground with a continent-spanning tale about the so-called "honour killing" of a woman accused of bringing shame on her family.

Latife Tekin *Berji Kristin: Tales from the Garbage Hills*. The hard underbelly of Turkish life is shown in this surreal allegory set in a shantytown founded on an Istanbul rubbish dump. By the same author, *Dear Shameless Death* examines how rural families cope with the move to the big city.

FOREIGN LITERATURE SET IN TURKEY

Stella Duffy *Theodora*. This racy but literate historical romp traces the rise of the Theodora from circus-performer cum whore to consort of the Emperor Justinian – putting loving flesh on the bones of the character vilified in Procopius' *The Secret History*.

★ Jason Goodwin *The Janissary Tree*. A very palatable entry into a nineteenth-century Istanbul on the verge of the Tanzimat reforms, this racy historical thriller has all kinds of skulduggery being uncovered by Yashin, a eunuch detective. The successful formula spawned three sequels.

Joseph Kanon *Istanbul Passage*. Gripping, atmospheric thriller set in a down-at-heel city that has just about survived World War II as a neutral non-participant. Terse dialogue, believable characters and an authentic evocation of Istanbul in 1945.

Pierre Loti *Aziyade*. For what's essentially romantic twaddle set in nineteenth-century Ottoman Istanbul, this is surprisingly pacy, with good insights into Ottoman life and Western attitudes to the Orient.

Barbara Nadel Her Istanbul-set Inspector İkmen mysteries include *A Chemical Prison*, *Arabesque* and *Harem*. Some people love the tales of doughty, chain-smoking Inspector İkrem and various associates trawling through the city's underworld, others find them a tad unconvincing. They're well worth a try, though, conjuring up a side of the city barely imaginable to the average visitor.

Barry Unsworth *The Rage of the Vulture*. Set in the twilight of the Ottoman Empire, with the paranoid Sultan Abdülhamit, during the last year of his reign, being observed by a troubled British officer-with-a-past stationed in Istanbul.

Language

English is widely studied in Turkish schools and has a great cachet, but away from tourist-dominated Sultanahmet or, to a lesser extent, sophisticated Beyoğlu, you won't come across many people who speak very much of it. It pays to learn as much Turkish as you can; even cosmopolitan Istanbulites greatly appreciate foreigners who show enough interest and courtesy to learn at least basic greetings. The main advantages of the language from the learner's point of view are that it's phonetically spelt and (almost always) grammatically regular. The disadvantages are that the vocabulary is unrelated to any language you're likely to have encountered (unless you're conversant in Arabic or Persian), and the grammar, relying heavily on suffixes, gets more alien the further you delve into it. Concepts like vowel harmony further complicate matters; trying to grasp at least the basics, though, is well worth the effort.

Phrasebooks and dictionaries

For a straightforward **phrasebook**, look no further than *The Rough Guide Phrasebook: Turkish*, with useful two-way glossaries and a brief and simple grammar section. To learn more, David Pollard and Asuman Çelen-Pollard's *Teach Yourself Turkish* is very good, and has an accompanying CD. Alternatively, there's the slimmer and cheaper *Turkish in Three Months*. The best series published in Turkey is a set of three textbooks and tapes, *Türkçe Öğreniyoruz (Engin Yayınevi)*, available in good bookshops in Istanbul.

Among widely available Turkish **dictionaries**, the best are probably the Langenscheidt/Lilliput miniature or coat-pocket sizes, or the *Concise Oxford Turkish Dictionary*, a hardback suitable for serious students. In Turkey, locally produced Redhouse dictionaries are the best value, though their fine print can be hard to read.

Pronunciation

Pronunciation in Turkish is worth mastering, since once you've got it the phonetic spelling helps you progress fast. The following letters differ significantly from English pronunciation.

Aa short a similar to that in far.

Ee as in b**e**t.

Iı unstressed vowel similar to the vestigial sound between the **b** and **l** of probable.

İi as in sk**i**.

Oo as in n**o**te.

Öö like ur in b**ur**n.

Uu as in bl**u**e.

Üü like ew in f**ew**.

Cc like j in jelly.

Çç like ch in **ch**at.

Gg hard g as in **g**et.

Ğğ generally silent, but either lengthens the preceding vowel or, when between two vowels approximates a **y** sound.

Hh as in **h**en, never silent.

Jj like the s in pleasure.

Şş like sh in **sh**ape.

Vv soft, somewhere between **v** and **w**.

Vowel harmony

Turkish generally tries to adhere to the principle of **vowel harmony**, whereby words contain either the so-called "back" vowels a, ı, o and u, or the "front" vowels e, i, ö and ü, but rarely mix the two types. A small number of native Turkish words (eg *anne*, mother; *karded*, brother) violate the norms of vowel harmony, as do compound words, eg *bugün*, "today", formed from *bu* (this) and *gün* (day), and foreign (mainly from Arabic, Persian and French) loan words.

Words and phrases

BASICS

Mr (follows first name)	Bey	I'm English/Scottish/	İngilizim/İskoçyalım/
Miss (precedes first)	Bayan	Welsh/Irish/	Gallerliyim/İrlandalıyım/
Mrs (literally lady; polite	Hanım	American/	Amerikalıyım/
Ottoman title; follows		Australian/	Avustralyalım/
first name)		from New Zealand	Yeni Zelandlıyım
Good morning	Günaydın	I live in ...	...'de/da oturuyorum
Good afternoon	İyi günler	Today	Bugün
Good evening	İyi akşamlar	Tomorrow	Yarın
Good night	İyi geceler	The day after tomorrow	Öbür gün/Ertesi gün
Hello	Merhaba	Yesterday	Dün
Goodbye	Allahaısmarladık	Now	Şimdi
Yes	Evet	Later	Sonra
No	Hayır	Wait a minute!	Bir dakika bekle!
No (there isn't any)	Yok	In the morning	Sabahleyin
Please	Lütfen	In the afternoon	Oğle'den sonra
Thank you	Teşekkür ederim/Mersi/	In the evening	Akşamleyin
	Sağol	Here/there/over there	Bur(a)da/Şur(a)da/Or(a)da
You're welcome/that's OK	Bir şey değil	Good/bad	İyi/Kötü, Fena
How are you?	Nasılsınız? Nasılsın?	Big/small	Büyük/Küçük
	Ne haber?	Cheap/expensive	Ucuz/Pahalı
I'm fine (thank you)	(Sağol) İyiyim/İyilik sağlık	Early/late	Erken/Geç
Do you speak English?	İngilizce biliyormusunuz?	Hot/cold	Sıcak/Soğuk
I don't understand	Anlamadım/Türkçe	Near/far	Yakın/Uzak
(Turkish)	anlamıyorum	Vacant/occupied	Boş/Dolu
I don't know	Bilmiyorum	Quickly/slowly	Hızlı/Yavaş
I beg your pardon, sorry	Affedersiniz	With/without (milk)	(Süt)lü/(Süt)süz
Excuse me (in a crowd)	Pardon	With/without (meat)	(Et)li/(Et)siz
		Enough	Yeter

SOME COMMON SIGNS

Entrance/exit	Giriş/Çıkış	Foreign exchange	Kambiyo
Free/paid entrance	Giriş ücretsiz/Ücretlidir	Beware	Dikkat
Gentlemen	Bay(lar)	First aid	İlk yardım
Ladies	Bayanlar	No smoking	Sigara içilmez
WC	WC/Tuvalet/Umumî	Stop, halt	Dur
Open/closed	Açık/Kapalı	Military Area	Askeri bölge
Arrivals/departures	Varış/Kalkış	Entry Forbidden	Girmek yasaktır
Pull/push	Çekiniz/İtiniz	No entry without a woman	Damsız girilmez
Drinking water	İçilebilir su	Please take off	Lütfen ayakkabılarınızı
To let/for hire	Kiralık	your shoes	çıkartınız

ACCOMMODATION

Hotel	Hotel/otel	Do you have a double	Bir/iki/üç gecelik çift
Pension/inn	Pansiyon	room for one/two/	yataklı odanızvar mı?
Do you have a room?	Boş odanız var mı?	three nights?	
Single/double/triple	Tek/çift/üç kişilik	With a double bed	Fransız yataklı

| With a shower | Duşlu | Can I see it? | Bakabilirmiyim? |
| Hot water | Sıcak su | I have a booking | Reservasyonum var |

QUESTIONS AND DIRECTIONS

Where is the … ?	… nerede?	How far is it to … ?	… 'a/e ne kadar uzak?
When?	Ne zaman?	What time does it open?	Kaçta açılıcak?
What/What is it?	Ne/Ne dir?	What time does it close?	Kaçta kapanacak?
How much (does it cost)?	Ne kadar?	What's it called in Turkish?	Türkcesi ne dir?/Turkin
How many?	Kaç tane?		Turkçe nasıl söylersiniz?
Why?	Niye?	Left	Sol
What time is it?	Saat kaç?	Right	Sağ
How do I get to … ?	… 'a/e nasıl giderim?	Straight ahead	Doğru, direk

TRAVELLING

Aeroplane	Uçak	Return	Gidiş-dönüş
Bus	Otobus	What time does it leave?	Kaçta kalkıyor?
Train	Tren	Can I book a seat?	Reservasyon yapabilirmıyım?
Car	Araba		
Taxi	Taksi	How many kilometres is it?	Kaç kilome tredir?
Bicycle	Bisiklet	How long does it take?	Ne kadar sürer?
Ferry	Feribot, vapur	Which bus goes to …?	Hangi otobus … 'a gider?
Catamaran, sea bus	Deniz otobüsü	Which road leads to …?	Hangi yol … 'a çıkar?
Hitchhiking	Otostop	Can I get out at a	Müsait bir yerde
On foot	Yaya	convenient place?	inebilirmiyim?
Airport	Havalimani/havaalanı	Parking/No parking	Park yapılır/Park yapılmaz
Bus station	Otogar	One-way street	Tek yön
Train station	Gar, tren ıstasyonu	No entry	Araç giremez
Ferry terminal/jetty	İskele	No through road	Çıkmaz sokak
Harbour	Liman	Slow down	Yavaşla
A ticket to …	… 'a bir bilet	Road closed	Yol kapalı
One-way	Gidiş, sadece		

DAYS OF THE WEEK, MONTHS AND SEASONS

Sunday	Pazar	June	Haziran
Monday	Pazartesi	July	Temmuz
Tuesday	Salı	August	Ağustos
Wednesday	Çarşamba	September	Eylül
Thursday	Perşembe	October	Ekim
Friday	Cuma	November	Kasım
Saturday	Cumartesi	December	Aralık
January	Ocak	Spring	İlkbahar
February	Subat	Summer	Yaz
March	Mart	Autumn	Sonbahar
April	Nisan	Winter	Kış
May	Mayıs		

NUMBERS

1	Bir	8	Sekiz
2	İki	9	Dokuz
3	Üç	10	On
4	Dört	11	On bir
5	Beş	12	On iki
6	Altı	13	On üç
7	Yedi	20	Yirmi

30	Otuz	700	Yedi yüz
40	Kırk	1000	Bin
50	Elli	100,000	Yüz bin
60	Altmış	500,000	Beşyüz bin
70	Yetmiş	1,000,000	Bir milyon
80	Seksen	The most important ordinals, as in class of train,	
90	Doksan	restaurant, etc, are:	
100	Yüz	First	Birinci
140	Yüz kırk	Second	İkinci
200	İki yüz	Third	Üçüncü

TIME CONVENTIONS

(At) 3 o'clock	Saat üç(ta)	It's 8.10	Sekizi on geçiyor
2 hours (duration)	İki saat	It's 10.45	On bire çeyrek var
Half-hour (duration)	Yarım saat	At 8.10	Sekizi on geçe
5.30	Beş büçük	At 10.45	On bire çeyrek kala

Food and drink

BASICS

Bal	Honey	Şeker	Sugar
Bulgur	Cracked wheat	Sirke	Vinegar
Buz	Ice	Su	Water
Dereotu	Dill	Süt	Milk
Ekmek	Bread	Tereyağı	Butter
Karabiber	Black pepper	Tuz	Salt
Makarna	Pasta (noodles)	Yağ	Oil
Mısır	Corn	Yoğurt	Yoghurt
Nane	Mint	Yumurta	Eggs
Pilav, pirinç	Rice		

USEFUL WORDS

Bakarmısınız!	Polite way of getting the waiter's attention	Garsoniye	"Waiter's" charge
		Hesap	Bill, check
Bardak	Glass	Kaşık	Spoon
Başka bir...	Another...	Peçete	Napkin
Bıçak	Knife	Servis ücreti	Service charge
Çatal	Fork	Tabak	Plate

COOKING TERMS

Acı	Hot, spicy	Peynirli, kaşarlı	With cheese
Etli	Containing meat	Pilaki	Vinaigrette, marinated
Etli mi?	Does it contain meat?	Pişmemiş	Raw
Etsiz yemek var mı?	Do you have any meatless food?	Sıcak/soğuk	Hot/cold
		Soslu, salçalı	In red sauce
Ezme	Paste; any mashed or crushed dip	Sucuklu	With sausage
		Tava, sahanda	Deep-fried, fried
Fırında(n)	Baked	Yoğurtlu	In yoghurt sauce
Haşlama	Meat stew without oil, sometimes with vegetables	Yumurtalı	With egg (eg *pide*)
		Zeytinyağlı	Vegetables cooked in their own juices, spices and olive oil (*zeytin yağı*), then allowed to steep and chill
Izgarada(n), ızgarası	Grilled		
Kıymalı	With minced meat		
Kızartma	Fried then chilled		

SOUP (ÇORBA)

Düğün	"Wedding": egg and lemon	Tarhana	Yoghurt, soured grain and spice
Ezo gelin	Rice and vegetable broth		
İşkembe	Tripe	Tavuk	Chicken
Mercimek	Lentils	Yayla	Similar to *tarhana*, with mint
Paça	Trotters	Yoğurt	Yoghurt, rice and celery greens

APPETIZERS (MEZE OR ZEYTINYAĞLI)

Antep/acılı ezmesi	Hot chilli mash with garlic, parsley, lettuce, onion	Mantar sote	Sautéed mushrooms
		Mücver	Courgette fritters
Barbunya	Red kidney beans, marinated	Patlıcan ezmesi	Aubergine pâté
		Piyaz	White haricots, onions and parsley vinaigrette
Beyin salatası	Lamb-brains salad		
Börülce	Black-eyed peas, in the pod	Rus salatası	"Russian" salad – potatoes, peas and gherkins in mayonnaise
Cacık	Yoghurt, grated cucumber and herb dip		
Çoban salatası	Chopped tomato, cucumber, parsley, pepper and onion salad	Semizotu	Purslane, usually mixed into yoghurt
		Sigara böreği	Cheese-filled pastry "cigarettes"
Deniz börülce	Sea samphire		
Deniz otu	Rock samphire	Tarama	Pink fish-roe
Haydarı	Yoghurt and garlic dip	Turşu	Pickled vegetables
İçli köfte	Usually meat in a spicy bulgur crust	Yaprak dolması/yılancı dolması	Stuffed vine-leaves
İmam bayıldı	Cold baked aubergine, onion and tomato	Yeşil salata	Green salad
		Zeytin	Olives

MEAT (ET) AND POULTRY (BEYAZ ET)

Adana kebap	Spicy Arab-style kebab	Karışık ızgara	Mixed grill
Beyti	Minced kebab wrapped in pitta	Keçi	Goat
		Kiremit kebap	Meat served on a hot ceramic tray
Billur/koç yumurtası	Testicle		
Böbrek	Kidney	Köfte	Meatballs
Bonfile	Small steak	Koyun	Mutton
Ciğer	Liver	Kuzu	Lamb
Çöp kebap	Literally, "rubbish kebab": tiny chunks of offal or lamb	Pastırma	Cured, spicy meat
		Piliç	Roasting chicken
Dana eti	Veal	Pirzola	Lamb chop, cutlet
Dil	Tongue	Saray kebap	Rissoles baked with vegetables
Döner kebap	Fatty lamb from a rotisserie		
İnegöl köfte	Mince rissoles	Sığır	Beef
İskender or Bursa kebap	*Döner* drenched in yoghurt and sauce	Şiş kebap	Shish kebab
		Tandır kebap	Side of tender, boneless lamb baked in an outdoor oven
Kaburga	Spare ribs, or ribs stuffed with *pilaf* rice		
Kağıt kebap	Meat and vegetables baked in wax paper	Tavuk	Boiling chicken
		Yürek	Heart
Kanat	Chicken wing		

FISH (BALIK) AND SEAFOOD

Ahtapod	Octopus	Barbunya, tekir	Red mullet, small and large respectively
Alabalık	Trout		

Çinekö	Baby bluefish; not very esteemed	Kılıç	Swordfish
Çipura	Gilt-head bream	Kolyoz	Club mackerel
Hams	Anchovy (Black Sea)	Levrek	Bass; usually farmed
İsparoz	Annular bream	Lüfer	Bluefish
İstakoz	Aegean lobster	Mercan	Pandora or red bream; wild
İstavri	Horse mackerel	Mezgit	Whitebait
Kalamar	Squid	Midye	Mussel
Kalkan	Turbot	Orfoz	Giant grouper
Karagöz	Two-banded bream	Palamut, torik	Small/large bonito respectively
Karides	Prawns	Sardalya	Sardine
Kefal	Grey mullet (Aegean)	Yengeç	Crab

VEGETABLES (SEBZE)

Acı biber	Hot chillis	Marul	Lettuce
Bakla	Broad beans	Maydanoz	Parsley
Bamya	Okra or lady's finger	Nohut	Chickpeas
Bezelye	Peas	Patates	Potato
Domates	Tomato	Patlıcan	Aubergine, eggplant
Enginar	Artichoke	Roka, tere	Rocket greens
Havuç	Carrot	Salatalık	Cucumber
Ispanak	Spinach	Sarımsak, sarmısak	Garlic
Kabak	Courgette, zucchini	Sivri biber	Skinny peppers, hot or mild
Karnabahar	Cauliflower	Soğan	Onion
Kuru fasulye	White haricots	Taze fasulye	French beans
Kuşkonmaz	Asparagus	Tere	Similar to, but hotter than, rocket
Lahana	Cabbage (usually stuffed)		
Mantar	Mushrooms	Turp	Radish

SNACKS

Badem	Almonds	Lavaş	Flat bread, usually served hot and "puffed-up" with dips as a starter
Börek	Rich layered pastry with varied fillings		
Çerez	Bar nibbles	Leblebi	Roasted chickpeas
Çeviz	Walnuts	Midye dolması	Mussels stuffed with rice, allspice and pine nuts
Cezer(i)ye	Carrot, honey and nut bar		
Çiğ börek	"Inflated" hollow turnovers	Mısır	Roasted and spiced corn
Dürüm	Pitta-like dough roll used to wrap meat for takeaway	Pestil	Sheet-pressed dried fruit
		Pide	Elongated Turkish "pizza"
Fındık	Hazelnuts	Poğaça	Soft bread, plain or stuffed with cheese or spicy potato
Gözleme	Village flat bread with various savoury fillings		
		Antep/Şam fıstık	Pistachios
Kestane	Chestnuts	Simit	Bread rings studded with sesame seeds
Kokoreç	Mixed innard roulade		
Kuru üzüm	Raisins	Su börek	"Water börek" – steamed, lasagne-like cheese pie
Lahmacun	Round Arabic "pizza"		
		Yer fıstığı	Peanuts

TYPICAL DISHES

Güveç	Meat and vegetable clay-pot casserole	Lahana sarma	Black-Sea version of stuffed vine-leaves, with baby cabbage leaves
İç pilav	Spicy rice		
Karnıyarık	Aubergine and meat dish, firmer than mussaka	Mantı	Mince-stuffed "ravioli" topped with yoghurt and chilli oil

Menemen	Stir-fried omelette with tomatoes and peppers	Sebze turlu	Vegetable stew
Saç kavurma	"Wok"-fried medley	Tas kebap	Meat and vegetable stew
Şakşuka	Aubergine, tomato and other vegetable fry-up	Türlü sebze	Another name for *tas kebap*

CHEESE (PEYNIR)

Beyaz	White; like Greek feta	Otlu peynir	Herb-flavoured cheese
Çerkez	Like Edam	Tulum	Dry, crumbly cheese made in a goatskin
Dil	Like mozzarella		
Kaşar	Kasseri, variably aged		

FRUIT (MEYVE)

Ahududu	Raspberry	Kavun	Persian melon
Armut	Pear	Kayısı	Apricot
Ayva	Quince	Kiraz	Sweet cherry
Böğürtlen	Blackberry	Limon	Lemon
Çilek	Strawberry	Mandalin	Tangerine
Dut	Mulberry	Muz	Banana
Elma	Apple	Nar	Pomegranate
Erik	Plum	Portakal	Orange
Hurma	Persimmon or date	Şeftali	Peach
İncir	Figs	Üzüm	Grape
Karpuz	Watermelon	Vişne	Sour cherry

SWEETS (TATLI)

Acı badem	Giant almond biscuit	Krem karamel	Crème caramel
Aşure	Pulse, wheat, fruit and nut "soup"	Kurabiye	Generic term for dry, shortbread-type biscuit
Baklava	Layered honey-and-nut pie	Lokum	Turkish delight
Dondurma	Ice cream	Muhallebi	Rice flour and rosewater pudding
Fırın sütlaç	Baked rice pudding		
İrmik helvası	Semolina and nut *helva*	Mustafakemalpaşa	Syrup-soaked dumpling
Kabak tatlısı	Baked orange-fleshed squash topped with nuts and *kaymak*	Pasta	Any pastry or cake
		Süpangile	Ultra-rich chocolate pudding, with sponge or a biscuit embedded
Kadayıf	"Shredded wheat" in syrup		
Kadın göbeği	Doughnut in syrup	Sütlaç	Rice pudding
Kaymak	Clotted cream	Tahin helvası	Sesame-paste *helva*
Kazandibi	Browned residue of *tavukgöğsü*	Tavukgöğsü	Chicken fibre, milk and semolina toffee
Keşkül	Vanilla-almond custard	Yaz helvası	Semolina-based *helva*, often chocolate-flavoured
Komposto	Stewed fruit		

DRINKS

Ada çayı	Sage tea	Memba suyu	Spring water (non-fizzy)
Ayran	Salted yoghurt drink	Musluk su	Tap water
Bira	Beer	Meyva suyu	Fruit juice
Boza	Fermented millet drink	Papatya çayı	Camomile tea
Çay	Tea	Rakı	Aniseed-flavoured spirit
Kahve	Coffee	Sahlep	Orchid-root-powder drink
Maden suyu	Mineral water (fizzy), often called soda	Şarap	Wine

Glossary

Many of the **Turkish terms** below will change their form according to their grammatical declension (eg *ada*, island, but *Edek Adası*, Donkey Island); the genitive suffix is displayed in brackets, or the form written separately when appropriate.

GENERAL MEDIEVAL AND MODERN TURKISH TERMS

Ada(sı) Island.

Ağa A minor rank of nobility in the Ottoman Empire, and still a term of respect applied to a local worthy; follows the name (eg Ismail Ağa).

Ayazma Sacred spring.

Bahçe(si) Garden.

Bekçi Caretaker or warden at monument.

Belediye(si) Municipality – both the corporation and the actual town hall, for a community of over 2000 inhabitants.

Bey Another minor Ottoman title, like *ağa*, still in use; follows the first name.

Cami(i) Mosque.

Çarşaf A bedsheet – or the full-length, baggy dress-with-hood worn by religious Turkish women.

Çarşı(sı) Bazaar, market.

Çay(ı) 1) Tea, the national drink; 2) a stream or small river.

Çeşme(si) Street-corner fountain.

Dağlar(ı) Mountains.

Dolmuş Literally "filled" – the shared-taxi system; (see p.27).

Eski Old (frequent modifier of place names).

Ezan The Muslim call to prayer.

Gazi Warrior for the (Islamic) faith; also a common epithet of Atatürk.

Gazino Open-air nightclub, usually adorned with coloured lights and featuring live or taped *arabesk* or taverna music.

Gecekondu Literally "founded-by-night" – a reference to the Ottoman law whereby houses begun in darkness that had acquired a roof and four walls by dawn were inviolable.

Gişe Ticket window or booth.

Göl(ü) Lake.

Hacı Honorific of someone who has made the pilgrimage to Mecca.

Hamam(ı) Turkish bath.

Han(ı) Traditionally a tradesmen's hall, or an urban inn; now can also mean an office block.

Harem The women's quarters in Ottoman residences.

Hastane(si) Hospital.

Hicri The Muslim dating system, beginning with Mohammed's flight to Medina in 622 AD, and based on the thirteen-month lunar calendar; approximately six centuries behind the Miladî calendar. Abbreviated "H." on monuments and inscriptions.

Hittite First great civilization (c.1800–1200 BC) to emerge in Anatolia.

Hoca Teacher in charge of religious instruction for children.

Imam Usually just the prayer leader at a mosque, though it can mean a more important spiritual authority.

Irmak River, eg Yeşilırmak (Green River).

İl(i) Province, the largest administrative division in Turkey, subdivided into *ilçes* (counties or districts).

İskele(si) Jetty, dock.

Janissary One of the sultan's praetorian guard, levied exclusively from the Christian communities of the Balkans between the fifteenth and eighteenth centuries; *yeniceri* in Turkish. Famous for their devotion to the Bektaşi order, outlandish headgear and marching music.

Kaplıca Developed hot springs, spa.

Kilim Flat-weave rug without a pile.

Kilise(si) Church.

Konak Large private residence, also the main government building of a province or city; genitive form *konağı*.

Lokanta Restaurant; rendition of the Italian *locanda*.

Mahalle(si) District or neighbourhood.

Meydan(ı) Public square or plaza.

Meyhane Tavern where alcohol and *meze*-type food are served together.

Miladî The Christian year-numbering system; abbreviated "M." on inscriptions and monuments.

Muezzin Man who pronounces call to prayer (*ezan*) from the minaret of a mosque.

Namaz The Muslim rite of prayer, performed five times daily.

Nehir (Nehri) River.

Otogar Bus station.

Ramazan The Muslim month of fasting and prayer.

Saz Long-necked, fretted stringed instrument central to Turkish folk ballads and Alevi/Bektaşi devotional music.

Sema A dervish ceremony; thus *semahane*, a hall where such ceremonies are conducted.

Sufi Dervish – more properly an adherent of one of the heterodox mystical branches of Islam. In Turkey the most important sects were (and to some extent still are) the Bektaşi, Mevlevî, Helveti, Nakşibendi, Cerrahi and Kadiri orders.

Sultan valide The Sultan's mother.

Şehzade Prince, heir apparent.

Şeyh Head of a Sufi order.

Tuğra Monogram or seal of a sultan.

Ulema The corps of Islamic scholars and authorities in Ottoman times.

Vezir Vizier The principal Ottoman minister of state, responsible for the day-to-day running of the empire.

Vilayet(ı) Formal word for province; also a common term for the provincial headquarters building itself.

ARCHITECTURAL/ARTISTIC TERMS

Apse Curved or polygonal recess at the altar end of a church.

Arasta Marketplace built into the foundations of a mosque, a portion of whose revenues goes to the upkeep of the latter.

Bedesten(ı) Covered market hall for valuable goods, often lockable.

Camekân Changing rooms in a *hamam*.

Eyvan Domed side-chamber of an Ottoman religious building; also applies to three-sided alcoves in secular mansions.

Göbek taşı Literally "navel stone" – the hot central platform of a *hamam*.

Hararet The hottest room of a *hamam*.

Hisar Castle, fort.

İmaret(ı) Soup kitchen and hostel for dervishes and wayfarers, usually attached to a *medrese*.

Kale(si) Castle, fort.

Kapı(sı) Gate, door.

Kemer Series of vaults, or an aqueduct.

Köşk(ü) Kiosk, pavilion, gazebo, folly.

Kubbe Dome, cupola.

Kule(si) Tower, turret.

Kurna Hewn stone basin in a *hamam*.

Külliye(si) Building complex – term for a mosque and dependent buildings taken as a whole.

Loge Screened-off booth or balcony where the sultan could pray in private.

Medrese(si) Islamic theological academy.

Mescit Small mosque with no *mimber*; Islamic equivalent of a chapel; genitive *mescidi*.

Mezar(i) Grave, tomb; thus *mezarlık*, cemetery.

Mihrab Niche in a mosque indicating the direction of Mecca, and prayer.

Mimber Pulpit in a mosque, from where the *imam* delivers homilies; often beautifully carved in wood or stone.

Minare(si) Turkish for "minaret", the tower from which the call to prayer is delivered.

Pendentive Curved, triangular surface, by means of which a dome can be supported over a square ground plan.

Pier A mass of supportive masonry.

Porphyry A hard red or purple rock containing mineral crystals.

Revetment Facing of stone, marble or tile on a wall.

Saray(ı) Palace.

Sebil Public drinking fountain, either free-standing or built into the wall of an Ottoman structure.

Selamlık Area where men receive guests in any sort of dwelling.

Son cemaat yeri Literally "Place of the last congregation" – a mosque porch where latecomers pray.

Synthronon Semicircular seating for clergy, usually in the apse of a Byzantine church.

Şadırvan Ritual ablutions fountain of a mosque.

Şerefe Balcony of a minaret.

Tabhane Hospice for travelling dervishes or *ahis*, often housed in an *eyvan*.

Tekke(si) Gathering place of a Sufi order.

Türbe(si) Free-standing, usually domed, tomb.

Tympanum The surface, often adorned, enclosed by the top of an arch; found in churches or more ancient ruins.

Verd-antique Type of green marble.

Yalı Ornate wooden residence along the Bosphorus.

Zaviye Mosque built specifically as a hospice for dervishes, usually along a T-plan.

ACRONYMS AND ABBREVIATIONS

AKP *Adalet ve Kalkınma Partisi* or Justice and Development Party; Islamist movement headed by Recep Tayyip Erdoğan, which currently dominates parliament with a two-thirds majority.

Bul Standard abbreviation for *bulvar(ı)* (boulevard).

Cad Standard abbreviation for *cadde(si)* (avenue).

CHP *Cumhuriyetçi Halk Partisi* or Republican People's Party (RPP).

IDO *Istanbul Deniz Ötöbüsleri*; company running Istanbul's car ferry and sea bus services.

KDV Acronym of the Turkish VAT.

MHP *Milliyet Hareket Partisi* or National Action.

PKK *Partia Karkaris Kurdistan* or Kurdish Workers' Party.

PTT *Post Telefon ve Telegraf*; the joint postal, telegraph and (formerly) phone service in Turkey.

Sok Abbreviation for *sokak (sokağı)* or street.

THY *Türk Hava Yolları*; Turkish Airways.

TRT Acronym of *Türk Radyo ve Televizyon*; the Turkish public-broadcasting corporation.

Small print and index

A ROUGH GUIDE TO ROUGH GUIDES

Published in 1982, the first Rough Guide – to Greece – was a student scheme that became a publishing phenomenon. Mark Ellingham, a recent graduate in English from Bristol University, had been travelling in Greece the previous summer and couldn't find the right guidebook. With a small group of friends he wrote his own guide, combining a highly contemporary, journalistic style with a thoroughly practical approach to travellers' needs.

The immediate success of the book spawned a series that rapidly covered dozens of destinations. And, in addition to impecunious backpackers, Rough Guides soon acquired a much broader readership that relished the guides' wit and inquisitiveness as much as their enthusiastic, critical approach and value-for-money ethos.

These days, Rough Guides include recommendations from budget to luxury and cover more than 120 destinations around the globe, as well as producing an ever-growing range of ebooks.

Visit **roughguides.com** to find all our latest books, read articles, get inspired and share travel tips with the Rough Guides community.

Rough Guide credits

Editors: Emma Gibbs, Matt Milton
Layout: Jessica Subramanian
Cartographers: James MacDonald, Ed Wright
Picture editor: Emily Taylor
Proofreader: Karen Parker
Managing editor: Keith Drew
Assistant editor: Payal Sharotri
Production: Nicole Landau

Cover design: Nicole Newman, Jessica Subramanian
Photographer: Roger Mapp
Editorial assistant: Rebecca Hallett
Senior pre-press designer: Dan May
Programme manager: Gareth Lowe
Publisher: Joanna Kirby
Publishing director: Georgina Dee

Publishing information

This third edition published May 2015 by
Rough Guides Ltd,
80 Strand, London WC2R 0RL
11, Community Centre, Panchsheel Park,
New Delhi 110017, India
Distributed by Penguin Random House
Penguin Books Ltd,
80 Strand, London WC2R 0RL
Penguin Group (USA)
345 Hudson Street, NY 10014, USA
Penguin Group (Australia)
250 Camberwell Road, Camberwell,
Victoria 3124, Australia
Penguin Group (NZ)
67 Apollo Drive, Mairangi Bay, Auckland 1310,
New Zealand
Penguin Group (South Africa)
Block D, Rosebank Office Park, 181 Jan Smuts Avenue,
Parktown North, Gauteng, South Africa 2193
Rough Guides is represented in Canada by Tourmaline
Editions Inc. 662 King Street West, Suite 304, Toronto,
Ontario M5V 1M7
Printed in Singapore

MIX
Paper from
responsible sources
FSC
www.fsc.org FSC™ C018179

Help us update

We've gone to a lot of effort to ensure that the third
edition of **The Rough Guide to Istanbul** is accurate
and up-to-date. However, things change – places get
"discovered", opening hours are notoriously fickle,
restaurants and rooms raise prices or lower standards. If
you feel we've got it wrong or left something out, we'd like
to know, and if you can remember the address, the price,
the hours, the phone number, so much the better.

Please send your comments with the subject line
"**Rough Guide Istanbul Update**" to @mail@uk.
roughguides.com. We'll credit all contributions and send a
copy of the next edition (or any other Rough Guide if you
prefer) for the very best emails.
Find more travel information, connect with fellow
travellers and plan your trip on ⓦroughguides.com.

ABOUT THE AUTHORS

Terry Richardson has lived in Turkey for over thirteen years. He first visited Istanbul in 1978 and has been an author of *The Rough Guide to Turkey* for a decade and a half. He contributes regular Turkey-related travel features to UK and Turkish newspapers, leads specialist history tours around Istanbul, and helped set up two long-distance walking trails in Turkey. When not travelling or climbing, Terry devotes rather too much time to following Middlesbrough FC.

Rhiannon Davies visited Istanbul for a week in autumn of 2012, was swept up by the rich art, music and culinary scenes and never quite managed to leave. She spent 18 months working as Arts and Culture Editor for *The Guide Istanbul* magazine, which allowed her to get under the skin of her new favourite city, before breaking out into freelance writing. She delights in discovering obscure regional Turkish dishes, and dicing with death by exploring Istanbul on a bicycle.

Acknowledgements

Terry would like to thank Seyhun Aktoprak, an Istanbulite and superb guide, for his valuable insights into this great city. Thanks also to Angelis Nanos of Istanbul Eats for bringing to life Istanbul's great street cuisine scene. My eldest son Doug again helped check out the Beyoğlu bars in return for free beers, and surprised himself by thoroughly enjoying a great walk along the land walls of Theodosius and cycling around the Princes' Islands. My youngest, Jake, did his bit too en route to Georgia. Thanks to Rhiannon for adding some fresh young blood to the guide. Lem, as ever, kept me sane through the updating and editing process. And finally thanks to Emma and Matt at Rough Guides for their firm but fair editing.
Rhiannon's thanks go to her stepfather and lovely mum for introducing her to Istanbul and imbuing her with their love for Turkey. Thanks also to Dilara Apa and her family for giving me a chance to get to know the city inside out with *The Guide Istanbul*; to Raz for always being there to accompany me on a new exploratory adventure; and to Apo for providing translation assistance and support.

Readers' updates

Thanks to all the readers who have taken the time to write in with comments and suggestions (and apologies if we've inadvertently omitted or misspelt anyone's name):

Jim Ainsworth, Xili Fernandez, Isabel Fletcher, Bill and Clare Fox, George Grimes, Simon and Avril Hillyard, John Lazarus, Nihan Vural and Boyd Wright.

Index

Maps are marked in grey

Map index

Listings key

- ■ Accommodation
- ● Cafés & Restaurants
- ■ Bars, Clubs & Live Music
- ● Shop

City plan

The **city plan** on the pages that follow is divided as shown:

N

0	250

metres

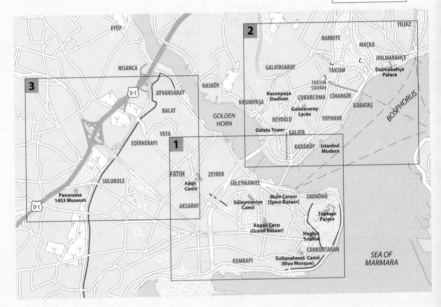

Map symbols

——— Road	★ Bus/dolmuş stop
▓▓▓ Motorway	▲ Peak
⌇⌇⌇ Road tunnel	⊠ Gate
⌇⌇⌇⌇⌇ Road under construction	✈ Airport
— - Ferry route	◆ Point of interest
Ⓜ Light railway/metro	ⓘ Tourist office
—Ⓣ— Tram	⊤ Fountain
⚓ Ferry terminal (regional map)	⍓ Lighthouse
- - - - Cable car	⊞ Hospital
⌇⌇⌇⌇ Funicular	⊠ Post office

@ Internet access	♱ Church (regional map)
♙ Castle	⊟ Church (town map)
∴ Ruins	▨ Building
♦ Museum	⬭ Stadium
⊙ Statue	⊞ Christian cemetery
♜ Mosque	⊻ Jewish cemetery
✡ Synagogue	▨ Park/forest
♒ Monument	▢ Beach
⚓ Swimming pool	
━━━ Wall	

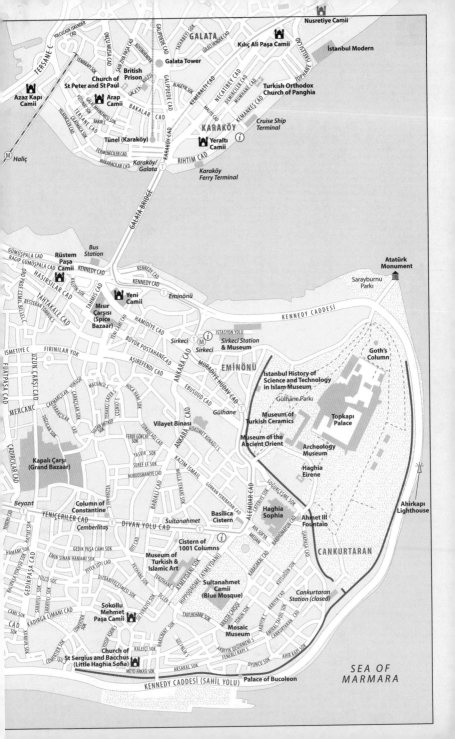

Nusretiye Camii

GALATA

Kılıç Ali Paşa Camii

İstanbul Modern

Galata Tower

British Prison

Church of St Peter and St Paul

Turkish Orthodox Church of Panghia

Azaz Kapı Camii

Arap Camii

KARAKÖY

Cruise Ship Terminal

Tünel (Karaköy)

Yeraltı Camii

Haliç

RIHTIM CAD

Karaköy/ Galata

Karaköy Ferry Terminal

GALATA BRIDGE

Atatürk Monument

Bus Station

Rüstem Paşa Camii

Sarayburnu Parkı

KENNEDY CAD

KENNEDY CAD

Eminönü

KENNEDY CADDESİ

Yeni Camii

Mısır Çarşısı (Spice Bazaar)

HAMİDİYE CAD

BÜYÜK POSTAHANECAD

Sirkeci

Goth's Column

Sirkeci

ISTASYON YOLU

Sirkeci Station & Museum

EMİNÖNÜ

Istanbul History of Science and Technology in Islam Museum

AŞİREFENDİ CAD

EBUSUUD CAD

MURADİYE HUDAY CAD

Gülhane

Gülhane Parkı

Museum of Turkish Ceramics

Topkapı Palace

Vilayet Binası

HÜKÜMET KONAĞI S

Museum of the Ancient Orient

Archeology Museum

Kapalı Çarşı (Grand Bazaar)

KAZIM İSMAİL

MOLLA FENARİ SOK

Haghia Eirene

Beyazıt

Column of Constantine

NURUOSMANIYE CAD

VEZİRHAN CAD

BABIALİ CAD

GÜRKAN YEREBATAN S

ALEMDAR CAD

Ahirkapı Lighthouse

YENİÇERİLER CAD

Çemberlitaş

DIVAN YOLU CAD

Sultanahmet

Basilica Cistern

Haghia Sophia

Ahmet III Fountain

AYA SOFYA MEYDANI

BABIHUMAYUN CAD

İŞKARPAŞA CAD

CANKURTARAN

Cistern of 1001 Columns

KABASAKAL CAD

Museum of Turkish & Islamic Art

Sultanahmet Camii (Blue Mosque)

HIPPODROME (ATMEYDANI)

Cankurtaran Station (closed)

Sokollu Mehmet Paşa Camii

Mosaic Museum

Church of St Sergius and Bacchus (Little Haghia Sofia)

KENNEDY CADDESİ (SAHİL YOLU)

Palace of Bucoleon

SEA OF MARMARA

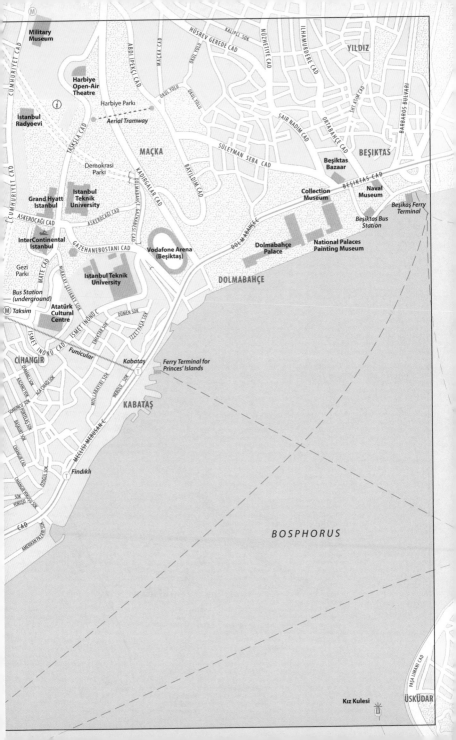

(M)

Military
Museum

Harbiye
Open-Air
Theatre

Harbiye Parkı

İstanbul
Radyoevi

Aerial Tramway

MAÇKA

Demokrasi
Parkı

Grand Hyatt
İstanbul

İstanbul
Teknik
University

InterContinental
İstanbul

Gezi
Parkı

İstanbul Teknik
University

Bus Station
(underground)

(M) Taksim

Atatürk
Cultural
Centre

CİHANGİR

Funicular

Kabataş

Fındıklı

KABATAŞ

Ferry Terminal for
Princes' Islands

Vodafone Arena
(Beşiktaş)

DOLMABAHÇE

Dolmabahçe
Palace

National Palaces
Painting Museum

Collection
Museum

Beşiktaş
Bazaar

BEŞİKTAŞ

Naval
Museum

Beşikaş Ferry
Terminal

Beşiktaş Bus
Station

YILDIZ

BOSPHORUS

Kız Kulesi

ÜSKÜDAR

CUMHURİYET CAD

ABDİ İPEKÇİ CAD

MAÇKA CAD

HÜSREV GEREDE CAD

KALIPCI SOK

OKUL YOLU

OKUL YOLU

NÜZHETIYE CAD

İLHAMÜRDERE CAD

ŞAIR NADIM CAD

ORTABAHÇE CAD

SAIT ASIM CAD

BARBAROS BULVARI

TAŞKLA CAD

KADIRGALAR CAD

DOLMABAHÇE GAZHANESI CAD

SÜLEYMAN SEBA CAD

BAYILDIM CAD

ASKEROCAĞI CAD

ASKEROCAĞI CAD

GAZHANEBOSTANI CAD

MATE CAD

MIRALAY ŞEFIKBEY SOK

BEŞİKTAŞ CAD

DOLMABAHÇE

İSMET İNÖNÜ CAD

İSMET İNÖNÜ CAD

İZZETTAŞA SOK

DÜMEN SOK

EDİBOĞLU SOK

MOLLABAYIRİ SOK

İNEBOLU SOK

MECLİSİ MEBUSAN C

OSMANLI SOK

KAZANCI YOK

AĞA CAMIİ SOK

SOMUNCU SOK

PÜRTELAS SOK

BAŞERE SOK

ÇIHANGIR CAD

ÖZOĞUL SOK

ÇIHANGIR YOKUŞU SOK

CAD

AMERIKAN PAZARI SOK

PAŞA LIMANI CAD

PUBLIC TRANSPORT

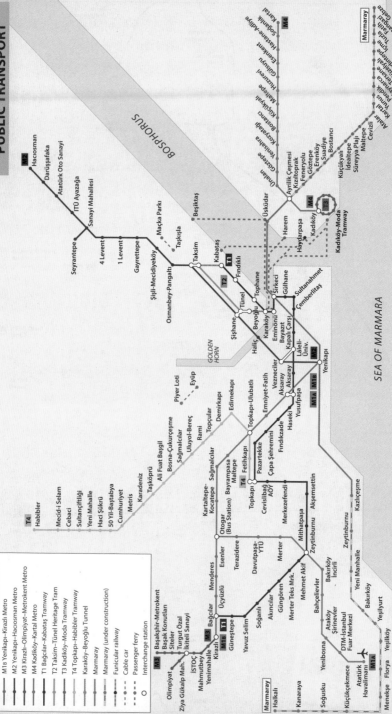

BOSPHORUS

SEA OF MARMARA

GOLDEN HORN

M1A Yenikapı–Atatürk Havalimanı Metro
M1B Yenikapı–Kirazlı Metro
M2 Yenikapı–Hacıosman Metro
M3 Kirazlı–Olimpiyat–Metrokent Metro
M4 Kadıköy–Kartal Metro
T1 Bağcılar–Kabataş Tramway
T2 Taksim–Tünel Heritage Tram
T3 Kadıköy–Moda Tramway
T4 Topkapı–Habibler Tramway
Karaköy–Beyoğlu Tünel
Marmaray
Marmaray (under construction)
Funicular railway
Cable car
Passenger ferry
Interchange station

SO NOW WE'VE TOLD YOU HOW TO MAKE THE MOST OF YOUR TIME, WE WANT YOU TO STAY SAFE AND COVERED WITH OUR FAVOURITE TRAVEL INSURER

WorldNomads.com

keep travelling safely

GET AN ONLINE QUOTE

roughguides.com/travel-insurance

MAKE THE MOST OF YOUR CITY BREAK